TELLING & DUXBURY'S

PLANNING LAW AND PROCEDURE

TELLING & DUXBURY'S PLANNING LAW AND PROCEDURE

FOURTEENTH EDITION

Edited by

RMC DUXBURY LLB, BARRISTER

Principal Lecturer in Law, Nottingham Law School, Nottingham Trent University

OXFORD
UNIVERSITY PRESS

Great Clarendon Street, Oxford OX2 6DP

Oxford University Press is a department of the University of Oxford.
It furthers the University's objective of excellence in research, scholarship,
and education by publishing worldwide in

Oxford New York

Auckland Cape Town Dar es Salaam Hong Kong Karachi
Kuala Lumpur Madrid Melbourne Mexico City Nairobi
New Delhi Shanghai Taipei Toronto

With offices in

Argentina Austria Brazil Chile Czech Republic France Greece
Guatemala Hungary Italy Japan Poland Portugal Singapore
South Korea Switzerland Thailand Turkey Ukraine Vietnam

Published in the United States
by Oxford University Press Inc., New York

First published 2009

British Library Cataloguing in Publication Data
Data available

Library of Congress Cataloging in Publication Data
Data available

Typeset by Cepha Imaging Private Ltd, Bangalore, India
Printed in Great Britain
on acid-free paper by
Ashford Colour Press Ltd, Gosport, Hampshire

ISBN 978-0-19-955320-4

1 3 5 7 9 10 8 6 4 2

PREFACE TO THE FOURTEENTH EDITION

The previous edition of this book featured the reforms introduced by the Planning and Compulsory Purchase Act 2004. Although the reform of development plans introduced by that Act has progressed reasonably well, it has taken over four years for many of the other measures in that Act to be implemented by means of various amendment orders and regulations. Clearly, planning legislation is a protracted process in these complicated times.

The year 2008 saw further fundamental and radical change. Based largely on the Government's 2007 White Paper, *Planning for a Sustainable Future*, the Planning Act 2008 introduces a self-standing development consent system for nationally significant infrastructure projects ('NSIPs') such as major airport terminals and power plants. Applications to develop such projects have in the past been frustrated by the delays inherent in the inquiry process and the Act sets up an independent commission, the Infrastructure Planning Commission, to examine and determine such applications within a period of nine months. The framework for the decisions of the Commission will be national policy statements in relation to the particular type of development promulgated by the Secretary of State.

The new Act also paves the way for the introduction of the Government's long awaited solution to the problem of infrastructure charges, which is to be a Community Infrastructure Levy. The provisions in the Act regarding the levy are skeletal and will be fleshed out in due course by regulations made by the Secretary of State. Other reforms to the planning system to be introduced by the Act include changes to the law relating to Local Development Frameworks, Tree Preservation Orders and planning appeals. Under the Act, there are also to be changes to the development control powers of local planning authorities. These include the power to make non-material changes to planning permission.

It must be stressed that many of the provisions of the Act of 2008 will come into force not immediately but on such a day as the Secretary of State may by order appoint and this will be done by means of statutory instruments. At the time of writing, no firm timetable has been published for the implementation of these provisions. Those sections of the Act that came into force on the day the Act was passed are set out in Appendix 2 of the book, where I have reproduced the commencement section of the Act.

Another recent statutory reform which is considered in this edition is the Greater London Authority Act 2007 which enhances the planning powers of the Mayor of London in various respects. There has also been, since the previous edition, a considerable number of important and interesting judicial decisions covering a range of matters including the meaning of development, the abandonment of existing uses, the enforcement of planning control, and listed buildings law. Space has been found to incorporate these new developments.

At a late stage in the publication process of this book a private members' measure, the Planning and Energy Act 2008, was passed. It enables local planning authorities in England and Wales to include in their development plans certain policies. These are policies imposing reasonable requirements for a proportion of energy used in development in the authority's area to be energy from renewable sources and low carbon energy, obtained locally. Policies may also be imposed reasonably requiring development in the area to comply with energy efficiency standards exceeding the energy requirements of the building regulations. Such policies must not be inconsistent with relevant national policies.

Although the arrangement of the chapters remains the same as the previous edition, chapter 8 is now in two parts; Part 1 deals with express planning permission granted by the local planning authority, and Part 2 with the new development consent regime for large infrastructure projects introduced by the Act of 2008. Other changes brought about by the new Act have been inserted into the relevant chapters.

I would like to thank the many people who have assisted me in one way or another in the preparation of this new edition, including my friend and colleague Sandra Morton for advising me on various aspects of European environmental law. I do not hesitate to add that any deficiencies in the text remain my responsibility alone. I would also like to record my gratitude to the publishers, Oxford University Press, for their support and assistance. As ever, the greatest debt of gratitude is owed to my wife, Jenny, whose tolerance of my various writing ventures knows no bounds.

Robert Duxbury
Nottingham Law School
December 2008

CONTENTS–SUMMARY

CONTENTS

TABLE OF CASES

UNITED KINGDOM

EUROPEAN

TABLE OF LEGISLATION

UNITED KINGDOM

EUROPEAN

TABLE OF ABBREVIATIONS (LEGISLATION)

Advertisement Regulations	Town and Country Planning (Control of Advertisements) Regulations 2007, SI 2007 No 783, as amended
COMAH Regulations	Planning (Control of Major-Accident Hazards) Regulations 1999, SI 1999 No 981, as amended
CROWA 2000	Countryside and Rights of Way Act 2000
Determination by Inspectors Rules	Town and Country Planning Appeals (Determination by Inspectors) (Inquiries Procedure) (England) Rules 2000, SI 2000 No 1625
Development Plans Direction	Town and Country Planning (Development Plans and Consultation) (Departures) Direction 1999, in DETR Circular 7/99
EA 1995	Environment Act 1995
EIA (Amendment) Regulations	Town and Country Planning (Environmental Impact Assessment) (England and Wales) (Amendment) Regulations 2000, SI 2000 No 2867, as amended
Environmental Impact Assessment Regulations	Town and Country Planning (Environmental Impact Assessment) (England and Wales) Regulations 1999, SI 1999 No 293, as amended
General Development Procedure Order	Town and Country Planning (General Development Procedure) Order (GDPO) 1995, SI 1995 No 419, as amended
General Permitted Development Order	Town and Country Planning (General Permitted Development) Order (GDPO) 1995, SI 1995 No 418, as amended
General Regulations	Town and Country Planning General Regulations 1992, SI 1992 No 1492, as amended
GLAA 1999	Greater London Authority Act 1999
GLAA 2007	Greater London Authority Act 2007
Hazardous Substances Regulations	Planning (Hazardous Substances) Regulations 1992, SI 1992 No 656, as amended
Hearings Rules	Town and Country Planning (Hearings Procedure) (England) Rules 2000, SI 2000 No 1626
HRA 1998	Human Rights Act 1998
HRA 2008	Housing and Regeneration Act 2008
Inquiries Procedure Rules	Town and Country Planning (Inquiries Procedure) (England) Rules 2000, SI 2000 No 1624
LGPLA 1980	Local Government, Planning and Land Act 1980

Listed Buildings Regulations	Town and Country Planning (Listed Buildings and Buildings in Conservation Areas) Regulations 1990, SI 1990 No 1519, as amended
Local Development Regulations	Town and Country Planning (Local Development) (England) Regulations 2004, SI 2004 No 2204, as amended
MTCPA 1943	Minister of Town and Country Planning Act 1943
Nature Conservation Regulations	Conservation (Natural Habitats, etc) Regulations 1994, SI 1994 No 2716, as amended
NERCA 2006	Natural Environment and Rural Communities Act 2006
NPACA 1949	National Parks and Access to the Countryside Act 1949
PA 2008	Planning Act 2008
P(HS)A 1990	Planning (Hazardous Substances) Act 1990
P(LBCA)A 1990 (or LBA 1990)	Planning (Listed Buildings and Conservation Areas) Act 1990
PCA 1991	Planning and Compensation Act 1991
PCPA 2004	Planning and Compulsory Purchase Act 2004
Planning Obligations Regulations	Town and Country Planning (Modification and Discharge of Planning Obligations) Regulations 1992, SI 1992 No 2832
Regional Planning Regulations	Town and Country Planning (Regional Planning) (England) Regulations 2004, SI 2004 No 2203
SDS Regulations	Town and Country Planning (London Spatial Development Strategy) Regulations 2000, SI 2000 No 1491
SEA Regulations	Strategic Environmental Assessment of Plans and Programmes Regulations 2004, SI 2004 No 1633
TCP(M)A 1981	Town and Country Planning (Minerals) Act 1981
TCPA 1947	Town and Country Planning Act 1947
TCPA 1954	Town and Country Planning Act 1954
TCPA 1962	Town and Country Planning Act 1962
TCPA 1968	Town and Country Planning Act 1968
TCPA 1971	Town and Country Planning Act 1971
TCPA 1990	Town and Country Planning Act 1990
Tree Preservation Regulations	Town and Country Planning (Trees) Regulations 1999, SI 1999 No 1892, as amended
Use Classes Order	Town and Country Planning (Use Classes) Order 1987, SI 1987 No 764, as amended
WCA 1981	Wildlife and Countryside Act 1981
Written Representations Regulations	Town and Country Planning (Appeals) (Written Representation Procedure) (England) Regulations 2000, SI 2000 No 1628

TABLE OF ABBREVIATIONS (OTHER)

AONB	Area of Outstanding Natural Beauty
BAT	Best Available Techniques
BATNEEC	Best Available Techniques Not Entailing Excessive Cost
BCN	Breach of Condition Notice
CIL	Community Infrastructure Levy
CIS	Community Involvement Scheme (Wales)
CLEUD	Certificate of Lawfulness of Existing Use or Development
CLOPUD	Certificate of Lawfulness of Proposed Use or Development
DCLG	Department for Communities and Local Government
DCMS	Department of Culture, Media and Sport
DEFRA	Department for the Environment, Food and Rural Affairs
DETR	Department for the Environment, Transport and the Regions
DPD	Development Plan Document
DTLR	Department for Transport, Local Government and the Regions
EC	European Community
ECHR	European Convention on Human Rights
ECtHR	European Court of Human Rights
ECJ	European Court of Justice
EU	European Union
EIA	Environmental Impact Assessment
GDPO	General Development Procedure Order
GPDO	General Permitted Development Order
HCA	Homes and Communities Agency
IPC	Infrastructure Planning Commission
IPC	Integrated Polllution Control
IPPC	Integrated Pollution Prevention and Control
LDD	Local Development Document
LDF	Local Development Framework
LDO	Local Development Order
LDP	Local Development Plan (Wales)
LDS	Local Development Scheme
LPA	Local Planning Authority
MAFF	Ministry of Agriculture, Fisheries and Food
MPA	Minerals Planning Authority
MPG	Minerals Policy Guidance Note
MWDS	Minerals and Waste Development Scheme
NPS	National Policy Statement
NSIP	Nationally Significant Infrastructure Project

ODPM	Office of the Deputy Prime Minister
PGS	Planning Gain Supplement
PPG	Planning Policy Guidance Note
PPS	Planning Policy Statement
RDA	Regional Development Agency
ROMP	Registration of Old Mining Permissions
RPB	Regional Planning Body
RPG	Regional Planning Guidance
RSS	Regional Spatial Strategy
SAC	Special Area of Conservation
SEA	Strategic Environmental Assessment
SCI	Statement of Community Involvement
SDP	Statement of Development Principles
SDS	Spatial Development Strategy (for Greater London)
SPA	Special Protection Area
SPD	Supplementary Planning Document
SPZ	Simplified Planning Zone
TPO	Tree Preservation Order
TSN	Temporary Stop Notice
UCO	Use Classes Order
UDP	Unitary Development Plan
WHS	World Heritage Site
WSP	Wales Spatial Plan

1

HISTORICAL DEVELOPMENT OF PLANNING LAW

Introduction

1.01 The problems of town and country planning in Britain arise mainly from the profound revolution through which the country has passed in the last 200 years. The most important feature of the revolution has been the enormous growth in the population, especially during the nineteenth century. In 1800 the population was about 10.5 million; by 1850 it had increased to nearly 21 million and by 1900 it had nearly doubled again to 37 million. Since then the rate of increase has been considerably less but even so the population has grown to over 60 million. Such an increase could not fail to alter the physical appearance of the country and to bring in its train a whole host of problems.

1.02 It is doubtful whether the country could have sustained so large a growth in the population but for the industrial revolution which changed Britain from a predominantly agricultural nation to an industrial one. The early industrial revolution was centred on the coalfields and on the wool and cotton towns of the north, and was assisted by the building first of canals and later of railways. The result was to concentrate the population in certain parts of the country, chiefly the north of England, the Midlands and South Wales. The industrial towns grew in size more dramatically even than the general population and people left the countryside to find work in the new factories. During the first half of the nineteenth century the number of people in the countryside increased since the growth in population was greater than the migration to the towns; but with the decline in agriculture after 1850 the population of the countryside declined absolutely.

1.03 Conditions in the new industrial towns were often appalling. Factories and houses sprang up side by side without any attempt at zoning; although it must be remembered that until the coming of the railways, most people had to live within walking distance of their work. Still worse, there was no attempt even to control standards of building construction and sanitation. Although the housing conditions of the skilled artisan and the miners were often better than is now realized, conditions generally were very bad.[1] The foul state of the houses encouraged the spread of disease and there were serious outbreaks of cholera and typhoid in the 1830s and 1840s. Local boards of health had been set up after the cholera epidemic of 1831–3 but were allowed to lapse. In 1838 the Poor Law Commissioners published a report showing evidence obtained when they employed a number of doctors to inquire into the causes of death and destitution in London. They then commissioned the energetic public health reformer Edwin Chadwick to carry out a similar investigation over the whole country. The publication of the results of this in 1842 led to the appointment of a Royal Commission on the Health of Towns, which published its first report in 1844 (to a considerable extent the work of Chadwick) and its second report in 1845. These reports were followed in 1848 by two Acts of Parliament, which although very limited in scope and effect, are significant as laying the foundations of permanent statutory restrictions on the freedom of landowners to build as they pleased. The Public Health Act 1848 set up a General Board of Health with powers to create local boards on the petition of 10 per cent of the inhabitants of a district and to enforce boards where the death rate was above 23 per 1,000. The boards were given powers to ensure that both new and existing houses were provided with water and drainage: the building of new houses was not to be commenced until the board had been given notice of the position of privies and drains. The Nuisance Removal and Disease Prevention Act 1848 applied throughout the country and made it an offence to build a new house to drain into an open ditch. This Act was replaced in 1855 by the Nuisances Removal Act, which enabled the local authority to complain to the justices where any premises were in such a state as to be a nuisance or injurious to health. The justices' order could require the provision of sufficient privy accommodation, means of drainage, and ventilation to make the house safe and habitable, and, if the house were unfit for habitation, could prohibit its use for that purpose. The Act of 1855 was extended by the Sanitary Act 1866, which inter alia enabled the local council or board of health to deal with houses lacking proper drainage by

[1] For a general account of conditions in the towns, see for instance: J L and Barbara Hammond, *The Town Labourer and The Bleak Age*; and J H Clapham, *An Economic History of Modern Britain* vol I.

compelling their connection with a public sewer (if within 100 feet) or with a cesspool or some other place.

1.04 At the same time, the more enterprising municipalities were obtaining extended powers by petitioning Parliament for local Acts. These local Acts were of special significance in that they paved the way for the great Public Health Act 1875. This consolidated the earlier public general Acts and gave national application to provisions previously found only in local Acts. Local authorities were given power not only to secure proper standards of drainage and closet accommodation, but also to make byelaws regulating the size of rooms, the space about the houses, and the width of the street in front of them; provision was also made for the making up and sewering of unadopted streets at the expense of the frontages.

1.05 Builders were anxious to get as many houses as possible to the acre, and the byelaw minimum became accordingly the maximum and the minimum at once. The result was the sea of uniform rows of streets and houses which surrounds the centre of many of our industrial towns and whose dreary and unbroken regularity is too well known to require description. Nevertheless, byelaw control was an important step forward.

1.06 The powers of local government in the field of public health were supplemented by housing legislation beginning with the Artizans and Labourers' Dwelling Act 1868, which gave powers to deal with individual insanitary houses. This was followed in 1875 by powers to undertake slum clearance[2] and in 1890 by powers to build tenements and cottages for the housing of the working classes.[3]

1.07 This activity in the fields of public health and housing was followed by a sweeping reform of local government. Outside the boroughs, local government was entrusted to a patchwork of authorities often of an ad hoc character such as the local boards of health. These were replaced by the establishment of county councils in 1888, and urban and rural district councils in 1894.

1.08 Thus, by the end of the century, there existed an effective system of local government with substantial powers in the fields of public health and housing. It soon became apparent, however, that something more was necessary. The possibility of more satisfactory conditions of living and working was being demonstrated by the building of such places as Bournville and Port Sunlight by enlightened industrialists. About the same time, Ebenezer Howard wrote the famous book *Garden Cities of Tomorrow*, which may be taken as the starting point of the new towns movement, as well as the immediate inspiration for the first 'garden city' of Letchworth started in 1903.

---

[2] Artizans and Labourers' Dwelling Improvement Acts 1875 and 1879.
[3] Housing of the Working Classes Act 1890.

The development of regulatory planning

The Acts of 1909 to 1943

1.09 The first Planning Act was passed in 1909.[4] It authorized the preparation by local councils of planning schemes for any land 'which is in course of development or appears likely to be used for building purposes', ie suburban land. Such schemes were to be prepared with the object of ensuring 'that in future land in the vicinity of towns shall be developed in such a way as to secure proper sanitary conditions, amenity and convenience in connection with the laying out of the land itself and any neighbouring land'.

1.10 Thus to the search for good sanitary conditions, which had characterized the nineteenth century reforms, there were added the claims of amenity and convenience. The planning scheme was far more ambitious and flexible than the byelaw. Not only could it regulate the number of buildings on a site and the space about them, but it could provide both for the control of their appearance and the way in which they might be used. The scheme might also define zones in which only certain specific types of building use would be permitted, and it could list types of development which could not be undertaken without specific application to the local authority.

1.11 The preparation and approval of a scheme was necessarily a lengthy process, and an Act of 1919[5] introduced the concept of interim development control: that is during the period from the passing by the council of a resolution to prepare a scheme until the scheme became effective. Under interim control, a developer was not obliged to apply for permission but if his development conflicted with the scheme as ultimately approved he could not obtain compensation. On the other hand, if he obtained interim development consent, he was safeguarded.

1.12 The next major step forward was the Act of 1932[6] which enabled local authorities to prepare planning schemes for any land in England and Wales and not merely for suburban land as hitherto. The Act of 1932 was purely permissive, but it was supplemented in 1935 by the Restriction of Ribbon Development Act which made new building within 220 feet of classified roads, or roads made the subject of a resolution under the Act, subject to control. And in 1943 (when 73 per cent of the land in England and 36 per cent of the land in Wales had become subject to interim control under the Act of 1932) it was provided that all land in England

---

4 Housing, Town Planning, &c Act 1909.
5 Housing, Town Planning, &c Act 1919.
6 Town and Country Planning Act 1932.

and Wales should be deemed to be subject to interim control whether or not the local authority had passed a resolution to prepare a scheme.[7]

New problems

1.13 The Acts of 1909 to 1943 had all been based on the concept of the planning scheme. Such schemes were undoubtedly useful in ensuring that new development conformed to certain standards of amenity and convenience and in controlling changes in the use of existing buildings. But new problems were coming into prominence and it soon became apparent that the planning scheme was unsuitable for dealing with these. The population continued to grow substantially although less dramatically than in the nineteenth century. The advent of road transport and a cheap supply of electric power were changing the face of the country. These influences resulted in a new growth in the size of towns and cities and of many places beyond their boundaries. Industry was no longer tied to the coalfields and railways, and between the two wars a major relocation of the nation's industrial power took place. Some of the older industrial areas went through a period of prolonged and at times severe depression which led to the appointment of Commissioners for Special Areas. The Commissioners, while emphasizing that economic considerations must in the main determine the location of industry, drew attention to the dangers involved in the continued haphazard growth of the Metropolis and considered that much of the growth was not based on strictly economic factors.[8] The result was the appointment of the Royal Commission on the Distribution of the Industrial Population (the Barlow Commission).

1.14 The Barlow Report,[9] after lengthy examination of the advantages and disadvantages of the swollen state of the cities, came to the definite conclusion that:[10] 'the disadvantages in many, if not in most of the great industrial concentrations, alike on the strategical, the social, and the economic side, do constitute serious handicaps and even in some respects dangers to the nation's life and development, and we are of opinion that definite action should be taken by the Government towards remedying them.'

1.15 The Report also commented on the serious loss of agricultural land which it said:[11] 'since 1900 has been so rapid that it is stated to have covered with bricks and mortar an area equal in size to the counties of Buckingham and Bedford combined. Alike in urban extensions and in expropriation of land by Government

---

[7] Town and Country Planning (Interim Development) Act 1943.
[8] Third Report of the Commissioners for Special Areas 1936 (Cmd 5303).
[9] Cmd 6153.
[10] Cmd 6153, para 413.
[11] Cmd 6153, paras 36 and 37.

Departments for military, Royal Air Force, or other national requirements, regard must be had to the agricultural needs of the country.'

1.16 Nor is it merely the agricultural needs of the country that should be borne in mind. Providence has endowed Great Britain not only with wide tracts of fertile soil, but with mineral wealth in the form of tin, lead, iron-ore, and, above all, coal; with abundant supplies of water, hard and soft, corresponding to the various needs of industry; with rivers and harbours apt for transport and for both foreign and internal trade; and last, but by no means least, with amenities and recreational opportunities, with hills and dales, with forests, moors, and headlands—precious possessions for fostering and enriching the nation's well-being and vitality.

1.17 Publication of the Barlow Report was followed by the appointment of a Committee on Land Utilization in Rural Areas under the chairmanship of Lord Justice Scott. Both the Barlow Report and the Scott Report[12] urged that more effective action should be taken to control the siting of development and both pointed to the weaknesses of the Act of 1932. As the Barlow Report put it:[13]

> While present statutory town planning tends towards producing a more pleasant, healthier and more convenient local environment, it is not adapted to check the spread of great towns or agglomerations, nor, so long as their growth continues, to arrest the tendency to increasing central density and traffic congestion . . . Present town planning does not concern itself with the larger question of the general and national grouping of the population.

1.18 To remedy the situation both reports recommended the establishment of a central planning authority, the immediate extension of planning control to all parts of the country, and the formulation of a national plan for the location of industry and population.

1.19 The immediate results were the passing in 1943 of two Acts concerned with planning. The first provided for the appointment for the first time of a Minister 'charged with the duty of securing consistency and continuity in the framing and execution of a national policy with respect to the use and development of land throughout England and Wales'.[14] The other Act[15] extended, as already explained, interim control under the Act of 1932 to the whole country: legislation more suited to the control of land use generally, as distinct from local amenity and environment, did not come until the passing of the Town and Country Planning Act (TCPA) 1947.

[12] Cmd 6378.
[13] Cmd 6153, para 219.
[14] Minister of Town and Country Planning Act 1943, s. 1.
[15] Town and Country Planning (Interim Development) Act 1943.

Problems of redevelopment

The Act of 1944

1.20 In the meantime another problem had come into prominence: the redevelopment of older built-up areas. Existing planning legislation was concerned only with the preparation of schemes for regulating the activities of developers. These developers would normally be private individuals and companies, though there was a certain amount of development by local and other public authorities which was equally subject to the regulatory control of the planning scheme. Although the scheme would indicate what was desirable, it could not compel development to take place.

1.21 The limits of the approach became obvious during the Second World War when a good deal of thought was given to the physical reconstruction of older cities and towns. Although the immediate stimulus to this new thinking came from the opportunities created by the bombing, people were soon thinking of bolder schemes of reconstruction. For this purpose something more than regulatory planning was wanted, namely, publicly organized schemes of redevelopment. Although town improvement schemes had been authorized in part by local Acts, local authorities had no general powers to carry out redevelopment schemes until 1944.

1.22 The Town and Country Planning Act of that year[16] gave local authorities power to designate for general reconstruction areas which had been heavily bombed, or had been badly laid out and whose development was now obsolete. These were known as 'declaratory areas' and the local authority could compulsorily purchase any land in a declaratory area and carry out their development either themselves or by disposing of their land to private developers for approved schemes.

[16] Town and Country Planning Act 1944.

2

BASIS AND OBJECTS OF MODERN PLANNING LAW

2.01 In this chapter we will consider the principal primary legislation concerned with town and country planning in this country before going on to consider other legislation related to planning. We will then examine the wider legislative context in which planning law operates—European environmental law and the human rights legislation. The chapter concludes with a discussion of some challenges facing the planning system.

Planning legislation

The planning Acts

2.02 The framework of the modern system of planning law was established with the passing of the TCPA 1947. It repealed all previous legislation (with the exception of the Minister of Town and Country Planning Act (MTCPA) 1943) and made a completely new start with effect from 1 July 1948.

2.03 In setting up the new system, Parliament was plainly guided to a large extent by the recommendations of the Barlow and Scott reports. For instance the TCPA 1947 set up a powerful system of central administration. Although the Act did not create a 'central planning authority' as recommended by the reports, the Minister was given very strong powers which, taken with his general duties under the MTCPA 1943, enabled him to act to all intents and purposes as a central planning authority. The recommendations of the Barlow Report about the location of population and industry were given effect by providing that the applications for planning permission to build all but the smallest factories should require the support of the Board of Trade. Certain powers were also given to the Minister of Transport.

2.04 The TCPA 1947 also strengthened local administration. Under the previous Acts, non-county boroughs and district councils as well as county boroughs were entrusted with the preparation of planning schemes. The TCPA 1947 provided that the local planning authority should normally be the county council or county borough council, the former providing a larger and more realistic area for the preparation of development plans.

2.05 Each local planning authority was required under the TCPA 1947 to carry out a survey of the whole of its area and to prepare a development plan based on the results of the survey; the development plan was to be reviewed every five years from the date of approval in the light of a fresh survey of the area. By requiring that development plans should be based on the results of a physical, social, and economic survey of the area, the Act moved away from planning primarily in terms of amenity and convenience to planning on the basis of securing proper control over the use of land. The plans embodied both concepts of planning as described in the previous chapter—regulatory and positive. In the sphere of positive planning, the Act provided for areas of comprehensive development similar to the declaratory areas of the TCPA 1944, but including areas which required total replanning for reasons other than extensive war damage.

2.06 With regard to regulatory planning, however, the development plan was materially different from the old planning scheme in that it did not confer any rights to develop. Henceforth, no development was to take place without planning permission; normally this would require an application to the local planning authority which would then decide whether to grant planning permission, with or without conditions, having regard to the provisions of the development plan and any other material considerations. There were additional powers of control in the case of buildings of architectural or historic interest, trees, and outdoor advertisements.

2.07 The TCPA 1947 also contained some complex provisions for dealing with the financial problems inherent in any comprehensive planning control. These will be discussed in a later chapter.[1] It will suffice to say here that normally no compensation was payable under the TCPA 1947 where permission was either refused or granted subject to conditions. However, where land had become incapable of reasonably beneficial use, certain persons falling within a somewhat artificial definition of 'owner' might serve a purchase notice.

2.08 The following years were to see a number of amending Acts. The Acts of 1953 and 1954 radically altered the financial provisions of the TCPA 1947. The Acts of 1959 and 1960 made some improvements in the system of planning control without disturbing the framework of physical planning established by the TCPA 1947: the concept of the purchase notice was extended to cases of planning blights, provision was made for appeals to the courts on points of law, and the system of enforcement was strengthened.

2.09 The TCPA 1947 and the subsequent amending legislation were repealed and consolidated in the TCPA 1962. But it was not long before further changes were made. The Civic Amenities Act 1967 introduced the conservation area and strengthened the earlier provisions regarding trees and buildings of special architectural or historic interest.

2.10 In the meantime, the Minister had appointed a Planning Advisory Group to review the system of town and country planning and to see what changes were required to meet the needs of the next 20 years and beyond. The Group reported in 1965 that the system of control was effective, but that control was based on plans which were out of date and technically inadequate. In 1948 it had been assumed that the population of Great Britain would become static round about 1953; this assumption had proved entirely false, and the more conservative estimates were suggesting an increase to over 70 million by the year 2000. Again, in 1948, no one forecast the enormous increase in the volume of motor traffic. In the light of these two trends, the Planning Advisory Group saw the need for a much more flexible type of development plan; they would recommend that there should be broad structure plans which would require the approval of the Minister, and

[1] See ch 21 below.

local plans which would not require ministerial approval. These, together with some other changes, were put into effect by the TCPA 1968.

2.11 The TCPA 1962 and subsequent legislation were then repealed and consolidated in the TCPA 1971. This Act was in its turn amended by several Acts passed between 1972 and 1986. As a result, another consolidation took place in 1990; the existing legislation was consolidated in three separate Acts: the Town and Country Planning Act 1990, the Planning (Listed Buildings and Conservation Areas) Act 1990, and the Planning (Hazardous Substances) Act 1990. These Acts were supplemented by the Planning (Consequential Provisions) Act 1990 which is mainly concerned with the repeal of the pre-1990 legislation and with consequential amendments to some other legislation.

2.12 The consolidation of 1990 was followed almost immediately by the introduction of the Planning and Compensation Bill which received the Royal Assent in July 1991. The Planning and Compensation Act 1991 made important changes to planning law with regard to development plans, the meaning of development, enforcement notices, planning appeals, listed buildings, and other miscellaneous matters. In particular, the Act introduced for the first time a requirement for district-wide local plans and, implementing many of the proposals of the Carnwath report, strengthened the enforcement powers of local planning authorities. The Act also introduced reforms to the law of compulsory purchase and compensation.

2.13 The Environment Act 1995, which established a single unified Environment Agency for England and Wales, brought into existence new National Park authorities to act as local planning authorities for the area of the park. These replaced the existing National Park boards. The Environment Act 1995 also provided for the initial review and updating of mineral permissions granted from 1948–82, and the periodic review of all mineral permissions.

2.14 The Planning and Compulsory Purchase Act (PCPA) 2004 introduced fundamental reforms. In this respect it has been compared with TCPA 1968. PCPA 2004 received the Royal Assent in May 2004 and has been brought into force in stages by the Secretary of State. The Government's initial proposals for reforming the system were contained in the 2001 Planning Green Paper, *Delivering a Fundamental Change*. This was followed by a policy statement in July 2002, *Sustainable Communities: Delivery through Planning*, and other statements on regional and local planning and on compulsory purchase.

2.15 PCPA 2004 abolishes structure and local plans and replaces them with a two-tier system of a new kind, that is Regional Spatial Strategies for the English regions—these are based on regional planning guidance and revised by Regional Planning Bodies—and Local Development Frameworks made by local planning authorities. In Wales, there is to be a Wales Spatial Plan, made by the Assembly, and local development plans made by local planning authorities.

2.16 Under the 2004 Act, those exercising functions in relation to these new plans must do so with the objective of contributing to the objectives of 'sustainable development'. This concept is a fundamental purpose of the legislation and will be considered more fully when dealing with planning policy in chapter 3 below.[2] In addition, PCPA 2004 introduced a number of reforms designed to speed up and improve the efficiency of the system of development control. Further, the 2004 Act contains provisions abolishing, to an extent, the immunity historically enjoyed by the Crown in matters of planning control; it also amended the procedures relating to compulsory purchase.

2.17 The most recent piece of primary legislation involving the planning system is the Planning Act (PA) 2008. The Act is largely based on the White Paper, *Planning for a Sustainable Future*, 2007, which set out proposals to reform the system for obtaining planning permission and other consents for nationally significant infrastructure, such as power stations and major airport terminals, and proposed other measures to improve the planning system. The White Paper was the Government's response to two influential reports, the *Review of Land Use Planning*, 2006, and *The Eddington Transport Study*, also 2006. In the first of these, the Government had commissioned Kate Barker to consider how the planning system could better serve the national economy in a way that was consistent with the objective of sustainable development; in the second, Sir Rod Eddington was asked to advise on the long-term linkage between transport and economic performance and how the delivery mechanisms for transport infrastructure could be improved within the context of the goal of sustainable development.

2.18 Parts 1–8 of PA 2008 are taken up with the creation of a new system of development consent for Nationally Significant Infrastructure Projects (NSIPs). This new self-standing regime covers a range of projects in the fields of energy, transport, water, waste water and waste development. The Act sets up a new independent body, the Infrastructure Planning Commission (IPC) which will be responsible for examining applications for NSIP development thus removing the need for an application for planning permission to the local authority and for consents under other legislation. In some cases, the decision to grant a development consent order will be taken by the Commission, in others by the Secretary of State. The categories of NSIP development requiring consent are set out in the Act and are subject to various thresholds. Decisions are to be taken on the basis of policies set out in National Policy Statements (NPSs) made by the Secretary of State relating to relevant NSIP development. The Act also contains provisions relating to the enforcement of the regime, ie where development is carried out without consent or in breach of a development consent order.

[2] See para 3.20.

2.19 Part 9 of PA 2008 provides for compensation where land is subject to planning blight caused by an NPS or in connection with a development consent order. A number of other miscellaneous reforms are made by Part 9 which include amendments to the law relating to Local Development Frameworks, Tree Preservation Orders, and planning appeals. Reforms to development control include the power to make non-material changes to planning permission. Part 10 adds certain matters within the field of town and country planning to the legislative competence of the Welsh Assembly. Part 11 makes provision for the introduction of a Community Infrastructure Levy (CIL), the purpose of which is to ensure that the costs incurred in providing infrastructure to support the development of an area can be wholly or partly funded by landowners, the value of whose land may increase as a result of obtaining planning permission for development.

2.20 Despite the extensive changes introduced by PCPA 2004 and PA 2008, TCPA 1990 remains the principal planning Act, pending any future consolidation of the enactments.

Central administration

2.21 The current legislation continues the principle of a strong system of central administration, even though some detailed controls over the local planning authorities have been relaxed in recent years. The Secretary of State has a very wide range of powers and duties which enable him to control the policies of the local planning authorities and also to initiate policies; indeed, it is his duty to secure consistency in planning policies.[3] The extent to which he actually initiates policy will depend partly on the state of public opinion as to the desirability of forceful action by Whitehall and partly on the personality of the particular minister. Some aspects of planning policy—eg the moving of population and industry from London and the 'green belts'—owe much to a strong lead by ministers.

2.22 There have been changes in the central administration of the planning system in recent years. Following the general election of 2001, there was a transfer of ministerial functions. The old Department of Environment, Transport and the Regions (DETR) was broken up and responsibility for planning was vested in the Department for Transport, Local Government and the Regions (DTLR) and functions relating to environmental protection fell under the remit of the Department for the Environment, Food and Rural Affairs (DEFRA). The latter ministry absorbed the former Ministry of Agriculture, Fisheries and Food (MAFF).

2.23 The resignation of the Secretary of State for Transport, Local Government and the Regions in 2002 prompted yet another departmental reorganization in Whitehall.

---

[3] This derives from the Minister of Town and Country Planning Act 1943.

A Secretary of State for Transport was appointed to lead a single ministry devoted to transport, while planning became the responsibility of a new department, the Office of the Deputy Prime Minister (ODPM). The then Deputy Prime Minister, who led this department, was entitled 'the First Secretary of State'.

2.24 In May 2006, in yet another ministerial reshuffle, a new department, the Department for Communities and Local Government (DCLG) replaced the ODPM. The DCLG assumed responsibility for the planning system; and, in addition, local government, housing and urban regeneration. It should be noted that the Secretary of State for Culture, Media and Sport also has important functions under current planning legislation.

2.25 Throughout this book, the principal planning minister will be referred to as the 'Secretary of State' (unless the reference is to matters occurring before 1970, when the reference will be to the 'Minister'). This will be the case even in those exceptional cases where planning functions are exercised by a minister other than the Secretary of State for Communities and Local Government. The reference will be to the 'Secretary of State'.

Local authorities

2.26 Until 1974 the local planning authority was usually the county council or the county borough council. On 1 April 1974 a new system of local government was introduced. Outside Greater London, the whole country was divided into metropolitan counties and non-metropolitan counties, each county having two tiers of local authorities concerned with town and county planning. Some planning functions—notably the preparation of the structure plans—became the responsibility of the county council as 'county planning authority', but many matters were entrusted to the district councils. However, now that PCPA 2004 has abolished structure plans and replaced them in England with Regional Spatial Strategies, the role of county councils has diminished. Nevertheless, amendments to the Planning and Compulsory Purchase Bill made at the insistence of the House of Lords have ensured a greater role than that originally envisaged by the government. These matters will be discussed in chapter 5.

2.27 Further radical changes in local government came into effect on 1 April 1986; the Greater London Council and the metropolitan county councils were abolished with the result that in Greater London and the metropolitan areas, all aspects of town and country planning were entrusted to the Greater London borough councils and the metropolitan district councils. With regard to the non-metropolitan areas of England, the Local Government Commission was established in order to examine the existing two-tier structure and make possible recommendations as to the creation of new 'unitary', that is, single tier authorities. This it began to do in 1992. As a result the Secretary of State issued a number of structural change orders reorganizing local authorities in specific areas—these came into effect on 1 April 1996. But in other areas the existing two-tier structure is to remain. In Wales, the Local Government (Wales) Act 1994 abolished the two-tier system of local government and replaced it with a system of 21 unitary authorities. These changes also took effect on 1 April 1996.

2.28 Further fundamental constitutional change has taken place in Wales. Under the Government of Wales Act 1998, elections for a Welsh Assembly were held on 6 May 1999. The leader of the Assembly is the First Secretary. Once the Assembly came into being there was a transfer of powers from the Secretary of State for Wales to the Assembly by means of Order in Council. Among the powers to be transferred were powers in relation to town and country planning, historic buildings, and transport.

2.29 The metropolis experienced further structural change with the coming into force of the Greater London Authority Act 1999. The Act created a strategic Greater London Authority, a London Assembly, and the office of Mayor. The Mayor is required to publish a Spatial Development Strategy which is subject to processes of public participation and examination in public. Under the Act, the Mayor is given certain powers of direction over London borough planning authorities whereby they may be required to refuse planning permission in a particular case. The Act of 1999 has been amended in various respects by the Greater London Authority Act 2007, which received the Royal Assent on 23 October 2007. The new Act gives the Mayor additional planning powers which will be discussed in chapter 3.[4]

Development plans

2.30 The former system of structure and local plans was introduced into different parts of the country at different times. When provision for the system was first made by the TCPA 1968, the Minister invited a number of authorities to prepare structure plans for certain specified areas. The first formal orders were made in 1972 to enable the authorities concerned to embark upon the statutory procedures for public participation and the submission of the plans to the Secretary of State. By 1974 all the authorities concerned (normally the county planning authorities) had been requested to prepare structure plans and eventually all the original structure plans were approved. In Greater London and the metropolitan areas further changes took place. Structure and local plans were replaced by unitary development plans for the London boroughs and metropolitan districts.

2.31 Structure plans were in the nature of policy documents concerned with the main planning problems of the area and the best way of dealing with these problems. The detailed solutions, including land allocations, were found in the local plans.

---

[4] See para 3.65.

An important feature of the system was the emphasis laid on the positive aspects of planning. In preparing plans, the local planning authorities were specifically required to include proposals for conserving the natural beauty and amenity of the land, for the improvement of the physical environment, and the management of traffic. As mentioned earlier in this chapter, PCPA 2004 introduced a new system of development plans with effect, in England, from 28 September 2004. The development plan in that country, outside Greater London, will comprise the Regional Spatial Strategy and the Development Plan Documents adopted or approved for the area and prepared by the local planning authorities. Initially, the Regional Spatial Strategy is to be based on regional planning guidance made by Regional Planning Bodies. Further revisions will be made by the Regional Planning Bodies.

2.32 In Greater London, the development plan is the Spatial Development Strategy, to which reference was made earlier in this chapter, and the adopted or approved Development Plan Documents.

2.33 In Wales, as we have seen, the legislation provides for a Wales Spatial Plan which will be the development plan in conjunction with Local Development Plans prepared by local planning authorities.

2.34 Although not defined in PCPA 2004, 'spatial' planning is intended to be a concept which goes beyond traditional land use planning and integrates other policies and programmes. The aim is to co-ordinate regeneration strategies, regional economic and housing strategies, community development, and local transport plans with town and country planning development plans.

2.35 The second tier of plans in England is the Local Development Scheme prepared by local planning authorities comprising Local Development Documents including Development Plan Documents, the latter being part of the statutory development plan. Some of the Local Development Documents will be Supplementary Planning Documents which expand upon policies set out in Development Plan Documents. This will place what have in the past been termed 'bottom drawer' plans on a statutory footing for the first time. As with the old local plans, the Local Development Scheme is to be based on a survey, including the principal physical, economic, social, and environmental characteristics of the area.

2.36 The Local Development Scheme, together with the local planning authority's Statement of Community Involvement, will comprise the 'Local Development Framework' for the area. The Statement of Community Involvement is a statement of the authority's policy as to the involvement of persons having an interest in matters relating to development in their area.

2.37 The Local Development Framework—a non-statutory term—is designed to be a 'portfolio' of documents which will encompass all the components of the new local planning system.

2.38 Although PCPA 2004 abolished structure, local, and unitary development plans, there were transitional arrangements. Existing adopted plans were 'saved' for a period of three years. Draft plans which had reached a certain stage in the adoption process were saved for three years after their adoption.

2.39 As with the old plans, the new strategies and schemes will be of fundamental importance in regulatory planning; in considering an application for planning permission, for instance, the local planning authority will need to consider the policies laid down in the regional strategy and the more detailed provisions of Local Development Scheme in force in the locality concerned.

Development control

2.40 The requirements as to planning permission are the king-pin of the whole system of regulatory planning. They depend on the definition of development in TCPA 1990, s. 55—namely, the carrying out of building, engineering, mining, or other operations or the making of any material change in the use of buildings or other land. This definition is not as simple as might appear[5] and has given rise to a large number of High Court actions as well as numerous appeals to the Secretary of State. Any person who is in doubt as to whether a proposed operation or change of use would be lawful may apply to the local planning authority for a certificate to that effect and, if dissatisfied with their decision, may appeal to the Secretary of State; there is also a further right of appeal to the High Court.[6]

2.41 Where planning permission is required it is sometimes granted by the Secretary of State by development order and there are a few cases in which planning permission is deemed to be granted. Otherwise application should be made to the local planning authority; if the applicant is aggrieved by their decision he may appeal to the Secretary of State whose decision is final except for an appeal to the High Court on points of law.[7]

2.42 Where the land has become incapable of reasonable beneficial use, or the chances of selling it are adversely affected by planning proposals, certain categories of owner may serve a purchase notice.[8]

2.43 If development is carried out without planning permission or in breach of conditions attached to the permission, the local planning authority may issue an enforcement notice. There are certain rights of appeal to the Secretary of State but, once the notice takes effect, failure to comply with it is an offence

---

5 This definition is discussed fully at para 6.01.
6 See para 6.179.
7 See para 20.07.
8 See para 14.01.

punishable by fine and the planning authority have certain additional powers of enforcement.[9]

2.44 Even where planning permission has not been obtained, development may become immune from enforcement through the passage of time. In some cases the qualifying period is four years, in others it is 10. After this, the particular development is regarded as lawful. Any person wishing to ascertain the lawfulness of any existing development may apply to the local planning authority for a certificate of lawfulness; in the case of a refusal of a certificate, the applicant may appeal to the Secretary of State. A further appeal lies to the High Court.[10]

2.45 A grant of planning permission may be revoked or modified before it is acted upon[11] and the local planning authority have certain powers to require the removal or alteration of existing buildings and uses.[12]

Controls over amenity

2.46 The importance of conserving and where possible of enhancing the physical environment is recognized by giving local planning authorities certain additional powers of control which are not dependent upon the definition of development. These relate to the preservation of trees and woodlands, the control of advertisements and the tidying up of waste land, the control of hazardous substances,[13] and the preservation of buildings of special architectural and historic interest.[14] The local planning authority may also designate conservation areas in which special attention will be paid to conservation and improvement.

Other legislation related to planning

2.47 The consolidating Acts passed in 1990, as amended by the PCA 1991 and PCPA 2004, PA 2008 provide the main statutory framework for town and country planning in England and Wales. There have been in addition some other Acts dealing with special problems associated with planning, including notably: the New Towns Act 1981 (re-enacting earlier legislation on new towns); the National Parks and Access to the Countryside Act 1949; the Wildlife and Countryside Act 1981; the Environment Act 1995; and the Countryside and Rights of Way Act 2000.

---

9 See para 12.01.
10 See para 12.161.
11 See para 11.01.
12 See para 11.15.
13 See para 15.81.
14 See para 16.01.

New towns

2.48 The genesis of the new towns movement is to be found in Ebenezer Howard's *Garden Cities of Tomorrow*, published in 1899. It led to the formation of the Garden Cities Association[15] and two voluntary experiments in the building of garden cities at Letchworth and Welwyn. The importance of garden cities was recognized by the Acts of 1925 and 1932 which gave the Minister power to acquire land required for garden city development by compulsory purchase, although these powers were in fact never used. Fresh impetus to the movement was given by the Barlow and Scott Reports[16] which drew attention to the importance of securing the decentralization of urban areas without at the same time creating fresh suburban sprawl. Finally, it was recognized that the redevelopment of older towns, on account of war damage or for other reasons, would inevitably create an over-spill problem. In 1945 a government committee on new towns was appointed 'to consider the general question of the establishment, development, organization and administration that will arise in the promotion of new towns in the furtherance of a policy of planning decentralization from congested urban areas; and in accordance therewith to suggest guiding principles on which such towns should be established as balanced communities for work and living'. In the first interim report[17] the committee came to the conclusion that the most effective agencies for the purpose would be state-appointed development corporations.

2.49 This recommendation was adopted and the New Towns Act 1946 was passed 'to provide for the creation of new towns by means of development corporations and for purposes connected therewith'.[18] The current legislation for the establishment of new towns is contained in the New Towns Act 1981. Twenty-three new towns were designated between 1946 and 1970; none has been designated since then.

2.50 When the development of a new town is complete, the development corporation will be wound up. Originally, the law provided for the assets to be transferred to the Commission for New Towns which was set up for the purpose of taking over, with a view to its eventual disposal, holding, managing, and turning to account the property previously vested in the development corporation for a new town. However, the Housing and Regeneration Act 2008 has abolished the Commission and its functions will be carried out in England by a newly created Homes and Communities Agency (HCA). The objectives of the HCA are stated to be: (a) to improve the supply and quality of housing; (b) to secure the regeneration or development of land or infrastructure; (c) to support in other ways the creation, regeneration

15 Later known as the Town and Country Planning Association.
16 See paras 1.14 and 1.17.
17 Cmd 6759.
18 NTA 1946.

or development of communities or their continued well-being; and (d) to contribute to the achievement of sustainable development and good design.[19]

2.51 The Government's current initiative to establish a number of 'eco-towns' is discussed at the end of this chapter.[20]

Urban development areas

2.52 In the 1980s the emphasis changed from the development of new towns to the regeneration of major areas of social and industrial decay. The Secretary of State is empowered to designate any area of land as an urban development area if of opinion that it is in the national interest to do so. Designation is achieved by an order confirmed by both Houses of Parliament.[21]

2.53 The Secretary of State is empowered by the LGPLA 1980 to establish an urban development corporation for each such area with the object of the regeneration of the area. The development corporation can submit a specific development plan for the area for the approval of the Secretary of State. The Secretary of State is then enabled to make a special development order granting planning permission for any development in accordance with the plan. The development corporation can be made, by order of the Secretary of State, the local planning authority for development control purposes under Part III of the TCPA 1990 and for a number of other functions. PCPA 2004 amended the Act of 1980 so as to permit the planning functions conferred on the corporation by s. 149 of the 1980 Act to be exercised by specified members of the corporation—the corporation can therefore delegate its planning functions in the same way as may be done by a local planning authority.

2.54 Originally, only two urban development areas were designated; Merseyside and London Docklands. Several more were designated later including Birmingham Heartlands, Plymouth, Teeside, Trafford Park, and Tyne and Wear. In 1998, however, the eight remaining urban development corporations in England were wound up and their assets and liabilities transferred to local authorities. The corporations were dissolved on 1 July 1998.

2.55 A new urban development area was designated in 2004. In that year, the Secretary of State designated two areas in the London Thames Gateway as an urban development area and established an urban development corporation to regenerate the area.[22] An additional urban development corporation was later designated in Northamptonshire.

---

19 Housing and Regeneration Act 2008, s. 2(1).

20 See para 2.174.

21 LGPLA 1980, s. 134.

22 London Thames Gateway Development Corporation (Area and Constitution) Order 2004, SI 2004 No 1642. The order came into force on 26 June 2004.

2.56 A similar model to the urban development corporation is to be seen in the Olympic Delivery Authority set up by the London Olympic Games and Paralympic Games Act 2006. The Act, which gives the Authority similar planning powers to an urban development corporation, requires the Authority to deliver the public infrastructure necessary for the holding of the 2012 London Olympic Games.

Urban regeneration

2.57 A fresh approach to the problem of vacant and derelict land was to be found in Part III of the Leasehold Reform, Housing and Urban Development Act 1993. Such land has proved an intractable problem:

2.58 Much land that was once useful and productive has become waste land, particularly in the inner cities and mining areas. It is unsightly, unwanted and, at worst, derelict and dangerous. The planning system is not designed to deal with such land easily: its essential characteristic is to allocate land between competing uses. Where there are no pressures for development, there is a severe limit to what a local authority can do.[23]

2.59 The Urban Regeneration Agency was established by the 1993 Act. The main object of the Agency was to secure the regeneration of land in England suitable for regeneration and was one or more of the following: (a) vacant or unused; (b) under-used or ineffectively used in an urban area; (c) contaminated, derelict, neglected, or unsightly; or (d) likely to become derelict, neglected, or unsightly by reason of underground working other than for coal. The general powers of the Agency included powers of acquisition, management, and disposal of land, the carrying out of development within the objectives of the Act, and the giving of financial assistance to other persons.

2.60 The Secretary of State was empowered to designate urban regeneration areas. The main consequence of such designation was that certain functions of the local planning authority could be transferred to the Agency by order of the Secretary of State so that it became the local planning authority for the whole or part of the designated area.

2.61 The Urban Regeneration Agency was abolished by the Housing and Regeneration Act 2008 and its functions will now be carried out by the Homes and Communities Agency (HCA). The new Act, in ss. 13–15, contains similar powers enabling the Secretary of State to make designation orders providing for the HCA to be the local planning authority for the whole or part of the designated area.

---

[23] Cullingworth and Nadin, *Town and Country Planning in Britain* 1994.

National parks

2.62 The National Parks and Access to the Countryside Act 1949 (NPACA) established a National Parks Commission, which in 1968 was re-named the Countryside Commission, and in 1999 the Countryside Agency. It was concerned not only with national parks; it also had duties in connection with the preservation and enhancement of the beauty of the countryside and encouraging the provision of facilities for the enjoyment of the countryside. The achievement of these objectives was not left solely to the Agency: the legislation gave important powers and duties to local authorities. The year 2006 brought further reform. Under the Natural Environment and Rural Communities Act 2006 (NERCA), the functions of the Countryside Agency were assumed by the body 'Natural England', the general purpose of which is 'to ensure that the natural environment is conserved, enhanced and managed for the benefit of present and future generations, thereby contributing to sustainable development.'[24] The Environmental Protection Act 1990, s. 130, established a separate commission for Wales, called the Countryside Council for Wales. Its functions are in parallel to Natural England although additionally it must afford opportunities for the study of nature and have regard to the social and economic interests of rural areas in Wales.

2.63 Natural England may, by order submitted to and confirmed by the Secretary of State (of Environment, Food and Rural Affairs), designate an extensive tract of countryside as a national park, with a view to preserving and enhancing the natural beauty of the area[25] and to promoting its enjoyment by the public.[26] It must be an area which affords opportunities of open air recreation[27] by reason of its character and its position in relation to centres of population.[28]

2.64 The responsibility for seeing that these objects are carried out rests on the national park authorities (as local planning authorities) rather than Natural England.[29] This will be done in three ways. First, there will be a strict control over development; some permitted development rights are reduced and others withdrawn entirely.[30] A national park will not be exclusively devoted to enjoyment by the public. The life of the area is to go on and the various authorities are to have due regard to the needs of agriculture and forestry.[31] Other land uses, such as mineral

---

24 NERCA 2006, s. 2(1).

25 Includes flora, fauna, and geological and physiographical features: NPACA 1949, s. 114(2), amended by the Countryside Act 1968.

26 The statutory purposes of national parks have been redefined by the EA 1995, see para 2.68.

27 'Open air recreation' does not include organized games: NPACA 1949, s. 114(1).

28 NPACA 1949, s. 5, as amended by NERCA 2006, s. 59(1).

29 As to planning authorities in a national park, see para 3.49.

30 See para 7.01.

31 NPACA 1949, s. 84.

development, may be permitted in exceptional circumstances.[32] A national park will in fact be an area of special control in which amenity considerations will be predominant but not necessarily decisive.

2.65 Secondly, the national park authority may provide various facilities for public enjoyment such as accommodation, meals and refreshment, camping sites, and parking grounds; and they may compulsorily acquire land for these purposes.[33] They may also improve waterways for sailing, bathing, or fishing.[34]

2.66 Thirdly, the Act provides for extended government grants to encourage the national park authorities to use their powers to preserve and enhance the natural beauty of the area. Thus an authority wishing to make an order under TCPA 1990, s. 102 for the removal of an authorized use[35] in a national park would get a special grant for the purpose.

2.67 Part III of the Environment Act 1995 made some important changes to the original provisions relating to national parks.

2.68 The purpose of national parks was redefined to take account of the problems caused by, inter alia, the number of visitors to the parks. Accordingly, such parks are to be for the purpose (a) 'of conserving and enhancing the natural beauty, wildlife and cultural heritage' of the designated areas and (b) 'of promoting opportunities for the understanding and enjoyment of the special qualities of those areas by the public'.[36] In the case of conflict between (a) and (b), (a) is to prevail. And in pursuing these objectives, national park authorities are to 'seek to foster the economic and social well-being of local communities within the national park, but without incurring significant expenditure in doing so, and shall for that purpose co-operate with local authorities and public bodies whose functions include the promotion of economic and social development' within the park.[37] In 1992 the Government announced that it had accepted independent advice that the national parks would more effectively fulfil their purposes if run by independent authorities rather than by, as had been the case since 1949, planning boards or committees of constituent councils. Parliament gave effect to this proposal by enacting the Environment Act 1995, s. 63; this enabled the Secretary of State by order to establish a national park authority to replace an existing authority for a national park or following the

32 See the Minister's statement on the Second Reading of the Bill: 463 H of C Official Report (5th series) col 1492.

33 NPACA 1949, s. 12.

34 NPACA 1949, s. 13.

35 See para 11.15.

36 NPACA 1949, s. 5, as amended by s. 61 of the EA 1995. See also NERCA 2006, s. 59(1) amending NPACA 1949, s. 5, which takes account of 'possible' opportunities for promoting public understanding and enjoyment.

37 NPACA 1949, s. 11A(1), as inserted by s. 62 of the EA 1995.

designation of a new park. Such authorities will be the local planning authority for the park. The EA 1995 imposed an obligation on the new authorities to prepare and publish a National Park Management Plan within three years of their being set up: the plan must formulate their policies for the management of the park and for the carrying out of their functions.[38] Having now been established by the Secretary of State, the new national park authorities began to exercise planning functions as follows: in England, as from 1 April 1997, Dartmoor, Exmoor, the Lake District, Northumberland, North Yorkshire Moors, the Peak District, and the Yorkshire Dales; in Wales, as from 1 April 1996, the Brecon Beacons, the Pembrokeshire Coast, and Snowdonia. A proposed new national park for the South Downs has gone to public inquiry but the designation has yet to be confirmed.

Areas of outstanding natural beauty (AONBs)

2.69 Areas of Outstanding Natural Beauty are areas of high landscape value and the designation as such is intended to conserve and enhance the natural beauty of the land. Originally, AONBs were designated under NPACA 1949, s. 87 but the AONB provisions of NPACA were replaced by the Countryside and Rights of Way Act 2000 (CROWA). AONBs cover about 14 per cent of the land area of England and Wales and include such well-known areas of scenic beauty as the Northumberland Coast, the Cotswolds, the Isles of Scilly, the Isle of Wight, and the Gower peninsula.

2.70 Under CROWA 2000, s. 82, Natural England may designate as AONBs such areas as appear to them as of such natural beauty that special controls should apply. The designation must be confirmed, after consultation, by the Secretary of State. The management of AONBs falls largely upon the relevant local planning authorities who have similar responsibilities to national park authorities within the national parks. The local planning authorities in AONBs are empowered to take all such action as appears to them 'expedient for the accomplishment of the purpose of conserving and enhancing the natural beauty' of the area.[39]

2.71 The Secretary of State may establish conservation boards to manage the AONB.[40] Where such a board is set up, local authority functions may be transferred to it, other than powers relating to development plans and planning control. Thus, unlike national parks, the local planning authorities remain unchanged in such areas. As with national parks, however, certain permitted development rights are restricted. Under CROWA 2000, there is a duty on the local authority or conservation board to prepare a management plan for the AONB and keep it under review.[41]

---

38 EA 1995, s. 66.
39 CROWA 2000, s. 84(4).
40 Ibid, s. 86.
41 CROWA 2000, s. 89.

Sites of special scientific interest (SSSIs)

2.72 A Site of Special Scientific Interest is an area of land which is of special interest because of its 'flora, fauna or geological or physiographical features'. Originally, the designation of such sites was provided for under NPACA 1949 but the relevant law is now contained in the Wildlife and Countryside Act 1981 (WCA) as amended by CROWA 2000 and NERCA 2006. SSSIs are significant in that there are over 6,000 sites covering approximately seven per cent of the land area of Great Britain.

2.73 If Natural England (or, in Wales, the Countryside Council) is of the opinion that an area of land is of special interest by reason of its flora, fauna, or geological or physiographical features, they are under a duty to notify that fact to (a) the local planning authority in whose land the area is situated; (b) every owner and occupier of the land; and (c) the Secretary of State.[42] The notification is to specify the features by which the land is of special interest and any 'operations' likely to damage the flora, fauna, etc. Natural England must also state their views as to the management of the site, including any views they might have regarding its conservation and enhancement.

2.74 Owners and occupiers of the site then have a period of three months in which they can object or make representations about the notification. Natural England must decide within a period of nine months from the original notification whether to confirm the notification of the SSSI. If they do not so confirm, with or without modifications, the notification will lapse.

2.75 It should be noted that the concept of 'operations' does not have the same meaning under the SSSI legislation as it does under s. 55 TCPA 1990[43] which lays down the meaning of development requiring planning permission. The meaning is much wider under the SSSI code. It can include, eg agricultural activities which would normally be excluded from the definition of development. Thus activities such as ploughing might well be very damaging to the scientific interest of the site and can therefore be prevented.

2.76 Once the site is notified, owners and occupiers are not permitted to carry out any of the operations specified in the notification unless the owner has given written notice of the proposal to Natural England and (a) that body has consented in writing; or (b) the operation is carried out in accordance with a management agreement under NPACA 1949, s. 16 or WCA 1968, s. 15; or (c) the operation is carried out in accordance with a management scheme under WCA 1981, s. 28J, or a management notice under WCA 1981, s. 28K. However, the operation

---

42 WCA 1981, s. 28(1).
43 For operational development under s. 55, see para 6.02.

may be carried out where it is authorized by an express grant of planning permission or was an operation carried out in an emergency, the details having been given to Natural England as soon as possible after it was commenced.[44] If Natural England refuse consent for the operation, the owner or occupier may appeal to the Secretary of State. There is also a right of appeal against the imposition of conditions.

2.77 The carrying out of operations in breach of the requirement of notice and without reasonable excuse constitutes an offence punishable by a fine of £20,000 on summary conviction or an unlimited fine on indictment.[45] Likewise an offence is committed, subject to the same penalties, where an owner or occupier fails to give effect to the provisions of an agreed management scheme and Natural England serves a management notice.[46]

2.78 Obligations are imposed on public authorities and statutory undertakers to take reasonable steps to further the conservation and enhancement of the flora, fauna, etc of the SSSI. Such bodies are required to notify Natural England of operations likely to be damaging to the SSSI; the public body has 28 days before deciding to authorize or proceed with the operations once it has notified Natural England.[47]

2.79 Natural England has the power to denotify all or part of an SSSI if the site is no longer of special interest and, where this occurs, the land will cease to be an SSSI.[48]

2.80 The SSSI status has proved controversial since although the regime provides enforcement powers against potentially damaging operations, it nevertheless remains the fact that the legislation provides a 'reasonable excuse' for carrying out such an operation where the local planning authority have granted express planning permission. Nevertheless, the planning system does provide some measure of protection for such sites in that development plans must contain policies regarding SSSIs; permitted development rights may be restricted;[49] and Natural England must be consulted on applications for planning permission affecting an SSSI.

2.81 It should be noted that an SSSI may also be protected under European legislation and international conventions, such as a Special Protection Area (SPA) under the Birds Directive; or a Special Area of Conservation (SAC) under the Habitats Directive. The effect of these designations is considered in chapter 18.

---

44 WCA 1981, s. 28 P (4)(a) and (b).
45 Ibid, s. 28P(1).
46 Ibid, s. 28P(8).
47 Ibid, s. 28 I.
48 Ibid, s. 28E.
49 For permitted development, see para 7.01.

Planning law: the wider legislative context

2.82 So far in this book, we have examined the historical development of planning law, the current planning Acts, and other legislation related to planning, such as that providing for national parks and other special areas. These statutory measures do not exist in isolation—there is a wider legislative context.

2.83 There are three 'external' sources of law that have reshaped the contours of modern domestic planning law. First, the UK's membership of the European Union has had a significant impact, particularly in the environmental assessment of projects and plans; and in the law relating to nature conservation. Thus European environmental law and policy plays an important part in many development control decisions in this country, especially regarding large scale development. Secondly, the Human Rights Act 1998, which incorporated the provisions of the European Convention of Human Rights (ECHR) into national law has opened up the possibility of planning decisions and procedures being challenged on human rights grounds before the domestic courts. Although such challenges have not often been successful, the human rights jurisprudence has become an important and pervasive part of planning law. Thirdly, the planning system is of significance in other areas of environmental regulation such as waste management and pollution prevention and control. Thus developments such as major landfill sites will require a specialized permit under environmental law as well as planning consent. There is inevitably some overlap between the planning and environmental regimes and this issue is considered in chapter 18 below.

2.84 We now turn to a consideration of the role of European Community environmental law and policy, followed by a discussion of the significance of the Human Rights Act 1998.

European Community environmental law and policy

2.85 We begin the consideration of European environmental law with an introductory guide to European Community law and its relationship with UK domestic law. In order to appreciate the role of EC environmental law, which includes town and country planning measures, it is necessary first to examine the institutions of the EC and their function.

Institutions of the European Union

2.86 The leading organs are: (i) the Commission; (ii) the Council of Ministers; (iii) the Parliament; and (iv) the European Court of Justice (ECJ).

The Commission

2.87 This is the policy-making body whose main function is to draft the initial proposals for EC legislation, which is then passed to the Council and Parliament for amendment, rejection, or adoption. In some respects, the Commission, which is based in Brussels, resembles a civil service. The Commission is also entrusted with enforcing EC law either in response to complaints received or on its own initiative. After investigating alleged breaches of EC law, it may initiate proceedings under Article 226 of the Treaty of Rome.[50] The Commission is composed of several 'Directorates General'—environmental matters are covered in the main by the Environment Directorate General ('DG Env'). The commissioners are appointed by governments of the member states.

The Council of Ministers

2.88 The Council is the leading political institution of the EU. Each of the 27 member states is represented on the Council by its own representative at ministerial level according to the subject under discussion. The presidency of the Council is held by member states for a six-month period on a rotational basis. It is also based in Brussels and is the major institution for legislative decisions and the adoption of new legislation.

European Parliament

2.89 Members (MEPs) are directly elected to this institution for a term of five years by nationals of member states. Full meetings of the Parliament are held in Strasbourg. The UK has 78 MEPs out of a total of 785. Historically, this institution was merely a consultative body under the traditional 'consultation procedure' of introducing legislation. It would deliver an opinion to the Council before the Council took its final decision on the enactment of the legislation. However, Parliament's powers in the legislative process were increased under the Single European Act 1987, which introduced the 'co-operation procedure' involving Parliament and the Council. This process involved qualified majority voting in the Council. The Maastricht Treaty 1992 introduced a new 'co-decision procedure' under which Parliament was given greater powers of involvement in the legislative process including the power of veto. The Treaty of Amsterdam has made further changes, increasing the number of occasions when the co-decision procedure is to be used. The co-decision procedure is the method now normally used for purely environmental measures.

50 See para 2.117.

European Court of Justice (ECJ)

2.90 This is the judicial body situated in Luxembourg and consisting of 27 judges. Eight advocates-general make reasoned submissions to the court so as to provide assistance in the performance of its tasks. The ECJ is the ultimate power in interpreting EC law under the provisions of Articles 220–45 of the Treaty of Rome and it settles disputes whether brought by member states, EU institutions, private sector companies, or individuals. The ECJ has developed the doctrine of the supremacy of EC law and of 'direct effect', 'indirect effect', and the *Francovich* principle, which will be discussed below.[51] Article 228 of the Treaty, as amended, gives the ECJ the power to award a lump sum or penalty against a member state which has not taken the necessary measures to comply with its earlier judgment in the case.

Sources of EC legislation

2.91 The Treaty of Rome 1957 (as amended) is the primary source of EC legislation. The Treaty provides for secondary sources of law under Article 249 which provides that the Parliament, acting jointly with the Council and Commission, may 'make regulations, issue directives, take decisions, make recommendations or deliver opinions'. These instruments require further explanation.

2.92 *Regulations*—'regulations' are directly applicable to everyone in all member states and have binding effect in their entirety, without the need for transposing legislation by national Parliaments. Where there is conflict between an EC regulation and an existing or future national law, the regulation prevails. It should be noted, however, that the regulation is not the method normally adopted for environmental measures.

2.93 *Directives*—'directives' are binding on member states as the result to be achieved. The choice of form and methods of implementation is left to each national government. They are required to implement the measure within the time limit specified in the directive, usually one or two years. Most environmental legislation is made by means of directives and, in the UK, the Government will implement the directive either by primary or secondary legislation. There is, however, a distinction between 'formal' and 'actual' compliance with a directive. Compliance is said to be 'formal' where the domestic law is changed by the introduction of an Act of Parliament or statutory instrument transposing the directive. This may not amount to 'actual' compliance since a regulator may exercise a discretion granted to it not to enforce the law laid down in the statute.

---

[51] See para 2.11.

2.94 *Decisions, recommendations, and opinions*—'decisions' are binding in their entirety on those to whom they are addressed, ie a particular member state, company, or individual. They have the force of law without any need for implementation, however, they are rarely used in environmental law. 'Recommendations' and 'opinions' have no binding effect, being merely the views of the institution issuing them.

Principles of EC environmental legislation

2.95 The original Treaty of Rome did not have any environmental provisions as such—it was concerned fundamentally with trade between member states. However, in the early years, some legislation addressed environmental concerns as a subsidiary issue—for example, Directive 70/220 was principally concerned with harmonizing the measures to be taken against motor vehicle emissions throughout member states, principally an economic objective. In 1973, the EEC adopted its first environmental policies with an Action Programme[52] which informed the development of Community law. However, it was not until the Single European Act 1986 that the environment was formally adopted into community policy when (what are now) Articles 174–176 were incorporated into the Treaty.

2.96 Article 174 provides that community policy on the environment should contribute to the pursuit of the following objectives:

Preserving, protecting, and improving the quality of the environment;
protecting human health;
prudent and rational utilization of resources;
[and] promoting measure at national level to deal with regional or worldwide environmental problems.

2.97 Article 175 provides for the Council to decide what measures should be taken by the Community to achieve the above-mentioned objectives and for general Action Programmes setting out priority objectives, which are discussed below. Article 176 enables member states to introduce more stringent measures to protect the environment, providing they are compatible with the Treaty. The environmental provisions were further enforced by the Maastricht Treaty (1992) and the Treaty of Amsterdam (1997). The latter, in particular, introduced 'sustainable development'[53] as a major EC policy objective in both Articles 2 and 6.

Action programmes on the environment

2.98 The development of European law and policy on the environment has been influenced by the Community Action Programmes. The first Action Programme on

52 See para 2.97.
53 'Sustainable development' is explained at para 3.20.

the environment, 1973–6, listed a number of principles which were subsequently repeated in the Programmes of 1977, 1983, and 1987. The principles included:

(1) The principle of prevention—it is better than cure.
(2) Environmental effects should be taken into account at the earliest possible stage in decision-making.
(3) The polluter pays for the cost of preventing and eliminating harm to the environment.
(4) Activities in one member state should not cause deterioration in the environment of another.
(5) The Community and member states should act together in promoting international environmental policy.
(6) Pollution control should be established at all levels, local, regional, national, EU, and international, at the level best suited to the type of pollution and the geographical zone to be protected.

2.99 The fifth Action Programme, 'Towards Sustainability', targeted five main economic areas, manufacturing, energy, transport, agriculture, and tourism, and set out specific performance targets and a list of actions to be taken. The sixth Action Programme sets priorities for 2000–10 in the following areas: climate change, biodiversity, environmental health, and the sustainable use of natural resources.

Methods of adoption of EC legislation

2.100 EC law is legislation by treaty and therefore any laws depend for their validity on being attributed to one or more treaty articles. Without such correct legal basis, proposed legislative measures, such as Directives, will fail and the ECJ may annul the particular provision. So far as environmental laws are concerned, there are two possibilities. First, Article 175, which was introduced by the Single European Act 1986, provides the basis for environmental measures. The Amsterdam Treaty introduced the co-decision procedure for this provision. Second, Article 95, which is concerned with the harmonization of the single market, could be used for the adoption of an environmental measure as, when introducing such measures, the Commission must 'take as a base a high level of [environmental] protection'. Again, the co-decision procedure gives the Parliament a greater role in formulating legislation.

In fact, the majority of environmental measures are based on Article 175.

Examples of EC environmental legislation

2.101 More than 500 items of environmental legislation have been adopted by the Community. They cover such issues as: water and air quality; emissions into the atmosphere; noise; packaging and packaging waste; end-of-life vehicles; waste electronic and electrical equipment; and energy efficiency and climate change.

2.102 Those Directives of particular relevance to town and country planning (and related topics) include the following: the Environmental Impact Assessment Directive;[54] the Strategic Environmental Assessment Directive;[55] the Habitats Directive;[56] the Waste Framework Directive;[57] and the Control of Major Accident Hazards Directives.[58] The EIA Directive is of particular importance as the domestic courts originally displayed a rather lukewarm attitude to the requirements of the Directive, but the turning point came with the decision of the House of Lords in the case of *Berkeley v Secretary of State for the Environment, Transport and the Regions (No 1)*[59] where a planning permission was quashed on the ground of the failure to carry out an environmental assessment as required by the Directive. The implementation of this Directive is considered in Part 1 of chapter 9, where there is an analysis of the developing case law on the topic.[60]

2.103 We now turn, in the next section, to the enforceability of EC law in member states.

Legal relationship between EC and national legislation

The doctrine of the 'direct effect' of Directives

2.104 As has already been observed, most EC environmental legislation is in the form of Directives. There is a duty on national governments to implement the Directive within (usually) two years after its adoption by the EC. It may be asked, what is the position where a member state chooses not to implement, or implement fully, the terms of a Directive? It was to deal with this situation that the ECJ developed the theory of the 'direct effect' of Directives. The pre-conditions that must exist before a Directive is directly effective are as follows: (i) the terms of the directive must be sufficiently clear and precise; (ii) the directive must be worded unconditionally leaving no room for discretion by the member state; and (iii) the time limit for the implementation of the Directive by the member State must have expired.

2.105 If the above pre-conditions are met, the Directive may be held to have direct effect in a national court and be applied over any inconsistent law. In *Pubblico Ministero v Ratti*[61] R was charged under Italian laws relating to the labelling of dangerous substances in the solvent industry. He contended that under the provisions of two EC harmonization directives, such practices were not illegal. These Directives had not been implemented in Italy—the date for the implementation of one of the

54 See para 9.01.
55 See para 9.65.
56 See para 18.39.
57 See para 18.10.
58 The 'Seveso' I and II Directives—see 15.81.
59 [2001] JPL 58.
60 See para 9.37.
61 [1979] ECR 1629.

Directives, 'A', had passed; however the time limit for implementing the other Directive, 'B', had not yet expired. The court held that R could escape liability under A as it was now directly effective. He could not rely on B because the time limit for its implementation had not yet expired.

2.106 It is necessary at this point to distinguish between 'vertical' and 'horizontal' direct effect.

Vertical direct effect

2.107 Vertical direct effect is illustrated by *Marshall v Southampton Health Authority*.[62] M was employed by the health authority and challenged the employers' compulsory retirement age of 60 for women and 65 for men. Although valid under UK law, the restriction was in breach of Equal Treatment Directive 76/207. The case was referred by the Court of Appeal to the ECJ under Article 177[63] which ruled that the compulsory retirement age was in breach of the Directive. The court stated:

> '[W]here a person involved in legal proceedings is able to rely on a Directive as against the State, he may do so regardless of the capacity in which the latter is acting, whether as employer or public authority.'

2.108 The vertical effect doctrine may also apply to local authorities—in *Fratelli Costanzo SpA v Commune di Milano*,[64] the ECJ held that where a Directive has direct effect and imposes obligations on local authorities, they are bound by it, even if it conflicts with national law. The courts have developed, in connection with the vertical effect doctrine, the concept of the 'emanation of the state'. In *Foster v British Gas Plc*,[65] the ECJ held that a Directive can be invoked against bodies carrying out functions on behalf of the State that are not actually 'the State' in any form, for example, a statutory corporation or an NHS Trust hospital. The court explained that an emanation of the State is 'a body, whatever its legal form, which has been made responsible, pursuant to a measure adopted by the State, for providing a public service under the control of the State and has for that purpose special powers beyond those which result from normal rules applicable between individuals.' In *Griffin v South West Water Plc*,[66] a water company was held to be an emanation of the State even following its privatization.

Horizontal direct effect

2.109 Let us suppose that a Directive, if implemented, would have given rights to a private employee against their private employer. The question that arises is whether

---

62 [1986] ECR 723.

63 See now Article 234—see para 2.122.

64 (1990) 3 CMLR 329.

65 [1991] 2 All ER 705.

66 [1995] IRLR 14.

the Directive can be invoked. It would seem not, because of the 'horizontal effect' of the Directive. Article 249, which confers the power to issue Directives, is binding only on the member state to which it is addressed, thus there is no obligation imposed by Directives on individuals to implement the terms of Directives. This was confirmed in *Faccini Dori v Recreb Srl.*[67]

The doctrine of the 'indirect effect' of Directives

2.110 The difficulties referred to in the previous section in relation to the horizontal effect of non-implemented Directives have led to the development of the doctrine of 'indirect effect'. In *Von Colson v Land Nordrhein Westfalen,*[68] Von Colson wished to bring a claim under the provisions of the Equal Treatment Directive 76/207 which had not been implemented in German law. She based her case on Article 5 of the Treaty of Rome which requires States to 'take all appropriate measures' to ensure fulfilment of their obligations, but the legislative organ of the State had failed to carry out this duty. The ECJ held that it was down to the national court to interpret the national law covering the topic in such a way as to give effect to the terms of the Directive. Thus the Directive was given effect *indirectly* through the interpretation of domestic law. It would seem that the doctrine rests on two factors. First, the national court being willing and able to apply such an interpretive approach; and secondly, there being some body of domestic law covering the same subject matter so that the court can adopt a purposive approach.

2.111 What is the position if there is no existing law covering the same topic before, and none is introduced after, the Directive should have been implemented? The situation arose in *Marleasing SA v LS Commercial Internacional de Alimentacion SA*[69] where the ECJ held that national courts in interpreting national law 'must do everything possible' in view of the wording and the objectives of the Directive to achieve the result laid down by it, in order to comply with Treaty obligations. The court held that the doctrine of indirect effect applies to national legislation, whether that legislation is adopted before or subsequent to the coming into effect of a Directive.

Compensation against the State: the Francovich principle

2.112 The strength of Directives has been further enhanced by the case of *Francovich v Italian Republic.*[70] In this case, the Italian government failed to implement Directive 80/987 harmonizing the laws relating to an employee's remuneration in the event of the employer's insolvency. Employees brought an action against the

---

67 [1994] ECR 1 3325.
68 [1984] ECR 1891.
69 [1992] 1 CMLR 305.
70 [1991] ECR1 5357.

State after the date for the implementation of the Directive claiming compensation payable under the Directive or alternatively, damages from the State. The court held that the Directive was not sufficiently clear as to the institution responsible for the payment of remuneration—it was not therefore directly effective. However, the ECJ considered that where a State had failed to fulfil its obligation to ensure compliance as to the result to be achieved by a Directive, there may be a right of compensation against the State, subject to certain criteria being fulfilled. The criteria are:[71]

(1) The Directive in question confers rights on individuals.
(2) The breach of the Directive is sufficiently serious.
(3) There is a causal link between the State's failure to fulfil its obligations and the damage suffered by the persons affected.

2.113 The right to claim damages is subject to a further proviso—the claimant must be able to show that they have sufficient interest ('locus standi')[72] under the legal rules of their national legal system in order to commence proceedings. One of the difficulties of invoking the *Francovich* principle in the environmental sphere is that few environmental Directives confer explicit rights on individuals.

Proportionality

2.114 The concept of 'proportionality' is a significant restriction on EC environmental measures. It is illustrated by the case of *EC Commission v Denmark*[73] (the 'Danish Bottles case').

2.115 Denmark enacted a law which required beer and soft drink containers to be returnable and re-usable with a refundable deposit. All such containers had to be approved by the country's national agency for environmental protection. The scheme was successful in that over 95 per cent of all such containers were returned and reissued up to 30 times. However, foreign producers were obliged to manufacture or purchase only approved containers which made the import of their products into Denmark costly and difficult. The Commission, supported by the UK, challenged the Danish law, arguing that it was a disguised discrimination against foreign manufacturers and a barrier to free trade under (what is now) Article 28. It was held by the ECJ that the protection of the environment was a mandatory requirement of the Treaty justifying an interference with the operation of the common market. However, the court further held that such interference must be proportionate to the objective pursued. Thus the deposit and return

[71] As amended by *Brasserie du Pecheur v Federal Republic of Germany* [1996] ECR 1 1029.
[72] See paras 20.28 and 20.34.
[73] (1988) ECR 4607.

scheme was acceptable but the restriction on the type of containers was not—it was disproportionate.

2.116 It follows that not only must environmental protection measures be necessary, they must be the least restrictive in the circumstances. Thus Denmark had failed to fulfil its obligations under the Treaty; the law was therefore in conflict with the Treaty and unenforceable. The Single European Act 1986 introduced (what is now) Article 174 which provides that Directives seeking to harmonize EU laws may include a safeguard clause permitting a member state to take provisional measures for environmental reasons. Such measures are subject to inspection by the Commission.

2.117 It should further be noted that Article 176, introduced in 1986, provides that even where an EC environmental measure has been adopted under Article 175, a member State may keep or introduce a later more stringent environmental protection measure, provided it is compatible with the Treaty, and notified to the Commission.

Methods of enforcing EC environmental law

2.118 The Treaty provides a number of mechanisms by which EC law can be enforced. These are discussed below.

Article 226—the Commission

2.119 Article 226 provides that if the Commission considers that a member State has failed to fulfil a treaty obligation, it shall deliver a reasoned opinion on the matter after giving the state concerned the opportunity to submit its observations. If the State concerned does not comply with the opinion within the period laid down by the Commission, the latter may bring the matter before the ECJ.[74] This procedure can be triggered by a complaint from a member State, an organization, or an individual.

Article 227—member States

2.120 Under Article 227 an aggrieved member state may complain to the Commission about an alleged infringement by another member State. Both governments are given the opportunity to make observations to the Commission which then delivers a reasoned opinion. At that stage, or three months after the initial complaint if the Commission does not deliver a reasoned opinion, the aggrieved Government can institute proceedings in the ECJ. It is a method not widely used by member States.

---

[74] See for example *EC Commission v United Kingdom* [1993] 1 Env LR 472 where complaints relating to Blackpool and Southport beaches were brought before the ECJ who held the UK to be in breach of the Bathing Water Directive 76/160.

Article 230—individuals

2.121 Article 230 enables the ECJ to review the legality of actions of EU institutions, including the Parliament, the Council, and the Commission. By this means the validity of Regulations, Directives, and decisions can be challenged within two months of publication of the measure or of its notification to or knowledge of by a claimant. Actions may be brought under this Article by a member State, the Council, the Commission, or the Parliament. Actions may also be brought by any individual (natural or legal) person who must have standing in that the matter must be of 'direct and individual' concern to them. Few environmental measures are likely to fulfil this criterion which will deprive claimants of standing in many cases.[75]

Article 234—preliminary rulings

2.122 Under this provision, any court of a member State may refer any matter of EC law to the ECJ for its interpretation of the law. The court will give a preliminary ruling—this is the method by which most nationals obtain the interpretation and application of EU law.[76] The procedure has played an important part in the expansion of EC environmental law and has enabled the ECJ to take a purposive approach to legislation. However, whether a reference is made is essentially at the discretion of the national court which may consider the EC measure to be sufficiently precise and clear so as not to require a reference. In this sense, the ECJ cannot really be classed as an 'appellate court' to which claimants have a right of appeal.

Human Rights Act 1998

2.123 The Human Rights Act (HRA) 1998, which came into force on 2 October 2000, incorporates the provisions of the European Convention of Human Rights (ECHR) into the domestic law of the UK.

2.124 Before the passing of the HRA 1998, it was only possible for individuals to petition the European Court of Human Rights (ECtHR) at Strasbourg if they had exhausted all domestic remedies. The right to take a case to the European Court still exists after the 1998 Act has been brought into force, but it is now possible for challenges to be made before the domestic courts.

[75] See *Stichting Greenpeace v EC Commission* [1999] Env LR 181 where the action failed on this ground.

[76] See for example *R v Secretary of State for the Environment, ex p RSPB* [1992] Env LR 431, where the House of Lords referred an issue under the Birds Directive to the ECJ.

Convention rights

2.125 Under the HRA 1998, the rights and fundamental freedoms set out in the ECHR and its protocols are defined as 'Convention rights',[77] and so far as it is possible to do so, primary and subordinate legislation must be read and given effect in a way which is compatible with Convention rights.[78] This provision applies to all legislation whenever enacted. It should be understood, however, that this does not give the judges a power to strike down primary legislation that is incompatible with the rights of the Convention, although they may do so in the case of subordinate legislation.

2.126 Under HRA 1998, s. 6, it is unlawful for any public authority[79] to act in a way which is incompatible with Convention rights, unless, as a result of primary legislation, the authority could not have acted differently. A person who is, or would be, the victim of such an unlawful act may bring proceedings against the authority concerned, or rely on the Convention right or rights in issue in any legal proceedings.[80]

2.127 Although, as we have seen, the courts cannot strike down incompatible primary legislation, they may make a 'declaration of incompatibility' where legislation is in conflict with Convention rights.[81] Such declarations do not affect the validity or continuance of the provision in question and are not binding on the parties to the proceedings in which they are made.[82] Nevertheless, the Government may, by statutory instrument, make such amendments to the legislation as are necessary to remove the incompatibility.[83] And HRA 1998, Sch 2 provides for such 'remedial orders', as they are called, to be approved by Parliament.

2.128 HRA 1998, s. 8 provides judicial remedies. In relation to any act (or proposed act) of a public authority which the court finds is (or would be) unlawful, it may grant such relief or remedy or make such order within its powers as it considers just or appropriate. Under this provision damages may be awarded by courts with the power to award damages.

Human rights and land use planning

2.129 The Convention rights which are the most relevant to land use planning are:

> **Article 6(1)**
> **Right to a Fair Trial**
> In the determination of his civil rights and obligations or of any criminal charge against him, everyone is entitled to a fair and public hearing within a reasonable time

77 HRA 1998, s. 1(1).
78 HRA 1998, s. 3(1).
79 A local planning authority is a 'public authority'.
80 HRA 1998, s. 7(1).
81 HRA 1998, s. 4(2).
82 HRA 1998, s. 4(6).
83 HRA 1998, s. 10(2).

by an independent and impartial tribunal established by law. Judgment shall be pronounced publicly but the press and public may be excluded from all or part of the trial in the interest of morals, public order, or national security in a democratic society, where the interests of juveniles or the protection of the private life of the parties so require, or to the extent strictly necessary in the opinion of the court in special circumstances where publicity would prejudice the interests of justice.

2.130 Article 6(2) provides that anyone charged with a criminal offence shall be presumed innocent until proved guilty; and Article 6(3) provides the defendant in a criminal case with certain minimum safeguards, such as the right to be informed of the case against him and to have legal representation.

Article 8
Right to Respect for Private and Family Life

1. Everyone has the right to respect for his private and family life and his correspondence.
2. There shall be no interference by a public authority with the exercise of this right except as is in accordance with the law and is necessary in a democratic society in the interests of national security, public safety or the economic well-being of the country, for the prevention of disorder or crime, for the protection of health or morals, or for the protection of the rights and freedoms of others.

First Protocol, Article 1
Protection of Property

Every natural or legal person is entitled to the peaceful enjoyment of his possessions. No one shall be deprived of his possessions except in the public interest and subject to the conditions provided for by law and by the general principles of international law.

The preceding provisions shall not, however, in any way impair the right of a state to enforce such laws as it deems necessary to control the use of property in accordance with the general interest or to secure the payment of taxes or other contributions or penalties.

2.131 Even before the HRA 1998 came into force, the ECtHR heard complaints from individuals alleging an infringement of the Convention in planning matters.

2.132 In *Bryan v United Kingdom*[84] the applicant had been served with an enforcement notice by the local planning authority alleging a breach of planning control and requiring him to demolish two brick buildings on his land.[85] The applicant appealed to the Secretary of State and an inspector was appointed to conduct an inquiry to determine the appeal; his appeal was dismissed and, after exhausting all domestic remedies, he alleged a breach by the UK of Article 6(1) of the Convention.[86] The applicant claimed he had not received a fair and public hearing by an independent and impartial tribunal.

84 [1996] JPL 386.
85 For enforcement notices see ch 12 below.
86 See above.

2.133 The application failed. The Court concluded that where an appeal against an enforcement notice was determined by an inspector, and his decision was challenged in the courts, there was compliance with Article 6(1). The procedure of the inquiry was quasi-judicial and the inspector was under a duty to act fairly and impartially—the court had the power to intervene if the inspector's reasoning was perverse or irrational. Although the scope of review by the High Court was considered to be sufficient it was held that the inspector himself was not independent or impartial enough to satisfy Article 6(1) because the Secretary of State could at any time recover jurisdiction from the inspector and determine the case himself.

2.134 Article 8 of the Convention was in issue in *Buckley v United Kingdom*.[87] The applicant, a gypsy, placed caravans, without planning permission, on a site that she had acquired. The local planning authority issued an enforcement notice requiring the removal of the caravans. Her appeal against the enforcement notice failed and she was fined for non-compliance. The applicant alleged a violation of Article 8 of the ECHR in that she was unable to live on her own land and provide her children with a stable upbringing and education free from disruption; and that she was a victim of discrimination as a gypsy. The Commission found that Article 8 had been violated and referred the case to the ECtHR which held that although Article 8 applied to the applicant's case, there had been no violation of the Article (by a majority of six votes to three).

2.135 There is no doubt that the cases of *Bryan* and *Buckley* served as an early warning that the planning procedures of the UK were susceptible to challenge on human rights grounds. The HRA 1998 was not long in force before the whole issue came before the courts.

The Alconbury *litigation*

2.136 In *R v Secretary of State for the Environment, Transport and the Regions, ex p Alconbury Developments Ltd*,[88] three (originally four) consolidated appeals came before the House of Lords from a ruling of the Divisional Court (Tuckey LJ and Harrison J) that the procedures whereby the Secretary of State recovered jurisdiction in planning appeals for his own determination were incompatible with Article 6(1) of the Convention. The court had taken the view that as the Secretary of State was the policy-maker, he could not also be an independent and impartial decision-taker without, in effect, being a judge in his own cause. If this decision had been upheld by the House of Lords, wide-ranging reform of long-established procedures for the determination of planning decisions would have been required. However, in May 2001 a unanimous House of Lords held that

---

87 [1996] JPL 1018.
88 [2001] JPL 920.

although Article 6(1) applied to the procedures in question, there was no conflict between these procedures and the Article itself, at least where a public inquiry was held. Thus the Secretary of State could be both policy-maker and decision-taker without infringing Article 6(1).

2.137 Lord Nolan expressed concern that any alternative to the existing procedures (of planning permission and judicial review) would involve the removal from the Secretary of State of his discretion over the grant of planning permission and its vesting in some other body constituting an 'independent and impartial tribunal' for the purposes of Article 6(1). He said: 'In the relatively small and populous island which we occupy, the decisions made by the Secretary of State will often have acute social, economic and environmental implications. A degree of central control is essential to the orderly use and development of town and country. Parliament has entrusted the requisite degree of control to the Secretary of State, and it is to Parliament that he must account for his exercise of it.'

2.138 As to the process of review by the courts, although the planning merits of the decision could not be reviewed, a review of the merits of the decision-making process was fundamental to the court's jurisdiction. Lord Nolan felt that a broad and generous approach had been adopted in the development of judicial review extending not only to points of law in the strict and narrow sense but to such matters as the rationality of the decision and the fairness of the decision-making process.[89] In allowing the appeals and declaring that the impugned powers were not incompatible with the HRA 1998, the House of Lords upheld the status quo and confirmed that the Secretary of State's role is not inconsistent with Article 6(1). In particular, their Lordships rejected the distinction made by the Divisional Court between a decision taken by an inspector and one taken by the Secretary of State, such as where the Secretary of State recovers jurisdiction. Lord Clyde considered that this difference was 'too slight to be of serious consequence'.[90]

Local authority decision-making

2.139 In the wake of the *Alconbury* cases, the focus of human rights challenges shifted to local authority decision-making processes, such as the determination of planning applications.

2.140 In a line of cases including *R (on the application of Vetterlein) v Hampshire District Council; Friends Provident Life* and *Pensions Ltd v Secretary of State for the Environment, Transport and the Regions;* and *R v Secretary of State for the Environment, Transport and the Regions, ex p Adlard* (the cases are discussed in chapter 10[91])

[89] At para 62.
[90] At para 162.
[91] See para 10.155.

the courts considered whether the planning process affords the parties a reasonable opportunity to put their case and whether the system enables decision-makers to be adequately informed.

2.141 Broadly speaking, the courts have upheld the procedures involved and consider that (as with *Alconbury*) the availability of judicial review constitutes an adequate safeguard that the parties receive a fair hearing. For example, it would seem that unless the case is exceptional, an objector would not necessarily have a right to an oral hearing before a planning committee for Article 6 to be satisfied.

Enforcement of planning control

2.142 A considerable number of the cases concerned with Article 8 have involved enforcement action taken by local planning authorities against gypsies who occupy land residentially without planning permission. The issue came before the House of Lords in *South Buckinghamshire District Council v Porter*[92] (which involved consolidated appeals in a number of linked cases) where their Lordships emphasized the requirement for 'proportionality' in cases under the Convention. Thus where injunctions were sought against gypsies occupying land without planning permission, the local planning authority were entitled to consider the personal circumstances of the occupiers. If the local planning authority had considered the hardship involved but nevertheless resolved to seek an injunction, the court would respect the balance which the authority had struck between public and private interests. It would weigh heavily in favour of granting injunctive relief. It is for the court to decide whether the remedy sought is just and proportionate in the circumstances.

2.143 The issue of gypsy sites has continued to exercise the courts post-*Porter*, notably in *First Secretary of State v Chichester District Council*.[93] Three gypsy sites were granted planning permission on appeal to the Secretary of State for the use of land as a residential site with mobile homes and associated outbuildings. Taking into account a local plan policy which permitted gypsy sites subject to strict criteria, the inspector held that permission should be granted even though the development would cause some planning harm. He also held that the local planning authority's refusal of planning permission violated the applicants' rights under Article 8, ie to respect for their private and family life. The local planning authority successfully appealed against the inspector's decision, Blackburne J holding, inter alia, that the inspector had erred in his interpretation of Article 8 in that he had said that it imposed a duty on the local authority to exercise its powers to provide an adequate number of gypsy sites.

[92] [2003] UKHL 26. The case is further discussed at para 12.129.

[93] [2004] EWCA Civ 1248.

2.144 The Court of Appeal held[94] that the inspector had not erred in his application of Article 8; it was clearly engaged in respect of the applicants' homes—the issue was whether interference by enforcement action[95] by the local planning authority was necessary and proportionate under Article 8(2). The inspector was entitled to balance the limited planning harm caused by the site against the personal circumstances of the applicants. The grant of planning permission was restored.

Proportionality

2.145 As we have seen with the *Porter* case discussed in the previous section, under ECHR jurisprudence, 'proportionality' is a key factor to be taken into consideration by decision-makers. Thus there is a balance to be struck between the rights of landowners and public concern for the environment and good standards of planning.

2.146 The striking of a fair balance was in issue in the decision of the Court of Appeal in *Lough v First Secretary of State*[96] where it was held that a dimunition in the value of property caused by neighbouring development did not constitute a separate or independent basis for alleging a breach of Article 8 and Article 1 of the First Protocol. Article 8 required respect for the home but did not give rise to any absolute right to the amenities enjoyed by the landowner or occupant. The role of the Article had to be viewed in the context of the competing rights of other landowners and the public as a whole.

Challenges facing the planning system

2.147 What is the purpose of all this planning legislation? In chapter 1 an outline was given of the development of the country's planning problems from the Industrial Revolution to the end of the Second World War. Many of these problems still exist and indeed have been intensified by current trends. Some problems, such as the concerns about climate change, have come into existence more recently.

The national economy

2.148 Until the downturn of 2008, the national economy enjoyed approximately a decade of growth and stability. But in fact for much of the time since the passing of the Act of 1947, the economy has been under strain. The promotion of exports has been a prime objective of governments. During the late 1970s and early 1980s the economy went through a severe depression; much of the country's

94 Auld LJ dissenting on the article 8 issue.
95 See para 12.01.
96 [2004] EWCA 2005.

manufacturing base disappeared as a result of overseas competition and new technology.

2.149 The town and country planning system cannot produce exports or create jobs; but in the formulation of statutory development plans, economic growth and employment are very important issues. As government policy has stated:[97]

> Planning authorities should have regard to the importance of encouraging industrial and commercial development if the national economy is to prosper, particularly when technological and other requirements of modern business are changing rapidly. All local economies are subject to change and the planning system must make adequate provision for this. Local authorities need to be alive to the future needs of local business. A flexible approach with a range of sites available to business should be provided in plans, and authorities will want to ensure that in allocating sites there is a reasonable expectation of development proceeding.

2.150 The need to encourage sustainable economic development is also a matter to be taken into account in deciding individual planning applications. Sometimes these economic considerations prevail over other planning objectives. An illustration is given below.

2.151 A company manufacturing steel castings sought permission to extend their factory to nearly twice the previous size. The local planning authority refused permission: the existing works constituted a serious injury to local amenities, and any extension would increase this injury; any reconstruction or extension should take place on the opposite side of the road on land which was likely to be zoned for industrial purposes.

2.152 On appeal, it was considered by the inspector that the company's objections to the use of the alternative site were well-founded. The factory was wrongly sited but its complete resiting could only be considered as part of a long-term project which might become practicable at some future date. In the meantime, there was immediate need for expansion of the existing works to enable the company to meet their commitments and satisfy export demands. The proposed development would also benefit amenity by improving the appearance of the works. The company's appeal was accordingly allowed by the Minister.[98]

2.153 Thus the planning system often has to strike a balance between competing objectives and interests.

---

97 PPG 12, 1992, para 5.44. The guidance note has been superseded but the advice is of continuing relevance.

98 Bulletin of Selected Appeal Decisions VIII/14.

Distribution of population and employment

2.154 In 1940 the Barlow Report had commented on the over-concentration of population and industry in the large conurbations and on the tendency of commerce and industry to move from some of the older industrial areas to London and the South-East. The tendency of industry to move to certain favoured areas is just as strong today; much of the new 'High Tech' industrial development is concentrated in the south of England. There is also a heavy concentration of new office buildings in London and some large provincial cities. The result is congestion, particularly in London and the home counties.

2.155 One of the major problems of planning, therefore, is to restrain these tendencies and try to steer new offices and factories to less crowded areas. This is largely a problem of 'regulatory planning'; the development plans will indicate where land is available for new development and planning authorities may also lay down density standards for new buildings.

The outward spread of towns: green belts

2.156 With a high level of development, there is a natural tendency for towns to spread outwards into the surrounding countryside. This outward spread has many disadvantages; those who live in the inner areas are further removed from the countryside; those who find homes further out have a long journey—often in crowded public transport—to their work; those who choose to drive to work add to the congestion on the roads; and in some cases towns may merge to form an almost continuous urban agglomeration.

2.157 One very important method of checking the unrestrained sprawl of towns is the establishment of green belts. Since 1955, local planning authorities have been urged formally to designate green belts originally by means of sketch plans and ultimately by incorporation in development plans. The green belts are correctly perceived as being one of the successes of post-war planning. The green belts serve five purposes: checking the unrestrained sprawl of large built-up areas, safeguarding the surrounding countryside from further encroachment, preventing neighbouring settlements from merging into one another, preserving the special character of historic towns, and assisting urban regeneration. They are also seen as having a positive role in providing access to the countryside for the urban population.

2.158 The establishment of green belts may assist in urban regeneration by encouraging investment in the improvement and redevelopment of older built-up areas. But there will almost certainly be demand for building land beyond the green belts and difficult decisions may have to be made about the location of new development.

Agriculture and the countryside

2.159 Two of the most important aims of planning over the years have been the need in the interests of food production to safeguard good agricultural land and also preserve the countryside for its own sake. Building in the open country away from existing settlements or areas allocated for development in development plans has therefore been strictly controlled.

2.160 These remain important aims, but with some change of emphasis. Post-war agricultural policy aimed to provide the country with a reasonably priced and reliable source of food, at the same time providing the farming industry with a reasonable return. These policies were reinforced when the UK joined the European Community with the result that there was an increase in output and food surpluses. In the early 1990s the government began to pursue a policy of curtailing support and protection to the industry and encouraging the role of market forces. This meant that, for the first time in the twentieth century, land was taken out of production. Landowners were required to consider a range of options for economically viable uses of their land, including recreation and leisure enterprises and the restoration of damaged landscapes and habitats. These changes in agriculture also resulted in a need to find acceptable alternative uses for redundant buildings.

Urban renewal

2.161 The late twentieth and early twenty-first centuries have seen a revival in the vitality of city centres as places to live, work, and enjoy cultural and recreational pursuits. Despite all that has been done to improve these areas, in some of the older conurbations there are still areas of industrial dereliction and housing decay. There is still scope for further redevelopment but this presents challenging problems of finance, administration, and land ownership. Private enterprise, however, has become involved in the provision of new homes in twilight areas; in many towns and cities, local authorities and private builders have entered into partnership agreements. But the problem remains formidable; the legal instruments available to authorities to tackle these problems were discussed earlier in this chapter.[99]

Minerals

2.162 Mineral deposits are a precious national asset. Since minerals must be worked where they are found, it is one of the objects of planning to ensure that valuable deposits are not sterilized by premature building or other forms of development. Mineral working, whether surface or underground, is a form of development for the purposes of TCPA 1990 and is thus subject to the ordinary processes of planning control: these are supplemented by special legislative provisions including the Minerals Act 1981, certain measures under the Environment Act 1995, and by special regulations.[100]

---

99 See paras 2.48–2.61.
100 See ch 17 below.

Traffic and access problems

2.163 In deciding upon the location of new development, it is important to consider the effect on traffic and access to roads. Certain types of building—offices, hotels, and places of public entertainment—obviously attract traffic and create problems of parking and access. Government policy encourages local planning authorities to implement their development policies in ways which help to reduce the length and number of motorized car journeys. An important part of this approach will be the promotion of alternative means of transport with less environmental impact. The theme of 'sustainable development' is reflected in general planning policy guidance which calls on the planning system to shape new development in a way which minimizes the need to travel.

Planning and the environment

2.164 One of the objects of planning control is to preserve and where possible improve the pleasant appearance of streets and buildings and of the countryside. There are several aspects to this problem.

2.165 First, to see that new buildings are of good design; thus planning permission may be refused for a building which is unattractive or is of poor design or which would be unsuitable in its surroundings. Conditions may be imposed requiring the use of certain materials; for instance, requiring a new house in the Cotswolds to be built of stone.

2.166 Secondly, planning permission may be refused for development which would be 'unneighbourly', such as development which would give rise to noise, smoke, smell, or dirt or which would interfere with the day-lighting of adjoining buildings, or which would obtrude upon the privacy of neighbouring residents. Noise, smoke, smell, and other interference with the comfortable enjoyment of land may constitute a nuisance at common law or may be regulated under other legislation such as the Environmental Protection Act 1990.[101] Planning permission does not, as a general rule, override common law rights or statutory restrictions[102] and so in some cases it may be reasonable to permit development in the knowledge that neighbouring residents or landowners are adequately protected. But in other cases, the planning authority may consider that common law rights or other statutes do not afford sufficient protection and accordingly may refuse permission or impose conditions.

---

101 The relationship between planning and other environmental regulatory controls is considered in ch 18.

102 Planning permission may, however, change the character of a neighbourhood for the purposes of the law of nuisance, see para 10.18.

2.167 Thirdly, it may be necessary to give permission for development even though it involves some loss of amenity; mineral workings are an example. In such cases conditions may be imposed in order to minimize the interference with amenity. The preservation and enhancement of the environment is not entirely a matter of regulatory planning, however. The designation of conservation areas[103] gives the planning authority the opportunity to promote positive measures for improving the physical environment in such areas.

Planning and economic competition

2.168 As mentioned earlier, planning has to take account of general economic needs, such as the promotion of exports or mineral supplies. It must also take account of local economic requirements, such as the need for shops or petrol stations. Where there is conflict with other planning objectives—eg the preservation of amenity—the planning authority will have to decide whether the need outweighs the objections. If there is an appeal, the appellant may have to satisfy the Secretary of State that the need exists. Where there is no objection on other planning grounds, the question of need should not be relevant.

2.169 There may, however, be circumstances in which the effects of competition are relevant to planning. For instance, a proposal for a superstore on the outskirts of a small town may threaten the viability of the town's traditional shopping centre; here the question is not the protection of individual businesses from competition, but the protection of the town centre. However, application of current policy, where possible, to locate major retail developments in town centres may mean that, in future, such 'out of centre' development will be less likely than has been the case in the past.

Climate change

2.170 There is compelling evidence that greenhouse gas emissions are bringing about a change in the world's climate. The government has proposed that targets for the reduction of greenhouse gases could be met by a range of sustainable development measures, including: encouraging energy-efficient buildings such as 'zero carbon' homes, locating new developments so as to reduce the need to travel, encouraging walking and cycling in the design of new developments, and supporting an integrated system of public transport.

2.171 Planning is also perceived as having a crucial role in speeding up the transition to renewable and low carbon forms of energy. No doubt the PA 2008, which has introduced a new 'fast track' system of development consent for nationally significant infrastructure including developments in the field of energy, will play a part in this.

---

[103] See para 16.100.

As part of its commitment to climate change policy, in 2007 the Government issued a Planning Policy Statement (PPS) on climate change, as a supplement to PPS 1, *Delivering Sustainable Development*.

Housing

2.172 During the 1960s and early 1970s there was a considerable boom in development schemes—its most outstanding feature was the demand for new homes created by rising levels of prosperity. At the same time, more and more people were able to take holidays away from home with the result that there was a great demand for holiday facilities. This placed considerable pressures on sensitive areas such as National Parks; the Lake District, in particular, is an example. Some of the demand for holiday accommodation was channelled into caravan sites, the location of which caused special problems for local planning authorities. In the mid-1980s and again, from the mid-1990s to the downturn in late 2008, there has been rising demand for land for new homes which has put considerable pressure on the countryside, especially in the South-East of England. Part of the Government's response to this demand has been to increase the proportion of new housing it wishes to see on previously developed land, ie 'brownfield' sites within existing urban areas; and to revise housing density standards.

2.173 In the Government's current view, there will be an increased demand for housing, especially good quality affordable housing. Indeed, on the Government's own estimate, unless the supply of housing is increased from the 2007 rate, the proportion of couples able to afford their own homes would drop from around 50 per cent to 30 per cent by 2026. This rising demand is the result of a number of factors, including an increase in population, a greater proportion of older people in the community, the rise in marital breakdown, and increasing prosperity. The biggest challenge facing the planning system will be finding the land.

Eco-towns

2.174 The 'Eco-towns' intiative is part of the Government's response to the challenges of climate change, the goal of more sustainable living, and the need, as discussed in the previous section, to increase the supply of housing. In 2007, the Government issued the *Eco-towns Prospectus* as an adjunct to the Housing Green Paper.[104] Eco-towns are seen by the Government as a major opportunity for local authorities, developers, and social landlords to collaborate in the building of small new towns. The concept is that the towns should be well-designed, well-serviced, and attractive places to live that connect well with larger settlements close by. They present, in the Government's vision, the opportunity to develop an entire town in order to

104 *Homes for the Future: More Affordable, More Sustainable*, DCLG, 2007.

achieve zero-carbon development. The notion is that this experience will, by example, influence other developments across the country.

2.175 According to the prospectus, the criteria for eco-towns is as follows:

(i) Eco-towns must be new settlements, separate and distinct from existing towns but well linked to them. They need to be additional to existing plans, with a minimum target of 5,000 homes.
(ii) The development as a whole should reach zero-carbon standards, and each town should be an exemplar in at least one other area of environmental sustainability.
(iii) Eco-town proposals should provide for a good range of facilities within the town—a secondary school, a medium scale retail centre, good quality business space, and leisure facilities.
(iv) Affordable housing should make up between 30 and 50 per cent of the total through a wide range and distribution of tenures in mixed communities, with a particular emphasis on larger family homes.
(v) A management body will help develop the town, provide support for people moving to the new community, for businesses, and to co-ordinate delivery of services and manage facilities.

2.176 Originally, the Government invited bids and in total 57 were received and 15 locations were shortlisted for further consideration. The shortlisted locations, according to a government statement, make significant use of brownfield land including former military bases, disused airfields, and previous industrial sites. It is understood that five eco-towns are to be completed by 2016, and up to 10 by 2020. Eco-town schemes will be subject to a planning application which is expected to be determined by the local planning authority. There is to be a Planning Policy Statement on eco-towns which will be an important material consideration in deciding applications—such proposals are likely to be subjected to a rigorous sustainability appraisal.

3

CENTRAL AND LOCAL ADMINISTRATION

3.01 The administration of town and country planning in England is the responsibility mainly of the Secretary of State for Communities and Local Government and the local planning authorities. The ministerial responsibility for the planning system has undergone a series of reorganizations under the period of Labour government which began in 1997.

3.02 In May 1997, as respects England, the former ministries of Environment and Transport were merged and the powers were assumed by the Secretary of State for the Environment, Transport and the Regions. However, in the wake of the General Election of June 2001, this super-ministry was divided into the Department for Environment, Food and Rural Affairs (absorbing the former Ministry of Agriculture, Fisheries and Food) and the Department for Transport, Local Government and the Regions. In 2002 there was a further reorganization and responsibility for planning was transferred to a new department, the Office of the Deputy Prime Minister (ODPM) from the short-lived DTLR.[1] A new Department of Transport was set up at the same time to take over responsibility for transport issues.[2] The year 2006 brought further change. In May of that year a new Department for Communities and Local Government (DCLG) was set up to replace the ODPM and assume responsibility for planning. At the time of writing the Secretary of State is the Rt Hon Hazel Blears MP whose remit, in addition to planning, also includes local government, urban regeneration, and neighbourhood renewal.

3.03 In Wales, planning functions were originally exercised by the Secretary of State for Wales. After 6 May 1999, on the coming into being of the Welsh Assembly under the Government of Wales Act 1998, s. 22, these functions were transferred to the Assembly.[3]

3.04 The Secretary of State for Culture, Media and Sport has certain responsibilities in connection with historic buildings.[4]

The Secretary of State

3.05 As the successor to the Minister of Town and Country Planning, the Secretary of State is charged by statute[5] with the duty of 'securing consistency and continuity in the framing and execution of a national policy with respect to the use and development of land'. It will be observed that his duty relates to the framing and execution of a national policy: he is not called upon to prepare a *plan* in the sense in which local planning authorities are required to do. Moreover, the Secretary of State has over the years laid down *policies* rather than a single policy statement. Thus, he has laid down policies with regard to the dispersal of population and industry from London and other urban centres, green belts, the preservation of agricultural land, and so on.

---

1 The departmental reorganization was legitimized by the Secretaries of State for Transport, Local Government and the Regions and for Environment, Food and Rural Affairs Order 2001, SI 2001 No 2568.

2 Transfer of Functions (Transport, Local Government and the Regions) Order 2002, SI 2002 No 2626.

3 National Assembly for Wales (Transfer of Functions) Order 1999 SI 1999 No 672. Under the Government of Wales Act 2006 the Assembly has primary legislative powers (subject to referendum) including town and country planning.

4 See para 16.01. These powers were formerly exercised by the Secretary of State for National Heritage.

5 Minister of Town and Country Planning Act 1943, s. 1. This section was repealed by the Secretary of State for the Environment Order 1970, SI 1970 No 1681, but that Order transferred the functions of the former Minister of Local Government (who had inherited the functions of the former Minister of Town and Country Planning) to the Secretary of State; it is at least arguable that the duty imposed by the MTCPA 1943, s. 1, still survives.

3.06 In fact, the real authority of the Secretary of State derives from his specific powers and duties under the Town and Country Planning Acts and other planning legislation. The nature and extent of these duties may be illustrated by a few examples.

Duties of the Secretary of State

(1) Making of regulations

3.07 The law of town and country planning is to be found not only in various Acts of Parliament but also in orders and regulations made by the Secretary of State in the form of statutory instruments relevant to planning. Their importance can hardly be exaggerated. The Use Classes Order,[6] for instance, excludes certain changes of use from the definition of development and thus removes them altogether from planning control. By the General Permitted Development Order, the Secretary of State has given a general planning permission for a wide variety of development with the result that it is not necessary in these cases to apply for permission to the local planning authority.[7]

(2) Approval

3.08 Some actions of the local planning authority require the approval of the Secretary of State. Thus, orders for the revocation or modification of planning permission[8] (with a few exceptions) and orders establishing areas of special control for outdoor advertisements[9] do not become effective unless and until they are confirmed by the Secretary of State. Until the Planning and Compensation Act 1991 changed the position, the same principle applied to structure plans.[10]

(3) Appeals

3.09 Other actions of the local planning authority do not require the approval of the Secretary of State, but persons affected may have a right of appeal to him. The most important example is the right of appeal against a decision of the local planning authority refusing planning permission or granting it subject only to conditions. Although the Secretary of State decides each case on its merits and does not move from precedent to precedent as does a judge in a court of law, his decisions nevertheless form something like a body of 'case law' which is invaluable to local authorities and developers in that it shows what policy the Secretary of State is likely to adopt in future cases.

---

6 See para 6.69.
7 See para 7.01.
8 See para 11.01.
9 See para 15.53.
10 See para 4.13.

(4) Powers of direction

3.10 In some cases the Secretary of State may give directions either of a general or a particular nature. An example of a general direction is the Development Plans and Consultation Direction 1999[11] which lays down the procedure to be followed where the planning authority wish to grant planning permission for development which does not accord with the development plan. The Secretary of State may also issue a direction to a local planning authority with regard to a particular matter: he may, for instance, 'call in' an application for planning permission so that he may give a decision himself;[12] this may be done where the proposed development would conflict with the development plan or where the development is of especial public interest such as the application for the processing of nuclear waste at Sellafield.

(5) Default powers

3.11 If the Secretary of State considers that a local planning authority have failed to fulfil some function under the TCPA 1990, he may himself take action. He may, for instance, revoke a planning permission,[13] issue an enforcement notice in respect of a breach of planning control,[14] or make a tree preservation order.[15]

(6) Judicial determinations

3.12 The whole machinery of planning control depends on the definition of 'development' in the TCPA 1990.[16] Under TCPA 1990, s. 192, as substituted by the Planning and Compensation Act 1991, the Secretary of State may, on appeal from the local planning authority, be called upon to certify as to whether any proposed operation or change of use would be lawful.[17] Under s. 191, he may be required to certify the lawfulness of any existing use or operations.[18] And, on an appeal against an enforcement notice in respect of a breach of planning control, he may have to decide whether the matters complained of in the notice constituted development.[19]

3.13 Obviously, the Secretary of State cannot exercise all these functions personally. Most of the decisions are made on his behalf and given in his name by senior civil servants; and, in the case of many planning appeals, the decision may be given by the inspector who conducted the inquiry. Nevertheless, the Secretary of State is

11 See para 8.45.
12 The power to do this is conferred by TCPA 1990, s. 77.
13 TCPA 1990, s. 100.
14 TCPA 1990, s. 182.
15 TCPA 1990, s. 202.
16 See para 6.01.
17 See para 6.179.
18 See para 12.157.
19 TCPA 1990, s. 174. See para 12.157.

responsible for every decision, and (except perhaps for the judicial determinations mentioned above) answerable for it in Parliament.

Framing of national policy by the Secretary of State

3.14 In addition to his statutory functions, the Secretary of State is able to shape planning policy through advice and information. Circulars are sent from time to time to local planning authorities on various aspects of planning control, and frequently contain statements of policy; these circulars are usually available to the public as well, so they are often of considerable assistance to landowners and their professional advisers in negotiations with the local planning authority and in conducting appeals to the Secretary of State. Where a circular contains a statement of the Secretary of State's policy on a particular matter, that statement is a 'material consideration' to be taken into account in deciding upon an application for planning permission: indeed, it has been stated to be binding upon the Secretary of State himself to the extent that, if he is seen to have departed from his policy without some good reason, his decision may be quashed by the court.[20]

3.15 For some years now, policy, information, and advice have also been conveyed through Planning Policy Guidance Notes (PPGs), handbooks, and other publications on such matters as the density of residential areas and the location of retail developments. PPGs, in particular, have become increasingly important. The modern tendency is for advice on law and procedure to be contained in circulars with PPGs being the main source of guidance on policy.

3.16 Until recently there were some 25 PPGs in place covering such matters as general planning policy (PPG 1); Green Belts (PPG 2); Town Centres and Retail Developments (PPG 6); Nature Conservation (PPG 9); Regional Planning (PPG 11); Development Plans and Regional Planning Guidance (PPG 12); the Historic Environment (PPG 15); and Enforcement (PPG 18).

3.17 PPGs are being progressively replaced by Planning Policy Statements (PPSs). Some PPSs are already in place. PPS 11 (Regional Spatial Strategies) has replaced the above-mentioned PPG 11; PPS 12 (Local Development Frameworks) has replaced PPG 12. These statements provide guidance on the new system of development plans introduced by the PCPA 2004. In February 2005, PPG 1 was replaced by PPS 1 (Delivering Sustainable Development) which is intended to set out the 'overarching' planning policies on the delivery of sustainable development through the planning system. The most recent PPS, PPS 25, on Development and Flood Risk, was made in 2006. In 2007, the government issued a supplement to PPS 1 on Climate Change.

---

20 *J A Pye (Oxford) Estates Ltd v West Oxfordshire District Council* [1982] JPL 577.

3.18 In addition to Planning Policy Guidance Notes and Planning Policy Statements, there are Minerals Policy Guidance Notes (MPGs) and Minerals Policy Statements (MPSs). Originally, there were Regional Policy Guidance Notes (RPGs) but these have been upgraded, under the provisions of the PCPA 2004, to statutory development plans in the form of Regional Spatial Strategies.

3.19 The Secretary of State is also responsible for framing the National Policy Statements under the NSIP development consent regime introduced by PA 2008.[21]

Sustainable development

3.20 PPS 1 affirms that sustainable development is the core principle underpinning planning, that is 'development that meets the need of the present without compromising the ability of future generations to meet their own needs', as defined by the World Commission on Environment and Development in 1987. The statement stipulates at paragraph 13 that the following key principles should be applied to ensure that development plans and decisions on planning applications contribute to the delivery of sustainable development:

(1) Development plans should ensure that sustainable development is pursued in an integrated manner, in line with the principles for sustainable development set out in the UK strategy. Regional planning bodies and local planning authorities should ensure that development plans promote outcomes in which environmental, economic, and social objectives are achieved together over time.

(2) Regional planning bodies and local planning authorities should ensure that development plans contribute to global sustainability by addressing the causes and potential impacts of climate change—through policies which reduce energy use, reduce emissions (for example, by encouraging patterns of development which reduce the need to travel by private car, or reduce the impact of moving freight), promote the development of renewable energy resources, and take climate change impacts into account in the location and design of development.

(3) A spatial planning approach should be at the heart of planning for sustainable development.

(4) Planning policies should promote high-quality inclusive design in the layout of new developments and individual buildings in terms of function and impact, not just for the short term but over the lifetime of the development. Design which fails to take the opportunities available for improving the character and quality of an area should not be accepted.

---

21 See para 8.158.

(5) Development plans should also contain clear, comprehensive, and inclusive access policies—in terms of both location and external physical access. Such policies should consider people's diverse needs and aim to break down unnecessary barriers and exclusions in a manner that benefits the entire community.
(6) Community involvement is an essential element in delivering sustainable development and creating safe communities. In developing the vision for their areas, planning authorities should ensure that communities are able to contribute to ideas about how that vision can be achieved, have the opportunity to participate in the process of drawing up the vision, strategy, and specific plan policies, and to be involved in development proposals.

Nature of the Secretary of State's decisions

3.21 The Secretary of State's decisions are of two kinds: policy decisions and judicial determinations.

Policy decisions

3.22 The most important examples arise in connection with planning appeals and development plans. When considering an appeal against a refusal of planning permission or in deciding whether or not to confirm policies in a development plan document which he has referred to himself for decision, the Secretary of State's concern is to achieve or uphold good standards of planning and to ensure that land is not used in a manner detrimental to the public interest. In other words, he is concerned with questions of policy rather than law. He must act within a legal framework—that is, he must not exceed the powers given him by the planning Acts and he must observe the relevant statutory procedures—and, if he fails in either of these respects, the decision may be challenged in the courts. But the courts will not go into the question of whether his decision represents good planning policy. Subject to his responsibility to Parliament, the Secretary of State is the final arbiter of what is good planning.

3.23 Before reaching the decision in any particular case, the Secretary of State usually has to give the parties concerned the opportunity of being heard by a person appointed for the purpose, usually an inspector from the Planning Inspectorate. The hearing by the inspector often takes the form of a public local inquiry at which the persons immediately affected—that is, the landowner (or developer) and the planning authority—will state their case and members of the public can make representations. The parties will often be represented by counsel or a solicitor, and will usually call witnesses on questions of fact or expert opinion. The hearing thus has some of the characteristics of a court of law. But the inspector is not a judge. At one time, the duty of the inspector was limited to making a report to the Secretary of State presenting the facts (as they have emerged from the evidence at the inquiry or from his own inspection of the land in question) together with his own conclusions and recommendations. The Secretary of State is not obliged to accept the report but will reach his own decision.[22] The role of the inspector has been enhanced in recent years and in the great majority of cases he now gives the actual decision on behalf of the Secretary of State.

3.24 Public inquiries of this kind have for many years formed part of the procedure for slum clearance schemes made under the Housing Acts and for compulsory purchase under a number of statutes. Over the years, however, there has been controversy as to their nature and purpose. In some quarters they have been regarded simply as part of the machinery by which Ministers collect information and opinion to enable them to make their decisions. This was described by the Franks Committee Report (1957) as the 'administrative' view.[23]

3.25 The courts have held, in cases under the Housing Acts, that the rules of natural justice must apply to the conduct of the inquiry and that the Secretary of State must not receive information from one party to the inquiry behind the back of the other.[24] It has always been assumed that the same principle applies to planning inquiries. But the courts have never questioned the right of Ministers to obtain information and opinion from other quarters, particularly from other government departments. The administrative school of thought considers it is both proper and reasonable for Ministers to obtain information in this way.

3.26 Diametrically opposed to the administrative view is what the Franks Committee called the 'judicial' view.[25] This regards a planning inquiry as a dispute between the local planning authority and the individual: the ensuing decision should be judicial in the sense that it should be based wholly and directly upon the evidence presented at the inquiry.

3.27 These two opposing views were considered by the Franks Committee, which came to the conclusion that neither provided a satisfactory analysis:[26]

> Our general conclusion is that these procedures cannot be classified as purely administrative or purely judicial. They are not purely administrative because of the provision for a special procedure preliminary to the decision—a feature not to be found in the ordinary course of administration—and because this procedure as we have shown involves the testing of an issue, often partly in public. They are not on the other hand purely judicial, because the final decision cannot be reached by the application of rules and must allow the exercise of a wide discretion in the balancing of public and

22 For a full account of the procedure at a public inquiry, see para 19.15.
23 Franks Committee Report, paras 262, 263.
24 The leading case is *Errington v Minister of Health* [1935] 1 KB 249.
25 Franks Committee Report, paras 262, 264.
26 Franks Committee Report, paras 272, 273, 274.

> private interest. Neither view at its extreme is tenable, nor should either be emphasized at the expense of the other.
>
> If the administrative view is dominant the public inquiry cannot play its full part in the total process, and there is a danger that the rights and interests of the individual citizens affected will not be sufficiently protected. In these cases it is idle to argue that Parliament can be relied upon to protect the citizen, save exceptionally. We agree with the following views expressed in the pamphlet entitled *Rule of Law*. 'Whatever the theoretical validity of this argument, those of us who are Members of Parliament have no hesitation in saying that it bears little relation to reality. Parliament has neither the time nor the knowledge to supervise the Minister and call him to account for his administrative decisions'.
>
> If the judicial view is dominant there is a danger that people will regard the person before whom they state their case as a kind of judge provisionally deciding the matter, subject to an appeal to the Minister. This view overlooks the true nature of the proceedings, the form of which is necessitated by the fact that the Minister himself, who is responsible to Parliament for the ultimate decision, cannot conduct the inquiry in person.

3.28 The Franks Committee endeavoured to find a reasonable balance between these two views by applying the tests of openness, fairness, and impartiality to the current practice.[27] The application of these tests led to the conclusion that some reforms were necessary, and the Franks Committee recommended among other things that the case for the planning authority should be properly notified in advance and supported at the inquiry,[28] that the inspector's report should be available to the parties to the inquiry,[29] that the Minister should submit to the parties for their observations any factual evidence which he obtains after the inquiry, whatever the source, and that he should give the reasons for the decision.[30] These recommendations have largely been put into effect, partly by legislation[31] and partly by administrative action.

3.29 These changes undoubtedly bring current practice much nearer the judicial school of thought. It should not, however, be thought that they are detrimental to the interests of the administrative school. On the contrary, they should strengthen administration by ensuring that only tested and proven information is relied upon in reaching a decision; insistence upon the giving of reasons should also discourage ill-thought-out decisions.

---

27 Franks Committee Report, paras 276, 277.

28 Franks Committee Report, paras 280 ff.

29 Franks Committee Report, para 344.

30 Franks Committee Report, paras 347 ff.

31 Tribunals and Inquiries Act 1992, replacing the Tribunals and Inquiries Acts of 1958 and 1971; Inquiries Procedure Rules 2000. See para 19.01.

Judicial determinations

3.30 Examples of judicial determinations by the Secretary of State have been mentioned above.[32] They involve a decision on a point of law and he must not consider questions of good planning policy. Before making his decision he must give the parties involved an opportunity to be heard, though often the parties agree to submit written representations instead. The Secretary of State's decision may be the subject of an appeal to the High Court.[33]

The Secretary of State's responsibility to Parliament

3.31 The Secretary of State is responsible to Parliament for the manner in which he carries out his functions under the Planning Acts. Questions may be put to him in Parliament and debates held. Parliament has not the time to exercise any detailed supervision, although in recent years Parliamentary Select Committees have had an increasingly influential role in scrutinizing ministerial decision-making. It was also suggested in the pamphlet *Rule of Law*[34] that Parliament lacks the necessary knowledge, but this does not seem to be the case. There have from time to time been important and useful debates, particularly on broader topics such as the conduct of planning inquiries. The Minister's decisions in the 'Essex chalkpit' case and over Stansted airport were specifically debated. Moreover, as an alternative to a formal parliamentary question, MPs often raise matters in correspondence with the Secretary of State.

3.32 There are, however, certain inherent difficulties about taking up individual cases with the Secretary of State. Four situations may arise:

(1) A planning application has been made to the local planning authority and awaits a formal decision. In this case, there is no particular difficulty. The matter can be freely debated in Parliament and the Secretary of State can 'call in' the application giving the parties an opportunity to be heard at a public inquiry.

(2) The local planning authority have refused permission, or granted it subject to conditions, and there is an appeal to the Secretary of State. Is it consistent with the principles laid down by the Franks Committee to express opinion in Parliament with the obvious intention of influencing the Secretary of State's decision? A former Lord Chancellor thought not. In the course of a debate in the House of Lords, a peer commented on the merits of an appeal then before the Minister. The Lord Chancellor rebuked him on the ground that the matter

[32] See para 3.12.
[33] See para 20.01.
[34] See para 3.27.

was sub judice.[35] The rule that there should be no comment on matters which are sub judice comes from the courts of law, and it can be argued that it does not strictly apply to the consideration of a planning application; indeed the Franks Committee mentioned the Minister's responsibility to Parliament as one of the reasons why the judicial view of planning decisions could not be wholly accepted.[36] But if statements can be made in Parliament with the intention of influencing the Secretary of State's decision, what happens to the principle laid down by the Franks Committee that he should only take into account information and opinions which were given at the inquiry or upon which the parties have had an opportunity to comment? Of course, there can be no objection to discussion after the Secretary of State has made his decision, but then it is too late to be of practical value.

(3) The local planning authority have granted permission. In this case there will be no appeal and no inquiry.[37] There can therefore be no objection to parliamentary discussion but it will be of little practical value unless the Secretary of State is prepared to direct the local planning authority to make a revocation order, but this can be very costly in terms of compensation.[38]

(4) The Secretary of State is called upon to give a judicial determination Here, it is submitted, the sub judice principle must apply.

3.33 Where the Secretary of State has called in an application for planning permission, he can, instead of making the final decision himself, make a special development order authorizing the development; the order must be laid before Parliament, thus giving the opportunity for debate. The Secretary of State has occasionally chosen that course, notably in the case of the Windscale (now Sellafield) development. This procedure may perhaps be inconsistent with the principles suggested by the Franks Committee, but there will from time to time be developments of such public concern that the final decision should be the responsibility of Parliament. It is significant that there are other instances where Parliament itself has the last word: for example the taking of land belonging to the National Trust for the construction of motorways.

3.34 Parliamentary control may to some extent have been strengthened by the Parliamentary Commissioner Act 1967. The Commissioner can investigate complaints of maladministration arising from the exercise by the Secretary of State of any of his administrative functions. 'Maladministration', however, probably refers to the manner in which the Secretary of State reaches his decision rather

[35] House of Lords Debates, 1 December 1960.

[36] Franks Committee Report, para 274.

[37] The only person who can appeal to the Secretary of State against the local planning authority's decision on an application for planning permission is the applicant himself: TCPA 1990, s. 78.

[38] For revocation procedure, see para 11.01.

than to its substance, and in some cases under the TCPA 1990 the courts afford redress against this type of maladministration; unless there are special reasons, the Commissioner must not investigate complaints which can be dealt with by the courts.[39]

Local planning authorities

3.35 At local level, the administration of town and country planning (including many of the initiatives in policy making) is the responsibility of the local planning authorities.

3.36 Prior to the reorganization of local government in 1974, the local planning authority (outside Greater London) was usually the county or county borough council. The Minister, however, could set up joint planning boards; these might be constituted for the area, or part of the area, of two or more counties or county boroughs. In fact, only two such joint boards were set up; these were for the Lake District and Peak District national parks. However, both these boards were wound up as from 1 April 1997.

3.37 Under the pre-1974 system a county council might delegate certain planning functions to borough and district councils, and a joint board might likewise delegate certain functions to its constituent authorities. In 1959 provision was made for the compulsory delegation of certain functions to district councils with populations of over 60,000.

3.38 The changes introduced by the Local Government Act 1972, with effect from 1 April 1974, were substantial. A comprehensive two-tier system of county and district councils was established for the whole of England and Wales, except for the Isles of Scilly, the 'all-purpose' county boroughs having been abolished. The Act divided England (exclusive of Greater London[40] and the Isles of Scilly) into six metropolitan counties and 39 non-metropolitan counties. The metropolitan counties were divided into 30 metropolitan districts with populations ranging from 180,000 to 1,100,000. The non-metropolitan counties, before reorganization in 1996, were divided into 333 non-metropolitan districts with populations mostly between 65,000 and 120,000. In Wales there were eight counties divided into 40 districts.

3.39 These districts were in most cases much larger than the former boroughs and county districts, and they were entrusted with direct (instead of delegated) responsibility for many planning matters.

---

39 See para 20.51.

40 Local Government Act 1972, Sch 1.

3.40 The Local Government Act 1985 brought further changes. The Greater London Council and the six metropolitan county councils were abolished, and, apart from Greater London (where there has been further reform), there is only one tier of local government in these areas.

3.41 The unitary model, established in the metropolitan districts, has now been extended to some of the non-metropolitan areas of England. The Local Government Act 1992 established a Local Government Commission charged with the responsibility of conducting a review of local government in the 'shire counties'. The Commission was empowered to make recommendations to the Secretary of State as to structural, boundary, or electoral changes, having regard to the need (a) to reflect the identities and interests of local communities, and (b) to secure effective and convenient local government.[41] The outcome of this review was the creation of some 44 unitary authorities. Some of these new authorities were carved out of existing counties and others resulted from the abolition of administrative counties created in 1974; for example on 1 April 1996 Cleveland County Council was abolished and replaced by four new unitary councils.[42]

3.42 The new unitary authorities were established progressively. The first was the Isle of Wight in 1994, then a further nine in 1996, 14 were scheduled for 1997 and others came after that. The average population of the unitary authorities is 185,000. The result, in the shires, is a patchwork of local authorities, some unitary but others retaining the existing two-tier structure established in 1974.[43] In 2007, the government announced the creation of a further five unitary councils in England to be up and running by 1 April 2009.

3.43 In Wales, the Local Government (Wales) Act 1994 abolished the two-tier structure and replaced it with 21 unitary councils as from 1 April 1996.

3.44 We can now consider the s ystem of local planning authorities under three headings: non-metropolitan England, Wales, and Greater London and the metropolitan counties.

Non-metropolitan England

3.45 Where the two-tier system of local government is retained, there are two tiers of local planning authorities; the county councils act as county planning authorities, and the district councils as district planning authorities. The Secretary of State may set up a joint board as the county planning authority for the area, or part of the area, of two or more counties; and he may also set up a joint board

41 Local Government Act 1992, s. 13.

42 Hartlepool; Redcar and Cleveland; Middlesbrough; and Stockton-on-Tees.

43 *Renewing Local Government in the English Shires*, A Report on the 1992–1995 Structural Review, HMSO.

as the district planning authority for the area, or part of the area, of two or more districts.[44]

3.46 The county planning authority have been responsible for the structure plan and for certain 'county matters' in regard to development control. However, with the abolition of structure plans and the move to statutory regional planning under PCPA 2004, the role of county councils will inevitably be diminished. Nevertheless, under the provisions of the Act, 60 per cent of the membership of each Regional Planning Body will be members of local authorities, including members of county councils. In addition, under PCPA 2004, the regional body is to consult county councils and other authorities with strategic planning expertise in the exercise of its functions relating to the Regional Spatial Strategy.

3.47 Historically, 'county matters' have been restricted to minerals and waste. Under PCPA 2004, county councils must, in respect of any part of their area where there is a district council, prepare a Minerals and Waste Development Scheme.

3.48 The district planning authority will be responsible for preparing local plans for its area; the district authority will also be responsible for administering the statutory provisions relating to the control of development.

3.49 In national parks, however, all planning functions were originally exercisable by the county planning authority (or joint board) with only a few minor exceptions. Where there was no joint or special planning board, however, the county council had to appoint a national park committee to exercise all planning functions except those relating to development plans, and the control of development which either conflicted with those plans or straddled the boundary of the park. However, under the EA 1995, s. 63, the Secretary of State was empowered to establish 'a National Park authority' to replace an existing authority for a national park, and this includes the joint and special boards referred to above.[45] Such authorities are the sole local planning authority for the area of the park.[46]

3.50 In the Norfolk and Suffolk Broads, the Broads Authority is the local planning authority for the exercise of many functions under the planning Acts, such as local plans, development control, listed building control, and conservation areas.[47]

3.51 Finally, where a new unitary authority is constituted in non-metropolitan England, the council will be the local planning authority for all purposes.

44 TCPA 1990, s. 2(1)
45 See para 2.62.
46 TCPA 1990, s. 4A, which prescribes some limited exceptions. See ch 2 above.
47 TCPA 1990, s. 5.

Wales

3.52 As a result of local government reorganization in Wales, from 1 April 1996, the local planning authority for all purposes will be the county or county borough council for each area.[48]

Greater London and the metropolitan counties

3.53 In these areas the local planning authority will normally be the London borough council[49] or the metropolitan district council as the case may be.[50]

3.54 In Greater London certain functions in respect of listed buildings and conservation areas can now be exercised by English Heritage.[51] The 1985 Act required the local planning authorities in Greater London to establish a joint committee to advise those authorities on matters of common interest relating to the planning and development of Greater London; the committee also informed the Secretary of State of the views of those authorities on such matters, including matters on which he had requested their advice. It had the function of informing local planning authorities in the vicinity of Greater London of the views of the authorities in London concerning matters of common interest relating to the planning and development of Greater London.[52] However, with the creation of the Greater London Authority and the office of Mayor under the Greater London Authority Act 1999, the responsibility for strategic planning in London passed to the Mayor and the joint committee was abolished. The reforms brought about by the GLAA 1999, as amended by the GLAA 2007, are discussed below.

Enterprise zones

3.55 In an enterprise zone, the enterprise zone authority will be the local planning authority to the extent mentioned in the order designating the zone.[53]

Urban development areas

3.56 Where an urban development area is designated, the urban development corporation specified in the order will be the local planning authority.[54]

---

48 TCPA 1990, s. 1(1B) as inserted by the Local Government (Wales) Act 1994.

49 The London borough councils were originally constituted by the London Government Act 1963.

50 TCPA 1990, s. 1.

51 See para 16.04.

52 TCPA 1990, s. 3, now repealed.

53 TCPA 1990, s. 6.

54 TCPA 1990, s. 7. See para 2.52.

Designated areas under the Housing and Regeneration Act 2008

3.57 Where an area is designated for regeneration under the HRA 2008, the Secretary of State may make an order designating the Homes and Community Agency (HCA) to be the local planning authority for the whole or part of the area.[55]

Housing action area

3.58 Where a housing action trust is set up for a housing action area under the Housing Act 1988, the Secretary of State may make an order designating the trust as the local planning authority for certain purposes.[56]

Local planning authorities: compulsory purchase for planning purposes

3.59 The implementation of the local planning authority's policies will in some cases depend upon the use of the powers of compulsory purchase for planning purposes contained in the TCPA 1990.

3.60 TCPA 1990, s. 226(1), as amended by PCPA 2004, s. 99,[57] provides that a local authority may compulsorily purchase any land in their area—

(a) the acquisition of which the authority think will facilitate the carrying out of development, redevelopment, or improvement on or in relation to the land;
(b) which is required for a purpose which it is necessary to achieve for the proper planning of the area in which the land is situated.

3.61 However, the authority must not exercise their powers under (a) above unless they think that the development, redevelopment, or improvement is likely to contribute to the provision or improvement of the economic well-being of the area, of its social well-being, or of its environmental well-being.

3.62 Where land is acquired under either (a) or (b) above, the local authority may also compulsory purchase (i) any adjoining land which is required for executing works to facilitate the development or use of the land which is the main subject of the compulsory purchase; (ii) land to replace common land and certain other special categories of land.[58]

3.63 Where land is acquired under TCPA 1990, s. 226, the authority may themselves develop the land (eg by erecting buildings to let) or they may sell or lease the land for private development.[59]

---

55 HRA 2008, ss. 13–15.
56 Housing Act 1988, s. 67; s. 8.
57 The PCPA 2004 amendment came into force on 31 October 2004.
58 TCPA 1990, s. 226(3).
59 Ibid, ss. 233 and 235.

There is an important provision in TCPA 1990, s. 233(5)–(7). If the authority dispose of any land acquired under TCPA 1990, s. 226(1)(a), they are to have regard to the needs of persons who were living or carrying on business or other activities in the area. So far as may be practicable, any such person is to be given the opportunity to obtain accommodation in the area on terms which have regard to the price at which his property was acquired from him. **3.64**

Greater London

3.65 The Greater London Authority Act 1999 created a Greater London Authority consisting of a directly elected Mayor and a 25-member elected Assembly.

3.66 The Authority has power to do anything which it considers will further its principal purposes, ie promoting, in Greater London, (a) economic development and wealth creation; (b) social development; and (c) the improvement of the environment.[60]

3.67 The Mayor is required to publish and keep under review a Spatial Development Strategy (SDS) containing his general policies in respect of the use and development of land in Greater London. The SDS is discussed more fully in a later chapter.[61] Neither the Mayor nor the Greater London Authority will constitute a local planning authority for the area and development control functions will remain primarily with the London boroughs, although in certain circumstances the Mayor can direct that he himself is the local planning authority; this is discussed below. The development plans of the boroughs must be in general conformity with the SDS and the Mayor is empowered to direct the local planning authority of a London borough to refuse planning permission in a particular case.[62] The circumstances in which this power may be exercised were set out originally in the Town and Country Planning (Mayor of London) Order 2000;[63] however this order has now been replaced by a new Mayor of London Order made in 2008.[64]

Applications of potential strategic importance (PSI applications)

3.68 The Mayor of London Order requires the local planning authority of a London borough to forward to the Mayor a copy of any planning application of 'potential strategic importance' (a 'PSI application').[65] The local planning authority may not grant planning permission unless they have sent to the Mayor a copy of the

60 GLAA 1999, s. 30(1) and (2).
61 See para 5.140.
62 GLAA 1999, s. 344 inserting a new s. 74(1B) and (1C) into the TCPA 1990.
63 SI 2000 No 1493.
64 SI 2008 No 580, which came into force on 6 April 2008.
65 Town and Country Planning (Mayor of London) Order 2008, art 5.

permission they propose to grant and the Mayor has indicated that he is content for the authority to grant permission; or 14 days have elapsed from when the Mayor notified the authority that he has received the copy of the proposed permission.[66]

3.69 If the Mayor considers that to grant planning permission on an application notified to him as above would be: (a) contrary to the SDS or prejudicial to its implementation; or (b) otherwise contrary to good strategic planning in London, he may (within the 14-day period to which reference was made above), direct the local planning authority to refuse the application.[67] Before giving such a direction the Mayor is to have regard to a wide range of matters as set out in article 6(2) of the Order, so far as material to the application. The Mayor must give reasons for his direction. Subject to any contrary direction by the Secretary of State, the local planning authority must refuse the application.[68]

3.70 With regard to PSI applications, the Greater London Authority Act 2007 has increased the Mayor's powers in certain respects. Thus the Mayor can direct that he is the local planning authority for a PSI application and determine it himself—in deciding whether to give such a direction, the Mayor must have regard to guidance issued by the Secretary of State. Such a direction must include the Mayor's reasons for giving it and a copy must be sent to the applicant and the Secretary of State. It should be noted that the Mayor will also be the local planning authority in relation to any 'connected applications' such as for listed building or conservation area consent, including any applications for variation or discharge of conditions under connected consents.[69]

3.71 The 2007 Act introduces a requirement for 'representation hearings'. Thus before deciding a PSI application himself[70], the Mayor must give the applicant and the local planning authority an opportunity to make oral representations and must publish a document setting out (i) those persons (other than the applicant or local planning authority) who may make representations at such a hearing; (ii) a procedure for the hearing; and (iii) arrangements for identifying information which must be agreed by persons making oral representations at the hearing. Persons making oral representations must be given at least 14 days' notice of the hearing. The provisions of the Local Government Act 1972 (relating to public admission to meetings and public access to documents) apply to representation hearings.

---

66 SI 2008 No 580, art 5. The Mayor may inform the local planning authority that he does not wish to be consulted pursuant to art 5.

67 SI 2008 No 580, art 6.

68 SI 2008 No 1493, art 6(7) and (8).

69 GLAA 2007, s. 31, inserting a new ss. 2A and 2B into TCPA 1990. Note that there are special rules in GLAA 2007, ss. 32–4 providing for the Mayor to negotiate a s. 106 planning obligation (see ch 13 below) where he is determining a PSI application himself. Such obligations will be enforceable by both the Mayor and the local planning authority.

70 GLAA 2007, s. 35, inserting a new s. 2F into TCPA 1990; Mayor of London Order, art 9.

3.72 We have seen that the local planning authority must notify the Mayor of applications of potential strategic importance. This means any application for planning permission which the local planning authority considers to fall within the schedule to the Mayor of London Order. If the local planning authority receive a planning application which they consider forms part of more substantial proposed development, they must treat the application as an application for planning permission for more substantial development.[71]

3.73 The Schedule to the Order is in four parts, covering: Part 1—large scale development; Part 2—major infrastructure; Part 3—development which may affect strategic policies; and Part 4—development on which the Mayor must be consulted by virtue of a direction of the Secretary of State.

Part 1—Large scale development

Category 1A

3.74 Development which comprises or includes the provision of more than 150 houses, flats, or houses and flats.

Category 1B

3.75 Development (other than purely residential) which comprises or includes the erection of a building or buildings: (a) in the City of London and with a total floorspace of more than 100,000 square metres; or (b) in Central London (other than the City of London) and with a total floorspace of more than 20,000 square metres; or (c) outside Central London and with a total floorspace of more than 15,000 square metres.

Category 1C

3.76 Development which comprises or includes the erection of a building in respect of which one or more of the following conditions is met: (a) the building is more than 25 metres high and is adjacent to the River Thames; (b) the building is more than 150 metres high and in the City of London; or (c) the building is more than 30 metres high and outside the City of London.

Category 1D

3.77 Development which comprises or includes the alteration of an existing building where: (a) the development would increase the height of the building by more than 15 metres; and (b) the building would, on completion of the development, fall within a description set out in paragraph 1 of Category 1C.

[71] Schedule to Town and Country Planning (Mayor of London) 2008 Order, paras 2 and 3.

Part 2—Major infrastructure

Category 2A

3.78 Development which comprises or includes mining operations where the development occupies more than 10 hectares.

3.79 *Category 2B*

1. Waste development to provide an installation with capacity for a throughput of more than (a) 5,000 tonnes per annum of hazardous waste; or (b) 50,000 tonnes per annum of waste; produced outside the land in respect of which planning permission is sought.
2. Waste development where the development occupies more than one hectare.

3.80 *Category 2C*

1. Development to provide: (a) an aircraft runway; (b) a heliport (including a floating heliport or a helipad on a building); (c) an air passenger terminal at an airport; (d) a railway station or tram station; (e) a tramway, an underground, surface or elevated railway; or a cable car; (f) a bus or coach station; (g) an installation for a use within Class B8 (storage or distribution) of the schedule to the Use Classes Order 1987 where the development would occupy more than four hectares; (h) a crossing over or under the River Thames; or (i) a passenger pier on the River Thames.
2. Development to alter an air passenger terminal to increase its capacity by more than 500,000 passengers per year.
3. Development for a use which includes the keeping or storage of buses or coaches where: (a) it is proposed to store 70 or more buses and/or coaches; or (b) the part of the development that is to be used for the keeping or storage of buses and/or coaches occupies more than 0.7 hectares.
4. For the purpose of paragraph 3(b), the area used for keeping or storing buses and/or coaches includes the area occupied by maintenance, administrative, and staff facilities connected with such use.

Category 2D

3.81 Waste development which does not accord with one or more provisions of the development plan in force in the area in which the application site is situated and which falls into one or more of these sub-categories: (a) it occupies more than 0.5 hectares; (b) it is development to provide an installation with a capacity for a throughput of more than: (i) 2,000 tonnes per annum of hazardous waste; or (ii) 20,000 tonnes per annum of waste.

Part 3—Development which may affect strategic policies

Category 3A

Development which would be likely to: (a) result in the loss of more than 200 houses, flats, or houses and flats (irrespective of whether the development would entail also the provision of new houses or flats); or (b) prejudice the residential use of land which exceeds four hectares and is used for residential use. **3.82**

Category 3B

Development (a) which occupies more than four hectares of land which is used for a use in Class B1 (business), B2 (general industrial), or B8 (storage or distribution) of the Use Classes Order 1987; and (b) which is likely to prejudice the use of that land for any such use. **3.83**

Category 3C

Development which is likely to prejudice the use as a playing field of more than two hectares of land which: (a) is used as a playing field at the time of the relevant planning application; or (b) has been used as such at any time in the preceding five years. **3.84**

Category 3D

Development: (a) on land allocated as Green Belt or Metropolitan Open Land in the development plan, in proposals for such a plan, or in proposals for the alteration or replacement of such a plan; and (b) which would involve the construction of a building with a floorspace of more than 1,000 square metres or a material change in the use of such a building. **3.85**

Category 3E

Development which (a) does not accord with the development plan; and (b) comprises or includes the provision of more than 2,500 square metres of floorspace for a use or uses falling within one of the following classes in the Use Classes Order 1987—(i) class A1 (retail); (ii) class A2 (financial and professional); (iii) class A3 (food and drink); (iv) class A4 (drinking establishments); (v) class A5 (hot food takeaways); (vi) class B1 (business); (vii) class B2 (general industrial); (viii) class B8 (storage and distribution); (ix) class C1 (hotels); (x) class C2 (residential institutions); (xi) class D1 (non-residential institutions); (xii) class D2 (assembly and leisure). **3.86**

Category 3F

Development for a use, other than residential use, which includes the provision of more than 200 car parking spaces in connection with that non-residential use. **3.87**

Category 3G

3.88 Development which: (a) involves a material change of use; (b) does not accord with the development plan; (c) where the application site is used or designed to be used wholly or mainly for the purpose of treating, keeping, processing, recovering, or disposing of refuse or waste materials; and (d) the application site: (i) occupies more than 0.5 hectares; or (ii) contains an installation with a capacity for a throughput of more than 2,000 tonnes per annum of hazardous waste; or (iii) contains an installation with a capacity for a throughput of more than 20,000 tonnes per annum of waste.

Category 3H

3.89 Development which: (a) comprises or includes the provision of houses and/or flats; (b) does not accord with the development plan; and (c) is on a site that is adjacent to land used for treating, keeping, processing, recovering, or disposing of refuse or waste materials with a capacity for a throughput of more than: (i) 2,000 tonnes per annum of hazardous waste; or (ii) 20,000 tonnes per annum of waste.

Category 3I

3.90 Development which: (a) involves a material change of use; (b) does not accord with the development plan; and (c) is either: (i) on a site that is used for keeping or storing 70 or more buses and/or coaches; or (ii) on a site on which an area of over 0.7 hectares is used for keeping or storing buses and/or coaches, which area includes the area occupied by maintenance, administrative, and staff facilities connected with such use.

Part 4—Development on which the Mayor must be consulted by virtue of a direction of the Secretary of State

Category 4

3.91 Development in respect of which the local planning authority is required to consult the Mayor by virtue of a direction given by the Secretary of State.

Planning officers, estoppel, and legitimate expectation

Delegation to officers

3.92 At one time it was the almost universal rule in local government that decisions could be taken only by the council itself or by a duly authorized committee. The officers might advise but they could not take decisions even in minor matters.

3.93 However, the TCPA 1968 introduced for the first time powers under which local authorities might delegate the power of decision-making in planning matters to their officers. These provisions authorized delegation to named officers of the power to decide upon applications for planning permission, for consent for outdoor advertising, for a determination as to the necessity for planning permission,[72] for an established use certificate,[73] and for any approval required by the General Development Order or by a condition attached to a planning permission.

3.94 As from 1 April 1974, these powers have been replaced by a much wider power under the Local Government Act 1972, s. 101. This provides that a local authority may arrange for the discharge of any of their functions by an officer of the authority. This must, however, be read subject to any other statutory provisions which in effect preclude delegation; for instance, the adoption of an old-style local plan required a formal resolution of the local planning authority.[74]

Estoppel

3.95 It is, of course, inevitable that, in the day-to-day conduct of affairs, landowners and developers should seek information and advice from planning officers. This is a desirable practice so long as all concerned recognize the position of the planning officer in such matters, where formal authority has not been delegated to him. Local authorities often consider that they are not bound by statements made by their officers in response to requests for information or advice.

3.96 The traditional rule of local government law has been that estoppel cannot operate to prevent or hinder a local authority in the performance of a statutory duty. The local planning authority have a discretion whether or not to serve an enforcement notice.[75] But in *Southend-on-Sea Corpn v Hodgson (Wickford) Ltd*,[76] the Divisional Court considered that the traditional rule applied to the exercise of a statutory discretion as well as to a statutory duty; it was held that the local planning authority were not estopped from serving an enforcement notice, even though the planning officer had written to the company saying that the land had existing use rights and that planning permission was not required.

3.97 The severity of this rule was modified to a limited extent in *Wells v Minister of Housing and Local Government*.[77]

3.98 The applicants, who were builders' merchants and had for many years made concrete blocks, applied in December 1962 for planning permission to erect a concrete

---

[72] This procedure no longer applies and has been replaced by certificates of lawfulness; see para 6.178.

[73] Ibid.

[74] TCPA 1990, s. 43(1).

[75] See para 12.01.

[76] [1962] 1 QB 416, [1961] 2 All ER 46.

[77] [1967] 2 All ER 1041, [1967] 1 WLR 1000.

batching plant 27 feet 6 inches high. In March 1963 the council's surveyor replied that the plant could be regarded as permitted development under class VIII of the General Development Order then in force and it was therefore proposed not to take any further action on the application for planning permission. The applicants then decided to erect a plant 48 feet high. Thinking that the plant would be covered by the council's letter, they applied only for byelaw consent. The local authority granted the byelaw consent and on the official notification deleted the words 'No action should be taken hereunder until the approval of the town planning authority and licensing authority have been taken'.

3.99 The appellants erected the 48 feet-high plant but the council served an enforcement notice requiring it to be taken down. The Minister upheld the enforcement notice.

3.100 The Court of Appeal decided that the letter of March 1963 was a valid determination under TCPA 1971, s. 53.[78] Although there had been no application for such a determination under that section, every application for planning permission contained an implied invitation to make such a determination. As Lord Denning put it: 'a public authority cannot be estopped from doing its public duty, but I do think it can be estopped from relying on technicalities'; in his Lordship's opinion the absence of a formal application for a determination under the Act was a technicality. But as regards the 48 feet-high plant, the council had not positively stated that planning permission was not required, and there had been no application for planning permission in respect of it. The council were therefore entitled to serve an enforcement notice, but the case was remitted to the Minister to consider whether planning permission should be granted having regard to the fact that the appellants had the right (as a result of the letter of March 1963) to erect a plant 27 feet 6 inches high.

3.101 The issue of estoppel also came up in *Lever Finance Ltd v Westminster (City) London Borough Council.*[79] In that case Lord Denning (with whom Megaw LJ concurred) appeared to have considerably extended the scope of estoppel to give some protection to developers who acted upon representations made by a planning officer or other appropriate officer of a local authority. For some years thereafter estoppel was recognized by the courts and the Secretary of State as a defence to an enforcement notice.[80]

---

[78] This was an application to the local planning authority for a formal declaration as to whether planning permission was required.

[79] [1971] 1 QB 222, [1970] 3 All ER 496.

[80] See the decisions of the Divisional Court in *Norfolk County Council v Secretary of State for the Environment* [1973] 3 All ER 673, [1973] 1 WLR 1400; and *Brooks and Burton Ltd v Secretary of State for the Environment* (1976) 35 P & CR 27. For decisions of the Secretary of State see those reported in [1975] JPL 609, 614.

3.102 Since then, however, there has been a return to the traditional doctrine. In *Western Fish Products Ltd v Penwith District Council*,[81] the plaintiffs alleged that a letter from the planning officer had amounted to confirmation that they had an existing use right which covered the uses contemplated by their scheme. The Court of Appeal held that the letter could not reasonably be understood in that sense and that accordingly no estoppel could be founded on it. That finding would have been sufficient to have disposed of the case, but the court also held that as a matter of law the council could not be estopped from performing their statutory duties. The court was prepared to recognize only two exceptions. First, where the planning authority acting as such delegate to an officer authority to determine specific matters, any decision that he makes pursuant to the authority cannot be revoked. This, it is submitted, has nothing to do with the law of estoppel; the officer's decision is made on behalf of the authority and is binding on the authority even if the developer has not yet acted upon it.[82] The second exception recognized by the court related to cases like that which arose in *Wells v Minister of Housing and Local Government*.[83] The court insisted that there must have been (as in *Wells*) an application for planning permission, and were not prepared to accept any greater degree of informality.

3.103 In fact, it is difficult to reconcile the *Western Fish* decision with the reasoning of the majority of the Court of Appeal in *Lever Finance Ltd v Westminster (City) London Borough Council*.[84]

3.104 In the subsequent case of *Newbury District Council v Secretary of State for the Environment*,[85] the House of Lords had to consider whether a developer who had taken up a planning permission was estopped from asserting later on that no such permission was necessary. The House of Lords decided that the developer was not estopped. It is of interest here that Lord Fraser of Tulleybelton and Lord Scarman considered that the doctrine of estoppel should not be introduced into planning law.[86] Despite these sentiments, the *Lever Finance* decision continued to cast its spell many years after it was decided.

3.105 In *Camden London Borough Council v Secretary of State for the Environment*[87] the High Court upheld an inspector's decision on the basis that the facts were similar to *Lever Finance*. Planning permission for a roof extension and terrace was granted

[81] [1981] 2 All ER 204.

[82] Indeed the court itself seems to have doubted whether this was estoppel at all—see the judgment of the court at 209.

[83] See para 3.97.

[84] See para 3.101.

[85] [1981] AC 578, [1980] 1 All ER 731.

[86] At 607, 617 respectively.

[87] [1993] EGCS 83.

on appeal. The appellant's architect then wrote to the local planning authority seeking approval for a 'minor variation' in the approved plans. A planning officer responded that the variation would not constitute development requiring planning permission. The works were duly carried out but subsequently the authority contended that the works differed materially from the approved plans and an enforcement notice was issued. The notice was quashed on the basis that the council's response conveyed ostensible authority and the authority was therefore estopped.

3.106 However, as a result of the decision of the House of Lords *in R v East Sussex County Council, ex p Reprotech (Pebsham) Ltd*,[88] (discussed in the next section), it is extremely doubtful whether the exceptions recognized in the *Lever Finance* and *Wells* cases continue to apply.

Legitimate expectation

3.107 In *R v Leicester City Council, ex p Powergen UK Ltd*,[89] it was argued that letters sent by the local planning authority to the developers, and the subsequent course of dealing, amounted to a clear and unequivocal representation that the developers could commence part of the development without having submitted and obtained approval of details on the remainder of the site.

3.108 The appellants did not base their case on estoppel, but on the public law doctrine of 'legitimate expectation'. However, Dyson J considered that the two principles were closely analogous. Under the doctrine of legitimate expectation, unfairness amounting to an abuse of power may be challenged in the courts where there has been conduct by a public body equivalent to a breach of contract or a breach of representations. To establish such unfairness, the applicant must be able to show that he relied on the representation to his detriment. Dyson J was in no doubt that if the arguments in *Western Fish* had been expressed in terms of legitimate expectation, rather than estoppel, the outcome would not have been any different. It was held that the representations in this case had not founded a legitimate expectation, and the developers were unable to show reliance. The officers did not have delegated powers to vary or waive the planning conditions, so any undertaking allegedly given by them could not be binding on the authority.

3.109 In *R v East Sussex County Council, ex p Reprotech (Pebsham) Ltd*,[90] the House of Lords considered estoppel to be an unhelpful concept in planning law. In *Reprotech*, Tucker J at first instance[91] granted declarations that the appellants had the right to generate electricity at a waste recycling plant on the basis, inter alia, that a

88 [2002] JPL 821.
89 (1999) EGCS 130.
90 [2002] JPL 821.
91 (2000) Env LR 263.

resolution by the council to vary a restriction on opening hours amounted to a determination under the (now repealed) s. 64 TCPA 1990 that planning permission was not required. The Court of Appeal[92] considered that Tucker J had been correct to hold that the resolution could constitute such a determination. This approach did not find favour with the House of Lords.

3.110 Lord Hoffmann (with whom Lords Nicholls, Mackay, Hope, and Scott agreed) did not consider it necessary to consider whether the decision in *Wells v Minister of Housing and Local Government*[93] was correctly decided although like Megaw LJ in Western Fish his Lordship considered that the dissenting judgment of Russell LJ was very powerful. Lord Hoffmann went further—he thought it unhelpful to introduce private law concepts of estoppel into planning law. Estoppels bind individuals on the ground that it would be unconscionable for them to deny what they have represented. These concepts of private law should not be extended into 'the public law of planning control which binds everyone'.[94]

3.111 His Lordship said:

> There is of course an analogy between a private law estoppel and the public law concept of a legitimate expectation created by a public authority, the denial of which may amount to an abuse of power: see *R v North and East Devon Health Authority, ex p Coughlan* [2001] QB 213. But it is no more than an analogy because remedies against public authorities also have to take into account the interests of the general public which the authority exists to promote. Public law can also take into account the hierarchy of individual rights which exist under the Human Rights Act 1998, so that, for example, the individual's right to a home is accorded a high degree of protection . . . while ordinary property rights are in general far more limited by considerations of public interest: see *Alconbury*.[95]
>
> It is true that in early cases such as the *Wells* case and *Lever Finance*, Lord Denning MR used the language of estoppel in relation to planning law. At that time the public law concepts of abuse of power and legitimate expectation were very undeveloped and no doubt the analogy of estoppel seemed very useful. In *Western Fish* the Court of Appeal tried its best to reconcile these invocations of estoppel with the general principle that a public authority cannot be estopped from exercising a statutory discretion or performing a public duty. But the results did not give universal satisfaction: see the comments of Dyson J in the *Powergen* case [2000] JPL 629, 638. It seems to me that in this area, public law has already absorbed whatever is useful from the moral values which underlie the private law concept of estoppel and the time has come for it to stand on its own two feet.

---

92 (2000) Env LR 381.

93 See para 3.97.

94 Lord Hoffmann adopted the words of Lord Scarman in *Newbury District Council v Secretary of State for the Environment* [1981] AC 578, 616.

95 See para 2.136.

4

DEVELOPMENT PLANS BEFORE THE PLANNING AND COMPULSORY PURCHASE ACT 2004

4.01 One of the most important features of the planning system in this country since 1947 has been the requirement that there should be for each area a development plan to provide a basis for both positive and regulatory planning. The nature of these development plans, however, has changed fundamentally over the years. The Act of 1947 resulted in a comprehensive system of development plans prepared by county councils and county borough councils and approved in each case by the Minister. These development plans were based on detailed maps: although there was also a written statement this was more in the nature of an accompaniment to the maps.

4.02 Following the recommendations of the Planning Advisory Group,[1] the Act of 1968 made provision for a quite different 'two-tier' system of development plans consisting of structure plans which deal with strategic issues and which (before the Planning and Compensation Act (PCA) 1991 came into force) required the approval of the Secretary of State, and local plans which have never normally required his approval. Both structure and local plans were essentially policy documents, maps and diagrams being only illustrative. The PCA 1991 maintained

[1] See para 2.10.

the two-tier system but made a number of reforms designed to improve the effectiveness of the system.

4.03 From 1986, in Greater London and the metropolitan areas structure and local plans were replaced by 'unitary development plans' (UDPs) which combined in single plans parts corresponding to structure and local plans; unitary development plans did not normally require the approval of the Secretary of State.

4.04 Parts 1 and 2 of PCPA 2004 have introduced a comprehensive reform of the system of development plans, replacing structure, local, and unitary plans with Local Development Frameworks made by local planning authorities and incorporating statutory Development Plan Documents. Regional planning guidance made by Regional Planning Bodies—which had hitherto been non-statutory—assumed development plan status, to be termed 'Regional Spatial Strategies'. In addition, under the reforms introduced by PCPA 2004, the Spatial Development Strategy for London became a statutory development plan together with the Development Plan Documents which have been adopted or approved by the relevant London Borough. And in Wales, under the 2004 Act, the Assembly must prepare and publish a Wales Spatial Plan and local planning authorities may prepare a Local Development Plan—these will comprise the statutory development plan for the area.

4.05 Although the provisions in TCPA 1990 regarding development plans have been repealed, Schedule 8 of PCPA 2004 contained transitional arrangements for existing development plans and those that were in the course of preparation. These measures are discussed in more detail in chapter 5[2] but in general terms existing adopted plans were to be 'saved' for three years[3] as were draft plans which had reached a certain stage in their adoption process.

4.06 It will therefore be necessary to discuss the 'old' system of plans, and those involved in planning will need to be familiar with both the old and new regimes. The new system, introduced by PCPA 2004, will be considered in chapter 5.

The system of structure and local plans

4.07 The structure and local plans were very different both in concept and presentation from the original 1947 Act development plans. The structure and local plans set out policies and proposals in written form, any maps and diagrams being illustrative of the text rather than the basis of the plan; they were much more concerned with the implementation—in land use and environmental terms—of social and

---

2 See para 5.153.

3 From the coming into force of Parts 1 and 2 of PCPA 2004.

economic policies. The structure plan dealt with the major planning issues for the area and set out broad policies and proposals. Local plans elaborated these broad policies and proposals in more detail, relating them to precise areas of land and thus providing the detailed basis for both positive and regulatory planning.

4.08 The system was introduced gradually. Shortly after the Act of 1968 was passed, the Minister invited 26 authorities[4] to prepare structure plans. Later more authorities were invited to do so, and following local government reorganization in 1974 the remaining county councils were likewise invited. By September 1981 all the original structure plans had been submitted to the Secretary of State for approval and most had been approved with or without modification. The original structure plans, except in the case of two of the old national parks, were prepared by the county councils; they usually related to the whole of a county. Since local plans represented the detailed implementation of the broad policies and proposals of the structure plan, local plans could not normally be formally adopted before the structure plan had been approved; it was thus only later that local plans came forward in any significant numbers for adoption.

4.09 It became clear that the procedures for the approval and adoption of the system of structure and local plans were prone to delay. This was recognized by a White Paper[5] which, echoing the Secretaries' of State concern, noted that, in 1988, outside the Metropolis, only 20 per cent of England and Wales (by population) was covered by a formally adopted local plan. The Paper proposed that the system should be replaced by (at county level) statements of county planning policy, and (at district level) by a comprehensive district development plan. The latter would cover the whole of the district planning authority's area and the preparation of such plans would be mandatory. But these proposals were abandoned in favour of reforming the existing two-tier system of structure and local plans. This was to be achieved by legislation.

4.10 The Planning and Compensation Act 1991 introduced fundamental reforms to the procedures for the adoption of structure and local plans with the object of simplifying and streamlining those procedures. County councils were given the power to adopt their own structure plans; in addition, the PCA 1991 placed a *duty* upon district planning authorities in non-metropolitan areas to prepare a district-wide local plan for the whole of their area.

4.11 Both structure and local plans were kept under review. Proposals for the alteration or replacement of structure and local plans could be made by the relevant authority at any time—indeed, the authority could be directed to do so by the

[4] Some of these were county boroughs under the pre-1974 system of local government.
[5] 'The Future of Development Plans' 1989 (Cm 569).

Secretary of State. Both types of plan had to be based on the results of a survey. Under TCPA 1990, it was the duty of each local planning authority to 'keep under review the matters which may be expected to affect the development of that area or the planning of its development', and they could at any time carry out a fresh survey examining these matters.

4.12 Now that the relevant parts of PCPA 2004 have come into force, a similar obligation to carry out surveys by the body preparing plans arises in connection with the new local development schemes and plans.[6]

Structure plans

4.13 The structure plan was essentially a written statement of the local planning authority's general policies and proposals in respect of the use and development of land in their area. The plan could contain diagrams or other illustrative matter but these had not to be based on a scale map. The procedures for the adoption of structure plan proposals were largely contained in the TCPA 1990 and in the Plans Regulations 1999. The procedures were not markedly different from the procedures for draft revisions of the new spatial strategies discussed in the next chapter.

4.14 After a period of consultation and public participation, the structure plan proposals were put before an 'examination in public' (EIP) held by the local authority. It was for the Secretary of State, however, to select the person or persons who were to conduct the EIP. It was a feature of this procedure that no authority or person—not even the local planning authority that prepared the proposals—had any right to be heard at the EIP. The procedure was thus designed to 'put more emphasis on a broad examination of the strategic issues, while not excluding a consideration of the detailed objections'.[7]

4.15 The panel which conducted the EIP reported to the local planning authority, whose decision to adopt the structure plan proposals was final except for a limited right of challenge in the High Court on matters of law or procedure. The Secretary of State, however, retained considerable supervisory control. Thus, if it appeared to him that the proposals were unsatisfactory, he could, at any time before the local planning authority adopted the proposals, direct the authority to modify them. The Act also provided him with extensive powers to 'call in' all or any part of the proposals, ie refer them to himself for approval or rejection. He could exercise this power at any time from when the plan was placed on deposit until it was adopted.

---

6 See para 5.53 and, in connection with Wales, see para 5.116.
7 325 HL Official Reports (5th series) col 762.

Local plans

4.16 The local plan set out detailed policies and specific proposals for the development and use of the land, and guided most day-to-day planning decisions. Under the system in force from 1968 and before it was amended by the Act of 1991, structure plans were supplemented by any number of local plans, usually prepared by district councils. But the local plan-making powers were discretionary; in particular there was no requirement to prepare a plan or plans for the whole of the local planning authority's area. This resulted in the patchy and often inadequate coverage to which reference was made earlier, and to the practice of local planning authorities relying on non-statutory plans in the development control process. Accordingly, the 1991 Act imposed a duty on local planning authorities in non-metropolitan areas to prepare a single district-wide local plan.

4.17 In addition to a written statement, the local plan had to consist of a map—called the 'proposals map'—illustrating each of the detailed policies and also such diagrams, illustrations, or other descriptive or explanatory matter in respect of the policies as were to be prescribed by the Secretary of State or as the authority thought appropriate. The proposals map was prepared on an ordnance survey base; no scale was prescribed, although policies for any part of the authority's area could be illustrated on a separate map on a larger scale than the proposals map, called an inset map. The requirement that a local plan had to include a scale map is in contrast with the provisions as to structure plans described above.

4.18 In drawing up a local plan, the local planning authority had to see that it conformed to the structure plan, and they were to have regard to such information and other considerations as the Secretary of State prescribed, or in a particular case directed.

4.19 The procedure for the making and adoption of local plans differed from structure plans in that the authority could not adopt the proposed plan unless they had caused a public local inquiry or other hearing to be held for the purpose of considering objections. The presiding inspector was normally appointed by the Secretary of State, and after the inquiry, he reported to the local planning authority. The authority's decision to adopt the plan was final, except for a limited right of challenge in the High Court on similar grounds as to structure plans, as mentioned above. Some plans were challenged in this way.

4.20 A leading case of statutory challenge was the decision of the House of Lords in *Great Portland Estates v City of Westminster*.[8] In this case, the City of Westminster

[8] [1984] 3 All ER 744.

District Plan provided for the protection of certain specified industrial activities within the local planning authority's area. The council wished to safeguard long-established industrial firms who required a central location to maintain their services, but this central location made them vulnerable to pressure from other more profitable uses. Great Portland Estates challenged the validity of this policy. The Court of Appeal held that the council's real concern was the protection of existing occupiers, which was not a permissible consideration; the court therefore quashed the relevant passages in the District Plan.

4.21 The council appealed and the House of Lords allowed the appeal. Lord Scarman said that the test of what was a material consideration in the preparation of development plans or in development control was whether it served a 'planning purpose'; and a planning purpose was one which related to the use and character of the land. A genuine planning purpose was stated in the plan, namely the continuation of industrial uses considered important to the character, vitality, and functions of the area; inevitably this meant that existing occupiers would be protected, but this was not a *purpose* of the plan although it would be *a consequence*.[9]

4.22 This emphasis on the character of the use of the land does not preclude consideration of the human factors. Lord Scarman said that the personal circumstances of an occupier and the difficulties of businesses of value to the community were not to be ignored in the administration of planning control. In a well-known statement his Lordship said: 'It would be inhuman pedantry to exclude from the control of our environment the human factor.' But, as Lord Scarman explained, these factors can be given effect as exceptional or special circumstances; the existence of such cases might be mentioned in the plan, but this would only be necessary where it was prudent to emphasize that, notwithstanding the general policy, exceptions could not be wholly excluded from consideration in the administration of planning control. Although this case concerned an old-style local plan, it seems that the principles laid down on it applied equally to structure plans and to development plans generally, including those made under PCPA 2004.

4.23 Turning to the procedure for the making of the old local plans, there was some criticism that, in dealing with objections, the authority were acting as 'judge in their own cause'. Although this phrase is not wholly appropriate to what was essentially an administrative procedure, there was some force in the criticism. There was a risk, once they had determined on a particular course of action, that the authority would close their minds to possible alternatives as suggested by the objectors or as recommended by the inspector; and even where the authority had in fact given full consideration to possible alternatives, the public might not feel confident that this had been done.

---

9 Author's italics.

4.24 There were, however, safeguards. As with structure plan proposals, the Secretary of State could call in the plan at any time before the authority formally adopted it, and where it was left to the authority to decide whether or not to adopt the plan, objectors might require the authority to state their reasons for doing so; there was also the duty to publish a statement of their decisions on the various objections.

Minerals local plans and waste local plans

Minerals local plans

4.25 Before the reforms to the local plan system introduced by the PCA 1991, several mineral planning authorities[10] had prepared local plans dealing with policies in respect of development for the winning and working of minerals. But these were 'subject plans' of the old type and there was no duty on minerals planning authorities to prepare them. After 1991, however, such authorities came under a duty to prepare a county-wide minerals plan containing the authority's detailed proposals in respect of development consisting of the winning and working of minerals or involving the deposit of mineral waste.

4.26 A minerals local plan had to consist of a written statement and a map illustrating each of the detailed policies and proposals or such other matter as might be prescribed; it had to be in general conformity with the structure plan. The procedures for the making and adoption of minerals local plans were the same as for district-wide local plans discussed in the previous section. The Act specifically provided that minerals and minerals waste policies should be excluded from district-wide local plans. In metropolitan areas, such policies were to be included in the unitary development plans, discussed below.

Waste local plans

4.27 A waste local plan was a plan containing detailed policies in respect of development involving the deposit of refuse or waste materials, other than mineral waste. Originally, such policies were included in structure plans or in subject plans. The PCA 1991 inserted a new s. 38 into the TCPA 1990 requiring county planning authorities in non-metropolitan areas either to prepare a waste local plan or, alternatively, to include their waste policies in their minerals local plan.

4.28 In formulating their waste policies, local planning authorities had to have regard to the national waste strategy and to any 'waste management plan' for their area made under the Environmental Protection Act 1990, and they had to justify any inconsistency in their reasoned justification for the waste local plan.

10 In non-metropolitan areas, the minerals planning authority is the county council.

Waste management plans were the responsibility of the Environment Agency and covered the kinds and quantities of waste to be disposed of, the methods of disposal, and the Agency's policy on the granting of waste management licences.[11]

4.29 The main purpose of waste local plans was to consider the land use implications of the authority's waste policies, but plans could stop short of individual site identification where this was sensible, but still serve a valuable planning function by setting out general criteria against which applications would be considered, indicating the main environmental and geological constraints, and identifying broad areas of search for sites and facilities.

Minerals and waste under PCPA 2004

4.30 Under the reforms made by PCPA 2004, county councils are required to prepare a Minerals and Waste Development Scheme for any part of their area for which there is a district council. These matters are discussed in chapter 5.[12]

Unitary development plans (UDPs)

4.31 In Greater London and the metropolitan counties, structure and local plans were replaced by unitary development plans. Each local planning authority—that is in Greater London each of the London borough councils and in the metropolitan areas each of the metropolitan district councils—were required to prepare a UDP.

4.32 In Wales, the Local Government (Wales) Act 1994 required each unitary council, as local planning authority, to prepare a UDP to replace existing structure and local plans.[13] Following local government reorganization in England, the Secretary of State could direct a unitary authority to prepare a UDP plan for its area. The UDP was in two parts:

(a) Part I consisted of a written statement formulating the authority's general policies in respect of the development and use of land in their area.
(b) Part II consisted of:
   (i) a written statement in such detail as considered appropriate (and so as to be readily distinguishable from other contents of the plan) of their proposals for the development and use of land in their area;
   (ii) a map showing these proposals on a geographical basis;

11 Waste management licences have now been replaced by environmental permits; see ch 18 below.

12 See para 5.113.

13 Local Government (Wales) Act 1994, s. 20, inserting a new s. 10A into the TCPA 1990. The National Parks in Wales (but not England) were required to prepare UDPs.

(iii) a reasoned justification of the general policies in Part I and of the proposals in Part II;
(iv) such diagrams etc as the authority thought appropriate or the Secretary of State prescribed.

4.33 Part I of a UDP was very similar to the structure plan for a non-metropolitan county. Part II consisted of a number of separate parts each similar in effect to a local plan. Although the structural and local elements were included in a single unitary plan, it was not necessary to defer publication and adoption of a unitary plan until every locality had been considered in detail; additional 'parts' could be added from time to time. Although Part I of a UDP was the equivalent of a structure plan, a UDP would not normally be submitted to the Secretary of State for approval; but he had power to call in for approval either the whole or any part of such a plan.

4.34 The procedures for the preparation and adoption of UDPs were modelled closely on the procedures for local plans discussed above. Subject to the Secretary of State's power to call in the plan for his own consideration, it fell to the local planning authority to consider the objections and for this purpose they had to arrange for a local inquiry or other hearing at which objectors had the right to appear. It was of course implicit that the local planning authority gave proper consideration to any recommendations made by the inspector, and they were expressly required to give reasons for their decisions. The local planning authority's decision to adopt a UDP was final subject to the possibility of High Court challenge on substantive or procedural grounds.

4.35 UDPs retained development plan status as saved plans for a period of three years from the coming into force of Parts 1 and 2 of PCPA 2004. Draft plans which had reached the public consultation stage on commencement of Parts 1 and 2 were saved for three years after adoption. Such plans were subject to the procedures in the Development Plans Regulations 1999 which continued to apply for the purpose of the transitional arrangements.[14]

Meaning of 'development plan' under TCPA 1990

4.36 TCPA 1990, s. 54, contained provisions prescribing what plans constituted the 'development plan' for a particular area. Although these provisions have been repealed in relation to England,[15] they are reproduced below, as these plans may

[14] T & CP (Transitional Arrangements) (England) Regulations 2004, SI 2004 No 2205, reg 4. See para 5.153.
[15] PCPA 2004, Sch 9.

have remained in force for some time as saved plans under the transitional arrangements in PCPA 2004.[16]

4.37 In England outside Greater London and the metropolitan counties 'the development plan' was to be taken as consisting of:

(a) the structure plan in force for the time being for the area;
(b) any alterations to the structure plan;
(c) the provisions of the local plan and any minerals local plan or waste local plan for the time being in operation for the area;
(d) any alterations to the plans specified in (c) above;

together with the resolutions of the authority who made or altered the plan, or as the case may be, the Secretary of State's notice of approval.

4.38 In London and the metropolitan counties in England the development plan consisted of:

(a) the provisions of the UDP in force for that area (or the relevant part of the plan) together with the local planning authority's resolution of adoption or the Secretary of State's notice of approval as the case may be;
(b) any alteration to the plan together with the resolution of adoption (or the notice of approval).

4.39 In Wales, until the changes brought about by PCPA 2004 are implemented:[17]

(a) the provisions of the UDP in force for that area (or the relevant part of the plan) together with the local planning authority's resolution of adoption or the Secretary of State's notice of approval as the case may be;
(b) any alteration to the plan together with the resolution of adoption (or the notice of approval).

Development plans under PCPA 2004

4.40 We are now in a position to examine the new development plans regime introduced by PCPA 2004, which is discussed in the next chapter.

---

16 See para 5.153.
17 See para 5.116.

5

DEVELOPMENT PLANS AFTER THE PLANNING AND COMPULSORY PURCHASE ACT 2004

5.01 Parts 1 and 2 of the Planning and Compulsory Purchase Act 2004, which came into force on 28 September 2004, introduced a new system of development plans for England and Wales. In England outside Greater London, the statutory development plan will comprise the Regional Spatial Strategy for the particular region, together with the Development Plan Documents adopted or approved in relation to each local area. The regions are: the North-East; the East of England, the East Midlands, the South-East, the South-West, the West Midlands, Yorkshire and Humberside, and the North-West.[1]

5.02 In Greater London, the statutory development plan is the Spatial Development Strategy, as originally introduced by the Greater London Authority Act 1999 together with the adopted or approved Development Plan Documents of the London boroughs. The London Mayor's Spatial Development Strategy was not originally statutory but PCPA 2004 gave it that status.

5.03 In Wales, Part 6 of PCPA 2004 provides for a Wales Spatial Plan which will constitute the development plan along with the relevant Local Development Plan for the local area.

5.04 The impetus for these reforms lay in the government's concern that the process of updating plans had become expensive and time-consuming. Their essential objectives were stated as being to simplify the existing 'hierarchical' framework of plans, to speed up the system, to make the system more efficient and transparent, and to promote the objectives of sustainable development.[2] 'Spatial' planning, which is not defined in PCPA 2004, has been described as something going beyond traditional land use planning, bringing together and integrating land use policies with other policies and programmes which influence the nature of places and how they function. It would certainly seem to be a broader remit than that prescribed for structure plans over 30 years earlier.

5.05 According to government guidance, spatial plans should: (1) set a clear vision for the future pattern of development with appropriate objectives and strategies;

---

[1] As defined in the Regional Development Agencies Act 1998, Sch 1. National Parks, however, will be covered by a single RSS even where they cross the boundaries of regions.

[2] Green Paper, *Planning: Delivering a Fundamental Change*, DETR 2001; *Sustainable Communities: Delivering through Planning*, ODPM 2002.

(2) consider the needs and problems of the communities they cover and relate them to the use and development of land—this may include social, economic and environmental objectives; and (3) seek to integrate the wide range of activities relating to development and regeneration. This will apparently involve plans working alongside urban and rural regeneration strategies; regional economic and housing strategies; and community development and local transport plans. This will obviously require close co-operation with the bodies responsible for those strategies so as to ensure effective integration.[3]

5.06 Although PCPA 2004 abolished structure plans, local plans, and unitary development plans, there were transitional provisions. Existing adopted plans were saved for three years. Draft plans, providing they had reached a certain procedural stage on the appointed day, were saved for three years after their adoption.[4]

5.07 A most important provision is contained in s. 39, PCPA 2004. It provides that any person or body who exercises any function (a) in relation to the Regional Spatial Strategy; (b) in relation to Local Development Documents; or (c) in relation to the Wales Spatial Plan, must exercise the function with the objective of contributing to the achievement of sustainable development. For this purpose, the person or body must have regard to national policies and advice contained in guidance issued by, in England, the Secretary of State, and in Wales, the Assembly.[5] Although the concept of sustainable development has been a theme in planning policy guidance for some years, it is, for the first time, placed on a statutory footing.

5.08 PCPA 2004 requires that proposed planning documents under the new system must be subjected to a sustainability appraisal. In practice this obligation may be satisfied by meeting the requirements of Strategic Environmental Assessment—this is discussed in Part 2 of chapter 9 below.

5.09 The new planning regime will be covered in this chapter in seven parts: (1) regional planning in England; (2) local development planning in England; (3) development plans in Wales; (4) strategic planning in Greater London; (5) transitional arrangements as between the old system and the new; (6) the meaning of 'development plan' under PCPA 2004; and (7) High Court challenge.

---

3 PPS 1, *Delivering Sustainable Development*, ODPM 2005, para 32.

4 See para 5.151.

5 The section was brought into force in relation to England on 28 September 2004.

Part 1: Regional planning in England

Regional Spatial Strategies (RSS)

5.10 PCPA 2004, Part 1,[6] provides that for each region there is to be an RSS, setting out the Secretary of State's policies, however expressed, in relation to the use and development of land within the region.[7] To begin with, the RSS for a region will be so much of the Regional Planning Guidance (RPG) relating to the region as the Secretary of State prescribes.[8] In this way, regional planning policy is placed on a statutory basis.

Regional planning bodies

5.11 The RSS is effectively to be the responsibility of the Regional Planning Bodies (RPBs). The Secretary of State has the power to recognize a body as the RPB for the region.[9] For the time being at least, the RPBs are the Regional Chambers for the purpose of each region's Regional Development Agency (RDA).

5.12 In order to inject an element of democratic accountability, PCPA 2004 prescribes that not less than 60 per cent of the membership of the RPB must be members of (a) a district council; (b) a county council; (c) a metropolitan district council; (d) a National Park authority; or (e) the Broads authority whose area falls within the region.[10] This provision introduced a concession by the government. The government's aim was for directly elected regional assemblies to be RPBs, however the Regional Assemblies (Preparations) Act 2003 (which paved the way for elected assemblies) empowered Chambers to act as RPBs, unless and until an elected assembly is in place in the region. Where regional assemblies are not established, the existing arrangements are likely to be permanent. The Secretary of State may, at any time, give a direction withdrawing the recognition of a body as RPB and may himself carry out the functions of the RPB as he considers appropriate.[11]

---

6 Part 1 was brought into force by PCPA 2004 (Commencement No 1) Order 2004, SI 2004 No 2097 and PCPA 2004 (Commencement No 2, Transitional Provisions and Savings) Order 2004, SI 2004 No 2202, on 28 September 2004.

7 PCPA 2004, s. 1(1) and (2). If, to any extent, a policy set out in the RSS conflicts with any other statement or information in the RSS, the conflict must be resolved in favour of the policy: PCPA 2004, s. 1(4).

8 PCPA 2004, s. 1(5).

9 Ibid, s. 2(1).

10 Ibid, s. 2(3) and (4). More detailed criteria are set out T & CP (Regional Planning) (England) Regulations 2004 (the 'Regional Planning Regulations') SI 2004 No 2203, regs 4(1) and (2).

11 PCPA 2004, s. 2(5), (6) and (7).

5.13 Under a change made by PA 2008, s. 179, RPBs will be able to enter into an agreement with the RDA for its region, delegating any of the RPB's functions. In addition, where the Secretary of State has the power to exercise any of the functions of the RPB, these powers may also be delegated to the RDA by agreement.

Duties of the RPB in relation to review and monitoring of the RSS

5.14 The RPB must keep under review the RSS and the matters which may be expected to affect development in its region, or any part thereof, and the planning of that development.[12] It is under a duty to monitor the implementation of the RSS throughout the region, and consider whether the implementation is achieving the purposes of the RSS. Further, the RPB must prepare an annual monitoring report on the implementation of the RSS and submit it to the Secretary of State.[13]

Duties and powers of the RPB to other bodies in relation to the RSS

5.15 The RPB must advise any other body or person if it thinks that to do so will help to achieve the implementation of the RSS.[14]

5.16 The RPB is not to work in isolation. It is under a duty itself to seek advice as to the exercise of its functions under the RSS from county, metropolitan district and district councils and National Park authorities within its region. The authorities must advise the RPB to the extent that the exercise of the RPB's functions affect, directly or indirectly, the authorities' own functions.[15] There are also provisions enabling the RPB to arrange with local authorities to discharge, with certain exceptions, the duties of the RPB and to reimburse them for doing so.[16]

5.17 By the above measures the PCPA 2004 secures greater local authority involvement than the government had originally intended, especially involvement by county councils.

Revision of the RSS

5.18 PCPA 2004 contains provisions relating to the revision, either wholly or in part, of the RSS. There is, however, no timetable as such in the Act itself. When it appears necessary or expedient to do so, the RPB must, on giving notice to the Secretary of State, prepare a draft revision of the RSS. It must also prepare a draft

[12] Ibid, s. 3(1) and (2).

[13] Ibid, s. 3(3) and (4). The contents of the report are prescribed by the Regional Planning Regs, reg 5.

[14] PCPA 2004, s. 3(6).

[15] Ibid, s. 4(1) and (2).

[16] Ibid, s. 4(5)–(9).

revision at such time as prescribed by the Secretary of State or if directed by him to do so.[17]

Draft revision of the RSS: form and content

5.19 The form and content of a draft revision of the RSS are prescribed by the Regional Planning Regulations. A draft revision must contain a reasoned justification of the policies contained in it, the policies being clearly distinguished from the reasoned justification.[18] As with the old structure plans, a draft revision must contain a key diagram illustrating the policies contained in the revision.[19] It may also include an inset diagram, drawn to a larger scale than the key diagram, illustrating the application of policies to part of the area covered by the revision.[20] Neither the key diagram nor the inset diagram may be on a map base.[21]

5.20 In preparing a draft revision, the RPB must have regard to national policies and guidance issued by the Secretary of State; the RSS for each adjoining region; the Spatial Development Strategy for Greater London if any part of its region adjoins Greater London; the Wales Spatial Plan if any part of its region adjoins Wales; the resources likely to be available for implementation; and the following matters prescribed by the Regional Planning Regulations:[22]

(a) the strategy prepared for the region under s. 7, of the Regional Development Agencies Act 1998;
(b) the objectives of preventing major accidents and limiting the consequences of such accidents;
(c) the need, in the long term, to maintain appropriate distances between establishments and residential areas, buildings and areas of public use, major transport routes as far as possible, recreational areas and areas of particular natural sensitivity or interest; and
(d) where the region or part of the region for which the draft revision is being prepared adjoins Scotland, the National Planning Framework for Scotland.

5.21 The RPB is also to have regard to the desirability of making different provision for different parts of the region—if it decides to do so, the detailed proposals must first be made by a county council, metropolitan district or unitary authority, or National Park authority, ie authorities with expertise in strategic planning.[23]

---

17 Ibid, s. 5(1) and (2); s. 10(1).
18 Regional Planning Regs, reg 7(2) and (3).
19 See para 4.13.
20 Ibid, reg 9(1).
21 Ibid, reg 9(2).
22 PCPA 2004, s. 5(3); Regional Planning Regs, reg 10(1). Other relevant matters are outlined in PPS 11, paras 2.4 to 2.9.
23 PCPA 2004, s. 5(5).

But if the RPB and the authority in question agree, the detailed proposals may first be made by a district council which is not such an authority, or by the RPB.[24]

5.22 In order to meet the requirements of Strategic Environmental Assessment,[25] in preparing a draft revision, the RPB must carry out an appraisal of the sustainability of the proposals in the draft, and prepare a report of the findings of the appraisal.[26]

Draft revision of the RSS: pre-submission procedure

5.23 The Regional Planning Regulations provide[27] that before submitting a draft revision to the Secretary of State, the RPB must consult such of the 'specific consultation bodies' as are, in the opinion of the RPB, likely to be affected. Specific consultation bodies include local planning authorities whose area is within or adjoins the RPB's region; the RPB for each adjoining region; the Countryside Agency; English Heritage; English Nature; the Environment Agency; the Strategic Rail Authority; and a Regional Development Agency whose area is in or adjoins the local authority's region.[28]

5.24 They must also consult such of the 'general consultation bodies' as the RPB considers appropriate. General consultation bodies means—

(a) voluntary bodies some or all of whose activities benefit any part of the region, and bodies representing the interests of:
(b) different racial, ethnic, or national groups in the region;
(c) different religious groups in the region;
(d) disabled persons in the region; and
(e) persons carrying on business in the region.

5.25 The RPB must then prepare a statement setting out which of the specific and general consultation bodies the RPB have consulted; and how they and any others the RPB consulted, were consulted; a summary of the main issues raised in the consultations; and how those issues have been addressed in the draft revision.[29]

Submission of draft revision of RSS to the Secretary of State

5.26 Submission of the draft revision documents to the Secretary of State must be both in hard copy and electronic form.[30] Copies of the draft revision documents and

---

[24] Ibid, s. 5(6). Form and content for making such different provision are prescribed by the Regional Planning Regs, reg 8.
[25] See para 9.65.
[26] PCPA 2004, s. 5(4).
[27] Regional Planning Regs, reg 11.
[28] Ibid, regs 2 and 11(a).
[29] Ibid, reg 11(2).
[30] Regional Planning Regs, reg 12.

matters must be made available for inspection at the RPB's principal office and such other places within the region as the RPB considers appropriate, as well as publishing them on its website.[31] Local planning authorities within the region must make the documentation available for inspection in like manner unless the draft revision does not relate to any part of their area.[32]

5.27 The RPB must then send to the pre-submission consultees,[33] and such others as the RPB consider may wish to make representations—

(1) the draft revision;
(2) the sustainability appraisal report;
(3) the pre-submission consultation statement;
(4) such of the supporting documents as the RPB consider relevant;
(5) notice of the draft revision matters; and
(6) a statement that the draft revision documents are available for inspection and particulars of the places and times at which they can be inspected.[34]

5.28 Representations on a draft revision must be made within 12 weeks, unless the Secretary of State has informed the RPB that, in his opinion, a draft revision constitutes a minor amendment to the RSS, in which case the period is six weeks.[35] The Secretary of State is not required to have regard to a submission outside these time limits,[36] but he may entertain it should he choose to do so.

5.29 In order to ease the transition from Regional Planning Guidance (RPG) to the RSS, PCPA 2004[37] enables the Secretary of State to make an order specifying that steps taken in the revision of existing RPG should continue to have effect, once the RPG becomes the RSS, as if they were steps taken under PCPA 2004 in the revision of the RSS. Under these powers the Secretary of State has made the Town and Country Planning (Regional Planning Guidance as Revision of Regional Spatial Strategy) Order 2004.[38] This specifies which regional planning guidance should take effect as statutory spatial strategy as if it were made under PCPA 2004.

5.30 The RPB may withdraw a draft revision at any time before it submits the draft to the Secretary of State.[39]

---

31 Ibid, reg 13(1)(a) and (b).
32 Ibid, reg 13(2) and (3).
33 See para 5.23.
34 Regional Planning Regs, reg 13(c).
35 Ibid, reg 13(4) and (5).
36 Ibid, reg 13(6).
37 PCPA 2004, s. 10(7) and (8).
38 SI 2004 No 2208.
39 PCPA 2004, s. 5(9). Procedure is prescribed by the Regional Planning Regs, reg 18.

Community involvement

5.31 For the purpose of exercising its functions revising the RSS, the RPB must prepare and publish a statement of its policies for involving persons who appear to the RPB to have an interest. The RPB must keep those policies under review and from time to time revise the statement and publish it.[40] Further, the Regional Planning Regulations provide that in preparing the regional participation statement, the RPB must include in the statement policies in particular about (i) how and when persons who appear to the RSS to have an interest in its revision will be involved; and (ii) the identification and involvement of other persons to work with the RPB in the revision of the RSS. It must make the statement available for inspection at its principal office and elsewhere as appropriate and also on its website.[41]

5.32 The RPB is under a legal obligation to comply with the statement.[42] No doubt the RPB would be susceptible to legal challenge should it not abide by the policies.

Examination in public

5.33 When the Secretary of State receives a draft revision of the RSS, any persons may make representations upon it, and the Secretary of State may arrange for an examination in public to be held.[43]

5.34 In deciding whether an examination in public should be held, the Secretary of State must have regard to (a) the extent of the proposed revisions; (b) the extent and nature of the consultation on the draft before it was published; (c) the level of interest shown in the draft; and (d) such other matters as the Secretary of State thinks appropriate.[44]

5.35 These provisions make it clear that the Secretary of State is under no compulsion to hold an examination in public and, having regard to the criteria in (a)–(d) above, may proceed to approve the draft revision of the RSS.

5.36 If the Secretary of State decides to hold an examination in public, it will be a statutory inquiry for the purposes of the Tribunals and Inquiries Act 1992, s. 1(1)(c).[45] PCPA 2004 requires that the examination in public must be held before a person appointed by the Secretary of State[46]—in practice it seems that a panel will be appointed for the purpose. PPS 11 states that it may be sufficient for the panel to consist of the Chair and one or more planning inspectors. However a technical

40 PCPA 2004, s. 6(1) and (2).
41 Regional Planning Regs, reg 6.
42 PCPA 2004, s. 6(3).
43 Ibid, s. 7(2) and (3).
44 Ibid, s. 7(4).
45 PCPA 2004, s. 8(7).
46 Ibid, s. 8(2).

assessor may also be needed to provide specialist expertise if there are areas where the Chair or inspector may not have relevant knowledge or experience. By way of example, this may be necessary in order to assess very specialized information put forward on the technical aspects of waste management.[47]

5.37 As with public examinations into structure plan proposals,[48] no person has a right to be heard. Planning Policy provides:

> As the [examination in public] is not a forum for hearing all representations, there is no need to invite all those who objected to the proposals. Nor will it normally be necessary or appropriate to invite everyone who objected or made representations in respect of the selected matters. The panel will ensure that it invites sufficient participants to ensure an effective examination of the strategic issues. This may involve inviting participants who have not made representations in order to contribute to an understanding of the strategic issues. The aim will be to select participants who between them represent a broad range of viewpoints and have a relevant contribution to make thereby enabling an equitable balance of differing viewpoints to be achieved in discussion of the soundness of the revision.[49]

5.38 It seems that the invitation will normally be extended, as appropriate, to the following: the RPB; and possibly adjoining RPBs; the Government Office for the region; Government departments and agencies (including Regional Development Agencies); business and commercial organizations; environmental organizations; community groups; women's groups; and private interest groups or individuals.

5.39 Under the Regional Planning Regulations, the Secretary of State must publish on his website a statement of his decision to hold an examination in public, the address of the place it will be held, the date when it will start, and name of the person appointed by the Secretary of State to conduct the examination.[50]

5.40 If the Secretary of State decides not to hold an examination in public, he must notify that decision to the submission consultees and any other person who has made representations within the time allowed and not withdrawn them.[51] The Secretary of State must then consider the representations.[52]

5.41 Where an examination in public is held, the person appointed or the panel must make a report to the Secretary of State. The Secretary of State must publish the report, as must the RPB and the local planning authorities within the region and

---

47 PPS 11, Annex C, para 7.
48 See para 4.13.
49 PPS 11, Annex C, para 19.
50 Regional Planning Regs, reg 14(1)(a).
51 Ibid, reg 14(2).
52 PCPA 2004, s. 9(1).

any county councils whose area includes a district council.[53] As with the legislation regarding structure plans, there is provision in PCPA 2004 for the Secretary of State, after consultation with the Lord Chancellor, to make regulations with regard to the procedure to be followed at an examination in public.[54]

5.42 The Secretary of State must then consider the report and any representations which have not been considered by the person appointed to hold the examination in public.[55] Whether or not an examination in public has been held, at this point, if the Secretary of State proposes to make any changes to his draft, he must publish them together with his reasons,[56] and notify them in the same manner as the publication of the draft itself.[57] Any person may make representations on the proposed changes and the Secretary of State must consider them.[58]

Publication of the revised RSS

5.43 The Secretary of State must publish the revision of the RSS in its final form incorporating such changes as he thinks fit, with reasons.[59] It should be noted, however, that the Secretary of State may withdraw a draft revision of the RSS at any time before he publishes the RSS revision in accordance with the above procedure.[60]

5.44 As with the legislation regarding old-style development plans, the Secretary of State has default powers. He may prepare a draft revision of the RSS if the RPB have been directed to undertake one and failed to do so within the specified time—similar provisions apply as for draft revisions prepared by the RPB.[61]

5.45 If the Secretary of State considers it necessary or expedient, he may, under s. 10(5) PCPA 2004, at any time revoke the RSS as a whole, or such parts as he thinks appropriate. There is no corresponding power for the RPB to revoke an approved RSS.

National parks

5.46 PCPA 2004, s. 12(2), provides that the Secretary of State may by order direct that if the area of a National Park falls within more than one region, it is treated as falling within such region as is specified in the order. Thus National Parks are not to be divided between regions for the purpose of the RSS.

53 Regional Planning Regs, reg 15.
54 PCPA 2004, s. 8(4) and (5).
55 Ibid, s. 9(1).
56 Ibid, s. 9(2)(a) and (b).
57 Regional Planning Regs, reg 16.
58 PCPA 2004, s. 9(4) and (5).
59 Ibid, s. 9(6)(a) and (b); Regional Planning Regs, reg 17.
60 PCPA 2004, s. 9(7); Regional Planning Regs, reg 18.
61 PCPA 2004, s. 10(5); Regional Planning Regs, reg 23.

5.47 Under this provision the Secretary of State has made the Town and Country Planning (Regions) (National Parks) (England) Order 2004.[62] The order directs that the area of the North Yorkshire Moors National Park and the area of the Yorkshire Dales National Park (both of which fall within more than one region) are to be treated as falling wholly within the Yorkshire and Humber region. Likewise the Peak District National Park, which falls within no less than four regions, is treated as falling wholly within the East Midlands region.

Part 2: Local development planning in England

The Local Development Framework (LDF)

5.48 Part 2 of PCPA 2004 deals with local development planning in England.[63] Structure Plans, Local Plans, and Unitary Development Plans will be replaced by an LDF for each local area.[64] 'Local Development Framework' is a non-statutory designation which denotes a 'portfolio' of planning documents, only some of which will have statutory development plan status.[65] According to PPS 12, paragraph 1.8, local planning authorities are expected to adopt a 'spatial' planning approach to LDFs to ensure the most efficient use of land by balancing competing demands within the context of sustainable development.

5.49 The LDF will include a statutory Local Development Scheme (LDS) which is essentially a programme for the production of planning documents. One element of the LDF is the Statement of Community Involvement (SCI). The SCI is a statement of the authority's policy as to the involvement of members of the community in the development of the local area. Also included in the framework will be the annual monitoring report to the Secretary of State on the implementation of the LDS, and any Local Development Orders (LDOs)[66] and Simplified Planning Zone schemes (SPZs).[67]

5.50 The LDS is to be comprised of Local Development Documents (LDDs) including Development Plan Documents (DPDs), the latter being part of the statutory development plan. There will also be Supplementary Planning Documents (SPDs) which expand upon policies set out in DPDs and will no doubt include such matters as site development briefs and design statements.

---

62 SI 2004 No 2207.

63 The Secretary of State may direct that Part 2 does not apply to the area of an Urban Development Corporation: PCPA 2004, s. 33.

64 Transitional arrangements are discussed at para 5.153.

65 See generally, PPS 12, *Local Development Frameworks*, ODPM 2004.

66 See para 7.67.

67 See para 7.77.

5.51 The distinction between the DPDs and other LDDs is of crucial importance as DPDs are those LDDs which will have been formally approved as part of the statutory development plan for the purpose of s. 38(6) PCPA 2004. Under that provision, if regard is to be had to the development plan for the purpose of any determination under the planning Acts, the determination must be made in accordance with the plan unless material considerations indicate otherwise.

5.52 Thus the LDF, together with the RSS discussed in Part 1 of this chapter, provides the foundation for planning in the local authority's area. The result is a more structurally complex arrangement at the local level than was the case under the TCPA 1990 provisions, but it is to be hoped that the new system has the capacity to be more flexible and responsive to changing circumstances. The portfolio concept allows for parts of the plan to be revised and updated without waiting for a revision of the whole plan.

The survey

5.53 Local planning authorities must keep under review matters which may be expected to affect the development of their area or the planning of its development.[68] These matters include—

(a) the principal physical, economic, social, and environmental characteristics of the area of the authority;
(b) the principal purposes for which land is used in the area;
(c) the size, composition, and distribution of the population of the area;
(d) the communications, transport system, and traffic of the area;
(e) any other considerations which may be expected to affect those matters; and
(f) such other matters as may be prescribed or as the Secretary of State may direct.[69]

5.54 The matters include any changes which the authority think may occur in relation to any other matter and the effect such changes are likely to have on the development or planning of the area. The local planning authority may also keep under review and examine matters in relation to any neighbouring area if they affect the area of the local planning authority, in which case the local planning authority must consult with the local planning authority for the neighbouring area.[70]

68 Ibid, s. 13(1).
69 Ibid, s. 13(2).
70 Ibid, s. 13(4) and (5).

5.55 These provisions regarding the survey that must be carried out by local planning authorities resemble those in TCPA 1990 relating to structure plans,[71] although the scope of the matters to be kept under review has been widened to include social and environmental characteristics—this doubtless accords with the spatial approach to planning and the objectives of sustainable development.

5.56 A similar duty to survey their area falls upon county councils, which (in respect of so much of their area for which there is a district council) must keep under review matters which may be expected to affect development of the area or the planning of its development in so far as it relates to a county matter, or if directed by the Secretary of State to do so.[72] 'County matters' are essentially confined to minerals and waste matters.[73] Such a survey requires the relevant county council to keep under review the following matters:

(a) the principal physical, economic, social, and environmental characteristics of the authority;
(b) the size, composition, and distribution of the population of the area;
(c) the communications, transport system, and traffic of the area; and
(d) any other considerations which may be expected to affect those matters.[74]

5.57 The county council must make available the results of their review to any local planning authority any part of whose area lies within the area of the county council, and, if the relevant RPB so requests, the RPB.[75] These provisions reflect the reduced role of county councils in strategic planning consequent upon the abolition of structure plans.

The Local Development Scheme (LDS)

5.58 The local planning authority must prepare and maintain an LDS. The LDS is a public statement of the local planning authority's programme for the production of LDDs.

5.59 Local planning authorities were required to submit their first LDS to the Secretary of State within six months of the commencement of Part 2 of PCPA 2004, ie 28 March 2005. Planning guidance required the LDS to focus initially on the first three years from the commencement of PCPA 2004, and indicate in general

---

71 See para 4.13.
72 PCPA 2004, s. 14(1) and (2).
73 TCPA 1990, Sch 1, para 1.
74 T & CP (Local Development) (England) Regulations 2004, SI 2004 No 2204: 'The Local Development Regulations', reg 5(1).
75 Ibid, reg 5(2).

terms what future work is proposed beyond that three-year period, particularly in terms of reviewing or supplementing the documents proposed in the scheme.[76]

5.60 The LDS must specify:

(a) the documents which are to be LDDs;
(b) the subject matter and geographical area to which each document is to relate;
(c) which LDDs are to be DPDs—which will form part of the statutory development plan;
(d) which documents, if any, are to be prepared jointly with other LPAs;
(e) any matter or area in respect of which the LPA have agreed, or proposed to agree, to the constitution of a joint committee;
(f) the timetable for the preparation and revision of the documents; and
(g) such other matters as are prescribed.[77]

5.61 The local planning authority must prepare the LDS and submit it to the Secretary of State. A copy must also be sent to the RPB or Mayor of London as appropriate.[78] The Secretary of State may direct the local planning authority, with reasons, to amend the scheme and the local planning authority must comply with such a direction.[79] The LPA must revise the LDS when they consider it appropriate or when directed to do so by the Secretary of State.[80]

5.62 Under changes made by s. 30 of the Greater London Authority Act 2007 (amending PCPA 2004), when the Mayor of London receives the LDS from the local planning authority, the Mayor has power to make a direction requiring amendments to be made, having regard to guidance issued by the Secretary of State. A copy of this direction must also be sent to the Secretary of State, who has power to direct the local planning authority to disregard or modify the Mayor's direction. This new power gives the Mayor the possibility of having greater influence over local development policies in the London boroughs.

Local Development Documents (LDDs)

5.63 PCPA 2004 prescribes that the LDDs 'must (taken as a whole) set out the [local planning] authority's policies (however expressed) relating to the development and use of land in their area'. If, to any extent, a policy set out in an LDD conflicts

76 PPS 11, para 3.19.

77 See the Local Development Regs, reg 8.

78 As to Greater London, See para 5.140.

79 PCPA 2004, s. 15(1), (2), (3) and (4). Local Development Regs, regs 10 and 11, as amended by SI 2008 No 1371.

80 Ibid, s. 15(8).

with any other statement or information in the document, the conflict must be resolved in favour of the policy. The local planning authority must keep under review their LDDs having regard to the results of their survey of the area; a document is an LDD only so far as it, or any part of it, is adopted by resolution of the local planning authority or approved by the Secretary of State, as the case may be.[81]

5.64 The Local Development Regulations prescribe the documents which must be specified in the LDS as LDDs. These are (a) any document containing statements of:

(i) the development and use of land which the local planning authority wish to encourage during any specified period (a 'core strategy');
(ii) objectives relating to design and access which the local planning authority wish to encourage during any specified period;
(iii) any environmental, social, and economic objectives relevant to the attainment of the development and use of land mentioned in paragraph (i) above;
(iv) the authority's general policies in respect of the matters referred to in paragraphs (i) to (iii) above;

and (b) a 'submission proposals map'.[82]

5.65 In addition, the following must be specified as LDDs in the LDS—

any document which (i) relates to part of the area of the local planning authority; (ii) identifies that area as an area of specific change or special conservation; and (iii) contains the authority's policies relevant to areas of significant change or special conservation (an 'area action plan'), and (b) any other document which includes a site allocation policy.

5.66 Of the above-mentioned documents, the following must be DPDs, ie documents having development plan status:

(1) core strategies;
(2) site specific allocations and policies; and
(3) area action plans, where needed.

These will be discussed below.

Core strategy

5.67 The core strategy should set out the key elements of the planning framework for the area—a 'long term spatial vision for the authority's area and the strategic

81 Ibid, s. 17(3), (5), (6) and (8).
82 Local Development Regs, reg 6(1)(a) and (b). As to submission proposals map, see para 5.71.

policies required to deliver that vision'.[83] The core strategy will apply to the whole of the local planning authority's area or to locations within it, but should not identify individual sites. A key diagram will illustrate the broad strategy for the area, unless there are policies which need to be identified on an Ordnance Survey map. The timescale of the core strategy will be a period of at least 10 years from the date of adoption.

Site specific allocations

5.68 These are documents allocating land for specific uses and should not form part of the core strategy. If necessary, greater detail, eg as to design, may be included in an SPD.

Area action plans

5.69 These should be used to provide the planning framework for areas requiring significant change or conservation, for instance to stimulate the regeneration of an area. Local planning authorities could, in their core strategy, set criteria for identifying locations and priorities for preparing area action plans. Further guidance may be provided in SPDs.

5.70 Local planning authorities must include within the LDF an 'adopted proposals map' expressing geographically the development plan policies of the local planning authority. The map is to identify areas of special protection such as green belt, conservation areas, and Areas of Outstanding Natural Beauty, and illustrate in map form the site specific policies in the adopted DPDs.

5.71 Separate inset maps may be used to indicate policies for part of the local planning authority's area, eg area action plans, although these must also appear in their adopted proposals map. When local planning authorities submit their DPDs to the Secretary of State,[84] they must include a 'submission proposals map' to identify how the adopted proposals map will be amended or made subject to additions.

Statement of Community Involvement (SCI)

5.72 The local planning authority must prepare an SCI, that is, a statement of the authority's policy as to the involvement of persons who appear to have an interest in matters relating to development in their area; in the preparation and revision of LDDs; and in the carrying out of the authority's development control functions.[85] Under PCPA 2004 as originally enacted, the SCI was required to be subjected to

83 PPS 12, para 2.10.
84 Local Development Regs, reg 6(1)(b).
85 PCPA 2004, s. 18(1) and (2).

an independent examination,[86] but this requirement is to be removed by s. 180 of PA 2008. Nevertheless, local planning authorities must comply with the SCI when preparing LDDs, once the SCI has been adopted.[87] The SCI is not an LDD for the purpose of conformity with the RSS.[88] However under PCPA 2004, the SCI was required to be specified in the LDS as an LDD but this requirement will be removed by s. 180 of PA 2008.

5.73 Failure by the local planning authority to comply with their SCI could render the adopted document susceptible to legal challenge.

Preparation of Local Development Documents

5.74 PCPA 2004 provides that LDDs must be prepared in accordance with the LDS[89] and be in general conformity with the RSS,[90] or in Greater London, the SDS.[91]

5.75 In preparing an LDD, the local planning authority must have regard to:

(a) national policies and advice contained in guidance issued by the Secretary of State;
(b) the RSS for the region, the SDS for Greater London, the Wales Spatial Plan[92] as appropriate;
(c) the RSS for adjoining regions;
(d) the 'community strategy' prepared by the authority under s. 4 of the Local government Act 2000 and the community strategies for neighbouring authorities;
(e) any other LDD which has been adopted by the authority;
(f) the resources likely to be available for implementing the proposals in the document;
(g) such other matters as the Secretary of State may prescribe.[93]

5.76 The Secretary of State has prescribed the following additional matters to which the local planning authority must have regard:

(a) the strategy prepared under s. 7 of the Regional Development Agencies Act 1998 for the region;
(b) any local transport plan affecting the local planning authority's area;

---

86 See para 5.84.
87 PCPA 2004, s. 19(3).
88 Ibid, s. 18(3). See para 5.63.
89 Ibid, s. 19(1). Detailed requirements as to the form and content of LDDs are prescribed by the Local Development Regs, regs 13 and 14. See generally PPS 12, ch 2.
90 PCPA 2004, s 24.
91 See para 5.140.
92 See para 5.116.
93 PCPA 2004, s. 19(2).

(c) any other policies prepared under s. 108(1) and (2) of the Transport Act 2000 affecting the local planning authority's area;
(d) the objectives of preventing major accidents and limiting the consequences of such accidents;
(e) the need (i) in the long term to maintain appropriate distances between establishments and residential areas, buildings and areas of public use, major transport routes as far as possible, recreational areas and areas of particular sensitivity or interest, and (ii) in the case of existing establishments, for additional technical measures in accordance with Article 5 of Council Directive 96/82/EC on the control of major accident hazards involving dangerous substances so as not to increase the risks to people;
(f) the national waste strategy;
(g) where the authority's area adjoins Scotland, the National Planning Framework for Scotland.

5.77 Further, in preparing LDDs, the authority must, as we have seen, comply with their SCI[94] and must also carry out a sustainability appraisal and prepare a report of its findings.[95] The sustainability appraisal may incorporate the requirements of Strategic Environmental Assessment.[96]

Development Plan Documents: submission and adoption

5.78 DPDs are LDDs that will form part of the statutory development plan for the area and cannot be adopted by the local planning authority unless submitted to the Secretary of State for independent examination. PA 2008, s. 180, inserted a new provision into PCPA 2004 so as to place a duty on local planning authorities to include, in their DPDs, policies designed to secure that the development and use of land in their area 'contributes to the mitigation of, and adaption to, climate change'. This provision will reinforce the existing obligation under s. 19(2)(a) of PCPA 2004 to have regard to, in preparing LDDs, the Secretary of State's policy guidance. This now includes a PPS on climate change.

Pre-submission consultation and public participation

5.79 The Local Development Regulations require consultation and public participation before a proposed DPD is submitted to the Secretary of State.

---

94 See para 5.72.

95 PCPA 2004, s. 19(5). Note that PA 2008 s. 180 removes the requirement to carry out a sustainability appraisal of the proposals in an SPD.

96 See para 9.66.

Consultation

5.80 The local planning authority must consult (a) each of the 'specific consultation bodies' to the extent that the authority thinks that the proposed subject matter of the DPD affects the body, and (b) such of the 'general consultation bodies' as the authority consider appropriate.[97]

5.81 The specific consultation bodies means the RPB[98] and a number of other specified bodies including Natural England, the Environment Agency, English Heritage, the Secretary of State for Transport, Primary Care Trusts, and neighbouring local planning authorities.[99] The general consultation bodies means—

(a) voluntary bodies some or all of whose activities benefit any part of an authority's area; and bodies representing the interest of—
(b) different racial, ethnic, or national groups in the area;
(c) different religious groups in the area;
(d) disabled persons in the area; and
(e) persons carrying on business in the area.

Pre-submission public participation

5.82 Before the local planning authority prepare and submit a DPD to the Secretary of State, they must make copies of the proposals documents and a statement of the proposals matters available for inspection and publish them on their website. They must send the relevant documents to the consultees[100] and publish by local advertisement the fact they are available for inspection.[101]

5.83 Any person may make representations concerning the local planning authority's proposals for a DPD within six weeks from when the relevant documents and matters were made available for inspection. The local planning authority must not submit the DPD to the Secretary of State until they have considered any representations made in accordance with the regulations.[102]

Independent examination

5.84 The local planning authority must submit every DPD, but not every LDD, for independent examination.

---

97 If the document is the LPA's SCI the requirement referred to in (a) would be satisfied if the authority consult the RPB (in London the Mayor); neighbouring authorities; and the Highways Agency; Local Development Regs, reg 25(2)(a) and (b).

98 In Greater London, the Mayor.

99 Local Development Regs, reg 2(1), as amended by SI 2008 No 1371.

100 See para 5.81.

101 Local Development Regs, reg 26.

102 Ibid, reg 27.

5.85 They should not submit such a document unless they have complied with all the relevant requirements contained in the regulations and they think that the document is ready for independent examination. They must also submit the following documents: the sustainability report; the authority's SCI, if adopted; and a statement indicating how the local planning authority has addressed the issues raised in representations received on the proposed DPD.[103]

5.86 Representations including proposals for alternative site allocations must be published by the authority and representations invited. All representations on a development plan document that seek changes to it should specify precisely the changes sought.[104]

5.87 The examination must be carried out by an inspector appointed by the Secretary of State and the purpose of it is to determine whether the DPD satisfies the requirements of PCPA 2004, the regulations relating to the preparation of DPDs, and whether it is 'sound'.[105] Apparently, a DPD will be sound if it meets the following tests in PPS 12, paragraph 4.24:

> *Procedural*
> (i) it has been prepared in accordance with the LDS;
> (ii) it has been prepared in compliance with the SCI, or with the minimum requirements set out in the [Local Development] Regulations where no SCI exists;
> (iii) the plan and its policies have been subjected to a sustainability appraisal.
>
> *Conformity*
> (iv) it is a spatial plan which is consistent with national planning policy and in general conformity with the RSS for the region or, in London, the SDS and it has properly had regard to any other relevant plans, policies, and strategies relating to the area or adjoining areas;
> (v) it has had regard to the authority's community strategy;
>
> *Coherence, consistency, and effectiveness*
> (vi) the strategies/policies/allocations in the plan are coherent and consistent within and between DPDs prepared by the authority and by neighbouring authorities, where cross boundary issues are relevant;
> (vii) the strategies/policies/allocations represent the most appropriate in the circumstances, having considered the relevant alternatives, and they are founded on a robust and credible evidence base;
> (viii) there are clear mechanisms for implementation and monitoring; and
> (ix) the plan is reasonably flexible to enable it to deal with changing circumstances.

---

[103] PCPA 2004, s. 20(1), (2) and (3). Local Development Regs, reg 24(1), as inserted by SI 2008 No 1371.

[104] Local Development Regs, reg 28(3).

[105] PCPA 2004, s. 20(4) and (5).

5.88 It seems that the presumption that the DPD is sound unless it is shown to be otherwise has been dropped from the latest version of PPS 12.

5.89 Any person making representations about a DPD must, if they so request, be given an opportunity to appear before and be heard by the inspector appointed to carry out the examination.[106] If, however, none of those who have made representations wish to exercise their right to appear, the examination may take place using the written representations procedure, and a formal public examination need not be held.

5.90 It seems that the procedure at the examination should be as informal as possible. PPS 12, paragraph D41, states that it is for the inspector to decide how to conduct the proceedings and ensure that the examination is conducted impartially, fairly, and openly. The inspector will normally lead discussions and will set out in advance the matters he or she wishes to discuss based on the evidence submitted, the original representations to the submitted DPD, and on the need to consider the soundness of the plan. The independent examination is a novel procedure in planning law. It is not a public local inquiry; it bears some resemblance to the examination in public into structure plan proposals but with a right to be heard.

5.91 After the examination, the inspector must produce a report with recommendations, giving reasons, and the local planning authority must publish the recommendations and the reasons.[107] The report will be binding on the authority. The local planning authority therefore lose the freedom previously enjoyed under the old-style local plans to propose modifications to the plan contrary to the inspector's recommendations. Under the new system, the local planning authority must incorporate the changes required by the inspector before they adopt the DPD.

Adoption of development plan documents

5.92 Unless there is an intervention by the Secretary of State,[108] the local planning authority must adopt the DPD as soon as practicable after receiving the inspector's report. They must prepare an adoption statement which must state the date on which the DPD was adopted and refer to the right of persons aggrieved to apply to the High Court.[109]

5.93 The local planning authority must publicize that the DPD has been adopted and where and when it can be inspected, and send a copy of the adoption

106 PCPA 2004, s. 20(6). Under PCPA 2004, s. 32, the Secretary of State or LPA may disregard a representation if they think that it is, in substance, a representation or objection to certain orders under the Highways Acts 1959 and 1980 or under s. 1 of the New Towns Act 1981.

107 PCPA 2004, s. 20(7) and (8).

108 See para 5.96.

109 Local Development Regs, reg 24(2). See para 5.175.

statement to those who have asked to be notified. The local planning authority must make the report of the examination and the final sustainability report availale for inspection, informing those who have asked to be notified.[110]

Supplementary Planning Documents (SPDs)

5.94 Supplementary Planning Documents are LDDs but they are not to be DPDs and therefore do not have to be submitted to the Secretary of State for independent examination. SPDs may be adopted by the local planning authority by resolution of the authority as prescribed by Part 5 of the Local Development Regulations 2004, as amended. In a reform made by s. 180 of PA 2008, local planning authorities will no longer need to list SPDs in their LDS and they will be able to produce these documents without the agreement of the Secretary of State. Nevertheless, SPDs will continue to have LDD status and the Secretary of State will be able to require modification of SPDs before adoption, should the Secretary of State wish to do so.

5.95 Policy guidance in the original PPS 12, paragraph 2.43, stated that SPDs:

> 'may cover a range of issues, both thematic and site specific, which may expand policy or provide further detail to policies in a DPD. They must not be used, however, to allocate land. SPDs may take the form of design guides, area development briefs, master plan or issue-based documents which supplement policies in a DPD. The following principles apply to an SPD:
> (i) it must be consistent with national and regional planning policies as well as the policies set out in the DPDs contained in the LDF;
> (ii) it must be clearly cross-referenced to the relevant DPD policy which it supplements (or, before a relevant DPD has been adopted, a saved policy);
> (iii) it must be reviewed on a regular basis alongside reviews of the DPD policies to which it relates; and
> (iv) the process by which it has been prepared must be made clear and a statement of conformity with the SCI must be published with it.'

Local Development Documents: further provisions

Intervention by the Secretary of State

5.96 Under PCPA 2004, the Secretary of State has powers of intervention which are closely modelled on the provisions in TCPA 1990 relating to local plans. Thus, if he thinks that a proposed LDD is unsatisfactory, he may at any time before the

---

110 Ibid, reg 36.

document is adopted direct the local planning authority to modify the document, giving reasons. The local planning authority must comply with such a direction and must not adopt the document unless the Secretary of State gives notice that he is satisfied that they have complied with it.[111]

5.97 At any time before a DPD is adopted by the local planning authority, the Secretary of State may 'call in' the document, ie direct that the document, or any part of it, be submitted to him for approval.[112] In such a case, the local planning authority can take no further step in connection with the adoption of the document until the Secretary of State gives his decision—the document, or the relevant part of it, has no effect until approved by the Secretary of State.[113]

5.98 If the Secretary of State's decision—is given before the authority have submitted their document, the Secretary of State must hold an independent examination. If, however, the direction is given after the authority have submitted their document, but before the inspector has made his recommendations, he must make his recommendations to the Secretary of State.[114]

5.99 The Secretary of State must publish the recommendations made to him by the inspector with the reasons for them. In considering the document, or part thereof, the Secretary of State may take into account any matter which he thinks is relevant, and it is immaterial whether any such matter was taken account of by the local planning authority.[115] The Secretary of State may approve, approve subject to specified modifications, or reject the document, or part thereof; he must give reasons for his decision.[116]

5.100 In exercising these functions, the Secretary of State must have regard to the LDS.[117]

Withdrawal of LDDs

5.101 The local planning authority may withdraw an LDD at any time before it is adopted, but once a DPD has been been submitted for independent examination, it may be withdrawn only if the inspector so recommends and that recommendation is not overruled by the Secretary of State; or if the Secretary of State directs that the document be withdrawn.[118]

---

111 PCPA 2004, s. 21(1) and (2); Local Development Regs, reg 39.
112 Ibid, s. 21(4); Local Development Regs, regs 40–4.
113 Ibid, s. 21(5)(a) and (b).
114 Local Development Regs, s. 21(5)(c).
115 Ibid, s. 21(6), (7) and (8).
116 Ibid, s. 21(9).
117 Ibid, s. 21(10).
118 Ibid, s. 22(1) and (2).

Conformity with RSS

5.102 LDDs must be in general conformity with the RSS, or in Greater London, the SDS. In the case of DPDs, the local planning authority are required to seek the written opinion of the RPB, or in Greater London, the Mayor, as to their conformity with the relevant strategy.[119]

5.103 The authority may request the opinion of these bodies with regard to any other LDD. Whether or not the local planning authority request the opinion of the RPB or Mayor, as appropriate, the RPB or Mayor may give their opinion as to conformity.[120]

5.104 If in the opinion of the RPB or Mayor, a document is not in conformity with the RSS or SDS, as the case may be, they must be taken to have made representations seeking a change to the document.[121] There is an exception in the case of the RPB, where the Secretary of State can direct that this provision must be ignored.[122] The implication of these provisions is that the deemed representations will be made before the DPD is submitted for independent examination. The inspector will therefore come under a duty to take them into account.

Revocation of LDDs

5.105 The Secretary of State may at any time revoke an LDD at the request of the local planning authority, and he may prescribe descriptions of LDD which may be revoked by the authority themselves.[123] The Secretary of State may not therefore revoke an LDD on his own motion or at the behest of any other person or body.

5.106 The local planning authority have no power to revoke an LDD once it has been adopted by them, or approved by the Secretary of State.

Revision of LDDs

5.107 The local planning authority may at any time prepare a revision of an LDD, and the authority must do so if the Secretary of State directs them so to do, in accordance with such timetable as he directs. The revision of an LDD is subject to the same procedure as the preparation.[124]

---

119 Ibid, s. 24(2).
120 Ibid, s. 24(5).
121 Ibid, s. 24(6) and (7).
122 Ibid, s. 24(8).
123 Ibid, s. 25.
124 Ibid, s. 26(1), (2) and (3). There are specific provisions regarding Enterprise Zones—see PCPA 2004, s. 26(4)–(7).

Default powers of the Secretary of State

5.108 The Act confers default powers on the Secretary of State, thus if he thinks the local planning authority are failing in their duties with regard to the preparation, revision, or adoption of a DPD, he must hold an independent examination. He may, at the authority's expense, prepare or revise the document and approve it as an LDD, giving reasons.[125]

Joint LDDs and joint committees

5.109 Under the provisions of PCPA 2004, two or more local planning authorities may agree to prepare one or more joint LDDs.[126] Further, under s. 29 of PCPA 2004, if one or more local planning authorities agree with one or more county councils, the Secretary of State may by order constitute a joint committee to be the local planning authority for the area, or in respect of such matters as are prescribed. However the section restricts the committee's role to the functions under Part 2 of PCPA 2004, that is as to local development planning.

5.110 Under s. 30 PCPA 2004, the constituent authorities may agree that the joint committee is to be the local planning authority for an additional purpose or area, for the purposes of Part 2, and they must revise their LDS accordingly. A constituent authority may request the dissolution of a joint committee, and the Secretary of State may revoke the order.[127]

Annual monitoring report

5.111 Every local planning authority must make an annual monitoring report to the Secretary of State which must contain such information as is prescribed in relation to the implementation of the LDS, and the extent to which the policies set out in the LDDs are being achieved.[128]

5.112 The report must cover the period of 12 months commencing on 1 April each year, and it must be submitted within nine months of the end of the relevant period.[129]

---

125 PCPA 2004, s. 27(1)–(6). Local Development Regs, reg 45.
126 PCPA 2004, s. 28. Local Development Regs, regs 46 and 47.
127 PCPA 2004, s. 31.
128 PCPA 2004, s. 35: Local Development Regs, Part 8.
129 Local Development Regs, reg 48(1) and (2).

Minerals and Waste Development Scheme (MWDS)

5.113 Under the changes made by PCPA 2004, the residual planning functions of county councils are confined to minerals and waste matters.

5.114 PCPA 2004, s. 16 requires county councils to prepare an MWDS for any part of their area for which there is a district council.[130] In general, the provisions applying to the LDS discussed earlier in this chapter[131] also apply to the MWDS. The documents included in an MWDS must also, taken as a whole, set out the authority's policies, however expressed, in relation to development which is a 'county matter' under TCPA 1990.

5.115 County councils were required to submit their MWDSs to the Secretary of State within six months of the commencement of Part 2 of PCPA 2004, ie by 28 March 2004.

Part 3: Development plans in Wales

Wales Spatial Plan (WSP)

5.116 Part 6 of PCPA 1990 provides for a spatial plan for Wales, which must set out such of the Assembly's policies, however expressed, as appropriate in relation to the use and development of land in Wales.[132]

5.117 The Assembly must prepare and publish the WSP, keep it under review, and consider from time to time whether it should be revised. If the Assembly revises the plan, it must publish, as applicable, the whole plan as revised or only the revised parts.[133] The Assembly must consult such persons or bodies as it considers fitting in preparing or revising the Plan; the Plan and any revision of it must be approved by the Assembly—this function cannot be delegated.[134]

The survey

5.118 Local planning authorities in Wales must keep under review those matters which may be expected to affect the development or planning of their area. These matters include:

---

130 PCPA 2004, s. 16(1). The reference to a 'district council' means that the section will not apply to county councils which are unitary authorities who will include their minerals and waste policies as LDDs under the LDS.

131 See para 5.58.

132 Ibid, s. 60(1) and (2).

133 PCPA 2004, s. 60(3) and (4).

134 Ibid, s. 60(4)–(7).

(a) the principal physical, economic, social, and environmental characteristics of the area;
(b) the principal purposes for which land is used in the area;
(c) the size, composition, and distribution of the population of the area;
(d) the communications, transport system, and traffic of the area;
(e) any other considerations which may be expected to affect the above matters; and
(f) any other matter which may be prescribed or as the Assembly direct.

5.119 These matters may also include any changes which the local planning authority think may occur and the effect such changes are likely to have on the development of the area or the planning of such development.[135]

5.120 The local planning authority may also keep under review and examine the above matters in relation to any neighbouring area, in which case they must consult the local planning authority for the area in question.[136]

Local Development Plans (LDPs)

5.121 Every local planning authority in Wales must prepare an LDP for their area. The LDP must set out the authority's objectives in relation to the development and use of land in their area and their general policies for the implementation of those objectives. The plan may also set out specific policies in relation to any part of the authority's area.[137]

5.122 In preparing an LDP, the authority must have regard to:

(a) current national policies;
(b) the WSP;
(c) the RSS for any English region which adjoins the area;
(d) the community strategy prepared by the authority under s. 4 of the Local Government Act 2000;
(e) the community strategy for any other authority whose area comprises any part of the area of the local planning authority;
(f) the resources likely to be available for implementing the LDP; and
(g) such other matters as the Assembly prescribes.[138]

135 Ibid, s. 61(1), (2) and (3).
136 Ibid, s. 61(4) and (5).
137 Ibid, s. 62(1), (2) and (3).
138 PCPA 2004, s. 62(5).

5.123 The local planning authority must also carry out an appraisal of the sustainability of the plan and prepare a report of the findings of the appraisal.[139]

5.124 A plan is an LDP only if adopted by resolution of the local planning authority as such, and approved by the Assembly.[140]

5.125 Two or more local planning authorities may agree to prepare a joint LDP.[141] Save for the provisions regarding the WSP, the Assembly may direct that Part 6 of PCPA 2004 (relating to local development plans in Wales) does not apply to the area of an Urban Development Corporation.[142]

Community Involvement Scheme (CIS)

5.126 An LDP must be prepared in accordance with the authority's CIS and the timetable for the preparation and adoption of the LDP. The CIS is a statement of the authority's policy as to the involvement in the exercise of the authority's functions of such persons (a) as the Assembly prescribes; and (b) such other persons as appear to the authority to have an interest in development matters in the area.[143]

Independent examination

5.127 The local planning authority must submit their LDP to the Assembly for independent examination. They must not submit a plan unless they have complied with the relevant requirements and they think the plan is ready.[144]

5.128 The examination must be carried out by a person appointed by the Assembly. The purpose of the examination is to determine whether the LDP satisfies the relevant requirements and whether it is sound. As with the arrangements discussed earlier in this chapter regarding DPDs in England,[145] any person making representations seeking to change the plan must be given an opportunity to appear before and be heard by the appointed inspector.[146]

5.129 The inspector must make recommendations, with reasons, and the local planning authority must publish the recommendations and the reasons.[147]

---

139 Ibid, s. 62(6).
140 Ibid, s. 62(8).
141 Ibid, s. 72.
142 Ibid, s. 74.
143 Ibid, s. 63(1), (2) and (3).
144 Ibid, s. 64(1) and (2).
145 See para 5.78.
146 PCPA 2004, s. 64(4), (5) and (6). If the Assembly or LPA think that a representation made in relation to an LDP is, in substance, a representation or objection to certain orders or schemes under the Highways Acts 1961 and 1980 or under the New Towns Act 1981, they may disregard it; PCPA 2004, s. 73.
147 PCPA 2004, s. 64(7) and (8).

Intervention by the Asssembly

5.130 If the Assembly think that an LDP is unsatisfactory, it may at any time before the plan is adopted, direct the local planning authority to modify the plan, stating its reasons. The local planning authority must comply with the direction and must not adopt the plan until the Assembly gives notice that it is satisfied they have complied with the direction.[148]

5.131 At any time before an LDP is adopted by the local planning authority, the Assembly may direct that the plan is submitted to it for approval. In such a case, the authority must not take any steps in connection with the adoption of the plan until the Assembly gives its decision. If the direction is given before the authority has submitted the plan, the Assembly must hold an independent examination; if the direction is given after, the inspector must make his recommendations to the Assembly. The recommendations and the reasons must be published.[149]

5.132 In considering a plan submitted to it, the Assembly may take account of any matter it thinks relevant—it is immaterial whether such a matter was taken account of by the authority. The Assembly may approve, approve subject to specified modifications, or reject the LDP, giving reasons.[150]

Withdrawal of LDP

5.133 The local planning authority may withdraw an LDP at any time before it has been adopted. However once a plan has been submitted for independent examination, it can only be withdrawn on the recommendation of the inspector or on the direction of the Assembly.[151]

Adoption of LDP

5.134 The local planning authority may by resolution adopt an LDP as originally prepared only if the inspector so recommends; they may only adopt a modified plan if he likewise so recommends. The local planning authority cannot adopt a plan if the Assembly directs them not to do so.[152]

5.135 The Assembly may at any time revoke an LDP at the request of the local planning authority.[153]

---

148 Ibid, s. 65(1) and (2).
149 Ibid, s. 65(1)–(6).
150 Ibid, s. 65(7), (8) and (9).
151 Ibid, s. 66.
152 Ibid, s. 67.
153 Ibid, s. 68.

Review and revision of LDP

5.136 The local planning authority must carry out a review of the LDP at such times as the Assembly prescribes and they must report to the Assembly the findings of the review. The review must be in the form, and published in the manner, as prescribed.[154]

5.137 The local planning authority may at any time prepare a revision of the LDP. They must do so if directed by the Assembly or if, following a review, they think the plan should be revised.[155]

5.138 If the Assembly thinks that the local planning authority are failing to carry out their duties in connection with the preparation, revision, or adoption of an LDP, the Assembly must hold an independent examination and publish the recommendations and reasons. The Assembly may prepare and revise the plan, as the case may be, and approve it as an LDP, giving reasons. The authority must reimburse the Assembly for expenditure incurred.[156]

5.139 Every local planning authority in Wales must make an annual report to the Assembly, which must contain as much information as prescribed as to the extent to which the objectives set out in the LDP are being achieved.[157]

Part 4: Strategic planning in Greater London

Spatial Development Strategy for Greater London (SDS)

5.140 As discussed in an earlier chapter,[158] the Greater London Authority Act (GLAA) 1999 established an Assembly and created the office of Mayor for the Greater London area. The authority has extensive responsibilities in relation to planning.

5.141 Under Part 8 of GLAA 1999, the Mayor is required to prepare and publish a document called a Spatial Development Strategy which must contain the Mayor's strategy for spatial development in London.

154 Ibid, s. 69.
155 PCPA 2004, s. 70.
156 Ibid, s. 71.
157 Ibid, s. 76.
158 See para 3.65.

Form and content of SDS

5.142 The SDS must include the Mayor's general policies in respect of the development and use of land and it must deal only with matters of strategic importance to Greater London.[159]

5.143 Although the SDS was not originally a statutory development plan, the pre-existing legislation tied the strategy into the framework of plans in Greater London. However PCPA 2004, s. 38(2) provides that for the purpose of any area in Greater London, the development plan is to comprise the SDS and the DPDs, taken as a whole, which have been adopted or approved in relation to the area.

5.144 The SDS must include statements of such of the other strategies mentioned in GLAA 1999, s. 41(1) as involve consideration of spatial development, and such of the Mayor's other policies or proposals as involve such considerations, whether or not the strategy or policy relates to the use and development of land. The strategies mentioned in s. 41(1) are: transport; the London Development Agency; the SDS itself; the London Biodiversity Action Plan; municipal waste management; the London air quality strategy; the London ambient noise strategy, and the culture strategy.[160]

5.145 The SDS must contain a reasoned justification of the Mayor's strategy and a key diagram; it may also contain a larger scale inset diagram but, as with the old structure plans, neither of these diagrams is to be on a map base.[161]

5.146 In formulating the SDS, in addition to the strategies in s. 41(1),[162] the Mayor shall have regard to the RSS for a region which adjoins Greater London; the Secretary of State's waste policies; the prevention of major accidents; and the need to maintain appropriate space between buildings.[163]

SDS procedure

5.147 The procedure for preparing and revising the SDS is as follows:

(1) Having prepared a draft of his proposals for the SDS, the Mayor must make the draft available to and consult with the Assembly and the 'functional bodies' (ie Transport for London; the London Development Agency; the Metropolitan Police Authority; and the London Fire and Emergency Planning

---

159 GLAA 1999, s. 334(1), (2), (3) and (4). The SDS is called the 'London Plan'.

160 GLAA 1999, s. 334(4).

161 Ibid, s. 334(7) and the T & CP (London Spatial Development Strategy) Regulations 2000, SI 2000 No 1491 (the 'SDS Regulations'), regs 4 and 5.

162 See para 5.144. Other matters to which the Mayor must have regard in formulating the strategy are prescribed by GLAA 1999, s. 41(4), (5) and (6).

163 GLAA 1999, s. 342(1), as amended by PCPA 2004, s. 118(2).

Authority), after which he must prepare a draft proposed SDS.[164] The GLAA 2007, s. 29[165] further provides that the Mayor must have regard to any comments made to him in response by the Assembly and the functional bodies. The Mayor must prepare and submit a written statement to the chair of the Assembly, (a) identifying which comments submitted by the Assembly are accepted for implementation in the strategy; and (b) setting out the reasons why any such comments so submitted are not accepted.

(2) The Mayor must then make copies of the proposed SDS, accompanied by the sustainability appraisal,[166] available for inspection. Copies must be sent to the Secretary of State; every London borough council; neighbouring local authorities; the Countryside Agency; the Environment Agency; English Heritage; and any other body the Mayor considers appropriate.[167]

(3) The Mayor must then advertise the availability of the proposals for public inspection and allow a period of 12 weeks (or six weeks in the case of minor alterations) for the making of representations.

(4) Before publishing the SDS, the Mayor, unless otherwise directed by the Secretary of State, must hold an examination in public. It is for the Secretary of State to appoint the person, or persons (the 'panel'), who are to conduct the examination in public and it is for the panel to select the issues to be examined. No person has the right to be heard, although the Mayor and any person invited by the panel may take part.[168]

(5) The panel must advertise the matters to be examined at least 12 weeks before the opening of the examination in public and allow 28 days for the making of representations.[169]

(6) After the examination in public has been held, the Mayor must make the panel's report available for public inspection within eight weeks of receiving it.[170] The Mayor must take the report into account but is not bound to follow its recommendations.

(7) The Mayor cannot publish the SDS unless he has sent a copy to the Secretary of State who has at least six weeks to consider it.[171] The Secretary of State may give the Mayor a direction not to publish the SDS unless modified to take account of inconsistency with national policy or guidance, or any detriment to the interests of an area outside Greater London.[172] The powers of the

164 GLAA 1999, s. 335(1) and (2).
165 Inserting new subsections (1A) and (1B) into the GLAA 1999, s. 335.
166 See para 9.66, under strategic environmental assessment.
167 GLAA 1999, s. 335(3); SDS Regs, reg 7.
168 GLAA 1999, s. 338.
169 SDS Regs, reg 8.
170 Ibid.
171 SDS Regs, reg 9.
172 GLAA 1999, s. 338(6), (7) and (8).

Secretary of State are limited to these grounds. The SDS will become operative on the date it is published by the Mayor.

5.148 The examination in public that must be held under the GLAA 1999 is similar, but not identical to, the examination which had to be held before the old structure plans could be adopted.[173] The selection of issues is entirely a matter for the panel; and the panel is not required to consider any written submission unless: (a) it concerns a matter selected to be examined; and (b) it is shorter than 2,000 words and the panel have received sufficient copies of it no later than three weeks before the opening of the examination.[174]

Review of SDS

5.149 The SDS must be kept under review by the Mayor and it may at any time be altered or replaced by him, either at his own instance or by direction of the Secretary of State.[175] The Mayor is also under a duty to monitor the implementation of the strategy and also the LDDs of each London borough.[176]

Conformity

5.150 Part 1 of the Unitary Development Plans (UDPs) of the London boroughs must be in general conformity with the SDS for the time being in force; and the proposals in Part 2 of these plans must be in general conformity not only with Part 1 but also with the SDS.[177] And where a London borough planning authority has prepared proposals for a UDP, they must apply to the Mayor for a written opinion as to whether the proposals are in general conformity with the SDS.

5.151 If the Mayor considers that the proposals are not in general conformity this will be treated as an objection;[178] but ultimately the UDP cannot be adopted unless Parts 1 and 2 are in general conformity with the SDS.[179] In putting forward UDP proposals, the London borough is entitled to assume that any proposed changes to the SDS have been operative as if published by the Mayor.[180]

5.152 Now that Parts 1 and 2 of PCPA 2004 have come into force, UDPs continue in force only as 'saved' plans under the transitional provisions of that Act,[181] and the

173 See para 4.14.
174 SDS Regs, reg 6.
175 GLAA 1999, ss. 339, 340 and 341.
176 Ibid, s. 346, as amended by PCPA 2004, s. 118(2); and s. 348.
177 GLAA 1999, s. 344(2) and (3).
178 Ibid, s. 344(4) and (5).
179 Ibid, s. 344(6).
180 Ibid, s. 344(7).
181 See para 5.153.

relevant local planning authorities must produce an LDS. As we have seen,[182] the DPDs of the relevant authorities must be in general conformity with the SDS.

Part 5: Development plans—transitional arrangements

5.153 Schedule 8 to the PCPA 2004 contains transitional arrangements relating to the transfer from the old to the new system of development plans contained in Parts 1 and 2 of the Act; that is, in England, the RSS for the region (in London the SDS) and the DPDs for each local area.

5.154 The governmental objectives which underlie the transitional arrangements are (i) to move as quickly as possible from the TCPA 1990 system to the new one; (ii) to maintain continuity in the system of development plans as a framework for development control; and (iii) to minimize the costs of transition.[183]

5.155 The transitional period is whichever is the earlier of a period of three years from the bringing into force of Parts 1 and 2 of PCPA 2004 (28 September 2004), or until a new policy expressly replacing an old policy is published, adopted, or approved.[184]

5.156 During the transitional period, the 'development plan' for an area is to mean (a) the RSS for the region, or in London the SDS; and (b) the old-style development plan under TCPA 1990, that is, the relevant structure, local, or unitary development plan.[185]

Structure plans

5.157 Structure plans will be 'saved' for a period of three years from the bringing into force of Parts 1 and 2 of PCPA 2004 or from the adoption of the structure plan, whichever the later, unless during that period:

- (i) RSS revisions are published which are expressed to replace the structure plan policies in whole or in part; or
- (ii) the Secretary of State directs that the three-year period does not apply to any structure plan policies as are specified in the direction.[186]

182 See para 5.74.
183 PPS 12, ch 5, para 5.1
184 PCPA 2004, Sch 8, para 1(2).
185 Ibid, Sch 8, para 1(1).
186 PCPA 2004, Sch 8, para 1(3).

5.158 If the RPB wish to replace saved structure plan policies with RSS policies, it should identify the relevant policies in their draft revision—this will then be tested at the examination into the RSS revision. If the RPB decides that it does not wish to replace the saved structure plan policies during the three-year period, the structure plan will cease to have effect at the end of that period, unless the Secretary of State otherwise directs. The RPB may consider that some policies in the saved plan should continue for longer than three years; where that is the case the RPB must put their case to the Secretary of State who will consider the issue according to the following criteria:

(i) the saved policies are consistent with national planning policy and in general conformity with the RSS;
(ii) the saved policies address an existing policy deficit and do not duplicate national or local policy;
(iii) the operation of policies to be saved for longer than three years is not materially changed by virtue of other policies in the old plan not being saved; and
(iv) even where the policies are not compliant with one or more of the above, the Secretary of State considers that it is appropriate for the policies to be saved for longer than three years.

5.159 If there is conflict between the RSS and a structure plan, whichever was adopted, approved, or published most recently takes precedence. For this purpose, where the Secretary of State prescribes that RPG should be treated as an RSS, its publication date will be the date the relevant RPG was published.

5.160 Any structure plan that is adopted or approved after the bringing into force of Parts 1 and 2 of PCPA 2004 will have been done so under TCPA 1990[187] and may not be in conformity with the RSS. The RPB must ensure it makes the necessary representations at the examination in public into the structure plan so that the plan is consistent with the RSS. Planning guidance urges RPBs, in co-ordination with regional Government Offices, to look for opportunities to move forward into the new system as quickly as practicable.[188]

Local plans and Unitary Development Plans

5.161 As with the arrangements for structure plans, adopted local plans and UDPs will retain development plan status as 'saved plans' for a period of three years from the bringing into force of Parts 1 and 2 of PCPA 2004.[189]

---

187 Ibid, Sch 8, para 2(2).
188 PPS 12, ch 5, paras 5.8–5.14.
189 PCPA 2004, Sch 8, paras 8–13.

5.162 Draft plans which have reached the public consultation stage on commencement of Parts 1 and 2 of PCPA 1990 are saved for three years after adoption. Again, as with structure plans, policies can be saved for longer than three years with the approval of the Secretary of State. The local planning authority should demonstrate to the Secretary of State that these policies are compliant with the following criteria:

(i) where appropriate, there is a clear and central strategy;
(ii) the policies have regard to the Community Strategy for the area;
(iii) the policies are in general conformity with the RSS and [in London] the SDS;
(iv) the policies are in general conformity with the core strategy DPD, where the core strategy has been adopted;
(v) there are effective policies for any parts of the authority's area where significant change in the use or development of land or conservation of the area is envisaged; and
(vi) the policies are necessary and do not merely repeat national or regional policy.[190]

5.163 During the three-year period, local planning authorities are expected to bring forward LDDs to replace all or parts of the saved plan in accordance with the LDS.

Plans in preparation

5.164 The local planning authority are required to take no further step in relation to a draft plan which, on commencement of Parts 1 and 2 PCPA 2004, has not reached the public participation stage.

5.165 Where the draft plan is at a more advanced stage, but an inspector has not yet been appointed to conduct the inquiry, the inspector's report will be binding on the authority and there will no longer be a modification stage, as there was under the old arrangements.[191] The entire plan, including any changes the authority wish to make, will have to be re-deposited in order to allow for further representations.

5.166 Regulations have been made[192] setting out the circumstances in which the Plans Regulations 1999 will continue to apply to development plans that were being prepared when the new system came into force. The regulations also contain provisions which have the effect of treating things done before the commencement of PCPA 2004, Part 2, as if they had been done after that Part came into force.

---

[190] PPS 12, ch 5, para 5.15.
[191] See para 4.19.
[192] T & CP (Transitional Arrangements) (England) Regulations 2004, SI 2004 No 2205.

5.167 The difficulties inherent in the transition from local plans to LDFs led to litigation in the case of *Wealdon District Council v Martin Grant Homes Ltd.*[193] The facts were that in 2003 the appellant local planning authority had commenced a review of its old-style (ie pre-PCPA 2004) local plan. With the onset of the new legislation, the authority decided in 2004 to discontinue work on its draft local plan and begin work on an LDF under PCPA 2004. The respondent developers sought judicial review of the council's decision to withdraw the emerging local plan. The High Court held that the local planning authority did not have the power to withdraw the plan by virtue of the transitional provisions in Schedule 8 of PCPA 2004.

5.168 On appeal to the Court of Appeal, the court acknowledged that the power of an authority to withdraw an emerging local plan was implicit in the legislation and confirmed by the case of *Persimmon Homes (Thames Valley) Ltd v North Hertfordshire District Council.*[194] The local planning authority had acted perfectly properly in withdrawing the plan when they did and for the reasons that they did.

5.169 Giving the judgment of the court, Mummery LJ explained the effect of the transitional provisions under Schedule 8. The scheme drew a line at the public participation stage, ie making copies of the revised plan available for inspection. If the local planning authority had not got to that stage, they could not proceed any further. In this case, however, the local planning authority had published the revised local plan before the commencement of Part 2 of PCPA 2004, but had not got to the inquiry stage. There was nothing in the transitional provisions that required the authority to continue with the old-style local plan review if they did not wish to. The power to withdraw was expressly preserved. The judge at first instance had made an error of law.

Part 6: The meaning of 'development plan' under PCPA 2004

Part 3 of PCPA 2004

5.170 Under Part 3 of PCPA 2004, in England, outside London, the 'development plan' is to be taken as consisting of:

(a) the RSS for the region, and
(b) the DPDs, taken as a whole, which have been adopted or approved in relation to the area.

---

193 [2005] EWCA Civ 221.
194 (2001) 31 EG 102(CS).

5.171 In London, the 'development plan' is:

(a) the SDS, and
(b) the DPDs, taken as a whole which have been adopted or approved in relation to the area.

5.172 For the purpose of any area in Wales, the 'development plan' will be the LDP adopted or approved in relation to the area.[195]

5.173 If, to any extent, a policy contained in a development plan conflicts with another policy in the development plan, s. 38(5) PCPA 2004 provides that the conflict must be resolved in favour of the policy which is contained in the last document to be adopted, approved, or published, as the case may be.

5.174 Section 38(6) PCPA 2004 states: 'If regard is to be had to the development plan for the purpose of any determination to be made under the planning Acts the determination must be made in accordance with the plan unless material considerations indicate otherwise.' This provision re-enacts s. 54A of TCPA 1990.[196]

Part 7: Development plans: High Court challenge

5.175 PCPA 2004, s. 113 provides that (a) a revision of the RSS; (b) the WSP and revisions thereof; (c) a DPD and revisions thereof; (d) an LDP and revisions thereof; (e) the SDS and alterations or replacements thereof must not be questioned in any legal proceedings, except in so far as provided for by PCPA 2004.

Grounds of challenge

5.176 The Act provides that any person aggrieved by one of the above-mentioned documents may apply to the High Court on the ground that the document is outside the appropriate authorizing powers,[197] and/or a procedural requirement has not been complied with.

5.177 The application must be made within six weeks of the publication, approval, or adoption of the relevant document, as the case may be.[198] If the High Court is satisfied that a relevant document is outside the appropriate power and/or the interests of the applicant have been substantially prejudiced by a failure to comply with

195 PCPA 2004, s. 38(1)–(4).
196 See para 8.57.
197 The 'appropriate power' in each case is set out in PCPA 2004, s. 113(9).
198 PCPA 2004, s. 113(11).

a procedural requirement, the High Court may quash the relevant document, either wholly or in part, generally or as it affects the applicant's property.[199]

5.178 A challenge to a new-style plan arose in *Ensign Group Ltd v First Secretary of State*[200] where the applicants sought to quash parts of an RSS published by the Secretary of State as a statutory development plan. The Secretary of State had made an error in that, inter alia, a specific allocation of 1,500 homes was omitted. In the High Court, the Secretary of State conceded that the strategic plan as published contained an error but argued that to quash parts of the plan would create a 'policy gap' that would not be in the public interest. He contended that a better course would be to issue a public statement indicating, in the light of errors, as to how the RSS should be read.

5.179 Sullivan J disagreed. It would be better for all concerned to quash those parts of the document containing errors and for the Secretary of State to issue guidance under s. 19(2)(a) of PCPA 2004.[201] The learned judge observed that it was unfortunate that the error could not be remedied by some form of declaratory relief, but s. 113 of PCPA 2004 did not enable the court to grant such relief. He added: 'The power to quash, in whole or in part, or not to quash, is a blunt instrument, made the more blunt by the fact that a procedural error, such as a failure to give reasons at the end of a lengthy statutory process, which may have been carried out in an impeccable manner throughout all the earlier stages, will result in the policy or policies being quashed, so that the process has to be recommenced from the beginning.'

5.180 These limitations of the power of the court, acknowledged in the *Ensign* case, have prompted the Government to introduce reform. PA 2008, s. 185, provides that the High Court may, instead of quashing, remit the relevant document to the authority that has prepared it with directions as to the action to be taken. Thus the High Court may direct that: the document be treated as an unapproved or unadopted draft; the document be sent back to any stage in its preparation process specifying which steps in the process have been taken satisfactorily or not, as the case may be; or require action to be taken by persons or bodies with functions relating to the preparation, publication, adoption or approval of the document.

5.181 These new powers of the High Court will apply to all the strategies, plans and documents listed in s. 113 PCPA 2004 as set out above.

---

199 Ibid, s. 113(6) and (7).

200 [2006] EWHC 255 (Admin). See also *R (on the application of Howsmoor Developments Ltd) v South Gloucestershire County Council* [2008] EWHC 262 (Admin) where a challenge to an SPD on the grounds of inadequate strategic environmental assessment failed.

201 That provision states that in preparing an LDD, the local planning authority must have regard to national policies and advice contained in guidance issued by the Secretary of State.

6

DEFINITION OF DEVELOPMENT

6.01 The whole system of planning control in this country depends on the definition of development[1]. If a particular operation or change of use[2] involves development as defined in the Act of 1990, it will (with a few exceptions)[3] require planning permission. If, however, the operation or change of use does not involve development, no planning permission is required. For the purpose of the planning Acts, development is defined[4] as the 'carrying out of building, engineering, mining, or other operations in, on, over, or under land, or the making of any material change in the use of any buildings or other land'.

Operations

6.02 It will be seen that there are two 'legs' to this definition of development—'operations' and 'uses'. It is important to grasp the distinction between the two. The essence of an 'operation' was explained by Lord Parker CJ in *Cheshire County Council v Woodward*;[5] it is some act which changes the physical characteristics of

[1] The definition of development has rightly been described as 'lynch pin'of the system.
[2] The concept of a change of use is considered below at para 6.43.
[3] See para 7.02.
[4] TCPA 1990, s. 55(1).
[5] [1962] 2 QB 126, [1962] 1 All ER 517.

the land, or of what is under it, or of the air above it. 'Use' refers to the purpose to which land or buildings are devoted. The difference between the two concepts has been explained by Lord Denning as follows: 'it seems to me that the first half, "operations", comprises activities which result in some physical alteration to the land which has some degree of permanence in relation to the land itself—whereas the second half, "use", comprises activities which are done in, alongside or on the land, but do not interfere with the actual physical characteristics of the land.'[6]

6.03 Unless the context otherwise requires, the word 'use' does not include the carrying out of building or other operations.[7] It follows that permission for the use of land for a particular purpose does not confer the right to erect buildings for that purpose. The point is illustrated by the case of *Sunbury-on-Thames UDC v Mann*.[8]

6.04 Mann had been granted permission for the continued use of certain land and buildings as a yard, workshop, and stores until 30 October 1957. In May 1957, he erected a new building on the site for use in connection with the maintenance and repair of engineering equipment. The council served an enforcement notice requiring the building to be pulled down.

6.05 Mann claimed that the erection of the building was permitted by what was then Class IV(1) of the First Schedule in the General Development Order, which permits the erection of buildings required in connection with building operations on adjoining land. Held, as Mann had permission only for the use of the land, he could not bring himself within Class IV(1) which refers to *operations*.

6.06 Whether a particular proposed activity amounts to development is said to be a matter of 'fact and degree' based on the facts before the decision-maker, whether it be the local planning authority or the Secretary of State on appeal. Thus it is not a question of law, although the decision-maker must take into account proper legal considerations. A reminder that the determination is one of fact and degree based on the individual circumstances is provided by the case of *Beronstone Ltd v First Secretary of State*.[9] Here the local planning authority alleged that development had taken place in that several hundred wooden posts had been erected in a field so as to define the boundaries of 40 plots of land. The inspector on appeal considered that the posts were of sufficient substance, scale, and type to amount to development and upheld an enforcement notice. Judge Mole QC rejected an argument that the inspector was under a duty to identify a threshold at which the fixing of the posts became development—he considered the contention to be irrelevant and unhelpful. The inspector was required to consider, as a matter of

---

[6] *Parkes v Secretary of State for the Environment* [1978] 1 WLR 1308 at 1311.

[7] TCPA 1990, s. 336(1).

[8] (1958) 9 P & CR 309.

[9] [2006] EWHC 2391 (Admin).

fact and degree, whether the works constituted development and he had done so in this case—his approach could not be impugned.

Building operations

6.07 For most purposes of the TCPA 1990, the word 'building' includes 'any structure or erection and any part of a building so defined, but does not include plant or machinery comprised in building'.[10] The use of the word 'includes' shows that this is not intended to be a complete definition. Its effect is to extend the ordinary meaning of the word 'building' to include structures which would not normally be regarded as buildings such as walls, fences, hoarding, masts. Machinery in the open will be a 'building' for the purposes of the TCPA 1990 so that its erection will be development, but not if housed in a building.

6.08 In *Buckinghamshire County Council v Callingham*,[11] it was held that a model village of buildings constructed to scale was a structure or erection and therefore subject to planning control. In *Cooper v Bailey*,[12] the question was whether advertisements displayed at a garage were erected on a 'building'. The garage consisted of a central building and petrol pumps with two walls on either side running from the building in a curve towards the road; in front of the walls was a kerb marking the limits of the pull-in. Some advertisement signs were fixed to the kerb or displayed on the concrete between the kerb and the wall. It was held that these advertisements were displayed on part of the building or structure of the garage.

6.09 It does not follow, however, that anything placed on land is to be treated as a building. Things like caravans and vending machines, which are comparatively easy to move, are not normally regarded as buildings for the purposes of planning control.[13] And in *Cheshire County Council v Woodward*,[14] the Divisional Court held that the Minister was quite entitled to find that the installation of a coal hopper some 16 to 20 feet high and a conveyor was not development.

6.10 There is apparently no simple test for determining whether some object or installation is a 'building'. In *Cheshire County Council v Woodward*,[15] Lord Parker CJ drew an analogy with the problem frequently encountered in real property law of deciding what fixtures pass with the freehold, and concluded that 'the Act is

---

[10] TCPA 1990, s. 336(1).

[11] [1952] 2 QB 515, [1952] 1 All ER 1166.

[12] (1956) 6 P & CR 261.

[13] The placing of caravans on land may, however, involve a material change in the use of the land. See para 7.07, fn 7.

[14] [1962] 2 QB 126, [1962] 1 All ER 517. See also *Bendles Motors Ltd v Bristol Corpn* [1963] 1 All ER 578, [1963] 1 WLR 247, in which the court held that the Minister was entitled to find that the installation of a free-standing egg-vending machine in the forecourt of a garage and petrol filling station involved a material change of use and therefore constituted development.

[15] See para 6.02.

referring to any structure or erection which may be said to form part of the realty and to change the physical character of the land'. But in *Barvis Ltd v Secretary of State for the Environment*,[16] the Divisional Court adopted a different approach.

6.11 The appellants—specialists in the erection of precast concrete structures—had erected at their depot a mobile tower crane some 89 feet high which ran on rails fixed in concrete. It had previously been used on contract work and they intended to use it again for contract work when required. The dismantling and re-erection of the crane was carried out by specialists; the whole operation took several days and cost about £2,000.

6.12 The Secretary of State—applying *Cheshire County Council v Woodward*—concluded that the erection of the crane with all that it entailed did alter the physical characteristics of the land and amounted to building, engineering, and other operations.

6.13 The Divisional Court, in dismissing an appeal against the Minister's decision, thought it unnecessary to go so far. Bridge J giving the first judgment[17] applied criteria suggested in *Cardiff Rating Authority and Cardiff Assessment Committee v Guest Keen Baldwin's Iron and Steel Co Ltd*,[18] where the question was whether under rating legislation certain apparatus was a building or structure. These criteria may be summarized as follows:

(1) A building or structure will be something of such size that it has either been in fact or would normally be built or constructed on the site as opposed to being brought on it ready made.[19]
(2) It will have some degree of permanence; once installed it will normally remain in situ and only be removed by pulling down or taking to pieces.
(3) The question whether the thing is or is not physically attached to the site is relevant but not conclusive.
(4) A limited degree of motion does not prevent it being a structure.

6.14 The degree of permanence (in (2) above) was recognized by the Court of Appeal in *R v Swansea City Council, ex p Elitestone Ltd*[20] as being a highly material factor. In that case the question arose as to whether some 27 self-built wooden chalets were 'buildings' for the purpose of planning law. It seems they were of varying

---

16 (1971) 22 P & CR 710.

17 It is perhaps worth noting that Lord Parker CJ was a member of the court and concurred with the judgment of Bridge J.

18 [1949] 1 KB 385, [1949] 1 All ER 27.

19 A thing is not necessarily removed from the category of building or structure because by some feat of engineering or navigation it is brought to the site in one piece—[1949] 1 All ER 27 at 36. And see the rating case of *Scaife v British Fermentation Products Ltd* [1971] JPL 711 (transport in one piece of fermenting vessel weighing 13 tons and over 57 feet high).

20 [1993] JPL 1019.

degrees of substance and some were little more than sheds—nearly all were suspended on pillars. Mann LJ (with Staughton LJ and Sir Thomas Bingham MR in agreement) concluded that the chalets were structures or erections; it could be assumed that they had been erected with a prospect of permanence, they had survived over many years and their erection had affected the physical quality of the land. However, 'permanent' does not necessarily mean that the object in question is intended to remain permanently on a permanent foundation—it is a matter of degree between the temporary and the everlasting. In *Skerritts of Nottingham Ltd v Secretary of State for the Environment, Transport and the Regions (No 2)*,[21] the Court of Appeal upheld an inspector's decision that the erection of a substantial marquee in the grounds of an hotel constituted development. The marquee stood on the lawn of the hotel between February and October each year.

6.15 In *R (on the application of Hall Hunter Partnership) v First Secretary of State*,[22] Sullivan J considered that the erection of a series of large interlinked walk-in plastic tunnels ('polytunnels'), for growing soft fruit, amounted to development. The tunnels had the requisite degree of permanence, size, and physical attachment. This decision of the High Court led the DCLG in 2007 to clarify the situation regarding the status of polytunnels. In a letter to chief planning officers, the Department stated that this decision did not mean that all polytunnels would necessarily need planning permission: the position would depend on the type and scale of the tunnels proposed. In other words, as we have already seen, each case is decided on its own particular facts.

6.16 The expression 'building operations' is also defined. It *includes* '(a) demolition of buildings; (b) rebuilding; (c) structural alterations of or additions to buildings; and (d) other operations normally undertaken by a person carrying on business as a builder'.[23] The effect of this very wide definition is cut down by TCPA 1990, s. 55(2)(a) which excludes from the definition of development 'the carrying out of works for the maintenance, improvement or other alteration of any building, being works which affect only the interior of the building or which do not materially affect the external appearance of the building'. It should be noted, however, that PCPA 2004 enabled the Secretary of State to specify, in a development order, the circumstances in which such works will amount to development by increasing the gross floorspace of a building by a specified amount.[24] This amendment was prompted by the practice of superstores inserting mezzanine floors into their

[21] [2000] JPL 1025. See also *R (on the application of Westminster City Council) v Secretary of State for the Environment, Transport and the Regions* [2001] EWHC Admin 270, [2002] 1 P & CR 99.

[22] [2006] EWHC 2482 (Admin).

[23] TCPA 1990, s. 55(1A) added by PCA 1991, s. 13(1). Note that not all demolition will be development: See para 6.35.

[24] TCPA 1990, s. 55(2A) and (2B) inserted by PCPA 2004, s. 49(1). For the circumstances in which the new subsections apply, see PCPA 2004, s. 49(2).

premises thereby greatly increasing the retail floorspace. In *Eastleigh Borough Council v First Secretary of State*,[25] it was held that the doubling of retail floorspace of a store by the insertion of such a floor did not amount to development as it was not a material change of use. The Secretary of State has implemented the provision in PCPA 2004. As from 10 May 2006 planning permission has been required for increases in gross floorspace of more than 200 square metres where the building is used for the retail sale of goods other than hot food; and the effect of the operations will be to provide additional floorspace which can be used for the retail sale of goods other than hot food.

6.17 It does not follow that something done to the exterior of a building which alters its external appearance will require planning permission; if what has been done does not amount to a building or other operation, planning permission will not be required. In *Kensington and Chelsea Royal London Borough Council v CG Hotels*,[26] the owners of an hotel installed floodlights in the basement area and on the first floor balconies. The council served an enforcement notice requiring the removal of the floodlights. On appeal, the inspector quashed the enforcement notice; he decided (i) that the 'works' did not amount to building or other operations and (ii) that in any case the floodlights were virtually invisible during daylight. The Divisional Court upheld the inspector's decision; even if the works amounted to development, they did not materially affect the external appearance. The real cause of complaint was probably the effect of the floodlighting at night, but the use of electricity is obviously not an operation within the definition of development.

6.18 In *Burroughs Day v Bristol City Council*,[27] the question arose as to whether some proposed roof alterations would materially affect the external appearance of a building. The works in question would have superimposed two areas of flat roof instead of slopes running down to a valley gutter. Richard Southwell QC, sitting as deputy judge, ruled that what must be affected is the 'external appearance' not the 'exterior'; thus all roof alterations which can be seen from any vantage point on the ground or from neighbouring buildings would be capable of affecting external appearance. Moreover, whether the alterations were material had to be judged by reference to the building as a whole and not by reference to a part taken in isolation. In the case itself, the alterations would not have been visible from any of the surrounding streets and the judge concluded that the works were not development.

---

[25] [2004] 24 EG 149 (CS). This case is further discussed at para 6.135.

[26] (1980) 41 P & CR 40.

[27] [1996] 19 EG 126. And see also [1997] JPL 107. It would seem that visibility from the air alone would not suffice, although the case does not specifically decide this point.

6.19 It is sometimes difficult to decide whether works on an existing building are works of maintenance or improvement for the purpose of TCPA 1990, s. 55(2)(a) or not. The difficulty is illustrated by the case of *Street v Essex County Council*.[28]

6.20 A demolition order on a building was stayed on Street's undertaking to carry out repairs approved under the building byelaws. Unfortunately, he found it necessary to demolish the existing building down to damp course and to rebuild from there.

6.21 The local authority served an enforcement notice alleging that Street had carried out development without planning permission and requiring him to remove what they said was a new building. The Minister upheld the enforcement notice. On appeal to the High Court, it was contended on behalf of Street that the work done did not constitute development; provided the design and some part, however small, of the original structure remained, the operations could be said to be works of maintenance.

6.22 Held: whether the works could fairly be said to amount to works of maintenance, or were properly called reconstruction, was a matter of fact and degree. In the circumstances the Minister was entitled to hold as a matter of fact that what took place was reconstruction and as such involved development.

6.23 In *Street's* case, the reality was that there was no longer a building to be maintained or improved. But where is the dividing line? The rebuilding of one or two walls may possibly be accepted as maintenance, but it is now clear that TCPA 1990, s. 55(2)(a) will not apply where two walls are pulled down and rebuilt and then the other two are rebuilt as part of the same programme of reconstruction. In *Larkin (CW) v Basildon District Council*[29] the local planning authority advised the developer that the rebuilding of two walls would not need planning permission; having rebuilt two walls, he went on, against the advice of the authority, to rebuild the other two. The authority served an enforcement notice in respect of the rebuilding of all four walls. In dismissing an appeal, the Secretary of State said: 'None of the external walls of the original building remain and new walls have been constructed as part of the operation and are unlike the walls of the original building: the construction of these walls, as distinct from the replacement of one or two of them, are not works of maintenance, improvement or other alteration of a building within the meaning of [TCPA 1990, s. 55] since the original building has virtually ceased to exist.'

6.24 The Divisional Court upheld the Secretary of State's decision. The fact that the new walls were 'unlike' the originals might in itself have put the works outside TCPA 1990, s. 55(2)(a) as materially affecting the external appearance, but that

28 (1965) 193 Estates Gazette 537.
29 [1980] JPL 407.

does not seem to have been the main point at issue. The principle that rebuilding by stages will normally be outside s. 55(2)(a) has been upheld by the Court of Appeal in *Hewlett v Secretary of State for the Environment*.[30]

6.25 These problems do not arise in connection with the restoration of war-damaged buildings because it is expressly provided that TCPA 1990, s. 55(2)(a) shall not apply to war damage repairs; the result is that any war-damage repairs, however trivial, are development.[31]

6.26 The provision of additional space below ground level, if begun after 5 December 1968, is also deemed to involve development.[32]

Engineering operations

6.27 The expression 'engineering operations' includes 'the formation or laying out of means of access to highways',[33] otherwise the expression is to be given its ordinary dictionary meaning[34] and includes building and maintenance of roads, the laying of sewers, water mains, and other public utility apparatus. The removal of earth embankments has been held to constitute an engineering operation.[35]

6.28 PCA 1991, s. 14, inserting a new TCPA 1990, s. 55(4A), extends the definition of an 'engineering operation' to include the placing or assembly of fish tanks (or cages) in inland waters for the purpose of fish farming.[36]

6.29 The following are excluded from the definition of development:

(a) the maintenance or improvement of a road by the [local] highway authority within the existing boundaries of the road[37]—however, where the works are not exclusively for the maintenance of the road, excluding any works which may have significant adverse effects on the environment;
(b) the inspection, repair, and renewal of sewers, mains, cables, etc, by a local authority or statutory undertaker.[38]

---

30 [1985] JPL 404.
31 Until 1988 the repair of war damage was permitted development.
32 TCPA 1990, s. 55(2)(a).
33 TCPA 1990, s. 336(1).
34 *Fayrewood Fish Farms Ltd v Secretary of State for the Environment* [1984] JPL 267—engineering operations are those of a type usually undertaken by, or calling for the skills of, an engineer.
35 *See Coleshill and District Investment Co Ltd v Minister of Housing and Local Government* [1969] 2 All ER 525, [1969] 1 WLR 746. See also para 6.35.
36 This provision is not retrospective; PCA 1991, s. 14(2). However the General Permitted Development Order 1995, Sch 2, Part 6 gives permitted development rights for floating tanks and cages outside national parks, subject to the local authority's right to exercise prior approval relating to siting and appearance.
37 TCPA 1990, s. 55(2)(b).
38 TCPA 1990, s. 55(2)(c).

The word 'local' in square brackets in paragraph (a) above was repealed by PCPA 2004.[39] **6.30**

Mining operations

There is no definition of mining operations as such in the TCPA 1990, but the word 'minerals' is defined as *including*[40] all minerals and substances in or under land of a kind ordinarily worked for removal by underground or surface working.[41] It is submitted that the expression 'mining operation' is to be interpreted in the light of the definition and that it would therefore include quarrying and other surface operations as well as underground mining. **6.31**

This interpretation of mining operations is extended by TCPA 1990, s. 55(4) which provides that mining operations shall *include* (a) the removal of material of any description from a mineral working deposit, from a deposit of pulverized fuel ash etc, or from a deposit of iron, steel, or other metallic slags; and (b) the extraction of minerals from a disused railway embankment.[42] **6.32**

Other operations

As already explained, the word 'operation' in this context means something which changes the physical characteristics of the land, or of what is under it or of the air above it.[43] There is, however, some uncertainty as to the meaning of the phrase 'other operations', since it can be interpreted in different ways. **6.33**

(1) It might be taken as meaning any operation affecting the physical characteristics of the land. But in that case why does s. 55(2) specifically refer to building, engineering, and mining operations?[44]
(2) Another approach would be to try to apply the *ejusdem generis* rule, that is, to limit the phrase to operations of the same class or genus as building, engineering, and mining. The difficulty here is to find any common genus to building, engineering, and mining.[45]

---

39 PCPA 2004, ss. 118(1), 120; Sch 6, paras 1, 2; Sch 9. The provision was brought into force as from 7 June 2006 by SI 2006 No 1281.

40 In this case, the word 'includes' must be interpreted as 'means and includes'.

41 TCPA 1990, s. 336(1); peat cut for purposes other than sale is excluded.

42 This extended definition of 'mining operations' was introduced by the Minerals Act and came into force in May 1986.

43 See above.

44 See the remarks of Lord Morris of Borth-y-Gest and Lord Pearson in *Coleshill and District Investment Co Ltd v Minister of Housing and Local Government* [1969] 2 All ER 525 at 529 and 543 respectively.

45 See the remarks of Lord Guest, Lord Wilberforce, and Lord Pearson, [1969] 2 All ER 525 at 532.

(3) There is a rule of interpretation known as *noscitur a sociis*; that is, the meaning of a word can be gathered from the words with which it is associated. If this rule were applied, 'other operations' would be restricted to operations similar to building, engineering, or mining, but in a less strict manner than would be required by the *ejusdem generis* rule.[46]

6.34 Even on the narrowest interpretation, the phrase 'other operations' must obviously include some matters which do not fall within the strict definitions of building, engineering, or mining. The removal of topsoil (which under some circumstances would appear to be development)[47] is probably an operation of this kind. Until the PCA 1991 there was uncertainty as to whether the demolition of a building fell within the category of 'other operations'. This question is dealt with below.

Demolition

6.35 For many years it was generally assumed that the demolition of a building did not of itself constitute development[48] and this view was supported by the judgment of Marshall J in *Howell v Sunbury-on-Thames UDC*.[49] In *Coleshill and District Investment Co Ltd v Minister of Housing and Local Government*,[50] the House of Lords held that an ammunition store and the surrounding concrete blast walls constituted a single structure. The proposed removal of the blast walls would have constituted a structural alteration materially affecting the external appearance of the building. The *partial* demolition of a building, therefore, may amount to operational development requiring planning permission. (Their Lordships further held that the removal of earth and rubble embankments surrounding the walls would be an engineering operation.) Significantly, the House of Lords refused to say whether *total* demolition constituted development and left the issue open. And in *Iddenden v Secretary of State for the Environment*[51] the Court of Appeal held that the demolition of some Nissen huts and a lean-to shed was not development. Lord Denning appeared to imply that whereas the demolition of relatively insubstantial structures was not development, the demolition of

---

46 See the remarks of Lord Pearson, ibid, at 543. This approach was endorsed by the Court of Appeal in *Cambridge City Council v Secretary of State for the Environment* [1992] JPL 644.

47 The Agricultural Land (Removal of Surface Soil) Act 1953 makes it an offence to remove topsoil without planning permission in any case where such operations would constitute development.

48 This was the government's view in Circular 67 (now replaced).

49 (1963) 15 P & CR 26. In *LCC v Marks and Spencer Ltd* [1953] AC 535, [1953] 1 All ER 1095, the House of Lords decided that demolition with a view to redevelopment amounted to 'works for the erection of a building' for the purposes of the TCPA 1947, s. 78. The House of Lords did not say that such demolition constituted development; this view of the case is confirmed by Glidewell LJ in *Cambridge City Council v Secretary of State for the Environment* [1992] JPL 644.

50 [1969] 2 All ER 525, [1969] 1 WLR 746.

51 [1972] 3 All ER 883, [1972] 1 WLR 1433.

much larger buildings might be such. Of course, it has always been recognized that demolition might be of such a scale and character that it amounts to an engineering operation.

6.36 Such was the state of the law when the matter came before David Widdicombe QC, sitting as deputy judge in *Cambridge City Council v Secretary of State for the Environment*.[52] The judge referred to the question of whether demolition was development as one which 'like a ghost has haunted planning law for many years'. Deciding to lay the ghost to rest, he held that the demolition of two dwelling-houses constituted development as an operation normally undertaken by a person carrying on business as a builder.[53] This decision created considerable uncertainty amongst developers and since the Planning and Compensation Bill was in the course of its passage through Parliament, the government took the opportunity to clarify the law.

6.37 Accordingly, TCPA 1990, s. 55(1A), inserted by PCA 1991, s. 13 extends the definition of building operations to include the demolition of buildings. However, the Act grants the Secretary of State the power to direct that the demolition of particular types of building is not development subject to planning control;[54] the Secretary of State's direction in this regard is dealt with below. The Court of Appeal[55] allowed an appeal against the decision of David Widdicombe QC in the *Cambridge* case; there was no material before the judge upon which he could find that the works in question were operations normally undertaken by a person carrying on business as a builder. However, the Court of Appeal went on to hold that demolition of itself was not an 'other operation' within the meaning of TCPA 1990, s. 55(1).

6.38 Before considering these controls, it should be borne in mind that demolition may still constitute development where it involves the partial demolition of a building, being a structural alteration and therefore a building operation. Nevertheless, the Secretary of State has by direction[56] excluded the demolition of certain types of building from the definition of development; that is to say, the demolition of these buildings shall not involve development:

(1) listed buildings, buildings in conservation areas, and scheduled monuments;[57]
(2) building of less than 50 cubic metres, measured externally;

52 [1991] JPL 428. In fact this decision was reversed by CA at [1992] JPL 644. See below.
53 Within the meaning of TCPA 1990, s. 336 as originally enacted.
54 TCPA 1990, s. 55(2)(g).
55 [1992] JPL 644.
56 T & CP (Demolition—Description of Buildings) Direction 1995, contained in circular 10/95. This was the government's fourth attempt at this particular piece of delegated legislation.
57 The demolition of these is controlled under other legislation: See para 16.37.

(3) any building other than a dwellinghouse or a building adjoining a dwellinghouse;
(4) the whole or any part of any gate, fence, wall, or other means of enclosure, unless in a conservation area.

6.39 The Secretary of State's direction defines 'dwellinghouse' (in (3) above) as including residential homes or hostels and a building containing one or more flats. Further, each house in a pair of semi-detached houses and every house in a row of terrace houses is to be regarded as a separate building, whether or not in residential use. If, therefore, a house has been converted to a non-residential use, it is only excluded from control where any adjoining house is not also in use as a dwelling. In addition, where the residential use of a dwellinghouse is ancillary[58] to a non-residential use of the building or site, for example a caretaker's flat in an office building, it is excluded from control under the above provisions.

6.40 The 1995 direction also provides that '"building" does not include part of a building'. The effect of this provision arose in *R (on the application of Hammerton) v London Underground Ltd*[59] in connection with the redevelopment of the historic Bishopsgate Goods Yard for the proposed extension of the East London Line. Part of the yard, the Braithwaite Viaduct, was listed as a building of special architectural and historic interest[60] in 2002. Such buildings cannot be demolished without a special form of consent known as 'listed building consent'. Applying the direction, Ouseley J considered that if the yard including the viaduct was a single building, planning permission would be required for the demolition of the unlisted part. If, on the other hand, the viaduct was a separate building, no planning permission would be required for the demolition of the rest of the goods yard. However, in the particular circumstances of the case, Ouseley J did not consider it necessary or appropriate to come to a finding as to whether there was one or more structures.

6.41 It can be seen, then, that these controls are aimed at the demolition of dwellinghouses and of buildings adjoining dwellinghouses, and that they do not apply to the demolition of very many types of buildings, whether they be shops, offices, factories, and so forth unless they are adjoining a dwellinghouse. However, the government's main concern is not so much to prevent the demolition of dwellinghouses as to have the means of regulating the details of demolition in order to minimize its impact on the amenity of a locality. Accordingly, the General Permitted Development Order (an order made by the Secretary of State granting planning permission for various classes of development discussed in chapter 7

58 Ancillary or incidental uses are discussed at para 6.74.
59 [2002] EWHC 2307 (Admin).
60 See para 16.01.

below), grants planning permission (with one exception) for the demolition of all buildings not excluded from these controls by virtue of the Secretary of State's direction.[61] However, in certain cases, the permission cannot be implemented until the local planning authority has determined whether it requires to give prior approval to the method of the proposed demolition.[62]

6.42 In *R (on the application of Magauran) v First Secretary of State*,[63] Davis J held that when a planning application necessarily involves the demolition of existing structures before a new build can take place, no separate planning application is required for the demolition. If planning permission is granted, it is implicit that the permission authorizes both the demolition of the existing buildings and the erection of new buildings. Of course, as we have seen, under paragraph (3) of the Secretary of State's Direction, the demolition of any building other than a dwellinghouse (or where one of the other paragraphs apply) is not development and therefore no planning application will be required for demolition in any event. The principle in the *Magauran* case applies, therefore, to those cases where demolition is development; this would include, for example, cases of partial demolition and those cases where the permitted development right, to which reference is made above, has been withdrawn by the Secretary of State.

Change of use

6.43 We may now consider the second 'leg' in the definition of development—namely 'the making of any material change in the use of any buildings or other land'. The buildings or land under consideration in any particular case are often referred to as 'the planning unit'; this is usually the unit of occupation, but in some cases buildings or land in the same occupation may be divided into two or more planning units.[64] Where the occupier carries on more than one activity within the same planning unit, the 'use' of the buildings or land comprised in it will depend on the nature of the activities. It is quite common for one activity to be ancillary to a primary activity; for instance, a factory may have an office block, or part of a retail shop may be used for storage in connection with the retailing activity. The right to use buildings or land for an ancillary activity may be regarded as included in the primary use; separate planning permission is not required for the commencement of an ancillary activity[65] but the right to use land for an ancillary activity will be lost

---

[61] The scope of this class of permitted development is discussed in at para 7.50.The exception is where the building has been made unsafe or uninhabitable through deliberate action or neglect.

[62] This procedure is discussed at para 7.52.

[63] [2005] EWHC 1751 (Admin).

[64] See at para 6.144.

[65] *Trio Thames Ltd v Secretary of State for the Environment and Reading Borough Council* [1984] JPL 183.

on the cessation of the primary activity.[66] The planning unit may, however, accommodate two or more activities neither of which is ancillary to the other; in such cases, the planning unit may be said to have a mixed or composite use.[67]

6.44 There will be no development unless the change of use is 'material'; that is, unless the change is of such a character that it matters having regard to the objects of planning control. As was said in *Marshall v Nottingham City Corpn*:[68] 'if the business of a retail dealer is being carried on in any building, it may be that there is a change of use if, for example, the business of a baker is substituted for a different business, for example, that of a grocer; but I am unable to see why or how such a change can be material from any point of view which could legitimately be taken by a planning authority.'

6.45 In many cases it will be obvious that a change of use is 'material' in this sense, eg where it is proposed to use a dwellinghouse as offices or to station a large number of caravans on a field hitherto used for agriculture. In other cases, however, it is far from easy to decide whether a change of use is material or not. Is there, for instance, a material change of use if a doctor uses two rooms in a dwellinghouse for his practice? Or if a family take in a lodger? If not, in this latter case, would it be material if they took in six lodgers? Is there a material change of use if an existing use is intensified, as for instance in *Guildford RDC v Penny*[69] where the number of caravans in a field was increased over a period of years from eight to 27?

6.46 Some help with this problem is given by TCPA 1990, s. 55 which lays down specific rules for certain cases. Apart from these, however, the question whether there is a material change of use must be decided in the light of all the circumstances. We will deal first with the statutory rules laid down in TCPA 1990, s. 55, and then with the general principles applicable to cases not covered by these rules.

The statutory provisions: matters declared to be a material change of use

6.47 The following are specifically declared to involve a material change of use:

(a) the conversion of a single dwellinghouse into two or more separate dwellings;[70]
(b) the deposit of refuse or other waste materials, including the extension of an existing tip, if the superficial area is extended or the height is extended above the level of the adjoining ground;[71]

66 *David W Barling Ltd v Secretary of State for the Environment* [1980] JPL 594.
67 See eg *Burdle v Secretary of State for the Environment* [1972] 3 All ER 240, [1972] 1 WLR 1207.
68 [1960] 1 All ER 659 at 665, per Flyn-Jones J.
69 [1959] 2 QB 112, [1959] 2 All ER 111.
70 TCPA 1990, s. 55(3)(a).
71 TCPA 1990, s. 55(3)(b).

(c) the display of advertisements on any external part of a building not previously used for that purpose.[72]

6.48 The intention is to make it clear beyond doubt that these changes of use constitute development and so require planning permission. There remain, however, difficulties of interpretation. For instance, what is meant in paragraph (a) by 'separate dwellings'?

6.49 In *Ealing Corpn v Ryan*,[73] three floors of a house were each occupied by different families; the kitchen was shared by all the families, and it was inferred that any bathroom and lavatory accommodation was also shared. The corporation served an enforcement notice requiring the use of the property as two or more separate dwellinghouses to be discontinued and later prosecuted the owners for non-compliance. The magistrates dismissed the case.

6.50 On appeal counsel for the corporation contended that if the people in the house were found to be living separately, the dwellings must be separate. The Divisional Court did not accept this contention. A house might well be occupied by two or more persons, who to all intents and purposes were living separately, without that house thereby being used as separate dwellings. Multiple occupation is not by itself enough to bring the statutory rule into operation[74]—the existence or absence of any form of physical reconstruction is also a relevant factor; another is the extent to which the alleged separate dwellings are self contained.

6.51 The effect of these provisions should not be misunderstood. For instance, multiple occupation of a dwellinghouse may constitute a material change of use even though the house has not been converted into separate dwellings; that is a matter to be decided by reference to general principles.[75] A similar point arises with regard to the tipping of refuse and other waste materials. Such tipping may constitute a material change of use even though the superficial area of the existing tip has not been extended, nor the height raised above the permitted level. Thus in *Alexandra Transport Co Ltd v Secretary of State for Scotland*,[76] the Court of Session considered that the backfilling of quarry refuse had been part of the use as a quarry; use thereafter as a 'dump' was a material change of use.

---

[72] TCPA 1990, s. 55(4). This is not likely to be of much practical significance as all outdoor advertisements require consent under the Control of Advertisements Regulations whether their display involves development or not—see para 15.53.

[73] [1965] 2 QB 486, [1965] 1 All ER 137.

[74] See the account of *Birmingham Corpn v Minister of Housing and Local Government and Habib Ullah* [1963] 3 All ER 668 at para 6.128.

[75] Use of a dwellinghouse by (a) a single person or people living together as a family, or (b) not more than six residents living together as a single household, is not development, by virtue of the Use Classes Order: see para 6.95.

[76] (1972) 25 P & CR 97.

The statutory provisions: uses excluded from definition of development

6.52 Certain uses of land are specifically excluded from the definition of development.

(1) The use of a building or other land within the curtilage of a dwellinghouse

6.53 The use of a building or other land within the curtilage of a dwellinghouse for any purpose incidental to the enjoyment of the dwellinghouse as such is not development.[77] It follows that the use of an existing garden shed as a garage for the owner's own car or as additional sleeping accommodation would not be development. But, since the word 'use' does not include the carrying out of building operations,[78] this paragraph does not authorize the erection of a building or shed for these purposes. This paragraph is a re-enactment of a provision originally contained in the TCPA 1947. At that time the concept of the use of land had not been the subject of judicial analysis and the concept of the planning unit had not emerged, and it may have been thought important to safeguard the incidental use of the curtilages of dwellinghouses. Nowadays, it is recognized that the incidental use of the curtilage, of a building does not require planning permission,[79] so the above paragraph seems little more than a statutory expression of a general principle. Moreover, since the planning unit may be larger than the curtilage, planning permission will probably not be necessary for the use of land outside the curtilage but within the same unit of occupation—for instance, a paddock—for purposes incidental to the enjoyment of the dwellinghouse.

6.54 In *Wallington v Secretary of State for Wales*,[80] a householder kept 44 dogs at her home, which made a considerable noise. The dogs were not kept commercially but as a hobby. Malcolm Spence, QC, as deputy judge, rejected a submission that just because a use was a hobby it was automatically incidental to the enjoyment of a dwellinghouse—'the occupier might well be enjoying him, or herself, in some way which was not related to the dwelling itself as a dwelling'. Accordingly, the use was not 'incidental' within the meaning of the provision.

6.55 In dismissing an appeal against this decision, Farquarson LJ in the Court of Appeal[81] recognized that the question was a difficult one but in approaching it, it was sensible to consider what would be a normal use of a dwellinghouse, although this was not the determinative factor. The word 'incidental' meant subordinate in land use terms to the enjoyment of a dwellinghouse as a dwellinghouse—a hobby

---

77 TCPA 1990, s. 55(2)(d).

78 See para 6.03; TCPA 1990, s. 336(1).

79 See eg *Kensington and Chelsea Royal Borough v Secretary of State for the Environment and Mia Carla Ltd* [1981] JPL 50: it was held in the case of a garden attached to a restaurant that planning permission was not required for the use of the garden for the purposes of the restaurant.

80 [1990] JPL 112.

81 [1991] JPL 942.

'might be of such a kind and requiring such space that the enjoyment of the dwellinghouse became incidental to the indulgence of the hobby'. The matters that the learned Lord Justice thought relevant to the question of whether a use was incidental to the enjoyment of a dwellinghouse included the location of the dwellinghouse, its size and how much ground was included within its curtilage, the nature and scale of the activity in question, and the disposition and character of the occupier. He felt that to pigeon-hole the test as being either a subjective or objective one merely served to complicate matters; Slade LJ, on the other hand, was more emphatic that an objective standard had to be applied. In this respect one was entitled to have regard to what people normally did in dwellinghouses.[82]

6.56 The objective standard was adopted by the Court of Appeal in a subsequent case, *Croydon London Borough Council v Gladden*.[83] Here, the householder placed a lifesize replica of a Spitfire on his house. Applying the *Wallington* case, Dillon LJ considered that what was 'incidental' under the provision involved an element of objective reasonableness and could not rest solely on the unrestrained whim of the occupier. Accordingly, 'no one could regard it as reasonable to keep 44 dogs in a dwellinghouse and likewise, no one could . . . regard it as reasonable to keep a replica Spitfire of the size of this replica on the land'. Moreover, personal pleasure derived from annoying the local planning authority had to be discounted—this was not 'enjoyment of the dwellinghouse as such'.

6.57 Although not concerned with residential user, the decision of Sullivan J in *Harrods v Secretary of State for the Environment, Transport and the Regions*[84] is of interest on the issue of incidental use. Harrods sought a certificate[85] that the proposed use of the roof of their department store, whereby the Chairman[86] could land his personal helicopter for no more than 10 landings a week, was lawful as being incidental to the primary use. The local planning authority's refusal to grant a certificate was upheld by the Secretary of State who considered that the proposed use could not, as a matter of fact and degree, be regarded as 'ordinarily' incidental to the main retail use. Sullivan J agreed, concluding that a restrictive formulation of the ancillary use test, so as to include the words 'ordinarily incidental', would give effect to Parliament's intention that material changes of use should, in general, be subject to planning control. The Secretary of State was entitled to have regard to 'ordinary and reasonable practice' or to what is normally done at inner city department stores in deciding whether the proposed use met the ordinarily

82 The enforcement notice limited the number of dogs that W could keep without planning permission to six.

83 [1994] JPL 723.

84 [2001] EWHC Admin 600, [2001] 31 EG 101 (CS).

85 Under TCPA 1990, s. 192; See para 6.179.

86 Mr Mohammed Al Fayed, memorably described in the inspector's report as a 'key worker in the planning unit'.

incidental test. In this respect, the judge specifically endorsed the approach taken in the *Wallington* case. This decision was subsequently upheld by the Court of Appeal.[87]

(2) Use for agriculture or forestry

6.58 The use of any land for the purpose of agriculture or forestry (including afforestation), and the use for any of these purposes of any building occupied with land so used, does not involve development.[88] The use of land for agriculture obviously involves the carrying out of a number of operations such as ploughing; in this context it is submitted that the word 'use' must include such operations as are essential to and inseparable from agriculture, but that it does not include such operations as the erection of farm buildings.

6.59 'Agriculture' is defined as *including*:[89] horticulture, fruit growing, seed growing, dairy farming, the breeding and keeping of livestock (including any creature kept for the production of food, wool, skins or fur or for the purpose of its use in the farming of land), the use of land as grazing land, meadow land, osier land, market gardens and nursery grounds, and the use of land for woodlands where that use is ancillary to the farming of land for other agricultural purposes. This definition has been the subject of some precise interpretation. In *Belmont Farm Ltd v Minister of Housing and Local Government*,[90] it was held that the breeding and training of horses for show jumping was not agricultural; such use was not covered by the words 'breeding and keeping of livestock' because those words were qualified by the parenthesis which refers to the keeping of creatures for the production of food. However, in *Sykes v Secretary of State for the Environment*,[91] it was held that the use of land for grazing some racehorses and point-to-point ponies was agricultural: because the reference in the statutory definition to the use of land as grazing land was not qualified by the words in parenthesis. The use of land for allotments has been held to fall within the statutory definition.[92]

6.60 Although the use of land for agriculture does not include operations such as the erection of buildings, it may include the placing on the land of caravans, vehicles, and pieces of equipment for purposes ancillary or incidental to agriculture. In *Wealden District Council v Secretary of State for the Environment and Day*,[93] D had placed a caravan on agricultural land for the purpose of providing a waterproof place for the storage and mixing of cattle food and to provide shelter for himself

---

87 [2002] EWCA Civ 412.
88 TCPA 1990, s. 55(2), (3).
89 TCPA 1990, s. 336(1).
90 (1962) 13 P & CR 417.
91 [1981] JPL 285.
92 *Crowborough Parish Council v Secretary of State for the Environment* [1981] JPL 281.
93 [1988] JPL 268.

and his wife. The council objected, apparently because of the visual effect, and issued an enforcement notice alleging a material change of use. On appeal, the inspector quashed the enforcement notice on the grounds that the caravan was used for animal feed preparation and shelter, such uses were ancillary to the agricultural use, and stationing the caravan was not a material change. The council unsuccessfully appealed to the High Court.

6.61 Kennedy J pointed out: 'The fact that an item which is brought on to the land is aesthetically objectionable does not of itself cast any light on the question of whether the land is being used for the purposes of agriculture and whether the item complained of is contributing to that purpose'.

6.62 Kennedy J's judgment was upheld by the Court of Appeal. Ralph Gibson LJ said:'There is, in planning law even with reference to the most beautiful parts of our countryside, no basis for excluding from the notion of ordinary equipment a useful and suitable article such as a caravan on the ground only that it was not traditional in construction or appearance for the particular purposes for which Mr Day had applied it.'

6.63 Two comments may be pertinent. First, the fundamental question was whether Mr Day's use of the caravan amounted to use for agriculture: since it did, the effect of what is now TCPA 1990, s. 55(2)(e) was to remove it from the definition of development. It was for this reason, it is submitted, that the question of the effect of the caravan on the amenities of the neighbourhood was irrelevant; in other cases the effect on amenity may be relevant in determining whether there is a material change of use.[94] Second, had Mr Day been seen using the caravan as living accommodation and not merely for shelter whilst working, the result would probably have been very different.

6.64 The issue of what constitutes a lawful agricultural use received further consideration by the Court of Appeal recently in *Millington v Secretary of State for the Environment, Transport and the Regions*.[95] In this case the applicant had a vineyard on his land and he also opened the site to the public, offering wine for sale and providing light refreshments. The local planning authority issued an enforcement notice alleging a material change of use from agriculture. On appeal, the Secretary of State granted planning permission for the production of wine but preventing its sale. The High Court upheld the enforcement notice. In addition, the Secretary of State refused to certify the use of the land for the sale of wine and public visits.

---

94 See para 6.136.
95 [2000] JPL 297.

6.65 The Court of Appeal rejected the Secretary of State's contention that when grapes were crushed so as to produce juice a new product was created and this process fell outside the permitted use of the land for the purposes of agriculture.

6.66 Schiemann LJ[96] said: 'To make the distinction between development and non-development turn on whether a new product is being created is pregnant with difficulty. Is a new product being created when grapes are put out to dry in order to become raisins; when honey in the honeycomb is separated from the wax; when the chaff is separated from the corn; when silage is being made?'

6.67 The learned Lord Justice considered that the proper approach was to consider whether what the applicant was doing could, having regard to ordinary and reasonable practice, be regarded as ordinarily incidental to the growing of grapes for wine; or, had it come to the stage where the operations could not reasonably be said to be consequential on the agricultural operations of producing the crop? He felt that this approach echoed the intention of Parliament in excluding agricultural uses from development control. Accordingly, Schiemann LJ held that the making of wine on the scale concerned was a perfectly normal activity for a farmer engaged in growing wine grapes.

(3) The Use Classes Order

6.68 No development is involved by a change of use from one purpose to another within one of the use classes specified in the use classes order made by the Secretary of State.[97] At present this means the Use Classes Order 1987. This order sets out 16 use classes, each of which groups together a number of similar uses. We will consider first the general purpose and effect of the Use Classes Order before setting out the separate use classes.

The Use Classes Order: its purpose and effect

6.69 Where a building or other land is used for a purpose within one of the use classes specified in the Use Classes Order made by the Secretary of State, the use of that building or other land (or of part thereof)[98] for another purpose within the same use class does not constitute development.[99] Thus, a change of use from say a bookshop to a travel agency will not be development because both fall within Class A1 (shops). But a change of use from a bookshop to a shop for the sale of hot food may be development because the latter is specifically excluded from Class A1; it does not follow, however, that this change must be development. The TCPA 1990 and the Use Classes Order say that a change from one purpose to another

96 Mantell LJ delivered a concurring judgment and Butler-Sloss LJ agreed.

97 TCPA 1990, s. 55(2)(f).

98 The reference to the use of part of a building is at present subject to one exception: see the discussion of Class C3 (dwellinghouse) at para 6.96.

99 TCPA 1990, s. 55(2)(f).

within the same use class does not involve development. They do not say that a change from something within a particular use class to something outside it (or vice versa) must be development; such cases must be considered in the light of all the facts, having regard to the general principles set out below.[100]

6.70 The current Use Classes Order was made in 1987, replacing that made in 1972. The use classes set out in 1972 were very similar to those originally formulated in 1948. The current order is a radical revision; by reducing the number of use classes and broadening the scope of many of the classes, it facilitates changes of use which might otherwise be deemed to be material and thus require planning permission.

6.71 There are many uses which do not fall within any of the use classes—the term *sui generis* is commonly used to describe these. Expressly excluded by virtue of article 3(6) of the order are: use as a theatre, amusement arcade etc, as a launderette, for the sale of fuel for motor vehicles, for the sale or display of motor vehicles, for taxi and car hire businesses, as a scrapyard, etc, for work registrable under the Alkali, etc Works Regulation Act 1906, as a hostel, for certain kinds of waste disposal operation. Two further uses were added to this list by the Town and Country Planning (Use Classes) (Amendment) (England) Order 2005.[101] These are: use as a retail warehouse club where goods are sold, or displayed for sale, only to persons who are members of that club; and use as a night club. In 2006, there was a further addition to the list—use as a casino was added.[102] Many other uses are not mentioned at all in the Use Classes Order, for instance, agriculture, transport depots.

6.72 The right to make a change of use within a particular use class does not arise until the premises have actually been used for a purpose within that class. Thus, if planning permission is granted for the use of premises as an office within Class B1, the right to change to another use such as light industry within that class does not arise until the premises have actually been used as offices. A mere token use may not be sufficient.[103]

6.73 It does not matter, however, that the initial use may have been unlawful in the sense that it was commenced without the necessary grant of planning permission. Thus, if there was an unauthorized change of use of a dwellinghouse to offices more than 10 years ago the office use will now be lawful and immune from enforcement action and the use can now be changed to light industry;[104] if the office use

100 *Rann v Secretary of State for the Environment* (1979) 40 P & CR 113 at 117.

101 SI 2005 No 84. The amendment came into force on 1 April 2005.

102 SI 2006 No 220. This amendment came into force on 6 April 2006.

103 *Kwik Save Discount Group Ltd v Secretary of State for the Environment* (1980) 42 P & CR 166, CA.

104 Assuming that the office use is within Class B1. For time limits on enforcement action, see para 12.34.

commenced within the last 10 years, the use can be changed to light industry but may be the subject of enforcement action because the office use has not become lawful.

6.74 When considering whether the Use Classes Order applies, it is important to distinguish between primary and ancillary uses. For instance, a farm will probably include buildings which are used for the storage of crops and farm equipment; the use of these buildings for storage is ancillary use to the primary use of the land for agriculture. Or there may be ovens for the baking of bread at the rear of a baker's shop: the baking of bread is an industrial process, but (unless the bread is also sold through other shops) is ancillary to the shop use.

6.75 It is a well-established principle that where a use is ancillary to the main use, it cannot be detached and turned into an independent use.

6.76 Thus, in *G Percy Trentham Ltd v Gloucestershire County Council*,[105] a firm of building and civil engineering contractors bought a farmhouse, yard, and farm buildings. This firm used some of the buildings (which had previously been used for housing farm machinery, etc) for the storage of building materials for their business. The county council having served an enforcement notice, the firm appealed on the ground that both uses fell within Class X of the Use Classes Order then in force relating to wholesale warehouses and repositories. The Court of Appeal considered that the farmer's use of these buildings for housing farm machinery was not use as a repository; but even if the buildings had been a repository, they could not be severed from the rest of the farmhouse and buildings; one had to look at the unit as a whole.[106]

6.77 A similar approach was adopted by the Court of Appeal in *Brazil (Concrete) Ltd v Amersham RDC and Minister of Housing and Local Government*.[107] A builders' yard with ancillary buildings had been used for storage in connection with a building contractor's business. In 1962 the premises were bought by R Brazil & Co Ltd and this company obtained planning permission to convert a big shed in the yard to various uses including a carpenter's shop. Brazil (Concrete) Ltd—a subsidiary company—then erected a ready mix concrete plant in the yard. It was contended on behalf of the company that they were entitled to do this because the big shed was now an industrial building for the purposes of the Use Classes Order, which meant that the land used with it fell within that category by virtue of

105 [1966] 1 All ER 701, [1966] 1 WLR 506.

106 [1966] 1 All ER 701 at 702. The decision of the Court of Appeal that use for housing farm machinery was not use as a repository has since been disapproved by the House of Lords in *Newbury District Council v Secretary of State for the Environment* [1981] AC 578, [1980] 1 All ER 731, but there was no suggestion that the court erred in any way in holding that the building could not be severed from the rest of the farm unit.

107 (1967) 18 P & CR 396.

article 2(3) of the order; that being so, the company were industrial undertakers and as such entitled by virtue of the General Development Order to erect the concrete plant.[108] The court rejected the basic contention that the big shed had become an industrial building for the purpose of the Use Classes Order; although articles were made in the carpenter's shop, that was incidental to the primary purpose of a builder's yard.

6.78 In the *Brazil (Concrete)* case Lord Denning MR gave an apt illustration of what is meant by an ancillary or incidental use:

> Take, for instance Harrods store, the unit is the whole building. The greater part is used for selling goods: but some parts are used for ancillary purposes such as for offices and for packing articles for dispatch. The character of the whole is determined by its primary use as a shop. It is within Class [A1] of the Use Classes Order [use as a shop]. The ancillary use of part as an office does not bring it within Class [B1—use as an office]: and the ancillary use of a part for packing does not make it a light industrial building within Class [B1—light industrial use].[109]

6.79 Reference was made to these words of Lord Denning MR by Malcolm Spence QC, sitting as Deputy Judge, in *Main v Secretary of State for the Environment.*[110] The judge held that a planning inspector had misunderstood and misapplied the word 'ancillary'. The inspector had treated the word as meaning 'relatively small' as opposed to being 'functionally related' to the use of the site. In the case, haulage activities and a skip hire operation which were only marginally connected with a scrap yard could not properly be said to be ancillary to the scrap yard merely because they were relatively small uses.

The Use Classes Order: the separate classes

6.80 Class A1 refers to use as a shop for all or any of the following purposes:

(a) for the retail sale of goods other than hot food;[111]
(b) as a post office;
(c) for the sale of tickets or as a travel agency;
(d) for the sale of sandwiches or other cold food for consumption off the premises;
(e) for hairdressing;
(f) for the direction of funerals;
(g) for the display of goods for sale;
(h) for the hiring out of domestic or personal goods or articles;

---

108 Successive General Development Orders have given permission for certain types of development by industrial undertakers, see para 7.48.

109 References to the current Use Classes Order have been substituted.

110 [1999] JPL 195.

111 The sale of fuel for motor vehicles and the sale or display for sale of motor vehicles are also excluded: see above.

(i) for the washing or cleaning of clothes or fabrics on the premises;[112]
(j) for the reception of goods to be washed, cleaned, or repaired;
(k) as an internet café; where the primary purpose of the premises is to provide facilities for enabling members of the public to access the internet;[113]

where the sale, display, or service is to visiting members of the public.

6.81 The purposes specified in Class A1 are very similar to those included in the definition of 'shop' for the purposes of Class I of the 1972 Order. The current Class A1 is, however, much simpler in form since it is not linked to a complicated definition of the word 'shop' as in the former Class I. However, it has been held that use as a 'shop' under Class A1 is confined to uses within buildings and so the Class does not apply to retailing carried out on open land.[114] If the main activity is the sale of goods by retail, any other uses such as storage being purely ancillary thereto, the 'use' of the building is quite clearly retailing and falls within Class A1. But if another main use wholly outside the use class, such as gaming machines, is carried on as well, there would appear to be a mixed or composite use which would suffice to remove the 'use' of the building from Class A1. In *Lydcare v Secretary of State for the Environment and Westminster City Council*,[115] the Court of Appeal held that premises were not used for the carrying on of a retail trade or business where there was a mixed use of the sale of goods by retail and for the viewing of films in coin-operated booths; although this was a decision on the definition of shop for the purposes of the 1972 Order, the principle, it is submitted, is still applicable.

6.82 Of course, each case will turn on its own particular facts. In *R v Maldon District Council, ex p Pattani*,[116] one of the issues was whether the operation of a pharmacy within a supermarket 'foodstore' constituted a material change of use requiring separate planning permission. The Court of Appeal upheld a decision of Collins J that the pharmacy was making a supply in circumstances corresponding to a retail sale. Thus, there was no distinction to be made, in planning terms, between the supply of medicines on prescription and their supply otherwise than on prescription.

6.83 The meaning of the words 'visiting members of the public' in Class A1 arose in *R v Thurrock Borough Council, ex p Tesco Stores Ltd*,[117] where a 'warehouse club' was held not to be a shop for the purpose of the provision. The club only sold goods to a restricted membership who were required to pay a subscription. Schiemann J

---

[112] As amended by T & P (Use Classes) (Amendment Order) 1991, SI 1991 No 1567 which substituted an amended para (i) and a new para (j).
[113] Added by SI 2005 No 84.
[114] *Crawley v Secretary of State for the Environment* [1990] JPL 742.
[115] (1984) 49 P & CR 186, CA.
[116] [1998] EGCS 135.
[117] [1994] JPL 328.

held that if there were a restriction on those who could come and buy, then the premises were not *prima facie* properly described as being used for the sale of goods to visiting members of the public.

6.84 Class A2 (financial and professional services) was entirely new in 1987. It refers to use for the provision of:

(a) financial services;
(b) professional services (other than health or medical services);
(c) any other services (including use as a betting office) which it is appropriate to provide in a shopping area;[118]

where the services are provided principally to visiting members of the public.

6.85 Class A2 thus embraces offices of a type—such as banks, building society branches, estate agents' offices—which the public expect to find in shopping areas.

6.86 It includes solicitors' offices as long as they provide services principally to visiting members of the public. In this respect it matters not that the office operates an appointment system.[119]

6.87 Although offices of this type are regarded as appropriate in shopping areas, they have been assigned to a separate use class with the intention as far as possible of maintaining control over the conversion of retail shops to office uses.[120] Offices not falling within Class A2 are in Class B1 along with light industrial uses, as explained below.

6.88 Class A3 as originally framed in 1987 was a broad use class comprising use for the sale of food for consumption on the premises or of hot food for consumption off the premises. It covered, for example, cafés, restaurants, wine-bars, and hot food takeaways. However, the proliferation of such establishments in recent years led to demands for a greater degree of control. Accordingly, the Use Classes Order has been amended[121] so as to substitute, for the old Class A3, the following:

Class A3. Restaurants and cafés
Use for the sale of food and drink for consumption on the premises
Class A4. Drinking establishments
Use as a public house, wine-bar or other drinking establishment
Class A5. Hot food takeaways

---

118 Amusement arcades are, however, excluded by virtue of art 3(6): see above.

119 *Kalra v Secretary of State for the Environment* [1995] NPC 164, CA. See also *Palisade Investments Ltd v Secretary of State for the Environment* [1993] 3 PLR 49—bureau de change within Class A2.

120 Circular 13/87, para 18 (now revoked and replaced by Circular 3/05).

121 Substituted by SI 2005 No 84; see Circular 3/05.

6.89 Use for the sale of hot food for consumption off the premises.

Class B1 (business) refers to use for all or any of the following purposes:

(a) use as an office[122] other than a use within Class A2;
(b) for research and development of products or processes;
(c) for any industrial process;[123]

being a use which can be carried on in any residential area without detriment to the amenity of that area by reason of noise, vibration, smell, fumes, smoke, soot, ash, dust, or grit.

6.90 This use class is perhaps the most radical of the changes made by the 1987 Use Classes Order. It brings into a single class many of the office uses and the light industrial uses which had been quite distinct classes in earlier Use Classes Orders, together with certain uses connected with research and development. It includes, for instance, the development and manufacture of computers, micro-engineering, biotechnology, pharmaceutical research and manufacture—provided always that such use could be carried on without detriment to the amenities of a residential area by reason of noise, vibration, smell, etc.

6.91 The proviso about detriment to the amenity of a residential area was an essential feature of light industrial use in the earlier Use Classes Orders, but the present Order makes one significant change. In the earlier Orders the test was whether the processes carried on or the machinery installed were such as could be carried on or installed in any residential area without detriment to the amenity of that area by reason of noise, vibration, smell, etc; provided the nature of the processes or the machinery satisfied the test, the actual use might be detrimental to the activities of a residential area. The new formula is intended, apparently, to enable consideration to be given to all aspects of the use judged by the specified criteria of noise, vibration, smell, etc.[124]

6.92 The effect of the words 'which can be carried on in any residential area' was considered in *Lamb (WT) Properties Ltd v Secretary of State for the Environment and Crawley Borough Council*.[125] In that case an industrial use was carried on in a building near to Gatwick Airport. It was held that the proximity of the airport was irrelevant. 'One had to imagine the effect of the noise and so on from these premises were they set in the middle of a residential area. The hypothetical residential area was not one within a short distance of a busy international airport'.

---

122 'Office' use is not confined to commercial office use and can include, eg governmental administration; *Inner London Education Authority v Secretary of State for the Environment* [1990] JPL 200.

123 For the definition of 'industrial process', see para 6.103.

124 Circular 13/87, para 20. See now Circular 3/05.

125 [1983] JPL 303.

6.93 Class B2 refers to general industrial use, that is, use for the carrying on of any industrial process[126] other than one falling within Class B1. The Order as originally drafted included special industrial classes B3 to B7—these classes have now been abolished.[127]

6.94 Class B8 refers to use for storage or as a distribution centre. This replaced the former Class X which referred to 'wholesale warehouse or repository'; the current Class B8 is apparently intended to be similar in scope and thus will not include use as a retail warehouse, but it is wider than the former Class X in that it includes the use of open land as well as of buildings.[128]

6.95 Class C1 is concerned with hotels where no significant element of care is provided, and Class C2 with various kinds of residential institutions. A new Class C2A—secure residential institutions—was inserted in 2006.[129] This provides for use 'for the provision of secure residential accommodation, including use as a prison, young offenders' institution, detention centre, secure training centre, custody centre, short-term holding centre, secure hospital, secure local authority accommodation or use as a military barracks'. This new class has been inserted as a consequence of the abolition of Crown immunity by PCPA 2004. Class C3 was wholly new in 1987, creating for the first time a use class comprising dwellinghouses as such; it refers to use as a single dwellinghouse (whether or not as a sole or main residence):

(a) by a single person or persons living together as a family; or
(b) by not more than six residents living together as a single household (including a household where care is provided for residents).

6.96 Class C3 is clearly intended to facilitate change of use from a single family house to sharing by unrelated persons living together as a household, eg a group of students or other young persons or by a group of people with disabilities who are in need of some element of care. Such a change of use would not necessarily involve development at all, but this use class removes all doubt provided the 'household' consists of not more than six people; where there are more than six people, the question whether there is a material change of use has to be decided on general principles in each case.

6.97 In *R v Kettering Borough Council, ex p Hossack,*[130] Lightman J held that, in order for residents to be regarded as living together as a single household, they had to

---

126 For the definition of 'industrial process', see para 6.103.

127 T & CP (Use Classes) Amendment Order 1992, SI 1992 No 610: T & CP (Use Classes) Amendment Order 1995, SI 1995 No 297.

128 Circular 13/87, para 23. See now Circular 3/05.

129 T & CP (Application of Subordinate Legislation to the Crown) Order 2006, SI 2006 No 1282, which came into force on 7 June 2006.

130 [2002] 27 EG 141 (CS).

be bound together by a relationship beyond that of a common need for accommodation, support, and resettlement. This decision was reversed by the Court of Appeal[131] who considered that the learned judge's test was too stringent. The court placed some reliance on Circular 13/87 which states that Class C3 is intended for small community care homes and other groups of people such as students who are not necessarily related to each other.

6.98 In *North Devon District Council v First Secretary of State,*[132] a semi-detached house in a residential area was being used to house two children who had been placed in care by local authorities. Care was provided by two non-resident staff who were, between them, on duty at all times. On appeal, the inspector held that the use was lawful as it was the use of a dwellinghouse by not more than six residents living together as a single household under Class C3(b). Collins J held that a 'household' under this class required more than just children, there had to be a proper functioning household—this meant that children and carers must reside on the premises.[133] The inspector had erred in treating this case as falling under Class C3(b) rather than Class C2. However, *North Devon* was a case involving children; in *R (on the application of Crawley Borough Council) v First Secretary of State,*[134] Richards J rejected the suggestion that where care is needed for those under a disability, C3 could only apply if the carers were in residence in the same property as those for whom they were caring. Each case had to be decided on its own facts as a matter of fact and degree.

6.99 It is important to note that Class C3 does not derogate from the rule that the conversion of a single dwellinghouse into two or more separate dwellings is a material change of use and thus requires planning permission.[135] Whether development occurs in the converse situation of the conversion of two or more separate dwellings into a single dwellinghouse is a matter of fact and degree. It is clear, however, from the decision in *Richmond upon Thames London Borough Council v Secretary of State for the Environment, Transport and the Regions*[136] that such a change does not fall under Class C3. The proposal in question was the conversion of a house divided into seven flats into a single family dwellinghouse. Christopher Lockhart-Mummery QC, sitting as Deputy Judge, rejected a contention that such a change came within the ambit of the Use Classes Order. This was because the word 'buildings' in the first part of TCPA 1990, s. 55(2)(f) did not refer to part of a building. A building that is divided into seven flats is not in 'use as a single

131 [2002] EWHC Civ 886.
132 [2003] EWHC 157 (Admin).
133 Disapproving *R v Bromley London Borough Council, ex p Sinclair* (1991) 3 PLR 60.
134 [2004] EWHC 160 (Admin).
135 See Use Classes Order, art 4.
136 [2001] JPL 84.

dwellinghouse' within Class C3 and therefore the Use Classes Order did not apply.

6.100 It would seem that, in London, Class C3 may be overidden by the Greater London (General Powers) Act 1973, s. 2 which provides that the use of residential accommodation in the metropolis for 'temporary sleeping accommodation' involves a material change of use. In *Hyde Park Residence Ltd v Secretary of State for the Environment, Transport and the Regions*,[137] the Court of Appeal held that, in London, GL(GP)A 1973, s. 3 prevailed over the Use Classes Order.

6.101 Class D1 brings into a single use a variety of non-residential uses such as the provision of medical or health services (except the use of premises attached to the residence of the consultant or practitioner), day nurseries and centres, provision of education, art galleries, museums, and so on. Class D2 is concerned with assembly and leisure and includes cinemas, concert halls, bingo halls, swimming baths, and so on. As originally drafted, this class included use as casino but this use was removed from Class D2 and became a *sui generis* use as from 6 April 2006. Theatres were included in Class XVII of the 1972 Order together with cinemas, music halls, and concert halls. They have been excluded from any of the use classes in the current order with the intention of protecting them from being sold off for other purposes[138] but the question remains whether a change from theatre to, say, cinema would be a material change of use.

6.102 In *Rugby Football Union v Secretary of State for the Environment, Transport and the Regions*,[139] Ouseley J upheld a decision of the Secretary of State that Twickenham rugby stadium could not be classed as a 'concert hall' under Class D2(b) of the Order as the physical characteristics of a concert hall were not present—it did not have a roof. As it was used for outdoor sport, Twickenham was within Class D2(e), which refers to 'a swimming bath, skating rink, gymnasium, or other indoor or outdoor sports or recreations, not involving motorised vehicles or firearms'. The judge considered that the words 'or other outdoor . . . recreations' covered physical activities rather than activities of an artistic nature, and so the Class did not extend to the holding of concerts at this particular venue. This decision was upheld by the Court of Appeal.[140]

'Industrial process'

6.103 As we have seen, Class B1 of the current Use Classes Order includes light industrial processes, and Class B2 is wholly concerned with various other industrial processes.

---

137 [1999] 3 PLR 1.

138 Circular 13/87, para 32. See now Circular 3/05.

139 [2001] EWHC 927 (Admin), [2001] 45 EG 139 (CS). For an amusing commentary on this case, see the *Encyclopaedia of Planning Law and Practice*, November 2001 Monthly Bulletin.

140 [2002] EWHC Civ 1169.

An industrial process is a process for, or incidental to, any of the following purposes:[141]

(a) the making of any article (including a ship or vessel, or a film, video, or sound recording);
(b) the altering, repairing, maintaining, ornamenting, finishing, cleaning, washing, packing, canning, adapting for sale, breaking up, demolition of any article;
(c) the getting, dressing, or treatment of minerals.

6.104 The 'process' must be one which is carried on in the course of trade or business, that is something which is an occupation rather than a pleasure.[142] It seems that a hobby, even though financially profitable, is not a trade or business; this appears to have been taken for granted in the case of *Peake v Secretary of State for Wales.*[143] But it is not essential to the concept of a business that it should be carried on with a view to making a profit; thus in *Rael-Brook Ltd v Minister of Housing and Local Government*,[144] use of a building as a cooking centre by a local authority for the provision of school meals was held to be industrial, so that planning permission was not thereafter required for a change to shirt making.

6.105 It might appear from this that the court adopts a liberal approach to the definition of 'industrial building'. The court has, however, recognized the danger that amateur workshops might be turned over to commercial industrial activity without any control by the planning authority. Accordingly, a relatively severe construction is to be placed on the terms of the order. There were some important remarks to that effect in *Rael-Brook Ltd v Minister of Housing and Local Government.*[145] These remarks were followed in *Tessier v Secretary of State for the Environment.*[146]

6.106 A sculptor used a dutch barn as a studio. In the barn there were six large benches with vices, casting pits, a forge, an anvil, and furnaces; stone masonry blocks of up to three-and-a-half tons would be cut out with drills, grinders, electric hammers, and hand chisels. The sculptor also used the studio as a showroom and for lectures. The Secretary of State held that the use was not industrial, but *sui generis.*

6.107 Held: the Secretary of State was entitled to take the view that an artist, expressing his art form and making articles in the process, even if they were sold, was not making them in the course of a trade or business.

141 Use Classes Order, art 2.
142 *Rolls v Miller* (1884) 27 Ch D 71 at 88, per Lindley LJ.
143 (1971) 22 P & CR 889. For an account of this case, See para 6.131.
144 [1967] 2 QB 65, [1967] 1 All ER 262.
145 Ibid.
146 (1975) 31 P & CR 161.

6.108 Difficulties sometimes arise where two or more uses are carried on together. For instance, manufacturing firms may carry on light industry in one building and general industry in a neighbouring building. Article 3(4) of the Use Classes Order provides that where land on a single site or adjacent sites is used by a single undertaking for two or more purposes within Classes B1 and B2, those classes may be treated as a single class provided the area occupied for general industrial purposes is not substantially increased. This facilitates changes of use within a group of buildings.

6.109 Interchangeability is also facilitated by article 3(3) which provides that a use which is ordinarily incidental to and included in a use specified in the order is not excluded from that use because it is specified elsewhere in the order as a separate use. The effect of this may be seen from *Vickers-Armstrong Ltd v Central Land Board*[147] which was decided on article 3(3) of the Use Classes for the Third Schedule Purposes Order 1948.[148]

6.110 An aviation works included an administration block; it was used partly as offices, but also by designers of blueprints and by draughtsmen, and in it technicians carried out important mechanical tests.

6.111 In connection with a claim for compensation the question arose as to whether this building could have been used for general industrial purposes without planning permission.

6.112 The Court of Appeal held that the building could have been so used without planning permission. 'Looked at as a whole, I should have thought that the appellants' works were clearly used as a general industrial building. It is true that the administration block was not wholly used for the carrying out of an 'incidental' process, but it plainly was, I should have thought, incidental use of the works within article 3(3) of the Order. That being so, it matters not that it cannot have been said wholly to have been used for the carrying out of processes; offices are clearly incidental to the use of a general industrial building.'

General principles

6.113 Where the statutory rules do not apply, the question whether there is a material change of use must be decided on general principles. As we have seen, a change is 'material' if it matters having regard to the objects of planning control. In this

[147] (1957) 9 P & CR 33.

[148] This Order provided a similar set of use classes, but for a different purpose (compensation).

connection the following points may arise:

(1) In most cases the first question to ask will be whether the change of use will completely alter the character of the land or buildings.
(2) Where an existing use is intensified it is necessary to ask whether there has been a complete change in the character of the land or buildings.
(3) If the change of use only partially alters the character of the land or building, it will be necessary to ask whether the change is material for some other reason.
(4) In some cases, the answer may depend on the unit of land or buildings under consideration.
(5) In some cases, it is necessary to consider whether existing use rights have been lost or abandoned.

We will consider each of these in turn.

(1) Will the change of use completely alter the character of the land or buildings?

6.114 The relevance of this test was emphasized in *Guildford RDC v Penny*.[149] On 1 July 1948 a field was used as a site for eight caravans. Over the years the number was increased to 27 and the local authority served an enforcement notice. On appeal, the magistrates held that this did not constitute a material change of use and quashed the enforcement notice. The Court of Appeal held that an increase or intensification of use might amount to a material change of use, but in this case the land had been used as a caravan site from first to last, and it could not be said that the magistrates had erred in law in finding that there had been no material change of use. The Court of Appeal was saying in effect that the increase in number was not so great that it was unreasonable for the magistrates to hold that there had been no real change in the character of the site.

6.115 It should be noted that the test is the character of the use and not the particular purpose of the particular occupier. This is illustrated by *Marshall v Nottingham City Corpn*.[150]

6.116 From 1912 to 1957 L owned a plot of land which he used for manufacturing and selling wooden portable buildings, garages, and wooden garden ornaments. The goods were made in a workshop and displayed in the open. There was a hut which he used as an office and from which he conducted sales. After 1939 the business dwindled and by 1957 was moribund though not dead.

6.117 In 1957 M bought the land from L so that a company of which she was managing director could use it for selling caravans and wooden portable buildings; the company did not manufacture any goods. The corporation served an enforcement

149 [1959] 2 QB 112, [1959] 2 All ER 111.
150 [1960] 1 All ER 659, [1960] 1 WLR 707.

notice alleging a material change of use by using the land for the display and sale of caravans and wooden buildings.

6.118 Glyn-Jones J held: (1) neither the fact that the company did not manufacture the goods which they sold, nor the fact that the company sold caravans which L had not sold, constituted a material change of use; (2) the increase in the intensity of the use had not been so great as to constitute a material change of use.

6.119 Similar considerations arose in *East Barnet UDC v British Transport Commission.*[151]

6.120 This case concerned some 30,855 sq yards of land belonging to the British Transport Commission near a railway station. The land was divided into seven parcels. Three parcels comprising nearly 20,000 sq yds had been used as coal stacking yards; one parcel of over 10,000 sq yds had been vacant for many years; two very small parcels consisted of buildings which had been used as workshops; the seventh parcel was a siding.

6.121 At different dates Vauxhall Motors took tenancies of all these parcels, and used the land as a transit depot for the handling and storage of crated motor vehicles nearly all of which were received and despatched by rail. In 1951 they applied for planning permission in respect of two of the parcels (one of them previously used for coal stacking, and the other the unused land) and the council granted permission subject to the condition that the use of all the land for this purpose would cease on 31 May 1958. The use continued after that date, and the council served enforcement notices.

6.122 On appeal, the magistrates quashed the enforcement notices on the ground that the use of the land did not constitute development.

6.123 The council thereupon took the case to the High Court. It was held, inter alia, that the magistrates were entitled to find that there had been no material change of use. The land had originally been a coal storage depot, the coal being brought in and taken away by rail. There would have been no material change of use if the British Transport Commission had changed the storage from coal to oil. 'The mere fact that the commodity changes does not necessarily mean that the land is being used for a different purpose nor, as it seems to me, is there any relevance in the fact that the purpose for which the land is used is effected by other hands, in this case by [Vauxhall Motors].'[152]

6.124 Put shortly, there was no material change of use because the land was used throughout as a storage and transit depot. As regards the unused parcel, the Divisional

[151] [1962] 2 QB 484, [1961] 3 All ER 878.
[152] Per Lord Parker CJ at 885.

Court said that it was proper to regard this not as a separate unit of land but merely as an unused portion of the whole unit.

6.125 That the test is the character of the use and not the particular purpose of the particular occupier was subsequently confirmed by the House of Lords in *Westminster City Council v British Waterways Board*.[153]

6.126 In *Secretary of State for Transport, Local Government and the Regions v Waltham Forest London Borough Council*,[154] it was held that what has to be compared, in deciding whether a proposed use is a material change, is the existing use and the proposed use. It is not permissible, as part of the decision-making process, to interpose some notional use. In this case, the Court of Appeal held that an inspector had erred in finding that because Class C3 of the Use Classes Order 1987[155] permits the use of a dwellinghouse by not more than six residents living together as a single household, there would be no material change of use if that number were exceeded by one or two residents. It seems the inspector arrived at this conclusion on the basis that the property could have been lawfully used by a large family of more than six persons—this was a notional, as opposed to the actual, use of the property.

6.127 Thus, the fact that no further permissions are required to move from the existing use A to the notional use B, or to move from the notional use B to the proposed use C, has no bearing on the decision whether the change from A to C is a material change of use. It might, however, be potentially relevant to the quite different question of whether planning permission ought to be granted for the proposed use.

(2) Where the existing use has been intensified, has there been a complete change in the character of the land or buildings?

6.128 It is now well established that a material change in the use of a building or other land can occur through intensification of the existing use. The question is whether the existing use has been intensified to such a degree that it has become materially different from what it was before. A good illustration is the case of *Birmingham Corpn v Minister of Housing and Local Government and Habib Ullah*.[156]

6.129 Two houses each of which had been in single family occupation were sold to new owners, and several families were installed in each house. The corporation served enforcement notices alleging that there had been a material change of use by changing the use of each from single dwellinghouse to house-let-in-lodgings. The Minister considered that there had been no material change of use since the houses were still residential.

---

153 [1985] AC 676, [1984] 3 All ER 737.
154 [2002] EWCA Civ 330.
155 See para 6.96.
156 [1964] 1 QB 178, [1963] 3 All ER 668.

Held: the Minister had erred in law in saying that because the houses remained residential there could not be a material change of use; whether there had been a material change of use, said Lord Parker CJ, was a matter of fact and degree in each case. The court remitted the cases to the Minister for reconsideration. **6.130**

Intensification may also occur through an increase in the amount of an activity. This form of intensification is illustrated by *Peake v Secretary of State for Wales*.[157] **6.131**

In 1950 following the grant of planning permission, P built a private garage. From then until 1968 he used it for the repair and servicing of motor vehicles as a spare-time activity or profitable hobby. In 1968 he began working full-time at the garage. The local planning authority served an enforcement notice. The Secretary of State, dismissing P's appeal, said that a material change of use had occurred in 1968. P then appealed to the High Court. **6.132**

Held: although a change in an activity from part-time to full-time could not of itself amount to a material change of use, the Secretary of State was entitled to conclude as a matter of fact and degree that P's use of the garage prior to 1968 was incidental to its designated use as a private garage but that after that date the use escalated to a degree where it could no longer be said to be incidental to use as a private garage and involved a material change of use. **6.133**

It must often be very difficult to decide at what point an intensification of use results in a material change of use, but this difficulty does not affect the general principle of law. It is worth emphasizing that it is not sufficient to say that the existing use has been 'intensified'; the vital question is the degree of intensification. In the case of *Kensington and Chelsea Royal Borough v Secretary of State for the Environment and Mia Carla Ltd*,[158] Donaldson LJ said it was much too late to suggest that the word 'intensification' should be deleted from the language of planners, but it has to be used with very considerable circumspection, and it had to be clearly understood by all concerned that intensification which did not amount to a material change of use was merely intensification and not a breach of planning control. His Lordship hoped that, where possible, those concerned with planning would get away from the term and try to define what was the material change of use by reference to the *terminus a quo* (that is, the starting point) and the *terminus ad quem* (that is, the end point). **6.134**

There will be some cases where the intensification of a use occurs but the intensified use remains in the same use class of the Use Classes Order as the **6.135**

[157] (1971) 22 P & CR 889. And see *Turner v Secretary of State for the Environment* [1991] JPL 547 where a change from private fishing to use as recreational fishing was held to be capable of being a material change of use. An appeal was allowed on other grounds: [1992] JPL 837.

[158] [1981] JPL 50.

pre-intensification user. In *Eastleigh Borough Council v First Secretary of State*,[159] it was held that an increase in the retail floorspace of a store was not a material change of use—the use of the premises had remained under Class A1 throughout and therefore no development had taken place. Whereas the principle in the case is one of general application, increases in floorspace have now, under PCPA 2004, been brought under planning control.[160]

(3) Where a change of use does not completely alter the character of the land or building is the change material for any other reason?

6.136 It would seem that a change of use will be 'material' if it completely alters the character of the land or building. However, there are many changes of use which only partially alter the character of the land or building. In such cases further questions must be asked. In *Guildford RDC v Penny*,[161] Lord Evershed said that a change of use might be material if it would involve a substantial increase in the burden of services which a local authority has to supply. The principle seems to be sound. Thus the conversion of large houses to multiple occupation will tend to increase the demand for services provided by public authorities, but cases of this sort will usually be considered to be material changes of use in any event by virtue of the statutory rule about the conversion of houses into more than one dwelling[162] or under the heading of intensification.[163]

6.137 Since planning control is to some extent concerned with the preservation of amenity, it may also be relevant to ask what effect a change of use will have on the neighbourhood. A change of use may well be 'material' if the nature of the use as changed is such that it is likely to involve a great increase in the number of persons calling at the premises or if it is likely to cause a great deal of noise. There have been some pronouncements which suggest that it is not permissible to take into account the effect on the neighbourhood[164] but these seem inconsistent with the opinions of the Divisional Court. Thus, in *Williams v Minister of Housing and Local Government*,[165] the owner of a nursery garden had used a timber building on the land for the sale of produce grown in the nursery garden; he then began selling imported fruit as well. The Divisional Court upheld an enforcement notice: the main ground for the decision was that the planning unit was the nursery garden and not the timber building, but Widgery J also said: 'there is clearly, from

159 [2004] 24 EG 149 (CS).
160 See para 6.16.
161 [1959] 2 QB 112, [1959] 2 All ER 111.
162 See para 6.48.
163 See para 6.128.
164 See Circular 67, issued in 1948. See also remarks by Sir Douglas Frank QC (sitting as a deputy judge) in *Rann v Secretary of State for the Environment* (1979) 40 P & CR 113.
165 (1967) 18 P & CR 514.

a planning point of view, a significant difference in character between a use which involves selling the produce of the land itself, and a use which involves importing goods from elsewhere for sale. All sorts of planning considerations may arise which render one activity appropriate in a neighbourhood and the other activity quite undesirable.'

6.138 Widgery J's point is illustrated by the case of *Blum (Lilo) v Secretary of State for the Environment and London Borough of Richmond upon Thames Council.*[166]

6.139 The site had been used as livery stables—that is stabling for the accommodation of privately owned horses—since 1950. In 1980–1 it began to be used in addition as a riding school; an enforcement notice was issued alleging a material change of use from livery stables to riding school and livery stables.

6.140 On appeal, the inspector held that there had been a material change of use. Although there were superficial resemblances, there were significant differences of purpose, function, and character; the character of the use was affected by the amount of additional staff and facilities, and there would be more horse traffic, more rides out, and more car traffic. He also referred to the introduction of a sanded paddock for instructional purposes.

6.141 In the High Court Simon Brown J upheld the inspector's decision. Although the inspector had referred to some of the factors involved in terms of intensification, a new use had been introduced.

6.142 It seems clear enough that this was not in reality the intensification of the existing use—the livery stables—but the introduction of a new use—the riding school: in deciding whether this additional use was a material change the environmental effects were clearly very relevant.

6.143 It may also be proper to ask what is the purpose of a particular change of use, eg whether it is incidental to the existing use of the premises or whether it is the establishment of a trade or business. This test must, however, be applied with care. The doctor who uses two rooms in his private residence for the purpose of his practice and the family who take in a lodger are both doing so for the purposes of gain, but it is probably true to say that in neither case is there a material change of use. Planning control is concerned with the use of land, not with personal motives.

(4) What is the unit under consideration?

6.144 TCPA 1990 refers to a material change in the use of 'any buildings or other land'. This is vague and in some cases can give rise to difficulty. In *East Barnet UDC v*

166 [1987] JPL 278.

British Transport Commission,[167] the question whether there had been a material change in the use of one parcel of land turned on whether that parcel should be regarded as a separate unit of land or merely part of a larger unit. Lord Parker CJ commented that the choice of unit was always a matter of difficulty but 'looked at *as a matter of commonsense* in the present case it seems to me that this was merely an unused part of the unit in question'.[168] In other words there can be no hard and fast rules as to the choice of unit: one must approach the problem in each case on commonsense lines.

6.145 In the later case of *Burdle v Secretary of State for the Environment*,[169] however, the Divisional Court attempted a more precise formulation, and suggested three possible criteria for determining the planning unit. First, whenever it is possible to recognize a single main purpose of the occupier's use of his land, to which secondary activities are incidental or ancillary, the whole unit of occupation should be considered. This would seem to cover the circumstances of the *East Barnet* case. Secondly, it may be equally apt to consider the entire unit of occupation even though the occupier carries on a variety of activities, and it is not possible to say that one is incidental or ancillary to another; eg, a composite use where the activities are not confined within separate and physically distinct areas. Third, within a single unit of occupation two or more physically distinct areas may be occupied for substantially different and unrelated purposes. In such a case each area used for a separate main purpose (together with its incidental and ancillary activities) ought to be considered as a separate planning unit.

6.146 These criteria are not absolute rules. In *Wood v Secretary of State for the Environment*,[170] a conservatory attached to a dwellinghouse was used for the sale of produce from a smallholding. The Secretary of State, in considering an appeal against an enforcement notice in respect of this use, treated the conservatory as a separate planning unit. The Divisional Court considered that the Secretary of State had approached the matter in the wrong way. Lord Widgery CJ said that it could rarely, if ever, be right to dissect a dwellinghouse and to regard one room in it as a separate planning unit. In other words, the Secretary of State should have considered whether the use of the conservatory for the sale of produce amounted to a material change in the use of the whole of the premises.

6.147 Lord Widgery's dictum in *Wood's* case is of considerable importance because of the large number of cases in which the resident occupier of a house uses one or two rooms for the purposes of his profession or business. There may, of course, be a

---

167 [1962] 2 QB 484, [1961] 3 All ER 878.
168 At 886, author's italics.
169 [1972] 3 All ER 240, [1972] 1 WLR 1207.
170 [1973] 2 All ER 404, [1973] 1 WLR 707.

material change of use in such cases, but the question is to be decided by looking at the house as a whole and not in separate parts.[171]

6.148 It seems that Lord Widgery's dictum is not to be extended to buildings other than single dwellings. In *Johnston v Secretary of State for the Environment*,[172] the Divisional Court considered that in the case of a block of flats in single ownership, but let to separate and different tenants, the planning unit would normally be the individual flat in question. Frequently, a single planning permission covers a complex of buildings—for example, a housing estate or commercial development. In *Hertsmere Borough Council v Secretary of State for the Environment*,[173] an office, which formed part of a larger complex of offices in multiple occupation, had been turned into a wholesale warehouse without planning permission. On appeal against the enforcement notice, the inspector took the planning unit to be the whole complex and he was led to this conclusion by the fact that the whole complex was covered by a single planning permission. David Widdicombe QC, as deputy judge, held that this conclusion was unreasonable and perverse—there is no reason to suppose that the grant of planning permission necessarily dictates the planning unit; 'a planning permission has no necessary relationship to the planning unit to be adopted in considering whether a material change of use has taken place. Many separate uses may be comprised in a single development—a block of flats is an example'.

6.149 There will also be cases in which a large business undertaking occupies two or more geographically separate sites. Even if these separate sites could properly be described as a single unit of occupation it would not be appropriate to treat them as a single planning unit. In *Fuller v Secretary of State for the Environment*,[174] the appellant farmed over 2,000 acres comprising a widely scattered number of farms. The local planning authority issued enforcement notices requiring discontinuance of the use of the land for the commercial storage of grain not grown on the appellant's own specified agricultural units. Dismissing appeals against the notices, the Secretary of State said that the separate farms could not reasonably be regarded as one planning unit 'any more than, say, the similarly scattered retail outlets of a local chain of shops, all in the same ownership and occupation and performing the same function, would be so regarded'. In the High Court Stuart Smith J upheld the Secretary of State's decision.

---

171 See, for instance, a decision of the Secretary of State concerning the use of part of a dwelling-house by a veterinary surgeon for the purposes of his practice: [1976] JPL 328.

172 (1974) 28 P & CR 424.

173 [1991] JPL 552.

174 [1987] JPL 854. And see *Thames Heliport v Tower Hamlets London Borough Council* [1997] JPL 448, considered at para 6.184.

Sub-division of the planning unit

6.150 There is some uncertainty as to whether the division of the planning unit into two or more separate units is a material change of use. As we have seen, the division of a single dwellinghouse into two or more separate dwellings is a material change of use by virtue of a specific statutory provision,[175] but what of other cases?

6.151 In *Wakelin v Secretary of State for the Environment*,[176] a large house set in two acres of grounds had always been used as a single residential unit. In 1965 the then owner, who needed accommodation for an elderly relative, was granted planning permission for 'additional residential accommodation and three garages' subject to the condition that the new building should not be occupied other than by a close relative or member of the household staff. Some years later, W, with a view to selling off the lodge, applied for planning permission for 'separate and unrelated occupancy'. Permission was refused. On appeal, the inspector concluded that changing from one unit of accommodation to two was a material change of use.[177] The Court of Appeal held that the inspector had quite properly concluded that the division of what was a single unit into two separate units was a material change of use.

6.152 It is clear enough that in this case the sub-division of the planning unit involved a material change of use because the use permitted in 1965 was of both buildings as a single unit. It is less certain that the Court of Appeal intended to lay down a general rule that sub-division of a planning unit would always be development; indeed Browne LJ expressly reserved his opinion on that point.

6.153 Subsequently, in *Winton v Secretary of State for the Environment*,[178] Woolf J after considering the judgments in *Wakelin* said that the subdivision of the planning unit did not in itself amount to a material change of use but that it would do so if it had 'planning consequences'. The *Winton* case concerned the sub-division of an industrial building into two separate units; the previous use and the subsequent uses all fell within Class IV of the then Use Classes Order. The local planning authority took enforcement action. On appeal, the Secretary of State held that there had been a material change of use and upheld the enforcement notice. Woolf J decided that the court could not interfere with the Secretary of State's decision that there had been a material change. There remained, however, the question whether this change of use was covered by the Use Classes Order; the learned judge held—perhaps surprisingly—that the Use Classes Order did not cover the

---

[175] See para 6.47.

[176] [1978] JPL 769.

[177] The case did not fall within what is now the TCPA 1990, s. 55(3)(a) because the single unit of accommodation consisted of more than one building.

[178] (1982) 46 P & CR 205.

division of a unit into sub-units. Since then, however, what was then TCPA 1990, s. 22(2)(f) has been amended and the sub-division of a unit into two or more units within the same use class will not constitute development.[179]

(5) Have existing use rights been lost or abandoned?

6.154 The question of how far existing rights should be considered to have been lost or abandoned has caused some difficulty. The circumstances in which this may happen may be classified under two main heads: (a) extinguishment, and (b) abandonment.

Extinguishment

6.155 It is a fairly obvious principle that existing use rights may be extinguished as a result of new development. In many cases the continuation of previous uses would be wholly inconsistent with the new development and often indeed impracticable. But there are cases in which the continuation of previous uses would not be impracticable and not necessarily inconsistent with the new development. Over the years there have been a number of cases in which previous uses have continued after some development has taken place, but it was not until the decision of the Court of Appeal in *Jennings Motors Ltd v Secretary of State for the Environment*[180] that a single consistent principle for deciding such cases was adopted.

6.156 It will, however, be useful to look first at some of the earlier cases. In *Petticoat Lane Rentals Ltd v Secretary of State for the Environment*,[181] a cleared bomb site had been used throughout the week as a market. The entire site was redeveloped by the erection of a building; the ground floor was open, the building being supported on pillars, and was to be used as a car park and loading area. Permission was given for the use of the ground floor as a market on Sundays, but in fact it continued to be used as a market throughout the week. The Divisional Court held that the previously existing land had merged in the new building, and a new planning unit had been created which had no previous planning permission (except on Sundays) and that there was therefore a breach of planning control.

6.157 The theory of the 'new planning unit' was applied in *Aston v Secretary of State for the Environment*[182] where a building was erected on part of the original planning unit. In 1952 A bought some land which he began to use for the keeping of pigs and also as a base for vehicles for his transport business. In 1956 he built a large barn which he used for both these purposes. The barn was blown down in a storm in 1961 and for some years there was no use for this part of the site. However, in

179 See para 6.69.
180 [1982] QB 541, [1982] 1 All ER 471.
181 [1971] 2 All ER 793, [1971] 1 WLR 1112.
182 (1973) 43 P & CR 331.

1969 he built a much larger barn without planning permission and claimed that he had the right to use it for the maintenance of his vehicles. The Divisional Court held that, where a new building is erected on part of the land, that part of the land becomes a new planning unit with no permitted uses apart from those derived from the planning permission, if any.

6.158 Alongside this theory of 'the new planning unit' a different but related theory had emerged—that of 'a new chapter' in the planning history. It began with *Prossor v Minister of Housing and Local Government*.[183] A garage proprietor applied for planning permission to rebuild a petrol service station; permission was granted on condition that no retail sales were to take place in the new building. Afterwards the appellant claimed that he had existing use rights for selling motor cars. Lord Parker CJ said that by adopting the permission granted in April 1964 the appellant's predecessor gave up any possible existing use rights in that regard which he may have had. 'The planning history of this site, as it were, seems to begin afresh on April 4, 1964 with the grant of this permission which was taken up and used.'[184]

6.159 This theory was later restated in *Newbury District Council v Secretary of State for the Environment*.[185] In that case temporary permission was granted for the use of two hangars as warehouses on the condition that the hangars should be removed when the temporary permission expired. Lord Lane said: 'The holder of planning permission will not be allowed to rely on any existing use rights if the effect of the permission when acted on has been to bring one phase of the planning history of a site to an end and to start a new one . . . In the present case there is no such break in the history.'

6.160 We can now turn to *Jennings Motors Ltd v Secretary of State for the Environment*.[186] The site had an established use as a taxi, car and coach hire business and for vehicle repairs and car sales. Most of the site was used for access and parking. There was a garage workshop in one corner occupying one-twelfth of the site; there was a showroom and office in another corner occupying one-thirteenth of the site. There had also been a second garage workshop, but the appellants pulled it down and put up a new building notwithstanding a refusal of planning permission to do so. The new building occupied about one seventeenth of the site, and the appellants began to use it for the repair and servicing of vehicles.

183 (1968) 67 LGR 109.

184 There is no change in the planning history of the site if the planning permission is not taken up, and it would perhaps be more logical to have chosen the date when the development began rather than the date of the planning permission.

185 [1981] AC 578, [1980] 1 All ER 731.

186 [1982] QB 541, [1982] 1 All ER 471.

6.161 The local planning authority did not take enforcement proceedings against the new building because it was better in appearance than that which it replaced. But enforcement proceedings were taken to prevent it being used for repair and maintenance work.

6.162 The Secretary of State upheld the enforcement notice. In the light of the *Petticoat Lane Rentals* case, he considered that when the new building was erected, a new planning history commenced in respect of it and the building on completion had a 'nil' use.

6.163 Held: (1) the erection of a new building did not necessarily create a 'new planning unit' nor give rise to a 'new chapter in the planning history'; (2) the question whether a new planning history was about to begin was one of fact and degree in each case; (3) in the present case there had been no change in the planning history and the appellants were entitled to the existing use rights attaching to the site inside the new building.

6.164 The Court of Appeal thus emphatically rejected the theory that the erection of a new building automatically extinguished previous use rights. The test now is whether, in the words of Lord Denning MR, 'there is a radical change in the nature of the buildings on the site or the uses to which they are put—so radical that it can be looked on as a fresh start altogether in the character of the site'.[187] This test is more flexible and, it is submitted, much fairer, but it will not always be easy to apply in practice. In the *Petticoat Lane Rentals* case the new test would have produced the same result, but different opinions have been expressed on the question whether the result would have been the same in *Aston*.[188]

Abandonment

6.165 The question whether existing use rights have been lost through abandonment arises where a use has ceased for a time and the land has not been used for any other purpose in the meantime; if the circumstances justify a finding that the use has been abandoned, the land will be deemed to have a nil use and a resumption of the previous use will require planning permission. It is not correct to say that a use has been 'abandoned' where it is immediately followed by another positive use;[189] if the latter amounts to a material change of use, it is unlikely that the previous use could thereafter be resumed without planning permission because a change from the latter to the former use would normally be a material change of use. The distinction is important because it may affect the right, given by the

187 [1982] 1 All ER 471 at 476.

188 Lord Denning thought that the result would have been different and that *Aston* was wrongly decided. Oliver and Watkins LJJ thought the result would have been the same.

189 *Young v Secretary of State for the Environment* [1983] JPL 465; affd [1983] JPL 677.

TCPA 1990, to resume a previous use where an enforcement notice is served in respect of a subsequent unlawful use.[190]

6.166 The question whether existing use rights have in fact been abandoned is a difficult one, and can usefully be considered under a number of headings suggested by Ashworth J in *Hartley v Minister of Housing and Local Government*.[191] '(1) If the sole use to which the land is put is suspended and thereafter resumed without there being any intervening different user, prima facie the resumption does not constitute development. As Lord Parker CJ put it in an earlier case[192] it is of course quite plain that a change from A to X and then from X to A does not involve development either way, if X is completely nil, no use at all'.

6.167 There are, of course, some uses of land which by their very nature are intermittent. Thus: 'a racecourse is perhaps used for a few days three or four times a year, but no one would suggest that it ceases to be used as a racecourse in the closed season, or that a new development occurs on the first day of the next meeting.'[193]

6.168 On the face of it Lord Parker's dictum goes wider than the case of the intermittent use and may well cover seasonal uses and cases where an activity is closed down and is then resumed after an interval.

6.169 (2) Nevertheless, there are circumstances in which the previous use will be deemed to have been abandoned. In *Hartley v Minister of Housing and Local Government*,[194] Lord Denning MR said that, if the land has remained unused for a considerable time in such circumstances that a reasonable man might conclude that the previous use has been abandoned, the tribunal[195] may hold it to have been abandoned. In other words if the circumstances justify such a conclusion, it is within the competence of the court to hold that the previous use has been abandoned. Lord Denning's guidance was applied by the Divisional Court in *Ratcliffe v Secretary of State for the Environment*.[196] From about 1920 to 1961 a quarry had been used by a local authority for tipping refuse. Thereafter there had been some sporadic tipping, but not by the local authority who had ceased tipping when their tenancy had run out, which had mainly involved the deposit of some lorry loads of clay and earth by a purchaser of the land who had been proposing to use it for chicken farming. In 1970 the land was acquired by the appellant who applied for a

---

190 See para 7.06.

191 [1969] 2 QB 46, [1969] 1 All ER 309.

192 *McKellen v Minister of Housing and Local Government* (1966) 198-Estates Gazette 683.

193 *Hawes v Thornton Cleveleys UDC* (1965) 17 P & CR 22 at 28, per Widgery J.

194 [1970] 1 QB 413, [1969] 3 All ER 1658. See also *R (on the application of Samuel Smith Old Brewery (Tadcaster) Ltd v Selby District Council* [2005] EWHC 3034 (Admin).

195 The 'tribunal' will normally be the court or the Secretary of State.

196 [1975] JPL 728. And see the CA decision in *White v Secretary of State for the Environment* [1989] JPL 692 where it was confirmed that the doctrine of abandonment could apply to a pre-1948 lawful use.

determination under what became section 64 of the TCPA 1990 as originally enacted as to whether filling the quarry for reclamation purposes would amount to development. The Secretary of State decided that the tipping use had been abandoned in 1961 and that resumption would be a material change of use.

6.170 The Divisional Court upheld the decision of the Secretary of State. Bridge J said that not only was the Secretary of State entitled so to find but applying the Hartley principles, he (Bridge J) could not see how he could have reached any other conclusion.

6.171 Presumably, in this case, Bridge J was saying that the 'reasonable man' looking at the circumstances would almost certainly have said that the use had been abandoned.

6.172 The Court of Appeal in *Hughes v Secretary of State for the Environment, Transport and the Regions*[197] has confirmed the objective approach in holding that the intentions of the owner, although relevant, could not be decisive, because the test must be the view taken by the reasonable man with knowledge of all the relevant circumstances. In the view of Kennedy LJ (with whom Thorpe LJ and Mance LJ agreed) this was a conclusion that accorded with common sense, '. . . otherwise a labourer's cottage which an emigrant and his family left 40 years ago, which has been in ruins for years, cannot cease to be regarded as a residence so long as its owner in America or Australia cherishes the dream that someday he will return to live there'.

6.173 There are, however, cases in which the intentions of the occupier must be considered. Thus in *Hall v Lichfield District Council*[198] Mrs H had spent the last 13 years of her life in hospital leaving her house empty and, it seems, no repairs were done; on her death, her personal representatives obtained a declaration that the residential use had not been abandoned. Intention is not the only factor which has to be taken into account, however. In connection with the issue of whether residential user has been abandoned, it seems that three other criteria are relevant—the physical condition of the building; the length of time for which the building has not been used; and whether it has been used for any other purposes.[199]

6.174 (3) Where land is put to a composite use the issues are more complex. The cessation of one of the component uses does not of itself constitute development; nor can it be said that the change from dual use to single use is of itself a material change of use. But there may be a material change in the use of the whole site if, after the cessation of one of the uses, the continuing use absorbs some or all of the

---

197 [2000] JPL 826.

198 [1979] JPL 425.

199 *Trustees of the Castell-y-Mynach Estate v Secretary of State for Wales* [1985] JPL 40.

remaining land.[200] It seems that there is no need to invoke the concept of abandonment in such a case.

6.175 (4) It may happen that one of the component uses is discontinued without any subsequent intensification of the other component use or uses. If the discontinued use is later resumed without planning permission it will be necessary to consider whether that use has in fact been abandoned. Relevant considerations will include the nature of the uses, what portion of the site was devoted to the discontinued use, what use if any was made of that portion during the period of discontinuance and how long the discontinuance lasted. Ultimately, said Ashworth J, the problem will resolve itself into the question: 'When the resumption occurred, was there a material change in the use of the land?'[201]

6.176 The decision of the House of Lords in *Pioneer Aggregates (UK) Ltd v Secretary of State for the Environment*[202] affirms the principle that an existing use may be lost by abandonment, but it also shows that there are limits to its application. It may happen that a use was begun in accordance with planning permission and subsequently suspended in circumstances which point to the use having been abandoned. If, however, the planning permission is still in force, the use can be resumed by virtue of that permission; a planning permission still capable of being implemented according to its terms cannot be extinguished by abandonment.[203] The question of whether the doctrine of abandonment applies to uses which become lawful through the passage of time under the new time limits introduced by the Planning and Compensation Act 1991 is discussed in chapter 12.[204]

6.177 The apparent breadth of the principle enunciated by the House of Lords in the *Pioneer* case was subjected to interpretation by the Court of Appeal in the later case of *Cynon Valley Borough Council v Secretary of State for the Environment*.[205] In that case, in 1958, the then occupier of premises obtained planning permission for a change of use to a fish and chip shop. Subsequently, the use of the premises was lawfully changed to use as an antiques shop in reliance on Class III of the then GDO. It was held that the premises could not later be used as a hot food take-away by reliance on the 1958 permission. That permission had been 'spent' upon implementation and could not be reverted to. The *Pioneer* case was explained on the basis that the planning permission authorized a mining operation where

---

200 See *Wipperman and Buckingham v London Borough of Barking* (1965) 17 P & CR 225; *Philglow Ltd v Secretary of State for the Environment and the London Borough of Hillingdon* [1985] JPL 318.

201 *Hartley v Minister of Housing and Local Government* [1969] 1 All ER 309 at 315.

202 [1985] AC 132, [1984] 2 All ER 358.

203 See para10.145.

204 See para 12.34.

205 [1986] 2 EGLR 191.

'each shovelful or each cut of the bulldozer is a separate act of development'. [206] Thus, once begun, the planning permission was not spent and was capable of implementation; it was of continuing effect. This interpretation was relied on by the High Court in *M & M (Land) Ltd v Secretary of State for Communities and Local Government* [207] where the court observed that most uses are not of this continuing nature—they can only be implemented once and therefore are susceptible to abandonment.

Cases of doubt

6.178 There will obviously be many cases in which it is not clear whether an operation or use of land involves development. TCPA 1990, s. 64 as originally enacted provided a procedure for dealing with such cases. Any person who proposed to carry out an operation or to change the use of land could apply to the local planning authority for a determination whether the proposed operation or change of use would constitute development and, if so, whether planning permission was required. But this procedure had become ineffective as a result of being restrictively interpreted by the courts. The Planning and Compensation Act 1991 repealed the procedure[208] and replaced it with one where any person wishing to ascertain whether any proposed use or operation would be lawful may apply to the local planning authority for a certificate—a certificate of Lawfulness of Proposed Use or Development (or CLOPUD).

6.179 TCPA 1990, s. 192(1) provides that if any person wishes to ascertain whether any proposed use of buildings or other land, or any operations proposed to be carried out in, on, over, or under land would be lawful, he may make an application for the purpose to the local planning authority specifying the land and describing the use or operations in question. The requirement that the application must 'describe' a use etc, may mean that the procedure cannot be used merely as a 'fishing expedition' to see what permission, if any, might be forthcoming; nor is the procedure available where the use etc, has already been carried out.

6.180 If the local planning authority are provided with information satisfying them that the use or operations described in the application would be lawful if instituted or begun at the time of the application, they shall issue a certificate to that effect; and

206 Per Lord Widgery CJ in *Thomas David (Porthcawl) Ltd v Penybont Rural District Council* [1972] 1 All ER 733.

207 [2007] EWHC 489 (Admin). The case is discussed in more detail at para 12.170. See also *James Hay Pension Trustees Ltd v First Secretary of State* [2005] EWHC 2713 (Admin).

208 PCA 1991, s. 10 introducing a new TCPA 1990, s. 192.

in any other case they shall refuse the application.[209] The authority's decision is a purely judicial one and, if they are satisfied that the applicant's case is made out, they must grant a certificate.

6.181 The certificate must specify the land to which it relates, describe the use, operations, or other matter in question and give reasons for determining them lawful.[210] The certificate may be issued in respect of the whole or part of the land specified in the application and where the application specifies more than one use etc, a certificate may be granted for all of them or one or more of them.

6.182 Under TCPA 1990, s. 192(4) the lawfulness of any use or operations for which a certificate is in force shall be conclusively presumed unless there is a material change, before the use is instituted or the operations are begun, in any of the matters relevant to determining lawfulness. There is a right of appeal to the Secretary of State where the applicant is aggrieved by the determination of the local planning authority.[211]

6.183 Another way of ascertaining whether a particular operation or change of use involves development is to apply for a declaratory judgment of the High Court. This method was available as an alternative to a section 64 determination[212] and remains available as an alternative in addition to the new procedure.

6.184 A case in which a declaration was sought is *Thames Heliport v Tower Hamlets London Borough Council*[213]—one of the most unusual cases in the planning field to come before the courts in recent years.

6.185 The plaintiff company had formulated plans for a floating heliport over the tidal River Thames; the defendant local authority headed a group of 10 riparian local planning authorities affected by the plaintiff's proposals. The plaintiff sought to establish whether, (1) helicopters taking off from a satellite-controlled vessel, floating, but not moored on the river would constitute operational development or a material change of use of land within the meaning of the TCPA 1990, and (2) whether, if the activity constituted development, the permitted development right under the GDO 1988, which authorizes the use of land for not more than

209 TCPA 1990, s. 192(2). See *R (on the application of Tapp) v Thanet District Council* [2001] EWCA Civ 559—it is not open to the LPA to require an application under s. 192 to be modified.

210 TCPA 1990, s. 192(3). It must also specify the date of the application for the certificate. In the case of a use falling within one of the classes of the Use Classes Order, the use must be identified by reference to that class.

211 TCPA 1990, s. 195.

212 *Pyx Granite Co Ltd v Ministry of Housing and Local Government* [1960] AC 260, [1959] 3 All ER 1.

213 [1995] JPL 526; revsd in part [1997] JPL 448, CA.

28 days total in any calendar year,[214] applied to each of the 22 proposed landing and take-off sites or the whole 10-mile stretch of the river containing the sites.

6.186 Sir Haydn Tudor Evans QC, sitting as deputy judge at first instance, considered that when deciding the extent of the meaning of the word 'land' under the Act the court was entitled to look at the purpose of the Act and the mischief it was designed to prevent, ie the mischief of uncontrolled development. He therefore accepted the submission of counsel for the defendant that the water of a river rested on land and so the use of it was the use of land. Thus when a helicopter was landing on or taking off from the vessel, that was not operational development but it was part of a material change in the use of land. This was particularly so where, as here, the vessel was to be moored to the bank for substantial periods.

6.187 On the question of the permitted development right the issue was whether the appropriate planning unit was the particular locations where the helicopters would land and take off or whether it was the length of the river. If the former it would greatly increase the scale of the permitted activity. The learned deputy judge placed reliance on the approach suggested by Diplock LJ in *G Percy Trentham Ltd v Gloucestershire County Council*[215] that the court should look at the whole area which was used for a particular purpose. Despite the geographical separation of the sites, all the activities on each site were linked; the planning unit was therefore the whole area.

6.188 The Court of Appeal confirmed that the proposal *could* constitute a change of use of land for the purposes of TCPA 1990 s. 55, but did not consider it right for the court to hold as a matter of law that a material change of use would occur. This was a matter of fact and degree for the local planning authority, as was the question of the appropriate planning unit. The latter was an issue for the local planning authority when taking enforcement action.[216] Schiemann LJ regarded it as inappropriate for the court to decide in an action for a declaration the boundaries of land to which permitted development applied. He also indicated that the courts should be extremely cautious in granting declarations before any evaluation of proposals had been made by the local planning authority.

6.189 The learned Lord Justice said: '[it] had to be borne in mind that Parliament had provided in [TCPA 1990, s. 192] [ie the CLOPUD] a mechanism for the citizen who wished to discover whether a proposed use . . . would be lawful under the planning legislation. In general it would be appropriate to use that method rather than come to the courts for an answer.'

---

214 Under Part 4, Class B of the 1988 order: now GPDO 1995, See para 7.34.

215 See para 6.76.

216 See para12.01.

6.190 In *James Hay Pension Trustees Ltd v First Secretary of State*,[217] the Court of Appeal held that s. 192 of TCPA 1990 is in mandatory terms and must be complied with for a CLOPUD to be valid. Article 24(11) of the GPDO 1995 provides that a certificate under s. 192 should be in the form set out in schedule 4 to the Order or 'in a form substantially to the like effect'. In this case, an inspector held that a document issued by the local planning authority that merely responded to specific questions was not a valid s. 192 certificate. The Court of Appeal agreed as there was no clear description in the document as to the use or operations in question and the local planning authority had failed to give any reasons for determining the lawfulness of the use. Nor was the document substantially to the like effect of the prescribed form.

217 [2007] 1 P & CR 23. Cf *Broads Authority v Secretary of State for the Environment, Transport and the Regions* [2001] PLCR 66.

7

PLANNING PERMISSION: PERMITTED DEVELOPMENT

7.01 The basis of planning control in England and Wales is TCPA 1990, s. 57(1) which provides that: 'Subject to the following provisions of this section, planning permission is required for the carrying out of any development of land.'[1]

7.02 There are certain exceptions to this rule, namely:

(1) Temporary use existing on 1 July 1948

7.03 Prior to 6 December 1968 permission was not required for the resumption of the normal use of land which on 1 July 1948 was temporarily used for another purpose. If the normal use had not been resumed by 6 December 1968, permission will be necessary.[2]

(2) Occasional use existing on 1 July 1948

7.04 Permission is not required in the case of land which on 1 July 1948 was normally used for one purpose and was also used on occasions for any other purpose, in

[1] This does not apply to development carried out before 'the appointed day', which was 1 July 1948, the day the 1990 Act came into force: TCPA 1971, Sch 24, para 12; Planning (Consequential Provisions) Act 1990, Sch 3, para 3.
[2] TCPA 1990, Sch 4, para 1.

respect of the use for that other purpose on similar occasions after that date provided the right had been exercised on at least one occasion between 1 July 1948, and the beginning of 1968.[3]

(3) Land unoccupied on 1 July 1948

7.05 Where land was unoccupied on 1 July 1948, but had before that date been occupied at some time on or after 7 January 1937, planning permission is not required in respect of any use of land before 6 December 1968, for the purpose for which it was last used before 1 July 1948.[4]

(4) Resumption of previous use

7.06 If planning permission has at any time been granted specifically for a limited period, or by a development order/subject to limitations, no permission is necessary to resume the use which was normal before that permission was granted, provided that the 'normal use' was not begun in contravention of planning control under TCPA 1990, Part III or the corresponding provisions of the previous Acts. Nor is permission necessary to resume the previous lawful use of land when an enforcement notice has been served in respect of any unauthorized development;[5] the previous use cannot be resumed if it also was begun in breach of planning control. If the previous use was unlawful, there is no right to revert to some earlier lawful use.[6] There would appear to be little, if any, practical significance for most purposes in the distinction between these classes of development and those matters which are excluded from the definition of development.

7.07 Except in the cases noted above[7] permission is required under TCPA 1990, Part III for all classes of development. That permission may be granted in five ways:

(a) by a development order made by the Secretary of State, or by a local development order made by the local planning authority;
(b) by an enterprise zone scheme;
(c) by a simplified planning zone scheme;
(d) by being 'deemed to be granted' in special cases as provided in TCPA 1990;
(e) as a result of an application to the local planning authority.

7.08 Each of these will now be considered in turn.

---

[3] TCPA 1990, Sch 4, para 2.

[4] TCPA 1990, Sch 4, para 3.

[5] TCPA 1990, s. 57(2)–(6). For development orders, see this chapter, below. For enforcement notices see para 12.01.

[6] *Young v Secretary of State for the Environment* [1983] 2 AC 662, [1983] 2 All ER 1105.

[7] Exceptions (2), (3) and (4) do not apply to the use of land as a *caravan site*, except where there was such a use at least once during the two years ending on 9 March 1960: TCPA 1990, Sch 4, para 4.

Permission under development order

7.09 This form of permission is provided for by TCPA 1990, s. 59. Development orders made by the Secretary of State may be either general orders applicable (subject to any exception specified therein) to all land in England and Wales, or special orders applying only to certain specified land.

7.10 Historically, general development orders made under TCPA 1990, s. 59 have served two principal purposes. They have prescribed some of the procedures relating to express planning permission and also granted planning permission for a range of 'permitted' development. The General Development Order (GPDO) 1988, which was discussed in the ninth edition of this book, conformed to that pattern. However, in 1995 the Government repealed the 1988 Order and enacted two separate Orders; the General Development Procedure Order and the General Permitted Development Order.[8] Although the process was largely a consolidation (the 1988 Order had been amended some 16 times) there were some changes and the most significant of these will be dealt with in this chapter.

7.11 In addition, PCPA 2004, s. 40, inserting new sections 61A–D into the TCPA 1990, has introduced a new procedure whereby local planning authorities may make local development orders (LDOs). This will allow local authorities to enlarge in their local area upon permitted development rights prescribed on a country-wide basis by general development orders.

The General Permitted Development Order

7.12 The General Permitted Development Order is of general application and by article 3 grants permission for a wide range of developments set out in Schedule 2 to the Order. Schedule 2 is divided into 40 parts most of which are divided into different classes; for instance, Part 1 (development within the curtilage of a dwellinghouse) is divided into eight classes lettered A to H. Thus, Schedule 2 sets out a considerable number of classes of development which can be carried out without applying to the local planning authority for express permission. Of course, this is not the same as excluding these matters from the definition of development, and nothing in the General Permitted Development Order is to operate so as to permit development contrary to a condition imposed on any other grant of permission under TCPA 1990, Part III.[9] Moreover, article 3(5), introduced by amendment to

---

[8] T & CP (GDP) Order 1995, SI 1995 No 419; T & CP (GPD) Order 1995, SI 1995 No 418. And see Circular 9/95.

[9] GPDO, art 3(4).

the previous General Development Order in 1992,[10] provides that permitted development rights may not be exercised if (a) in the case of permission granted in connection with an existing building, the operations involved in the construction of that building are unlawful, and (b) in the case of permission granted in connection with an existing use, that use is unlawful.

7.13 The Secretary of State and the local planning authority have certain powers under article 4 to withdraw in specific cases the benefit of a permission granted by the order: this power has been quite extensively used, but this would not have been possible if the matters in question had been excluded from the definition of development. Lastly, the Secretary of State can at any time make new development orders either extending or restricting the range of permitted developments.

7.14 Of the 40 categories of development permitted by the General Permitted Development Order, Parts 1 to 9, 21, 22, 27, 28, and 31 are of general interest; the remainder concern public bodies such as local authorities and English Heritage, and utilities such as water, gas, electricity, coal, telecommunications, and airports. As from 7 June 2006, new Parts 34–8 were inserted consequent upon the abolition of Crown immunity under PCPA 2004—these provisions relate to permitted development by or on behalf of the Crown.

7.15 In many cases the permitted development is subject to limits. For example, Class A of Part 1 (development within the curtilage of a dwellinghouse) permits the extension of a house, but does not permit an extension which, inter alia, would exceed a maximum projection for single storey rear extensions (4 metres for detached, 3 metres for other types of house); for two-storey rear extensions, 3 metres or within 7 metres of the rear boundary. This means that, if any part of the extension is in breach of any of these restrictions, the whole extension and not merely the excess is unauthorized and so liable to enforcement action.[11] In some cases, the permitted development is also subject to conditions; breach of a condition would not, it is submitted, invalidate the whole development, but the local planning authority would be entitled to take enforcement action to secure compliance with the condition.

7.16 There are some further restrictions which apply to all development permitted by the General Permitted Development Order:

(1) The order does not authorize any development[12] which involves the formation, laying out, or material widening of a means of access to a trunk or classified road, or which creates an obstruction to the view of persons using any road

10 T & CP General Development (Amendment) (No 5) Order 1992, SI 1992 No 1563.

11 See para 12.01.

12 Except in relation to development permitted by Parts 9, 11, 13, or 30.

used by vehicular traffic at or near any bend, corner, junction, or intersection so as to be likely to cause danger to such persons.[13]

(2) Development is not permitted by the order if an application for planning permission for that development would require an Environmental Impact Assessment.[14] A prospective developer may apply to the local planning authority for an opinion as to whether development which would otherwise be permitted requires an environmental assessment and therefore a planning application.

(3) The order is subject to regulation 60 of the Nature Conservation Regulations.[15] Regulation 60 imposes a condition on permission granted by the Order ensuring that development likely to have a significant effect on a 'European site' shall not begin without the local planning authority's approval—such approval may only be given where the authority, after consulting the relevant Nature Conservancy Council, have ascertained that the development will not adversely affect the integrity of the site.

Development within the curtilage of a dwellinghouse

7.17 Part 1 makes provision for the extension of a dwellinghouse[16] and for other development within the curtilage of a dwellinghouse. An amending order, coming into force in 1 October 2008, substituted a new Part 1.[17]

7.18 Class A permits the enlargement, improvement, or other alteration of a dwellinghouse.[18] The volume limitations in the old Part 1 have been removed, making it easier to enlarge a dwellinghouse under permitted development rights. The new permitted development right is subject to the following restrictions:

(a) Single storey rear extensions must not extend beyond the rear wall of the original dwellinghouse[19] by more than 4 metres for detached houses or 3 metres for the other types of house; nor must they exceed 4 metres in height.

(b) Extensions having more than one storey must not extend beyond the rear wall of the original dwellinghouse by more than 3 metres or be within 7 metres of the rear boundary.

---

13 GPDO, art 3(6).

14 See para 9.01.

15 See para 18.35.

16 'Dwellinghouse' does not include a building containing one or more flats, or a flat contained within such a building: GPDO, art 1(2).

17 T & CP (General Permitted Development) (Amendment) (No 2) (England) Order 2008, SI 2008 No 2362.

18 Other than alterations to its roof; the construction of a porch to an external door; the installation of a chimney, flue or vent; or the installation of a satellite antenna; separate provision for these forms of development is made by Classes B, D, G and H.

19 The 'original' dwellinghouse means the house as built on 1 July 1948 or, if built since that date, as so built: GPDO, art 12.

7.19 Further additional restrictions include the following:

(i) The height of the resulting building must not exceed the highest part of the roof of the existing dwellinghouse.
(ii) Only 50 per cent of the curtilage (excluding the ground area of the original dwellinghouse) may be covered by buildings.
(iii) If the house is in a National Park, Area of Outstanding Natural Beauty, conservation area, or other special area, cladding of the exterior is not permitted.
(iv) The resulting building must not extend beyond a wall which fronts the highway and forms either the principal or side elevation of the original dwellinghouse.
(v) The resulting building must not include the construction or provision of a veranda, balcony, or raised platform.

7.20 Various conditions are imposed by paragraph A3 including a condition that the material used in the exterior work (other than a conservatory) must be of a similar apperanace to the existing dwellinghouse.

7.21 Extensions to the roof of a dwellinghouse are permitted by class B subject to specific limits on volume—40 cubic metres for terraced houses and 50 cubic metres for other dwellinghouses; extension of a roof beyond the roof face fronting a highway is a not permitted. No part of the dwellinghouse should, as a results of the works, exceed the height of the existing roof. There are conditions imposed by paragraph B2 including a condition that the material used must be similar in appearance to the existing dwellinghouse. Class B dose not apply in National Parks and other special areas.

7.22 Any other alteration to a roof is permitted by Class C subject to restrictions including a requirement that the highest part of the alteration must not exceed the height of the original roof.

7.23 Class D deals with erection of porches to external doors. Class E provides for any building or enclosure, swimming or other pool required for a purpose incidental to the enjoyment of the dwellinghouse.[20] Class F is concerned with the provision of domestic hardstanding—under the 2008 amendment where these exceed 5 square metres at the frontage they must be porous, unless rainwater is diverted elsewhere within the property.[21] Class G permits the installation, alteration, or replacement of a chimney, flue, or soil and vent pipe on a dwellinghouse. Class H allows the installation, alteration, or replacement of a microwave antenna on a dwellinghouse or within the curtilage of the dwellinghouse. Classes D to H are subject to restrictions.

---

20 The Class also permits a container used for domestic heating and the storage of oil or liquid petroleum gas.

21 This is to alleviate flood risk.

Minor operations

7.24 Class A of Part 2 permits the erection of gates, fences, walls, or other means of enclosure not exceeding one metre in height where adjacent to a highway[22] used by vehicular traffic, or two metres in other cases. It also permits maintenance, improvement or alteration of a gate, fence etc within these limits of height or the original height, whichever is the greater.

7.25 In *Prengate Properties Ltd v Secretary of State for the Environment*,[23] the Divisional Court held that the words 'gate, fence or wall' are governed by the words 'other means of enclosure'; that is, the construction of eg a wall is not authorized unless it has some function of enclosure. Lord Widgery said that the permission would not extend to someone who erected a freestanding wall in the middle of his garden in circumstances in which it did not play any part in enclosing anything. But what is meant by saying that the structure must serve some function of enclosure? It seems that in most cases, the court will regard this as a question of fact and degree to be determined, in the event of an appeal, by the Secretary of State or his inspector. In *Ewen Developments Ltd v Secretary of State for the Environment and North Norfolk District Council*,[24] the court refused to interfere with an inspector's finding that some embankments within a caravan site were not enclosures for the purposes of what is now Class A of Part 2 even though each embankment formed a continuous ring and so in one sense did enclose land; presumably the embankments were intended merely as landscaping. The implication seems to be that, to qualify under Class A, the structure must be required as a means of preventing or restricting access to or from an area of land.

7.26 Class B of Part 2 permits the making of an access to a highway, which is not a trunk or classified road, where that access is required in connection with other development permitted by the General Permitted Development Order.[25]

7.27 Class C permits the exterior painting of buildings otherwise than for the purposes of advertisement, announcement, or direction. The permission is only required where such painting would materially affect the external appearance of the building; in other cases it will not be development at all.[26] Perhaps the real value of Class C is that it avoids arguments as to whether development is involved.

---

22 The use of the expression 'adjacent to' (instead of 'abutting upon' used in earlier GDOs) is, no doubt, intended to emphasize that the rule applies even if the structure does not touch the boundary of the highway.

23 (1973) 25 P & CR 311.

24 [1980] JPL 404.

25 Except development permitted under Part 2, Class A.

26 See para 6.01.

Change of use

7.28 As we have seen in an earlier chapter, a change of use from one purpose to another within the same use class does not constitute development and so does not require planning permission.[27] Classes A to D, F, and G of Part 3 of Schedule 2 of the General Permitted Development Order permit development consisting of a change of use from one use class to another in certain cases. Consequent upon the amendment to the Use Classes Order 1987 made by the Town and Country Planning (Use Classes) (Amendment) (England) Order 2005,[28] the Government made the Town and Country Planning (General Permitted Development) (Amendment) (England) Order 2005.[29] The effect of this change is to remove the former permitted development right for motor car showrooms to change to A1 shop use.

7.29 Part 3 is summarized in the following table.

Change permitted

By GPDO	From UCO Class	To UCO Class
A	A3 (restaurants and cafés) A4 (drinking establishments) A5 (hot food takeaways)	A1 (shops) A1 (shops) A1 (shops)
AA	A4 (drinking establishments) A5 (hot food takeaways)	A3 (restaurants and cafes) A3 (restaurants and cafes)
B(a)	B2 (general industrial)	B1 (business)
B(a)	B8 (storage and distribution)	B1 (business)*
B(b)	B1 (business)	B8 (storage and distribution)*
B(b)	B2 (general industrial)	B8 (storage and distribution)*
C	A3 (restaurants and cafés) A4 (drinking establishments) A5 (hot food takeaway)	A2 (financial and professional) A2 (financial and professional) A2 (financial and professional)
D	Premises within A2 (financial and professional) with display window at ground floor level	A1 (shops)
F(a)	A1 (shops)	Mixed A1 (shops) and single flat uses other than a flat at ground floor level
F(b)	A2 (financial and professional)	Mixed A2 (financial and professional) and single flat uses, other than a flat at ground floor level

27 See para 6.69.
28 See para 6.71.
29 SI 2005 No 85, which came into force on 28 April 2005.

By GPDO	From UCO Class	To UCO Class
F(c)	Premises within A2 (financial and professional) with display window at ground floor level	Mixed A1 (shops) and single flat uses other than a flat at ground floor level
G(a)	Mixed A1 (shops) and single flat uses	A1 (shops)
G(b)	Mixed A2 (financial and professional) and single flat uses	A2 (financial and professional)
G(c)	Premises of mixed A2 (financial and professional) and single	A1 (shops)
H	Flat uses with display window at ground floor level Casino (*sui generis*)	D2 (assembly and leisure)

* Not permitted where change of use relates to more than 235 square metres of floor space in the building.

7.30 The phrase 'development consisting of a change of use' is significant: the changes of use mentioned above are not excluded from the definition of development by virtue of the Use Classes Order and they will constitute development if they amount to a material change of use. A change of use from a warehouse (use Class B8) to a light industrial use (which falls within use Class B1) is almost certainly a material change of use, but is permitted within certain limits by the General Permitted Development Order as shown above. Whether a change from a 'take away' selling hot food (use Class A5) to an ordinary retail shop (use Class A1) is a material change of use is arguable; the General Permitted Development Order permits the change of use and so makes argument unnecessary.

7.31 Class E of Part 3 introduces a measure of freedom to change to alternative uses originally permitted by a grant of planning permission. It has always been possible for a planning authority to grant planning permission in a form which would enable a developer to take up one of a number of specified uses. For example, permission might be given for the use of a large house as offices or as a hotel; if the developer then used it for offices, the planning permission was implemented and would not cover a subsequent change to a hotel. Class E now permits a change of use from one specified in a planning permission, and implemented, to any other use specified in that permission. Class E does not apply (a) if the application for the planning permission was made before 5 December 1988; (b) if the change of use would be carried out more than 10 years after the grant of planning permission; or (c) if it would result in the breach of any condition, limitation, or specification contained in that planning permission in relation to the use in question.

7.32 Classes F and G (see table above) were introduced in 1995 and incorporated in the consolidation of that year; they provide further flexibility. It will be seen that Class F permits a change of use of premises used either as shops or for financial and professional services (Classes A1 or A2) to a mixed use as a single flat and Class A1 or A2 uses. Class G permits a change of use in the reverse direction to Class F. It should be remembered, however, that apart from these provisions in Part 3, no use class is specified in the Use Classes Order for mixed uses. Class H was introduced in 2006 consequent upon the removal of use as a casino from Class D2 and its categorization as a *sui generis* use.

Temporary buildings and uses

7.33 Class A of Part 4 gives permission for the provision on land of buildings, moveables, structures, works, plant, or machinery required temporarily in connection with and for the duration of operations being or about to be carried out on, in, under, or over the land or on land adjoining that land. An imaginative interpretation of the permitted development right was arrived at in *North Cornwall District Council v Secretary of State for Transport, Local Government and the Regions.* [30] In this case, trading from a temporary structure on the forecourt of a shop, pending refurbishment of the shop, was held to fall under Class A of Part 4. Class A does not apply if (a) the operations referred to are mining operations, or (b) planning permission is required for those operations but is not granted or deemed to be granted. It is a condition of Class A that the buildings etc, shall be removed when the operations have been carried out and that any adjoining land be reinstated to its former condition.

7.34 Class B gives permission for a temporary use of land[31] for any purpose on not more than 28 days in any calendar year (of which not more than 14 days in total may be for the holding of markets, motor car, and motor cycle racing)[32] and the provision of moveable structures on the land for the purpose of the use. The provision is often relied on for such temporary uses as fairs, markets, and camping. The use of land as a caravan site is excluded from Class B; the temporary use of land for caravans is provided for by Part 5 of Schedule 2. Further, where the land is within an area of special scientific interest (as notified under the Wildlife and Countryside Act 1981), Class B development is not permitted for motor sports, clay pigeon shooting, or any war game. 'War game' is defined as an enacted, mock, or imaginary battle conducted with weapons which are designed not to injury, excluding activities organized under the aegis of the Ministry of Defence. In *Ramsey v Secretary of State for the Environment*,[33] agricultural land was used for the purpose of motorcycle scrambling. Although used for this purpose only intermittently, the land retained throughout the physical features of the use—tyres embedded in the ground, fencing marking out the track, and mounds forming an obstacle course. The inspector's conclusion that the use was a permanent one was upheld by the

30 [2003] 1 P & CR 25.
31 Class B does not apply to buildings or land within the curtilage of a building.
32 Including trials of speed and practising.
33 [1998] JPL 60. And see [1971] JPL 1073.

court as being a decision that was open to him as a matter of fact and degree. Subsequently, the operators applied for a certificate of lawfulness[34] relating to an adjacent parcel of land for vehicular sports not exceeding 28 days in any one year; the Secretary of State's refusal to grant the certificate was upheld in the High Court by Scott-Baker J.[35] However, that decision was reversed by the Court of Appeal in *Ramsey v Secretary of State for the Environment, Transport and the Regions*,[36] the Court holding that if the physical changes to the site did not prevent reversion to the normal use of the land, it could not be said that the rights under Part 4 of the General Permitted Development Order were not available. The Secretary of State and the judge had erred in attaching significance to the character of the site—since it was possible to revert the site to its normal use, ie sheep grazing, the rights granted by Part 4, Class B of the development order were available.

Agricultural buildings and operations

7.35 As we have seen, the use of land for agriculture is not development and so does not require planning permission.[37] The carrying out of building and other operations in connection with agriculture, however, does require planning permission because the word 'use' in the TCPA 1990 does not include operations.[38] In many cases the necessary planning permission for agricultural buildings and operations is given by Part 6 of Schedule 2 to the General Permitted Development Order.

7.36 Part 6 of the General Development Order 1988 as originally enacted was substituted by an amendment in 1991[39] and the amended version is now contained in the current General Permitted Development Order. The old Part 6 granted a single planning permission for the carrying out on agricultural land comprised in an agricultural unit of 0.4 hectares or more of certain building operations or engineering operations reasonably necessary for the purpose of agriculture within the unit. However, the revised Part 6 divides such general agricultural development into Classes A and B.

7.37 Class A applies to an agricultural unit of an area of five hectares or more. It permits, on agricultural land[40] comprised in such a unit, (a) works for the erection, extension, or alteration of a building; or (b) any excavation or engineering operations,

34 See para 12.157.
35 [2001] All ER (D) 124 (Apr).
36 [2002] All ER (D) 16 (Feb).
37 See para 6.58.
38 See para 6.03.
39 T & CP General Development (Amendment) (No 3) Order 1991, SI 1991 No 2805.
40 'Agricultural land' means land used for agriculture and which is so used for the purpose of a trade or business: GPDO, Sch 2, Part 6, para D1.

which are reasonably necessary for the purposes of agriculture. Class A does not include the erection or alteration of a dwellinghouse, nor the provision of a building not designed for the purposes of agriculture. There are several important limitations and conditions including the following:

(1) The ground area of any building must not exceed 465 square metres, and if the building would be within 90 metres of another building (other than a house) belonging to the same farm and erected within the last two years, the area of that building must be deducted from the maximum of 465 square metres.
(2) The height of any building within three kilometres of the perimeter of an aerodrome must not exceed three metres nor 12 metres in any other case.
(3) No part of the development must be within 25 metres of the metalled portion of a trunk or classified road.
(4) Excavations and engineering operations which are connected with fish farming are not permitted where the land is within national parks or certain areas of high landscape value specified in Schedule 1, Part 2 of the Order.
(5) There are restrictions on the siting of buildings or excavation for the accommodation of livestock or for the storage of slurry or sewage sludge. And where the development involves the extraction of minerals or the removal of any mineral from a mineral-working deposit, the mineral shall not be moved off the agricultural unit.

7.38 Further, where the development consists of:

(i) the erection, extension or alteration of a building in national parks or certain areas of high landscape value specified in Schedule 1, Part 2 of the Order and elsewhere if the alteration or extension is significant;[41]
(ii) the formation or alteration of a private way;
(iii) the carrying out of excavations or the deposit of waste material;
(iv) the placing or assembly of a tank in any waters;

the developer must give the local planning authority a written description and plan of the proposed development. The authority then have 28 days in which to notify the developer that the development must not commence without prior approval of the siting, design and external appearance of the building, the siting and means of construction of the private way, the siting of the excavation or deposit, or the siting and appearance of the tank, as the case may be. If the authority have not required

[41] 'Significant' means any extension or alteration which would exceed the cubic content of the original building by more than 10 per cent or the height of the original building would be exceeded.

prior approval, the development is to be carried out in accordance with the written description and plan.[42]

7.39 Class A contains a significant change of terminology from what was Class VI of the 1977 Order. The old Class VI referred to the carrying out on agricultural land comprised in an agricultural unit of building or engineering operations requisite for the use of the land for the purposes of agriculture. As we have seen in an earlier chapter, in *Fuller v Secretary of State for the Environment*[43] Stuart-Smith J held that an agricultural unit could comprise several planning units; in consequence, planning permission was required for the use of buildings on one farm for the storage of grain produced on another farm within the same agricultural unit. The reference in the new Class A to the creation of buildings reasonably necessary 'for the purposes of agriculture within that unit' is apparently designed to permit storage within buildings erected under Class A of produce from other farms in the same agricultural unit. This extension of permitted development rights is likely to result in the further concentration of buildings on the 'home farm'.

7.40 The meaning of 'reasonably necessary for the purposes of agriculture' in Part 6 was considered by the Court of Appeal in *Clarke v Secretary of State for the Environment.*[44] It seems that in the case of the erection of a building, the proper test to be applied is whether the building in question is reasonably necessary for, and if so is it designed for, the purposes of the agricultural activities which might reasonably be conducted on the unit in question. Allowing an appeal against a decision of Malcolm Spence QC (sitting as deputy judge) the court held that the inspector had not erred in law in considering whether the building was reasonably necessary for, and designed for, a sheep unit. As Glidewell LJ put it, 'the inspector was not obliged to cast about to contemplate some possible but unlikely agricultural activity on the land which had not been suggested by or on behalf of [the appellant]'.

7.41 Class B of the amended Part 6 permits certain development on agricultural units of less than five hectares but not less than 0.4 hectares in area. The permitted development consists of—

(a) the extension or alteration of an agricultural building;
(b) the installation of additional or replacement plant or machinery;
(c) the provision, rearrangement or replacement of sewer, main, pipe, cable, or other apparatus;
(d) the provision, rearrangement, or replacement of a private way;
(e) the creation of a hard surface;
(f) the deposit of waste; or

42 GPDO, Sch 2, Part 6, para A2(2).
43 (1987) 56 P & CR 84, [1987] JPL 854.
44 [1992] 42 EG 100.

(g) the carrying out of certain operations in connection with fish farming including the repairing and dredging of ponds and the replacement of tanks where reasonably necessary for the purposes of agriculture within the unit.

7.42 Class B is subject to limitations and conditions, some of which are the same as, or similar to, those applying to Class A. Thus there are similar restrictions as to the siting of buildings or structures, as to the ground area to be covered by the development and as to the proximity to trunk or classified roads. In particular, the external appearance of the premises must not be materially affected and if the development relates to fish farming it is restricted to associated works outlined in paragraph (g) above—it cannot involve the placing of tanks on land or waters not previously used for such a purpose or an increase in the size of any tanks or ponds. Further, there are detailed limitations relating to buildings under paragraph (a) and machinery under paragraph (b)—any works to a building must not involve the extension, alteration, or provision of a dwelling. In national parks and areas of high landscape value specified in Schedule 1, Part 2 of the Order, permitted development involving a building or a private way is subject to a notification and possible 'prior approval' procedure similar to that which applies to some development under Class A discussed above.

7.43 In 1997 the Government amended Classes A and B (above) by imposing conditions on permitted development rights for the erection etc, of buildings where the use of such development for agricultural purposes permanently ceases within 10 years of substantial completion. Unless planning permission has been granted for some purpose other than agriculture within 10 years of permanent cessation, the development can be required to be removed by the local planning authority and the land restored to its former condition.[45]

7.44 Class C of Part 6 permits the winning and working of minerals reasonably necessary for agricultural purposes, from agricultural land or land held therewith, comprised within the same agricultural unit.

Forestry buildings and operations

7.45 Although the use of land for forestry is not development, the carrying out of building and other operations connected with forestry is development and requires planning permission. Part 7 permits the carrying out on land used for the purposes of forestry[46] of development reasonably necessary for those purposes consisting of:

(a) the erection, extension, or alteration of buildings but not dwellinghouses;
(b) the formation, alteration, or maintenance of private ways;

---

45 T & CP (General Permitted Development) (Amendment) Order 1997, SI 1997 No 366.
46 Including afforestation.

(c) operations on that land or land held therewith to obtain minerals for the formation, etc of private ways;
(d) other operations (but not engineering or mining operations).

7.46 The height of any buildings within three kilometres of an aerodrome must not exceed three metres, and no part of any development permitted by Part 7 must be within 25 metres of the metalled portion of a trunk or classified road.

7.47 Where the land is in a national park or certain areas of high landscape value (as specified in Schedule 1, Part 2 of the Order), or elsewhere if the works to a building are significant,[47] any person proposing to erect or alter a building, or to form or alter a private way, must give the local planning authority a written description and plan of the development; the authority then have 28 days in which to notify the developer that the development shall not be begun without prior approval of the siting, design, and external appearance of the building, or the siting and means of construction of the private way. If the authority have not required prior approval, the development is to be carried out in accordance with the written description and plan.

Industrial and warehouse development

7.48 Class A of Part 8 permits additions to industrial buildings and warehouses[48] within the curtilage of the undertaking concerned. The additions may take the form of extensions or new buildings up to certain limits of size and other limitations:

(1) In national parks, areas of outstanding natural beauty, conservation areas and certain other special areas[49] the additions must not exceed 10 per cent of the cubic content of the original building,[50] and the total aggregate floor space must not be increased by more than 500 square metres; elsewhere the cubic content must not be increased by more than 25 per cent and the floor space by more than 1,000 square metres.
(2) The building as extended or altered must be used for the purposes of the undertaking.
(3) The building must be used for the purpose of carrying out an industrial process[51] or, in the case of a warehouse, for storage or distribution.

---

47 'Significant' means any extension or alteration which would exceed the cubic content of the original building by more than 10 per cent or the height of the original building would be exceeded: GPDO Sch 2, Part 7, para A3.

48 Ie any building used for any purpose within Class B8 of the Use Classes Order: see para 6.94, above, but excluding a building associated with a mine: GPDO, art 1(2), Sch 2, Part 8, para E.

49 GPDO, Sch 1.

50 Ie as built on 1 July 1948 or, if built since that date, as so built: GPDO, art 1(2); where two or more original buildings are in the same curtilage and are used for the same undertaking, they are to be treated as one in making any measurement.

51 As defined in GPDO, art 1(2). The definition is similar to that in the Use Classes Order: See para 6.103.

(4) The height of the original building must not be exceeded, and the external appearance of the whole of the premises must not be materially affected.
(5) The extension or new building must not come within five metres of the boundary of the curtilage.
(6) There must be no reduction in the space available for parking or turning vehicles.

7.49 Part 8 also gives permission for various works and installations on land used for industry or warehousing.

Demolition of buildings

7.50 Class A of Part 31[52] grants planning permission for any building operation consisting of the demolition of a building. This permission does not apply to the demolition of buildings excluded from control by the Secretary of State's direction,[53] which means, in effect, that it applies to dwellinghouses, as defined by the Secretary of State, and to buildings adjoining dwellinghouses.

7.51 However, the permitted development right will not apply where a building has been rendered unsafe or uninhabitable, either deliberately or through neglect, by anyone having an interest in the land on which the building stands, and it is practicable to make the building secure through temporary repairs or support. With certain exceptions (given below), the permitted development right cannot be exercised until the local planning authority has determined whether it is required to give prior approval to the method of the proposed demolition and any proposed restoration of the site.

7.52 Where such a determination is required, the developer must apply to the local planning authority and the application must be accompanied by a written description of the proposed demolition. The local planning authority then have a period of 28 days to consider whether they wish to give prior approval. If the local planning authority do not notify the developer that prior approval of details is required within the 28-day period, he may proceed to demolish in accordance with the details submitted in the application or to those otherwise agreed. If the local planning authority respond that prior approval is required before demolition may proceed, the developer may appeal to the Secretary of State (i) if approval is refused; or (ii) if a decision on the details is not given within eight weeks. However, there is no right of appeal to the Secretary of State against a decision by the authority to require approval to details. Demolition must be carried out in accordance with the details agreed by the local planning authority; enforcement action[54] may be taken

52 As introduced by the GDO (Amendment) (No 3) Order 1992, SI 1992 No 1280.
53 See para 6.37.
54 See para 12.01.

where the developer fails to comply with such details. The proposed demolition may be carried out within a period of five years of the approval, or where prior approval was not required, within five years of the date of the application.

7.53 In certain cases, the determination referred to above is not required. Thus a determination will not be required where demolition is urgently necessary in the interests of health and safety, provided the developer gives a written justification of the demolition to the local planning authority as soon as reasonably practicable after the demolition has taken place. Nor will one be needed where the demolition is required under other legislation, eg a demolition order under the Housing Acts, or where demolition is required by some order or notice under the Planning Acts.[55]

7.54 Class B of Part 31 grants permitted development rights for the demolition of gates, fences, walls, and other means of enclosure in conservation areas.[56]

7.55 If the local planning authority wish to prevent demolition under Part 31 from taking place, they may only do so by means of an article 4 direction, discussed below.

Domestic microgeneration equipment

7.56 Article 2(3) of the Town and Country Planning (General Permitted Development) (Amendment) (England) Order 2008[57] inserted a new Part 40 of Schedule 2 to the GPDO. The new Part confers permitted development rights for the installation of specified types of microgeneration equipment on or within the curtilage of a dwellinghouse. 'Dwellinghouse', for this purpose, includes a building consisting wholly of flats or which is used for the purposes of a dwellinghouse.

7.57 Class A permits the installation, alteration, or replacement of solar PV or solar thermal equipment on a dwellinghouse or on a building within the curtilage. The equipment, where installed on an existing wall or roof, must not protrude more than 200 millimetres beyond the plane of the wall or roof slope and no part of the equipment should be higher than the highest part of the roof, excluding any chimney.[58] So far as practicable, the equipment must be sited in such a way as to minimize its effect on the external appearance of the building or the amenity of the area. If and when the equipment is no longer needed, it must be removed as soon as reasonably practicable.

---

55 Including an enforcement notice (see para 12.01), a discontinuance order (see para 11.01), or a planning obligation (see para 13.01).

56 Class B applies only to building operations, not engineering operations: *Caradon District Council v Secretary of State for the Environment, Transport and the Regions* [2001] PLCR 299.

57 SI 2008 No 675, which came into force on 6 April 2008.

58 There are additional restrictions in the case of conservation areas, World Heritage Sites, and listed buildings. See Class A, art A.1, paras (c) and (d).

7.58 Class B permits the installation, alteration, or replacement of stand alone solar within the curtilage of a dwellinghouse. 'Stand alone solar' is solar PV or solar thermal equipment which is not installed on a building. Only one stand alone solar is permitted within the curtilage, and no part of the device must exceed four metres above ground level or be within five metres of the boundary. The surface area of the solar panels forming part of the stand alone must not exceed nine square metres nor must any dimension of its array exceed three metres, including any housing. Stand alone solar cannot be situated within the curtilage of a listed building.[59] Once again, the equipment must be so sited as to minimize the effect on amenity and, if no longer needed, removed as soon as practicable.

7.59 Classes C and D permit the installation, alteration, or replacement of a ground source heat pump and a water source heat pump respectively within the curtilage of a dwellinghouse. Class E allows the installation, alteration, or replacement of a flue forming part of a biomass heating system, on a dwellinghouse, provided the height of the flue does not exceed the highest part of the roof by one metre or more.[60] Class F grants a permitted development right for the installation, alteration of a flue forming part of a combined heating and power system, subject to the same restrictions as Class E.

Article 4 directions

7.60 Article 4 of the General Permitted Development Order provides that the Secretary of State or the local planning authority may direct either (i) that all or any of the developments permitted by any Part, class, or paragraph in Schedule 2 of the Order shall not be carried out in a particular area without specific permission, or (ii) that any particular development shall not be carried out without specific permission.[61] Such directions are often referred to as 'article 4 directions'. An article 4 direction by a local planning authority requires the consent of the Secretary of State unless it relates only to buildings of special architectural or historic interest[62] and does not affect certain specified operations of statutory undertakers. Directions relating to development within Parts 1 to 4 of Schedule 2 may take effect for six months without the Secretary of State's approval. Notice of a direction affecting an area of land must be published in at least one local newspaper; where the direction is for a particular development, notice must be served on the owner and occupier.

---

59 In the case of conservation areas and WHSs, there is an additional restriction in art B.1(b)(ii).

60 In the case of conservation areas and WHSs, there is an additional restriction in art F.1 (b).

61 Article 4 is not applicable to Class B of Part 22 or Class C of Part 23, relating to certain forms of mineral development, but a similar procedure is provided by GPDO, art 7.

62 See ch 16 below.

7.61 In effect, therefore, an article 4 direction withdraws the permission granted by the General Permitted Development Order and makes it necessary to apply to the local planning authority for permission. If permission is refused or granted subject to conditions, the owner is entitled to compensation on the footing that permission already granted has been revoked or modified.[63] Article 4 directions have been extensively used so as to withdraw the permission given under what is now Part 4 for temporary markets.

7.62 It would seem that an article 4 direction may not be made after the development authorized by the permission has been completed. In *Cole v Somerset County Council*[64] land, which before the war had formed part of a golf course, had been used since 1950 as a caravan site for members of the Caravan Club. This use was at that time permitted development under Class V of the General Development Order 1950. In 1954 the county council served on the owner of the land an article 4 direction approved by the Minister. In 1956 the county council served an enforcement notice requiring the owner to discontinue the use and remove the caravans. On appeal, it was held that neither the Minister nor the planning authority had power under article 4 to withdraw permission which had already been given and acted upon. The enforcement notice was therefore invalid.

7.63 Article 4(2)—which appears for the first time in the 1995 Order—gives local planning authorities enhanced powers to restrict, selectively, certain permitted development rights relating to dwellinghouses in conservation areas.[65] This may apply where the development fronts a 'relevant location', that is, a highway, waterway, or open space.

Special development orders (SDOs)

7.64 Planning permission may also be granted by special development order. For instance, in the urban development areas[66] planning permission was granted by special development orders[67] for development which was in accordance with the general plans for those areas as approved by the Secretary of State; the permission covered both public and private development, but where the development was not being carried out by the development corporation, it may have been necessary to obtain the approval of the corporation of the details. Somewhat similar provision has been made for development within new towns.[68] In all these cases there was

---

63 TCPA 1990, s. 108. See ch 11 below.

64 [1957] 1 QB 23, [1956] 3 All ER 531.

65 See para 16.116.

66 See para 2.52.

67 See eg the T & CP (Merseyside Urban Development Area) SDO 1981, SI 1981 No 560; T & CP (London Docklands Urban Development Area) SDO 1981, SI 1981 No 1082.

68 See the T & CP (New Towns) SDO 1977, SI 1977 No 815.

power to make directions similar to those made under article 4 of the General Permitted Development Order. These orders all facilitate development by making it unnecessary to apply to the local planning authority for express permission; in the past, some special development orders have been made to modify the effect of General Development Orders in sensitive areas such as the national parks, but these modifications are now set out in the General Permitted Development Order itself.

7.65 Some orders give permission for specific projects. The proposals for reprocessing nuclear waste at Windscale (now Sellafield, Cumbria) were originally the subject of an application to the local planning authority; the application was called in and, after public inquiry, the Secretary of State decided to make a special development order[69] to allow opportunity for parliamentary debate. A similar procedure was adopted with proposals for office and housing development on a very large riverside site in London.[70]

Local development orders (LDOs)

7.66 PCPA 2004 enables local planning authorities to make Local Development Orders. As originally enacted, the legislation provided that an LDO could only be made to implement policies contained in DPDs, or in Wales, the LDP. However, PA 2008, s.189, removes the requirement that an LDO can only be made to implement such policies.

7.67 An LDO may grant planning permission for a specific development or for a class of development. It may relate to a specific site or all, or any part, of the local authority's area. Different provision may be made for different descriptions of land.[71] As with development orders made by the Secretary of State, planning permission granted by an LDO may be granted unconditionally or subject to conditions and limitations. Where planning permission is granted for development of a specified description, the LDO may enable the authority to direct that the permission does not apply in relation to development in a particular area; or any particular development.[72]

7.68 There is an important provision in s. 61A(5) of TCPA 1990, as inserted by PCPA 2004, that the Secretary of State may, by development order, specify any area or class of development for which an LDO must not be made. This has enabled the Secretary of State to specify that an LDO may not apply to development affecting a listed building, development where Environmental Impact Assessment

69 T & CP (Windscale and Calder Works) SDO 1978, SI 1978 No 523.
70 See the T & CP (Vauxhall Cross) SDO 1982, SI 1982 No 796.
71 TCPA 1990, s. 61A(2), (3) and (4).
72 Ibid, s. 61C(1) and (2).

is mandatory, and development affecting natural habitats under the Nature Conservation Regulations.[73]

Intervention by the Secretary of State

7.69 PCPA 2004 gives the Secretary of State[74] considerable powers of intervention. Thus at any time before an LDO is adopted by the authority the Secretary of State may direct that the order, or any part of it, is submitted to him for approval.[75] Where the Secretary of State does this, the local planning authority must not take any further steps in connection with the adoption of the LDO until the Secretary of State gives his decision, and the order has no effect until approved by the Secretary of State.[76] If the Secretary of State thinks that the LDO is unsatisfactory he may, at any time before adoption, direct the local planning authority to modify it, giving reasons.[77] The local planning authority must comply with any such direction and cannot adopt the LDO until informed by the Secretary of State that he is satisfied that they have complied with it.[78]

Revocation of LDO

7.70 The local planning authority, or the Secretary of State, may at any time revoke an LDO.[79] In such a case, planning permission granted by the LDO is withdrawn, although the order may include provision that if planning permission is withdrawn after the development has started, the development may be completed.[80]

LDO procedure

7.71 PCPA 2004 inserts a new Schedule 4A into the TCPA 1990[81] prescribing the procedure for the preparation and revision of LDOs. Thus:

(1) A development order made by the Secretary of State may include provision as to the preparation, submission, approval, adoption, revision, revocation, and withdrawal of an LDO; notice, publicity, and inspection by the public; consultation; and the making and consideration of objections.
(2) The local planning authority may at any time prepare a revision of an LDO. An authority must prepare a revision of an LDO if the Secretary of State (in Wales, the Assembly) directs them to do so, and in accordance with such timetable as directed.

---

73 See further SI 2006 No 1062, art 5.
74 In Wales, the Assembly.
75 TCPA 1990, s. 61B(1).
76 Ibid, s. 61B(1).
77 Ibid, s. 61B(2).
78 Ibid, s. 61B(6).
79 Ibid, s. 61B(7).
80 Ibid, s. 61A(6) and s 61B(8).
81 Ibid, s. 61D(1) and (3).

(3) If a DPD (in Wales an LDP) is revised or revoked, an LDO made to implement the policies in the document must be revised accordingly.
(4) An LDO is of no effect unless it is adopted by resolution of the local planning authority. The local planning authority's annual monitoring report must include a report as to the extent to which the LDO is achieving its purposes.

Enterprise zones (EZs)

7.72 The concept of the enterprise zone was introduced in 1980 as a means of reviving the local economy in areas of high unemployment.

7.73 The Secretary of State may invite a district council, a new town corporation, or urban development corporation to prepare a scheme for the development of an area with a view to the area being designated as an enterprise zone.[82] The authority may then prepare a draft scheme 'in accordance with the terms of the invitation': adequate publicity must be given to the draft scheme so that members of the public may make representations about it within a specified time. The authority may then adopt the scheme or modify it to take account of any representations.[83] Subject to any challenge in the High Court as to the validity of the scheme, the Secretary of State may then designate the area as an enterprise zone.[84]

7.74 The designation order grants planning permission for development specified in the scheme or for particular classes of development so specified.[85] The designation order is thus akin to a special development order by permitting the carrying out of development without the express permission of the local planning authority.

7.75 Under the Environmental Impact Assessment Regulations[86] any order designating an enterprise zone shall only have effect to grant planning permission to the extent that it is not development requiring an environmental assessment. This does not affect any development begun before the commencement of the Regulations, which came into force on 14 March 1999.

Simplified planning zones (SPZs)

7.76 An SPZ is defined as an area in which a simplified planning zone is in force.[87] The effect of such a scheme is to grant planning permission for either some specific development, or a class of development specified in the scheme; such planning permission may be unconditional or subject to conditions, limitations,

---

82 Local Government Planning and Land Act 1980, Sch 32, para 1.
83 A scheme may not be modified in any way inconsistent with the Secretary of State's invitation; LGPLA 1980, Sch 32, para 3(3).
84 LGPLA 1980, Sch 32, paras 2 to 5.
85 LGPLA 1980, Sch 32, Part III.
86 See para 9.01.
87 TCPA 1990, s. 82(1).

or exceptions.[88] These schemes have been aptly described as 'local general development orders made by local planning authorities', and there is indeed some overlap with the LDOs as introduced by PCPA 2004, discussed above.[89] But the scheme must not restrict the right of any person (a) to do anything not amounting to development, or (b) to carry out development for which permission is not required or for which planning permission has been granted otherwise than under the scheme, eg by the General Permitted Development Order.[90]

7.77 The coming into force of the original legislation[91] imposed on every local planning authority the duty to consider, as soon as practicable, whether the making of one or more simplified planning zones would be desirable and thereafter to keep that question under review. Where the authority concluded that such a scheme was desirable, it became their duty to prepare a scheme.[92] However, these provisions have now been replaced by PCPA 2004.[93] If the RSS[94] identifies the need for an SPZ in a local planning authority's area, the authority must keep under review the question for which part or parts of their area an SPZ scheme is desirable. They must make such a scheme if they decide it is desirable to do so. The SPZ scheme must be in conformity with the RSS.[95] Under the provisions regarding SPZs originally contained in TCPA 1990, any person could request the local planning authority to make or alter a scheme, thereby triggering the procedure—this has been removed by PCPA 2004.[96]

7.78 Simplified planning zone schemes cannot be made for certain environmentally sensitive areas, namely any land in a national park, conservation area, the Broads, area of outstanding natural beauty, approved green belt, or an area of special scientific interest under the Wildlife and Countryside Act 1981.[97]

7.79 Since the SPZ legislation was first introduced, very few local authorities have taken advantage of the powers granted to them to make such schemes. At one time, the Government felt that one reason for this was that the procedure for the making and adoption of such schemes was too lengthy and cumbersome. Accordingly, the Planning and Compensation Act 1991, s. 28 and Schedule 5

---

88 TCPA 1990, ss. 82(2), (3), 84(1), (2).

89 House of Lords Debates, 13 October 1986.

90 TCPA 1990, s. 84(3).

91 Ie the 1986 Act which came into force as regards simplified planning zones on 2 November 1987.

92 TCPA 1990, s. 83(1), (2).

93 PCPA 2004, s. 45(2) inserting a new s. 83 into the TCPA 1990.

94 In Wales, the Assembly.

95 TCPA 1990, s. 83 (2), (2B).

96 PCPA 2004, s. 45(8).

97 TCPA 1990, s. 87.

introduced a more streamlined procedure. These provisions are now to be found in TCPA 1990, Schedule 7, as amended by PCPA 2004.

7.80 The procedure for making and adoption of such a scheme, as amended, is as follows:

(1) The local planning authority should notify the Secretary of State and he has the power to call in the making of the scheme at any stage prior to formal adoption.
(2) The authority must consult such persons as the regulations[98] require them to consult.
(3) The authority must give publicity to their proposals and consider any representations received in accordance with the regulations. Under the amended provisions publicity and consultation requirements are effectively reduced thus shortening the time required for this process.
(4) The authority then prepare the scheme and make it available for inspection indicating the time within which objections may be made.
(5) The authority then have, subject to the direction of the Secretary of State, a discretion to hold either a local inquiry or to have the objections considered in writing by a person appointed by the Secretary of State or appointed by the authority.
(6) The authority must then consider the report of the inspector who conducted the inquiry or hearing; and publish a statement of their decisions including their reasons.
(7) The authority may then resolve to adopt the scheme. Unless challenged in the High Court in the meantime,[99] the scheme will come into force six weeks thereafter.

7.81 The scheme will remain in force for 10 years, but may be altered at any time.[100] The procedure for altering a scheme is the same as for the making and adoption of a scheme as set out above. However, if the Secretary of State[101] feels that, after holding an inquiry or other hearing, the local planning authority are not taking the steps required to make or alter a scheme, the Secretary of State may himself make or alter the scheme, providing the RSS identifies the need for such a scheme in the local area.[102]

[98] T & CP (Simplified Planning Zone) Regulations 1992, SI 1992 No 2414.
[99] TCPA 1990, s. 288.
[100] TCPA 1990, s. 85, as amended by PCPA 2004, s. 45(5).
[101] In Wales, the Assembly.
[102] TCPA 1990, Sch 7, as amended by s. 45(7) PCPA 2004.

7.82 Under the Environmental Impact Assessment Regulations[103] any order designating a simplified planning zone shall only have effect to grant planning permission to the extent that it is not development requiring an environmental assessment. This does not affect any development begun before the commencement of the Regulations, which came into force on 14 March 1999.

7.83 In the belief that planning delays can be a significant obstacle to the development of leading edge technology companies, the Government had originally intended to introduce Business Planning Zones (BPZs) where no planning permission would be necessary for development. In the event, the SPZ regime has been revived, but with little change from the original statutory procedures. Indeed, SPZs are very similar to LDOs discussed earlier in this chapter. Both schemes grant planning permission but the basis of the LDO is in local development planning whereas the basis of the SPZ will be the RSS.

Permission 'deemed to be granted' under the Act

7.84 In certain cases no application for planning permission is required because permission is deemed to have been granted under the TCPA 1990. For instance, there is a deemed planning permission for the carrying out of development for which planning permission was granted after 21 July 1943 under the pre-1947 planning legislation but which had not been carried out by 1 July 1948.[104] Likewise, where works for the erection of a building had been begun but not completed before 1 July 1948 there is a deemed planning permission for the erection of the building.[105] In both cases, the deemed planning permission will now have lapsed if the development was not begun before 1 April 1974.[106]

7.85 There is also deemed permission relating to outdoor advertisements. The display of advertisements does not of itself constitute development, but the erection of an advertisement hoarding will be development because the hoarding is a 'building'[107] and the use for the display of advertisements of any external part of a building not normally used for that purpose is a material change of use.[108]

---

103 See para 9.01.

104 TCPA 1990, Sch 13, para 7; TCPA 1990, Sch 24, para 1(3). Planning (Consequential Provisions) Act 1990, Sch 3, para 3.

105 TCPA 1990, Sch 13, para 8; TCPA 1990, Sch 24, para 1(3). Planning (Consequential Provisions) Act 1990, Sch 3, para 3. The effect of this deemed permission was considered in *LCC v Marks and Spencer Ltd* [1953] AC 535, [1953] 1 All ER 1095 (clearance of site preparatory to erection of building held to be 'works for erection of a building').

106 TCPA 1990, Sch 24, para 19(1). Planning (Consequential Provisions) Act 1990. Sch 3, para 3. See para 10.115 as to when the development is begun.

107 See the definition of 'building' in the TCPA 1990, s. 336, discussed at para 6.07.

108 TCPA 1990, s. 55(4).

All outdoor advertisements require consent under the Control of Advertisements Regulations,[109] whether development is involved or not. The TCPA 1990 provides that where the display of advertisements in accordance with the regulations involves development, planning permission shall be deemed to have been granted.[110]

109 See para15.53.
110 TCPA 1990, s. 222.

8

PLANNING PERMISSION AND NATIONALLY SIGNIFICANT INFRASTRUCTURE DEVELOPMENT CONSENT

Part 1: express planning permission granted by the local planning authority under TCPA 1990

8.01 As explained in chapter 7 there are some forms of development which do not require planning permission under TCPA 1990; some are permitted by development orders or have the benefit of deemed permission. In every other case, application should be made to the local planning authority for express permission.

8.02 The applicant need not be the owner of an interest in the land, nor is it necessary to obtain the consent of the owner.[1]

Publicity for applications

8.03 Under the law as it was before the coming into force of PCA 1991,[2] there was no general requirement for applicants to give notice to the public but there was an exception in the case of so-called 'bad neighbour' development under the former article 11 of the General Development Order 1988. This included developments such as the construction of public conveniences, waste disposal sites, scrap yards, funfairs, Turkish baths, zoos, and the like.

8.04 PCA 1991, s. 16 introduced a new TCPA 1990, s. 65 enabling provision to be made by development order ensuring that the local planning authority provides some publicity for all planning applications. The General Development Procedure Order 1995[3] sets out the statutory requirements for different categories of development. In essence, the General Development Procedure Order provides for three basic types of publicity. These are as follows:

(1) The display of a site notice.
(2) Publication of a notice in a local newspaper.
(3) Neighbour notification to owners and occupiers of adjoining properties.

1 *Hanily v Minister of Local Government and Planning* [1952] 2 QB 444, [1952] 1 All ER 1293.
2 TCPA 1990, ss. 65–68 as originally enacted.
3 T & CP (GDPO) 1995, SI 1995 No 419. Guidance is given in Circular 9/95.

8.05 Which one or more of the above is required depends upon which category of development it falls into under article 8 of the General Development Procedure Order. For this purpose development is classified as follows:

Paragraph (2) applications

8.06 Applications for planning permission for development[4] which (i) is accompanied by an environmental statement;[5] (ii) does not accord with the provisions of the development plan; or (iii) would affect a public right of way[6] must be publicized by the local planning authority by the display of a site notice for not less than 21 days *and* by publication of a notice in a local newspaper. The form of the notice is prescribed by the General Development Procedure Order[7] and must give particulars of a place where the public may inspect copies of the application, the plans, and any other documents submitted with the application.

Applications for major development

8.07 Major development is development which does not fall under paragraph (2) above and which involves one or more of the following:

(a) the winning and working of minerals or the use of the land for mineral-working deposits;
(b) waste development, ie development involving the treating, storing, processing, or disposing of refuse or waste materials;
(c) the provision of dwellinghouses where the number of houses is 10 or more, or where the site has an area of 0.5 hectares or more and the number of houses is not known;
(d) the provision of a building or buildings where the floor space to be created by the development is 1,000 square metres or more; or
(e) development carried out on a site having an area of one hectare or more.

8.08 In the case of major development, the local planning authority must publicize the application by (a) *either* the display of a site notice for not less than 21 days *or* by serving notice on any adjoining owner or occupier *and* (b) by publication of a notice in a local newspaper. Again, the notice must be in the form prescribed by the GDPO.

Applications for minor development

8.09 Minor development is a residual category which is neither paragraph (2) development nor major development. In this instance the local planning authority must

4 Listed in para 2, art 8 GDPO.
5 See Para 9.01.
6 Under the Wildlife and Countryside Act 1981, Part III.
7 GDPO, Sch 3, or in a form substantially to the like effect.

publicize the application in the prescribed form by either the display of a site notice for not less than 21 days or serving notice on any adjoining owner or occupier. It should be noted that these requirements are minima and that in appropriate cases additional publicity may be desirable. The relevant circular[8] cites some examples including developments attracting crowds, traffic, and noise in a quiet area.

8.10 In the case of all three of the classes of development above, members of the public may make representations to the local planning authority. Where the notice has been given by site display or by notification of adjoining owners or occupiers, representations must be made within 21 days from when the notice was first displayed or the adjoining owners or occupiers had notice served on them. If the notice has been given by advertisement in a local newspaper, the relevant period is 14 days from the date when the notice was first published.

8.11 Additionally, in the case of development affecting the setting of a listed building, or the character or appearance of a conservation area, the local planning authority must publish a notice in a local newspaper and display a site notice for not less than seven days, affording the public the opportunity to make representations within a period of 21 days.[9] There may be, therefore, an element of duplication in the statutory requirements; in such a case the more demanding of the publicity requirements will apply.[10]

8.12 What is the position where the local planning authority fail to publicize the application in accordance with the requirements set out above? That such failure affords a possible ground for quashing a grant of planning permission was confirmed in the case of *R (on the application of Gavin) v Haringey London Borough Council*.[11] However, although the applicant for judicial review in this case had been prejudiced by the failure to comply with the publicity requirements, there had been undue delay in bringing proceedings and quashing the permission would have caused substantial hardship to the developers. Accordingly, Richards J exercised his discretion not to invalidate the planning consent. Where no prejudice has been caused and there has been substantial compliance with the procedural requirements, the court is unlikely to accede to an argument that the permission should be quashed. In *R (on the application of Wembley Fields Ltd) v Brent London Borough Council*,[12] a notice was placed in a local newspaper (in

[8] Circular 15/92.

[9] LBA 1990, ss. 67, 73, as amended by PCPA 2004, s. 118, Sch 6, paras 23 and 24. See Planning (Listed Buildings and Conservation Areas) (Amendment) (England) Regulations 2004, SI 2004 No 2210, which were brought into force on 28 September 2004. Note that special publicity arrangements apply in the London Borough of Camden. For listed buildings and conservation areas, see para 16.01.

[10] Circular 15/92, para 20.

[11] [2003] EWHC 2591 (Admin).

[12] [2005] EWHC 2978.

accordance with article 8 GDPO) inviting representations on a planning application for the redevelopment of a school. The claimants made representations concerning the proposed development but the planning committee resolved to grant planning permission on the 21st day of the statutory 21-day period. The claimants contended that the required consultation period had not expired until one minute to midnight on the final day of the relevant period and therefore the authority's decision was invalid. The court, however, concluded that the purpose of the regulations had been substantially complied with and, in the absence of prejudice, the local planning authority's decision was upheld.

Notification of owners

8.13 The publicity requirements discussed above are the responsibility of the local planning authority; under article 6 of the General Development Procedure Order, the *applicant* for planning permission must give notice of the application to any other person who, on the day 21 days before the date of the application, is an owner of the land to which the application relates. He must also notify tenants of agricultural holdings on such land.[13]

8.14 The form of the notice is prescribed by the General Development Procedure Order[14] and it must be served on every owner etc, whose name and address is known to him. There are additional requirements in the case of applications for development consisting of the winning and working of minerals underground. In such a case, in addition to serving notice on owners etc, the applicant must publish notice in a local newspaper and display a site notice.[15]

8.15 Owners and tenants of agricultural holdings then have 21 days from when notice was served on them to make representations to the local planning authority.

Form of application

8.16 TCPA 1990, s. 62, as originally enacted provided that the application for planning permission had to be made on a form issued by the local planning authority and accompanied by a plan sufficient to identify the land and such other plans and drawings necessary to describe the development. The authority could require the applicant to submit such further information as required for the purposes of giving a

13 TCPA 1990, s. 65(2) as substituted by PCA 1991, s. 16. 'Owner' is a person having a freehold or leasehold with at least seven years to run.

14 Sch 2, or in a form substantially to the like effect.

15 GDPO, art 6(2).

decision. Under these provisions, for many years the Government allowed local planning authorities to produce their own application forms and this resulted in variations in different local authority areas in the information required of applicants. The Government, however, came to the view that a standardized planning application form would speed up the process and provide more certainty at the outset as to what information was required by the authority. There was also a perceived need to simplify the procedures, so that one application form could be used for a variety of different forms of consent, such as advertisement consent,[16] or listed building consent.[17]

8.17 Accordingly, PCPA 2004 paved the way for new standardized planning application forms—a new s. 62 of TCPA 1990, substituted by PCPA 2004, s. 42(1), provides for the form and content of planning applications to be prescribed by development order made by the Secretary of State. In consequence, the Secretary of State has made an amending order to the GDPO[18] which came into force on 6 April 2008. After that date, applications for planning permission must be made on the Standard Application Form ('1 APP')[19] and local planning authorities will refuse to accept applications not made in this way. Although the standard form can be submitted on paper, the government wishes to encourage the submission of planning applications electronically. The information required by the local planning authority to make a valid application for planning permission is specified by article 4E of the amended GDPO. To comply with this provision, the application must:

(a) be made in writing on the form published by the Secretary of State (currently 1 APP), in paper or electronic form;
(b) include the particulars specified or referred to on the form;
(c) be accompanied by a plan identifying the relevant land, and any other plans, drawings, and information necessary to describe the proposed development; and
(d) (except where the application is made electronically) consist of the original form and accompanying documents plus three copies, or fewer if the local planning authority so indicate.

8.18 In addition, article 5 of the GDPO requires that a valid application must include a certificate of ownership (discussed below in the next section); a design and access statement, if required (discussed below); any particulars or evidence required by the authority, as published on their website before the application is made; and the appropriate fee.[20] It should be noted that there may be slightly different requirements

16 See para 15.53.
17 See para 16.37.
18 T & CP (GDP)(Amendment)(England) Order 2008, SI 2008 No 550. See also Circular 2/08.
19 1 APP can be accessed through the Planning Portal http://www.planningportal.gov.uk.
20 Planning fees are discussed at para 8.32.

for the validity of other types of application, such as for listed building consent; these requirements are set out in Annex A of Circular 2/08.

8.19 Further, there are certain applications which are not covered by the requirement for a Standard Application Form—these include planning applications for mining operations or the use of land for mineral working deposits; and applications for hazardous substances consent.[21] Such applications should therefore continue to be made on a form issued by the relevant authority.

8.20 Local planning authorities are encouraged to validate planning applications as soon as reasonably practicable after receipt—according to Circular 2/08, para 33, applications for minor and small scale development should be validated within three to five working days and applications for major development within 10 working days. Notice should be given in writing confirming the validity of the application and the commencement date of the period within which the local planning authority must determine the application. It seems that if the authority do not consider the application to be valid because it lacks the requisite information, they may decline to determine the application. The applicant may then appeal to the Secretary of State against such non-determination in the normal way under s. 78 TCPA 1990. This provides a right of appeal when the authority fail to determine an application within the statutory time limit, which, as we shall see, is either eight or 13 weeks.[22]

8.21 *Design and access statements* A further reform made by PCPA 2004 provided for a development order to require that planning applications of such description as specified must be accompanied by (a) a statement about the design principles and concepts that have been applied to the development; (b) a statement about how issues relating to access to the development have been dealt with.[23] This measure has now been implemented—article 4C of the amended GDPO requires that such a statement must accompany planning applications, whether full or outline, although there are some important exceptions. Thus a design and access statement is not required for planning applications for engineering or mining operations; additions to dwellinghouses outside designated areas (ie National Parks, SSSIs, conservation areas, AONBs, World Heritage Sites, and the Broads); and material changes of use, unless also involving operational development.

8.22 The design and access statement is intended to be a brief report supporting a planning application justifying the proposed development and illustrating the processes that have led to the application. According to Circular 1/06, it seems

---

21 See para 15.81.
22 See para 8.106.
23 TCPA 1990, s. 62(5) as substituted by PCPA 2004, s. 42(1). The provision came into force on 10 August 2006 under SI 2006 No 1062.

that the purpose is to better inform not only the decision maker but other interested parties—in a non-technical manner—as to the design and access rationale underpinning the application. The GDPO, article 4C(3), requires that a design and access statement shall (a) explain the design principles and concepts that have been applied to the following aspects of the development: (i) amount; (ii) layout; (iii) scale; (iv) landscaping; and (v) appearance; and (b) demonstrate the steps taken to appraise the context of the development and how the design of the development takes that context into account in relation to its proposed use and each of the aspects specified in (a) above. Under article 4C(5), 'amount' means, in relation to residential development, the number of proposed housing units; and in relation to all other development, the proposed floorspace for each proposed use. 'Context' is defined as meaning the physical, social, economic, and policy context of the development.

8.23 Compliance with the new requirements introduced by PCPA 2004 is mandatory, as s. 327A TCPA 1990[24] provides that the local planning authority must not entertain an application that fails to comply with any legal requirement as to the form and manner in which an application is made; or the form and content of any document or other matter accompanying the application.

8.24 *Certificates of ownership* The application must be accompanied by a certificate in a form prescribed by the General Development Procedure Order[25] that the applicant has satisfied the requirements of article 6 of the General Development Procedure Order as to the notification of owners etc, discussed above.[26] There are four alternative certificates to cover the following situations:

(1) On the day 21 days before the date of the application, nobody except the applicant was the owner of any part of the land to which the application relates (Certificate A).
(2) The applicant has given the requisite notice to everyone else who, on the day 21 days before the date of the application, was the owner of any part of the land to which the application relates. Such owners must be listed. (Certificate B).
(3) The applicant is unable to issue Certificate A or B (above) but the applicant has given the requisite notice to the persons specified in the certificate who on the day 21 days before the date of the application were owners of any part of the land to which the application relates. This certificate will be used where the applicant is unable to discover all the persons with an interest in the land—the applicant must certify that he has taken all reasonable steps to ascertain the other owners but has been unable to do so (Certificate C).

---

24 Inserted by PCPA 2004, s. 42(5).
25 Art 6 and Sch 2.
26 See para 8.13.

(4) The applicant cannot issue Certificate A and is unable, after taking all reasonable steps, to ascertain the names of any of the persons who on the day 21 days before the date of the application were owners of any part of the land to which the application relates (Certificate D).

8.25 In the case of (3) and (4), above, the steps that the applicant is required to take include the circulation of a notice in a local newspaper. In all cases, the applicant must also certify either that none of the land to which the application relates is, or is part of, an agricultural holding or that notice has been given to every person who on the day 21 days before the date of the application was a tenant of an agricultural holding on all or part of the land to which the application relates.

8.26 What is the position where the certificate of ownership contains factual error? First, under s. 65(6) TCPA 1990 an offence may be committed if a person, knowingly or recklessly, issues a certificate which is false or misleading; on conviction a fine not exceeding level 5 on the standard scale may be imposed. A more fundamental issue however, where there is factual error, is whether any planning permission subsequently granted is valid. In *R v Bradford-on-Avon Urban District Council, ex p Boulton*,[27] the Divisional Court held that a planning permission could be valid even though granted on the strength of a certificate of ownership containing factual error. Thus the mere existence of factual error in the certificate did not deprive the local planning authority of jurisdiction. The court expressed concern that third parties, such as purchasers, ought to be able to rely on a grant of planning permission as running with the land. If purchasers were required to investigate the circumstances in which a planning application had been made in order to be able to rely on it, this would place undue obstacles in the way of the conveyancing transaction.

8.27 In a later case, *Main v Swansea City Council*,[28] the Court of Appeal took a different approach. The court held that a factual error in a certificate could, in an appropriate case, entitle the court to exercise its discretion to quash the subsequent grant of planning permission. Relevant factors in the exercise of such discretion include the identity of the person bringing proceedings, any lapse of time, the effect on other parties and on the public interest. In the case itself, a person whose identity was unknown had an interest in the relevant land and the wrong certificate was submitted. Although acknowledging that in certain circumstances the defect was sufficient to afford grounds for relief, the court exercised its discretion not to quash the grant of planning permission on the grounds, inter alia, of delay. An application to quash a planning permission on the ground of non-compliance with the notice requirements succeeded in *R (on the application of Pridmore)*

[27] [1964] 1 WLR 1136.

[28] [1985] JPL 558.

v Salisbury District Council. In this case, D submitted a planning application to build a house certifying that all land included in the application was in his ownership. This was not the case as some of the adjacent land, owned by the claimants, was included. On the advice of the local planning authority, D submitted an amended plan accompanied by Certificate B certifying that the claimants had been informed. Unaware that this was not the case, the local planning authority granted planning permission for the revised proposal. Newman J quashed the permission, holding that the local planning authority had made an error of law in treating the original application as valid and that they should have required D to submit a fresh application. To allow the permission to stand would have undermined the mandatory scheme of the legislation—the claimants had suffered prejudice and it was appropriate for the court to quash the permission.

8.28 There is a danger that a landowner who is not informed of a planning application may dispose of his land for less than its market value. In *English v Dedham Vale Properties Ltd*,[29] a planning application was submitted in the vendor's name without his knowledge. In the Chancery Division, Slade J held that the applicant had to account to the vendor for the profits derived from the increased value of the land owing to the grant of planning permission. The basis of the decision was that the applicant had become the self-appointed agent of the vendors, thereby giving rise to a fiduciary relationship.

Outline planning permission

8.29 Where the applicant seeks permission for the erection of a building or buildings, he may apply in the first instance for outline planning permission with a view to obtaining permission in principle before going to the expense of preparing detailed plans. Outline planning permission is granted with the reservation for subsequent approval by the local planning authority of 'reserved matters'. For many years, the legislation provided that these matters were: siting, design, external appearance, access, and landscaping. However, as from 10 August 2006 (under powers introduced by PCPA 2004), the list of reserved matters changed to: access, appearance, landscaping, layout, and scale.[30]

8.30 The local planning authority may decline to entertain an outline application if they consider that the application ought not to be considered separately from the reserved matters specified above; in this event, the applicant may either furnish particulars of these details or appeal to the Secretary of State.[31] A permission on an

29 [1978] 1 WLR 93.

30 T &CP (General Development Procedure)(Amendment)(England) Order 2006, SI 2006 No 1063.

31 GDPO, arts 2, 23.

outline application is a valid planning permission even though the applicant must obtain further approvals before acting upon it. An outline permission can be revoked only in accordance with the statutory procedures; these normally require the consent of the Secretary of State and the payment of compensation.[32]

8.31 Concerns as to whether outline planning permission could be reconciled with the requirements of Environmental Impact Assessment[33] led the government to include in the Planning and Compulsory Purchase Bill 2004 a proposal for a 'Statement of Development Principles' (SDP). An SDP would in effect be a statement by the local planning authority that a particular proposed development was in principle permissible which would then become a material consideration in determining the planning application proper. But it would not have had the certainty of an outline planning consent and, not being legally binding, could have been displaced by changes in policy. There was considerable opposition to the SDP, not surprisingly from the development industry. During the passage of the Bill, an amendment to omit the relevant clause was carried and the Government abandoned the idea.

Planning fees

8.32 TCPA 1990, s. 303 enables the Secretary of State to make regulations requiring the payment of fees to the local planning authority in respect of applications for planning permission and other matters.

8.33 The regulations which the Secretary of State has made[34] provide that, with a few exceptions, every application for planning permission (or for consent for matters reserved by an outline permission)[35] shall be accompanied by the fee prescribed by the regulations. If the application is not accompanied by the requisite fee, the statutory period within which the planning authority are required to give notice of their decision on the application does not begin until the correct fee has been received.[36]

8.34 Although the payment of planning fees has been required for some time, it has hitherto been the position that the local planning authority were not allowed to charge the applicant for any pre-application advice they may have given him.[37]

---

32 *Hamilton v West Sussex County Council* [1958] 2 QB 286, [1958] 2 All ER 174.

33 See para 9.01.

34 Town and Country Planning (Fees for Applications and Deemed Applications) Regulations 1989, SI 1989 No 193, as amended. The most recent amending regs are SI 2008 No 958.

35 See para 8.29.

36 GDPO, art 20.

37 *McCarthy & Stone (Developments) Ltd v London Borough of Richmond-upon-Thames* [1992] 2 AC 48.

However, s. 53 of PCPA 2004[38] permits the Secretary of State[39] to make regulations allowing the authority to require the payment of a charge or a fee for the performance of any of their functions, and for anything which facilitates, or is conducive or incidental to, the performance of such functions.[40] This enhanced power has been used in connection with charging fees for visits to landfill sites in order for the local planning authority to monitor compliance with site conditions attached to planning permission.

8.35 The PA 2008, s. 199, substitutes a new s. 303 of TCPA 1990 relating to planning fees. The section provides that the Secretary of State may make regulations providing for the payment of a fee or charge to the local planning authority in respect of (a) the performance by the local planning authority of any function they have; and (b) anything done by them that is calculated to facilitate, or is conducive or incidental to, the performance of such functions. The regulations may make provision as to a range of matters in connection with the payment of fees or charges under the regulations. In relation to Wales, the section enables the Welsh ministers to make like provision.

Reference of applications to the Secretary of State

8.36 Normally, the decision on an application for planning permission will be made by the local planning authority. But, as mentioned earlier,[41] the Secretary of State has power under TCPA 1990, s. 77 to 'call in' any application for planning permission: that is, to direct that it shall be referred to him for decision. Where an application is called in, the parties have the right to be heard at a public local inquiry or other hearing.

8.37 It is entirely within the discretion of the Secretary of State whether or not an application is called in; the court will intervene only if he misconstrues his powers in some way—perhaps by taking into account some irrelevant matter—or if he exercises his discretion in a wholly unreasonable manner.[42]

8.38 The present policy of the Secretary of State is to be very selective in calling in applications. The proposed development must, in general, involve planning issues of more than local importance or it may have engendered widespread public controversy; examples have been the processing of nuclear waste at Sellafield and coalmining in the Vale of Belvoir. But an application may also be called in because

---

[38] Amending s. 303 of TCPA 1990. The measures came into force, to the extent they were not already in force, on 7 March 2005: Planning and Compulsory Purchase Act 2004 (Commencement No 4 and Savings) Order 2005, SI 2004 No 204, art 2.

[39] In Wales, the Assembly.

[40] TCPA 1990, s. 303 as amended by TCPA 1990, s. 53(2).

[41] See para 3.10.

[42] *Rhys Williams v Secretary of State for Wales* [1985] JPL 29.

it involves a departure from the development plan, or because it would involve a serious loss of agricultural land.

Consultations by local planning authority

8.39 On receiving an application for planning permission, the local planning authority may have to consult various government departments and other authorities. Thus, in the case of development affecting trunk roads and certain other major highways (whether existing or proposed), the local planning authority must on receipt of the application consult the Secretary of State[43] who may direct the authority either to refuse permission or to impose conditions.

8.40 Other consultations are prescribed by article 10 of the General Development Procedure Order or by directions made by the Secretary of State under article 10. In these cases consultation is not automatically required; the duty to consult arises if the local planning authority, having given some consideration to the application, are minded to grant permission. For instance, the local planning authority must not grant planning permission for development within three kilometres of Windsor Castle, Windsor Great Park, or Home Park, or 800 metres of any other royal palace or park which might affect the amenities of that palace or park without first consulting the Secretary of State; and the Secretary of State must be consulted before permission is granted for development which is likely to result in a material increase in the volume or a material change in the character of traffic entering or leaving a trunk road.[44] The Coal Authority is to be consulted in a case of development which involves the provision of a building or pipe-line in an area of coal working notified by the authority to the local planning authority.

8.41 PCPA 2004[45] amends TCPA 1990, Schedule 1, so as to bring the consultation arrangements on planning applications between local planning authorities and county councils into line with the changes introduced by the new Act. It also introduces provision for RPBs to be statutory consultees on certain planning applications; thus the RPB must be consulted on any development which would be of major importance for the implementation of the RSS or a relevant regional policy, by reason of its scale, nature, or location. Further, each RPB may notify

---

[43] GDPO, art 15. These provisions apply to (a) the formation, laying out or alteration of any means of access to the highway; (b) any other development within 67 metres from the middle of the existing or proposed highway.

[44] It is apparently for the local planning authority to decide whether there is likely to be a material increase in volume or material change in character.

[45] PCPA 2004, Sch 6, para 16(4). The provision was brought into force on 25 July 2005 by SI 2004 No 2081.

local planning authorities of other descriptions of development in relation to which it wishes to be consulted.

8.42 An amendment to article 10 of the General Development Procedure Order was made in 2003 which introduced a requirement to consult, in England, the relevant RDA before the grant of planning permission for certain categories of development, ie strategic infrastructure projects; and development likely to affect regional investment or employment policies.[46] The amending Order also introduced an additional exception to the requirement to consult a statutory consultee, before the grant of planning permission, where a local planning authority consider that the development proposed is subject to any up-to-date standing advice issued by the relevant consultee.[47]

8.43 There can be no doubt that the statutory consultation procedure has been a major source of delay in the planning process. Accordingly, s. 54 of PCPA 2004 imposes a statutory duty upon consultees to give a substantive response to any consultation with which the Secretary of State[48] or local planning authority must comply before granting planning permission or other approvals or consents under the planning Acts as prescribed. Any person may, in relation to a proposed development, consult the consultee on any matter of which the Secretary of State is, or the local planning authority are, required to consult. The Secretary of State may require the statutory consultees to submit a report to him on their performance under these provisions.[49]

8.44 As had been indicated in a consultation paper,[50] the period prescribed for the purpose of the duty is 21 days starting with the day on which the statutory consultee receives notice of an application from a prospective developer or the local planning authority. A different period may be agreed in writing between the parties—this is a potential weakness in the measure.

8.45 The local planning authority must not grant planning permission for development which does not accord with the provisions of the development plan (a 'departure application') without first going through the procedure laid down by the Town and Country Planning (Development Plans and Consultation) (Departures) Directions 1999.[51] Departure applications are, of course, subject to the statutory publicity requirements of article 8 of the General Development Procedure Order.[52]

[46] T & CP (General Development Procedure) (England) (Amendment) Order 2003, SI 2003 No 2047, art 3.

[47] Ibid, art 4.

[48] In Wales, the Assembly.

[49] PCPA 2004, s. 54(1)–(4) and (6). The provision was brought into force as from 24 August 2005 by SI 2005 No 2081.

[50] *Changes to the Development Control System*, ODPM, November 2004.

[51] Published in Circular 7/99.

[52] See para 8.03.

8.46 The Directions require that where a departure application which a local planning authority do not propose to refuse is for:

(a) development which consists of or includes the provision of:
  (i) more than 150 houses or flats; or
  (ii) more than 5,000 square metres of retail, leisure, office, or mixed commercial floorspace measured externally;

(b) development of land of an interested planning authority, or for the development of any land by such an authority, whether alone or jointly with any other person;[53] or

(c) any other development which, by reason of its scale or nature or the location of the land, would significantly prejudice the implementation of the development plan's policies and proposals; the authority shall send to the Secretary of State:
  (i) a copy of the application, including copies of any accompanying plans and drawings;
  (ii) a copy of the notice required by article 8 of the General Department Procedure Order;[54]
  (iii) a copy of any representations made to the authority in respect of the application;
  (iv) unless contained in the officer's report, a statement of the material considerations which the authority consider indicate otherwise for the purposes of TCPA 1990 s. 54A;
  (v) a statement of the issues involved in the decision and of any views expressed on the application by a government department, another local planning authority, or parish council.

8.47 Once this procedure has been complied with and the Secretary of State has notified the local planning authority that he has received the documents at (i)–(v) above, the local planning authority are free to grant planning permission after the expiry of 21 days. This gives the Secretary of State the opportunity to call in the application or issue a direction restricting the grant of planning permission. The procedure will not apply to a departure application if the authority impose such conditions on the permission as will, in their opinion, ensure that if the development is carried out in accordance with those conditions it will be in accordance with the development plan.[55]

8.48 The 1981 Direction applied the notification procedure to applications for development which the local planning authority considered would conflict with or

---

53 See para 17.40.
54 See para 8.03.
55 Development Plans Direction, para 2(2).

prejudice the implementation of the development plan. The current Direction, and the previous version made in 1992, are intended to supplement section 54A of the TCPA 1990 (now s. 38(6) of PCPA 1990) which is designed to enhance the status of the development plan.[56]

8.49 What would be the position if the local planning authority granted planning permission without observing the procedure outlined above? Would such permission be valid? In *Co-operative Retail Services Ltd v Taff-Ely Borough Council*,[57] Ormrod and Browne LJ considered that the procedure laid down by the Direction then in force was merely directory and not mandatory. In the subsequent case of *R v St Edmundsbury Borough Council, ex p Investors in Industry Commercial Properties Ltd*,[58] the council failed to advertise a departure application as required by the 1981 Direction. Stocker J held that the reasoning of Ormrod and Browne LJ in the earlier case was not obiter, and that the failure to comply with the Direction did not render the grant of planning permission null and void.

8.50 The above-mentioned authorities should now be seen in the light of the decision in *R v Restormel Borough Council, ex p Parkyn*.[59] Here George Bartlett QC, sitting as deputy judge, ruled that certain planning permissions were unlawful on the basis, inter alia, that the applications should have been referred to the Secretary of State by virtue of the Direction of 1992. The wording of the 1992 Direction contained a clear prohibition—in framing the Direction in this way, it could be assumed that the Secretary of State had taken into account the views of the Court of Appeal in the *Co-operative Retail Services* case. This conclusion was not challenged when the case came before the Court of Appeal.[60]

8.51 From time to time, the Secretary of State has made other Directions restricting the grant of planning permission by the local planning authority without first referring the application to the Secretary of State. Concern about the loss of playing fields to development led the Secretary of State to make the Town and Country Planning (Playing Fields) (England) Direction 1998. Under the terms of the Direction, where the Sports Council (as statutory consultee) object to proposed development involving the loss of a playing field, but the local authority are minded to grant permission, the authority must notify the Secretary of State to give him the opportunity to call in the application. The Direction applies to planning applications made on or after 23 December 1998.[61] The Secretary of State

56 See para 8.57.
57 (1979) 39 P & CR 223 at 245, 246 and 253, 254, 255; affd sub nom *A-G (ex rel Co-operative Retail Services Ltd) v Taff-Ely Borough Council* (1981) 42 P & CR 1.
58 [1985] 3 All ER 234, [1985] 1 WLR 1168.
59 [2000] EGCS 105.
60 2 March 2001, unreported.
61 And see Circular 9/98.

has also over the years made Directions applying to planning applications relating to the development of 'greenfield' sites, residential density in the south-east of England; the development of the green belt, and major retail development. A more recent example is the Town and Country Planning (Flooding) (England) Direction 2007.

8.52 Under the 2007 Flooding Direction, where the local planning authority is minded to grant planning permission for major development in a flood risk area, but the Environment Agency has objected on flood risk grounds, all relevant parties must discuss and agree a course of action which would enable the Agency to withdraw its objection. If, after discussion, the Agency is unable to withdraw its objection, it should advise the local planning authority accordingly. 'Major development' is defined as (a) residential development where the number of dwellings to be provided is 10 or more, or the site area is 0.5 hectares or more; or (b) non-residential development where the floor space to be provided is 1,000 square metres or more, or the site area is one hectare or more. If the local planning authority is minded to grant planning permission for such development, even after the discussions to which reference was made above, the authority must notify the Secretary of State, who may consider whether to call in the application.

8.53 The government has issued a consultation paper reviewing 'call in Directions'[62] recommending that all existing Directions be withdrawn and a single new call in Direction be issued with five requirements for referral to the Secretary of State: playing fields, green belt, flooding, town centres, and World Heritage Sites.

Consideration by local planning authority

8.54 In reaching their decision the local planning authority must, of course, comply with any directions given by the Secretary of State. They must have regard to the views of any government departments or other public authorities with whom they have been required to consult and to any representations received from interested parties under the General Development Procedure Order or the Listed Buildings Act.

8.55 The local planning authority must always have regard to the provisions of the development plan and to any other material considerations.[63]

Provisions of the development plan

8.56 The provisions of the development plan have always been regarded as being of primary importance. Nevertheless, both ministerial policy pronouncements and

---

62 Review of call in Directions, DCLG, 2008.

63 TCPA 1990, s. 70(2).

the decisions of the courts adhered to the view that the development plan was one, but only one, of the material considerations that must be taken into account in dealing with planning applications.[64] Moreover, ministerial policy guidance over the years emphasized that there was a presumption in favour of development unless it could be shown that the particular proposal would cause demonstrable harm to interests of acknowledged importance[65] and this was even endorsed by the courts as a statement of the statutory position.[66]

8.57 The Planning and Compensation Act 1991, s. 26, which inserted a new TCPA 1990, s. 54A, represented a major departure from the above position. This provided that where, 'in making any determination under the Planning Acts, regard is to be had to the development plan, the determination shall be made in accordance with the plan unless material considerations indicate otherwise'. It has been described as a shift to a 'plan-led' planning system and this theme was reflected by the former Planning Policy Guidance Note 1, 1997 which provided that in all cases where the development plan is relevant, it will be necessary to decide whether the proposal is in accordance with the plan and then to take into account other material considerations. This will no doubt continue to be the case, particularly since PCPA 2004 has re-enacted s. 54A in virtually identical terms. PCPA 2004, s. 38(6) provides that, 'If regard is to be had to the development plan for the purpose of any determination to be made under the planning Acts the determination must be made in accordance with the plan unless material considerations indicate otherwise'.

8.58 TCPA 1990, s. 54A first came before the courts in *St Albans District Council v Secretary of State for the Environment*.[67] David Widdicombe QC (sitting as deputy judge) held that undoubtedly the section did set up a presumption in favour of the development plan but he rejected the submission that the plan should prevail unless there were strong contrary planning grounds. The judge felt that such an interpretation would put a gloss on the statute—he preferred to adhere to the words of the section which made it clear that the presumption in favour of the development plan may be rebutted if there were material considerations which 'indicated otherwise'.

8.59 In *R v Canterbury City Council, ex p Springimage Ltd*,[68] a planning permission was held ultra vires for failure to comply with the duty under s. 54A. Nevertheless,

64 *Simpson v Edinburgh Corpn* 1960 SC 313 at 319 per Lord Guest in dealing with the Scottish equivalent of s. 70(2). These remarks were adopted in *Co-operative Retail Services Ltd v Taff-Ely Borough Council* (1979) 39 P & CR 223, CA.

65 PPG 1, 1988, successively replaced by PPG 1, 1992, PPG 1, 1997, and PPS 1, 2005.

66 *Cranford Hall Parking Ltd v Secretary of State for the Environment* [1989] JPL 169; cf *Pehrsson v Secretary of State for the Environment* [1990] JPL 426.

67 [1993] 1 PLR 88.

68 [1994] JPL 427. And see *James v Secretary of State for the Environment* [1998] 1 PLR 33.

the court exercised its discretion not to quash the decision, there being no real possibility of the decision being decided differently if it were reconsidered. In this case the Chief Planning Officer reported to the planning committee that TCPA 1990, s. 54A required local authorities to 'have regard to the provisions of the development plan . . . in determining planning applications, unless material considerations indicate otherwise'. David Keene QC (sitting as deputy judge) had no doubt that s. 54A increased the importance of the development plan in the decision-making process, however the passage quoted above mis-stated the approach embodied in that section. The officer, in his report, had conflated two requirements: (1) to have regard to the development plan and any other material considerations under s. 70(2), a duty from which there was no escape; and (2) the duty under s. 54A to make its determination in accordance with the plan unless material considerations indicated otherwise. He had thus mis-stated both obligations and it was probable that the planning committee had been misled.

8.60 The Scottish equivalent of TCPA 1990, s. 54A—the Town and Country Planning (Scotland) Act 1972—has received attention from the House of Lords. In *City of Edinburgh Council v Secretary of State for the Environment*,[69] their Lordships ruled that the presumption which TCPA 1990, s. 54A laid down (ie in favour of the development plan) was a statutory requirement but in essence was a presumption of fact for the decision maker. The section did not increase the power of the courts to intervene in planning decisions. Indeed, the function of the courts was to see whether the decision maker had had regard to the presumption, not to assess the weight given to it in the face of other material considerations.

8.61 The opinions of Lords Hope and Clyde in the *City of Edinburgh* case (above) were accepted by the Court of Appeal in *R v Leominster District Council, ex p Pothecary*[70] as representing English law. Thus, TCPA 1990, s. 54A had not changed the remit of the courts, who will not readily interfere with decisions which Parliament had entrusted to local authorities. Schiemann LJ appositely remarked that in many cases each side 'will be able to cite policies in the same or different plans in support of their contentions. In many cases the relevant policies will contain within themselves value judgments upon which reasonable persons may differ'.

8.62 It may be asked; what material considerations would justify a decision which is not in accordance with the development plan? One obvious such consideration is whether the development plan policies are up to date. Ministerial guidance[71] has given the example of where policies and proposals in the plan have been superseded by more recent planning guidance issued by the Government, or developments since the plan became operative have rendered certain policies or proposals in the

69 [1998] JPL 224.
70 [1998] JPL 335.
71 PPG 1, 1997, para 54. PPG 1 was replaced by PPS 1, 2005.

plan incapable of implementation. These would be material considerations. Indeed this view of the position was endorsed by the Court of Appeal in *Loup v Secretary of State for the Environment*[72] where Glidewell LJ, in dealing with the effect of TCPA 1990, s. 54A, described the similarly worded predecessor to the above as 'important guidance'. By the same token he recognized that when a development plan was newly approved, the policies in it would have more weight in the scale than policies the relevance or force of which had been overtaken by events.

8.63 It might be the case that the development plan does not contain a policy at all relating to a particular development proposal or the plan contains contradictory policies—in such cases the application will have to be determined on its merits in the light of all the material considerations.[73]

8.64 When considering an application for planning permission the local planning authority may also have to take account of emerging plans, ie proposals for the amendment of existing plans or new plans in the course of preparation. It may be difficult in these circumstances to come to a decision which is fair to all concerned; if the proposed development is in accordance with the emerging plan, the authority may think it right that planning permission should be granted but to do so might pre-empt objections to the plan and the public inquiry. Some guidance on these problems has been given in *R v City of London Corpn, ex p Allan*.[74]

8.65 The Corporation had prepared a draft local plan known as the Smithfield Local Plan. Objections had been lodged and were due to go to public inquiry. However, an application had been received for planning permission for the redevelopment of a large part of the area. The Corporation referred the application to the Secretary of State but he declined to call it in. It seemed likely that the Corporation would grant permission, so the applicants sought an order of prohibition to prevent the grant of permission at this stage.

8.66 Woolf J said that once a planning authority had publicized proposals in a draft plan, the authority should have regard to that plan; if there were objections which would lead to an inquiry, the authority should take those objections into account and should consider whether it would be appropriate to deal with the application at this stage or to refuse permission on the ground that the application was premature. His Lordship concluded that there was nothing to suggest that the Corporation would not give proper consideration to the relevant matters and he dismissed the application for an order of prohibition.

---

[72] [1996] JPL 22.

[73] PPG 1, para 55. PPG 1 was replaced by PPS 1, 2005.

[74] (1980) 79 LGR 223. Followed by CA in *Davies v London Borough of Hammersmith* [1981] JPL 682; and in *R v South Norfolk District Council, ex p Pelham Homes Ltd* (2 August 2000, unreported).

8.67 It should be noted, however, that an emerging plan would not be part of the development plan for the purposes of s. 54A until the plan were adopted; it is nevertheless a material consideration. In *Nottinghamshire County Council and Broxtowe Borough Council v Secretary of State for the Environment, Transport and the Regions*,[75] Sullivan J recognized that there was a clear difference between a statutory obligation to determine an appeal in accordance with the development plan and an obligation to have regard to emerging policies as material considerations, even if the emerging policies are accorded considerable weight.

Other material considerations

8.68 It is an obvious principle that these considerations must be related to the objects of planning legislation. The difficulty is to say precisely what are these objects. In *Stringer v Minister of Housing and Local Government*, Cooke J said[76] that any consideration which related to the use and development of land was capable of being a planning consideration, its materiality depending on the circumstances. This dictum of Cooke J was said in the more later case of *Northumberland County Council v Secretary of State for the Environment and British Coal Corpn*[77] to be 'still good law'. The question of whether a particular issue was or was not material has come before the courts on numerous occasions, and the courts have in general adopted a liberal approach.

Cost of development

8.69 Cooke J's point in *Stringer* that the materiality of a particular issue may depend on the circumstances is well illustrated by the question of whether the economics of a proposed development should be taken into account. In *J Murphy & Sons Ltd v Secretary of State for the Environment*,[78] the issue was whether the cost of developing the site was a relevant consideration.

8.70 The Camden London Borough Council proposed to build flats on a site which was far from ideal because on one side it adjoined a railway and on another adjoined Murphy's industrial works; the Council considered it could be made suitable although it would be very expensive. Murphy's wanted to acquire the site and objected to the Council's proposals. The Secretary of State said that the cost of developing the site for a particular purpose was an irrelevant consideration in determining a planning application.

8.71 Ackner J in upholding the Secretary of State said, 'What the planning authority is concerned with is how the land is going to be used. . . . The planning authority

75 [1999] EGCS 35.
76 [1971] 1 All ER 65 at 77.
77 [1989] JPL 700.
78 [1973] 2 All ER 26, [1973] 1 WLR 560.

exercises no paternalistic or avuncular jurisdiction over would-be developers to safeguard them from their financial follies.' That seems to be a sound approach, but the learned judge appears to have overstated matters when he held 'as a matter of law' that the Secretary of State was not entitled to have regard to the cost of developing the site.[79] Certainly Forbes J disagreed in *Sovmots Investments Ltd v Secretary of State for the Environment*;[80] the Secretary of State must, he said, be entitled to bear in mind the likelihood of the development being carried out: 'Cost may or may not be a relevant consideration depending on the circumstances of the case; all that the court has to do is to say that cost can be a relevant consideration and leave it to the Secretary of State to decide whether in any circumstance it is or it is not.'

8.72 These remarks were adopted by Woolf J in *Sosmo Trust Ltd v Secretary of State for the Environment and London Borough of Camden*.[81] Nevertheless the Secretary of State may be overruled if his opinion as to the relevance of economic factors is unreasonable. In *Sosmo* the appellants had contended that nothing less than an office development of at least six storeys would be economically viable and that if permission were not granted the site would be left derelict; the inspector considered that the financial aspects were irrelevant and dismissed the appeal. Woolf J held that the inspector could not reasonably have come to this conclusion and remitted the case for reconsideration.

8.73 The prospective cost of development was also found to be relevant in *Niarchos (London) Ltd v Secretary of State for the Environment*.[82] The development plan provided that temporary planning permission which had been granted for office use should not be renewed in respect of houses which could 'reasonably be used or adapted for use for residential occupation': it was held that in deciding whether the premises could reasonably be used or adapted, the Secretary of State should have regard to the cost of re-converting the houses to residential use.

8.74 The whole question of the relevance of financial considerations came before the Court of Appeal in *R v Westminster City Council, ex p Monahan*.[83] The trustees of the Royal Opera House (ROH) had applied for planning permission to redevelop part of Covent Garden. The central objective was to extend and improve the ROH, but the application also included the erection of office accommodation on part of the site. The modernization of the ROH was an important feature of the local plan, but the proposal to erect offices was contrary to the plan. The City Council, albeit

---

[79] Ackner J in fact acknowledged in a later case that he 'might have stated the general proposition too widely': *Hambledon and Chiddingfold Parish Council v Secretary of State for the Environment* [1976] JPL 502.

[80] [1977] QB 411, [1976] 1 All ER 178.

[81] [1983] JPL 806.

[82] (1977) 35 P & CR 259.

[83] [1989] JPL 107.

reluctantly, accepted the need to erect offices on the ground that the funds necessary to improve the ROH were unobtainable by any other means.

8.75 The Covent Garden Community Association challenged the Council's decision on two grounds: first, that to permit the commercial development of part of the site for purely financial reasons, whatever their purpose, was not a material consideration which the Council was entitled to take into account; alternatively, that the Council was bound to investigate whether the erection of the offices was in fact necessary to achieve the objectives relating to the ROH.

8.76 Held: (1) the fact that the finances made available from the commercial development would enable the improvements to be carried out was capable of being a material consideration, that is, a consideration which related to the use and development of land, particularly as the proposed commercial development was on the same site as the ROH and the commercial development and the improvements to the ROH all formed part of one proposal; (2) that in fact the Council had adequately investigated the question whether the office development was necessary to achieve the improvements.

8.77 The judgments in this case must now be regarded as a definitive statement of the law on this question as the House of Lords refused leave to appeal.

Enabling development

8.78 The *Royal Opera House* case thus sanctions the principle that it is lawful to grant planning permission for development 'A' in order to provide the funds necessary to carry out development 'B', although 'A' would otherwise have been refused. This is sometimes referred to as 'enabling development'. In the *Royal Opera House* case, development 'B' was a central feature of the local plan, and both 'A' and 'B' were included in a composite application for planning permission. But suppose there had been no physical contiguity and the sites were some distance apart? That point was discussed in the Court of Appeal. Kerr LJ concluded that such a case 'would involve questions of fact and degree rather than of principle'. Staughton LJ suggested that the justification for permitting development 'B' must be that it fairly and reasonably related to development 'A'. In the subsequent case of *Northumberland County Council v Secretary of State for the Environment and British Coal Corpn*,[84] the connection between 'A' and 'B' seems to be more questionable than in the *Royal Opera House* case; Mr Malcolm Spence QC, sitting as deputy judge, held that the Secretary of State had not erred in law in permitting an opencast mine because of the financial benefit to deep mining, even though no particular deep mine had been identified.[85]

---

[84] [1989] JPL 700.

[85] Clearly there must be *some* rational connection between the two elements—see *Barber v Secretary of State for the Environment* [1991] JPL 559.

8.79 The decision of the local planning authority to grant planning permission for enabling development can be a finely balanced one. But it seems that the Court is not empowered to make a judgment as to the conflicting desiderata which faced the authority when they made the decision. In *R v West Dorset District Council, ex p Searle*,[86] the local planning authority granted planning permission for the erection of eight houses in the grounds of a listed building[87] on the basis that no development should commence until the listed building had been repaired and restored. It was contended that the authority should have tested the developer's financial case by engaging an outside expert—in not doing so they had failed to take into account a material consideration. A majority of the Court of Appeal (Aldous LJ dissenting) upheld a decision of Latham J that the authority had not so failed.

Planning policy

8.80 It is well established that 'other material considerations' include the Secretary of State's policy statements as contained, for instance, in the Department's circulars and Planning Policy Guidance Notes and Statements.[88] There may, of course, be circumstances in which it is proper for the local planning authority to decide not to follow a particular policy statement[89] but in that event they must give clear reasons for not doing so.[90]

8.81 A frequent bone of contention between the would-be developer and the local planning authority is whether the development is needed. Whether this issue is material depends, it is submitted, on the circumstances. The absence of need is not relevant if there are no other objections; but if there are other objections, the local planning authority may well consider whether the need for the development is sufficient to overcome those objections. Thus the need for additional farm dwellings may be sufficient to overcome the general policy objection to building isolated dwellings in the open countryside.

Existing planning permissions

8.82 The fact that there are permitted development rights under the General Permitted Development Order and existing planning permissions for similar, but not identical, development should be taken into account.[91]

---

86 [1999] JPL 331.

87 See para 16.01

88 See eg *J A Pye (Oxford) Estates Ltd v West Oxfordshire District Council* (1982) 47 P & CR 125, [1982] JPL 577.

89 A good illustration is to be found in *Camden London Borough Council v Secretary of State for the Environment and PSP (Nominees)* [1989] JPL 613.

90 *Gransden & Co Ltd v Secretary of State for the Environment* [1986] JPL 519; affd [1987] JPL 365, CA; *Carpets of Worth Ltd v Wyre Forest District Council* (1991) 62 P & CR 334.

91 *Wells v Minister of Housing and Local Government* [1967] 2 All ER 1041, [1967] 1 WLR 1000; and see the account of this case in ch 3 above.

Personal circumstances

8.83 It seems that the personal circumstances of the applicant may be a material consideration but they will only be peripheral; if there are substantial planning objections to the proposed development, those objections must obviously prevail, but where a case is more finely balanced, a genuine plea of hardship may tip the scales in the applicant's favour.[92]

Precedent

8.84 It is not uncommon for the local planning authority, or on appeal the Secretary of State, to state as a ground of refusal that a grant of planning permission would create a precedent which might make it difficult to refuse a similar application. This has been recognized as a material consideration. In *Collis Radio Ltd v Secretary of State for the Environment*,[93] Lord Widgery CJ said: 'Planning is something which deals with localities and not individual parcels of land and individual sites. In all planning cases it must be of the greatest importance to ask what the consequences in the locality will be—what are the side effects which will flow if such a permission is granted.' The law on this point has now been refined to some extent. In *Poundstretcher Ltd v Secretary of State for the Environment and Liverpool City Council*,[94] Mr David Widdicombe QC, sitting as deputy judge, said that mere fear or generalized concern about creating a precedent was not enough; there had to be evidence of one form or another for reliance on precedent. The learned deputy judge added, however, that in some cases the facts might speak for themselves: for instance, in the case of the rear extension of one house in a terrace of houses, it might be obvious that other owners in the terrace would want extensions if one was permitted.

8.85 The issue of precedent arose in *R (on the application of Chisnell) v Richmond-upon-Thames Borough Council*,[95] where the local planning authority had refused two previous applications for an extension to a house on the basis that the extension could be used as a separate dwelling. The developer submitted a third application which was the same externally as the previous one, save that the proposed extension could not be used as a separate dwelling. Objectors complained, as they had on the two previous occasions, as to the effect on the amenity of their neighbouring properties. The local planning authority were of the view that, as the previous refusals had not been based on amenity issues, they could not rely on any ground of refusal other than use as a separate dwelling. Planning permission was

---

[92] *Tameside Metropolitan Borough Council v Secretary of State for the Environment* [1984] JPL 180; *Westminster City Council v Great Portland Estates* [1985] AC 661, sub nom *Great Portland Estates plc v Westminster City Council* [1984] 3 All ER 774.

[93] (1975) 73 LGR 211, 29 P & CR 390.

[94] [1989] JPL 90.

[95] [2005] EWHC 134 (Admin).

granted but the decision was subsequently quashed by Newman J. Although the position arrived at in previous decisions was a material consideration, the principle that consistency was required in decision making did not mean that the council was bound by previous decisions.

Merits of application

8.86 It is not a material consideration that planning permission has already been granted for another form of development; a landowner is entitled to make as many applications as he pleases, and the local planning authority must consider each application on its merits.[96]

8.87 The duty to consider each application on its merits is further illustrated by the case of *Stringer v Minister of Housing and Local Government*.[97] In this case there was an agreement between Cheshire County Council, the rural district council, and Manchester University that development in certain areas in the neighbourhood of the Jodrell Bank telescope was to be resisted; the district council, in pursuance of that agreement, refused permission for development of a site in one of those areas. It was held that the agreement was ultra vires the planning authority and that there had been no proper determination on the application for planning permission; there would, however, have been no objection to arrangements for consulting the University provided they did not fetter the freedom of the local planning authority to have regard to all material circumstances.

Fears of local residents

8.88 The impact of proposed development on the occupiers of neighbouring land can clearly be material. In *West Midland Probation Committee v Secretary of State for the Environment*,[98] planning permission was refused for the expansion of a bail hostel in a residential area. There was evidence of disturbing and intrusive incidents such as robberies and car thefts caused by the existing bailees; it was accepted that the local residents had a genuine and justified fear of crime.

8.89 It was argued for the Probation Committee that apprehension and fear were not material considerations, since they did not relate to the character of the use of the land. Upholding the refusal, the Court of Appeal held that justified public concern about emanations from land as a result of proposed development may be a material consideration. To put it another way, the behaviour of the bailees did relate to the character of the use of the land, it did not merely arise because of the identity of the particular occupier or particular residents.

---

96 *Pilkington v Secretary of State for the Environment* [1974] I All ER 283, [1973] 1 WLR 1527.
97 [1971] 1 All ER 65, [1970] 1 WLR 1281.
98 [1998] JPL 388. And see *R v Broadlands District Council, ex p Dove* [1998] JPL B84; *Wood-Robinson v Secretary of State for the Environment* [1998] JPL 976.

8.90 The *West Midland Probation Committee* case was distinguished by the Court of Appeal on the facts in *Smith v First Secretary of State*.[99] Here, in refusing planning permission for a gypsy caravan park, an inspector took into account evidence of crime and fears that criminality would continue. The trial judge upheld the reasoning of the inspector and his decision. On appeal to the Court of Appeal, it was considered that the judge had erred—fear of crime could only be a material consideration where the apprehension was based on an extrapolation from past events rather than, in this case, an assumption not supported by the evidence. In fact, the number of reported incidents of crime had diminished. Criminal incidents had to be attributable not merely to the individuals concerned but also to the use of the land. Buxton LJ observed that 'a caravan site is not like a polluting factory or a bail hostel, likely of its very nature to produce difficulties for its neighbours.'

8.91 A few years before the decision in the *West Midlands* case, Glidewell LJ[100] had said in a case: 'Public concern is, of course . . . a material consideration . . . but if, in the end that public concern is not justified, it cannot be conclusive. If it were, no industrial—indeed very little development of any kind—would be permitted.'

8.92 Nevertheless, in *Newport County Borough Council v Secretary of State for Wales*,[101] the majority of the court appear to have taken a slightly different line in holding that public concern, even if not objectively justified, may be a material consideration. The case involved an order for costs against the council[102] on the basis that they had behaved unreasonably in refusing planning permission for a clinical waste plant. The basis of the refusal was the local planning authority's view that the proposed development was perceived by the local community to be contrary to the public interest. This view was contradicted by the opinions of experts. Staughton LJ, although he dissented on the issue of whether the inspector had erred in law, nevertheless considered that fears which are not justified could rank as part of the human factor referred to by Lord Scarman in *Great Portland Estates v City of Westminster*.[103] Of course, public opposition per se would not, without more, amount to a material consideration.

Planning and pollution control

8.93 A question that can arise is the extent to which matters regulated by other legislation can be a material consideration under the Planning Acts. The issue has arisen in relation to the controls over pollution in the Environmental Protection

99 [2005] EWCA Civ 859.

100 *Gateshead Metropolitan Borough Council v Secretary of State for the Environment* [1994] JPL 255, 263.

101 [1998] JPL 377. See also *R v Tandridge District Council, ex p Mohamed Al Fayed* [1999] JPL 825.

102 Under TCPA 1990, s. 320(2); and see Circular 5/87.

103 [1985] AC 661.

Act 1990: the case in question being the decision of the Court of Appeal in *Gateshead Metropolitan Borough Council v Secretary of State for the Environment.*[104]

8.94 The developers wished to construct and operate an incinerator for the disposal of clinical waste. Planning permission was required for the construction and use of the plant, whereas authorization under Part I of the Environmental Protection Act was required for the incineration process. Such authorization was the responsibility of HM Inspectorate of Pollution [now the Environment Agency]. An outline planning application was refused on several grounds; the local planning authority considered that the overall effects on the environment, especially health risk, had not been fully investigated. The developer's appeal to the Secretary of State against this decision was allowed, contrary to the inspector's recommendations. The Secretary of State considered that the controls under the Environmental Protection Act were adequate to deal with the concerns of the inspector. The local authority applied to the High Court to challenge the decision of the Secretary of State. Jeremy Sullivan QC (sitting as deputy judge) dismissed the application and the local authority appealed to the Court of Appeal. Held: whereas the potential for environmental pollution from the proposed plant, including health risks, was a material consideration, so was the existence of controls under the Environmental Protection Act. The Secretary of State had therefore not erred in law in concluding that the pollution controls under that Act meant that there would be no unacceptable discharges on adjacent land.

8.95 Glidewell LJ (with whom Hoffmann and Hobhouse LJJ agreed) recognized that the decision to be made on appeal to the Secretary of State lay in the area in which the regimes of control under the Planning Act and the Environmental Protection Act overlapped. However '[i]f it had become clear at the inquiry that some of the discharges were bound to be unacceptable so that a refusal by HMIP to grant an authorization would be the only proper course, the Secretary of State following his own express policy should have refused planning permission. But that was not the situation (here)'. Conversely, the grant of planning permission should not inhibit HMIP from refusing authorization under the Environmental Protection Act if they decided in their discretion that that was the proper course.

8.96 In the case of *R v Bolton Metropolitan Council, ex p Kirkman,*[105] the relationship between planning and pollution control was considered again. Here the local planning authority had granted planning permission for a waste recovery system. It was contended that, in granting permission, the local planning authority had failed to address properly questions concerning potentially hazardous air emissions. It was also argued that they had misunderstood or failed to apply a number of other

104 [1994] JPL 255.
105 [1998] JPL 787.

policies and duties imposed on them by the waste legislation, including whether the proposals represented the 'Best Practicable Environmental Option' (BPEO).

8.97 The Court of Appeal agreed with a decision of Carnwath J to dismiss an application for leave to bring judicial review proceedings. The impact of air emissions was capable of being a material consideration but the planning authority is entitled to take account of the existence of dedicated controls under the Environmental Protection Act—there had been no breach of duty in this regard by the local planning authority. Similarly, BPEO was also capable of being a planning consideration but the court was satisfied that the authority had had regard to this concept—it did not matter that they did not have the detailed figures before them.

Alternative proposals

8.98 The relevance of alternative proposals for a site the subject of planning permission arose in the case of *Mount Cook Land Ltd v Westminster City Council.*[106] The appellant company was the freehold owner of a building in a conservation area for which planning permission had been granted to a tenant under a 99-year lease. The development in question involved relatively minor external alterations. Prior to consideration of the tenant's planning application, the appellant had submitted detailed design options to the council which it claimed would further enhance the conservation area. The claimant's proposals were not the subject of a planning application and the planning committee of the council was advised that they were irrelevant; they were thus disregarded in arriving at the decision. The Court of Appeal declined to quash this decision and held that the appellant's alternative proposals were not material considerations. Auld LJ said: 'In my view, where application proposals, if permitted and given effect to, would amount to a preservation or enhancement in planning terms, only in exceptional circumstances would it be relevant for a decision maker to consider alternative proposals, not themselves the subject of a planning application . . . Even in an exceptional case, for such alternative proposals to be a candidate for consideration as a material consideration, there must at least be a likelihood or real possibility of them eventuating in the foreseeable future if the application were to be refused.'

Alternative sites

8.99 Can the existence of alternative and possibly more suitable sites for a proposed development be a material consideration? It seems that the answer to this question is (tentatively) in the affirmative, but this does not mean that the local planning authority is under any duty to search for suitable alternative sites.[107] The position was summarized by Simon Brown J in *Trusthouse Forte Hotels Ltd v Secretary of*

---

[106] [2003] EWCA Civ 1346.

[107] *Rhodes v Minister of Housing and Local Government* [1963] 1 WLR 208.

State for the Environment,[108] where it was made clear that land can be developed in any way that is acceptable in planning terms and that the fact that there exists other land that would be more suitable will not justify a refusal of permission. However, where there are objections on clear planning grounds to the development of the application site, it may be appropriate to consider whether there is a more appropriate site elsewhere. 'This [according to Simon Brown J] is particularly so when the development is bound to have significant adverse effects and where the major argument advanced in support of the application is that the need for the development outweighs the planning disadvantages inherent in it.' The judge considered that examples of such developments include airports, coalmines, nuclear power stations, and gypsy encampments. In contrast are cases where planning permission is sought for developments such as dwellinghouses, offices, and superstores. Nevertheless, the court recognized that there may be cases where it would be unnecessary to go into questions of comparability, even though the proposed development contained the characteristics referred to in the quotation above. This would clearly be the case where the environmental impact was relatively slight and the planning objections not particularly strong.

8.100 Inevitably, there will be some cases where a comparison between sites is not only necessary but desirable. Thus in *R (on the application of Chelmsford Car and Commercial Ltd) v Chelmsford Borough Council*[109] there were two separate planning applications submitted by two different developers, each to build 12 units of affordable housing on opposite sides of a road. There was a need in the locality for no more than 12 such dwellings. When planning permission was granted to one of the developers, the other challenged the decision on the ground that the local planning authority should have carried out an assessment of the comparative merits of the two sites. Sullivan J agreed—'common sense' suggested that a comparison between the two sites would be a material consideration. As the local planning authority had not carried out such an exercise the permission was quashed. The point raised in the *Mount Cook* case (discussed above in the previous section), that the alternative site is not the subject of a planning application, is inapplicable here.

The local planning authority's decision

8.101 The decision of the local planning authority may take one of three forms. They may grant permission unconditionally or they may grant permission subject to such conditions as they think fit or they may refuse permission.[110] Although the

108 [1986] JPL 834.
109 [2005] EWHC 1705 (Admin).
110 TCPA 1990, s. 70(1).

TCPA 1990 permits the authority to attach such conditions 'as they think fit', such conditions must serve some useful purpose having regard to the objects of planning legislation[111] and they must not offend against the general law, eg a condition requiring a payment of money to the planning authority would be invalid.[112] Within these limits, however, the local planning authority have a very wide discretion[113] and in particular they may attach conditions;[114]

(a) regulating the development or use of any land under the control of the applicant[115] (whether or not it is the land in respect of which the application has been made) provided the condition is reasonably related to the permitted development.
(b) requiring the permitted works to be removed or the permitted use to be discontinued at the expiry of a specified period, that is, in effect a permission granted for a limited period only.

8.102 TCPA 1990, ss. 91 to 93 as originally enacted provided that each planning permission shall be subject to a deemed condition that development shall be commenced within five years. The local planning authority could fix a period either shorter or longer than five years. However, s. 51 of PCPA 2004 amends TCPA 1990, s. 91, by providing that planning permission will normally be subject to a condition that the development must be begun within three years, unless a longer or shorter period is agreed. TCPA 1990, s. 92, is also amended in that where outline permission has been granted, application for approval of reserved matters must be made within three years and the development must be begun within two years of final approval of reserved matters. The overall time limit of five years disappears. These provisions will be considered in more detail in chapter 10.[116]

8.103 If the local planning authority refuse permission or impose conditions, they must state clearly and precisely their full reasons in the notice of their decision.[117] The duty to give full reasons was imposed as a statutory obligation for the first time in a previous General Development Order, but it had in fact been required by the courts at a much earlier stage in the development of planning law that the

[111] *Pyx Granite Co Ltd v Ministry of Housing and Local Government* [1960] AC 260, [1959] 3 All ER 1; *Fawcett Properties Ltd v Buckingham County Council* [1961] AC 636, [1960] 3 All ER 503; *Newbury District Council v Secretary of State for the Environment* [1981] AC 578, [1980] 1 All ER 731.

[112] *A-G v Wilts United Dairies* (1922) 91 LJKB 897.

[113] For further discussion on the local planning authority's powers see ch 10 below.

[114] TCPA 1990, s. 72(1).

[115] The land need not be in the ownership of the applicant; it suffices that he has the necessary right over the land to comply with the proposed conditions: *George Wimpey & Co Ltd v New Forest District Council and Secretary of State for the Environment* [1979] JPL 314.

[116] See para 10.113. PCPA 2004, s. 51 was brought into force by SI 1005 No 2081 as from 24 August 2005.

[117] GDPO, art 22.

authority should give all their reasons and not merely some of them.[118] But a developer is not entitled to claim that a condition is void merely because the local planning authority omitted to state any reason.[119]

8.104 Where the local planning authority give notice that planning permission is granted, is granted subject to conditions, or is refused, they must include a summary of their reasons and of the policies and proposals in the development plan which are relevant to their decision. In the case of the imposition of conditions, they must state their full reasons for each condition imposed.[120]

8.105 It should be noted here that as from 30 October 1994, the Nature Conservation Regulations may restrict the grant of planning permission for development likely to have a significant effect on a 'European site'. The regulations, which implement European legislation on habitat protection, are considered in chapter 18.

Time for giving decision

8.106 Article 20 of General Development Procedure Order provides that the local planning authority shall notify the applicant of their decision within eight weeks, unless the applicant agrees in writing to an extension of time. In the case of major development, the period has been extended to 13 weeks. The definition of 'major development' for this purpose is given above in relation to publicity for planning applications.[121]

8.107 If the authority do not give their decision within the proper time, the applicant can, appeal to the Secretary of State as if permission had been refused.[122] In certain circumstances, the statutory period within which the local planning authority must make their decision can be extended—this provision is contained in a new s. 78A of TCPA 1990, inserted by s. 50 of PCPA 2004. It is considered below.[123] Appeals are dealt with later in this chapter and considered more fully in chapter 19.

8.108 What happens if the local planning authority issue a decision out of time? The point first came up for consideration in *Edwick v Sunbury-on-Thames UDC*.[124]

8.109 The council served an enforcement notice on E requiring him to discontinue the unauthorized use of land for the display and sale of second-hand cars. Before the

---

118 *Hamilton v West Sussex County Council* [1958] 2 QB 286, [1958] 2 All ER 174.

119 *Brayhead (Ascot) Ltd v Berkshire County Council* [1964] 2 QB 303, [1964] 1 All ER 149.

120 GPDO, art 22, as substituted by art 5 of T & CP (General Development Procedure) (England) Order 2003, SI 2003 No 2047, as from 5 December 2003.

121 See para 8.07. This reform was introduced by SI 2006 No 1062 which came into force on 10 May 2006. Note that in the case of EIA development, the period is increased to 16 weeks see para 9.25.

122 TCPA 1990, s. 78(2).

123 See para 8.129.

124 [1962] 1 QB 229, [1961] 3 All ER 10.

notice took effect, E applied for planning permission and (under the law as it then was) this had the effect of suspending the operation of the enforcement notice pending a decision on the application. More than two years later, the council notified E that permission was refused. If this decision were valid, the enforcement notice would have come into effect, but Salmon J held that the statutory direction as to the time within which the local authority should give their decision was mandatory and accordingly the notice of decision was invalid.

8.110 The law relating to enforcement notices has now been changed, and the circumstances of the *Edwick* case cannot occur again, but Salmon J's reasoning would apply to any decision of a local authority on an application for planning permission. This is not likely to be of any practical consequence where the decision is in the form of a refusal, but might have serious consequences where the decision purports to grant permission.

8.111 However, in *James v Minister of Housing and Local Government*,[125] the Court of Appeal disapproved of the decision in *Edwick's* case and held that the prescribed time limit was not mandatory but directory. Lord Denning MR said that a grant or refusal of permission out of time is 'not void, but at most voidable'; by that his Lordship meant that a decision out of time would not be automatically void, but that in certain circumstances it might be treated as void. In the House of Lords,[126] the decision of the Court of Appeal was in part overruled, but three of their Lordships disapproved of *Edwick* and the others did not discuss the point; no reference was made to the suggestion that a grant or refusal of permission out of time might be treated as voidable.[127]

8.112 It is clear therefore that a grant or refusal of permission out of time is not void, but the question whether it is voidable has not yet been finally resolved. Even if such a decision is voidable, the opportunities for voiding it will be limited; for, as Lord Denning explained, it will be too late to void a grant of permission once it has been accepted and acted upon, or if an appeal is lodged against any conditions attached to the permission.[128] The question might, however, arise in disputes between vendor and purchaser or the assessment of compensation for compulsory purchase. It seems that the option to void a planning permission is for the court, not the parties;[129] in other words, the planning permission remains in force until declared void by the court.

125 [1965] 3 All ER 602.

126 Sub nom *James v Secretary of State for Wales* [1968] AC 409, [1966] 3 All ER 964.

127 In *London Ballast Co v Buckinghamshire County Council* (1966) 18 P & CR 446, Megaw J said that a grant or refusal of permission out of time might be voidable: all the circumstances must be looked at.

128 [1965] 3 All ER 602 at 606.

129 *Co-operative Retail Services Ltd v Taff-Ely Borough Council* (1979) 39 P & CR 223 at 246, per Ormrod LJ.

8.113 It is submitted, however, (i) that there is no logical reason for treating a planning permission as voidable merely because the local planning authority have not complied with the provisions of what is now article 20 as to the time within which they should give notice of their decision; (ii) that the purpose of article 20 is to fix a period after which, in the absence of a decision, the applicant can appeal to the Secretary of State.

When is planning permission granted?

8.114 A question of some practical importance is whether planning permission is effectively granted when the local planning authority make their decision by way of a resolution of the council or a duly authorized committee.[130] At one time it was generally assumed that planning permission was granted at that date with the result that the decision could not thereafter be changed except by making a formal order for the revocation or modification of the planning permission, which might impose upon the authority a liability for substantial compensation.[131]

8.115 However, in *R v Yeovil Borough Council, ex p Trustees of Elim Pentecostal Church*,[132] the Divisional Court took a different view. The council had resolved to authorize the town clerk to grant planning permission for a youth hostel when evidence of an agreement about car parking facilities had been received. Before the town clerk had received satisfactory evidence, the council changed their mind and resolved to refuse permission. The court held that, on the facts, there was no question of planning permission having been granted at any time before the town clerk had expressed a view with regard to the adequacy of the evidence submitted to him. This would have been sufficient to dispose of the case, but the court also decided that there could in law be no planning permission until written notice of the council's decision had been given to the applicant. The court appear to have relied on the decision of the Court of Appeal in *Slough Estates Ltd v Slough Borough Council (No 2)*[133] but that was a decision on the different wording of the Town and Country Planning Act 1932.

8.116 Subsequently, in *Co-operative Retail Services Ltd v Taff-Ely Borough Council*,[134] the Court of Appeal adopted the same view that the planning permission does not come into existence until formal notification is given to the applicant. Here again the point was not essential to the decision in the case: the point was not expressly dealt with by the House of Lords in their decision on the case.[135]

---

130 (1979) 39 P & CR 223.
131 See para 11.01.
132 (1971) 23 P & CR 39.
133 [1969] 2 Ch 305, [1969] 2 All ER 988.
134 (1979) 39 P & CR 223.
135 Sub nom *A-G (ex rel Co-operative Retail Services Ltd) v Taff-Ely Borough Council* (1981) 42 P & CR 1.

Planning registers

8.117 Every local planning authority must maintain a register, in such a manner and containing such information as is prescribed by development order, with respect to planning applications submitted to the authority. The register must be kept open for public inspection at all reasonable hours.[136]

8.118 GDPO 1995[137] prescribes that the register must be kept in two parts. Part I must contain a copy of every planning application and application for approval of reserved matters submitted to the authority and not finally disposed of, with the relevant plans and drawings. Part II must contain in respect of every planning application:

(a) a copy (which may be photographic) of the application and of the submitted plans and drawings;
(b) particulars of any direction given under TCPA 1990 or the GDPO 1995 in respect of the application;
(c) the decision, if any, of the local planning authority in respect of the application, including details of any conditions imposed, the date of the decision, and the name of the local planning authority;
(d) the reference number, the date, and effect of any decision of the Secretary of State in respect of the application, whether on appeal or call in under s. 77 of TCPA 1990;
(e) the date of any subsequent approval (whether approval of reserved matters or any other approval required) given in relation to the application.

8.119 The registers also contain certain other information, eg as to SPZ schemes.

8.120 PCPA 2004 substitutes a new s. 69 of TCPA 1990[138] which expressly requires the local planning authority to maintain a register containing such information as may be prescribed by development order as to (i) applications for planning permission; (ii) LDOs;[139] and (iii) SPZ schemes.[140]

Appeals to the Secretary of State

8.121 If the applicant is aggrieved by the decision of the local planning authority, or by their failure to give a decision within the proper time, he may appeal to the

136 TCPA 1990, s. 69(1), (2) and (5).
137 Art 25.
138 PCPA 2004, s. 118, Sch 6, para 3. The provision was brought into force as from 6 August 2004 by SI 2004 No 2097.
139 See para 7.66.
140 See para 7.76.

Secretary of State.[141] No one else has the right to appeal. Unless the Secretary of State agrees to an extension of time, the applicant should give notice of appeal within six calendar months of receiving the local planning authority's decision or (where the appeal is against their failure to give a decision) within six months of the date by which they should have done so.[142] The appellant must notify the parties he is required to notify by virtue of TCPA 1990, s. 54 and articles 6 and 7 of the General Development Procedure Order.[143] Originally, it was the case that, unless the Secretary of State agreed to an extension of time, the applicant should give notice of appeal within six months of receiving the local planning authority's decision or (where the appeal was against their failure to give a decision) within six months of the date they should have done so. However, the time limit for lodging appeals was reduced in December 2003 to three months. The change was made in order to give greater certainty about whether an appeal was to be made. But the amendment soon clogged up the appeals system and, as from 14 January 2005, the six-month time limit was reinstated.[144]

8.122 The Secretary of State must offer the appellant and the local planning authority the opportunity to present their cases to an inspector at an oral hearing; this may take the form of a public local inquiry, although the Secretary of State may, if the issues are sufficiently straightforward, offer the parties the alternative of an informal hearing. Indeed in the year 2000, the Secretary of State announced that, in future, hearings are to be preferred rather than inquiries[145] and, for the first time, made statutory rules governing their procedure.[146] However, if the parties agree, the appeal can be dealt with by written representations; this method is also encouraged and, nowadays, most appeals are dealt with in this way.[147]

8.123 Where there is to be an inquiry, the local planning authority and the appellant must provide statements of their cases before the hearing.[148]

8.124 Until 1968 the inspector never gave a decision, but reported to the Minister whose decision was made known in due course. However, in 1968 Parliament empowered the Minister to make regulations authorizing the inspector to give a decision in specified classes of appeals. The first regulation[149] authorized the inspector to

---

[141] TCPA 1990, s. 78(1), (2).

[142] GDPO, art 23.

[143] TCPA 1990, s. 79(4). This applies the same procedure as in applications at first instance to the local planning authority. See para 8.13.

[144] TCP (General Development Procedure) (Amendment) (England) Order 2004, art 2.

[145] Circular 5/00. See generally ch 19 below.

[146] T & CP (Hearings Procedure) (England) Rules 2000, SI 2000 No 1626. Hearings were previously conducted according to a code of practice in Circular 2/88.

[147] It should be noted that the Secretary of State retains and sometimes exercises the right to hold a public inquiry even though the parties have indicated a preference for written representations.

[148] See para 19.17.

[149] Town and Country Planning (Determination of Appeals by Appointed Persons) (Prescribed Classes) Regulations 1968, SI 1968 No 1972.

give a decision in a limited number of cases, but the list was later extended[150] so that by 1981 inspectors were deciding about 80 per cent of all appeals. The 1981 regulations[151] delegated to the inspector the power to decide all appeals against refusal of permission or conditions attached to permissions, with the exception of some appeals by statutory undertakers.

8.125 The current regulations[152] extend the powers of inspectors to determine to include appeals concerned with advertisement consents,[153] appeals concerned with certificates of lawfulness,[154] and certain listed building appeals.[155] The Secretary of State has, however, power to reserve the decision to himself in any specific instance[156] and this will be done in appeals of exceptional importance or unusual difficulty.

8.126 The inspector is empowered to deal with the appeal as if it had to come to him in the first instance.[157] Among other things, this means that in the case of an appeal against a condition attached to a planning permission the inspector can attach other conditions or even refuse permission altogether.

8.127 The inspector's decision is final,[158] except for the possibility of challenge under TCPA 1990, s. 288. Section 288 enables an application to be made to the High Court on the ground either that the decision was outside the powers conferred by the Planning Acts or that some procedural requirement of these Acts had not been complied with. It should be possible therefore to question the decision on the ground that he had taken into account considerations not relevant to planning, that he had failed to take into account relevant considerations, or that he had imposed or upheld an improper condition or that there was some breach of the rules of natural justice in the handling of the appeal. Planning appeals and the scope of section 288 are more fully dealt with in chapters 18 and 19 respectively.

Dual jurisdiction

8.128 PCPA 2004, s. 50(1) inserts a new s. 78A into TCPA 1990. We have seen that if the local planning authority do not give their decision on a planning application within the statutory eight-week period, the applicant is entitled to appeal to the

[150] Town and Country Planning (Determination of Appeals by Appointed Persons) (Prescribed Classes) Regulations 1972, SI 1972 No 1652.
[151] Town and Country Planning (Determination of Appeals by Appointed Persons) (Prescribed Classes) Regulations 1981, SI 1981 No 804 as amended by SI 1989 No 1087 and SI 1995 No 2259.
[152] Town and Country Planning (Determination of Appeals by Appointed Persons) (Prescribed Classes) Regulations 1997, SI 1997 No 420, as amended.
[153] See para 15.69.
[154] See para 12.157.
[155] See para 16.60.
[156] 1990 Act, Sch 6, para 3.
[157] TCPA 1990, s. 79(1).
[158] TCPA 1990, s. 79(5).

Secretary of State as if permission has been refused.[159] Rather than lodging an appeal in these circumstances, some applicants have submitted two identical or very similar applications, and, when the eight-week time limit expires without a decision having been made, lodged an appeal on one application while continuing to negotiate with the authority on the other. The practice is known as 'twin-tracking'. PCPA 2004, s. 43, introduces a new s. 70B into TCPA 1990 allowing local planning authorities to refuse to determine a twin-tracked application, which will be discussed later in this chapter.[160]

8.129 The new provisions in s. 78A are designed to remove the need for the practice of twin-tracking by giving the local planning authority and Secretary of State dual jurisdiction over cases where the authority have not determined the application within the time limit for an additional period where the case has gone to appeal. This will mean that the local planning authority have longer to make a decision—the applicant may receive a quicker decision than if the case goes to appeal; and the planning inspectorate have the opportunity to begin processing an appeal. The 'additional period' is to be prescribed by development order.[161]

8.130 Thus, where an applicant for planning permission appeals against the local planning authority's failure to determine, the additional period would commence. If within this period, the authority give notice refusing permission, that appeal becomes an appeal against this refusal, rather than the deemed refusal. In such a case, the Secretary of State must give the appellant the opportunity to revise the grounds and mode of appeal.[162] Alternatively, if the local planning authority decide to give notice granting a conditional planning permission, the appeal becomes an appeal against the imposition of conditions, should the applicant wish to continue with the appeal. If the applicant does continue with the appeal, he will have the same choices as referred to above in the case of a refusal.[163]

Major infrastructure projects

8.131 Planning applications for major infrastructure projects, for example the redevelopment of airports, have in the past often involved very lengthy inquiries.[164] There is a wide range of issues to be considered and there are likely to be many objectors. One means of reducing the time spent on the inquiry would be to examine a number of issues simultaneously rather than sequentially.

---

[159] See para 8.121.
[160] See para 8.140.
[161] TCPA 1990, s. 78A(6) as inserted by PCPA 2004, s. 50(1). The provisions were brought into force in England as from 24 August 2005 by SI 2005 No 2081.
[162] TCPA 1990, s. 78A(3)(a)–(c).
[163] Ibid, s. 78A(4)(a)–(c).
[164] The inquiry into the proposals for Heathrow's terminal 5 is a recent example.

8.132 Accordingly, s. 44 of PCPA 2004 inserts new ss. 76A and 76B into TCPA 1990. Under these provisions, the Secretary of State may call in a planning application if he thinks that the development to which the application relates is of national or regional importance.[165] He may also direct that any other application under the planning Acts which he thinks is connected to the application must also be referred to him.[166] He must appoint a 'lead inspector'.[167] The applicant is required to prepare an 'economic impact report' which must be submitted to the Secretary of State.[168] The content is to be prescribed by development order but it is likely to require the applicant's estimates of the overall economic impact of the project at local, regional, and national level.

8.133 The Secretary of State may direct the lead inspector to consider such matters relating to the application as are prescribed and to make recommendations on those matters.[169] After considering the representations of the lead inspector, the Secretary of State may appoint such number of additional inspectors as he thinks appropriate. This enables the simultaneous examination of issues to which reference was made above. The additional inspectors must consider such matters relating to the application as the lead inspector decides[170] and must comply with any directions as to procedure as the lead inspector gives and report to him on the matters he is appointed to consider.[171]

Power to decline to determine subsequent and twin-tracked applications

8.134 It is not uncommon for developers, faced with an initial refusal of planning permission, to submit repeat applications for the same development in the hope of wearing down the resistance of both the local planning authority and the local community. Such tactics have often proved successful and planning permission has been ultimately granted.

8.135 There is also the practice of 'twin-tracking' to which reference was made earlier in this chapter.[172] It may be recalled that here, two identical (or nearly identical) planning applications, A and B, are submitted to the local planning authority. The developer seeks determination of A while lodging an appeal against the

165 TCPA 1990, s. 76A(1) and (2).
166 Ibid, s. 76A(3).
167 Ibid, s. 76A(4); s. 76B(1).
168 Ibid, s. 76A(5).
169 Ibid, s. 76B(2).
170 Ibid, s. 76B(3).
171 Ibid, s. 76B(4).
172 See para 8.128.

non-determination of B after eight or 13 weeks—the statutory time limits. He will only proceed expeditiously with the appeal on B if planning permission is ultimately refused for A. If permission is granted for A, his appeal on B may be withdrawn. Such tactics place an unnecessary burden on local planning authorities and the planning inspectorate.

8.136 In an attempt to deal with the first of the above-mentioned problems, s. 17 of PCA 1991 originally introduced s. 70A into the TCPA 1990, providing for the local planning authority to decline to determine a subsequent application in certain circumstances. However, under s. 43 of PCPA 2004, s. 70A has been redesigned and a new s. 70B has been introduced, the latter a measure intended to address twin-tracking. The government has indicated that it will not bring s. 70B into force until local authorities improve their performance in the time taken to handle planning applications.

Subsequent applications

8.137 TCPA 1990, s. 70A now provides that the local planning authority may decline to determine a planning application[173] if (a) in the period of two years ending with the date on which the application for planning permission has been received (i) the local planning authority have refused more than one similar application and there has been no appeal to the Secretary of State against the refusal; or (ii) the Secretary of State has dismissed an appeal against the refusal of a similar application or failure to determine; or (iii) the Secretary of State has refused a similar application which has been referred to him;[174] and (b) the authority think there has been no significant change in the development, so far as material, and any other material considerations since either the refusal of a similar application or the dismissal of an appeal by the Secretary of State. By making the provision apply (at (i) above) where 'more than one' such application has been refused, applicants will be able to address reasons for the refusal of the first application in their second application.

8.138 An application for planning permission is 'similar' to another application if, and only if, the authority think that the development and the land to which the applications relate are the same or substantially the same.[175]

8.139 Schedule 7 of PA 2008 introduces amendments to the effect that s. 70A will also apply where an appeal to the Secretary of State has been lodged but withdrawn

[173] Or an application for design, etc approval in pursuance of s. 60(2) TCPA 1990 under the GPDO: s. 70A(5)(b).

[174] Under s. 76A (major infrastructure projects) or s. 77 (called in applications); see paras 8.132 and 8.36.

[175] TCPA 1990, s. 70A(8). The provision was brought into force as from 24 August 2005 by SI 2005 No 2081.

before being determined; and where there has been an enforcement appeal and the earlier application is a deemed application arising from the appeal.[176]

Twin-tracked applications

8.140 The reforms in PCPA 2004 regarding twin-tracking inhibit rather than forbid the practice. Under s. 70B the local planning authority are entitled, if they wish, to decline to determine a planning application if (i) a similar application is under consideration by the local planning authority and the determination period for that application has not expired; or (ii) a similar application is under consideration by the Secretary of State because it has been referred to him[177] or is on an appeal and the Secretary of State has not issued his decision; or (iii) that a similar application has been granted by the local planning authority, has been refused by them, or has not been determined by them within the determination period, and the time within which an appeal could be made to the Secretary of State has not expired.

8.141 Schedule 7 of PA 2008 amends s. 70B so that its provisions also apply to applications received by the local planning authority on the same day; and also that the section applies to deemed planning applications arising out of enforcement appeals.

8.142 As with s. 70A, a planning application under s. 70B is 'similar' to another if, and only if, the local planning authority think that the development and the land to which the applications relate are the same or substantially the same.[178]

8.143 The provisions in s. 70B should be read together with s. 78A of TCPA 1990 which provides for a period of dual jurisdiction.[179] As already mentioned, PCPA 2004, s. 43 has been brought into force only to the extent to which it relates to the power to decline subsequent applications but not to the extent to which it relates to twin-tracked applications.

Part 2: development consent for nationally significant infrastructure projects under the Planning Act 2008

Introduction

8.144 The Planning Act 2008 introduces a new development consent system for Nationally Significant Infrastructure Projects (NSIPs). The types of project

176 See para 12.88.

177 Under s. 67A (major infrastructure projects) or s. 77 (called in applications); see paras 8.132 and 8.36.

178 TCPA 1990, s. 70B(5).

179 See para 8.128.

concerned are set out in the Act and the list covers developments in the fields of energy, transport, water, waste water, and waste projects. The specific projects are defined in some detail in Part 3 of the Act and include, as one might expect, major infrastructure projects such as power stations, major gas facilities, highways, railways and rail freight interchanges, harbours, hazardous waste facilities, and major airport development. It is for precisely these types of project, especially nuclear power stations and airport terminals, that the planning process has in the past proved to be cumbersome and prone to delay, and the inquiry process slow, often taking several years to come to a decision. As Baroness Andrews put it when introducing the second reading of the Planning Bill in the House of Lords:[180]

> '[W]e have struggled for years with a system more akin to Jarndyce and Jarndyce than one fit for a modern economy. The system puts the difficult questions off until the last stage; it forces inquiries to spend enormous amounts of time debating what government policy is, and whether there is a need for infrastructure. The result is costly and there is uncertainty for communities as well as for developers.'

8.145 The Government's solution to this indisputable problem is radical. In order to speed up the process, the Act sets up the Infrastructure Planning Commission (which will be referred to variously as 'the IPC' or 'the Commission') as the body which determines applications for consent to carry out NSIP development. The members of the Commission will be appointed by the Government and naturally there has been criticism that the Commission is an 'unelected quango' lacking democratic accountability. Nevertheless, it is the Government's view that the provisions in the Act regarding consultation and publicity, at both the policy-making stage and in the handling of individual applications for consent, will enable the public and interested parties to be involved in decisions about key infrastructure. The procedure for examining applications for consent by the IPC does not normally involve cross-examination and will in the first instance involve the taking of evidence by means of written representations but the IPC will have to hold an 'open floor' hearing where an interested party requests one. The procedure therefore bears little resemblance to the traditional local inquiry. Normally, the IPC must complete its examination of the application within six months and the Commission must decide the application within nine months.

8.146 The Act introduces the concept of the National Policy Statement (NPS)—this is a statement made by the Secretary of State setting out national policy in relation to one or more types of NSIP development. Before an NPS comes into effect, the Secretary of State must carry out appropriate consultation and publicity and a sustainability appraisal. The statement is also subject to parliamentary scrutiny. The NPS is subject to judicial review in the courts.

---

[180] Hansard, 15 July 2008, col. 1160.

8.147 Development consent will be required in order to carry out NSIP development. Delay in handling major infrastructure applications has in the past been caused by a multiplicity of overlapping consent regimes. The Heathrow Terminal 5 application—a byword for planning delay—required 37 applications under seven separate pieces of legislation. The 2008 Act therefore aims to unify the consent regimes. Thus NSIP development consent removes the need for planning permissions granted by the local planning authority; for listed building and conservation area consents;[181] for scheduled ancient monument consent; and for a range of specified consents or authorizations in relation to each NSIP. Thus, for example, a pipe-line construction authorization is no longer required for the construction of a cross-country pipe-line, as the development is now an NSIP. A development consent for an NSIP also removes the need for various orders under the Harbours Act 1964, the Transport and Works Act 1992, and the Gas Act 1965.

8.148 In arriving at a decision on an application for an NSIP development consent order, the IPC must, except in certain specified circumstances, have regard to the relevant NPS. The Secretary of State can intervene in an application if, inter alia, there has been a significant change in the circumstances since the NPS was first published, which was not anticipated at the time, and there is an urgent need for the application to be decided. Where this occurs, the IPC will complete the examination and report to the Secre-tary of State who must decide it within a specified period. Decisions made in relation to NSIP development consents are subject to judicial review by the courts.

8.149 We will now examine the legislation in greater detail.

Infrastructure Planning Commission (IPC)

8.150 The Planning Act 2008, s. 1, sets up the Infrastructure Planning Commission to consider applications for NSIP development consent. Part 1 and Schedule 1 of the Act deal with the constitution of the Commission and related matters. We will consider this first before going on to examine National Policy Statements (Part 2 of the Act); the categories of NSIP development consent (Part 3); the requirement for development consent (Part 4); applications for orders granting development consent (Part 5); determining applications for orders granting development consent (Part 6); and development consent orders (Part 7).

Infrastructure Planning Commission: constitution

8.151 The members of the Commission are appointed by the Secretary of State who is responsible for appointing a chair and two deputies. The chair, deputies and

---

181 See paras 16.37 and 16.119.

other Commissioners hold and vacate office in accordance with the terms of their appointments; Commissoners must be appointed for a fixed term of not less than five or more than eight years. The Secretary of State can remove a Commissioner from office, but only if satisfied that he is unable or unwilling to perform his duties; has been convicted of a criminal offence; or is otherwise unfit to perform the duties of the office.

The Council

8.152 There has to be a body of Commissioners known as the Commission's Council ('the Council'). The Council consists of the chair of the Commission, each deputy, and Commissioners appointed to be ordinary members of the Council. The functions of the Council include deciding applications for development consent referred under s. 83 PA 2008 (following the report of a single Commissioner) and responding to consultation.

Staffing

8.153 The Secretary of State is responsible for appointing a chief executive of the Commission, who must not be a Commissioner but a member of the Commission's staff. The Commission can appoint such other staff as it thinks appropriate, but Commissioners cannot be members of the staff. The Secretary of State's approval must be obtained as to the overall number of staff that the Commission appoints and their terms and conditions.

Delegation

8.154 The Commission has the power to delegate, to any one or more of the Commissioners, certain of its functions relating to applications for orders granting NSIP development consent. The Commission is also allowed to delegate any of its other functions to any one or more of the Commissioners; the chief executive and any other member of its staff. Further, the chief executive may authorize, generally or specifically, any other member of staff to do anything done by the chief executive.[182]

Annual report

8.155 The Commission must prepare a report relating to the performance of its functions in respect of each financial year. The report should give details of any orders granting NSIP development consent during the year which have authorized compulsory acquisition of land; and such other matters as the Secretary of State may direct. The Commission is required to arrange for the publication of the report and the

[182] There is an exception in the case of the chief executive's role in the certification of the Commission's annual accounts.

Secretary of State must lay a copy of the report before Parliament. If the Secretary of State so requests, the Commission must provide the Secretary of State with a report of any information concerning any aspect of the Commission's functions.

Other matters

8.156 The Commission and its staff are not, under the terms of the Act, to be regarded as the servants or agents of the Crown, or to enjoy any status, immunity or privilege deriving therefrom. The Commission is subject to investigation by the Parliamentary Commissioner in the event of maladministration, and Commissioners are disqualified from membership of the House of Commons or Northern Ireland Assembly

8.157 Under s. 2 of the 2008 Act, the Commission must issue a code of conduct expected of commissioners in the performance of the Commission's functions, requiring each Commissioner to disclose financial and other interests. The code of conduct must be published and it must be kept under review. Under s. 3 PA 2008, the Commission must establish a register of Commissioner's interests and arrange for the entries to be published. By virtue of s. 4 PA 2008, the Secretary of State may make regulations to allow the Commission to charge fees in connection with the performance of any of its functions.

National policy statements

8.158 As noted at the beginning of this chapter, the National Policy Statements (NPSs) are a crucial element in the NSIP development consent regime. They are a novel concept; they have some of the elements of a statutory development plan[183] and some of the elements of the Secretary of State's planning policy statements.[184] Under Part 2 of the Act, the Government is empowered to designate a statement of policy as an NPS, and the Secretary of State must, in exercising this function, do so with the objective of contributing to sustainable development. For the purposes of the Act, under s. 5 PA 2008, an NPS must be issued by the Secretary of State and set out 'national policy in relation to one or more specified descriptions of development'.

8.159 Before designating a statement as an NPS, the Secretary of State must carry out a sustainability appraisal, and must comply with requirements as to consultation and publicity in s. 7 PA 2008; and the 'parliamentary requirements' in s. 9 PA 2008, which are discussed below.[185] There are provisions in s.12 PA 2008 which

[183] See paras 4.01 and 5.01.

[184] See para 3.14.

[185] See paras 8.164 and 8.166.

provide that the Secretary of State may, in certain circumstances, designate a statement as an NPS even if issued before the 2008 Act came into force, or if it refers to another statement issued before that time. The Secretary of State may likewise treat a sustainability appraisal as meeting the requirements of the Act even if carried out before the date of commencement of the Act.

8.160 The types of policy which may be set out in an NPS are set out in s. 5 PA 2008 and may include the following:

(a) in relation to a specified description of development, the amount, type or size of development of that description which is appropriate nationally or for a specified area;
(b) the criteria to be applied in deciding whether a location is suitable for a specified description of development;
(c) the relative weight to be given to specified criteria;
(d) the identification of locations as suitable or unsuitable for a specified descriptions of development;
(e) the identification of statutory undertakers as appropriate persons to carry out a specified description of development; and
(f) the circumstances in which it is appropriate for a specific action to mitigate the impact of specific development.

8.161 An NPS must give reasons for the policies set out and the Secretary of State must arrange for the publication of the NPS, and lay the policy before Parliament. The reasons must include a statement as to how climate change policies have been taken into account.

Review

8.162 Under s. 6 PA 2008, the Secretary of State must review each NPS whenever the Secretary of State thinks it appropriate, and after completing the review must either amend it, withdraw it or leave it as it is. Before amending the statement, unless the amendment is non-material, a further sustainability appraisal must be carried out and the consultation/publicity and parliamentary requirements must again be complied with. A review may relate to all or part of an NPS. If the Secretary of State amends an NPS, the Secretary of State must first arrange for it to be published and the amended statement must be laid before Parliament.

8.163 There is provision in s. 11 of the 2008 Act for suspension of the NPS pending review—the Secretary of State may suspend the operation of all or part of the NPS until a review of the statement has been completed. This the Secretary of State may do if the Secretary of State decides that since the NPS was first issued or last reviewed, there has been a significant change in the circumstances which was not anticipated at the time.

Consultation and publicity requirements

8.164 The Secretary of State must carry out consultation and arrange for publicity as the Secretary of State thinks appropriate in relation to the proposed NPS or amendment of an NPS. The Secretary of State must consult such persons as may be prescribed by regulations, and if the proposal identifies suitable locations for a specified development, the Secretary of State must ensure there is appropriate publicity. In deciding what is appropriate in this regard the Secretary of State must consult relevant local authorities as specified in s. 8 of the 2008 Act.

8.165 The Secretary of State must have regard to the responses to consultation and publicity in deciding whether to proceed with the proposed NPS.

Parliamentary requirements

8.166 Under s. 9 of the 2008 Act, the Secretary of State must lay the proposed NPS or amendment before Parliament. If, during the period specified in advance by the Secretary of State, either House of Parliament makes a resolution, or a committee of either House makes recommendations concerning the proposal, the Secretary of State must have regard to the recommendation or proposal. The Secretary of State's response must be laid before Parliament.

Legal challenge

8.167 Section 13 of the 2008 Act provides that legal challenges in relation to NPSs can only be brought by way of a claim for judicial review and only within a period of six weeks. This procedure is essentially a hybrid, mixing elements of statutory review under TCPA 1990 (the six week period) with judicial review (the procedure).

Nationally significant infrastructure projects (NSIPs)

8.168 Section 14(1) of PA 2008 lists those categories of projects which are NSIPs under the Act requiring development consent granted by order of the IPC. The Secretary of State may amend the categories of NSIPs at any time; however, new types of project may only be added if they are works in the fields of: energy; transport; water; waste water; waste; and in the case of projects in the field of energy, within a Renewable Energy Zone. NSIPs are any of the following projects if situated in England.[186]

[186] There are variations for Wales and Scotland.

Energy

8.169 **Generating stations** The construction or extension of a generating station which when constructed or extended is expected to be onshore with a capacity of more than 50 megawatts; or which is offshore and has a capacity of more than 100 megawatts.

8.170 **Electric lines** The installation of an electric line above ground except a line with a nominal voltage expected to be less than 32 kilovolts; or a line which is within the premises of the person responsible for its installation. 'Premises' includes any land, building, or structure.

8.171 **Underground gas storage facilities** Operations creating underground gas storage facilities or starting to use such facilities where the working capacity is expected to be at least 43 million standard cubic metres, or the maximum flow rate is expected to be at least 4.5 million standard cubic metres. The carrying out of operations for the purpose of altering underground gas storage facilities is also included if the effect of the alteration is expected to be an increase in the working capacity or maximum flow rate subject to the same thresholds as above. 'Underground storage facilities' is defined as including facilities for the storage of gas underground in cavities or in porous strata.

8.172 **LNG facilities** The construction of liquid natural gas facilities if the storage capacity is expected to be at least 43 million standard cubic metres, or the maximum flow rate is expected to be at least 4.5 million standard cubic metres a day. The alteration of an LNG facility is also included if the effect of the alteration is expected to be an increase in storage capacity or maximum flow rate subject to the same thresholds as above. An 'LNG' facility is defined as a facility for the reception of liquid natural gas from outside England; the storage of LNG; and the regasification of LNG.

8.173 **Gas reception facilities** The construction of a gas reception facility if when constructed the maximum flow rate of the facility is expected to be at least 4.5 million standard metres a day; and the alteration of such a facility where the increase is subject to the same threshold. 'Gas reception facilities' is defined as facility for receiving natural gas from abroad; and the handling of natural gas, other than its storage.

8.174 **Gas transporter pipe-line** The construction of a pipe-line by a gas transporter meeting specified criteria and conveying gas to supply at least 50,000 customers.

8.175 **Other pipe-lines** The constructruction of a pipe-line other than by a gas transporter which is a cross-country pipe-line the construction of which would (but for PA 2008) require authorization under s. 1(1) of the Pipe-lines Act 1962; and which crosses between England and Wales or, in the case of an oil or gas pipe-line, between England and Scotland. The definition of a cross-country pipe-line in the Act of 1962 is a pipe-line over 10 miles long on land, including associated apparatus and works. The construction of a diversion to a pipe-line is treated as the construction of a separate pipe-line. However, if the pipe-line to be diverted is nationally significant, the proposed construction of the diversion is treated as the 'construction of a pipe-line', whatever the length of the diversion.

Transport

8.176 **Highways** Highway related development which is the (a) construction of a highway for which the Secretary of State will be the highway authority; (b) the improvement of a highway for which the Secretary of State is the highway authority and the improvement is likely to have a significant effect on the environment; or (c) the alteration of a highway where the alteration is to be carried out by or on behalf of the Secretary of State and the alteration is for a purpose connected with a highway for which the Secretary of State is, or will be, the highway authority.

8.177 **Airports** The construction of an airport capable of providing air passenger services for at least 10 million passengers a year; or air cargo transport services for at least 10,000 air transport movements of cargo aircraft per year. The alteration of an airport is also included if it leads to an increase in passengers or air transport services subject to the same thresholds as above. The same principles apply to an increase in the permitted use of an airport, such as where a condition is relaxed but there is no physical development. An 'alteration', in relation to an airport, includes the construction, extension, alteration of a runway, building or radio/ radar antenna or other apparatus.

8.178 **Harbour facilities** The construction of harbour facilities capable of handling, in the case of container ships, 500,000 TEU (twenty foot equivalent unit); in the case of facilities for ro-ro ships 250,000 units; and in the case of cargo ships of any other description, 5 million tonnes. The alteration of harbour facilities is also included if the effect of the alteration is to bring about an increase subject to the same thresholds as above. In the case of facilities for more than one of the types of ship mentioned, s. 25 of the 2008 Act contains fractions for calculating the thresholds.

8.179 **Railways** The construction or alteration of a railway which will, when constructed, be part of a network operated by an approved operator and the construction or alteration is not permitted development. 'Approved operator' is defined as a person who is authorized to be the operator of a network by licence granted under s. 8 of the Railways Act 1993; or a wholly-owned subsidiary of a company which is such a person; and in either case who is designated in an order made by the Secretary of State. In practice, this means Network Rail or its subsidiaries.

8.180 **Rail freight interchanges** The construction of a rail freight interchange on land of at least 60 hectares in area and capable of handling consignments of goods from more than one consignor to more than one consignee and at least four goods trains per day. The rail freight interchange must be part of the railway network and must include warehouses to which goods can be delivered from the railway network either directly or by another means of transport. Also included is the alteration of a rail freight interchange where the alteration is expected to increase by at least 60 hectares the area of land on which the interchange is situated.

Water

8.181 **Dams and reservoirs** The construction (or alteration) of a dam or reservoir where the works will be carried out by more than one water undertaker and the volume (or additional volume) of water to be held back or stored exceeds 10 million cubic metres.

8.182 **Transfer of water resources** Development relating to the transfer of water resources by one or more water undertakers where the volume of water to be transferred is expected to exceed 100 cubic metres per year. The development must be one which enables the transfer of water resources between river basins; between water undertakers' areas; or between a river basin and a water undertaker's area; and the development must not relate to the transfer of drinking water.

Waste water

8.183 **Waste water treatment plants** The construction of a waste water treatment plant having a capacity exceeding a population equivalent of 500,000. Also included is the alteration of such a plant where the effect of the alteration is expected to be an increase by the same amount. 'Waste water' is defined as including domestic, industrial, and urban waste water.

Waste

8.184 **Hazardous waste facilities** The construction of a hazardous waste facility where the main purpose of the facility is expected to be the final disposal or recovery of hazardous waste where the capacity is, in the case of landfill or deep storage, more than 100,000 tonnes per year; in any other case, more than 30,000 tonnes per year. Also included is the alteration of such a facility where the increase is subject to the same thresholds.

NSIP development consent

8.185 Under the provisions of s. 31 PA 2008, development consent is required for development which is or forms part of a nationally significant infrastructure project, as set out above in the previous section. In this context, 'development' has the same meaning as it does in TCPA 1990[187] but for the purposes of the PA 2008, certain

[187] PA 2008, s. 32. For the definition of development, see para 6.01.

matters constitute a material change of use (and therefore development). These are:

(a) the conversion of a generating station to use crude liquid petroleum, a petroleum product, or natural gas;
(b) starting to use a cavity or underground strata for the storage of gas; and
(c) an increase in the permitted use of an airport.

8.186 In addition, for the purposes of the Act, certain matters are taken to be development, to the extent that they would not be otherwise:

(a) works for the demolition of a listed building or its alteration or extension in a manner which would affect its character as a building of special architectural or historic interest;
(b) demolition of a building in a conservation area; and
(c) certain works or operations in connection with scheduled ancient monuments.

Unification of consent regimes

8.187 The provisions discussed in the previous section above operate in conjunction with PA 2008, s. 33, which provides that where a project requires NSIP development consent, it will no longer require consent under other established regimes. These include: planning permission under TCPA 1990; listed building consent under LBA 1990; conservation area consent under LBA 1990; a pipe-line construction authorization under the Pipe-lines Act 1962; a gas storage authorization under the Gas Act 1965; a consent for the construction of a generating station under the Electricity Act 1989; and a consent or notice under the Ancient Monuments and Archaeological Areas Act 1990.

8.188 With regard to highways, the Highways Act 1980 provides the Secretary of State with the ability to make or confirm various orders in connection with the construction, improvement, or alteration of a highway. PA 2008, s. 33(4) enacts that where the relevant works require NSIP development consent, the Secretary of State may not make or confirm such orders.

Directions in relation to projects of national importance

8.189 Where an application is made to the relevant authority for one of the consents or authorizations mentioned above under s. 33 of the 2008 Act, the Secretary of State may direct that the application should be referred to the Infrastructure Planning Commission, which will then treat it as an application for NSIP development consent.

8.190 There are restrictions, however, in that (i) the Secretary of State may only make such a direction if the project falls into one of the following fields: energy; transport; water; waste water; and waste; and (ii) the Secretary of State must consider that the project is of national significance, either by itself or when considered with one or more other projects in the same specified field. Thus a series of projects that may be below the NSIP threshold can be considered collectively.

8.191 If the Secretary of State decides to give such a direction, reasons must be given for the decision.

Applications for orders granting NSIP development consent

8.192 An application for an order granting NSIP development consent must be made to the IPC and it must: specify the development to which it relates; be made in the prescribed form; be accompanied by the report of the consultation carried out in connection with the application;[188] and it must be accompanied by such documents and information as prescribed.[189]

8.193 The IPC may give guidance in connection with the application.The 2008 Act introduces a novel pre-application process which requires developers to consult with the local community, to have regard to the views expressed and demonstrate that they have done so. Before accepting the application, the IPC must make sure that these requirements have been met.

Consultation

8.194 Before submitting an application for a development consent order, under s. 42 PA 2008 the applicant must consult the following about the proposed application:

(a) such persons as may be prescribed;
(b) the local authority of the area in which the land is situated and adjoining local authorities;
(c) the Greater London Authority if the land is in Greater London;
(d) an owner, lessee, tenant (of whatever tenancy period) or occupier of the land. Included in paragraph (d) are persons whom the applicant thinks, if the development consent order sought were implemented, might be entitled to make a relevant claim as a result of the implementation of the order, or as a result of the use of the land once the order has been implemented.[190]

8.195 When consulting a person under the above provisions, the applicant must notify each consultee of a deadline for responding to consultation; this must be not less

---

188 See para 8.194.
189 PA 2008, s. 37.
190 'Relevant claim' refers to compensation for compulsory purchase and for depreciation under the Land Compensation Act 1973.

than 28 days from receipt of the consultation documents. The applicant must also supply the IPC with a copy of the consultation documents.[191]

Public participation

8.196 Under s. 47 PA 2008, the applicant must prepare a statement setting out how he proposes to consult people living in the vicinity of the land about the application. The applicant must consult with each relevant local authority about the contents of the statement, and the authority must reply within 28 days. In preparing the statement, the applicant must have regard to any responses from the local authority.

8.197 Once the applicant has prepared the statement, he must publish it. The consultation must be carried out in accordance with the proposals set out in the statement. The applicant must have regard to guidance issued by the Secretary of State or IPC about pre-application procedure.

Publicity and advice

8.198 The applicant, under s. 48 PA 2008, must publicize the proposed application as prescribed and regulations may make provision for publicity to specify a deadline for responses. Under s. 49 PA 2008, the applicant must consider any relevant responses received to the consultation and publicity before submitting the application to the IPC.

8.199 The IPC may give advice, under s. 51 PA 2008, to applicants and others about applying for an order for development consent or making representations about an application. The IPC may not, however, give advice about the merits of a particular application or proposed application.

Interests in land and rights of entry

8.200 In order to obtain information about interests in land, the IPC, under s. 52 PA 2008, may authorize the applicant to serve notice on the following persons:

(a) an occupier;
(b) a person who has an interest in the land as a freeholder, mortgagee or lessee;
(c) a person who directly or indirectly receives rent from the land;
(d) a person who, by agreement with a person interested in the land, is authorized to mange or arrange the letting of it.

8.201 The notice must require them to give the applicant details of any person who is owner, lessee, tenant, or occupier of the land; or a person having power to sell, convey, or release the land to which the application relates.

---

191 PA 2008, ss. 45 and 46.

8.202 Section 53 of the 2008 Act confers rights of entry.[192] The IPC may authorize a person to enter land for the purposes of surveying and taking levels in connection with:

(a) an application for an order granting development consent that has been accepted by the IPC;
(b) a proposed application for an order granting development consent; or
(c) an order granting development consent that includes authorisation for the compulsory purchase of land, or an interest in land.

It is an offence to obstruct wilfully a person exercising a right of entry under these provisions.

Determining applications for orders granting NSIP development consent

Handling of applications

Acceptance of applications

8.203 When the IPC receives an application for NSIP development consent, they must decide within 28 days whether or not to accept it.[193] They may only accept the application if they are satisfied as to the form and content of the application; that it relates to development requiring NSIP development consent; and that the pre-application procedure[194] has been complied with. The IPC must also be satisfied that the applicant has given reasons for not following any advice given by the IPC. If the IPC accepts the application, it must notify the applicant of the acceptance.

Notification of acceptance of application

8.204 PA 2008, ss. 56 and 57, specify the persons who must be notified of the acceptance of the application. The categories of persons are closely similar to those that the applicant is required to consult as part of the pre-application under s. 42 of PA 2008.[195] The applicant must, under s. 56(7) of the 2008 Act, publicise the application in the manner prescribed by the Secretary of State, allowing a period for persons to notify the IPC of their interest in, or objections to, the proposal. Under PA 2008, s. 58, the applicant must certify that he has complied with the above-mentioned notification requirements.

192 Note that under s. 54 PA 2008, rights of entry in relation to Crown land are modified.
193 PA 2008, s. 55.
194 See para 8.192.
195 See para 8.192.

Local impact report

8.205 Once the IPC has accepted the application, it must notify, under PA 2008 s. 60, relevant local authorities and in Greater London, the GLA, inviting them to submit a 'local impact report'. This is a report in writing giving details of the likely impact of the proposed development in the local authority's area. The notice must specify a deadline for the receipt by the IPC of the report.

Initial choice of Panel or single Commissioner

8.206 By virtue of s. 61 of the 2008 Act, when the IPC has accepted the application the chair must decide whether the application is to be handled by a Panel or single Commissioner. In making this decision, the chair must have regard to guidance issued by the Secretary of State and consult with other members of the Commission, having regard to the views expressed. Under PA 2008, s. 62, where an application for development consent is being handled by a single Commissioner, the chair may instead decide that the application should instead be handled by a Panel. Once again, in coming to this decision, regard must be had to any guidance from the Secretary of State and the views of the Commission.

Panel procedure

8.207 Once an application for a development consent order has been accepted, and the chair has decided it will be handled by a Panel, a Panel will be appointed. Under PA 2008, s. 65, the Panel is to consist of three Commissioners (of which one will chair the Panel) appointed by the chair of the IPC.

8.208 Where an effective NPS in respect of the type of development to which the application relates is in place, under s. 74 PA 2008, the Panel is responsible for examining and deciding the application. In any other case, the Panel must examine the application and make a report to the Secretary of State setting out their findings and their recommended decision on the application. In such a case, the Secretary of State will be responsible for deciding the application.

8.209 Panel decisions are made by majority vote and the lead member has a second (or casting) vote. By virtue of s. 76 of the 2008 Act, the Panel may allocate part of the examination to any one or more of its members. Where this occurs, the member or members are empowered to do anything the Panel as a whole could have done and their findings will be taken to be those of the Panel.

Single Commissioner procedure

8.210 Where it is decided that a single Commissioner is to decide the application, the chair of the IPC must appoint a Commissioner to the task. Before making such an appointment, the chair of the IPC must consult and have regard to the views of other members of the Commission.

8.211 Under s. 83 PA 2008, the single Commissioner must examine the application and make a report setting out their findings and recommendation as to the decision. Where an NPS has effect in relation to the type of development in question, the report is made to the Commission, who should refer it to the Council; in any other case, to the Secretary of State. Where the decision is made by the Council, at least five members of the Council must participate in any decision requiring majority agreement, with the chair of the Council having a second (casting) vote.

Examining of applications

8.212 Where the application for a development consent order is dealt with by a Panel, the Act refers to it as the 'Examining authority'; likewise a single Commissioner dealing with an application is also termed the 'Examining authority'.

8.213 Under PA 2008, s. 87, it is for the Examining authority to decide how to examine the application, and is so doing must comply with any procedural rules laid down by the Lord Chancellor under s. 97 of the 2008 Act, and any guidance given by the Secretary of State or the Commission. The Examining authority may disregard any representations that are vexatious or frivolous; relate to the merits of a policy set out in an NPS; or relate to compensation for compulsory purchase.

8.214 The Examining authority, under PA 2008 s. 88, must make an initial assessment of the principal issues arising on the application, and then hold a meeting with the applicant and each other interested party. The purpose of the meeting is to enable representations to be made as to how the application should be examined, or to discuss any other matter that the Examining authority wishes. In the light of this discussion, the Examining authority under s. 89 PA 2008 may make procedural decisions as to how the application is to be examined and interested parties must be informed.

Written representations

8.215 Under s. 90 PA 2008, the Examining authority's examination of the application will normally take the form of considering written representations about the application, subject to any requirement that a hearing should be held (in circumstances discussed below) or to a decision of the Examining authority that it should take a different form, such as the inclusion of a site visit.

Hearings

8.216 If the Examining authority considers under s. 91 PA 2008 that it is necessary for the examination of a specific issue to include oral representations, it must arrange a hearing in order to ensure: (a) an adequate examination of the issue; or (b) that an interested party has a fair chance to put their case. At the hearing, each interested party is entitled to make oral representations, subject, of course, to the Examining authority's powers of control over the conduct of the hearing.

8.217 By virtue of s. 92 of the 2008 Act, if the application involves a request for the compulsory purchase of land, the Examining authority must inform affected parties who have a right to request a hearing, which must be held if the request is received within the prescribed deadline.

8.218 If at least one of the interested parties informs the Examining authority of their wish to be heard at an 'open-floor hearing' within a specified deadline, the authority must arrange such a hearing. At an 'open-floor hearing', each interested party is entitled to make oral representations about the application, subject, once again, to the authority's powers of control over the conduct of the proceedings.[196]

8.219 At a hearing, the Examining authority may refuse to allow representations which relate to the merits of a policy set out in an NPS.

Timetable for decisions

8.220 Section 98 of the 2008 Act provides that the Examining authority is under a duty to complete its examination of the application within six months of the last day of the preliminary hearing. Where the Examining authority is required to make a report to the Secretary of State or the Commission's Council, ie where these bodies are responsible for making the decision, they must do so within nine months of the preliminary hearing. The chair of the Commission may extend these deadlines; if he does so, he must inform the Secretary of State and give his reasons for doing so.

The decision on the application

Decisions of the Panel and Council

8.221 Under s. 104 PA 2008, where a Panel or the Council is responsible for deciding the application, it must have regard to:

(a) any relevant NPS;
(b) any local impact report;
(c) any matters prescribed in relation to development of the description to which the application relates; and
(d) any other matters which the Panel or Council thinks are both important and relevant.

8.222 The Panel or Council must decide the application in accordance with any relevant NPS but this is subject to exceptions in s. 104(4)–(8) of the Act of 2008.

---

196 PA 2008, s. 93.

Subsection (7) in particular permits a departure from the NPS policy if the Panel or Council is satisfied that the adverse impact of the proposed development would outweigh its benefits.

Decisions of the Secretary of State

8.223 Where it is the Secretary of State who decides the application, the Secretary of State must, under s. 105 PA 2008, have regard to any local impact report; any matters prescribed; and any other matters the Secretary of State thinks are both important and relevant.

Timetable for decisions

8.224 The decision-maker[197] is under a duty prescribed by s. 107 of the 2008 Act to decide the application for a development consent order within a period of three months. If the decision-maker is the Panel or Council, this period begins from the end of the examination; if the decision-maker is the Secretary of State, it starts from the day the Secretary of State receives the IPC's report. The appropriate authority has the power to extend the deadline under PA 2008, s. 107.

Interventions by the Secretary of State

8.225 In certain circumstances the Secretary of State may intervene and decide an application for a development consent order instead of the IPC. Under s. 109(2) PA 2008 the Secretary of State may intervene if satisfied that since the relevant NPS was first published, there has been a significant change in the circumstances on which the policy was originally decided. The change of circumstances must not have been anticipated at the time; or if the change had been anticipated, the relevant policy would have been materially different and would be likely to have had a material effect on the IPC's decision on the application. Further, there must be an urgent need in the national interest for the application to be decided before the NPS can be reviewed. Under s. 110 PA 2008, the Secretary of State may also intervene in the interests of defence or national security.

8.226 If the Secretary of State does intervene, under s. 112 of the Act of 2008, the Secretary of State must issue a direction, giving reasons, within four weeks after the end of the preliminary hearing. In exceptional circumstances, the direction may be given later. The effect of the intervention is that the Secretary of State has the function of examining the application and deciding it. Schedule 3 of PA 2008 makes further provision in relation to the Secretary of State's functions in examining an application in these circumstances.

[197] Ie the Panel, when it is responsible for deciding the application; the Council or the Secretary of State when they are responsible: s. 103 PA 2008.

The decision: grant or refusal

8.227 Once the decision has been made, the decision-maker must, by virtue of s. 114 PA 2008, either make an order granting development consent[198] or an order refusing it. Under s. 115 of the 2008 Act, development consent may be granted for development which is not only the development applied for but associated development. This will presumably cover the kinds of ancillary operations or activities that arise on any major development project, but it does not include the construction of one or more dwellings.

8.228 The decision-maker must, under s. 116 PA 2008, prepare a statement of its reasons for the decision to grant, or as the case may be, refuse consent; copies of the statement must be provided to interested parties and published.

Legal challenges

8.229 Section 118 of the Act of 2008 provides for legal challenges relating to orders granting development consent. It provides that certain specified decisions or actions can only be challenged by means of a claim for judicial review brought in accordance with the provisions of the section. The relevant decisions or actions are:

(a) an order granting development consent—such a challenge must be made within six weeks of the order or of the publication of the statement of reasons, if later;
(b) a refusal of development consent—such a challenge must be made within six weeks of publication of the statement of reasons for refusal;
(c) a decision not to accept for examination an order granting development consent—such a challenge must be made within six weeks of the day on which the IPC notifies the applicant of its decision;
(d) a decision in relation to a correction or omission—such a challenge must in general be made within six weeks of the correction notice;
(e) a decision in relation to the change or revocation of a development consent order[199]—such a challenge must in general be made within six weeks of the notice of the change or revocation being given.

8.230 In addition, a challenge may be made in respect of anything else done by the IPC or Secretary of State in relation to an application for a development consent order. Such a challenge must be brought within six weeks of the 'relevant day'. Relevant day means: the day on which the application is withdrawn; the day on which the

[198] PA 2008, s. 114(2) provides that the Secretary of State may make regulations regarding the procedure to be followed if the decision-maker proposes to make an order on terms materially different from those proposed in the application.

[199] See para 8.240.

order granting development consent is published, or, if later, the publication of the statement of reasons; or the day on which the statement of reasons for the refusal of development consent is published.

8.231 It should be noted that although the claim is by means of judicial review, the period within which the claim must be brought is not the usual maximum of three months for judicial review but six weeks. The six week period is the one traditionally applicable to statutory review under s. 288 TCPA1990 whereby the legality of a decision of the Secretary of State in a planning appeal is challenged in the courts.[200] PA 2008, s. 118 introduces a hybrid procedure—given the magnitude of the developments involved under the NSIP regime, it is not surprising that the legislature has opted for a shorter time limit.

Correction of errors

8.232 There are provisions in Schedule 4 of the 2008 Act by which the decision-maker can correct errors in decision documents relating to an order for development consent, whether the document grants consent or refuses it.[201] An error is only correctable if it is part of the decision document that records the decision and is not part of the statement of reasons.

8.233 The appropriate authority[202] may correct the error or omission only if two conditions are satisfied. These are: (1) that before the end of a period of six weeks from the date of the decision the appropriate authority has been requested to correct the error or omission; or the appropriate authority has sent a written statement to the applicant explaining the error or omission and proposing to make the correction; (2) the appropriate authority must inform each relevant local planning authority that the request referred to above has been received, or the statement has been sent, as the case may be.

8.234 If the appropriate authority is requested to, or proposes to, make a correction in the above-discussed circumstances, it must issue a 'correction notice'. The authority must give the correction notice to: the applicant; interested parties; relevant local planning authorities; and if the correction was requested by another person, that person. Once a correction has been made, the relevant document remains valid, but is treated as corrected from date of issue of the correction notice.

---

200 See para 20.01.

201 The provisions are similar to those in Part 5 of PCPA 2004 relating to the correction of errors in certain decisions under TCPA 1990.

202 The 'appropriate authority' is the Commission, where the decision-maker is the Panel or the Council; the Secretary of State where the decision-maker is the Secretary of State.

NSIP development consent orders

Content of development consent orders

8.235 A development consent order under PA 2008 is essentially a type of planning permission authorising particular types of development. However, such orders go beyond the scope express planning permission granted by a local planning authority under TCPA 1990 and may authorize matters which, under general planning control, could only be achieved under other statutory powers. The NSIP development consent is therefore a rather more comprehensive legal instrument than a planning permission.

8.236 PA 2008, s. 120, provides that a development consent order may impose requirements in connection with the development corresponding to conditions attached to planning permission[203] or attached to any consent or authorization which would have been required but for the enactment of PA 2008. As may be expected, a development consent order may make provision for matters ancillary to the development and Schedule 5, Part 1 contains a non-exhaustive list of ancillary matters which may be included in the development consent order. This specifies a wide range of matters including the following:

(a) the acquisition of land, compulsorily or by agreement;
(b) the creation, suspension or extinguishment of, or interference with, interests in, or rights over land, either compulsorily or by agreement;
(c) the abrogation or modification of agreements relating to land;
(d) the sale, exchange or appropriation of Green Belt land;
(e) the protection of the property or interests of any person;
(f) carrying out surveys or taking soil samples;
(g) carrying out civil engineering or other works;
(h) the stopping up or diversion of highways.

8.237 The list also includes matters specific to the type of NSIP development consent sought, such as: the operation of a generating station; the use of underground gas storage facilities; the operation and maintenance of a transport system; and the creation of a harbour authority. A development consent order may also apply, modify, or exclude statutory provisions and amend, repeal, or revoke the provisions of a local Act of Parliament if it appears necessary or expedient to the decision-maker in connection with the order. However, there are certain things an order granting development consent cannot do, ie it may not make byelaws, create criminal offences or change existing powers to make byelaws or create offences.

203 See para 10.25.

8.238 To the extent that a development consent order can, as we have seen, exclude or modify statutory provisions, s. 121 of the 2008 Act requires that, before the Panel or Council exercise such powers, they must send a draft of the proposed order to the Secretary of State. If the Secretary of State thinks that any provision of a draft order would contravene European Community law or Convention rights under the Human Rights Act 1998, the Secretary of State may direct the Panel or Council to make changes so as to prevent the contravention from arising. Such a direction must be made by the Secretary of State within 28 days of receiving the draft order.

Duration of development consent order

8.239 Under s. 154 of the 2008 Act, when a development consent order is granted, the development must be begun before the end of the period prescribed by the Secretary of State or such other period as specified in the order. If the development is not begun before the end of the prescribed period, the development consent order will lapse. Development is taken to have begun, according to s. 155 PA 2008, as soon as any material operation comprised in, or carried out for the purposes of, the development is started to be carried out. There are similar provisions in TCPA 1990 relating to planning permission.[204]

Modification and revocation of development consent orders

8.240 Provisions relating to the modification and revocation of development consent orders are contained in Schedule 6 to the 2008 Act. The appropriate authority[205] may make a change to a development consent order if satisfied that the change is non-material. The power conferred to make such changes may only be exercised on an application by a restricted group of persons including the applicant, a person with an interest in the land, or a person for whose benefit the order has effect. There are consultation and publicity requirements.

8.241 Paragraph 3 of Schedule 6 to the 2008 Act gives the appropriate authority further and more general powers to modify or revoke an order, including changes that the appropriate authority would consider material. Application may only be made by the categories of parties referred to in the previous paragraph, and in certain circumstances, the relevant local planning authority or the Secretary of State.[206] The power may be exercised without an application if the appropriate authority is satisfied that the order contains a significant error and it would inappropriate to correct it under the powers contained in Schedule 4.[207]

204 See para 10.113.
205 Either the Commission or the Secretary of State, as the case may be.
206 This would be where the appropriate authority is the IPC.
207 See para 8.232.

8.242 If the development consent order is changed or revoked under these powers in paragraph 3 of the Schedule, the appropriate authority must give notice to such persons as may be prescribed. The power may not be exercised after four years from when the development was substantially completed, but this time limit does not apply where the changes are to requirements imposed by the order or where the order is to be revoked. Compensation may be payable where an order is changed or revoked to persons with an interest in the land or for whose benefit the order has effect.[208]

Development consent orders: compulsory purchase

8.243 Under the provisions of s. 122 PA 2008, a development consent order can only authorize compulsory acquisition if the decision-maker is satisfied that the land: (a) is required for development to which the development consent order relates; (b) is required to facilitate or is incidental to that development; or (c) is replacement land which is to be given in exchange for the order land. There must also be a compelling case in the public interest for the land to be so acquired.

8.244 Further, under s. 123 PA 2008, the decision-maker can only authorize the compulsory acquisition of order land if satisfied that one of the following conditions is met:

(a) that the application for the order included a request for the compulsory acquisition of that land;
(b) that all persons with an interest in the land consent to the inclusion of this provision; and
(c) that the prescribed procedure has been followed in relation to that land.[209]

8.245 Under s. 124 PA 2008, the Secretary of State may issue guidance about orders authorising compulsory purchase. Section 125 of the Act applies the provisions of Part 1 of the Compulsory Purchase Act 1965, with modifications, to any order involving compulsory acquisition. However, the order itself may make contrary provision, except with regard to compensation.

8.246 There are special provisions in the Act of 2008 relating to development orders which authorize the compulsory acquisition of statutory undertakers' land,[210] National Trust land,[211] commons and open spaces,[212] and Crown land.[213]

208 These provisions are contained in paras 6 and 7 of Sch 6.
209 There is an equivalent provision in the Acquisition of Land Act 1981.
210 PA 2008, ss. 127 and 128.
211 Ibid, s. 130.
212 Ibid, ss. 131 and 132.
213 Ibid, s. 135.

Enforcement of the NSIP development consent regime

8.247 The enforcement of the new regime, such as where development is carried out without consent, or in breach of a development consent order, is discussed in chapter 12.[214]

214 See para 12.177.

9

ENVIRONMENTAL IMPACT ASSESSMENT AND STRATEGIC ENVIRONMENTAL ASSESSMENT

Part 1: Environmental Impact Assessment

9.01 The protection of the environment from pollution and nuisance is an obvious objective of planning control. It has been said that, in principle, the established system of control should be capable in most cases of securing that the effect on the environment of any development project is evaluated before planning permission is granted. Nevertheless, in the mid-1980s, European Community Directive No 85/337 imposed special requirements for certain public and private projects. In these cases there has to be an assessment of the environmental effects before the project may proceed—this is what is meant by Environmental Impact Assessment (EIA).

9.02 The original 1985 Directive was implemented in English Law as a set of planning regulations; the Town and Country Planning (Assessment of Environmental Effects) Regulations 1988.[1] However in 1997 the 1985 Directive was amended by Directive No 97/11. This led the UK Government to make new regulations which came into force on 14 March 1999. These are the Town and Country Planning (Environmental Impact Assessment) (England and Wales) Regulations 1999 (the EIA Regulations).[2]

9.03 Whereas the EIA Regulations are the main set of regulations, a number of other regulations implement the Directive and are concerned with such matters as highways, forestry, land drainage, harbour works, offshore petroleum production, pipelines, and the Channel Tunnel Rail Link. Amending regulations were introduced in 2000 to bring the review of old mining permissions within the scope of EIA requirements.[3]

9.04 The EIA regulations were further amended in 2006 for the purpose of implementing article 3 of Directive 2003/35/EC (the Public Participation Directive), which amends the EIA Directive mainly with regard to public participation provisions. The amendments introduced by the Town and Country Planning (Environmental Impact Assessment) (Amendment) Regulations 2006[4] include the application of EIA requirements to planning permission granted by Local Development Orders,[5] the provision of publicity using electronic means, the extension of the scope of interested parties to non-governmental organizations promoting environmental protection, and the replacement of the blanket exemption for projects serving national defence purposes with an exemption applying on a case-by-case basis, where compliance with EIA requirements would have an adverse effect on national defence.

What is environmental impact assessment?

9.05 EIA is best seen as a process whereby, if EIA is required, an applicant for planning permission must submit to the local planning authority an 'environmental statement'. The statement will consist of one or more documents providing information enabling an assessment to be made of the likely impact of the proposed development on the environment. Where significant adverse effects are identified, the statement must contain a description of the remedial measures which the

1 SI 1988 No 1199 as amended; now revoked by SI 1999 No 293.
2 EIA Regs 1999, SI 1999 No 293. as amended by SI 2000 No 2867, and see Circular 2/99.
3 See para 17.90.
4 SI 2006 No 3295, which came into force on 7 January 2007.
5 See para 7.66.

developer proposes. The submission of this statement will set in motion publicity and consultations with a view to building up a body of 'environmental information' which must be taken into account before planning permission is granted. 'Environmental information' includes the environmental statement and any further information and representations duly made about the environmental effects of the proposed development.[6] When determining an EIA application, the regulations require the local planning authority or Secretary of State to inform the public of their decision and the main reasons on which it is based, whether refused or granted.[7]

9.06 The regulations forbid the granting of planning permission for development to which the regulations apply unless the EIA procedures have been followed.[8]

9.07 The 1999 regulations increase the range of projects that are subject to EIA and also introduce applicable thresholds and criteria. There have also been a number of procedural changes designed to improve the effectiveness of the system—these will be considered below. A further innovation is provision for consultation between member states where development is likely to have transboundary effects.[9]

EIA development

9.08 The cases in which an environmental statement is required (EIA development) are specified in Schedules 1 and 2 of the regulations. Such a statement will always be necessary for development falling within Schedule 1 unless exempted by a direction of the Secretary of State.

9.09 Schedule 2 development is defined as development of a type listed in Schedule 2 which (a) meets the criteria or exceeds the thresholds specified in Schedule 2 for the relevant development,[10] or (b) is located in a 'sensitive area'; this includes Sites of Special Scientific Interest, National Parks and areas of outstanding natural beauty, World Heritage Sites, and European Sites under the Nature Conservation Regulations.[11] However, even where conditions (a) and (b) above are not satisfied, the Secretary of State may direct that a particular development is EIA development.[12]

6 EIA Regs, reg 2(1).
7 EIA Regs, reg 21.
8 EIA Regs, reg 3.
9 EIA Regs, regs 27 and 28.
10 EIA Regs, reg 2(1).
11 EIA Regs, reg 2(1).
12 EIA Regs, reg 4(8).

9.10 Schedule 2 development is EIA development if likely to have significant effects on the environment by virtue of factors such as its nature, size, or location. The Secretary of State has power to direct that a particular development be exempted; the grounds upon which he may do so include where the development comprises national defence purposes and the Secretary of State considers that compliance with the regulations would have an adverse effect on those purposes.[13]

Schedule 1 development

9.11 As stated above, Schedule 1 development requires an EIA in every case. Schedule 1 contains detailed criteria; the headings are as follows:

1. Crude-oil refineries and some installations for the gasification and liquefaction of coal or bituminous shale.
2. Major thermal power stations, nuclear power stations and other nuclear reactors, other than certain research installations.
3. Installations carrying on certain processes involving nuclear fuel and radioactive waste, involving final disposal and storage.
4. Works for the initial smelting of cast-iron and steel and for the production of non-ferrous crude metals.
5. Processes involving asbestos.
6. Integrated chemical installations, including the production of fertilisers, pharmaceutical products, and explosives.
7. Construction works, including long-distance railway lines, airports, and major roads.
8. Inland waterways and ports, trading ports, and piers for vessels over 1,350 tonnes.
9. Waste disposal installations for the incineration, chemical treatment of landfill of hazardous waste.
10. Waste disposal installations for the incineration or chemical treatment of non-hazardous waste.
11. Groundwater abstraction or recharge schemes of 10 million or more cubic metres of water per annum.
12. Major works for the transfer of water resources, other than piped drinking water.
13. Waste water treatment plants with a capacity exceeding 150,000 population equivalent.
14. Extraction of petroleum and natural gas for commercial purposes above certain thresholds.

[13] EIA Regs, regs 2(1) and 4(8).

15. Dams and water storage installations above a certain capacity.
16. Pipelines, over a certain size, for the transport of gas, oil, or chemicals.
17. Installations, over a certain capacity, for the intensive rearing of poultry and pigs.
18. Industrial plants for the production of pulp; and for the production of paper and board exceeding 200 tonnes per day.
19. Quarries and open-cast mining where the surface of the site exceeds 25 hectares, or peat extraction where surface of the site exceeds 150 hectares.
20. Installations for the storage of petroleum, petrochemical, or chemical products with a capacity of 200,000 tonnes or more.
21. Any change or extension to development listed in Schedule 1 where such a change or extension meets the thresholds, if any, or description of development set out in Schedule 1.[14]

Schedule 2 development

9.12 Schedule 2 comprises development which is EIA development if likely to have significant effects on the environment by virtue of factors such as nature, size, or location.

1. *Agriculture and aquaculture*
   Use of uncultivated land for intensive agriculture (exceeding 0.5 hectare); water management projects (exceeding 1 hectare); intensive livestock installations other than Schedule 1 (exceeding 500 metres new floorspace); intensive fish farming (producing more than 10 tonnes of fish per year); any development involving reclamation of land from the sea.
2. *Extractive industry*
   Quarries, open-cast mining, peat extraction other than Schedule 1 and underground mining (excluding buildings not exceeding 1,000 metres new floorspace); extraction of minerals by fluvial dredging; deep drilling (exceeding 1 hectare); surface industrial installations for the extraction of coal, petroleum, natural gas, ores, and bituminous shale (exceeding 0.5 hectares).
3. *Energy industry*
   Industrial installations for electricity, steam, and hot water production, other than Schedule 1 (exceeding 0.5 hectares); industrial installations for carrying gas, steam, and hot water (exceeding 1 hectare); surface storage of natural gas, underground storage of combustible gases, and surface storage of fossil fuels (new buildings etc exceeding 500 metres or sited within 100 metres of controlled waters); industrial briquetting of coal and lignite (exceeding 1,000 metres

[14] Added by SI 2006 No 3295.

new floorspace); hydroelectric energy production (producing more than 0.5 megawatts); wind farms (more than two turbines or exceeds specified height threshold).

4. *Production and processing of metals*
   Installations for the production of pig iron or steel; installations for the processing of ferrous metals; ferrous metal foundries; non-ferrous metal processes; surface treatment of metals and plastics using electrolytic or chemical process; motor vehicle and engine manufacturing; shipyards; construction and repair of aircraft; manufacture of railway equipment; swaging by explosives; roasting and sintering of metallic ores (all categories exceeding 1,000 square metres new floorspace).
5. *Mineral industry*
   Coke ovens; manufacture of cement; production of asbestos other than Schedule 1; glass and glass fibre manufacture; smelting mineral substances; manufacture of ceramic products including bricks, tiles, and porcelain (all categories exceeding 1,000 metres new floorspace).
6. *Chemical industry*
   Treatment of intermediate products and production of chemicals, pesticides, pharmaceuticals, paint, varnishes, elastomers, and peroxides (exceeding 1,000 square metres new floorspace); storage of petroleum and related products (new building exceeding 0.5 hectare or more than 200 tonnes to be stored).
7. *Food industry*
   Manufacture of vegetable and animal oils and fats; packing and canning of foods; dairy products; brewing and malting; manufacture of confectionery and syrup; installations for the slaughter of animals; industrial starch manufacture; fish meal and fish oil factories and sugar factories (all categories exceeding 1,000 square metres new floorspace).
8. *Texile, leather, wood, and paper industries*
   Production of paper and board, other than Schedule 1; pre-treatment or dyeing of fibres and textiles; tanning of hides and skins; cellulose processing and production installations (all categories exceeding 1,000 square metres new floorspace).
9. *Rubber industry*
   Manufacture and treatment of elastomer-based products (exceeding 1,000 square metres new floorspace).
10. *Infrastructure projects*
    Industrial estate development project, urban development project, construction of intermodal trans-shipment facilities unless included in Schedule 1 (exceeding 0.5 hectares); construction of railways unless included in Schedule 1 (exceeding 1 hectare); construction of airfields unless included in Schedule 1 (involving an extension to a runway or exceeding 1 hectare); construction of roads unless included in Schedule 1 (exceeding 1 hectare).

Construction of harbours and port installations including fishing harbours, unless included in Schedule 1 (exceeding 1 hectare); inland waterways not included in Schedule 1, canalization, flood-relief works, dams, and water storage unless included in Schedule 1 (exceeding 1 hectare).

Tramways and similar railways used for passenger transport (exceeding 1 hectare); oil and certain gas pipeline installations unless included in Schedule 1, long-distance aqueducts (exceeding 1 hectare); any coastal protection works excluding maintenance and reconstruction; groundwater abstraction and recharge not included in Schedule 1, transfer of water resources not included in Schedule 1 (exceeding 1 hectare); motorway service areas (exceeding 0.5 hectares).

11. *Other projects*
Permanent racing and test tracks for motorized vehicles (exceeding 1 hectare); waste disposal unless included in Schedule 1 (incineration or exceeding 0.5 hectares or within 100 metres of controlled waters); waste water treatment plants unless included in Schedule 1 (exceeding 1,000 square metres); sludge deposition and storage of scrap (exceeding 0.5 hectares or within 100 metres of controlled waters); test bench for engines etc, manufacture of artificial mineral fibres, recovery or destruction of explosives, knackers yards (exceeding 1,000 square metres new floorspace).

12. *Tourism and leisure*
Skiing-related developments (exceeding 1 hectare or building exceeding 15 metres); marinas (exceeding 1,000 square metres enclosed water surface); holiday villages, hotel complexes, and theme parks (exceeding 0.5 hectares); camping and caravan sites (exceeding 1 hectare); golf courses and associated developments (exceeding 1 hectare).

13. *Changes to existing development and testing of new products*
Any change to or extension of development within Schedule 1 (other than a change falling within para 21 of that Schedule); or within Schedule 1, paragraphs 1–12, where that development is already authorized, executed, or in the process of being executed and the change or extension may have significant adverse effects on the environment.

In relation to Schedule 1 development there are additional thresholds and criteria for changes or extensions prescribed in Schedule 2, paragraph 13, column 2. In relation to Schedule 2 development the thresholds and criteria are the same as for new development. In either case, they apply to the change or extension and not to the development as changed or extended.

All development in Schedule 1 undertaken exclusively or mainly for the development and testing of new methods or products and not used for more than two years.

The need for EIA for Schedule 2 development

9.13 The local planning authority must 'screen' applications for Schedule 2 development in order to decide whether an environmental statement is required.

9.14 Schedule 3 to the regulations contains selection criteria for screening Schedule 2 development; that is, to decide whether it is likely to have significant effects on the environment. These include the characteristics of the development (eg its size, use of natural resources, production of waste, pollution, and nuisances); the location of the development (eg the environmental sensitivity of the areas likely to be affected); and the characteristics of the potential impact (eg the extent, magnitude, probability, and duration of the potential impact).

9.15 The Secretary of State, in Circular 2/99, expresses the view that in the light of the above criteria, EIA will be needed for Schedule 2 developments in three main types of case:

(a) for major developments of more than local importance;
(b) for developments which are proposed for particularly environmentally sensitive or vulnerable locations; and
(c) for developments with unusually complex and potentially hazardous environmental effects.

9.16 With regard to the criteria and thresholds in Schedule 2, the Circular emphasizes that they are only indicative. The question should be considered on a case-by-case basis. Developments falling below these thresholds may give rise to significant effects, especially where the development is in an environmentally sensitive location. And development which exceeds the thresholds would not in every case require EIA. The thresholds are to be used in conjunction with the general guidance set out in the Circular.[15]

9.17 The question whether Schedule 2 applies so as to require EIA will be a matter of judgment in the first instance for the local planning authority. Their decision may come under review by the Secretary of State and the courts.[16]

Screening

9.18 The question of whether EIA is required may come up for decision in a number of ways:

(1) The prospective developer may request a 'screening opinion' from the local planning authority before submitting a planning application. The authority

[15] Circular 2/99, para 44.
[16] See the cases discussed at para 9.37 .

should respond within three weeks or such longer period as may be agreed. If the authority fail to do so or if the developer is dissatisfied with the authority's opinion, he may request the Secretary of State to make a 'screening direction'.[17] The Secretary of State should make such a direction within three weeks or such longer period as he may reasonably require.[18] Where a screening opinion is adopted by the local planning authority, or a screening direction is made by the Secretary of State to the effect that EIA is required, full reasons must be given and notified to the applicant.[19]

(2) Where the local planning authority receive an application for planning permission without an environmental statement which the authority consider to be necessary, they should notify the applicant within three weeks or such longer period as may be agreed, giving their full reasons. The applicant then has three weeks in which to inform the authority either (i) that he accepts their opinion and will be submitting an environmental statement; or (ii) that he is applying to the Secretary of State for a screening direction on the matter. If the applicant fails to reply within three weeks, the application will be deemed to have been refused and no appeal to the Secretary of State will be possible.[20]

(3) A planning application may have been referred to the Secretary of State for decision by him under TCPA 1990, s. 77, or there may have been an appeal to him under TCPA 1990, s. 78. If he considers that EIA is required, he should so inform the applicant within three weeks or such longer period as he may reasonably require, giving his reasons. The applicant then has three weeks in which to notify the Secretary of State that he will be providing an environmental statement. Also, it may occur to the inspector deciding an appeal that an environmental statement should have been submitted, in which case he should ask the Secretary of State for a screening direction. If the Secretary of State directs that EIA is required, the inspector is precluded from determining the appeal until the appellant submits an environmental statement.[21]

(4) It is possible that a developer submits an environmental statement with a planning application without having obtained a screening direction to the effect that one is required. If the applicant expressly refers to the statement as an environmental statement for the purpose of the regulations, the application must be treated as an EIA application by the local planning authority.[22] On the other hand, if he does not refer to the information as constituting an environmental statement for the purpose of the regulations, the local planning authority should, if they have not already done so, adopt a screening opinion.

---

17 EIA Regs, reg 5.
18 EIA Regs, reg 6.
19 EIA Regs, reg 4(6).
20 EIA Regs, reg 7.
21 EIA Regs, reg 9.
22 EIA Regs, reg 4(2)(a).

(5) Even in the absence of an application to him, the Secretary of State has powers to make a screening direction, including a power to direct that development listed in Schedule 2 is EIA development even if it does not satisfy the conditions in relation to Schedule 2 development.[23] And, as we have seen,[24] he has wide powers to exempt proposed development from EIA, even though listed in the Schedules to the regulations. According to Circular 1/99 the Secretary of State does not foresee any circumstances in which this power would be used, although such circumstances may arise.

Scoping

9.19 The 1999 regulations permit a prospective developer to seek a formal opinion from the local planning authority as to the scope of an environmental statement, ie as to what information should be contained in it. This process is referred to as 'scoping'.

9.20 Before adopting a 'scoping opinion', the authority must consult the 'consultation bodies'[25] and the developer. The authority must adopt a scoping opinion within five weeks of receiving the request, or within such longer period as agreed. Such an opinion must be available for public inspection for a period of two years.[26]

9.21 If the local planning authority fails to adopt a scoping opinion within five weeks or such longer period as may have been agreed, the developer may apply to the Secretary of State for a 'scoping direction'.[27] He must make such a direction within five weeks, or such longer period as he may reasonably require, after having consulted the consultation bodies and the applicant.[28]

9.22 The 'consultation bodies', referred to above, are: statutory consultees under article 10 of the General Development Procedure Order[29] and (if not already included under article 10) any principal council for the area if not the local planning authority; Natural England; the Environment Agency; and other bodies designated by statutory provision as having specific environmental responsibilities which the local planning authority or Secretary of State consider likely to have an interest.

---

23 See para 9.12.
24 See para 9.09.
25 See para 9.22.
26 EIA Regs, regs 10 and 20.
27 EIA Regs, reg 10(7).
28 EIA Regs, reg 11(4).
29 See para 8.39.

Procedure on submission of an application for planning permission

9.23 Where a planning application is accompanied by a statement that the applicant refers to as an environmental statement, the applicant must submit three copies of the statement for transmission to the Secretary of State (within 14 days) and further copies for the consultation bodies and the public.[30] The local planning authority is then required to publicize the application[31] and the environmental statement allowing 21 days for written representations to be made to the local planning authority. The local planning authority must also consult the consultation bodies.

9.24 Where the environmental statement is submitted after the planning application, the responsibility for publicizing the statement falls on the applicant.[32] The procedures are the same as outlined above, although the applicant must certify that he has complied with the publicity requirements.

9.25 The local planning authority have 16 weeks in which to determine an EIA application, as opposed to the usual period of eight weeks (or 13 weeks in the case of major development).[33] The period runs from the date of receipt of the statement.[34]

9.26 The result of the publicity and consultations will be the assembly of a body of 'environmental information' comprising the environmental statement, representations made by the consultation bodies, and any representations duly made by any other person about the environmental effects of the development.[35] Before determining an EIA application the local planning authority or Secretary of State must take the environmental information into consideration, and state in their decision that they have done so.[36] What this means in effect is that the environmental information is one of the material considerations[37] to be taken into account in deciding whether to grant planning permission for proposed development. There is also an obligation to inform the Secretary of State and the public of the decision and the main reasons for it, and if planning permission has been granted, the main measures to avoid or mitigate the major adverse effects on the environment.[38]

---

30 EIA Regs, regs 13, 17 and 18.
31 See para 8.03.
32 EIA Regs, reg 14.
33 EIA Regs, reg 32.
34 EIA Regs.
35 EIA Regs, reg 2.
36 EIA Regs, reg 3. If planning permission is granted in breach of reg 3, the validity of the permission may be challenged in the High Court under TCPA 1990, s. 288.
37 See para 8.68.
38 EIA Regs, reg 21.

9.27 An innovation of the 1999 regulations is that the obligation to provide reasons for the decision applies to cases where planning permission has been granted as well as to where it has been refused.

9.28 It should be noted that the 1999 EIA Regulations have been amended by the EIA (Amendment) (England) Regulations 2008[39] so as to apply EIA requirements to applications for approval of reserved matters under outline planning permission, and to applications for the approval of conditions attached to planning permission, termed in the regulations as 'subsequent applications'.

Permitted development

9.29 It may be recalled from a previous chapter that a wide range of developments are permitted.[40] The majority of permitted development is of a minor nature and so the need for EIA is unlikely in most cases.

9.30 The EIA Regulations amend the General Permitted Development Order to provide that Schedule 1 or 2 development is not permitted development[41] unless the local planning authority has adopted a screening direction to the effect that the development is not EIA development; the Secretary of State has made a screening direction to like effect; or the Secretary of State has given a direction that the development is exempt from the application of the EIA Regulations.[42]

9.31 Similar provisions have been introduced relating to the grant of planning permission by Local Development Order for EIA development under the 1999 regulations.[43]

The environmental statement

9.32 The EIA Regulations make no provision as to the form an environmental statement should take. However, Schedule 4 of the regulations specifies the information to be included in such a statement.

9.33 Schedule 4 is in two parts. The regulations provide that the environmental statement should include such of the information in Part I of the Schedule as is reasonably required to assess the environmental effects and which the applicant

---

39 SI 2008 No 2093.

40 See para 7.01.

41 With some exceptions in art 3(12) GPDO.

42 EIA Regs, reg 35.

43 T &CP (EIA)(Amendment) Regs 2006, SI 2006 No 3295, inserting a new art 24A into the 1999 regulations.

can be reasonably required to compile but it should include at least the information in Part II of the Schedule.

Part I **9.34**

1. Description of the development, including in particular—
   (a) a description of the physical characteristics of the whole development and the land-use requirements during the construction and operational phases;
   (b) a description of the main characteristics of the production processes, for instance, nature and quantity of the materials used;
   (c) an estimate, by type and quantity, of expected residues and emissions (water, air, and soil pollution, noise, vibration, light, heat, radiation, etc) resulting from the operation of the proposed development.
2. An outline of the main alternatives studied by the applicant or appellant and an indication of the main reasons for his choice, taking into account the environmental effects.
3. A description of the aspects of the environment likely to be significantly affected by the development, including, in particular, population, fauna, flora, soil, water, air, climatic factors, material assets, including the architectural and archaeological heritage, landscape, and the inter-relationship between the above factors.
4. A description of the likely significant effects of the development on the environment, which should cover the direct effects and any indirect, secondary, cumulative, short, medium and long-term, permanent and temporary, positive and negative effects of the development, resulting from:
   (a) the existence of the development;
   (b) the use of natural resources;
   (c) the emission of pollutants, the creation of nuisances, and the elimination of waste,and the description by the applicant of the forecasting methods used to assess the effects on the environment.
5. A description of the measures envisaged to prevent, reduce, and where possible offset any significant adverse effects on the environment.
6. A non-technical summary of the information provided under paragraphs 1 to 5 of this part.
7. An indication of any difficulties (technical deficiencies or lack of know-how) encountered by the applicant in compiling the required information.

Part II **9.35**

1. A description of the development comprising information on the site, design, and size of the development.
2. A description of the measures envisaged in order to avoid, reduce, and, if possible, remedy significant adverse effects.

3. The data required to identify and assess the main effects which the development is likely to have on the environment.
4. An outline of the main alternatives studied by the applicant or appellant and an indication of the main reasons for his choice, taking into account the environmental effects.
5. A non-technical summary of the information provided under paragraphs 1 to 4 of this Part.

9.36 It is the responsibility of the developer to prepare an environmental statement. Where the local planning authority or Secretary of State are of the opinion that additional information is required, they have powers to require the applicant to submit further information. Any such information submitted must be subject to publicity and consultation; the requirements are similar to the environmental statement itself.[44]

Non-compliance with EIA requirements

9.37 Initially, the UK courts displayed an inconsistent approach to the requirements of the EIA Directive, in some instances refusing to treat the Directive, or parts of it, as having direct effect.[45] There was also, perhaps, a readiness to accept that the established machinery of planning control was a sufficiently effective vehicle for meeting the requirements of the Directive.

9.38 In *R v Swale Borough Council, ex p Royal Society for the Protection of Birds*,[46] the RSPB sought judicial review of a grant of planning permission which had been issued without an environmental impact assessment having been carried out. Simon Brown J held that the decision whether any particular development is within the scheduled descriptions is exclusively for the planning authority, subject only to *Wednesbury* challenge[47]—the issue is essentially one of fact and degree, not law. In particular, he considered that the court should not effectively act as an appeal court so as to reach its own conclusion as to whether the obligations of the European Union had been properly discharged.

9.39 More recently, the courts have signalled a less conservative approach. In *Berkeley v Secretary of State for the Environment, Transport and the Regions (No 1)*,[48] the

44 EIA Regs, reg 19.

45 See *Wychavon District Council v Secretary of State for the Environment* [1994] Env LR 239. 'Direct effect' is discussed in chapter 3.

46 [1991] JPL 39.

47 See para 10.68.

48 [2001] JPL 58.

Secretary of State had called in a planning application for the redevelopment of part of Fulham FC's ground, Craven Cottage. He did not, however, require the club to produce an environmental statement under the Regulations of 1988.[49] An inquiry was held in which environmental evidence was heard and planning permission was granted. The applicant, Lady Dido Berkeley, sought to quash the decision under TCPA 1990, s. 288[50] on the ground that it was ultra vires because no EIA had been undertaken.

9.40 In the High Court it was held that even if an EIA was required, the court would, as a matter of discretion, refuse to quash the permission since the absence of an EIA had no effect on the outcome of the inquiry. The Court of Appeal upheld this decision. On appeal to the House of Lords, it was common ground between the parties that the Secretary of State's action was a breach of regulation 4(2) of the 1988 Regulations which provided that the Secretary of State should not grant planning permission pursuant to a Schedule 2 application unless the information obtained by an EIA had been taken into account. The Secretary of State also accepted that his breach could not be justified on the ground that the outcome would have been the same even if he had required and considered an EIA. Instead, he argued that there had been substantial compliance with the requirements of the Directive, and that the equivalent of an environmental statement could be found in the inquiry proceedings.[51]

9.41 The House of Lords held that although the case of *EC Commission v Germany*[52] established that an EIA by any other name would do as well, their Lordships did not accept that the 'paper chase' of the inquiry could be treated as the equivalent of an environmental statement. Lord Hoffmann did not think it complied with the terms of the Directive: 'The point about the environmental statement contemplated by the Directive is that it constitutes a single accessible compilation, produced by the applicant at the very start of the application process, of the relevant environmental information and the summary in nontechnical language.'

9.42 A unanimous House of Lords[53] quashed the planning permission. It has been said that the practical consequence of the *Berkeley* decision is that developers cannot hope that the need for an EIA will go unnoticed by the planning authority as the failure to carry out EIA 'will be like an undetected mine, ready to go off and blow up the development project'.[54]

49 Now superseded by the 1999 Regulations.
50 See para 20.07.
51 As to the inquiry procedure, see ch 19 below.
52 [1995] ECR I-2189.
53 Lords Hope, Hutton, and Millett agreed with the speeches of Lords Bingham and Hoffmann.
54 Editorial comment at [2000] JPL 987.

9.43 A claim that the UK Government had failed properly to transpose the EIA Directive was rejected by the Court of Appeal in *Berkeley v Secretary of State for the Environment, Transport and the Regions (No 2)*.[55] The case concerned planning applications for some 30 flats on two sites at Mortlake—as such the proposals fell under the category of 'urban infrastructure projects' in Annex II of the Directive. However, since neither development exceeded the 0.5 hectare threshold in the regulations or was in a sensitive area, the inspector considered that he had no power to require an EIA.

9.44 It was submitted that since it was possible to accommodate projects with significant environmental effects on sites of less than 0.5 hectares (eg the London Eye), the regulations did not properly transpose the Directive. Rejecting that submission, the Court held that although in choosing thresholds, the Government had to have regard to criteria other than simply size, it did not follow that the resulting thresholds had to refer to each or all of the criteria referred to in the Directive. Simply because a situation could arise in which a particular development could have serious environmental effects without requiring an EIA did not mean that the regulations had not properly transposed the Directive. The decision serves as a reminder that, where a proposal falls below the criteria in the regulations, or is not in a sensitive area, it is only the Secretary of State who can require an EIA and that decision is discretionary. The fact that the proposal may be environmentally detrimental affords, of itself, insufficient grounds for the power to be exercised. In this case, the court displayed a more cautious approach than that adopted by the House of Lords in the earlier *Berkeley* decision, discussed above.

9.45 Outline planning permission and EIA requirements were at issue in the well-known 'Tew' litigation. In *R v Rochdale Metropolitan Borough Council, ex p Tew*,[56] a bare outline planning permission was granted for a business park and associated development on a site lying between the built-up area of Rochdale and the M62. An illustrative Master Plan and indicative schedule of uses accompanied the application and it was submitted with an environmental statement. It was common ground that the development required an environmental assessment under the 1988 Regulations. The objectors argued that planning permission could not be granted unless a description of the proposed development comprising, at minimum, information as to the design and size or scale of the project, as well as data necessary to identify the main environmental effects of the proposal, was included in the application. Indeed, they argued that these requirements made it impossible for outline planning permission ever to be lawfully granted for projects falling within the environmental effects regulations. Sullivan J, although reluctant

---

55 [2001] EWCA Civ 1012, [2002] 1 P & CR 264.
56 [1999] JPL 54.

to go that far, held that the general description of the development in the present case was inadequate to comply with the regulations and the planning permission was accordingly quashed.

9.46 Following that decision of Sullivan J a revised planning application and environmental statement were submitted and planning permission was granted by the local planning authority. In this second case[57] (known as *Milne*) objectors argued in the High Court that, in relation to the description of the proposed development, there had been a failure to comply with the EIA Regulations of 1999. The objectors also argued that there had been a failure to comply with development plan policy. Once again the matter came before Sullivan J. He acknowledged that it was not expected that the business park would be completely occupied until 2013. There was a contrast between projects such as the present one and most of the other descriptions of development in Schedule 2 of the EIA regulations, which were either industrial projects for particular processes, or 'one-off' infrastructure projects—roads, tramways, dams, or pipelines. These, by their very nature, had to be defined in considerable detail at the outset. The present project was not fixed at the outset but was expected to evolve over a number of years depending on market demand. Sullivan J held that there was no reason why a 'description of the project' for the purposes of the Directive should not recognize that reality and found for the respondent local planning authority. There was 'full knowledge' in the sense of there being as much information as could reasonably be expected at the particular stage. As a result of this case, it seemed possible to be able to reconcile outline planning permission with EIA requirements, even in the case of long-term projects.

9.47 However, this approach requires reconsideration as a result the case of *R (on the application of Barker) v Bromley London Borough Council*,[58] where the local planning authority granted outline planning permission for a development on Crystal Palace Park in south London. No consideration had been given at that point as to whether an EIA should be carried out. When the application for the approval of reserved matters was submitted, a number of councillors indicated that they wished a formal EIA to be carried out before approval. However, the planning committee was advised by the borough secretary that, as a matter of law, an EIA could not be required at the approval of reserved matters stage. On this basis, the application was approved without an EIA being carried out. The applicant, a local resident, sought to challenge the decision. In 2003, the House of Lords referred to the ECJ the issue of whether domestic law could preclude the carrying

57 *R v Rochdale Metropolitan Borough Council, ex p Milne* (2000) EGCS 103.

58 [2006] UKHL 52.

out of an EIA at the approval of reserved matters stage, where outline planning permission had been granted.

9.48 The ECJ determined that EIA was required if, in the case of a development consent comprising more than one stage, it became apparent, after the first stage, that the project was likely to have significant effects on the environment by virtue of, inter alia, its size, nature, and location. The EIA regulations were deficient in that they did not provide for an EIA at the stage of reserved matters in any circumstances; thus the regulations failed fully and properly to implement the Directive. On the basis of this ruling, the House of Lords in a 2006 hearing quashed the approval of reserved matters—the local planning authority had proceeded upon a misdirection of law. The House of Lords confirmed that the position was that, in the case of development falling under Schedule 2, the local planning authority must decide at the outset whether an EIA is required. Providing sufficient information was given at the outset, it should be possible for the authority to determine whether an assessment at that stage would take account of the likely environmental effects as the application proceeded. If it did not become apparent until a later time that the proposal was likely to have significant effects on the environment, the EIA would have to be carried out at the stage of reserved matters.[59]

9.49 In *R (on the application of Goodman) v London Borough of Lewisham*,[60] the Court of Appeal held that Tucker J had been wrong to hold that the local authority's decision whether a development was a Schedule 2 development could only be challenged on the ground of *Wednesbury* unreasonableness.[61] A company called The Big Yellow Property Co applied for planning permission to construct a 'self-storage' facility on a site exceeding more than 0.5 hectares. The application was not accompanied by an environmental statement. Residents in the locality contended that the development was an 'infrastructure project' and 'urban development project' within paragraph 10(b) of Schedule 2 to the EIA Regulations.[62] The residents applied for judicial review of the authority's decision to grant planning permission.

9.50 The Court of Appeal held that determination as to whether a project does or does not fall within one of the categories in the Schedules was not simply a finding of fact or of discretionary judgment. Rather it involves the application of the authority's understanding of the meaning in law of the expressions used in the regulations.

---

59 In *R (on the application of Mortell) v Oldham Metropolitan Borough Council* [2007] EWHC 1526 the court emphasized that it is only where the likely environmental effects cannot be identified or anticipated at the outline stage that they can be considered at the reserved matters stage.

60 [2003] EWCA Civ 140.

61 See para 10.68.

62 See para 9.12.

If the authority reaches an understanding of those expressions that is wrong as a matter of law, then the court must correct the error. If it decided that the development was Schedule 2 development, then the authority had to consider a further question, namely whether EIA was required because of its likely impact—this was an inquiry to which the *Wednesbury* principle did apply. Thus the council's officer's view in this case that storage did not fall under paragraph 10(b) was not right as a matter of law. The grant of planning permission was quashed.

9.51 The view that the decision as to whether development was likely to have significant environmental effects was a matter of judgment and opinion for the local planning authority (and reviewable only on *Wednesbury* grounds) was endorsed by the Court of Appeal in a later case; *R (on the application of Jones) v Mansfield District Council*.[63]

9.52 There will be cases where the developer offers remedial measures to mitigate the significant effects to the environment. In *Bellway Urban Renewal Southern v Gillespie*,[64] the Court of Appeal held that in considering whether an EIA was required the Secretary of State was not as a matter of law required to ignore proposals for remedial measures. Where the remedial measures were modest in scope or easily achievable, the Secretary of State could properly hold that the project would not be likely to have significant effects on the environment. However, in more complex cases where the effectiveness of such proposals could not be certain, such a decision could not properly be arrived at.

9.53 The meaning of 'development consent' in the EIA Directive arose in *R (Prokopp) v London Underground Ltd*.[65] The Court of Appeal held that a decision by a local planning authority not to take enforcement action[66] against unauthorized development did not amount to a development consent within article 1(2) of the EIA Directive and therefore did not attract the requirement of an environmental assessment.

EIA and mineral development

9.54 In a further group of cases, the statutory regimes for the deemed grant of old mining permissions and the review of minerals permissions have been challenged on the basis of non-compliance with the EIA Directive. This litigation led to the introduction of amending regulations to meet the requirements of the Directive.[67]

---

63 [2003] EWCA Civ 1408.
64 [2003] EWCA Civ 400.
65 [2003] EWCA Civ 961.
66 See para 12.01.
67 See para 17.90.

Under a regime introduced by the Planning and Compensation Act 1991, owners of old mining permissions granted between 1943 and 1948 under 'Interim Development Orders' (IDOs)[68] were required to register such permissions with the local planning authority. If registration was accepted, the local planning authority could impose fresh conditions and the planning permission could be implemented. Unless registered by a certain date, such permissions lapsed without compensation. The IDO regime came before the House of Lords in connection with EIA in *R v North Yorkshire County Council, ex p Brown*.[69]

9.55 Planning permission was granted in 1947 for limestone quarrying on the site in question and was not subject to any conditions or time limit. The PCA 1991, s. 22 and Schedule 2 gave the council, as minerals planning authority, the power to impose conditions on the operation of the quarry. The council advertised its intention to determine the conditions and consulted widely but it failed to undertake an EIA in accordance with Directive 85/337. In June 1995 the council determined the conditions and local residents sought judicial review to quash the determination on the ground that no EIA had been carried out. Before the House of Lords the council claimed that no EIA was required because the imposition of conditions was not a 'development consent' within the meaning of the Directive. Held: the council's appeal would be dismissed.

9.56 In the House of Lords, Lord Hoffmann said that the effect of the 1991 Act provisions was that, although the determination of conditions did not decide whether the developer may proceed, it does decide the manner in which he may proceed and is a necessary condition for his being entitled to proceed at all. This was sufficient to bring it within the European concept of development consent. The purpose of the Directive is to ensure that planning decisions which may affect the environment are made on the basis of full information. His Lordship went on to state that:

> A decision as to the conditions under which a quarry may be operated may have a very important effect on the environment. It can protect it by imposing limits on noise, vibration and dust, requiring the preservation of important natural habitats or the reinstatement of damage to the landscape and in many other ways. Without such conditions the unrestricted operation of the quarry might well have a significant effect on the environment. It cannot therefore be said that the environmental effect of the quarry was determined once and for 1947 [when planning permission was originally granted]. One of the purposes of the [PCA 1991] was to allow minerals planning authorities to assess those effects in the light of modern conditions.

9.57 The determination of the conditions was accordingly quashed.

---

[68] The IDO regime is discussed at para 17.72.

[69] [1999] JPL 616.

9.58 The decision of the Court of Appeal in *R v Durham County Council, ex p Huddleston*[70] raised a different aspect of the IDO regime. In this case, Sherburn (S) had a dormant planning permission to extract minerals at a site for which the council was the minerals planning authority. This was therefore an 'old mining permission' which, in order to quarry the site, required registration under PCA 1991, s. 22, subject to conditions set by the council.

9.59 PCA 1991, Schedule 2, para 2(6) (the 'deeming provision') provides that if the council had not determined the conditions within three months of S's application to register, the council was to be treated as having determined that the permission was to be subject to the conditions proposed by the developer in the application.

9.60 On 15 February 1999 S applied for registration and submitted conditions satisfactory to itself but tendered no environmental statement. In reliance on the *Brown* decision, discussed above, the council initially insisted on an EIA but later moderated its stance, accepting that it could not of its own motion treat the Directive as effective, or the deeming provision as ineffective—the position with regard to the deeming provision was an issue which the House of Lords had felt it unnecessary to decide. S informed the council that, as three months had elapsed without the council having determined the conditions, there was a deemed determination of the conditions put forward by S. The applicant sought an order that permission should not be implemented without an EIA.

9.61 Reversing a decision of Richards J, the Court of Appeal gave direct effect to the Directive so as to require EIA before the deeming provision could apply. In the view of the court, the applicant was entitled to complain that the State had not set up the requisite machinery to give him the opportunity which should have been afforded him if the Directive had been properly implemented. The decision in *Huddleston* raised a general concern in relation to the planning legislation; that is, the inconsistency between the provisions which deem planning permission to be granted and the need for the environmental effects of the development to be considered before the development proceeds. Indeed, when the Court of Appeal handed down its decision in the earlier *Brown* case, the Government announced its intention to introduce regulations to amend the procedures in PCA 1991 so as to enable the requirement of an EIA. These regulations came into force on 15 November 2000.[71] As they concern also the regime under the Environment Act 1995, Schedules 13 and 14, dealing with minerals permissions granted from

[70] [2000] 1 WLR 1484. See also *R v Somerset County Council, ex p Morris and Perry (Gurney Slade Quarry) Ltd* [2000] PLCR 117.

[71] SI 2000 No 2867.

1948 to 1982, the regulations will be considered in chapter 17 under mineral development.[72]

9.62 The ECJ further ruled on the IDO regime in the case of *R (on the application of Wells) v Secretary of State for Transport, Local Government and the Regions*[73] Once again, the meaning of 'development consent' under the Directive was in issue.

9.63 An old mining permission had been registered under PCA 1991 and, following an inquiry, the conditions were determined by the Secretary of State. No EIA had been carried out at any stage and the applicant, Delena Wells, argued that an EIA should have been carried out at the stage when conditions were imposed. Further, since there had been non-compliance with EIA requirements, a breach of European law had taken place and it was contended that the planning permission should be revoked. The Secretary of State's case was that if EIA was required, it should have been carried out at the stage of registration because this was the 'development consent' under the Directive. The ECJ did not agree with the case put forward by the Secretary of State.

9.64 The court held that: (1) the decisions adopted by the competent authorities (ie the local planning authority and the Secretary of State) whose effect was to permit the resumption of mining operations comprised, as a whole, a 'development consent', so that there was a requirement to carry out an EIA. (2) The EIA had to be carried out before consent was granted. In a consent procedure involving several stages, one a principal decision and the others involving implementing decisions which could not extend beyond the parameters of the principal decision, the assessment had to be carried out as soon as it was possible to identify all the environmental effects—this would normally be at the principal decision stage. (3) Individuals may invoke the provisions of the Directive before national courts—the fact that this may have adverse repercussions on the rights of third parties, eg developers, did not prevent an individual invoking those provisions. (4) Member States are obliged to take, within their sphere of competence, all measures necessary to ensure that where EIA has not taken place as it should, the consent is revoked or suspended to allow for an EIA to be carried out, and to make good any harm caused by the failure to carry out such an assessment. The court considered that the detailed rules for achieving this are a matter for member States.[74] The court in *Wells* also ruled that the fact that some considerable time had elapsed since the

---

72 See para 17.76.

73 [2004] Env LR 27.

74 Revocation of planning permission under domestic law is possible under s. 97 TCPA 1990, on payment of compensation.

development consent was granted did not mean that the revocation of the consent was contrary to legal certainty.[75]

Part 2: Strategic environmental assessment

9.65 Directive 2001/42/EC on Strategic Environmental Assessment (the 'SEA Directive') had to be implemented by member states by 21 July 2004. The Directive has introduced an obligation to take environmental considerations into account in the preparation of plans and programmes. It extends not only to land use development plans but also to programmes in other fields such as energy, transport, and telecommunications.

9.66 In terms of town and country planning, the obligations imposed by the Directive will apply to all development plans.[76]

9.67 The SEA Directive has been implemented by the Environmental Assessment of Plans and Programmes Regulations 2004[77] which came into force on 20 July 2004. The regulations implement the Directive as regards plans and programmes relating to England—there are separate regulations for Wales.[78]

What is SEA?

9.68 SEA, like EIA, is essentially a process or 'generic tool' the purpose of which 'is to provide for a high level of protection for the environment and to contribute to the integration of environmental considerations into the preparation and adoption of plans and programmes with a view to promoting sustainable development'.[79]

9.69 SEA applies to certain plans and programmes, including those co-financed by the European Community, as well as any modifications to them, which are required by legislative, regulatory, or administrative provisions and are either: (a) subject to preparation or adoption by an authority at national, regional, or local level; or

---

[75] In *R (on the application of the Noble Organisation) v Thanet District Council* [2005] EWCA Civ 782, the Court of Appeal held that this reasoning does not apply to challenges to the validity of *decisions*. See also *R (on the application of Hardy and Maille) v Pembrokeshire County Council* [2005] EWHC 1872 (Admin).

[76] See paras 4.01 and 5.01.

[77] SI 2004 No 1633—the 'SEA Regs'. The Government has issued guidance: *The Strategic Environmental Assessment Directive; Guidance for Planning Authorities*, ODPM, 2003.

[78] Environmental Assessment of Plans and Programmes (Wales) Regulations 2004, SI 2004 No 1656.

[79] SEA Directive, art 1.

(b) prepared by an authority for adoption through a legislative procedure by Parliament or Government.[80]

Requirement for environmental assessment

9.70 Where the first formal preparatory act in relation to a plan or programme to which the regulations apply takes place on or after 21 July 2004, the plan or programme cannot be adopted or submitted for adoption unless it has been subjected to an 'environmental assessment'.

9.71 The requirement for environmental assessment may also apply where a plan or programme in relation to which the first formal preparatory act occurred before 21 July 2004 has not been adopted before 22 July 2006. If an environmental assessment would have been required if the first formal preparatory act occurred on 21 July 2004, the plan or programme must be subjected to environmental assessment unless the responsible authority directs that this is not feasible and informs the public to that effect.[81]

9.72 An environmental assessment is defined by the Directive as the 'preparation of an environmental report, the carrying out of consultations, the taking into account of the environmental report and the results of the consultations in decision-making and the provision of information on the decision in accordance with [the Directive]'.[82]

9.73 More specifically the requirement for environmental assessment applies to any plan or programme which is prepared for agriculture, forestry, fisheries, energy, industry, transport, waste management, water management, telecommunications, tourism, town and country planning, or land use which sets the framework for future development consent of projects listed in Annexes I and II of the EIA Directive,[83] and to any plan or programme which, in view of the likely effect on sites, has been determined to require an assessment pursuant to articles 6 and 7 of the Habitats Directive.[84]

9.74 There are, however, exceptions for plans and programmes that determine the use of a small area at local level if the responsible authority has determined that there are unlikely to be significant environmental effects,[85] unless the Secretary of

---

80 SEA Regs, reg 2(1).

81 Ibid, reg 5(1) and reg 6. The 'responsible authority' is the authority responsible for preparing the plan or programme.

82 SEA Directive, art 2(b).

83 For EIA, see Part 1 of this chapter, at para 9.01.

84 SEA Regs, reg 5(2) and (3).

85 Ibid, reg 5(6).

State directs otherwise. Within 28 days of receiving such a direction, the responsible authority must accord it publicity.

9.75 Environmental assessment may also be required for other plans and programmes which set the framework for future development consent of projects if the responsible authority determine that the plan or programme is likely to have significant environmental effects,[86] unless the Secretary of State directs.[87] Within 28 days of receiving such a direction, the responsible authority must accord it publicity.

9.76 The criteria for determining the likely significance of effects on the environment are set out in Schedule 1 to the regulations:

(1) The characteristics of plans and programmes, having regard, in particular, to—
  (a) the degree to which the plan or programme sets a framework for projects and other activities, either with regard to the location, nature, size, and operating conditions or by allocating resources;
  (b) the degree to which the plan or programme influences other plans and programmes including those on hierarchy;
  (c) the relevance of the plan or programme for the integration of environmental considerations in particular with a view to promoting sustainable development;
  (d) environmental problems relevant to the plan or programme; and
  (e) the relevance of the plan or programme for the implementation of Community legislation on the environment (for example, plans and programmes linked to waste management and water protection).

(2) Characteristics of the effects and of the area likely to be affected, having regard, in particular, to—
  (a) the probability, duration, frequency, and reversibility of the effects;
  (b) the cumulative nature of the effects;
  (c) the transboundary nature of the effects;
  (d) the risks to human health or the environment (for example, due to accidents);
  (e) the magnitude and spatial extent of the effects (geographical area and size of population likely to be affected);
  (f) the value and vulnerability of the area likely to be affected due to— (i) special natural characteristics or cultural heritage; (ii) exceeded environmental quality standards or limit values; or (iii) intensive land-use; and
  (g) the effects on area or landscapes which have a recognized national, Community, or international protection status.

---

86 Ibid, regs 10(3) and 11(3).

87 Ibid, regs 5(4) and 9(1).

9.77 Within 28 days of making such a determination, the responsible authority must consult the 'consultation bodies' and publish details of their decision.[88]

9.78 The bodies to be consulted are the Countryside Agency, English Heritage, English Nature, and the Environment Agency. In respect of the part of a plan or programme (to which the regulations apply) that relates to any part of Northern Ireland, the Department of the Environment for Northern Ireland will be a consultation body. Where part of such a plan relates to any part of Scotland, the Scottish Ministers, the Scottish Environmental Protection Agency, and Scottish National Heritage will also be consultation bodies. Where part of such a plan relates to any part of Wales, the Assembly and the Countryside Agency for Wales will also be consultation bodies.[89]

The environmental report

9.79 Where an environmental assessment is required by the regulations, the responsible authority must prepare an environmental report. The report must identify, describe, and evaluate the likely significant effects on the environment of implementing the plan or programme, and the reasonable alternatives, taking into account the objectives and geographical scope of the plan or programme.

9.80 The report must take account of current knowledge and methods of assessment; the content and level of detail in the plan or programme; the stage of the plan or programme in the decision-making process; and the extent to which certain matters are appropriately assessed at the different levels in that process in order to avoid duplication of the assessment.[90]

9.81 When deciding on the scope and level of detail of the report, the responsible body must consult the consultation bodies, who have a period of five weeks within which to respond.[91]

9.82 The information that the environmental report must contain is prescribed by Schedule 2 to the regulations as follows:

(1) An outline of the contents and main objectives of the plan or programme, and of its relationship with other relevant plans and programmes.
(2) The relevant aspects of the current state of the environment and the likely evolution thereof without implementation of the plan or programme.
(3) The environmental characteristics of areas likely to be significantly affected.

---

88 Ibid, regs 10(3) and 11(3).
89 Ibid, reg 4.
90 Ibid, reg 12(1), (2) and (3).
91 Ibid, reg 12(5) and (6).

(4) Any existing environmental problems which are relevant to the plan or programme including, in particular, those relating to any areas of a particular environmental importance, such as areas designated pursuant to Council Directive 79/409/EEC on the conservation of wild birds in the Habitats Directive.
(5) The environmental protection objectives, established at international, Community, or member state level, which are relevant to the plan or programme and the way those objectives and any environmental considerations have been taken into account during its preparation.
(6) The likely significant effects on the environment, including short, medium and long-term effects, permanent and temporary effects, positive and negative effects, and secondary, cumulative, and synergistic effects, on issues such as—
  (a) biodiversity;
  (b) population;
  (c) human health;
  (d) fauna;
  (e) flora;
  (f) soil;
  (g) water;
  (h) air;
  (i) climatic factors;
  (j) material assets;
  (k) cultural heritage, including architectural and archaeological heritage;
  (l) landscape; and
  (m) the inter-relationship between issues referred to in sub-paragraphs (a) to (l).
(7) The measures envisaged to prevent, reduce, and as fully as possible offset any significant adverse effects on the environment of implementing the plan or programme.
(8) An outline of the reasons for selecting the alternatives dealt with, and a description of how the assessment was undertaken including any difficulties (such as technical deficiencies or lack of know-how) encountered in compiling the required information.
(9) A description of the measures envisaged concerning monitoring in accordance with regulation 17.[92]

Consultation

9.83 Every draft plan or programme and its accompanying environmental report (the 'relevant documents') must be made available for the purposes of consultation.[93]

92 Reg 17 of the SEA Regs is discussed at para 9.91.
93 SEA Regs, reg 13(1).

9.84 As soon as reasonably practicable after the preparation of the relevant documents, the responsible authority must—

(a) send a copy of the documents to the consultation body;
(b) take such steps as it considers appropriate to bring the preparation of the relevant documents to the attention of the persons who, in the authority's opinion, are affected or are likely to be affected by, or have an interest in, the decisions involved in the assessment and adoption of the plan or programme concerned required under the SEA Directive (the 'public consultees');
(c) inform the public consultees of the address (which may include a website) at which a copy of the relevant documents may be viewed, or from which a copy may be obtained—a reasonable charge may be levied for this; and
(d) invite the consultation bodies and the public consultees to express their opinion on the relevant documents, specifying the address to which, and the period within which, opinions must be sent. The period in question must be long enough so as to ensure that the consultation bodies and public consultees are given an effective opportunity to express their opinion on the relevant documents.

9.85 The responsible authority must keep a copy of the relevant documents available at its principal office for inspection by the public at all reasonable times and free of charge.[94]

Transboundary consultations

9.86 As with EIA,[95] there is provision in the SEA Regulations for transboundary consultations for draft plans and programmes prepared in another member state which are likely to have significant effects on the environment in any part of the UK.[96]

9.87 Thus where the Secretary of State receives a draft plan or programme from another member state he must indicate to that state whether the UK wishes to enter into consultation regarding—(a) the likely transboundary environmental effects of implementing the plan or programme; and (b) the measures envisaged to eliminate or reduce those effects.[97]

---

94 Ibid, reg 13(2)–(5).
95 For EIA, see Part 1 of this chapter, at para 9.01.
96 SEA Regs, reg 14.
97 Ibid, reg 15.

Post-adoption Procedures

9.88 As soon as reasonably practicable after the adoption of the relevant plan or programme for which an environmental assessment has been carried out, the responsible authority must make a copy of the plan or programme and its accompanying environmental report available for inspection, with due publicity.

9.89 At the same time, the responsible authority must inform the consultation bodies and public consultees (and where the responsible body is not the Secretary of State, the Secretary of State) that the plan or programme has been adopted, the date of adoption, and the location at which a copy of the relevant documents may be viewed. The authority must also indicate how environmental considerations have been integrated into the plan or programme, how the environmental report has been taken into account, and how the opinions of the consultees and representations by members of the public have been taken into account. There must also be an indication of the reasons for choosing the plan or programme as adopted in the light of other reasonable alternatives; and the measures to be taken to monitor the significant environmental effects of the implementation of the plan or programme.[98]

9.90 In the case of transboundary consultations, the Secretary of State must provide a member state, with which consultations have taken place in relation to a plan or programme, with the same information as referred to in the above paragraph.

Monitoring

9.91 The responsible authority must monitor the significant environmental effects of the implementation of each plan or programme. The purpose is to identify unforeseen adverse effects at an early stage, with a view to taking appropriate remedial action.[99]

---

98 SEA Regs, reg 16.

99 Ibid, reg 17. The responsible authority's monitoring arrangements may comprise arrangements established otherwise than for the express purpose of complying with reg 17.

10

PLANNING PERMISSION: FURTHER CONSIDERATIONS

Effect of permission

10.01 A grant of planning permission, unless it provides to the contrary, enures for the benefit of the land and of all persons interested in it.[1] It is thus possible to grant permission for the sole benefit of a particular individual.

10.02 The Secretary of State considers that the use of personal permissions is seldom desirable; a personal permission may be appropriate, however, where it is proposed on compassionate or other personal grounds to grant planning permission for the use of a building or land for some purposes which would not normally be

[1] TCPA 1990, s. 75(1).

allowed at the site.[2] In practice, the desired result can often be met by granting planning permission for a temporary period only. The Secretary of State's policy may be illustrated by a number of cases.

10.03 K lives in a large house in the Metropolitan Green Belt. He equipped and used two rooms exclusively as offices for his business, which was concerned with the sale of dehydrated foods; he employed one secretary. An enforcement notice was served. On appeal the inspector considered that there was no justification for terminating this use of the two rooms; however, the use of the rooms as offices by another organization, or any expansion of the present business beyond these two rooms, could attract additional traffic and activity. The Secretary of State granted planning permission for the use of the two rooms as an office in connection with the sale of dehydrated foods subject to conditions that the permission should enure only for the benefit of K so long as he lived there and that no other part of the dwellinghouse or curtilage should be so used.[3]

10.04 In another case the owner of a smallholding applied for permission for a caravan required to accommodate B whose help was wanted in the running of the smallholding. The Minister was satisfied that it would take some time to bring the land into production and that there were exceptional difficulties in connection with B reaching the smallholding. He accordingly allowed the appeal to the extent of granting permission for a caravan for Mr and Mrs B for a period of five years.[4]

10.05 But where a student at a theological college had taken part-time charge of a nonconformist church for the duration of his studies and needed a site for a caravan, the Minister on appeal granted permission for a caravan in the church grounds for a temporary period: it was evidently not considered necessary to make the permission a personal one.[5]

10.06 A planning permission obtained by a planning authority for their own development under the procedures introduced in 1976 and amended by the PCA 1991 is personal to that authority and does not enure for the benefit of the land.[6]

10.07 A grant of permission is effective only for the purposes of development control. It does not override listed building control. It does not relieve the developer of the necessity of complying with other legislation affecting the use or development of land such as the regulations governing the construction of buildings or the legislation relating to the control of pollution. Nor does it override restrictions imposed on the land under the general law such as easements or restrictive covenants.

---

2 Circular 11/95, para 93.
3 [1978] JPL 338.
4 Ministry ref 2381/40620/122.
5 Ministry ref 781/40620/29.
6 General Regs, reg 9. See further at para 17.40.

Although there is machinery for securing the removal or modification of restrictive covenants, the fact that planning permission has been granted is normally no ground on which a restrictive covenant can be revoked or modified.[7]

10.08 The grant of a planning permission does not revoke any previous planning permissions which have not been taken up. It has been said to be trite law that any number of planning permissions can validly co-exist for the development of the same land even though they are mutually inconsistent.[8] So where there are two or more planning permissions, none of which has been acted upon, a developer can choose which he will take up.

10.09 But what happens where there are mutually inconsistent permissions, and one of them is acted upon? The leading case on the point is *Pilkington v Secretary of State for the Environment*.[9]

10.10 The owner of land was granted planning permission to build a bungalow on part of it, site 'B'. It was a condition of the permission that the bungalow should be the only house to be built on the land. He built the bungalow. Later, he discovered the existence of an earlier permission to build a bungalow on another part of the same land, site 'A'. That permission contemplated the use of the rest of the land as a smallholding. He began to build a second bungalow when he was served with an enforcement notice.

10.11 Held: The effect of building on site 'B' was to make the development authorized in the earlier permission incapable of implementation; the bungalow built on site 'B' had destroyed the smallholding and the erection of two bungalows on the site had never been sanctioned.

10.12 The case of *Durham County Council v Secretary of State for the Environment*[10] provides further clarification. In 1947 planning permission for quarrying on a site was granted and it continued until 1956. In 1957 planning permission was granted for the tipping of household refuse and this continued until 1976; 42 per cent of the site subject to the 1947 permission had been tipped. In 1986 Tarmac Ltd began extraction operations relying on the 1947 permission. Were they entitled to do so?

---

[7] The principal method of obtaining a removal of a restrictive covenant is by application to the Lands Tribunal under the Law of Property Act 1925, s. 84.

[8] *Pioneer Aggregates (UK) Ltd v Secretary of State for the Environment* [1985] AC 132, [1984] 2 All ER 358, per Lord Scarman at 365.

[9] [1974] 1 All ER 283, [1973] 1 WLR 1527. The decision of the Divisional Court in this case has been approved by the House of Lords *in Pioneer Aggregates (UK) Ltd v Secretary of State for the Environment;* see fn 8, above. *See also Prestige Homes (Southern) Ltd v Secretary of State for the Environment* [1992] JPL 842; *Regent Lion Properties Ltd v Westminster City Council* [1991] JPL 569; and *Staffordshire County Council v NGR Land Developments Ltd* [2002] EWCA Civ 856.

[10] [1990] JPL 280.

10.13 Neill LJ explained that in the case of development which consisted of the making of any material change in the use of the land, the permission was 'spent' when the change of use was implemented. Accordingly an owner could not subsequently make use of this permission if the land was later used for some purpose not covered by this permission.[11] Permission for operational development, on the other hand, was not 'spent' when the development began; this was the case here where the mining operations permission needed to remain in force to authorize the moving of every shovelful of material.[12] He said the question for consideration was: 'was it possible to carry out the development covered by the permission on which it was now sought to rely having regard to that which had been done or authorized to be done under the permission which had already been implemented?' On the facts, it was so possible—the inspector found that the extraction of sand and gravel from areas covered by subsequently tipped material and by natural overburden would be both practicable and viable—thus the 1947 planning permission was still capable of being implemented.[13]

10.14 Another type of case where two planning permissions are not incompatible is where a developer is able to rely on one permission as regards one part of the land and on another permission as regards the other part of the land. This possibility is illustrated by *F Lucas & Sons Ltd v Dorking and Horley RDC*.[14]

10.15 In 1952 the plaintiffs were granted permission to develop a plot of land by the erection of 28 houses in a cul-de-sac layout; the layout showed 14 houses on the north side and 14 houses on the south side of the cul-de-sac. In 1957 the plaintiffs obtained permission to develop the same land by building six detached houses each on a plot fronting the main road; the plaintiffs built two houses in accordance with this permission. The council contended that the 1952 permission was no longer valid or effective. The plaintiffs sought a declaration that it was effective and entitled them to carry out all or any of the building or other operations to which it related.

10.16 Granting the declaration, Winn J said that the 1952 permission was not conditional upon the developer completing the whole of the approved development; it was a permission for any of the development comprised therein.

10.17 The learned judge pointed out that TCPA 1962, s. 12 (now TCPA 1990, s. 55) forbids development without planning permission, so it is more natural and

[11] *Young v Secretary of State for the Environment* [1983] 2 AC 662, [1983] 2 All ER 1105, HL; *Cynon Valley Borough Council v Secretary of State for Wales* (1986) 53 P & CR 68.

[12] *Thomas David (Porthcawl) Ltd v Penybont RDC* [1972] 3 All ER 1092, [1972] 1 WLR 1526.

[13] The *Durham* case was followed by the CA in *Camden London Borough Council v McDonald's Restaurants Ltd* (1992) 65 P & CR 423.

[14] (1964) 17 P & CR 111.

more likely to have been the intention to look at any particular development to see whether or not it is unpermitted than to look at the contemplated project for the achievement of which the planning authority has granted a planning permission. This was perhaps an exceptional case, but it is important in that it shows that the taking up of a planning permission does not necessarily render other permissions incapable of implementation. The local planning authority can prevent this kind of situation arising by attaching a condition that the later permission is not to be exercised in addition to or in combination with the earlier permission.[15]

Planning permission and nuisance

10.18 The case of *Gillingham Borough Council v Medway (Chatham) Dock Co Ltd*[16] illustrates that one of the effects of a planning permission can be to alter the character of a neighbourhood so as to render innocent activities which, prior to the implementation of the permission, would have constituted an actionable nuisance:

10.19 Planning permission was granted to redevelop the former Chatham Royal Navy Dockyard as a commercial port. The council were aware that the only access to the port ran through a residential area and that the port would be operational on a 24-hour a day basis. They considered, however, that the possible adverse effects of the development would be outweighed by the economic benefits. When the port became operational, the substantial increase in heavy goods traffic led the local residents to complain of noise and pollution problems. The local planning authority sought a declaration that the use of the access road amounted to a public nuisance and an injunction to restrain such use.

10.20 Held: there was no nuisance in law since the access road was now in a neighbourhood of a commercial port.

10.21 Buckley J said: 'I must judge the present claim in nuisance by reference to the present character of the neighbourhood pursuant to the planning permission'. He also indicated that a change in the development plan might have the same effect as the planning permission in this case. The planning permission was granted in 1983 before the coming into force of the regulations concerning environmental assessment.[17] Such an assessment might today provide an additional safeguard although the council might still have granted planning permission if they felt that the residents' interests were outweighed by the perceived economic benefits of the development.

10.22 The *Gillingham* case does not mean, however, that the carrying out of development in accordance with a planning permission will provide immunity from liability in

15 *F Lucas & Sons Ltd v Dorking and Horley RDC*, discussed at para 10.14.
16 [1992] JPL 458.
17 See para 9.01.

nuisance. In *Wheeler v JJ Saunders*,[18] the defendants were granted planning permission for the construction and use of two pig houses, each containing 20 pens capable of taking 20 pigs. The plaintiffs owned a holiday cottage situated some 11 metres from the development and alleged that the smell caused by the pigs constituted an actionable nuisance. The Court of Appeal rejected the defendants' argument that since they had obtained planning permission, any smell emanating from the pigs could not amount to a nuisance. The Court affirmed the principle that a planning permission could not authorize a nuisance; such an extinction of private rights would be the equivalent of statutory authority. Nevertheless, a planning authority can, as acknowledged in the *Gillingham* case, alter the character of a neighbourhood through its development plans and decisions. However, this had not happened in the instant case—the defendants' land remained a pig farm with merely an intensified use of part of it.

10.23 In *Hunter v Canary Wharf Ltd*,[19] local residents brought an action in nuisance against building owners for interference caused to domestic television reception by the presence of Canary Wharf tower. One of the issues before the Court of Appeal was whether implementation of permission to erect a building itself granted immunity in nuisance. Drawing a distinction with nuisance caused by activities, the court answered this question in the negative.[20]

10.24 It seems reasonable to suggest that the effect of the above ruling, and that in *Wheeler v JJ Saunders*,[21] is to limit the *Gillingham* principle to the effect caused to a locality by major developments.

Validity of conditions

10.25 As already explained,[22] the power to impose conditions on a grant of planning permission is not unlimited.

10.26 The provision in the TCPA 1990 that the planning authority may impose such conditions 'as they think fit' must be read subject to the requirements of the general law. Of these perhaps the most important is the long-established rule that statutory powers must be exercised only for the purpose of the statute concerned.

10.27 Thus, in *Pilling v Abergele UDC*[23] the local authority refused a licence for a caravan site under the Public Health Act 1936, s. 269, on the ground that the

18 [1995] JPL 619.
19 [1996] 1 All ER 482, [1996] 2 WLR 348.
20 The case proceeded to the House of Lords on different grounds.
21 See para 10.22.
22 See para 8.101.
23 [1950] 1 KB 636, [1950] 1 All ER 76.

caravans would be detrimental to the amenities of the locality; it was held that s. 269 was concerned with sanitary matters, and that the authority were not entitled to consider questions of amenity.

10.28 This principle was specifically considered in relation to planning control in *Pyx Granite Co Ltd v Ministry of Housing and Local Government*[24] and subsequently in *Fawcett Properties Ltd v Buckingham County Council.*[25]

10.29 The latter case provided the House of Lords with the opportunity of considering a number of points relating to the validity of conditions. As a result the following principles appear to have been established:

(1) A condition must serve some useful planning purpose.
(2) A condition must 'fairly and reasonably relate to the permitted development'.
(3) A condition must not be manifestly unreasonable.
(4) A condition may be imposed restricting the user of premises according to the personal circumstances of the occupier.
(5) A condition may be declared invalid on the ground that its meaning is uncertain.

10.30 The first three of these principles were re-affirmed by the House of Lords in *Newbury District Council v Secretary of State for the Environment*,[26] but the others are also important and we will consider all five in turn.

Condition must serve some useful planning purpose

10.31 This principle is based on the long-standing rule that statutory powers must be exercised only for the purpose of the statute concerned. Thus, a condition which does not serve a useful planning purpose must be ultra vires. In the *Newbury* case[27] Lord Scarman explained the point by saying that 'the condition must fairly and reasonably relate to the provisions of the development plan and to planning considerations affecting the land'. His Lordship referred specifically to the duty of the local planning authority, in dealing with an application for planning permission, to have regard to the provisions of the development plan and to any other material considerations.[28]

10.32 A condition might be void under this heading if it could be shown to serve some ulterior social or political objective beyond the scope of land use planning. The issue arose in *R v Bristol City Council, ex p Anderson*[29] where planning permission

24 [1958] 1 QB 554, [1958] 1 All ER 625; revsd in part [1960] AC 260, [1959] 3 All ER 1.
25 [1961] AC 636, [1960] 3 All ER 503.
26 [1981] AC 578, [1980] 1 All ER 731.
27 [1981] AC 578, [1980] 1 All ER 731.
28 TCPA 1990, s. 70(2); see discussion at para 8.68.
29 [2000] PLCR 104.

was granted for student accommodation subject to a condition requiring arrangements relating to the supervision, welfare, and support of students (including car parking arrangements) to be approved by the local authority. In proceedings for judicial review, Collins J held that the condition was 'too uncertain and in part at least has little or nothing to do with planning purposes'.

10.33 The Court of Appeal allowed an appeal against this decision—the Court considered that the amenities provided for the student occupiers would have consequences for the impact of the development on the neighbourhood. The condition clearly fulfilled a planning purpose and was not uncertain.[30]

Condition must relate to the permitted development

10.34 A condition will be void if it does not 'fairly and reasonably relate to the permitted development'. The phrase is a dictum of Lord Denning in *Pyx Granite Co Ltd v Ministry of Housing and Local Government*[31] and was adopted by the House of Lords in *Fawcett Properties Ltd v Buckingham County Council*.[32] It goes further than the simple requirement that conditions must serve the broad purposes of planning legislation.

10.35 A condition may serve some useful planning purpose, but nevertheless be invalid because it is not relevant to the particular development permitted by the planning permission.

10.36 This is well illustrated by the case of *Newbury District Council v Secretary of State for the Environment*.[33]

10.37 In 1962 the International Synthetic Rubber Co Ltd applied for planning permission to use two hangars on a disused airfield as warehouses for the storage of synthetic rubber. Planning permission was granted subject to two conditions, one being that the buildings should be removed by 31 December 1972.

10.38 ISR did not remove the buildings by that date, and the local planning authority served an enforcement notice. On appeal, the inspector was of the opinion that the hangars were large, prominent, and ugly in what must have been, and could be, a pleasant rural scene, and ought to be removed. Nevertheless, he considered that the condition was void.

10.39 The condition that two such substantial and existing buildings should be removed would appear to flow from a general wish to restore the area rather than from any

---

[30] As to uncertainty, see para 10.76.
[31] [1958] 1 All ER 625 at 633.
[32] [1961] AC 636, [1960] 3 All ER 503.
[33] [1981] AC 578, [1980] 1 All ER 731. See also *Delta Design and Engineering Ltd v Secretary of State for the Environment* [2000] JPL 726; and *Tarmac Heavy Building Materials United Kingdom v Secretary of State for the Environment, Transport and the Regions* [2000] PLCR 157.

planning need arising from the actual purpose for which the permission was sought. It was not necessary to that purpose, nor the protection of the environment in the fulfilment of that purpose; it was a condition extraneous to the proposed use.

10.40 The Secretary of State accepted his inspector's opinion and quashed the enforcement notice. The case went ultimately to the House of Lords where the Secretary of State's decision was upheld.

A condition must not be manifestly unreasonable

10.41 Even if conditions serve some useful planning purpose they may be quashed if they are unreasonable. But it is the well-settled policy of the courts to interfere only if the condition is wholly unreasonable; that is, such as could find no justification in the minds of reasonable men.[34] Or, as it was put in another case:[35] 'The task of the court is not to decide what it thinks is reasonable but to decide whether the condition imposed by the local authority is one which no reasonable authority acting within the four corners of their jurisdiction could have decided to impose.'

The Shoreham and Hillingdon cases

10.42 It is impossible to give an exhaustive catalogue of what might be considered un reasonable in this sense. But it is clear that it is wholly unreasonable for a local planning authority to impose a condition which requires a developer to take on part of the authority's duties under other legislation. Two cases illustrate this particular point.

10.43 The first of these cases was *Hall & Co Ltd v Shoreham-by-Sea UDC*.[36] The company applied for planning permission to develop some land for industrial purposes. The land adjoined a busy main road, and in granting permission the council imposed a condition requiring the company to construct an ancillary road over their own land along the entire frontage and to give rights of passage over it to and from the adjoining land on either side. The Court of Appeal considered that the condition was unreasonable because it required the company to construct a road and virtually to dedicate it to the public without paying any compensation; 'a more regular course' was open to the council under the Highways Act 1959,[37] that is the council should acquire the land paying proper compensation and then construct the road at public expense.[38]

---

34 *Kruse v Johnson* [1898] 2 QB 91 at 99.

35 *Associated Provincial Picture Houses Ltd v Wednesbury Corpn* [1947] 2 All ER 680 at 684.

36 [1964] 1 All ER 1.

37 Now the Highways Act 1980.

38 In fact today such an objective would be more likely to be achieved by requiring the developer to enter into a planning obligation (see ch 12 below). See also the interesting remarks of Lord

10.44 In *R v Hillingdon London Borough Council, ex p Royco Homes Ltd*,[39] Royco applied for planning permission to develop land for residential purposes. The council granted permission but imposed conditions, among others, that the houses when erected should be occupied at first by persons on the council's housing waiting list, and should for 10 years be occupied by persons enjoying the protection of the Rent Act 1968. The Divisional Court held that these conditions were unreasonable since they were the equivalent of requiring Royco to take on at their own expense a significant part of the duty of the council as a housing authority.

Land not included in the application

10.45 The question of unreasonableness also arises where the local planning authority wish for sound planning reasons to impose a condition affecting land not included in the application. As we have seen, TCPA 1990, s. 72 specifically authorizes the imposition of a condition affecting other land under the control of the applicant,[40] but what if the land is not under the control of the applicant? In most cases such a condition will be unreasonable. Thus in *Peak Park Joint Planning Board v Secretary of State for the Environment and ICI*,[41] Sir Douglas Franks QC, sitting as deputy judge, upheld a decision of the Secretary of State that a condition on a planning permission for quarrying which would have required extensive landscaping would be ultra vires in so far as it affected land not under the control of the applicants. In *Bradford City Metropolitan Council v Secretary of State for the Environment*,[42] the Court of Appeal held that a condition of this sort will be invalid even if the applicant has indicated a willingness to accept it.

10.46 The council had granted planning permission for residential development subject to a condition requiring the widening of an existing road; it seems that the applicants in effect invited the condition by including the land required for that purpose in a revised plan. Subsequently, they appealed on the ground that they did not own all the land affected by the condition. The Secretary of State held that the condition was ultra vires. The Court of Appeal upheld the Secretary of State.

10.47 Lloyd LJ explained the position in this way: 'If the proposed condition was manifestly unreasonable then it was beyond the powers of the planning authority to impose it; and if it was beyond the powers of the planning authority to impose

---

Hoffmann on this case in *Tesco Stores Ltd v Secretary of State for the Environment* [1995] 2 All ER 636, [1995] 1 WLR 759, HL.

39 [1974] QB 720, [1974] 2 All ER 643.

40 See para 8.101.

41 (1979) 39 P & CR 361, [1980] JPL 114.

42 (1986) 53 P & CR 55, [1986] JPL 598.

the condition, then it was beyond their powers to agree to impose it, even if the developer consented . . . Vires could not be conferred by consent.'

10.48 The unlawfulness of this type of condition can create a dilemma since the planning authority may find it undesirable to grant planning permission for development unless, say, access to the site is improved. The difficulty has in practice often been overcome by imposing a 'negative' condition to the effect that the development shall not be commenced until the access has been improved. The principle of the negative condition was approved by the House of Lords in *Grampian Regional Council v City of Aberdeen District Council.*[43] Here, planning permission for industrial development was granted subject to a condition that the developer was not to proceed until a nearby road had been closed. The site of the road formed no part of the application. The House of Lords held the condition valid; according to Lord Keith a condition requiring the developer to take steps to secure the stopping up of the highway would have been invalid as a positive obligation which was outside his powers to guarantee. But a condition phased in strictly negative terms could be perfectly valid, precise, and enforceable. However, in a later case, *Jones v Secretary of State for Wales,*[44] the Court of Appeal took the view that such a condition would be invalid if there was no reasonable prospect of its requirements being fulfilled.

10.49 *Jones v Secretary of State for Wales* was overruled by the House of Lords in *British Railways Board v Secretary of State for the Environment.*[45]

10.50 BRB applied for planning permission to develop a site partly owned by the Hounslow Borough Council. It was proposed that an access road should be built over land owned by the council. On appeal, the inspector recommended that permission should be granted subject to the council entering into an agreement with BRB providing for the construction of the road. However, the council refused to enter into such an agreement on environmental grounds; they considered that the site had a nature conservation interest and public amenity value. The Secretary of State took the view that, as a result of the *Grampian* case, he was precluded in law from granting permission subject to a condition which appeared to have no reasonable prospect of fulfilment within the life of the permission. BRB's application to the High Court was dismissed and that decision was affirmed by the Court of Appeal. The developers appealed to the House of Lords.

10.51 Held: a negative condition was not unreasonable merely because there was no reasonable prospect of it being fulfilled. The appeal was allowed.

43 (1983) 47 P & CR 633.
44 [1990] JPL 907.
45 [1994] JPL 32.

10.52 Lord Keith (who had given judgment in the *Grampian* case itself) placed considerable reliance on the fact that the Planning Act clearly contemplated that a planning application could be made by a person who did not own the land to which it related. The owner might well object and be unwilling that the development should go ahead; however, the mere fact of such objection could not in itself necessarily lead to a refusal. By the same token, the mere fact that 'a desirable condition appeared to have no reasonable prospects of fulfilment did not mean that planning permission must necessarily be refused. Something more was required before that could be the correct result'.

10.53 Notwithstanding the decision in the *British Railways Board* case, a footnote to paragraph 40 of Circular 11/95 states that the judgment leaves open the possibility for the Secretary of State to maintain, as a matter of policy, [that for the imposition of a negative condition], there should be at least reasonable prospects of the action in question being performed within the time-limit imposed by the permission. In *Millington v Secretary of State for the Environment, Transport and the Regions,*[46] Rich J thought that the footnote to paragraph 40 was mistaken, holding that the unlikelihood of the action being performed was not a sufficient reason to refuse planning permission, and 'allowing it to be a policy cannot make it so'. However, in *R v Secretary of State for the Environment, Transport and the Regions, ex p Kohlerdome Corpn,*[47] Dyson J appeared to take a line somewhat at variance with Rich J in the earlier case, holding that the Secretary of State was entitled as a matter of planning judgment to refuse planning permission for the relocation of Luton Town FC's ground on the basis that there was no prospect of the M1 motorway being widened. But in *Merritt v Secretary of State for the Environment, Transport and the Regions,*[48] Robin Purchas QC, sitting as deputy judge, quashed a decision where the policy had been applied mechanically without scope for discretion.

10.54 The validity of a negative condition relating to land both outside the application site and not under the control of the applicant arose in *Davenport v London Borough of Hammersmith and Fulham.*[49]

10.55 Planning permission in connection with motor vehicle repairs was granted subject to a condition that 'no vehicles which have been left with or are in the control of the applicant shall be stored or parked in Tasso Road'. The condition was imposed to avoid obstruction of the surrounding streets and to safeguard their amenity. Tasso Road was a public highway and thus not owned or controlled by the appellant. The Divisional Court upheld the validity of the condition; it was

46 [1999] JPL 644.
47 [1999] JPL 816.
48 [2000] JPL 317.
49 [1999] JPL 1122.

entirely reasonable—the appellant was perfectly able to comply with it and it fairly and reasonably related to the permitted development.

10.56 It would seem there is a general power under TCPA 1990, s. 70 to impose such conditions despite the existence of an express power under TCPA 1990, s. 72.[50] Of course, it might have been very different had the condition required the applicant to carry out works on land not included in the application nor within his control. In *Mouchell Superannuation Fund Trustees v Oxfordshire County Council*,[51] Glidewell LJ asserted in no uncertain terms that such a condition was outside the powers of the Act.

Derogation from the grant

10.57 Lord Keith, in the *British Railways Board* case (above), appeared expressly to leave open the possibility that a condition might be unlawful if it derogated from the grant of permission in some way. This is interesting because there is some authority that a condition may be unreasonable if it enables a third party to frustrate the planning permission. In *Kingsway Investments (Kent) Ltd v Kent County Council*,[52] the defendants had granted outline permission subject to the conditions (i) that detailed plans should be submitted to and approved by them before any work was begun, and (ii) that the permission should cease to have effect after three years unless within that time such approval had been notified. The plaintiffs submitted detailed plans, but they were not approved, and the three years ran out. The Court of Appeal, by a majority, held that the second condition was void. Davies LJ pointed out that the permission might lapse without any default on the part of the plaintiffs; 'the defendants are taking away with one hand that which they have purported to grant with the other and are thus evading the revocation procedure'. This, therefore, lends some support to the view that a condition is unreasonable if it puts certain matters out of the control of the developer, but it may be that in the final analysis the learned Lord Justice was basing himself on the point about the revocation procedure. Winn LJ held the condition to be invalid on different grounds, but made this significant remark: 'Nonetheless the characteristic of deprivation of ability to secure by his own efforts full enjoyment of the fruits of the permission granted to him is an important feature of the condition challenged.'

10.58 The House of Lords—again by a majority—found a somewhat ingenious method of holding the condition valid thereby reversing the decision of the Court of

50 See para 8.101.
51 [1992] 1 PLR 97.
52 [1969] 2 QB 332, [1969] 1 All ER 601.

Appeal.[53] It is submitted, however, that the reasons adduced were entirely consistent with the views quoted above.

10.59 The principle that a planning permission must not derogate from the grant of the original permission has been applied by the Court of Appeal in *Redrow Homes Ltd v First Secretary of State*.[54] In 1957 outline planning permission was granted for commercial and industrial development which allowed for the construction of access points onto a public highway, subject to a condition that they were not to be built until approved by the local planning authority. The developer applied for approval of access points but that application was not considered within the requisite time limit and so the developer appealed to the Secretary of State against a deemed refusal. Approval was given but the use of the access points was limited to public service vehicles. The developer challenged that decision and it was held in the High Court that the imposition of the limitation was an error of law because it substantially modified and derogated from the permission of 1957. The Court of Appeal upheld that decision. Such a modification of a planning permission can normally only be achieved under statutory powers and on payment of compensation.[55]

Restriction of existing use rights

10.60 There is also the question whether the local planning authority can impose conditions which deprive a landowner of existing use rights. Of course, there will be many cases in which the proposed development cannot be carried out without destroying existing use rights. The problem arises where the local planning authority seek to impose conditions restricting existing use rights which are not necessarily incompatible with the proposed development. The point is illustrated by *Allnatt London Properties Ltd v Middlesex County Council*[56] in which planning permission was granted for an extension to a factory subject to conditions which restricted occupation of the existing factory to firms already established in the locality. It was held that these conditions were void as being unreasonable.

10.61 This was followed by the decision of the House of Lords in *Minister of Housing and Local Government v Hartnell*[57] where their Lordships relied on the principle that a statute should not be held to take away private rights of property without compensation unless the intention to do so is expressed in clear and unambiguous terms. On the basis of these authorities it seemed reasonable in some earlier editions of this book to suggest that a local planning authority should not attempt

53 [1971] AC 72, [1970] 1 All ER 70. And see para 10.96.
54 [2004] EWCA Civ 1375.
55 See para 11.01.
56 (1964) 15 P & CR 288.
57 [1965] AC 1134, [1965] 1 All ER 490.

to restrict existing use rights by attaching conditions to a grant of planning permission; the more regular course would be for the authority to make an order under what is now TCPA 1990, s. 102, paying compensation accordingly.

10.62 However, it appears in the light of subsequent case law that this proposition may not be correct. In the case of *Kingston-upon-Thames Royal London Borough Council v Secretary of State for the Environment*[58] Lord Widgery CJ said that there is no principle of planning law which requires a local planning authority to refrain from imposing conditions abrogating existing use rights.

10.63 The British Railways Board applied for planning permission for the reconstruction of a railway station. Permission was granted subject to the condition that a certain piece of land should be made available at all times for car parking and should be used 'for no other purpose'.

10.64 A main electric traction cable ran across this piece of land. When the Board failed to remove the cable, the council served an enforcement notice. On appeal the Secretary of State quashed the notice; the condition was ultra vires in that it prevented the lawful use of land without compensation.

10.65 Held: the Secretary of State had erred in law, and the case should be remitted to him for further consideration of the merits of the condition.

10.66 This decision might appear to be quite contrary to the decision of the House of Lords in *Minister of Housing and Local Government v Hartnell*[59] but the Divisional Court considered that that case had been decided on special facts relating to an application under the Caravan Sites and Control of Development Act 1960.

Unenforceable conditions

10.67 What is the position where a condition is unenforceable in the sense that the local planning authority have no power to secure compliance with it? In British Airports Authority v Secretary of State for Scotland,[60] the Secretary of State imposed a condition on a planning consent for airport development which was designed to control the direction of take-off and landing of aircraft. The applicants had no control over these matters since the power to prescribe the direction of flights lay with the Civil Aviation Authority. Since the applicants had no power over the Authority to bring about the desired result, other than persuasion, the condition was incapable of enforcement and the local planning authority had no power to enforce it.

---

58 [1974] 1 All ER 193, [1973] 1 WLR 1549.

59 See para 10.61.

60 1979 SC 200. The decision was approved by the House of Lords *in Grampian Regional Council v City of Aberdeen District Council* (1983) 47 P & CR 633. Enforceability was also in issue in *R v Rochdale Metropolitan Borough Council, ex p Tew* [1999] JPL 54.

General principles

10.68 As mentioned above, the courts will interfere only if the condition is wholly unreasonable. For instance, the courts will not consider whether a condition is unduly burdensome or whether a different condition might not have been reasonable in the circumstances. It might well be asked why the courts should not quash a condition if it is unreasonable in this more general sense. The courts will consider the question of reasonableness or the merits of some action where a statute specifically requires a public authority to act reasonably or where a statute provides a right of appeal to the courts against the decision of a local authority. But where (as in the case of the Planning Act and many other statutes) there is no specific mention of reasonableness, it is the general policy of the courts not to intervene. Thus, in *Associated Provincial Picture Houses Ltd v Wednesbury Corpn*,[61] the proprietors of a cinema had applied to the local authority under the Sunday Entertainments Act 1932 for a licence to open on Sundays. The licence was granted subject to a condition that children under 15 should not be admitted whether accompanied by an adult or not. The plaintiffs sought a declaration that the condition was invalid. The Court of Appeal held that it was lawful for the corporation to take into consideration matters affecting the well-being and the physical and mental health of children. That, said the court, ended the matter: 'Once that is granted, counsel must go so far as to say that the decision of the authority is wrong because it is unreasonable, and then he is really saying that the ultimate arbiter of what is and is not reasonable is the court and not the local authority. It is just there, it seems to me, that the whole argument entirely breaks down. It is perfectly clear that the local authority are entrusted by Parliament with the decision on a matter in which the knowledge and experience of the authority can best be trusted to be of value.'[62]

10.69 The courts have adopted a similar policy in relation to byelaws made by local authorities. Although it is said that the validity of a byelaw may be questioned on the grounds of unreasonableness, it is clear that a byelaw will only be held to be unreasonable if it is manifestly unjust or oppressive[63] or if its application in a particular case would serve no useful purpose.[64] Byelaws made by local authorities being bodies of a public representative character entrusted by Parliament with delegated authority should be supported if possible.[65]

---

61 [1948] 1 KB 223, [1947] 2 All ER 680.

62 Per Lord Greene MR at 683.

63 *Kruse v Johnson* [1898] 2 QB 91.

64 See for instance *Repton School Governors v Repton RDC* [1918] 2 KB 133; and *A-G v Denby* [1925] Ch 596—both cases concerning the application of building byelaws as to space about buildings.

65 *Kruse v Johnson*, (1898) 2 QB 91.

10.70 The idea that the local authority are likely to be the best judges of what is reasonable has been expressed in a number of cases. It is not, however, the invariable policy of the courts to trust the local authority. For instance, the court will consider whether local authority expenditure is reasonable—even where statute empowers authorities to pay such wages as 'they think fit'[66]—apparently on the ground that local authorities have a fiduciary responsibility to their ratepayers.

10.71 Finally, it may be noted that the courts are no more likely to question the reasonableness of a condition imposed by the Secretary of State (or his inspector) on a grant of planning permission. Indeed, in *Sparks v Edward Ash Ltd*[67]—a case in which it was contended that certain traffic regulations were unreasonable—the Court of Appeal said that, 'If it is the duty of the courts to recognize and trust the discretion of local authorities, much more must it be so in the case of a Minister directly responsible to Parliament.'

Condition restricting use of premises according to personal circumstances of occupier

10.72 An example is the condition imposed in *Fawcett Properties Ltd v Buckingham County Council*[68] restricting the use of the cottages to agricultural occupants. The validity of such conditions was expressly upheld in that case.

10.73 It should be noticed that there is a difference in principle between a condition of this type and a personal planning permission. In the one case the permission runs with the land, although subject to a condition as to the persons who may occupy it; in the other, the permission itself is personal and does not run with the land.

10.74 Personal occupancy conditions can, however, give rise to difficult problems of construction. In *Knott v Secretary of State for the Environment*,[69] planning permission was granted for the erection of a house in rural Cornwall, subject to a condition that the permission 'shall enure solely for the benefit of Mr and Mrs A Knott'.

10.75 The intention of the local planning authority had been that only the Knotts should occupy the building. Although finding for the Secretary of State on the basis that he would have arrived at the same decision despite the error of law, Rich J considered that the form of the condition was not appropriate to meet the authority's desired objective. The learned judge held that the condition was 'spent' upon implementation and could not control the building's subsequent use—occupancy by someone other than the Knotts would not involve a material change of use.[70]

---

66 *Roberts v Hopwood* [1925] AC 578.

67 [1943] 1 KB 223, [1943] 1 All ER 1.

68 [1961] AC 636, [1960] 3 All ER 503.

69 [1997] JPL 713.

70 The court arrived at this (perhaps surprising) result by applying *Cynon Valley v Secretary of State for Wales* (1987) 53 P & CR 68 and *Wilson v West Sussex County Council* [1963] 2 QB 764, [1963] 1 All ER 751. A sequel to the *Knott* case is discussed at para 12.86.

Condition may be void for uncertainty

10.76 A condition will be void for uncertainty 'if it can be given no meaning or no sensible or ascertainable meaning'.[71] This involves more than ambiguity; if the wording of a condition is ambiguous (that is, capable of more than one meaning) the court can determine which is the correct meaning. But a condition may be so ill-worded that the court cannot resolve the doubt. Thus in *R v Secretary of State for the Environment, ex p Watney Mann (Midlands) Ltd*,[72] the local justices had made an order under the Public Health Act 1936, s. 94(2) requiring the abatement of nuisance caused by music played in a public house; the order required that the level of noise in the premises should not exceed 70 decibels. The Divisional Court considered that the order was void for uncertainty because it did not specify the position where the decibel reading was to be taken.

10.77 In *M J Shanley Ltd v Secretary of State for the Environment and South Bedfordshire District Council*,[73] in an attempt to overcome objections to development in the green belt, the appellants offered a condition that the first opportunity to buy the houses should be given to local people. The Secretary of State considered that this condition would be invalid and unenforceable. In the High Court Woolf J agreed that the condition would be invalid and unenforceable; it did not give any indication at all as to the method or terms upon which the first opportunity was to be offered.

10.78 In *Fawcett Properties Ltd v Buckingham County Council*,[74] the county council had granted planning permission for two cottages in the green belt subject to the condition that 'the occupation of the houses shall be limited to persons whose employment or latest employment is or was employment in agriculture as defined by TCPA 1990, s. 119(1)[75] or in forestry or in an industry mainly dependent upon agriculture and including also the dependants of such persons as aforesaid'. The House of Lords, by a majority, held that the condition was not void for uncertainty. It was not necessary to the validity of the condition to identify all the persons who might at any point be eligible to occupy the cottages, the owner's obligation was to satisfy himself that any proposed occupier would come within the definition.

10.79 It seems that in the borderline cases the benefit of the doubt will be given to the local planning authority.[76]

---

71 *Fawcett Properties Ltd v Buckingham County Council* [1960] 3 All ER 503 at 517, per Lord Denning.
72 [1976] JPL 368.
73 [1982] JPL 380.
74 See para 10.28.
75 Now TCPA 1990, s 336(1).
76 *Crisp from the Fens Ltd v Rutland County Council* (1950) 48 LGR 210.

Special types of condition

Conditions restricting use of buildings

10.80 A grant of permission for the erection of a building may specify the purposes for which the building may be used; and if no purpose is specified, the permission is to be construed as including permission to use the building for the purpose for which it is designed.[77]

10.81 The effect of this may be illustrated by some examples. In some cases it may be sufficient to incorporate the terms of the application in the grant of planning permission; thus, permission for a dwellinghouse may state that 'the local planning authority hereby grant planning permission for the erection of a dwellinghouse in accordance with the application and plans dated . . .' However, where application is made for permission to erect a building for industrial use, the planning authority may wish to impose a condition restricting such use to light industrial purposes. But, as we have seen, in the current Use Classes Order light industry falls within Class B1 (business) which also includes office and research and development.[78] This raises the question whether the planning authority can impose a condition to preclude the right to change from light industry to the other purposes comprised in Class B1, or even to restrict the industrial use to a particular type of manufacture such as micro-engineering. The difficulty about such a condition is that it attempts to prevent something which by the terms of the TCPA 1990 is not development at all, and it might be argued that planning control should not restrict matters which do not involve development. On the other hand, it seems reasonable that in permitting development the planning authority should be enabled to impose this type of condition provided it fairly and reasonably relates to the permitted development. This view of the matter was upheld by Talbot J in *City of London Corpn v Secretary of State for the Environment*[79] and in the case of *Camden London Borough Council v Secretary of State for the Environment*[80] it appears to have been taken for granted that a condition could be imposed to preclude the right under Class B1 to change from light industry to offices. Indeed, the argument that planning control should not restrict matters which are not development was firmly rejected by Sir Graham Eyre QC (sitting as deputy judge) in *Mirai Networks Ltd v Secretary of State for the Environment*.[81] Here a condition which potentially restricted the carrying out of works which are not under

77 TCPA 1990, s. 75(2), (3).
78 See para 6.89.
79 (1971) 23 P & CR 169.
80 [1989] JPL 613.
81 [1994] JPL 337.

development under TCPA 1990, s. 55(2)(a)[82] was upheld. The learned deputy judge considered that the condition in question related to a legitimate planning objection of importance.

10.82 Where such conditions as considered above are imposed, application can always be made for permission for the retention of the building or the continuance of the use without complying with the condition.[83]

Conditions restricting permitted development

10.83 A somewhat similar problem arises in connection with conditions restricting the right to carry out development permitted by the General Permitted Development Order. For instance, a planning authority might wish when granting permission for building a new house to impose a condition excluding the right to extend it under Part 1 of the Order. Or, on a grant of permission for mineral working, the authority might wish to impose conditions as to the siting of plant and machinery required for the treatment of the excavated mineral, thus restricting the mineral operator's rights under Part 19.

10.84 Such conditions appear to be authorized by article 3(4) of the General Permitted Development Order, which provides that 'nothing in this order permits development contrary to any condition imposed by any planning permission granted or deemed to be granted under Part III of the Act otherwise than by this order'.

10.85 The legality of restricting permitted development rights was implicitly recognized in *Dunoon Developments v Secretary of State for the Environment*.[84] However, it seems that for a condition to achieve the effect of restricting General Permitted Development Order rights, it must be worded in clear and unequivocal language.

10.86 In *Dunoon* planning permission was granted in 1956 for the erection of a car showroom subject to a condition that the use of the premises should be 'limited' to the display and sale of cars and associated activities; no heavy repairs or noisy activities were to be carried out. This was to preserve the amenities of a residential area. In 1990 the site was acquired by D who opened an indoor market, relying on Part 3 of the GDO 1988 which permitted a change of use from use for the sale etc, of motor vehicles to use as a shop under Class A1.

10.87 Held: the condition did not have the effect of excluding Part 3 of the GDO. The condition made no express exclusion of the GDO, nor could it be implied from the words themselves, in the context they were used.

---

82 See para 6.16.

83 TCPA 1990, s. 73. See para 10.99.

84 [1992] JPL 936, CA; see also *Carpet Decor (Guildford) Ltd v Secretary of State for the Environment* [1981] JPL 806; *Gill v Secretary of State for the Environment* [1985] JPL 710.

10.88 Sir Donald Nichols V-C said that the condition in question delimited or circumscribed the ambit of the permitted use, but no more; it was not apt to negative development under any existing or future General [Permitted] Development Order.

Conditions limiting period of permission

10.89 As we have seen, conditions may be imposed limiting the period for which permission is granted (a 'term consent'). The proper form of such a condition is indicated by TCPA 1990, s. 72(1)(b); namely, it should require the buildings or works to be removed or the use to be discontinued at the expiration of a specified period. This form is not always adopted in practice; for instance, the Secretary of State's decision on an appeal may state that 'the Secretary of State hereby gives permission for a period of five years'. The effect of such words was considered by the Court of Appeal in *Francis v Yiewsley and West Drayton UDC*,[85] in which the Minister on appeal granted permission for the retention of some unauthorized caravans 'for a period of six months from the date of this letter'. It was held that there was an implied condition that the caravans should be removed at the end of the six-month period.

10.90 Such a conclusion as above may not be tenable in light of the decision in *I'm Your Man Ltd v Secretary of State for the Environment*.[86] In this case it was held by Robin Purchas QC, sitting as deputy judge, that a planning permission 'for a temporary period of seven years' was effectively a permission for an unlimited period, ie the limitation carried no force. The basis of this was the court's conclusion that the legislation gave no power to impose limitations other than by development order.[87] Further, the local planning authority had failed to impose the condition under s. 72(1)(b) of TCPA 1990. The statute provided a procedure for achieving the objective sought by the local planning authority and they had not used that procedure.

10.91 On the expiry of a temporary permission, application may be made under TCPA 1990, s. 73A for permission to retain the buildings or works or continue the use in question. Alternatively, the previous normal use of the land may be resumed without applying for permission, provided the previous use was not instituted in breach of planning control.[88]

---

85 [1958] 1 QB 478, [1957] 3 All ER 529.
86 (1998) 77 P & CR 251.
87 This aspect of the decision is considered more fully at para 10.111.
88 TCPA 1990, s. 57(2), (5), (6). See also para 7.06.

Effect of striking out conditions

10.92 Although it is clear that the courts will in suitable cases declare a condition invalid, the effect on the permission is uncertain. Does the permission remain in force shorn of the condition, or does the permission itself fall with it?

10.93 There seem to be three possible answers to this question. There are dicta which appear to suggest that, if a condition is declared void, the permission automatically falls with it. At the opposite extreme there are some dicta which suggest that the permission should always stand. But the weight of opinion appears to be in favour of an intermediate position, that is, that the permission will fall if the offending condition is of fundamental importance but not if it is trivial or unimportant.

10.94 In *Pyx Granite Co Ltd v Minister of Housing and Local Government*, Hodson LJ was of the opinion that 'it would not be open for the court to leave the permission shorn of its conditions or any of them'.[89] But since the Court of Appeal were unanimous in holding that permissions were required and that the condition was proper, the point did not require decision by the court. The House of Lords subsequently held that permission was not required, so that the validity of the condition did not arise and there was no discussion on the possible effect of invalidating it.

10.95 These remarks of Hodson LJ were adopted by the Court of Appeal in *Hall & Co Ltd v Shoreham-by-Sea UDC*:[90] in that case, however, it was obvious that the conditions in question were fundamental to the whole of the planning permission, and the council were granted a declaration that the permission was consequently null and void. But in some later cases, the permission has been allowed to stand. Moreover, the judgments in that case recognized that it might be permissible to sever an offending condition if it were merely trivial or unimportant. So in *Allnatt London Properties v Middlesex County Council*,[91] Glyn-Jones J considered himself free in the circumstances of that case to hold that the planning permission should stand, shorn of the offending condition.

10.96 Such was the state of the authorities when the matter came up again in *Kent County Council v Kingsway Investments (Kent) Ltd*.[92] The Court of Appeal, having declared the condition void, held that the permission remained in force.[93] The condition in question related, said Davies LJ, not to the development itself but to matters preparatory or introductory to the permission; it was unimportant to the

[89] [1958] 1 QB 554, [1958] 1 All ER 625 at 637.
[90] [1964] 1 All ER 1.
[91] (1964) 15 P & CR 288.
[92] [1971] AC 72, [1970] 1 All ER 70.
[93] [1969] 2 QB 332, [1969] 1 All ER 601.

development itself. Winn LJ went further: 'if it [the condition] is void it can have no effect on the force of the permission itself'.

10.97 However, in the House of Lords, the majority of their Lordships held that the condition was valid. They nevertheless went on to consider whether the permission would have stood if they had decided that the condition was void. Lord Morris of Borth-y-Gest and Lord Donovan said that there might be cases in which unimportant or incidental conditions were superimposed on the permission; if such conditions were held to be void, the permission might be allowed to survive. But in the present case the condition was not trivial or unimportant. It would seem therefore that their Lordships did not accept the distinction drawn by Davies LJ between conditions relating to the development itself and conditions of a preparatory nature. And Lord Guest seems to have thought that the permission would always fail, even apparently where the offending condition was unimportant.[94]

10.98 It seems that the correct approach is to consider whether the condition is fundamental to the permission; in other words would the planning authority have granted permission without the condition in question.

10.99 There may be, however, a means by which a developer may avoid the loss of a planning permission due to a condition being held to be fundamental. This is by submitting an application under TCPA 1990, s. 73.

10.100 TCPA 1990, s. 73 permits an application for planning permission for the development of land without complying with conditions subject to which a previous planning permission was granted. The crucial point is that the local planning authority must consider *only the question of the conditions* to which the subsequent permission should be granted. On such an application, the local planning authority may grant permission subject to different conditions, grant permission unconditionally, or they may refuse the application. In the case of a refusal, the planning permission stands subject to the conditions previously attached. Under TCPA 1990, s. 78 the developer may appeal to the Secretary of State and under TCPA 1990, s. 288 there is a right of challenge on a point of law in the High Court.[95] Although the local planning authority may impose different conditions on a new permission under TCPA 1990, s. 73, it seems that the conditions must be such that they do not amount to a fundamental alteration of the original application. In *R v Coventry City Council, ex p Arrowcroft Group plc*,[96] the original permission allowed for a food superstore, a variety superstore, and smaller shop units. The application under TCPA 1990, s. 73 sought variation of the conditions with a

---

94 The approach of Lord Morris in the *Kingsway* case was applied by the Court of Appeal in *Fisher v Wychavon District Council* [2001] JPL 694.

95 See para 20.07.

96 [2001] PLCR 113.

different food operator and up to six comparison stores instead of a variety superstore. Sullivan J quashed the authority's resolution to grant planning permission; whatever the planning merits of the new proposal, the authority had no power under TCPA 1990, s. 73 to vary the conditions in this manner.

10.101 TCPA 2004, s. 73 has been amended by PCPA 2004, s. 51(3) so as to provide that planning permission cannot be granted under s. 73 so as to change an existing condition by extending the time within which the development must be started or an application for approval of reserved matters must be made. The case law giving rise to this amendment is discussed later in this chapter.[97]

Limitations

10.102 A grant of planning permission may be circumscribed not only by the conditions attached to it, but also by limitations inherent in the permission itself. The principle was first recognized in relation to the permissions granted by general development orders. To take one example: Class I of the 1977 Order permitted the extension of a dwellinghouse so long as the cubic content was not exceeded by certain limits, although some express conditions were attached, the restriction relating to cubic content was not a condition but was contained in the words whereby the permission was granted. (The current General Permitted Development Order has moved away from limits on volume.[98])

10.103 In the past, the courts have recognized that the principle applied to planning permissions granted on an application. In *Wilson v West Sussex County Council*,[99] planning permission had been granted for an 'agricultural cottage . . . in the terms of and subject to compliance with the details specified in plan and application No LG/2/56a submitted to the council on 23 July 1959, and any relevant correspondence'. The Court of Appeal, having regard to the wording of the planning permission and the application and correspondence specifically incorporated, held that the phrase 'agricultural cottage' limited the user of the building; the first occupant must therefore be someone engaged in agriculture. The court was not prepared to say whether subsequent occupation by a person not engaged in agriculture would be a material change of use.

10.104 In the later case of *Kwik Save Discount Group Ltd v Secretary of State for Wales*,[100] the Court of Appeal looked at the whole context of the application in deciding that the planning permission was subject to a limitation.

---

97 See para 10.136.
98 See para 7.17.
99 [1963] 2 QB 764, [1963] 1 All ER 751.
100 (1980) 42 P & CR 166.

10.105 A petrol station and garage included a large building used as a workshop. Planning permission was granted for 'alterations and extensions to Swifts Service Station . . . in accordance with the plan and application submitted to the council'. The application included 'Conversion of existing workshops to retail show room . . . Existing showroom to shop for retail of motor vehicle accessories and petroleum products'. No express restriction was placed on the character or nature of the goods that could be sold in the retail showroom. Subsequently the appellants acquired an interest in the workshop though not in the remaining part of the garage premises; they proceeded to use it as a retail supermarket for the sale of groceries, bread, meat, etc. The Secretary of State dismissed an appeal against an enforcement notice requiring the discontinuance of the use as a supermarket.

10.106 In the Court of Appeal counsel for the Secretary of State conceded that the appeal building was not to be used for a purpose ancillary to the service station but contended that it was to be used as a constituent part of it or of the overall site.

10.107 The application had been made by Esso: it was for the use of the appeal building as a retail showroom: the plans showed that it was designed as a car showroom: what was permitted were alterations and extensions to the service station; one of those was to one building on a site that was part of a larger site with other buildings being altered and extended.

10.108 The Court of Appeal held that these items in the application and grant pointed to the permission being limited to the use of the retail showroom for the sale of cars.

10.109 The TCPA 1990 expressly provides that the local planning authority may issue an enforcement notice in respect of failure to comply with any limitation subject to which planning permission has been granted.

10.110 Thus, if it is the intention of the local planning authority when granting planning permission that the use of land or buildings should be restricted, it is better to impose an express condition than to rely on any apparent restrictions inherent in the permission; a well-worded condition will prevent arguments about the interpretation of the permission and will also make it clear that the restriction is binding on subsequent occupants.[101]

10.111 In some previous editions of the book it was suggested that this reference to limitations lent support to the proposition that the limitations could be imposed on an express grant of planning permission. Such a theory requires re-examination in the light of the decision in *I'm Your Man v Secretary of State for the Environment*.[102]

---

[101] See for example *Northampton Borough Council v First Secretary of State* [2005] 7 EGCS 142. Cf the decision of the same judge (Sullivan J) in *Sevenoaks Borough Council v First Secretary of State* [2005] 1 P & CR 13.

[102] See para 10.90.

10.112 In that case the court examined the history of the enforcement provisions in the planning legislation and concluded that there was no power in the TCPA 1990 to impose limitations on the grant of planning permission pursuant to an application. Consequently, the references to breaches of limitation in the enforcement provisions under TCPA 1990, Part VII were to limitations inherent in permitted development rights granted by development order.

Duration of permissions

10.113 Prior to 1969 a planning permission might remain unused indefinitely unless a condition had been attached requiring work to be commenced within a specified period. Although such conditions might lawfully be imposed local planning authorities made little use of them; and in some areas unused planning permissions accumulated to the extent of becoming a serious problem. The local planning authority had no means of knowing whether the land would in fact be developed and, if so, when; developers complained that the planning authority were acting unreasonably in refusing permission to develop other land.

10.114 The TCPA 1968 introduced provisions designed to overcome these problems, and these are to be found in the TCPA 1990. As originally enacted, these provisions provided that every new planning permission was deemed to be subject to a condition that development should be commenced within five years or such other period as the planning authority may expressly impose. However, the relevant provision of TCPA 1990 has been amended by PCPA 2004, s. 51, with the effect that the time limit has been reduced from five years to three years or such other period as the authority might impose.[103] This reduction in the life of planning consents proved highly controversial and encountered fierce opposition from the development industry. The government's stated purpose in the reform was to encourage development to take place at an early stage; however the three-year period may be wholly inadequate for some developments, especially those requiring extensive measures before works can begin, eg environmental clean-up, land assembly, or the stopping up or diversion of highways. In such cases, local planning authorities may wish to use their powers to vary the time limit, particularly in the case of larger-scale development. In the case of outline permissions, the deemed condition under the old law was to the effect that application for approval of reserved matters had to be made within three years, and that the development must be begun within five years of the date on which the outline permission was granted or within two years of the grant of approval, whichever was the later;

[103] TCPA 1990, s. 91 as amended. The provision was brought into force in relation to England by SI 2005 No 2081.

here again the planning authority might impose different periods. Under PCPA 2004[104] the reference to an overall time limit of five years is dispensed with, but the period of three years for applying for approval of reserved matters remains—the development must be begun within two years of their final approval. Planning permissions granted before 1969 were made subject to retrospective conditions and have now lapsed if they remained unused after a transitional period.[105] The period within which the development must be begun will be extended by one year if legal proceedings are brought to challenge the validity of the planning permission. This is a new provision introduced by PCPA 2004.[106]

10.115 Under s. 56 of TCPA 1990, development will be deemed to have been commenced when a start is made on any of the following 'material operations':[107]

(a) Any work of demolition of a building;[108]
(b) Any work of construction in the course of the erection of a building;
(c) The digging of a trench which is to contain the foundations, or part of the foundations, of a building;
(d) The laying of any underground main or pipe to the foundations, or part of the foundations, of a building or to any such trench as is mentioned above;
(e) Any operation in the course of laying out or constructing a road or part of a road;
(f) Any change in the use of any land, where that change constitutes 'material development'.[109]

10.116 In *United Refineries Ltd v Essex County Council*,[110] planning permission for the development of 262 acres for an oil refinery was granted subject to the condition that 'the building and other operations hereby permitted' should be commenced by a specified date. The plaintiffs had constructed a temporary access road and stripped topsoil in preparation for the erection of some buildings; it was held that the plaintiffs had complied with the condition. It may even be sufficient to start digging a trench for the foundation of a building, and it is easy to imagine that there will be cases in which a trench will be dug and nothing more done for a

104 TCPA 1990, s. 92 as amended by PCPA 2004, s. 51(2)(a).
105 TCPA 1971, Sch 24, para 18; Planning (Consequential Provisions) Act 1990, Sch 3, para 3.
106 TCPA 1990, s. 91, ss (3A)–(3C) as inserted by PCPA 2004, s. 51(1).
107 TCPA 1990, s. 56(1), (2), (4).
108 Inserted by PCA 1991, Sch 7, para 10. See *Field v First Secretary of State* [2004] EWHC 147 (Admin)—demolition occurring before PCA 1991 came into force was held to be a material operation as the demolition was authorized by the LPA.
109 'Material development' means: (a) any development permitted by the current General Permitted Development Order; (b) certain forms of development falling within TCPA 1990, Sch 3, paras 1, 3 and 5; (c) any other development prescribed by the Secretary of State: TCPA 1990, s. 56(5).
110 [1978] JPL 110.

number of years. If this happens, the local planning authority will be able to serve a 'completion notice', stating that the planning permission will cease to have effect if the development is not completed within such period as may be specified. This is discussed below.

10.117 Until recently, it seemed that the correct test to be applied to establish whether a 'material operation' had been started was not whether by his actions the developer intended to keep the permission alive, but whether he intended to go on with the development.[111]

10.118 This approach was taken in several cases, including *R v Arfon Borough Council, ex p Walton Commercial Group Ltd.*[112]

10.119 Planning permission to develop a site for housing had been granted in 1958 and 1967. In early 1967 a trench was dug and a road constructed. Evidence was adduced that these works had been carried out in order to establish the value of the land under the [since repealed] Land Commission Act 1967—the purpose being to minimize liability for betterment levy. The works were not carried out in order to commence development.

10.120 The applicant claimed that these works were sufficient to preserve the permissions, as being development commenced before the beginning of 1968, the material date for keeping the permissions alive.

10.121 Held: the application failed. Where works were done simply in order to fix the value of the land for statutory purposes, rather than to commence the actual development, such works could not constitute the commencement of the development.

10.122 Placing some reliance on the decision of the Court of Appeal in *Malvern Hills District Council v Secretary of State for the Environment*,[113] Buxton J considered that the purpose of the statutory provisions was that existing permissions were not kept in abeyance forever without being implemented. He said: '[a] planning authority which gave permission to something in 1958 may well have a different view of planning circumstances in 1995. If that is right, it would be rather surprising if commencement of development could be satisfied purely by digging a ditch in 1967, thereby freezing the planning situation on a very large site for . . . some 28 years.'

10.123 What was required, therefore, was an ongoing intention to develop, rather than an intention simply to extend the life of the permission.[114]

---

111 *Hillingdon London Borough Council v Secretary of State for the Environment* [1990] JPL 575.

112 [1997] JPL 237.

113 [1983] 46 P & CR 58.

114 The court also held that the works did not suffice because they were in breach of condition and that implementation would have been physically impossible.

10.124 In the slightly later case of *Agecrest Ltd v Gwynedd County Council*,[115] the facts were similar in that works were carried out in 1967 in pursuance of a planning permission granted in 1964, the owners wishing to avoid the effect of impending legislation which would have limited the life of the permission. They also wished to avoid the impact of betterment levy. Collins J held that there must be an intention to develop for works to constitute the implementation of a planning permission and this intent must not be 'colourable'. However, the intention to develop need not be immediate. Of course, as the learned judge said: '. . . the longer the time that elapses the less chance there will be that a court will accept that there was an intention to develop at the material time or that what was done was genuinely done for the purpose of carrying out the development.'

10.125 On the evidence, Collins J was satisfied that work was being done after 1967 to progress the development—accordingly, he granted a declaration that the planning permission of 1964 was still valid.

10.126 However the decision of David Vaughan QC, sitting as deputy judge, in *Riordan Communications Ltd v South Buckinghamshire District Council*,[116] represents a fresh and, perhaps, welcome departure. The learned deputy judge effectively followed a unanimous decision of the Inner House of the Court of Session in Scotland dealing with similar provisions in the Scottish planning legislation. In *East Dunbartonshire Council v Secretary of State for Scotland*,[117] the Scottish court rejected the notion that, in order to keep a planning permission alive, the works must be genuinely done for the purpose of carrying out the development. The statute provided what works needed to be done on the site in order to keep the permission alive, and that was all that was required. In *Riordan* the deputy judge thought that there was no justification in the terms or structure of the legislation for the ill-defined requirement that the operation should be carried out with some particular intention. Thus the test is an objective one—the subjective intention of the developer is irrelevant on the question of whether development has commenced.[118]

10.127 In practice, the possibility of saving planning permissions under TCPA 1990, s. 56 is limited by the principle that the works in question must not contravene the conditions of the planning permission itself—the so-called 'Whitley' principle.[119]

---

115 [1998] JPL 325, [1996] NPC 106.

116 [2000] 1 PLR 45.

117 [1999] 1 PLR 53.

118 David Vaughan QC placed considerable reliance on the HL decision in *Pioneer Aggregates (UK) Ltd v Secretary of State for the Environment* [1985] AC 132, [1984] 2 All ER 358; see para 10.145.

119 *Whitley & Sons Co Ltd v Secretary of State for Wales* [1992] JPL 856. And see the CA decisions in *Daniel Platt Ltd v Secretary of State for the Environment* [1997] JPL 349 and *Staffordshire County Council v Riley* [2002] PLCR 75.

Thus, it is not uncommon for planning permission to be granted subject to a condition that no working should be carried out except in accordance with a scheme to be agreed by the local planning authority. This is particularly common in relation to minerals permissions. If the developers are unable to reach agreement with the authority, then the permission cannot be saved by works purporting to rely on TCPA 1990, s. 56. Such works would not comply with the planning permission and would constitute a breach of planning control.

10.128 The courts have in the past been prepared to recognize certain exceptions to the Whitley principle. First, where the local planning authority agree to allow the development to commence without full compliance with conditions, it has been held that the works may amount to a commencement of the development.[120] Secondly, the condition in question may have in substance been complied with but the formalities, eg a written notice of approval, have not been fulfilled by the time works commence on site. In such circumstances the local planning authority may decide not to take enforcement action.[121] Thirdly, the developer may have applied for approval before the relevant date and the approval was subsequently granted so that no enforcement action could be taken in respect of the works in question.[122]

10.129 However, a warning note was sounded regarding the exceptions by Richards J in *Coghurst Wood Leisure Park Ltd v Secretary of State for Transport, Local Government and the Regions.*[123] He said that it could not be assumed that the exceptions to the Whitley principle previously found to exist would still apply as any exceptions to that principle required reappraisal in the light of the *Powergen* and *Reprotech* cases.[124] It may be recalled that these cases established that it is unhelpful to introduce private law concepts into planning law, for example the notion that a local planning authority could be estopped by their conduct from taking enforcement action.

10.130 These issues came up in *R (on the application of Hammerton) v London Underground Ltd*[125] where planning permissions and listed building consents[126] had been granted for the construction of the East London extension line. The applicant contended that the consents had lapsed as no material operations had been carried out by January 2002, or that such works as had commenced were in breach of condition. The scheme was controversial as it involved works of demolition to the

120 *Agecrest Ltd v Gwynedd County Council*, discussed at para 10.124.

121 *R v Flintshire County Council, ex p Somerfield Stores Ltd* [1998] EGCS 53.

122 Recognized in *Leisure GB plc v Isle of Wight Council* [2000] PLCR 88. In this case the court considered that any exceptions to the *Whitley* principle should be on a clearly identifiable basis and not simply because the court considered it unfair on the merits to apply the general principle.

123 [2002] EWHC 1091 (Admin).

124 The cases are discussed at paras 3.106 and 3.107.

125 [2002] EWHC 2307 (Admin).

126 Listed building controls are discussed in ch 16 below.

historic Bishopsgate Goods Yard. Ouseley J held that although some of the material operations had commenced within the time limit, there was undoubted non-compliance with one of the conditions attached to the planning permission. This meant, prima facie, that the commencement of the development was unlawful; however, whether or not enforcement action by the local planning authorities would be lawful depended on whether the goods yard was a single building or several buildings. (This aspect of the case is discussed in chapter 6.)[127] However, the learned judge considered that this was a decision for the local planning authorities concerned—the court was prepared only to declare the commencement of the development unlawful. The authorities in question subsequently decided that the goods yard was a single building and therefore the planning permission had lapsed.

10.131 With regard to the exceptions to the Whitley principle, Ouseley J did not consider the *Powergen* and *Reprotech* cases as removing public law control from the exercise of a discretionary power to issue an enforcement notice where the circumstances warrant its intervention—'if after the expiry of the five year period, [ie the life of a planning permission] it is possible to conclude that enforcement action is not lawfully possible, I see no reason why development which cannot be enforced against should not be regarded as effective to commence development.' These views were endorsed by the Court of Appeal in *R (on the application of Prokopp) v London Underground Ltd.*[128]

10.132 The issue of whether a planning permission had been implemented within the time limit arose in *Henry Boot Homes Ltd v Bassetlaw District Council.*[129]

10.133 In August 1995 the local planning authority granted outline planning permission for residential development subject to conditions requiring, inter alia, the approval of reserved matters. The latter was given on 5 December 1995 subject to conditions requiring certain actions to be carried out before development commenced. Works sufficient in physical terms to fall under s. 56 TCPA 1990 were begun on 16 January 1996, but these works were commenced without compliance with the conditions of the outline planning permission or the reserved matters approval. There then followed discussions between the parties regarding the regularization of the development but in 1999 it was suggested that the planning permission had never been implemented. In the High Court, Sullivan J held that as the works were not authorized by the planning permission and no authorized development had begun before 2 August 2000, five years after the grant of planning permission, the planning permission no longer existed. The developers appealed, arguing that

127 See para 6.40.
128 [2003] EWCA Civ 961.
129 [2002] EWCA Civ 983.

they had a legitimate expectation, based on representations made on behalf of the local planning authority, either that the permission would be treated as having been implemented, or that compliance with the conditions had been waived.

10.134 Held: by the Court of Appeal—the planning code is a comprehensive one and the scope for the variation or discharge of planning conditions by non-statutory methods is extremely limited. The interests of the public and third parties reduce the potential for legitimate expectation to arise; the developers' expectation that its works would be treated as lawful implementation was not a legitimate expectation and there was no lawful waiver of conditions.

10.135 Keene LJ (with whom the other members of the court agreed) said that included in the statutory code was the s. 73 procedure[130] which operates by providing that an application for planning permission may be made without certain conditions previously imposed, it imports the safeguards for third parties and the public generally that apply to planning applications—thus 'although it is right that an application seeking approval under a condition does not attract the statutory provisions concerning publicity and consultation, an appeal under s. 73 does . . . [so] the public is engaged in the statutory process.'

Extension of time

10.136 It may be recalled that under TCPA 1990, s. 73[131] a developer may apply to the local planning authority for the development of land without complying with conditions subject to which a previous planning permission was granted.

10.137 In *R v Secretary of State for the Environment, ex p Corby Borough Council*,[132] was held that an application can be made under TCPA 1990, s. 73 so as to extend the time limit for the approval of reserved matters, even though the time limit originally fixed for such approval had expired.[133] This would not, however, be permissible (under TCPA 1990, s. 73(4)) if the previous planning permission was granted subject to a condition as to the time within which the development to which it related had to be begun and that time had expired without the development having been begun.

10.138 The question of the proper approach to be taken by local authorities in dealing with applications to extend time has exercised the courts. In *Allied London Property Investment Ltd v Secretary of State for the Environment*,[134] Christopher Lockhart-Mummery QC, sitting as deputy judge, held that TCPA 1990, s. 73(2) restricted

130 See para 10.99.
131 See para 10.99.
132 [1995] JPL 115.
133 For time limits on approval of reserved matters, see para 8.102.
134 [1997] JPL 199.

the decision maker to consider only the question of the conditions subject to which planning permission should be granted. It could not be used for the ulterior purpose of considering the acceptability of the proposed development in principle. But in an earlier decision, unknown to the court at the time of the *Allied London Property* hearing, a contrary position was adopted. In the case of *R v London Docklands Development Corpn, ex p Sister Christine Frost*,[135] Keene J considered that the question to be asked by the decision maker was: should this planning permission be allowed to continue in force beyond the original dates? In other words, the decision maker's enquiry may extend to the principle of the development and its appropriateness at the time of the application under TCPA 1990, s. 73. These decisions are not easily reconciled.

10.139 Some resolution of the conflict was achieved in the shape of a judgment of Sullivan J in *Pye v Secretary of State for the Environment*.[136] Here, outline planning permission having been granted, an application was made under TCPA 1990, s. 73 to extend the three-year period for approval of reserved matters as required by the permission. The local planning authority concluded that the effect of granting the permission under TCPA 1990, s. 73 would be to extend the life of the original permission for at least another two years. The application was refused on the basis that it did not accord with current planning policies. The decision was upheld by the Secretary of State on appeal.

10.140 Sullivan J, in the High Court, preferred to apply the approach taken in the *Sister Christine Frost* case.[137] The decision maker was entitled to apply the policy guidance which applied to an application for renewal of planning permission (in Circular 11/95, para 60) and could therefore take into account material changes in policy circumstances. Thus the local planning authority will be acting perfectly lawfully if, having regard to the development plan and any other material considerations including current policies, they resolve to refuse the application under TCPA 1990, s. 73 to extend time.[138]

10.141 The issue in the above-discussed cases may have been resolved by legislative reform. PCPA 2004 has amended TCPA 1990 to provide that planning permission must not be granted under s. 73 to the extent that it has the effect to change a condition subject to which a previous planning permission was granted by extending the time within which a development must be started or an application for approval of reserved matters under an outline planning permission must be made.[139]

---

135 (1997) 73 P & CR 199.

136 [1998] JPL B135.

137 See para 10.138.

138 This was confirmed by the CA in *Powergen UK plc v Leicester City Council* [2000] EGCS 64.

139 TCPA 1990, s. 73(5) as inserted by PCPA 2004, s. 51(3). The provision was brought into force in relation to England by SI 2005 No 2081 as from August 25 2005.

Completion notices

10.142 As we have seen, a planning permission will lapse if the development is not begun within the prescribed period.[140] If the development has begun but has not been completed within that period, the local planning authority—if of opinion that the development will not be completed within a reasonable period—may serve a completion notice. The notice will state that the planning permission will cease to have effect if the development is not completed within such further period (not less than 12 months) as may be specified. The notice will take effect only if and when confirmed by the Secretary of State, and before confirming the notice he must give to the persons upon whom it has been served the opportunity of appearing at a public local inquiry or other hearing.

10.143 If at the end of the period specified in the completion notice, the development has not been completed, the planning permission will be invalidated.[141] In effect, therefore, a completion notice gives the developer the choice of completing the development or of letting the planning permission lapse. It is a particularly useful procedure where a developer has kept a planning permission alive by doing only a minimal amount of preliminary work.[142] The procedure has also been used in less obvious cases; the Secretary of State has, for instance, confirmed a notice where one of two houses authorized by a planning permission had been built but not the other.[143] But the Secretary of State refused to confirm a notice in respect of a 10-acre site because he was satisfied that, since acquiring the site, the objectors had taken reasonable steps to press forward with the development having regard to some problems with access and the uncertain state of the property market.[144]

10.144 TCPA 1990, s. 95(4) provides that if a completion notice takes effect, the planning permission referred to in the notice shall become invalid at the expiration of a period specified in the notice. However, under the terms of s. 95(5), '[subsection (4)] shall not affect any permission so far as development carried out under it before the end of the [specified] period . . . is concerned.' The meaning of s. 95(5) arose in the case of *Cardiff City Council v National Assembly for Wales*[145] where a developer was granted planning permission for the erection of a garage and commenced the works. Part of the way through the development, the developer ceased working and ultimately the local planning authority served a completion notice. The issue before the court was whether, under s. 95(5), the planning permission became

140 See para 10.113.
141 1990 Act, ss. 94, 95.
142 See para 10.113.
143 [1985] JPL 125. The single house was 'an unsympathetic intrusion in a street scene of high visual qualities'.
144 [1970] JPL 184.
145 [2007] JPL 60.

entirely invalid as a result of the service of the completion notice, including the works already carried out prior to the expiry of the notice. Alternatively, did the works carried out before the expiry of the notice amount to works authorized by a planning permission? Adhering to the literal meaning of the wording of the subsection, Davis J held that the latter interpretation prevailed. The decision confirms what was widely believed to be the case; however the effect of it is far from satisfactory. Given that partially completed works are likely to be unsightly, there would appear to be no power to remove them other than the service of a revocation notice or discontinuance order,[146] which may involve the payment of compensation since such works are authorized development.

10.145 It seems that a planning permission may not be extinguished by abandonment. The judgments at first instance and in the Court of Appeal in *Slough Estates Ltd v Slough Borough Council (No 2)*[147] had suggested that where an owner or occupier of land had evinced an unequivocal intention to abandon planning permission, such permission would be extinguished by abandonment; the House of Lords disposed of the case in question on the ground that the document which had been relied on as a planning permission was not an effective permission, and the question of abandonment was left open. In the later case of *Pioneer Aggregates (UK) Ltd v Secretary of State for the Environment*,[148] the House of Lords emphatically rejected the view that a valid planning permission can be abandoned.

10.146 Planning permission had been granted in 1950 to Hartshead Quarries Ltd for the mining and working of limestone on an area of land which included the appeal site. Hartshead had extracted minerals from the land from 1950 to 1966. In September 1966 they wrote to the Peak Park Joint Planning Board giving notice that they would cease quarrying by the end of that year; in 1967 the Board wrote to Hartshead informing them that the restoration conditions had to be met to their satisfaction.

10.147 In 1978 Pioneer became interested in the land and asked the Board whether planning permission to quarry was needed. The Board replied that the 1950 permission had been abandoned.

10.148 To test the matter, Pioneer fired one blast to remove some stone; the Board served an enforcement notice. On appeal the Secretary of State upheld the enforcement notice.

10.149 The House of Lords held that there was no principle of planning law that a valid planning permission capable of being implemented according to its terms can be abandoned. Lord Scarman explained that planning control is a creature of statute;

---

146 See para 11.01.

147 [1969] 2 Ch 305, [1969] 2 All ER 988.

148 [1985] AC 132, [1984] 2 All ER 358.

it is an imposition in the public interest of restrictions upon private rights of ownership of land. It is a field of law in which the courts should not introduce principles or rules derived from private law unless they be expressly authorized by Parliament or necessary to give effect to the purpose of the legislation.

10.150 It was the clear implication of TCPA 1990, s. 33(1), TCPA 1990, s. 75(1) that only the statute or the terms of the planning permission could stop the permission enuring for the benefit of the land and of all persons for the time being interested therein.

10.151 The abandonment of an existing use, Lord Scarman pointed out, was a quite separate matter which had nothing whatever to do with the extinguishment of planning permission. This distinction can be explained by saying that in cases like *Hartley v Minister of Housing and Local Government*[149] the issue is simply one of fact: what is the use of the land at the date of resumption? It should be noted that the apparent breadth of the principle laid down by the House of Lords in *Pioneer* has been subject to a more restrictive interpretation in subsequent cases; see the discussion in chapter 6.[150]

Non-material changes to planning permission

10.152 A new s. 96A is inserted into TCPA 1990 by virtue of PA 2008, s. 190 Under this provision, local planning authorities in England may make a non-material change to a planning permission relating to land in their area. In deciding whether a change is material, the local planning authority must have regard to the effect of the change (together with any previous changes made under this section) on the planning permission as previously granted. The power conferred on the local planning authority includes the power to impose new conditions; and to remove or alter existing conditions.

10.153 The power in s. 96A will only be exercisable where the application has been made by a person with an interest in the land to which the application relates. Where a person has an interest in some, but not all, of the land to which the application relates, the application may only be made in respect of that part of the land in which the person has an interest.

10.154 The Secretary of State may by development order prescribe the form and manner in which applications under s. 96A must be made, including requirements as to consultation and publicity.

149 [1970] 1 QB 413, [1969] 3 All ER 1658.
150 See para 6.177.

Planning permission and human rights

10.155 It was suggested in an earlier chapter that a decision by a local planning authority to grant planning permission might be susceptible to challenge under the Human Rights Act 1998 at the instance of a third party.[151] The basis of this proposition is that a grant of planning permission to another may amount to a determination of the third party's civil rights under article 6(1) of the ECHR, and it may involve his right to a private and family life under article 8.[152]

10.156 Under the case law of the ECtHR, for such an application to succeed, there must be a 'dispute' over a 'right' arguably recognized under domestic law. The dispute must be genuine and serious; it may relate not only to the actual existence of the right but also to its scope and the manner of its exercise. The outcome of the proceedings must be directly decisive for the right in question—mere tenuous connections and remote consequences will not suffice.[153]

10.157 Such a challenge was mounted by the claimant in *R (on the application of Vetterlein) v Hampshire County Council*.[154] The claimant lived in close proximity to the site of a proposed waste incineration and energy recovery facility. Having received a report on the application by the county planning officer, the local planning authority decided to grant permission. Before the council determined the application, the claimant was allowed to address the planning committee for 10 minutes.

10.158 The claimant argued that the officer's report was erroneous as to the health risks of the proposed development and as a result of this false premise, the local planning authority had failed to acknowledge that there was a potential breach of the right to respect for the claimant's private and family life under article 8. Further, in the absence of a public inquiry in which evidence could be tested, the claimant argued he had been denied a fair and public hearing to which he and others were entitled under article 6(1).

10.159 Dismissing the application to quash the grant of planning permission, Sullivan J held that the report was not misleading, but even if it were, the challenges under articles 8 and 6(1) would fail. The claimant's concern was no more than a generalized concern which did not engage article 8; his connection with the decision to grant planning permission was tenuous and the environmental consequences remote so that the question of a fair hearing did not arise. Even if it did, the totality of the procedures adopted, including the public meeting, met such a requirement.

---

[151] See para 2.123.
[152] See para 2.129.
[153] See para 2.125.
[154] [2002] Env LR 8.

Sullivan J said: 'A 'fair' hearing does not necessarily require an oral hearing, much less does it require that there should be an opportunity to cross-examine. Whether a particular procedure is fair will depend on all the circumstances, including the nature of the claimant's interest, the seriousness of the matter for him and the nature of any matters in dispute.'

10.160 In *Friends Provident Life and Pensions Ltd v Secretary of State for the Environment, Transport and the Regions*,[155] Forbes J held that the claimants' civil rights and obligations were in play. The claimants, Friends Provident, owned a shopping centre in Norwich. They opposed the grant of planning permission by the City Council to Lend Lease for a major retail development. The claimants argued that the development would be commercially detrimental to their own holding. The court considered that the claimants' right to use and enjoy their own property was directly affected.

10.161 The claimants argued that the council's determination of the planning application was a breach of their rights under article 6(1), as was the Secretary of State's failure to call in the application. Forbes J said: '[I]n the light of the decision of the House of Lords in *Alconbury*,[156] I am of the view that there is no reason in principle, in an appropriate case, why the scope of article 6 should not extend to the administrative decision-making process relating to the third party's objection to the grant of planning permission, providing it directly affects that third party's civil rights.' Nevertheless, the court went on to hold that the composite process of the council's decision-making combined with the High Court's power of review met the requirements of article 6; and the same applied to the Secretary of State's refusal to call in the application. The judge did, however, make the obiter suggestion that the safeguard of the quasi-judicial process of the public inquiry before an independent inspector may well be required where findings of fact have to be made, such as in enforcement cases.[157]

10.162 The *Friends Provident* case was considered by the High Court in *R v Secretary of State for the Environment, Transport and the Regions, ex p Adlard*[158] where Collins J held there was no breach of the Convention where the Secretary of State refused to call in applications for the demolition and rebuilding of Fulham FC's ground. This decision was upheld by the Court of Appeal. Similarly, in *R v Camden London*

---

[155] (2001) EWHC 820 (Admin), (2001) 44 EG 147 (CS).

[156] See para 2.136.

[157] See para 12.01 Richards J expressed a similar view concerning local authority decision-making processes in *R (on the application of Alan Kathro) v Rhondda Cynon Taff County Borough Council* [2001] EWHC 527 (Admin), [2001] 4 PLR 83. See also *British Telecommunications plc v Gloucester City Council* (26 November 2001, unreported).

[158] [2002] EWHC 7 (Admin), [2002] All ER (D) 77 (Jan).

Borough Council, ex p Cummins,[159] Ouseley J decided that the Secretary of State's policy of refusing to call in applications with only local importance, and the relevant primary legislation, were not incompatible with article 6(1) of the ECHR.

10.163 In *R (on the application of Rose Malster) v Ipswich Borough Council*,[160] there was a challenge to the grant of planning permission for the redevelopment of the north stand at Ipswich Town's stadium at Portman Road, the effect of which would be to cast a shadow over nearby housing in which the claimant lived. Placing reliance on his own earlier decision in *Vetterlein*,[161] Sullivan J rejected submissions based on article 6(1). A further ground was that the proposed development infringed the claimant's rights under article 8[162] because of the severity of the overshadowing. Sullivan J said that whereas severe environmental pollution may result in a breach of article 8,[163] it was doubtful whether the shadowing effect on the claimant's garden crossed that threshold, in view of the fact that the Council's own standards were not infringed. But even if the threshold were crossed, the right to respect for private and family life was not absolute; article 8(1) required the authority to carry out a balancing exercise between the claimant's interest in her own home and the public interest in providing improved sporting facilities. The Court found that the Council had done this—it made no difference that the Council had not referred to article 8 in their committee report.

10.164 These cases leave open the possibility that even after the House of Lords decision in the *Alconbury* case[164] there may be circumstances in which a third party may be able to challenge successfully planning decisions on the basis of a breach of the ECHR.

Delay in decision-making

10.165 Article 6(1) of the Convention entitles the citizen, inter alia, to a fair hearing 'within a reasonable time'.[165]

10.166 We have seen that where a local planning authority fail to determine a planning application within the proper time, there is a right of appeal to the Secretary of State.[166] However, in other situations, such as where a planning application has been called in, there can be considerable delay.

---

159 (21 December 2001, unreported). This case is further discussed at para 17.46.
160 [2001] EWHC 711 (Admin), [2001] All ER (D) 107 (Aug).
161 See para 10.157.
162 See para 2.130.
163 See *Lopez Ostra v Spain* (1994) 20 EHRR 227.
164 See para 2.136.
165 See para 2.129.
166 See para 8.121.

10.167 This issue arose in *UK Coal Mining Ltd v Secretary of State for Transport, Local Government and the Regions*[167] where the applicant sought to quash a refusal of planning permission by the Secretary of State for opencast mining. The application had originally been submitted in September 1997 and was called in by the Secretary of State; he did not issue his decision letter until March 2001, some two and a half years after the delivery of the inspector's report. Ouseley J considered that the delay was inordinate, unreasonable, and involved a breach of the human rights of the claimant.

10.168 Clearly, what is a 'reasonable time' will depend upon the circumstances—there may well be valid reasons for delay in matters of great complexity and technicality. In the event, the decision in this case was quashed on other grounds although the court recognized there would have been no value in quashing the Secretary of State's decision on the basis of delay alone. Either the claimant would get a new letter in the post a day or so later saying the same thing; or if there were new factors requiring consideration, that would add to the delay.

10.169 In the case of *Lafarge Redland Aggregates Ltd v The Scottish Ministers*,[168] the petitioner sought judicial review (inter alia) of the failure of the respondent ministers to determine a planning application for quarrying development that had been called in by the Secretary of State for Scotland. The application had been submitted to the local planning authority in March 1991 and called in in January 1994, but it still had not been determined by July 2000. The petitioner contended that the failure to determine the application constituted inordinate delay and was a breach of article 6 of ECHR. Lord Hardie in the Outer House held that the petitioner had a legitimate expectation that its application would be decided in a reasonable time. The delay in this case was considered by the court to be 'scandalous' and ministers were in breach of article 6 of the Convention.

Stopping up and diversion of highways

10.170 Powers exist under the TCPA 1990 enabling the stopping up and diversion of highways, footpaths, and bridleways in connection with development.

Stopping up by the Secretary of State

10.171 Under TCPA 1990, s. 247 the Secretary of State may make an order to stop up or divert a highway if it is necessary to do so in order to enable development to be carried out in accordance with a grant of planning permission or by a government

[167] (2001) EWHC 912 (Admin).
[168] (2001) SC 298.

department. And under TCPA 1990, s. 251 the Secretary of State may make an order to stop up any public right of way over land held for planning purposes by a local authority[169]—he must be satisfied that an alternative right of way has been or will be provided, or that an alternative right of way is unnecessary.[170]

Stopping up and other action by local authorities

10.172 Under TCPA 1990, s. 257 a footpath or bridleway may be stopped up or diverted by order of the local planning authority for the purpose of enabling development to be carried out in accordance with a grant of planning permission or by a government department. TCPA 1990, s. 258 enables a local authority to make an order stopping up any footpath or bridleway over land held by them for planning purposes; the authority must be satisfied that an alternative right of way has been or will be provided, or that an alternative right of way is unnecessary.[171]

169 See para 3.59.

170 The procedure for orders under ss. 247 or 251 is prescribed by TCPA 1990,s. 252.

171 The procedure for orders under TCPA 1990, ss. 257 and 258 is prescribed by TCPA 1990, s. 259 and Sch 14.

11

REVOCATION OR MODIFICATION OF EXISTING RIGHTS

Revocation or modification of planning permission

11.01 Although a grant of planning permission is intended, in the absence of conditions to the contrary, to ensure permanently for the benefit of the land,[1] in certain circumstances it may be revoked or modified. The local planning authority may, if they consider it expedient, having regard to the development plan and to any other material considerations, make an order for this purpose; with some exceptions, the order must be submitted to the Secretary of State for confirmation.[2] The Secretary of State may make such an order himself, but only after consulting and after giving formal notice to the local planning authority.[3] If the order becomes effective, the local planning authority will have to pay compensation for abortive expenditure and for the depreciation in the value of the land.

11.02 It is comparatively rarely that the Secretary of State or the local authority will consider it desirable to revoke or modify a permission and the liability to compensation may deter an authority from such action even where they consider it desirable.

---

[1] See para 10.01.

[2] TCPA 1990, ss. 97, 98.

[3] TCPA 1990, s. 100.

Extent of power to revoke or modify

11.03 The power of revocation or modification applies only to permissions granted on an application under TCPA 1990, Part III. The reference to 'an application' excludes any permission granted by a development order,[4] or any deemed permission arising under TCPA 1990, s. 90 or 222 concerning development by government departments and advertisements respectively.[5]

11.04 The power to revoke or modify applies only where the development has not been completed. This is made clear by TCPA 1990, s. 97(3) which reads:

> The power conferred by this section to revoke or modify permission to develop land may be exercised—
> (a) Where the permission relates to the carrying out of building or other operations, at any time before those operations have been completed;
> (b) Where the permission relates to a change of the use of any land, at any time before the change has taken place.

11.05 Furthermore, the revocation or modification of permission for the carrying out of building or other operations will not affect so much of those operations as has been previously carried out.[6]

11.06 If the local planning authority wish to remove or modify development completed in conformity with planning permission they must make a 'discontinuance order' under TCPA 1990, s. 102.[7] Two procedures are available for the making of an order to revoke or modify. First, there is what may be called the standard procedure which involves submitting the order to the Secretary of State for confirmation. Secondly, there is the procedure which may be used where the local planning authority do not expect objections to the order.

The standard procedure

11.07 The local planning authority submit the order to the Secretary of State, and give notice to the owner[8] and occupier of the land and to any other person likely to be affected.

11.08 Any person receiving the notice has the right to be heard by the Secretary of State either at a public local inquiry or other hearing, before the Secretary of State decides whether or not to confirm the order.[9]

---

[4] A permission granted under the General Permitted Development Order, however, may in effect be revoked or modified as a result of an 'Article 4 direction' (see para 7.60).

[5] See para 7.84.

[6] TCPA 1990, s. 97(4).

[7] See para 11.15.

[8] The 'owner' means a person, other than a mortgagee not in possession, who (whether in his own right or as trustee) is entitled to receive the rack-rent of the land or, where the land is not let as a rack-rent, would be so entitled if it were so let: TCPA 1990, s. 336(1). And see para 14.23.

[9] TCPA 1990, s. 98(3), (4).

11.09 Where the Secretary of State himself makes an order, he must similarly notify the persons affected, and give them an opportunity of being heard before coming to a final decision.[10]

Procedure for unopposed orders

11.10 This procedure is available where the owner and occupier of the land and all persons who, in the authority's opinion, will be affected by the order have notified the authority in writing that they do not object to the order.[11] This, of course, presupposes that the authority have given preliminary notification of their intention to make the order.

11.11 In these circumstances, the authority publish an advertisement in the local press reciting the above-mentioned matters and stating that any person affected by the order may notify the Secretary of State that he wishes to be heard by a representative of the Secretary of State at a public local inquiry or other hearing. A similar notice is to be served on the very persons who have already indicated that they do not object.[12]

11.12 The authority must then send a copy of the public advertisement to the Secretary of State, who has the right to call in the order. If at the end of a specified period no person claiming to be affected has requested a hearing and the Secretary of State has not called in the order, it takes effect.[13]

11.13 The validity of an order revoking or modifying planning permission, whether made under the standard procedure or under that for unopposed orders, may be questioned in High Court proceedings under TCPA 1990, s. 288 but not otherwise.[14]

11.14 If the effect of the order is to render the land incapable of reasonably beneficial use the owner may serve a purchase notice under TCPA 1990, s. 137.[15]

Discontinuance orders

11.15 As explained earlier in this chapter the power to revoke or modify planning permission does not apply where the development has already been carried out. TCPA 1990, s. 102 enables the local planning authority to make 'discontinuance

10 TCPA 1990, s. 100(4)–(7).

11 TCPA 1990, s. 99(1). This procedure cannot be used to revoke or modify a planning permission granted by the Secretary of State on a called-in application or on appeal, or to modify conditions as to the duration of a planning permission: TCPA 1990, s. 99(8).

12 TCPA 1990, s. 99(2)–(6).

13 TCPA 1990, s. 99(7).

14 See para 20.07.

15 For purchase notices, see para 14.01.

orders' in relation to existing buildings and uses without the authority having to acquire the land.

11.16 Compensation must be paid to the owner for the loss of the rights but at least the local authority are spared the added expense of acquiring land for which they would have no particular need. This is a particularly useful method of dealing with the comparatively small objectionable black spot such as 'back-garden' industry or a caravan site in the wrong place. Many such uses were, of course, established at a time when planning permission was not required; in some cases they have arisen since 1948 in contravention of planning control but the local planning authority have failed to serve an effective enforcement notice within the proper time.[16]

11.17 The local planning authority may take action under TCPA 1990, s. 102 if they consider it desirable for the planning of their area, including considerations of amenity; regard is to be had to the development plan and to any other material considerations. An order may be made:[17]

(a) Requiring any use of land to be discontinued or imposing conditions on the continuance of the use; or
(b) Requiring any buildings or works to be altered or removed.

11.18 The local planning authority may be prepared to sanction some other development of the land: if so, they may include in the order a grant of planning permission for that purpose.[18] If the order would result in the displacement of residents, the local planning authority may have to secure the provisions of alternative accommodation.[19]

11.19 If the Secretary of State considers that the local authority ought to have made an order he may make an order himself.[20]

11.20 An order of the local planning authority does not become effective unless and until it is confirmed by the Secretary of State.[21] Before the Secretary of State can confirm the order, the owner and the occupier of the land must be given an opportunity of being heard—usually at a public inquiry.[22] If the order is made by the Secretary of State he will give the persons affected a similar opportunity of being heard before he comes to a final decision.[23]

---

16 See para 12.34.
17 TCPA 1990, s. 102(1).
18 TCPA 1990, s. 102(2), (3).
19 TCPA 1990, s. 102(6).
20 TCPA 1990, s. 104.
21 TCPA 1990, s. 103(1).
22 TCPA 1990, s. 103(3)–(6).
23 TCPA 1990, s. 104.

11.21 The Secretary of State may confirm the order with or without modifications and he may include in the order a grant of planning permission for some other purpose.[24] The validity of the order may be challenged not later than six weeks after the Secretary's confirmation in High Court proceedings under TCPA 1990, s. 288 but not otherwise.[25]

11.22 If the order relates to the use of the land, failure to comply is an offence punishable by fine.[26] But if it requires the removal or alteration of buildings or works the remedy is for the local planning authority to carry out the requirements of the order and recover the cost from the owner.[27]

11.23 If the effect of the order is to render the land incapable of reasonably beneficial use the owner may serve a purchase notice under TCPA 1990, s. 137.[28]

Compensation for revocation or modification of existing rights

11.24 As stated earlier in this chapter, where a revocation, modification, or discontinuance order is made, compensation will be payable under TCPA 1990, s. 107 or s. 115.

11.25 There is also in effect a revocation or modification, of planning permission if permitted development rights granted by development order[29] are withdrawn by the revocation or amendment of the order or if a direction[30] is issued requiring an application to be made for express permission. If such permission is refused or is granted subject to any conditions other than those prescribed by the development order, compensation can be claimed under TCPA 1990, s. 107.[31] However, under TCPA 1990, s. 108(3A) compensation will not be payable if development under a planning permission granted by a development order or local development order is started before the permission is withdrawn, and the order includes a provision permitting the development to be completed after the permission is withdrawn. An amendment made by s. 189 of PA 2008 means that compensation will not be payable if the withdrawal of the permitted development right (granted by GPDO or LDO) is published 12 months or more before the withdrawal takes effect.

---

24 TCPA 1990, s. 103.
25 See para 20.07.
26 TCPA 1990, s. 102.
27 TCPA 1990, s. 103.
28 See para 14.04.
29 Eg the rights granted by the GPDO: see para 7.12.
30 Eg a direction under the GPDO, art 4: see para 7.60.
31 TCPA 1990, s. 108.

Compensation for orders revoking or modifying existing rights

11.26 Compensation under TCPA 1990, s. 107 may be claimed by any person interested in the land who can show that:

(a) The has incurred expenditure in carrying out work which has been rendered abortive by the revocation or modification; and
(b) The has otherwise sustained loss or damage which is directly attributable to the revocation or modification.

11.27 The words 'a person interested in the land' may include contractual licensees as well as those having a legal or equitable interest such as the freehold or tenancy.

11.28 In *Pennine Raceway Ltd v Kirkless Metropolitan Council*,[32] the claimants were promoters of motor car and motor cycle racing and had entered into an agreement with the owner of an airfield to equip the airfield with pits, car park, and safety fencing; after a trial year the consideration payable to the owner was to be £500 per meeting and this sum was to be reviewed every five years.

11.29 The local authority directed under article 4 of the then General Development Order that the use of the airfield for motor car or motor cycle racing should no longer be permitted. The company lodged a claim for compensation for abortive expenditure but the local authority denied liability on the ground that the company was not 'a person interested in the land'.

11.30 The Court of Appeal held that a person who like the appellants had an enforceable right against the owner of the land to use the land in the way which had now been prohibited was a person interested in the land within what is now [TCPA 1990], s. 107. The heads of claim are:

Abortive expenditure

11.31 This head includes expenditure on plans and other preparatory matters whether or not any physical work has actually been done.[33] With the exception of expenditure on plans etc, the expenditure must have been incurred after the grant of the permission which has been revoked or modified.

Other loss or damage

11.32 This head may include such items as expenses incurred in securing release from a building contract entered into after the grant of the permission which has been revoked or modified and may even include loss of profit on contracts which

---

32 [1983] QB 382, [1982] 3 All ER 628.
33 TCPA 1990, s. 107(2). *Holmes v Bradfield RDC* [1949] 2 KB 1, [1949] 1 All ER 381.

would almost certainly have been obtained but for the revocation of the permission.[34]

Depreciation in the value of the land

11.33 Loss or damage directly attributable to the revocation or modification may include depreciation in the value of an interest in the land, and in many cases this will be the most important item of claim. The amount of compensation for depreciation will be the difference between (a) the value of the interest with the benefit of the permission prior to its revocation or modification; and (b) the value of the land subject to the revocation or modification assuming that permission would be given for development falling within TCPA 1990, Schedule 3, Part I.[35]

11.34 The meaning of the above provision was considered by the House of Lords in *Canterbury City Council v Colley*.[36]

11.35 In 1961 outline planning permission was granted for the demolition of a house and the erection of a new dwelling on a site formerly known as Marley House, Whitstable. In 1987 the local planning authority made an order revoking that permission which the Secretary of State subsequently confirmed. The appellants claimed compensation under [TCPA 1990,] s. 164 (now [TCPA 1990, Sch 3]). The disputed claim for compensation came before the Lands Tribunal.

11.36 The Tribunal, in assessing compensation, disregarded the statutory assumption in TCPA 1971, s. 164(4) that planning permission would be granted for rebuilding the house (under what is now TCPA 1990, Schedule 3, Part I), on the ground that if the assumption was applied it would eliminate compensation for depreciation occasioned by the revocation and this could not possibly have been Parliament's intention. The Council's appeal to the Court of Appeal was successful; the appellants appealed to the House of Lords which upheld the decision of the Court of Appeal. Their Lordships unanimously held that the statutory assumption was, in terms, mandatory, and that it had to be applied even though the assumed permission was the very permission that had been revoked.

11.37 Lord Oliver, after outlining the legislative history, explained the position this way: 'The conclusion is not one which I embrace with any enthusiasm and it may well be that the particular circumstance of the revoked permission being the very permission comprehended in the statutory assumption was not one which the legislature foresaw as ever likely to occur. But, whilst this provides a sound reason for the hope expressed by Sir Donald Nicholls V-C that Parliament may look

---

[34] *Hobbs (Quarries) Ltd v Somerset County Council* (1975) 30 P & CR 286.

[35] TCPA 1990, s. 107(3), (4), as amended by TCPA 1990, s. 31(4) and Sch 6, PCA 1991. For Sch 3, see Appendix 1.

[36] [1993] AC 401, [1993] 1 All ER 591.

again at what he described as 'an anachronistic relic', it cannot provide an escape from the clear and express words of the section.'

11.38 The landowner, Mrs Colley, subsequently served a purchase notice on the local authority, which led to further litigation.[37]

11.39 The procedure for claiming compensation is as follows. Claims for compensation under TCPA 1990, s. 107 must be made to the local planning authority within 12 months from the date of the relevant decision, unless the Secretary of State agrees to an extension of time.

11.40 This is so whether the claim arises from:

(a) An order revoking or modifying planning permission;[38]
(b) A refusal or conditional grant of planning permission following the revocation or amendment of a development order.

11.41 The compensation is payable by the local planning authority.[39] Any dispute as to the payment of compensation may be referred to the Lands Tribunal.[40]

Compensation for discontinuance orders

11.42 Where a discontinuance order is made under TCPA 1990, s. 102[41] the local planning authority will be liable to pay compensation: (1) to any person who has suffered damage by the depreciation in the value of an interest in land to which he is entitled; (2) to any person who is disturbed in his enjoyment of the land.[42] Furthermore, any person who carries out work in compliance with the order, such as the removal of buildings or plant and machinery, is entitled to recover his expenses;[43] compensation may be reduced by the value to the claimant of any timber, apparatus, or other materials which he has removed.[44]

11.43 As regards (1) above, it would seem that the interest must be the freehold or a lease, including the equitable interest created by a binding contract for sale; a claim may be made by a mortgagee but not in respect of that interest as such, and

[37] *Colley v Secretary of State for the Environment* (1998) 77 P & CR 190. This case is discussed at para 14.10. For purchase notices generally, see para 14.10.
[38] General Regs 1992, reg 12.
[39] TCPA 1990, s. 107(1).
[40] TCPA 1990, s. 118. Note that the liability to compensation, in so far as it does not relate to the use and development of land, is not capable of amounting to a material consideration in deciding whether to revoke or modify a planning permission; *Alnwick District Council v Secretary of State for the Environment, Transport and the Regions* [2000] JPL 474. For material considerations, see para 8.68.
[41] See para 11.15.
[42] TCPA 1990, s. 115(2).
[43] TCPA 1990, s. 115(3).
[44] TCPA 1990, s. 117(4).

he must account to the mortgagor.[45] A claimant under (1) must be able to show that he has suffered damage by reason of the depreciation in the value of the land; so, where the discontinuance order contains a grant of planning permission for some other purpose,[46] that must be taken into account.(2) above presumably extends to persons occupying the land under a licence, and the reference to 'enjoyment' includes commercial as well as personal enjoyment.

11.44 Claims for compensation must be made within 12 months of the date of the order unless the Secretary of State agrees to an extension of time.[47] Disputes as to compensation will be referred to the Lands Tribunal.[48]

45 TCPA 1990, s. 117(3).
46 See para 11.18.
47 General Regs 1992, reg 12.
48 TCPA 1990, s. 118.

12

THE ENFORCEMENT OF PLANNING CONTROL

12.01 A system of enforcement is required to deal with cases in which development is carried out either without planning permission or in breach of the conditions or limitations attaching to a grant of planning permission. With some minor exceptions,[1]

[1] The display of advertisements without the necessary grant of consent under the Advertisement Regs and thus without any necessary grant of planning permission is an offence: TCPA 1990, s. 224(3), (4).

Parliament has always declined to make a simple breach of planning control an offence punishable by the courts. Instead, local planning authorities have been authorized to issue an enforcement notice requiring the owner or occupier of land or premises to remedy the situation. It is only when the enforcement notice is ignored that the local planning authority may prosecute the offender.

12.02 While the enforcement notice will remain the principal and most powerful weapon in the armoury of local planning authorities in dealing with unauthorized development, the Planning and Compensation Act 1991 gave authorities new and supplementary powers for dealing with such development. These include the power to serve a 'planning contravention notice' (PCN) and a 'breach of condition notice' (BCN). The former may be used where it appears that there may have been a breach of planning control and the local planning authority require information about activities on the land in order to secure the owner's co-operation; and the latter may be used where there has been a failure to comply with a condition or limitation attached to a grant of planning permission. As we shall see in this chapter, these procedures are optional and supplementary—their existence does not preclude the local planning authority, in an appropriate case, from proceeding directly with an enforcement notice.

12.03 In the years since 1947, the taking of successful enforcement action has proved difficult for local planning authorities. There are a number of reasons for this. First, it is not an easy matter to discover what is happening or has happened on a piece of land, particularly where the activities are not static. This can make the drafting of a valid enforcement notice a difficult exercise, where the legal requirements, despite amendments made by the Local Government and Planning (Amendment) Act 1981 and PCA 1991, have been seen as inflexible and over-technical. Second, prior to the introduction of the breach of condition notice by the PCA 1991, there had been no quick and effective way of dealing with breaches of condition as opposed to development without planning permission; an enforcement notice may be too cumbersome to deal with the former.[2] Third, there is the question of time limits. Under the TCPA 1947, the enforcement notice had to be served[3] within four years of the breach of planning control. If no notice was served within that time, the unauthorized development or breach of condition became immune from enforcement action. In 1968 it was decided to remove this time limit on the service of enforcement notices in respect of unauthorized changes of use[4]

[2] Since 1957 it has been recognized that an injunction may also be available for this purpose; see para 12.124.

[3] Since the PCA 1991, the local planning authority 'issue' an enforcement notice and serve copies of it on those concerned instead of as previously 'serving' notices on those concerned.

[4] Although it was retained in the case of operational development and changes of use to a single dwelling: see para 12.35.

occurring after the end of 1963.[5] The result was that unauthorized changes of use occurring before 1964 became the established use of the land and immune from enforcement. With the passage of time it became increasingly difficult to prove with any accuracy the planning history of the land in question. Nevertheless, this remained the position until the coming into force of the PCA 1991 which, in general, substituted a 10-year time limit after which no enforcement action can be taken against an unauthorized change of use which then becomes the lawful use of the land.[6]

12.04 The difficulties referred to in the previous paragraph were identified by the Carnwath Report.[7] Robert Carnwath QC was appointed by the Secretary of State to examine the effectiveness of the enforcement system and make recommendations for its improvement. Most of his recommendations as to the reform of the system were accepted and appeared in the PCA 1991.[8]

12.05 To the existing enforcement powers in TCPA 1990, PCPA 2004 has added a new one—the Temporary Stop Notice (TSN). This enables local planning authorities to bring an immediate stop, for a temporary 28-day period, to activities on land constituting a breach of planning control.

12.06 The final section of this chapter is devoted to the enforcement provisions contained in Part 8 of PA 2008 which are concerned with the position where development is carried out without NSIP development consent, where that is required.

Planning contravention notices (PCNs)

12.07 The planning contravention notice, introduced by the PCA 1991,[9] was designed to fill a particular gap in the system. There will be many cases where the local planning authority are aware of, or suspect, a breach of planning control in circumstances where they might have granted planning permission had an application been made to them. Even if they are not disposed to grant permission, it may be that what is required is a warning 'shot cross the bows' to persuade the developer to co-operate with the authority. And if further action is contemplated, the local planning authority needs to be in possession of the correct factual information.

---

[5] Approximately four years before the introduction of the bill for the TCPA 1968.

[6] TCPA 1990, ss. 171B(3) and 191(2)(a). Again, the four-year time limit applies to certain breaches; see para 12.34.

[7] 'Enforcing Planning Control', Robert Carnwath QC, 1989.

[8] These amendments are incorporated by reference to the TCPA 1990.

[9] TCPA 1990, ss. 171C and 171D. And see Circular 10/97. The PCN is intended to supplement the local planning authority's more limited power to obtain information under TCPA 1990, s. 330.

Service of planning contravention notice

12.08 A planning contravention notice may be served wherever it appears to the local planning authority that there may have been a breach of planning control in respect of any land.[10] For all purposes under the TCPA 1990, 'breach of planning control' means (a) carrying out development without required planning permission; or (b) failing to comply with any condition or limitation subject to which planning permission has been granted.[11] In *R v Teignbridge District Council, ex p Teignmouth Quay Co Ltd*,[12] Judge J held that it is a requirement, or pre-condition, for the service of a planning contravention notice that it must appear that a breach of planning control (as defined above) might be taking place or might have taken place. The learned judge considered that although the contravention notice procedure was less draconian than an enforcement notice, it was nevertheless an 'intrusive' procedure and compliance was mandatory if properly served. Hence, as in the case itself, the mere refusal by a landowner to co-operate with informal queries by the authority was not sufficient to satisfy the minimal statutory requirements without which the notice could not be served. The notice in question was quashed.

12.09 The planning contravention notice may be served on the owner or occupier of the land or on any person who has an interest in it; the notice may also be served on any person carrying out operations on the land or using it for any purpose.[13] The notice may require the recipient to provide information as to operations, uses, and any other activities being carried out on the land and also as to any matter relating to the conditions or limitations subject to which any planning permission in respect of the land has been granted.[14] The notice must specify the precise nature of the information required.

12.10 Without prejudice to the general power to obtain information outlined in the paragraph above, the planning contravention notice may require more specific information as to five matters, so far as the recipient is able.[15] These are as follows:

(1) Whether the land is in fact being used or operations or activities carried out as alleged in the notice, or whether it has been so used in the past.
(2) When any use, operation, or activity began.
(3) Particulars of any person known to use, or to have used, the land for any purpose, or to be carrying out, or have carried out, any operations or activities on the land.

---

[10] TCPA 1990, s. 171C. The Act makes it clear that the service of a planning contravention notice does not affect any other power exercisable in respect of any breach of planning control; TCPA 1990, s. 171C(7).

[11] TCPA 1990, s. 171A(1).

[12] [1995] JPL 828.

[13] TCPA 1990, s. 171C(1).

[14] TCPA 1990, s. 171C(2).

[15] TCPA 1990, s. 171C(3)(a)–(e).

(4) Any information about any planning permission in relation to the land or why the recipient contends planning permission is not needed.
(5) What interest the recipient has in the land and the particulars of anyone else known to have an interest.

12.11 It will be observed that these information-gathering powers are exceptionally wide and include the power to demand from the recipient particulars of third parties, although the local planning authority has no legal power to obtain information from those third parties. However, the procedure goes further than information gathering. The notice *may* invite the recipient to come forward with positive suggestions as to how to regularize the position by offering to apply for planning permission, to refrain from operations or activities, to undertake remedial work, or to make any representations about the notice.[16] Such offers or representations may be made in person.[17] The Act further provides that the recipient must be warned in the notice of the penalties for non-compliance with the notice and in particular that enforcement action may be taken.[18] A planning contravention notice is complied with by giving the required information in writing to the local planning authority.[19]

Penalties for non-compliance

12.12 The failure to comply with a planning contravention notice constitutes an offence which will be committed if, at any time after 21 days beginning with the day on which the notice was served, the recipient has not complied with any requirement of it.[20] An offence may be charged by reference to any day or longer period and a person may be convicted of a subsequent offence by reference to any period of time following the preceding conviction.[21] Although there is no appeal against the notice, it is a defence to prove that the recipient has a reasonable excuse for failing to comply.[22] Persons convicted under the above provision are liable on summary conviction to a fine.[23] It is also an offence for a person to make a false or misleading statement about the notice; this offence is also punishable by a fine on summary conviction.[24]

---

16 TCPA 1990, s. 171(4).

17 Circular 10/97, para 2.6 states that if the local planning authority think that no useful purpose would be served by a face-to-face discussion with the recipient, they would be justified in using the notice for the purpose of obtaining information only.

18 TCPA 1990, s. 171C(5). The notice must also warn the recipient that his entitlement to compensation for loss due to a stop notice (see para 12.141) may be affected.

19 TCPA 1990, s. 171C(6).

20 TCPA 1990, s. 171D(1).

21 TCPA 1990, s. 171D(2).

22 TCPA 1990, s. 171D(3).

23 TCPA 1990, s. 171D(4). A fine not exceeding level 3 on the standard scale.

24 TCPA 1990, s. 171D(5) and (6). A fine not exceeding level 5 on the standard scale.

12.13 The planning contravention notice has proved to be an important procedural weapon in the local planning authority's armoury. It should not be forgotten that service of the notice is discretionary and the local planning authority may proceed directly to issue an enforcement notice if they feel it is expedient for them to do so.[25] It should be noted, however, that a local planning authority may be penalized in costs if it issues and serves an enforcement notice without making basic prior inquiries. In *R (on the application of Cobbledick) v First Secretary of State*,[26] the local planning authority failed to make enquiries that would have shown that the enforcement notice was wholly unnecessary since the owner clearly intended to remove the offending structure before the notice could take effect. Sullivan J held that the local planning authority had acted unreasonably.

PCN and human rights

12.14 As we have seen, the planning contravention notice may be used as a means of discovering whether there are grounds for taking enforcement action. A problem may arise where information obtained as part of this process is used as a source of evidence in support of a subsequent prosecution. This is because article 6(1) of the ECHR[27] is regarded as importing an unqualified privilege from self-incrimination, or a 'right to silence'.[28]

12.15 It is unlikely that requiring owners and occupiers of land to provide information, or indeed to produce potentially incriminating documents, would infringe article 6(1).[29] It may, however, be a breach of that provision to use information obtained through coercive powers in any criminal proceedings against the person who provided the information. If this is correct, the use of planning contravention notices by local authorities would be perfectly legitimate but evidence obtained in the circumstances outlined above may have to be excluded in any criminal proceedings.[30]

Powers of entry

12.16 Although the planning contravention notice, discussed above, gives the local planning authority substantial powers to obtain information, there may be cases where they will need to enter on the land in order to investigate a breach of planning control.

---

25 Circular 10/97, para 1.3.

26 [2004] EWHC 1341 (Admin).

27 See para 2.127.

28 *Saunders v United Kingdom* (1996) EHRR 313.

29 *R v Hertfordshire County Council, ex p Green Environmental Industries* [2000] 2 AC 412, [2000] 1 All ER 773.

30 See further Beloff and Brown [1999] JPL 1069.

12.17 In fact, local authorities have always had a general power to enter the land for the purpose of surveying with a view to the preparation of development plans, in dealing with planning applications, and for various other purposes.[31] Although this power could be used in connection with breaches of planning control, it could only be exercised where the local planning authority actually proposed to take enforcement action. The Planning and Compensation Act 1991 excluded this power for enforcement purposes and inserted into the TCPA 1990 three new sections, 196A, 196B, and 196C, which give local planning authorities specific powers of entry where a breach of planning control is suspected and for other related purposes.

12.18 The Act provides that any person duly authorized in writing by the local planning authority may at any reasonable hour enter the land (a) to ascertain whether there has been a breach of planning control; (b) to determine whether, and if so how, the authority's enforcement powers should be exercised; and (c) to ascertain whether there has been compliance with powers already exercised in that regard.[32] There must, however, be reasonable grounds for entry.[33]

12.19 What if entry under the above power is refused? In such a case the Act further provides that if it can be shown to the satisfaction of a justice of the peace on sworn information in writing that there are reasonable grounds for entering the land for any of the purposes (a), (b), or (c) in the above paragraph, and admission has been refused, or a refusal is reasonably apprehended or the case is one of urgency, the justice may issue a warrant authorizing entry on the land.[34] Unless the case is one of urgency, entry must be at a reasonable hour. A warrant authorizes entry on one occasion only; entry must be within one month from the date of issue of the warrant.[35]

12.20 TCPA 1990, s. 196C contains a number of supplementary provisions relating to the above rights of entry. In particular it is made an offence wilfully to obstruct a person acting in the exercise of a right of entry,[36] and if any damage is caused in the exercise of a right of entry, compensation may be recoverable from the authority authorizing entry.[37]

[31] TCPA 1990, s. 324.
[32] TCPA 1990, s. 196A.
[33] In the case of a dwellinghouse, 24 hours' notice must be given: TCPA 1990, s. 196A(4).
[34] TCPA 1990, s. 196B(1).
[35] TCPA 1990, s. 196B(3).
[36] Secretary of State, s. 196C(2). The penalty on summary conviction is a fine not exceeding level 3 on the standard scale.
[37] TCPA 1990, s. 196C(3).

Breach of condition notices (BCNs)

Service of breach of condition notice

12.21 Until the coming into force of the Planning and Compensation Act 1991, breaches of condition (and of limitations) could either be acquiesced in by the local planning authority or be made the subject of an enforcement notice.[38] What was lacking was an effective and speedy way of dealing with breaches of condition and the result was that developers could risk being lax in complying with conditions, since, as we have seen, a breach of planning control is not in itself an offence.

12.22 TCPA 1990, s. 187A[39] applies where planning permission has been granted subject to conditions[40] and any condition has not been complied with. In such circumstances the local planning authority may serve a breach of condition notice on any person (the 'person responsible') who is carrying out or has carried out the development or is the person having control of the land. In the case of the latter, ie persons having control of the land, the notice may only relate to conditions regulating the use of the land. The person will be required to take the steps specified in the notice.[41] The notice must specify the steps which the authority consider ought to be taken, or the activities which the authority consider ought to cease, to secure compliance with the conditions specified in the notice.[42] The notice must also specify a period of not less than 28 days beginning with the date of service of the notice as the period for compliance. The period may be extended by a further notice.[43] It seems that the notice may be invalid if, although served on a person having control of the land, the condition it purports to enforce relates to other land not subject to the planning permission. Thus in *Davenport v London Borough of Hammersmith and Fulham*,[44] the conviction of John Davenport for failing to comply with a notice was quashed because although he was in control of the land, the condition in question disallowed the use of Tasso Road for the parking of vehicles; ie a public highway over which he had no control.

Non-compliance with a breach of condition notice

12.23 The most striking aspect of the breach of condition notice is that the Act does not provide for any appeal against the notice. This is not as draconian as at first sight

38 An injunction is also another possible remedy, see para 12.122.
39 Inserted by the PCA 1991, s. 2.
40 'Conditions' includes limitations: TCPA 1990, s. 187A(13)(a).
41 TCPA 1990, s. 187A(1)–(4).
42 TCPA 1990, s. 187A(5).
43 TCPA 1990, s. 187A(7).
44 [1999] JPL 1122. A different aspect of this case is discussed at para 10.54.

it may seem since the Act provides other methods for challenging planning conditions[45] and the decision to serve a breach of condition notice will be judicially reviewable.[46] It does, however, mean that the developer will have to comply with the notice even where, say, the condition in question is contrary to policy guidance and would not be upheld on appeal. Where the condition which the local planning authority seek to enforce is invalid according to the criteria discussed in a previous chapter[47] the position is not, at present, entirely clear. In *Dilieto v Ealing London Borough Council*,[48] Sullivan J, giving the main judgment in the Divisional Court, held that a person prosecuted for failure to comply with a breach of condition notice could contend by way of defence that the notice had been served out of time. This was because the contravention of the condition had begun more than 10 years previously and was therefore outside the time limit for enforcement.[49]

12.24 However, Sullivan J went on to indicate that an argument that a condition was unreasonable in the 'Wednesbury' sense[50] would not be appropriate in criminal proceedings before the magistrates. Such a matter, it was said, should proceed by way of judicial review proceedings.[51]

12.25 An offence will be committed if the breach of condition notice is not complied with by the person responsible, within the specified period or any extended period.[52] It will be a defence for the person responsible to show that he took all reasonable measures to secure compliance with the conditions specified in the notice, or, where relevant, that he no longer has control of the land.[53] An offence may be charged by reference to any day or longer period and a person may be convicted of a subsequent offence by reference to any period of time following the preceding conviction.[54] Persons convicted under the above provision are liable on summary conviction to a fine.[55]

---

45 Ie by appeal to the Secretary of State (TCPA 1990, s. 78) or by subsequent application (TCPA 1990, s. 73).

46 *R v London Borough of Ealing, ex p Zainuddin* [1995] JPL B27—BCN quashed on the basis of an error of law by the LPA.

47 See para 10.25.

48 [2000] QB 381, [1998] 2 All ER 885. The decision of the House of Lords in *R v Wicks* [1998] AC 92, [1997] 2 All ER 801 was distinguished. See para 12.119.

49 See para 12.34.

50 See para 10.68.

51 This view is a little difficult to reconcile with *Boddington v British Transport Police* [1999] 2 AC 143, [1998] 2 All ER 203 where the House of Lords took a broader view of what matters could be challenged by way of defence in the magistrates' court.

52 TCPA 1990, s. 187A(8) and (9).

53 TCPA 1990, s. 187A(11).

54 TCPA 1990, s. 187A(10).

55 TCPA 1990, s. 187A(12). A fine not exceeding level 3 on the standard scale.

12.26 The service of a breach of condition notice constitutes 'taking enforcement action' for the purposes of the Act[56] and it follows that the time limits on the taking of enforcement action introduced by the PCA 1991 apply.[57] However, the provisions relating to time limits do not prevent the service of a breach of condition notice if an enforcement notice in respect of the breach is in effect.[58] The local planning authority may withdraw the breach of condition notice by serving notice on the person responsible. Withdrawal does not prejudice the local planning authority's power to serve a further breach of condition notice in respect of conditions specified in the withdrawn notice.[59]

12.27 What is the effect of a subsequent planning permission on a breach of condition notice? The Act provides that where, after the service of a breach of condition notice, planning permission is granted for any development carried out before the grant of that permission, the notice shall cease to have effect so far as it is inconsistent with that permission. The notice will also cease to have effect where, after a breach of condition notice has been served, any condition to which the notice relates is discharged so far as it requires any person to secure compliance with the condition in question. However, the fact that a breach of condition notice has wholly or partly ceased to have effect under these provisions does not affect the liability of any person for an offence in respect of a previous failure to comply, or secure compliance, with the notice.[60]

12.28 There can be no doubt that developers need to take planning conditions more seriously now that local planning authorities have the option of serving a breach of condition notice. It follows that they need to take care both when volunteering conditions and when acquiring land burdened with existing conditions. The result is to place greater emphasis on section 73[61] applications especially where the circumstances have changed since planning permission was originally granted.

---

56 TCPA 1990, s. 171A(2)(b). Under para (a) of the subsection, the issue of an enforcement notice also constitutes taking enforcement action. See below.

57 See para 12.34.

58 TCPA 1990, s. 171B(4)(a). A further exception in para (b) of the subsection is discussed below, at para 12.37.

59 TCPA 1990, s. 187A(6).

60 TCPA 1990, s. 180(1), (2) and (3).

61 See para 10.99.

Enforcement notices

Issue and service of enforcement notices

12.29 The law relating to the issue of enforcement notices and the service of copies on those concerned is highly technical, but it may be reduced to the following rules:

12.30 (1) the local planning authority have the power to issue an enforcement notice where there has been a breach of planning control. We have seen that a 'breach of planning control' consists of:

(a) Carrying out development without the required planning permission; or
(b) Failing to comply with any condition or limitation subject to which planning permission has been granted.[62]

12.31 It seems that the local planning authority may not be able to proceed against a breach of *condition* where the development as a whole has not been carried out in accordance with the approved plans. In *Handoll v East Lindsey District Council*,[63] planning permission had been granted to erect a bungalow subject to an agricultural occupancy condition. In fact the property was erected some 90 feet to the west of the location approved by the local planning authority. As a result the Court of Appeal held that the construction of the bungalow was not authorized by the permission and that the occupancy condition could not therefore be enforced. McCowan LJ accepted the contention of counsel for the appellants that the wrongdoer in such circumstances would not get a benefit; in fact he would be worse off because he had no permission to use the building and was susceptible to enforcement action in respect of a material change of use.

12.32 (2) The local planning authority should not automatically issue an enforcement notice in respect of every breach of planning control. They should be satisfied that it is expedient to issue the notice, having regard to the provisions of the development plan and to any other material considerations.[64] This suggests that the planning authority should ask themselves whether they would have granted planning permission had an application been made to them and, if so, whether they would have imposed conditions. If the local authority do not issue an enforcement notice the Secretary of State may himself issue such a notice.[65] In deciding whether to

---

62 TCPA 1990, s. 171A(1).

63 [1995] JPL 930, overruling the decision in *Kerrier District Council v Secretary of State for the Environment* [1981] JPL 193. See also *Sparkes v Secretary of State for the Environment, Transport and the Regions* [2000] 3 PLR 39.

64 TCPA 1990, s. 172(1)(b). The status of the development plan has been enhanced by TCPA 1990, s. 54A; see para 8.57.

65 TCPA 1990, s. 182.

take enforcement action, consideration must be given to the personal circumstances of the occupiers of the land.[66]

12.33 Policy pronouncements on behalf of the Secretary of State[67] have emphasized the discretionary nature of the local planning authority's power of enforcement; in considering any enforcement action, the decisive issue for the local planning authority should be whether the breach of control would unacceptably affect public amenity or the existing use of the land and buildings merit protection in the public interest. Local planning authorities are advised that enforcement action should always be commensurate with the breach of planning control to which it relates; it will usually be inappropriate to take formal enforcement action against a trivial or technical breach of control which causes no harm to amenity. Although authorities should attempt to resolve breaches of control by negotiation, particularly where small businesses or self-employed people are concerned, if the unauthorized development is causing serious harm to public amenity and immediate remedial action is required, an enforcement notice should normally be issued.[68]

12.34 (3) In certain cases the Act imposes time limits for issuing an enforcement notice. As explained at the beginning of this chapter these provisions were substantially amended by the Planning and Compensation Act 1991. The time limits apply to the taking of enforcement action, which is defined by the Act as (a) the issue of an enforcement notice, or (b) the service of a breach of condition notice.[69] When the time limit for taking enforcement action has expired, uses and operations become lawful.

12.35 Where a breach of planning control consists of the carrying out without planning permission of building, engineering, mining, or other operations, no enforcement action may be taken after the end of a period of four years beginning with the date on which the operations were substantially completed.[70] Further, where there has been a breach of planning control consisting in the change of use of any building to use as a single dwellinghouse, no enforcement action may be taken after the end of a period of four years commencing with the date of the breach.[71] However, in the case of any other breach of planning control, no enforcement action may be taken after the end of the period of 10 years beginning with the date

66 *R v Kerrier District Council, ex p Uzell* [1996] JPL 837.

67 Planning Policy Guidance Note No 18, para 5.

68 PPG 18, paras 5 and 13.

69 TCPA 1990, s. 171A(2)(a) and (b).

70 TCPA 1990, s. 171B(1). As to the date when the time runs, the section gives statutory force to the decision in *Howes v Secretary of State for the Environment* [1984] JPL 439. The four-year period of immunity does not start to run until the building has been substantially completed both internally and externally—*Sage v Secretary of State for the Environment, Transport and the Regions* [2003] UKHL 22.

71 TCPA 1990, s. 171B(2).

of the breach.[72] The new 10-year immunity period, which was recommended by the Carnwath Report, was said to be 'long enough for any offending use to come to light', and 'short enough to enable evidence to be obtained without undue difficulty'.

12.36 Under the TCPA 1990 as originally enacted the 'four-year rule' mentioned in the previous paragraph also applied to breaches of condition (or limitation) in connection with operational development and to changes of use to use as a single dwellinghouse. But these provisions gave rise to considerable difficulties[73] and have been abolished with respect to the former. The result is that all breaches of condition (or limitation) are now subject to a 10-year time limit; the only exception is a breach of condition preventing a change of use of any building to use as a single dwellinghouse, which remains a four-year case. That this was the intention of the legislature in framing the statutory provisions was affirmed by the Court of Appeal in *First Secretary of State v Arun District Council*.[74] It was confirmed that the time limit for taking enforcement action in respect of the change of use of any building to use as a single dwellinghouse is four years irrespective of whether the breach consisted of development without planning permission or a breach of condition.

12.37 The Act further provides that the service of a breach of condition notice in respect of any breach of planning control is not prevented if an enforcement notice in respect of the breach is in effect;[75] and the taking of further enforcement action in respect of any breach of planning control is not prevented if, during the period of four years ending with that action being taken, the local planning authority have taken or purported to take enforcement action in respect of that breach. This provision provides the authority with a so-called 'second bite' and changes the position under the old law where developers were able to challenge the validity of an enforcement notice and, while they were doing so, time continued to run and possibly expire, preventing the issue of another notice.[76] In *Jarmain v Secretary of State for the Environment*,[77] the Court of Appeal held that the local planning authority were entitled to rely on the second bite provision to issue a second enforcement to correct an error in an earlier notice. The *Jarmain* case was followed in *Romer v Haringey London Borough Council*[78] where the local planning authority had served an enforcement notice on the wrong one of two properties owned by R. When the local planning authority realized they had made a mistake, another

72 TCPA 1990, s. 171B(3).
73 See, eg *Harvey v Secretary of State for Wales* [1990] JPL 420.
74 [2006] EWCA Civ 1172.
75 TCPA 1990, s. 171B(4)(a).
76 TCPA 1990, s. 171B(4)(b).
77 [2000] JPL 1063.
78 [2006] EWHC 3840 (Admin).

notice was served on the correct property. This was more than four years after the actual breach of planning control but less than four years after the first erroneous notice. R argued that as the notices did not refer to the same breach of planning control, the second bite provisions did not apply. Rejecting this argument, the High Court upheld the second enforcement notice. The second bite provisions could be used to cover the same actual breach of planning control which had been described in different ways, even where originally the wrong site had been identified. The court, however, made it clear that the provisions could not be used to cover two quite physically different developments. Similarly, in *Fidler v First Secretary of State*,[79] a new enforcement notice alleging a breach materially wider than breaches alleged in previous notices was held to be an invalid second bite notice.

12.38 The above-mentioned 10-year limitation period, as applied to the breach of an occupancy condition, arose in *Nicholson v Secretary of State for the Environment*.[80] It would seem that, where the breach of an occupancy condition ceases, ie there is a period of compliance, a further resumption of the breach will start the 10-year time limit running afresh. It is not permissible to add the period of one breach to that of a subsequent breach. The 10-year period was also an issue in *Panton v Secretary of State for the Environment, Transport and the Regions*[81] where the Secretary of State's inspector was held to have misunderstood the term 'existing use' for the purpose of the 10-year immunity. The deputy judge held that a *dormant* use which had arisen by way of material change of use could still exist in planning terms provided it had not been lost by operation of law, that is to say by abandonment, the formation of a new planning unit, or by way of material change of use.[82] In *Panton* there had been a material change of use of premises to business purposes in 1960–2 and there was therefore an 'established use'[83] as the use had not apparently been abandoned in the intervening years. The court found that the inspector had been wrong to refuse a certificate of lawfulness[84] in relation to the use on the basis that there was, at the time of the site visit, no physical evidence of the use being carried on.

12.39 However, in the later case of *Thurrock Borough Council v Secretary of State for the Environment, Transport and the Regions*,[85] Newman J appeared to endorse the

---

79 [2003] EWHC 2003 (Admin).

80 [1998] JPL 553. The case also establishes a point in relation to Certificates of Lawfulness; see para 12.166, below. See also *Fairstate Ltd v First Secretary of State* [2005] EWCA Civ 238, a case decided under the Greater London Council (General Powers) Act 1973, s. 25.

81 [1999] JPL 461.

82 See para 6.43.

83 See para 12.175.

84 See para 12.161.

85 [2001] EWHC 128 (Admin), [2001] 3 PLR 14.

Panton principle in relation to an accrued right, such as an established use, but questioned whether it could be applicable to an unlawful use. He held that in determining whether an unlawful use had occurred more than 10 years before the issue of an enforcement notice, it was necessary to pay particular regard to the character and intensity of the use over the whole period. If at any time during the 10-year period the local planning authority could not have taken enforcement action against the breach, because, for example, no breach was taking place, then any such period cannot count towards the rolling period of years which gives rise to the immunity.

12.40 Some uses of land may be of a seasonal nature, for example where land is put to some recreational or holiday use over the summer months, but the activity ceases for the rest of the year. The issue arose in the case of *North Devon District Council v First Secretary of State*[86] where a holiday home had been continuously occupied for more than 10 years in breach of a condition preventing occupation during the winter months. The local planning authority argued that in each year of occupation there had been a breach of planning control only in the winter months and therefore there had not been a continuous breach for more than 10 years. Sullivan J disagreed and held that the continuous occupation of the holiday home for more than 10 years did amount to a continuous breach so that no enforcement action could be taken. In each of the 10 years for which the property had been in use, the local planning authority could have enforced but they had not done so—consequently, on the application of 'common sense', the judge considered the breach to be immune. The *Nicholson* case (to which reference was made above) was distinguished as in that case the condition bit continuously throughout the year.

12.41 The question of the correct test for applying the time-limit rules arose in *Swale Borough Council v First Secretary of State*,[87] a case where the landowner was seeking to establish a four-year period of immunity relating to the residential use of a barn. Relying on the reasoning in the earlier case of *Panton*, the Court of Appeal held that the legally correct question is to ask whether the barn had been used for residential purposes continuously for a four-year period preventing the local planning authority from serving an enforcement notice. On the evidence before the court, the inspector had failed to apply the correct test and his decision was quashed. There were substantial periods where the premises were not occupied for residential purposes.

12.42 (4) A copy of the enforcement notice must be served on the owner or occupier of the land to which it relates and on any other person having an interest in the land

86 [2004] EWHC 578 (Admin).
87 [2005] EWCA Civ 1568.

being an interest which, in the opinion of the authority, is materially affected by the service of the notice.[88]

12.43 'Owner' presumably means the person entitled to receive the rack-rent or the person who would be entitled to receive it if the land were so let.[89] This would exclude, for instance, the owner of a freehold reversion subject to a lease at less than a rack-rent; such a person would nevertheless have an interest in the land and might be materially affected.[90]

12.44 The word 'occupier' clearly includes anyone occupying land under a lease or tenancy. And it seems clear—in spite of some earlier doubts[91]—that it may include a licensee. In *Stevens v Bromley London Borough Council*,[92] the Court of Appeal rejected the proposition that an occupier for this purpose must be someone who has an interest in the land; the intention of the legislature was to ensure that anyone who might be prejudiced by an enforcement notice should be served with a copy of it.

12.45 Not all licensees will be occupiers for this purpose. Whether they are or not will depend upon the circumstances. In *Stevens v London Borough of Bromley*,[93] a number of caravanners occupied sites under licences from the owner of the land. These caravans were the permanent homes of their owners, and many of them made gardens on the small plots surrounding the caravans; each caravan had mains water and electricity and its drains were connected to a common cesspool. The licences could not be revoked unless one month's notice was given. It was held that the caravanners should have been served with the enforcement notice. Where, however, the arrangements are of a more transitory nature—as in *Munnich v Godstone Rural District Council*[94]—licensees will not be regarded as 'occupiers' for this purpose, but this was obiter.

12.46 There are obvious pitfalls for the local planning authority. In *Mayes v Secretary of State for Wales*,[95] Graham Eyre QC held that it was 'extremely important that all reasonable steps should be taken to identify all persons entitled to be served with

---

88 TCPA 1990, s. 172(2)(a) and (b).

89 See definition of 'owner' in TCPA 1990, s. 336(1), and *London Corpn v Cusack-Smith* [1955] AC 337, [1955] 1 All ER 302; see para 14.23.

90 As a person interested in the land, such an owner would have the right to appeal against the enforcement notice: see para 12.88.

91 Lord Denning MR suggested that a licensee could not be an occupier: *James v Minister of Housing and Local Government* [1965] 3 All ER 602 at 605; *Munnich v Godstone RDC* [1966] 1 All ER 930, [1966] 1 WLR 427.

92 [1972] Ch 400, [1972] 1 All ER 712.

93 See para 12.44.

94 See fn 91 above. The report of this case does not state the degree of transience of the so-called occupiers, but Danckwerts LJ described them as 'birds of passage'.

95 [1989] JPL 848.

enforcement notices . . . and that they should be served'. Failure to serve someone who should have been served with the notice may invalidate the notice altogether. This may depend on the circumstances. In *McDaid v Clydebank District Council*,[96] the council had failed to serve the owners even though they knew of their identity: the Court of Session held that the notice was a nullity. In *R v Greenwich London Borough Council, ex p Patel*,[97] the Court of Appeal in England distinguished *McDaid* on the ground that the borough council did not know of the appellant's interest. No harm is done, however, by serving someone who is not perhaps entitled to be served.[98] TCPA 1990, s. 176(5) provides that the Secretary of State, in appeal against an enforcement notice, may disregard the fact that some person who ought to have been served with the enforcement notice has not been served, if neither the appellant nor that person has been substantially prejudiced.

12.47 (5) The law requires that the enforcement notice shall state:

(a) The matters which appear to the local planning authority to constitute the breach of planning control;[99] and
(b) Whether, in the opinion of the authority, the breach consists of the carrying out of development without the required planning permission or the failure to comply with any condition or limitation subject to which planning permission has been granted.[100] Further, the notice shall specify:
(c) The steps which the authority require to be taken, or the activities which the authority require to cease, in order (wholly or partly) to remedy the breach of planning control or to remedy any injury to amenity caused by the breach;[101]
(d) The date on which the notice is to take effect;[102]
(e) The period at the end of which the notice must have been complied with;[103]
(f) The reasons why the local planning authority consider it expedient to issue the notice;[104]

[96] 1984] JPL 579. See also *Caravans and Automobiles Ltd v Southall Borough Council* [1963] 2 All ER 533, [1963] 1 WLR 690; notice rendered invalid by a failure to serve all the occupiers.
[97] [1985] JPL 851.
[98] See *Scarborough Borough Council v Adams* [1983] JPL 673.
[99] TCPA 1990, s. 173(1)(a).
[100] TCPA 1990, s. 173(1)(b).
[101] TCPA 1990, s. 173(3)–(7). Considered more fully at para 12.68.
[102] TCPA 1990, s. 173(8). Subject to any appeal (see para 12.96 as to the effect of an appeal) it shall take effect on that date.
[103] TCPA 1990, s. 173(9). The notice may specify different periods for different steps or activities.
[104] TCPA 1990, s. 173(10); T & CP (Enforcement Notices and Appeals) Regulations 1991, SI 1991 No 2804, reg 3.

(g) The precise boundaries of the land to which the notice relates, whether by reference to a plan or otherwise.[105]

12.48 If the rules as to service and content are not complied with, the notice may be a nullity; and, even if it is not a nullity, it may be invalid in which case it may be quashed on appeal. The distinction between 'nullity' and 'invalidity' is important because it affects the rights of persons on whom copies of the enforcement notice are served. If the notice is a nullity, it is 'so much waste paper';[106] it is, strictly speaking, not an enforcement notice at all, and the recipient is entitled to ignore it or, if he wishes, he can seek a declaration that it is void. If, however, the notice is invalid, it cannot safely be ignored and (with some possible exceptions) the recipient must exercise his rights of appeal under the TCPA 1990.[107]

12.49 What constitutes a nullity in this context was explained by Upjohn LJ in *Miller-Mead v Minister of Housing and Local Government*.[108] It seems that a notice will be a nullity if it fails to specify one of the two periods mentioned in paragraph (5)(d) and (e) above. This happened in *Burgess v Jarvis and Sevenoaks RDC*.[109]

12.50 Jarvis had built a number of houses without permission and the local authority served an enforcement notice requiring him to demolish the houses. This notice did not separately specify the period after which it was to take effect. Burgess, who was the tenant of one of the houses, obtained a declaration that the notice was null.

12.51 A notice will also be a nullity if:[110] 'on its true construction it was ambiguous and uncertain so that the owner or occupier could not tell in what respect it was alleged that he had developed the land without permission or in what respect it was alleged that he had failed to comply with a condition or, again, that he could not tell with reasonable certainty what steps he had to take to remedy the alleged breaches.'

12.52 This dictum is illustrated by *Metallic Protectives Ltd v Secretary of State for the Environment*.[111]

12.53 The local planning authority served an enforcement notice alleging breach of a condition in a planning permission that no nuisance should be caused to residential properties in the area by reason of noise, smell, smoke, etc. The enforcement

---

[105] SI 1991 No 2804, reg 3. Reg 4 requires an explanatory note explaining the relevant statutory provisions and information as to the rights of appeal.

[106] *Miller-Mead v Minister of Housing and Local Government* [1963] 2 QB 196, [1963] 1 All ER 459, per Upjohn LJ.

[107] See para 12.88.

[108] [1963] 2 QB 196, [1963] 1 All ER 459.

[109] [1952] 2 QB 41, [1952] 1 All ER 592. In the Court of Appeal, all three Lords Justice described the notice as 'invalid', but presumably they meant 'null' or 'void'.

[110] *Miller-Mead v Minister of Housing and Local Government*, above, per Upjohn LJ.

[111] [1976] JPL 166.

notice required the occupier to install satisfactory sound proofing of a compressor and to take all possible action to minimize the effect created by the use of acrylic paint. On appeal, the Secretary of State accepted that the notice was far too imprecise; he therefore substituted precise requirements.

12.54 Held: the enforcement notice as originally served was so defective as to be a nullity from the start; the Secretary of State could not amend it and it must be disregarded.

12.55 Although the Secretary of State's powers to amend or vary the terms of an enforcement notice have since been enlarged by the Act of 1981, it remains the law that he cannot use these powers where the notice is a nullity. Thus in *Dudley Bowers Amusements Enterprises Ltd v Secretary of State for the Environment*,[112] the local planning authority issued an enforcement notice requiring the company to discontinue the use of land for the holding of markets 'on such Sundays which fall within the period of summer time in any year'. On appeal the inspector amended the notice by substituting a reference to the Summer Time Act 1972. In the High Court Mr David Widdicombe QC, sitting as a deputy judge, held the original wording was hopelessly ambiguous; the notice was therefore a nullity and there was no power to amend it.

12.56 It seems to be well enough established that the language of an enforcement notice must be given its ordinary or popular meaning and that extrinsic evidence, such as early planning applications and decisions are, not admissible as aids to construction; where the issue is the meaning of the words used, the court will not go beyond the four corners of the notice.[113]

12.57 However, the courts are nowadays less inclined to insist on strict adherence to formalities and are willing in appropriate circumstances to adopt a more empirical approach. This change of emphasis is illustrated by *Coventry Scaffolding Co (London) Ltd v Parker*.[114]

12.58 The company carried on business from two premises in Crystal Palace Road, London, nos 73 and 75. Having at first warned the company not to use the rear of 73 for parking vehicles and storing equipment, the local planning authority served an enforcement notice; the enforcement notice referred to the name of the street, not the number of the property. Some years later the company were prosecuted and convicted for non-compliance with the notice.

---

[112] (1985) 52 P & CR 365, [1986] JPL 689.

[113] *Miller-Mead v Minister of Housing and Local Government* [1963] 2 QB 196, [1963] 1 All ER 459, CA; *Dudley Bowers Amusements Enterprises Ltd v Secretary of State for the Environment* (1985) 52 P & CR 365, [1986] JPL 689.

[114] [1987] JPL 127. A similar approach was taken in *Pitman v Secretary of State for the Environment* [1989] JPL 831.

12.59 The Divisional Court held that the omission to refer to no 73 was not a material or fundamental error so as to render the notice a nullity because the company were fully aware of the land to which it related. Kerr J, delivering the judgment of the court, said that it was not the correct view that one might only have regard to the contents of the notice within its four corners in order to decide whether it was a nullity or not.

12.60 What had to be decided in each instance was whether, in the light of the surrounding circumstances, the recipient of the notice was sufficiently and clearly apprised of the effect of the notice, and of what he had to do pursuant to it to render it just or unjust to hold him to it.

12.61 Also, where an enforcement notice required compliance with a condition of planning permission that the occupation of a bungalow be limited to persons employed locally in agriculture, the Court of Appeal held that the word 'locally' had a perfectly intelligible meaning even if some doubtful cases might arise. The enforcement notice did not require the owner to permit occupation to persons who satisfied the provisions of the planning permission. If the proposed occupier was clearly inside or clearly outside the restriction, the owner could permit or refuse occupation as the case might be: if he was uncertain he could for his own safety refuse occupation.[115]

The alleged breach of planning control

12.62 The local planning authority must correctly identify the nature of the breach. For example, an enforcement notice may allege that development has been carried out without permission when in fact there has been a failure to comply with a condition or limitation. Before the PCA 1991 the courts had long taken the view that such an error rendered the notice invalid (but not a nullity).[116] In *Kerrier District Council v Secretary of State for the Environment*,[117] Lord Lane LCJ said: 'It is clearly established by many decisions that, if a planning authority wishes to serve an enforcement notice, it must decide whether the breach alleged is development without planning permission or failure to comply with some condition or limitation. If, on the facts of the particular case, the planning authority puts the case in the wrong pigeon-hole, the enforcement notice will be set aside.'

---

[115] *Alderson v Secretary of State for the Environment* [1984] JPL 429.

[116] *Francis v Yiewsley and West Drayton UDC* [1958] 1 QB 478, [1957] 3 All ER 529; *Kerrier District Council v Secretary of State for the Environment* [1981] JPL 193. See also *Copeland Borough Council v Secretary of State for the Environment* (1976) 31 P & CR 403.

[117] [1981] JPL 193; overruled by *Handoll v East Lindsey District Council* [1995] JPL 930 but not on this point.

12.63 Another example of this problem is to be seen in *FG Whitley & Sons Co Ltd v Secretary of State for Wales*[118] where planning permission was granted for the extraction of minerals subject to conditions requiring schemes for restoration, landscaping, etc, to be agreed before the working commenced. An enforcement notice was served by the local planning authority alleging development without planning permission. Disagreeing with the Secretary of State, Sir Frank Layfield QC (sitting as a deputy judge) held that the description of the breach was incorrect and the notice was defective.

12.64 However, under the present system of appeals which was introduced in 1960, the Secretary of State can correct defects in enforcement notices provided he is satisfied that this can be done without injustice. In 1981 the powers of amendment of the Secretary of State were reworded, with a further slight rewording in 1991. He is now empowered to correct any defect, error, or misdescription in the enforcement notice, or vary the terms of the notice, if he is satisfied that the correction or variation will not cause injustice to the appellant or the local planning authority.[119] The courts have regarded these provisions as enabling the Secretary of State to amend even fundamental mistakes by the local planning authority in describing the breach of planning control. An illustration is *R v Tower Hamlets London Borough Council, ex p Ahern (London) Ltd.*[120]

12.65 The company had planning permission for a waste skip transfer station subject to a condition that the use should cease on 31 August 1987. In September 1987 the council refused permission to continue the use and served an enforcement notice alleging a breach of planning control by making a material change of use without planning permission. On appeal the inspector decided that the notice was so defective as to be invalid and incapable of correction without injustice. He therefore quashed the notice. The company applied to the High Court to set this decision aside because they wanted a decision on the planning merits without having to go through the procedure again; they would, they said, have suffered no injustice had the substance of the appeal been dealt with, as they knew precisely what was being alleged against them and what steps the council required them to take.

12.66 Roch J held that the inspector was wrong in deciding that the error in the enforcement notice was incapable of correction; he was further wrong in holding that he was unable to be satisfied that no injustice would be caused. The learned judge considered that the law had progressed to the point where the pettyfogging had stopped, where artificial and nice distinctions understood by lawyers no longer prevailed, and the Act could be read so that it meant what it said, namely that the

118 [1990] JPL 678. An appeal to the CA on another ground is reported at [1992] JPL 856.
119 TCPA 1990, s. 176(1) as substituted by the PCA 1991, s. 23 and Sch 7, para 23.
120 [1989] JPL 757.

Secretary of State might correct any defect if he was satisfied that the correction could be made without injustice to either party.

12.67 The above decision anticipated the Planning and Compensation Act 1991 which sought to improve the position of local planning authorities in alleging a breach of planning control. As we have seen,[121] under the TCPA 1990 as amended by the PCA 1991 the enforcement notice shall 'state' the matters which appear to the local planning authority to constitute a breach of planning control—under the TCPA 1990 as originally enacted they were required to 'specify' these matters. This is presumably intended to be a less onerous requirement. Further, the notice must now state whether, *in the opinion* of the authority, the breach consists of carrying out of development without planning permission or the failure to comply with any condition or limitation attached to a planning permission. There is ground for thinking that, in future, if their opinion is wrong the enforcement notice will not be invalid[122] and the robust strictures of Lord Lane in the *Kerrier* case, quoted above,[123] should now be seen in the light of this. Finally, it is provided that a notice complies with the Act if it enables any person on whom a copy is served to know what the matters are which appear to the local planning authority to constitute a breach of planning control.[124] This is a statutory formulation of the test laid down in a number of cases over the years.[125]

The steps to remedy the breach

12.68 The TCPA 1971, as originally enacted, provided that the enforcement notice must specify the steps required by the local planning authority to remedy the breach of planning control; that was either (a) in the case of development without permission, steps for the purpose of restoring the land to its previous condition; or (b) in the case of a breach of condition or limitation, steps for securing compliance with that condition or limitation.

12.69 There was considerable doubt as to whether the local planning authority had much scope for discretion in specifying the steps to be taken. It was clear from *Iddenden v Secretary of State for the Environment*[126] that they did not have to insist on the land being restored to precisely its previous condition but there was uncertainty as to what extent the local planning authority might 'under-enforce'.[127]

---

[121] See para 12.46.

[122] *Co-operative Retail Services Ltd v Taff-Ely Borough Council* (1979) 39 P & CR 223 (per Browne LJ); matters for the opinion of the LPA are not appropriate for review by the courts.

[123] See para 12.62.

[124] TCPA 1990, s. 173(2).

[125] See, inter alia, *Coventry Scaffolding Co (London) Ltd v Parker* [1987] JPL 127.

[126] [1972] 3 All ER 883.

[127] See *Copeland Borough Council v Secretary of State for the Environment* (1976) 31 P & CR 403.

12.70 The 1981 amendments gave the local planning authority greater flexibility. Under these provisions (which were incorporated into the TCPA 1990 until the coming into force of the PCA 1991) the enforcement notice could specify[128] steps to be taken to make the development comply with the terms of any planning permission which had been granted in respect of the land or for removing or alleviating any injury to amenity which had been caused by the development. There is no doubt that these provisions gave the local planning authority an alternative to requiring the removal or discontinuance of the unauthorized development. Thus, if a fish and chip shop had been opened without planning permission, the local planning authority may have no objection to the development in principle, but they might wish to restrict the opening hours so that they do not cause unreasonable disturbance to neighbours. Or where buildings or works have been erected without planning permission, the local planning authority may be willing for them to remain provided a landscaping or tree planting scheme is carried out.[129]

12.71 The Planning and Compensation Act 1991 further amended and clarified the provisions referred to above. The TCPA 1990 now provides[130] that an enforcement notice shall specify the steps which the authority require to be taken, or the activities which the authority require to cease, in order to achieve, wholly or partly, any of the following purposes.[131] These purposes are:[132]

(a) Remedying the breach by making any development comply with the terms (including conditions and limitations) of any planning permission which has been granted in respect of the land, by discontinuing any use of the land or by restoring the land to its condition before the breach took place; or
(b) Remedying any injury to amenity which has been caused by the breach.

12.72 The above provisions broadly re-enact the previous law; however, the reference to 'wholly or partly', which is new, expressly authorizes action which only partly achieves the planning authority's purposes, ie 'underenforcement'. The Act then goes on to spell out in more detail than previously what an enforcement notice may require,[133] for example:

(a) The alteration or removal of any buildings or works;
(b) The carrying out of any building or other operations;
(c) Any activity on the land not to be carried on except to the extent specified in the notice; or

128 TCPA 1990, s. 173(2), (3), (4) as originally enacted.

129 As to whether planning permission is deemed to be granted when such steps have been carried out, see para 12.74.

130 TCPA 1990, s. 173 inserted by the PCA 1991, s. 5.

131 TCPA 1990, s. 173(3).

132 TCPA 1990, s. 173(4).

133 TCPA 1990, s. 173(5).

(d) The contour of a deposit of refuse or waste material on land to be modified by altering the gradient or gradients of its sides.

12.73 These examples are wider and more explicit than anything that has appeared previously. Paragraph (a) could be used to require the removal of part of a building (eg an additional storey) that did not feature in the approved plans, while paragraph (b) provides for positive works to be carried out to remedy the breach, for example the erection of a wall to mitigate a visual intrusion upon amenity. Paragraph (c) refers to 'activity', which is not the same as use, and is particularly apt to deal with cases of intensification.

12.74 Further, where an enforcement notice is issued in respect of a breach of planning control consisting of the demolition of a building, the notice may require the construction of a replacement building which is as similar as possible to the demolished building.[134] Providing all the requirements of the notice with respect to construction of the replacement building have been complied with, planning permission is to be treated as having been granted for that construction.[135] Similarly, planning permission is to be treated as having been granted where an enforcement notice in respect of any breach of planning control could have required any building or works to be removed, or any activity to cease, but does not do so and all the requirements of the notice have been complied with.[136]

12.75 The steps required by an enforcement notice should not exceed what is necessary to achieve the purposes set out in TCPA 1990, s. 173(3), namely, (a) to remedy the breach of planning control; or (b) to remedy any injury to amenity caused by the breach. Excessive requirements do not invalidate the enforcement notice, but the Secretary of State may amend the notice on appeal.

12.76 An important application of the principle that the requirements should not be excessive is to be found in *Mansi v Elstree RDC*.[137]

12.77 Land occupied by M was used as a plant nursery and contained a number of glasshouses. From 1922 onwards there was a subsidiary use of part of the land, including one of the glasshouses, for retail sales of nursery produce and other articles. In 1959, M intensified the latter use until the glasshouse became primarily a shop. The local planning authority served an enforcement notice requiring M to discontinue use for the sale of goods. On appeal the Minister upheld the enforcement notice.

---

134 TCPA 1990, s. 173(6). See also TCPA 1990, s. 173(7) which lays down certain requirements that a replacement building must comply with.

135 TCPA 1990, s. 173(12).

136 TCPA 1990, s. 173(11).

137 (1964) 16 P & CR 153.

12.78 Held: the Minister should have recognized that a notice requiring discontinuance of all sale of goods went too far; the notice should be amended to safeguard the established right to carry on retail trade in the manner and to the extent to which it was carried on in 1959.

12.79 The '*Mansi* principle' that legitimate use rights should be safeguarded has been followed in a number of cases.[138] Further confirmation that the *Mansi* principle is of application, even after the reforms of 1991, has been provided by the Court of Appeal in *Duguid v Secretary of State for the Environment, Transport and the Regions*.[139] In this case, however, the Court held that it was not necessary to amend an enforcement notice so as to safeguard the appellant's permitted development right to carry on a 14-day market;[140] the resumption of a permitted temporary use after the discontinuance of prohibited use is not a breach of planning control and so cannot be a breach of the enforcement notice.[141] However, it seems that the *Mansi* principle is not of universal—application thus an enforcement notice may in certain circumstances override lawful use rights under a certificate of lawfulness.[142]

12.80 Finally, although the local planning authority now have more flexibility than ever before in prescribing the steps to remedy the breach of planning control, it is vital that these steps be properly defined, otherwise the enforcement notice will be void.

The date on which the notice takes effect

12.81 The TCPA 1990, as amended,[143] provides that an enforcement notice shall specify the date on which it is to take effect,[144] and subject to any appeal it shall take effect on that date.[145] In specifying this date the local planning authority must have regard to TCPA 1990, s. 172(3) which requires them to serve a copy of the enforcement notice on the owner and occupier and any other person likely to be affected, not more than 28 days after its date of issue, and not less than 28 days before the date specified in it as the date on which it is to take effect.

12.82 These provisions are linked with the requirement that any appeal against the enforcement notice must be lodged with the Secretary of State before the notice

---

138 See eg *Trevors Warehouses Ltd v Secretary of State for the Environment* (1972) 23 P & CR 215; and *Newport v Secretary of State for the Environment and Bromley London Borough* (1980) 40 P & CR 261.

139 (2000) 82 P & CR 52.

140 See para 7.34.

141 *Metallic Protectives Ltd v Secretary of State for the Environment* [1976] JPL 166; see para 12.52.

142 *Staffordshire County Council v Challinor* [2007] EWCA Civ 864 discussed at para 12.171.

143 The PCA 1991, s. 5, inserts a new TCPA 1990, s. 173.

144 TCPA 1990, s. 173(8).

145 As to the effect of an appeal, see para 12.96.

takes effect; it is important therefore that anyone affected by the notice is given a minimum of 28 days in which to appeal. It seems, however, that the Secretary of State may in his discretion disregard the fact that an appellant has received less than 28 days' notice. In *Porritt v Secretary of State for the Environment*,[146] an enforcement notice was issued in respect of unauthorized development but P was served with a copy of it only 27 days before the date on which it was due to take effect; however, he lodged an appeal before that date. The Secretary of State decided to disregard the procedural defect because no injustice had resulted. There was no statutory provision which authorized the Secretary of State to do so, but the court nevertheless upheld his decision; an interesting example of the extent to which the courts have moved away from insistence upon the strict observance of formalities.

The period for compliance with the notice

12.83 The enforcement notice must specify the period at the end of which any steps are required to have been taken or any activities are required to have ceased and may specify different periods for different steps or activities.[147] There is no statutory minimum period, but the period or periods specified must be reasonable having regard to what is required.

12.84 Under TCPA 1990, s. 173A the local planning authority may withdraw an enforcement notice issued by them, or they may waive or relax any requirement of such a notice and, in particular, may extend the period specified for compliance. Moreover, they may exercise these powers whether or not the notice has taken effect;[148] if they do exercise any of them, they must give notice to every person who has been served with a copy of the notice, or who would, if the notice were re-issued, be served with a copy of it.[149] The withdrawal of San enforcement notice does not affect the power of the local planning authority to issue a further notice.[150]

Misuse of powers

12.85 A decision by a local planning authority to take enforcement action may be susceptible to challenge in the courts if it involves a misuse, by the authority, of their powers under the TCPA 1990.

---

146 [1988] JPL 414.

147 TCPA 1990, s. 173(9). The period for compliance starts at the date the notice takes effect—an enforcement notice that stated that the time for compliance 'immediately' was a nullity: *R v Berkshire District Council, ex p Lynes* [2002] EWHC 1828 (Admin).

148 TCPA 1990, s. 173A(1) and (2). Under the TCPA 1990 as originally enacted, the LPA could withdraw the notice at any time before it took effect, but not afterwards.

149 TCPA 1990, s. 173A(3).

150 TCPA 1990, s. 173A(4).

12.86 It may be recalled from an earlier chapter that in *Knott v Secretary of State for the Environment*[151] the High Court held that the occupancy of a house was unrestricted despite the fact that a planning condition purported to limit its occupancy to Mr and Mrs Knott. At this point, the local authority, acting on the Secretary of State's view that the decision to grant planning permission had been 'grossly wrong', resolved to make an order revoking the planning permission and also a discontinuance order relating to the uncompleted works.[152] It then emerged that the house had not been built in accordance with the approved plans. The council therefore decided to issue an enforcement notice on the grounds of a breach of planning control; if successful, this course of action would have relieved the council of liability to pay compensation.

12.87 The matter came before the High Court in *R v Caradon District Council, ex p Knott*.[153] Under TCPA 1990, s. 172(1) it must appear 'expedient' to the local planning authority to issue an enforcement notice. Sullivan J accepted the applicant's contention that the council's decision to take enforcement action was unlawful. It had apparently been made with the sole purpose of reducing the compensation payable to the applicants; as the learned judge said: 'The Council was not choosing between two statutory means of removing unauthorised development. The [revocation and discontinuance] orders were already in force that would remove the development from the land. So no further planning purpose would be served by issuing an enforcement notice to precisely the same effect.' Sullivan J also held that the council was estopped from taking enforcement action.

Rights of appeal

12.88 As originally enacted the TCPA 1947 provided two methods by which an enforcement notice might be challenged: (a) by applying to the local planning authority for planning permission and then appealing, if need be, to the Minister against the planning authority's decision; (b) by appealing to the local magistrates on certain limited grounds of law. In addition, it was possible under the general law to apply to the High Court for a declaration on any matter of law.

12.89 These provisions were not well designed. They provided considerable opportunities for delay and evasion which were sometimes well exploited; and, owing to ambiguous drafting, there were doubts as to the precise extent of the right of appeal to the magistrates. The Caravan Sites and Control of Development Act 1960 substituted a right of appeal to the Secretary of State, both on planning and legal grounds, by any person on whom the enforcement notice had been served or

---

151 [1997] JPL 713; see para 10.74.

152 See para 11.15.

153 (1999) 80 P & CR 154.

by any other person having an interest in the land. These provisions, with some changes in detail, were contained in the TCPA 1990 as originally enacted. The PCA 1991 has made some minor amendments—in particular, the grounds of appeal have been modified to reflect changes in the substantive law already discussed.

Who may appeal?

12.90 TCPA 1990, s. 174(1) confers a right of appeal upon any person having an interest in the land or a 'relevant occupier', whether or not a copy of this notice has been served on him; 'relevant occupier' means any person who occupies the land by virtue of a licence at the date on which the enforcement notice is issued and continues to do so at the time the appeal is brought. This provision (introduced in 1984 and amended in 1991) restores the right of appeal to some of the licensees upon whom a copy of the notice ought to be served.[154]

12.91 In *R v Secretary of State for the Environment, Transport and the Regions, ex p Benham-Crosswell,*[155] an enforcement notice was served in respect of land farmed by the applicants. Some 15 days later, on 28 October, their lease expired and they then brought an appeal against the enforcement notice on 17 November. Thus although the applicants had an interest in the land when the enforcement notice was served, their interest had ceased before the lodging of appeal and it was not proved that there was any arrangement for them to occupy the land under licence thereafter. Penry-Davey J, in the High Court, upheld the inspector's decision that the applicants had no statutory right to appeal. The Court confirmed that, under TCPA 1990, s. 174, an enforcement appeal could only be brought by a person having an interest in the land at the time the appeal was brought, or by a licensee who occupied the land both when the enforcement notice was served and when the appeal was lodged.

The grounds of appeal

12.92 TCPA 1990, s. 174(2), as amended by the PCA 1991, provides that an appeal may be brought on any of the following grounds:

(a) That, in respect of any breach of planning control which may be constituted by the matters stated in the notice, planning permission ought to be granted or, as the case may be, the condition or limitation concerned ought to be discharged;
(b) That those matters have not occurred;

[154] See para 12.44 As originally enacted the right of appeal of a relevant occupier was confined to those occupying by virtue of a licence 'in writing'. In *R v Secretary of State for the Environment, ex p Davis* (1989) 59 P & CR 306, it was held that the Secretary of State's decision to refuse an appeal to a party claiming title by adverse possession was not perverse, and would be upheld.

[155] [2001] EGCS 30.

(c) That those matters (if they occurred) do not constitute a breach of planning control;
(d) That, at the date when the notice was issued, no enforcement action could be taken in respect of any breach of planning control which may be constituted by those matters;[156]
(e) That copies of the enforcement notice were not served as required by TCPA 1990, s. 172;[157]
(f) That the steps required by the notice to be taken, or the activities required by the notice to cease, exceed what is necessary to remedy any breach of planning control which may be constituted by those matters or, as the case may be, to remedy any injury to amenity which has been caused by any such breach;
(g) That any period specified in the notice for compliance with the notice falls short of what should reasonably be allowed.

12.93 The question of where the burden of proof lies in enforcement appeals was discussed in *Nelsovil Ltd v Minister of Housing and Local Government*.[158] Widgery J said, 'I should have thought that a person given a right to appeal on certain specified grounds is the person who has to make good those grounds and is the person on whom that onus rests.' He also said, 'I can see no sort of hardship in requiring that the onus shall lie on the appellant in such a case.' In this case the point at issue was whether a material change of use had occurred more than four years before an enforcement notice was served; but the appellants failed to discharge their burden of proof, and the Minister's decision that (in effect) there was no evidence of the changed use dating back four years was upheld by the court. An appeal against an enforcement notice is a civil matter; the standard of proof is on the balance of probabilities, not the criminal law standard of beyond reasonable doubt.[159]

Procedure on appeal

12.94 The TCPA 1990, as amended by the PCA 1991,[160] provides that an appeal against an enforcement notice can be made either (a) by giving written notice to the Secretary of State before the date on which the enforcement notice is due to take effect; or (b) by sending notice to him in a properly addressed and pre-paid letter posted to him at such time that, in the ordinary course of post, it would be delivered to him before that date. Paragraph (b), above represents a relaxation of the position established by *Lenlyn Ltd v Secretary of State for the Environment*[161] where

156 See para 12.34 as to the time limit rules.
157 See para 12.41.
158 [1962] 1 All ER 423, [1962] 1 WLR 404. See also *Parker Bros (Farms) Ltd v Minister of Housing and Local Government* (1969) 210 Estates Gazette 825; and *O'Reilly v First Secretary of State* (2005) 24 EG 179 (CS).
159 *Thrasyvoulou v Secretary of State for the Environment* [1984] JPL 732.
160 PCA 1991, s. 6, inserting a new TCPA 1990, s. 174(3).
161 [1985] JPL 482.

it had been held that the relevant date was the date when the notice was received by the Secretary of State, rather than the date of posting. Nevertheless, it remains the position that the time limit is absolute and the Secretary of State has no jurisdiction to extend it.[162]

12.95 Procedures for enforcement appeals are contained in regulations made by the Secretary of State. New regulations relating to enforcement inquiries, hearings, and appeals by way of written representations were made in 2002. These are the Town and Country Planning (Enforcement Notices and Appeals) (England) Regulations 2002, SI 2002 No 2682; the Town and Country Planning (Enforcement) (Written Representations Procedure) (England) Regulations 2002, SI 2002 No 2683; the Town and Country Planning (Enforcement) (Hearings Procedure) (England) Rules 2002, SI 2002 No 2684; Town and Country Planning (Enforcement) (Inquiries Procedure) (England) Rules 2002, SI 2002 No 2685.

12.96 The giving of notice of appeal suspends the operation of the enforcement notice pending the final outcome of the appeal.[163] Subject to what has been said above, the appellant and the local planning authority have the right to be heard at a public local inquiry or other hearing.[164] The Secretary of State may uphold, quash, or vary an enforcement notice. In particular, he may grant planning permission for the development to which the notice relates; and he may determine lawfulness of any development on the land and issue a certificate of lawfulness accordingly.[165] And as we have seen,[166] the Secretary of State is empowered to correct any defect, error, or misdescription in the enforcement notice, or vary the terms of the notice, if he is satisfied that the correction or variation will not cause injustice to the appellant or the local planning authority.

12.97 Finally, whether or not appeal ground (a), above, is invoked by the appellant, there is deemed to be an application for planning permission for the development to which the enforcement notice relates.[167] The PCA 1991 provides for the situation where the appeal is under ground (a) and a fee is payable for the deemed application; if the fee is not paid after the Secretary of State has given notice specifying the period within which it must be paid, the appeal, so far as brought on that ground, and the application shall lapse at the end of that period.[168]

162 *R v Secretary of State for the Environment, ex p JBI Financial Consultants* [1989] JPL 365.

163 TCPA 1990, s. 175(4), as amended by PCA 1991, s. 5 which now makes the suspension subject to any order under TCPA 1990, s. 289(4A); discussed at para 12.112.

164 TCPA 1990, s. 175(3).

165 TCPA 1990, s. 177(1). For certificates of lawfulness, see para 12.161.

166 See para 12.55.

167 TCPA 1990, s. 177(5).

168 TCPA 1990, s. 177(5A), inserted by PCA 1991, s. 6(3).

12.98 To what extent should an inspector, when dealing with an enforcement appeal and having identified a breach of planning control, consider whether the development could be made acceptable in planning terms? As confirmed in *Tapecrown Ltd v First Secretary of State,*[169] it seems that the inspector may need to consider any proposed modifications to the appeal site and their impact in terms of planning policy and amenity. In this case, an inspector dismissed an enforcement appeal against the unauthorized erection of a building and adjacent hardstanding on the ground, inter alia, that the total development exceeded the tolerances allowed by the GPDO. The inspector rejected an argument that the hardstanding was temporary and dismissed the possibility of certain proposed alterations. The Court of Appeal quashed the enforcement notice. Although it was not the inspector's duty to make the developer's case for him, he should bear in mind that the proceedings are intended to be remedial not punitive, and so should have considered the appropriateness of the modifications. That this may require inviting the parties to make further comment was recognized by the court.

12.99 In *Thrasyvoulou v Secretary of State for the Environment,*[170] the House of Lords had to consider the extent to which a ruling of the Secretary of State in an enforcement appeal creates an estoppel which is binding in subsequent proceedings.

12.100 In 1981, the local planning authority had issued enforcement notices in respect of the properties concerned alleging a material change of use to use as an hotel or hostel. On appeal, the inspector had concluded that the use was an hotel use which had been carried on since 1960 and that this was an established use. In 1985 the council issued further enforcement notices in respect of the properties alleging a material change of use to use as a hostel for homeless families. It was common ground that there had been no change in the use of the properties since service of the 1981 notices. On appeal against the later enforcement notices it was argued that an 'issue estoppel' arose which prevented the council from alleging that the use was as a hostel. Before the inspector and the High Court this argument was rejected; however T's appeal to the Court of Appeal was successful, whereupon the Secretary of State appealed to the House of Lords.

12.101 The House of Lords held that although an issue estoppel could not arise out of any decision to grant or withhold planning permission for development, the determination in favour of an appellant in an enforcement appeal on any of the grounds (b) to (e) of TCPA 1990, s. 99(2) (now TCPA 1990, s. 174(2)(b)–(e)) does give rise to an issue estoppel. According to Lord Bridge (with whom the other members of the House agreed), this will arise 'whenever the determination of the

[169] [2006] EWCA 1744.

[170] [1990] 2 AC 273, [1990] 1 All ER 65. See also *Hammond v Secretary of State for the Environment* [1997] JPL 724.

ground decided in favour of the appellant on an appeal against one enforcement notice can be relied on in an appeal against a second enforcement notice which is in the same terms and is directed at the same alleged development as the first'.

Environmental impact assessment in enforcement appeals

12.102 The Environmental Impact Assessment Regulations[171] provide that the Secretary of State shall not grant planning permission in respect of 'EIA development' which is the subject of enforcement action unless he has first taken into account the environmental information, and he must state in his decision that he has done so.[172]

12.103 It will be recalled from chapter 8 that 'EIA development' means development that is either Schedule 1 development or is Schedule 2 development likely to have significant effects on the environment by virtue of factors such as its nature, size, and location.

12.104 Regulation 25 of the EIA regulations lays down the procedures involved. Under the regulations, where it appears to the local planning authority that the matters constituting the breach of planning control involve EIA development, they shall, before an enforcement notice is issued, adopt a screening opinion.[173] They should serve with a copy of the enforcement notice a notice (a 'regulation 25 notice') including the screening opinion together with a written statement of reasons and require persons who give notice of appeal against the enforcement notice to submit four copies of an environmental statement to the Secretary of State relating to that EIA development.[174] Copies of the regulation 25 notice must be sent by the authority to the Secretary of State and the consultation bodies.[175]

12.105 Any person on whom a regulation 25 notice is served may apply to the Secretary of State for a screening direction. The application must be accompanied by a copy of the regulation 25 notice, a copy of the enforcement notice, and any other information or representations the applicant may wish to provide or make; a copy of the application must be sent to the authority.[176] The Secretary of State may notify the applicant and the authority that he requires additional information; this must be provided within a reasonable period. If the Secretary of State directs that the matters alleged to constitute a breach of planning control do not comprise or include EIA development, he must send a copy of the direction to every person on whom a copy of the regulation 25 notice was served.

---

171 See para 9.01.
172 EIA Regs, reg 25(1).
173 EIA Regs, reg 25(2).
174 EIA Regs, reg 25(3).
175 EIA Regs, reg 25(4).
176 EIA Regs, reg 25(6)(a), (b).

12.106 There is a provision requiring the authority and consultees to make any information relevant to the preparation of an environmental statement available to the person on whom the regulation 25 notice was served, at the instance of that person.[177]

Appeal to the Secretary of State without a screening opinion or screening direction

12.107 The regulations provide for the situation where an appeal against an enforcement notice is made to the Secretary of State in respect of EIA development and no screening opinion has been adopted and no screening direction has been made in respect of the development. Here the Secretary of State may make a screening direction.[178] But if he considers that he has not been provided with sufficient information to make such a direction, he may notify the appellant and the authority requesting further information within a reasonable period. If the appellant fails to provide this information, the planning application shall lapse at the end of the period specified in the notice.[179]

Appeal to the Secretary of State without an environmental statement

12.108 The regulations also provide for the situation where the Secretary of State is considering an appeal against an enforcement notice in respect of EIA development and no environmental statement has been submitted. In such circumstances, the Secretary of State shall, within three weeks of receiving the appeal, or such longer period as he may require, notify the appellant that he must, within a specified period, submit to the Secretary of State four copies of an environmental statement relating to the unauthorized EIA development. Again, the planning application shall lapse in the case of non-compliance.[180]

Procedure where an environmental statement is submitted to the Secretary of State

12.109 If the Secretary of State receives, in connection with an enforcement appeal, a statement which the appellant refers to as an environmental statement, the Secretary of State must send a copy to the relevant planning authority and notify the persons on whom a copy of the regulation 25 notice was served, informing them that they may make representations.[181]

---

177 EIA Regs, reg 25(7).

178 EIA Regs, reg 25(9).

179 EIA Regs, reg 25(10), (11).

180 EIA Regs, reg 25(12)(a), (c), (e). The procedure does not apply if satisfactory documentation has already been submitted for the purposes of a section 78 appeal to be determined at the same time as the enforcement appeal; EIA Regs, reg 25(12)(b).

181 EIA Regs, reg 25(13).

12.110 The regulations also provide for publicity for environmental statements or further information submitted in accordance with these rules[182] and for the public inspection of documents.[183]

Challenge in the High Court

12.111 The Secretary of State's decision on any point of law may be challenged in High Court proceedings at the instance of the local planning authority, of the appellant, or of any other person on whom the enforcement notice was served; and the Secretary of State may at any stage state a case on his own initiative for the opinion of the High Court.[184]

12.112 We have seen that an appeal to the Secretary of State suspends the effect of an enforcement notice until final determination of the appeal.[185] In *R v Kuxhaus*,[186] the Court of Appeal (Criminal Division) held that the High Court challenge provided for by the Act was part of the enforcement appeal procedure since the court could remit the matter to the Secretary of State. While no doubt technically correct, this decision could only assist those developers who, usually for commercial reasons, are prepared to use High Court proceedings as a means of delaying matters.[187] Accordingly, the PCA 1991 inserted a new TCPA 1990, s. 289(4A) which attempts to deal with the problem. Under this provision the notice remains suspended by virtue of TCPA 1990, s. 175(4) pending final determination which includes an appeal to the High Court. However, the High Court[188] may, on such terms if any as the court thinks fit (which may include terms requiring the local planning authority to give an undertaking as to damages or any other matter), order that the notice shall have effect or have effect to such extent as specified in the order pending the final determination of those proceedings. Under subs (5A) rules of court provide for the High Court to give directions as to the exercise of any other powers in respect of the matters to which such a notice relates. But the most significant new provision is TCPA 1990, s. 289(6) which provides that no proceedings shall be brought in the High Court in connection with an enforcement notice without the leave of that court and no appeal to the Court of Appeal shall be brought except with leave of the Court of Appeal or High Court.[189]

---

182 EIA Regs, reg 25(14), (15), (16).

183 EIA Regs, reg 25(19).

184 TCPA 1990, s. 289(1), (3).

185 See para 12.96.

186 [1988] QB 631, [1988] 2 All ER 705.

187 In *Kuxhaus* the enforcement notice was delayed for nine years. The case may not be an authority where nullity is alleged so that TCPA 1990, s. 289 is not used.

188 Or the Court of Appeal as the case may be.

189 Formerly it was only in respect of an appeal to the Court of Appeal that leave was required. See Order 94 RSC, inserted by SI 1992 No 638.

12.113 There is an important provision in the TCPA 1990 that the validity of an enforcement notice shall not be questioned in any proceedings whatsoever on any of the grounds of appeal specified in TCPA 1990, s. 174(2) except by way of appeal to the Secretary of State.[190] This provision thus excludes the right which would otherwise be available at common law to by-pass the Secretary of State by applying to the High Court for a declaration on any point of law covered by the statutory grounds of appeal.

Effect of enforcement notice

12.114 As already explained[191] an enforcement notice requires the person on whom it is served to take specified steps to remedy the breach of planning control. The notice continues to be effective after it has been complied with.[192] Furthermore, it is effective against any subsequent owner, provided it has been registered as a local land charge.

Enforcement of enforcement notice

12.115 Where the enforcement notice has not been complied with, the local planning authority's remedies vary according to the circumstances. They may enter the land to secure compliance with the notice,[193] they may initiate a prosecution for contravention of the notice,[194] or they may seek an injunction.

Entry on the land

12.116 Under the TCPA 1990 as originally enacted, the local planning authority had no power to enter the land if the steps required to be taken by the enforcement notice were for the discontinuance of a use or for the compliance with any condition or limitation. However, as a result of PCA 1991,[195] the local planning authority have the power, where *any* steps required by an enforcement notice are not taken within the period for compliance, to enter the land and take the steps. They may recover from the person who is then the owner of the land any expenses reasonably incurred by them in doing so; if the owner is not himself in breach of planning

---

190 TCPA 1990, s. 285(1). There is one exception in TCPA 1990, s. 285(2): see para 12.119. And the rule is subject, of course, to the right to test the Secretary of State's decision in the High Court under TCPA 1990, s. 289.

191 See para 12.68.

192 TCPA 1990, s. 181(1). It continues to be effective where there is subsequent development reinstating buildings or works demolished or altered in compliance with the notice; see TCPA 1990, s. 181(3), (4).

193 TCPA 1990, s. 178. See *R (on the application of O'Brien) v Basildon District Council* [2006] EWHC 1346 (Admin).

194 TCPA 1990, s. 179.

195 Substituting a new TCPA 1990, s. 178(1).

control, he has the right to recover the sum from the guilty party.[196] Further, the Act provides that any person who wilfully obstructs a person acting in the exercise of the powers outlined above shall be guilty of an offence.[197]

Prosecution for contravention of the notice

12.117 Under TCPA 1990, s. 179 (as amended)[198] the local planning authority may launch a prosecution for the contravention of an enforcement notice where, at any time after the period for compliance, any step required by the notice to be taken has not been taken, or any activity required by the notice to cease is being carried on. The person who is then the owner of the land is in breach of the notice and is guilty of an offence.[199] In proceedings against him it will be a defence for him to show that he did everything he could be expected to do to secure compliance with the notice.[200] Further, a person who has control of, or an interest in, the land to which the enforcement notice relates (other than the owner) who carries on an activity which is required by the notice to cease, or causes or permits such an activity to be carried on, after the end of the period for compliance with the notice, is guilty of an offence.[201]

12.118 An offence under the provisions outlined in the previous paragraph may be charged by reference to any day or longer period of time and a person may be convicted of a second or subsequent offence by reference to any period of time following the preceding conviction for such an offence.[202] However the statute does provide a defence if the person charged can show that he was not aware of the existence of the enforcement notice, that he has not been served with a copy of it, and the notice is not contained in the appropriate register under TCPA 1990, s. 188.[203]

Validity of enforcement notice

12.119 The defendant cannot question the validity of the notice in criminal proceedings for non-compliance with an enforcement notice. However this will not apply if the person prosecuted has held an interest in the land since before the enforcement

---

196 TCPA 1990, s. 178(3).

197 TCPA 1990, s. 178(6) as substituted. The offence is a summary offence liable to a fine not exceeding level 3 on the standard scale.

198 By PCA 1991, s. 8.

199 TCPA 1990, s. 179(1) and (2).

200 TCPA 1990, s. 179(3). The bona fide sale of the land to a third party prior to the expiry of the period for compliance did not of itself provide a defence under this subsection: *Thompson v East Lindsay District Council* [2002] EWHC 416 (Admin).

201 TCPA 1990, s. 179(4) and (5).

202 TCPA 1990, s. 179(6). The maximum penalty on summary conviction is £20,000; on indictment there is no limit. The court may take into account any financial benefit which has accrued; TCPA 1990, s. 179(8), (9).

203 TCPA 1990, s. 179(7). s. 188 requires the LPA to maintain a register of enforcement and stop notices, available for public inspection.

notice was issued and satisfies the court (i) that he did not know and could not reasonably have been expected to know that the enforcement notice had been issued; and (ii) that his interests have been substantially prejudiced by the failure to serve him with a copy of it.[204]

12.120 The privative provision explained above was considered by both the Court of Appeal and the House of Lords in *R v Wicks*.[205] The defendant had erected a building without planning permission and an enforcement notice was served. The defendant's appeal against the notice was dismissed by the Secretary of State. In criminal proceedings for non-compliance the defendant sought to challenge the notice on the grounds that the decision to serve it had been made in bad faith and motivated by immaterial considerations. These matters had not been raised by the defendant on appeal to the Secretary of State, nor by possible High Court proceedings by way of judicial review.

12.121 In answer to two certified questions of public importance put forward by the Court of Appeal, the House of Lords ruled that:

(1) A defendant who is prosecuted for an offence contrary to TCPA 1990, s. 179(1) is not entitled as a matter of right, at that stage, to raise the defence that the enforcement notice was invalid on the grounds that the decision to issue it was ultra vires.
(2) Where a defendant is not permitted to raise such a defence as of right in criminal proceedings, there were no exceptions to the rule, even where the alleged invalidity arose as a result of *mala fides* on the part of the issuing authority.

12.122 In the House of Lords, Lord Hoffmann clearly enunciated the rationale of the ruling when he said:

> The history shows that over the years there has been a consistent policy of progressively restricting the kind of issues which a person served with an enforcement notice can raise when he is prosecuted for failing to comply. The reasons for this policy of restriction are clear: they relate, first, to the unsuitability of the subject matter for decision by the criminal court; second, the need for the validity of the notice to be conclusively determined quickly enough to enable planning control to be effective and to allow the timetable for the service of such notices in the Act to be operated; and, third, to the fact that the criminal proceedings are part of the mechanism for the securing of planning control in the public interest.

12.123 An attempt to avoid the *Wicks* principle was made in *Palacegate Properties Ltd v Camden London Borough Council*.[206] Having had their appeal against conviction for breach of an enforcement notice dismissed by the Crown Court, the appellants

---

204 TCPA 1990, s. 285(2).
205 [1998] AC 92, [1997] 2 All ER 801.
206 [2001] JPL 373.

brought the matter before the Divisional Court. They argued that although valid on its face, the notice could not be relied on as the basis of a prosecution because its issue had not been authorized by a resolution of the council; that it was a nullity on the ground of uncertainty; and that it was unlawful in that it contradicted the terms of the lease. Laws LJ and Longmore J were not persuaded by these arguments—all that was required of the Council was that they demonstrated that the notice was valid 'on its face' and this they had done. The decision of the Crown Court was upheld.

Injunction

12.124 There will be cases where, despite the remedies available to the local planning authority under the Planning Acts, outlined above, they are faced by a defendant who is prepared to flout the law deliberately and flagrantly. The possibility of obtaining an injunction to deal with this situation was recognized in *A-G v Bastow*[207] which was decided at a time when the local planning authority had no power to enter the land where the enforcement notice merely required the discontinuance of a use. In that case the owner of a caravan site ignored an enforcement notice requiring him to discontinue the use of land as a caravan site, he was prosecuted and fined on a number of occasions, but he still did not comply with the notice. The Attorney-General acting in the public interest then sought a High Court injunction requiring the defendant to comply with the enforcement notice. The injunction was granted. In other cases, the Attorney-General acting on behalf of the local authority has been able to bring injunctions on a county-wide basis to prevent defendants escaping the effects of an enforcement notice by moving caravans from site to site.[208]

12.125 The local planning authority have for some years been able, under the Local Government Act 1972, s. 222 to sue for an injunction in their own name instead of invoking the aid of the Attorney-General.[209] The action must be for the promotion or protection of the interests of the inhabitants of the local authority's area. Whether such an injunction will be granted will depend on the facts of each individual case.[210] But these powers are somewhat uncertain and subject to certain limitations existing under the general law. The doubts may have been removed by

---

207 [1957] 1 QB 514, [1957] 1 All ER 497.

208 See *A-G v Smith* [1958] 2 QB 173, [1958] 2 All ER 557; *A-G (ex rel East Sussex County Council) v Morris* [1973] JPL 429. See also *Wealden District Council v Krushandal* [1999] JPL 174 where a district-wide ban was upheld under s. 187B of the 1990 Act.

209 See *Westminster City Council v Jones* (1981) 80 LGR 241.

210 *Runnymede Borough Council v Ball* [1986] 1 All ER 629, [1986] 1 WLR 353; *City of London Corpn v Bovis Construction Ltd* [1989] JPL 263; *Doncaster Borough Council v Green* [1992] 2 LS Gaz R 32.

the introduction, by PCA 1991, s. 3, of a new TCPA 1990, s. 187B; the new provisions are intended to be specifically tailored to planning enforcement.

12.126 Under TCPA 1990, s. 187B, where a local planning authority considers it necessary or expedient for any actual or *apprehended*, ie threatened, breach of planning control to be restrained by injunction, they may apply to the court for that remedy, whether or not they have exercised or are proposing to exercise any of their other powers under the Act.[211] It is further provided that the court may grant such an injunction as it thinks appropriate for the purpose of restraining the breach.[212] Rules of court provide for such an injunction to be issued against a person whose identity is unknown.[213]

12.127 The provisions introduced by PCA 1991 were considered in *Harwood v Runnymede Borough Council* and *Croydon London Borough Council v Gladden*.[214] In the former case the Court of Appeal held that an injunction could be granted where the criteria under the section were satisfied; in particular an interlocutory injunction could be used to restrain a breach pending the outcome of enforcement proceedings—it could not have been intended that the power was only exercisable at trial. In the latter case, which was considered in an earlier chapter,[215] the court rejected the argument that the use of the word 'restrained' in s. 187B meant there was no power to grant a mandatory injunction requiring the removal of operational development.

12.128 It seems that the impecuniosity of the defendant is no bar to the granting of a mandatory injunction under TCPA 1990, s. 187B. In *Warrington Borough Council v Hull*,[216] landfill operators had been served with enforcement notices relating to breaches of planning control which had serious consequences in terms of visual amenity and public health. It was argued on their behalf that the court should decline to grant an injunction as the defendants' resources fell far short of the £2 million required to restore the site. The Court of Appeal upheld Bracewell J's decision to grant an injunction. The financial position of the defendants was irrelevant; although it might be relevant to the subsequent enforcement of the injunction.

---

211 TCPA 1990, s. 187B(1). An injunction under s 187B does not have to be confined to the area of land that was subject to the enforcement notice: *Slough Borough Council v Prashar* [2002] EWCA Civ 671.

212 TCPA 1990, s. 187B(2).

213 TCPA 1990, s. 187B(3). Order 110 RSC, inserted by SI 1992 No 638.

214 [1994] JPL 723. TCPA 1990, s. 187B(1). An injunction under s. 187B does not have to be confined to the area of land that was subject to the enforcement notice: *Slough Borough Council v Prashar* [2002] EWCA Civ 671.

215 See para 6.56.

216 [1999] Env LR 869.

12.129 The unauthorized residential use of land by gypsies has often given local planning authorities problems with regard to enforcement. The public interest in the proper enforcement of planning control has to be weighed against the hardship that eviction from the land may cause. The issue arose in *South Buckinghamshire District Council v Porter*[217] where gypsies lived in mobile homes on land they occupied in breach of planning control. In exercise of the power under TCPA 1990, s. 189B the court had granted injunctions requiring them to vacate the land. There was no dispute that the injunctions were an interference with the gypsies rights under article 8(1) of the ECHR[218] but the issue was whether the interference was in accordance with the law and pursued for the protection of the rights of others within article 8(2), that is, the preservation of the environment.

12.130 On appeal to the Court of Appeal against the granting of the injunctions, it was held that the judge under s. 189B was neither required nor entitled to reach his own independent view of the planning merits of the case. But he should not grant an injunction unless he would be prepared to contemplate committing the defendant to prison for breach of the order, having considered for himself the question of hardship, and the availability of suitable alternative accommodation. Thus an injunction should not be used to evict gypsies unless the need for such a remedy to protect the environment outweighs the occupiers' rights to respect for their home and family life under article 8 of the Convention. This decision was subsequently upheld by the House of Lords.[219]

Stop notices

12.131 As we have seen, the lodging of an appeal suspends the operation of an enforcement notice until such time as the appeal is finally disposed of or withdrawn. In the meantime, the operation or change of use can continue without penalty. The TCPA 1968 introduced the remedy of the 'stop notice' to prevent the continuance of operations pending the outcome of an appeal against an enforcement notice. Strangely, this procedure could not at first be used to stop a change of use, but this omission was remedied in 1977. The PCA 1991, on the recommendation of the Carnwath Report, made considerable changes to the legal framework under which a stop notice may be used. These will be considered below.

12.132 A stop notice is essentially a supplement to an enforcement notice and cannot be served unless an enforcement notice has been issued. Under TCPA 1990,

---

217 [2001] EWCA Civ 1549; [2003] UKHL 26. The case involved four consolidated appeals.
218 See para 2.132.
219 The *Porter* case was distinguished in *South Cambridgeshire District Council v Gammell* [2005] EWCA Civ 1429.

s. 183(1),[220] where the local planning authority consider it expedient that any 'relevant activity' should cease before the expiry of the period for compliance with an enforcement notice, they may, when they serve a copy of the enforcement notice or afterwards,[221] serve a stop notice. The stop notice may prohibit the carrying out of that activity on the land to which the enforcement notice relates. The 'relevant activity' referred to above means any activity specified in the enforcement notice as an activity which the local planning authority require to cease and any activity carried out as part of that activity or associated with it.[222] The concept of a 'relevant activity' is wider than the terms of the TCPA 1990 as originally enacted since an associated activity may now be caught. However, a stop notice may not be served where the enforcement notice has taken effect.[223]

12.133 Under the original terms of the TCPA 1990 there were three types of activity which could not be prohibited by a stop notice. These were:

(1) The use of any buildings as a dwellinghouse. This exception was preserved by the PCA 1991;[224]
(2) The use of any land as the site of a caravan occupied by a person as his only or main residence. This exception was abolished by the PCA 1991—it will therefore be possible for a stop notice to be served in such a case;
(3) The taking of any steps required by the enforcement notice to remedy the breach of planning control alleged in the enforcement notice. This does not appear in the TCPA 1990 as amended by the PCA 1991.

12.134 Further, under the pre-1991 Act provisions, a stop notice could not be served in respect of an activity which began more than 12 months earlier unless it was, or was incidental to, building, engineering, mining, or other operations, or the deposit of refuse or waste materials. Under the PCA 1991, the period after which a stop notice is prohibited has been extended from 12 months to more than four years ending with the service of the notice; also, nothing prevents a stop notice from prohibiting any activity which is, or is incidental to, building etc, operations or the deposit of refuse or waste materials. The four-year period applies whether the activity has been carried out continuously or otherwise, and for the purpose of

220 As substituted by PCA 1991, s. 9.

221 This confirms the CA decision in *R v Pettigrove* (1990) 62 P & CR 355 that the enforcement notice and stop notice could be served simultaneously. The LPA are entitled to decide at one and the same time to take enforcement action and to serve a stop notice: *Westminster City Council v Jones* (1981) 80 LGR 241.

222 TCPA 1990, s. 183(2).

223 TCPA 1990, s. 183(3).

224 TCPA 1990, s. 183(4). Note that the exception does not extend to caravan-dwellers; *R (on the application of Wilson) v Wychavon District Council* [2007] EWCA Civ 52.

calculating the four-year period, no account is to be taken of any period during which the activity was authorized by planning permission.[225]

12.135 Although a stop notice depends for its validity upon an enforcement notice, the stop notice can be served on any person interested in the land or carrying out any activity specified in the stop notice; a stop notice may therefore be served on a contractor as well as on the owners and occupiers of the land.[226] The local planning authority may also put up a site notice.[227] A stop notice must specify the date on which it is to take effect and it cannot be contravened until that date;[228] TCPA 1990, s. 184(3) provides that the date upon which a stop notice shall take effect (a) must not be earlier than three days after the date when the notice is served, unless the local planning authority consider that there are special reasons for specifying an earlier date; and (b) must not be later than 28 days from when first served. If they do decide upon an earlier date under (a) above, for example, in an emergency to prevent some activity such as tipping, a statement of their reasons must be served with the stop notice.[229]

12.136 It is obviously very important that the wording of a stop notice should state clearly what activities are prohibited. But where a stop notice relates to a change of use, absolute precision may be difficult to achieve, as was illustrated in *R v Runnymede Borough Council, ex p Seehra*.[230]

12.137 The council issued an enforcement notice alleging a material change in the use of Mr Seehra's house to mixed residential and religious purposes, and prohibiting the use of the land for the purposes of religious devotion 'otherwise than as incidental to the enjoyment of the dwellinghouse as such'. The council also served a stop notice requiring the premises to cease to be used for purposes other than those incidental to a dwellinghouse.

12.138 The problem here was that participation in religious devotions by visitors to the house may up to a point be incidental to the enjoyment of a private house. Mr Seehra complained that the stop notice left him to decide how to behave; if he came to the wrong judgment he might be prosecuted or, alternatively, he might act so carefully that he was being deprived of something which he would be entitled to do.

---

[225] TCPA 1990, s. 183(5). TCPA 1990, s. 183(5) reverses the decision in *Scott Markets Ltd v Waltham Forest London Borough Council* (1979) 38 P & CR 597, where the CA held that the 12-month rule applied to periods where the activity was covered by a temporary planning permission.

[226] TCPA 1990, s. 183(6).

[227] TCPA 1990, s. 184(6).

[228] TCPA 1990, s. 184(2).

[229] Under the TCPA 1990 as originally enacted, the stop notice could not take effect earlier than three days in any circumstances.

[230] (1986) 53 P & CR 281.

12.139 Schiemann J said that these were well-founded worries; he nevertheless held that the notices were not void and did, within the spirit of the decided cases, give an indication to the applicant of what he had and had not to do.

12.140 There is no appeal against a stop notice, and failure to comply with it is a punishable offence.[231] The PCA 1991 has substantially increased the penalties for failing to comply with the notice;[232] however it is a defence for the accused to prove that the stop notice was not served on him and that he did not know, and could not reasonably have been expected to know, of its existence.[233] Moreover the courts have held that the invalidity of a stop notice can be set up as a defence in prosecution proceedings.[234] It is not an offence under the stop notice procedure to continue the prohibited activity after the enforcement notice has come into effect; and, of course, the stop notice will cease to have effect if the enforcement notice is quashed or withdrawn.[235]

12.141 If the enforcement notice is quashed or withdrawn, the local planning authority may be liable to pay compensation to owners or occupiers of the land for any loss or damage directly attributable to the stop notice; this compensation will include any damages payable to contractors.[236] While this potential liability for compensation is an important safeguard for owners and others who might be affected by the notice, it is probably the main reason for stop notices being used relatively rarely by local planning authorities. Indeed Circular 10/97 counsels local authorities to undertake a quick but thorough cost benefit assessment before serving a stop notice.[237] The position with respect to compensation has been clarified and improved slightly in the local planning authority's favour by PCA 1991, s. 9[238] which provides that no compensation will be payable (1) in respect of any prohibition in a stop notice of an activity which, at the time when the notice is in force, constitutes or contributes to a breach of planning control, or (2) in the case of a

---

231 TCPA 1990, s. 187(1), (1A), (1B), (2), (2A), as substituted by PCA 1991, s. 9.

232 The maximum penalty on summary conviction is a fine of £20,000; there is no limit on indictment. The court may have regard to any financial benefit which has, or is likely to have, accrued.

233 TCPA 1990, s. 187(3).

234 *R v Jenner* [1983] 2 All ER 46, [1983] 1 WLR 873. It was held that the accused was entitled to call evidence, by way of a defence to a prosecution for non-compliance, that the activity had exceeded the then 12-month limitation on the service of a stop notice.

235 TCPA 1990, s. 183(7).

236 TCPA 1990, s. 186. A party with a mere right to use the land will not be entitled to compensation, there must be a legal or equitable interest; *International Ferry Traders Ltd v Adur District Council* [2004] EWCA Civ 288, where the court followed *Stevens v London Borough of Bromley*, see para 12.44.

237 Circular 10/97, Annex 3, paras 3.16–3.18. This procedure is not mandatory, however; *R v Rochester upon Medway City Council, ex p Hobday* [1989] 2 PLR 38; *R v Elmbridge Borough Council, ex p Wendy Fair Markets Ltd* [1995] JPL B36.

238 Substituting a new TCPA 1990, s. 186(5).

claimant who was required to provide information,[239] in respect of any loss or damage suffered by him which could have been avoided if he had provided the information or had otherwise co-operated with the local planning authority when responding to the notice.

12.142 One of the few decided cases to date on stop notice compensation is *Sample (Warworth) Ltd v Alnwick District Council*,[240] where the claimants were a building firm who had contracted to build a house for a Mr and Mrs W at a fixed price. The council served an enforcement notice alleging that the erection of the house had been undertaken without planning permission and requiring it to be demolished. A stop notice served on the same day prohibited any further building on the site. The council subsequently granted planning permission but did not withdraw the enforcement notice or the stop notice. The enforcement notice was subsequently quashed on appeal and as a result the stop notice ceased to be effective.

12.143 The Lands Tribunal awarded compensation to the claimants for (1) cost of idle time when the workforce was taken off construction of the house; (2) work needed to rectify deterioration caused by the delays; (3) loss of interest on the purchase price of the house pending the delay in completion; (4) a payment made by the claimants to Mr and Mrs W for temporary accommodation.

12.144 The council had contended that some of these items were not reasonably foreseeable, but the Lands Tribunal held that compensation was payable for any loss directly attributable to the stop notice.

12.145 Where the enforcement notice turns out to be a nullity, it follows that the stop notice was also a nullity. Strictly speaking, therefore, there never was a stop notice upon which a claim for compensation could be based. The remedy here would seem to be to seek an injunction ordering the local planning authority to withdraw the stop notice.[241]

Temporary stop notices (TSNs)

12.146 The PCPA 2004 has introduced a new procedure relating to enforcement, the Temporary Stop Notice (TSN). The 2004 Act inserts new sections 171E–171H into TCPA 1990.[242]

---

239 Eg under s. 171C (PCN) or s. 330 (requisition for information). See para 12.07.

240 [1984] JPL 670.

241 *Clwyd County Council v Secretary of State for Wales and Welsh Aggregates* [1982] JPL 696; affirmed on other grounds by the Court of Appeal in *Welsh Aggregates Ltd v Secretary of State for the Environment and Clwyd County Council* [1983] JPL 50.

242 Inserted by PCPA 2004, s. 52. The provisions came into force in England on 7 March 2005: Planning and Compulsory Purchase Act 2004 (Commencement No 4 and Savings) Order 2005, SI 2005 No 204, art 3. See also ODPM Circular 02/05.

12.147 The Government's rationale for the introduction of the TSN is to provide local planning authorities with the ability to bring about the immediate cessation of an activity for a temporary period without resorting to an injunction. Unlike the 'normal' stop notice, which is discussed above,[243] there is no need to wait for an enforcement notice to be issued.

12.148 TSNs could be used in a wide variety of circumstances, for example, the inappropriate change of use of a backyard to a paint spraying business, the storage of pallets on open land, or the construction of an extension without planning permission.

Issue and duration of TSN

12.149 The local planning authority may issue a TSN if they think there has been a breach of planning control in relation to any land, and it is expedient that the activity which amounts to a breach is stopped immediately. The TSN must be in writing and specify the activity which the authority think amounts to a breach and prohibit the carrying on of the activity in question. They must, in their notice, set out the reasons for issuing it.

12.150 The TSN must be served on the person the local planning authority think (a) is carrying on the activity; (b) is an occupier; or (c) has an interest in the land. A copy of the notice must be displayed on the land together with a statement of the effect of the notice and the offences for non-compliance. A TSN has effect from the time a copy of it is first displayed on the land—the notice will cease to have effect at the end of 28 days starting with the day it was first displayed, or at the end of such shorter period as is specified, or if it is withdrawn by the local planning authority.[244] Thus the TSN, if served, effectively allows the authority a 28-day pause, when they can consider what further enforcement action they might wish to take.

12.151 There is no appeal against a TSN although an application for judicial review will be available to challenge the validity of such a notice.[245]

Restrictions on TSN

12.152 A TSN cannot prohibit the use of a building as a dwellinghouse, the carrying out of such activities as may be prescribed by the Secretary of State, or the carrying out of any activity which has been carried on for more than four years, unless the activity consists of or is incidental to operational development or the deposit of refuse or waste materials.

---

243 See para 12.131.
244 TCPA 1990, s. 171E (1)–(7).
245 For judicial review, see para 20.30.

12.153 The Secretary of State has prescribed, in the Town and Country Planning (Temporary Stop Notice) (England) Regulations 2005,[246] that a TSN cannot prohibit the stationing of a caravan on land where the land is used for that purpose immediately before the issue of a TSN, and the caravan is at that time occupied by a person as his main residence, unless the authority consider that the risk of harm to a compelling public interest arising from the stationing of the caravan is so serious as to outweigh any benefit, to the occupier, in the stationing of the caravan for the period for which the TSN has effect. It is understood that the purpose of this restriction is to ensure that gypsy travellers are not treated unfairly in relation to other groups.

12.154 A second or subsequent TSN must not be issued in respect of the same activity unless the local planning authority has first taken some other enforcement action in relation to the breach in question. Enforcement action includes obtaining an injunction under s 187B of TCPA 1990.[247]

Offences

12.155 A person commits a criminal offence if he contravenes a stop notice which has been served on him or displayed on the land. Contravention includes causing or permitting the contravention of the notice. An offence may be charged by reference to a day or longer period of time and a person may be convicted of more than one offence in relation to the same TSN by reference to different days or periods of time. An offence will not be committed if a person can prove (a) that the notice was not served on him; and (b) that he did not know, and could not reasonably be expected to know, of its existence.[248]

Compensation

12.156 Persons with an interest in the land are entitled to compensation from the local planning authority in respect of any loss or damage directly attributable to the prohibition in the TSN if (a) the activity in question is authorized by planning permission; (b) if a certificate of lawfulness (CLEUD) in respect of the activity has been issued;[249] or (c) if the TSN is withdrawn. However, (a) in the preceding sentence does not apply if planning permission is granted on or after the date the TSN was first displayed and (c) does not apply if the TSN is withdrawn following the

[246] SI 2005 No 206.

[247] TCPA 1990, s. 171F(1)–(6). Injunctions are discussed at para 12.124.

[248] Ibid, s. 171G(1)–(5). On summary conviction the maximum fine is £20,000: there is no limit on indictment. The fine may reflect any financial benefit which has accrued to the person convicted; TCPA 1990, s. 171G(6) and (7).

[249] See para 12.161.

grant of planning permission on or after the date on which the notice was first displayed.[250]

Certificates of lawfulness (CLEUDs)

12.157 Under the TCPA 1990 as originally enacted, persons interested in land with the benefit of an established use could apply to the local planning authority for a certificate of established use. Although, of course, the owner or occupier of the land would have grounds for a successful appeal if an enforcement notice were served, the purpose of the certificate was to remove the uncertainty.

12.158 A use was said to be 'established' under these provisions[251] if it was begun before 1964 without planning permission and had continued since the end of 1963; or if it was begun before 1963 under a planning permission containing conditions which had not been complied with since the end of 1963; or if it was begun after the end of 1963 as a result of a change of use not requiring planning permission and there had been since the end of 1963 no change of use requiring planning permission.

12.159 The difficulty of proving the subsistence of an unauthorized use which allegedly started before 1964 was mentioned at the beginning of this chapter.[252] As we saw, the Planning and Compensation Act 1991 introduced a new system of time limits within which enforcement action may be taken against a breach of planning control. As a consequence, in 1991 established use certificates were replaced by new Certificates of Lawfulness of Existing Use or Development (CLEUDs).[253]

12.160 In addition, the procedure under what was TCPA 1990, s. 64 whereby any person could apply to the local planning authority for a certificate to determine whether any proposed operations or change of use would constitute development, and if so whether planning permission was required, was replaced by the Certificate of Lawfulness of Proposed Use or Development (CLOPUD).[254] This procedure was considered in chapter 6, above.[255]

250 TCPA 1990, s. 171H. The grounds of compensation are somewhat narrower than those specified for a 'normal' stop notice—see para 12.141.

251 TCPA 1990, s. 191 before substitution by PCA 1991, s. 10. The time limits are set out in TCPA 1990, s. 171B, as introduced by PCA 1991, s. 4. These are discussed at para 12.34.

252 See para 12.03.

253 TCPA 1990, s. 191 as substituted by PCA 1991, s. 10. See also Circular 10/97, Annex 8.

254 TCPA 1990, s. 192 as substituted.

255 See para 6.179.

Certificates of lawfulness of existing use or development

12.161 TCPA 1990, s. 191(1) provides that if any person wishes to ascertain whether:

(a) Any existing use of buildings or other land is lawful;
(b) Any operations which have been carried out in, over, or under land are lawful; or
(c) Any other matter, constituting a failure to comply with any condition or limitation subject to which planning permission has been granted is lawful;

he may apply to the local planning authority specifying the land and describing the use, operations, or other matter. If, on such an application, the local planning authority are satisfied with the lawfulness of the use, operations, or other matters described in the application, or that description as modified or substituted by them, they shall issue a certificate or refuse the application.[256] The certificate must specify the land to which it relates, describe the use, operations, or other matter in question, and give reasons for determining them lawful.[257] Further, the certificate may be issued in respect of the whole or part of the land specified in the application and where the application specifies more than one use etc, a certificate may be granted for all of them or one or more of them; and the certificate shall be in such form as may be prescribed by development order.[258]

For the purposes of the Act, uses and operations are 'lawful' at any time if:

(a) No enforcement action may then be taken in respect of them (whether because they did not involve development or require planning permission or because the time for enforcement action has expired or for any other reason); and
(b) They do not constitute a contravention of any of the requirements of any enforcement notice then in force.[259]

12.162 The Act further provides that in respect of a failure to comply with any condition or limitation subject to which planning permission has been granted, any matter constituting such a failure is lawful at any time if:

(a) The time for taking enforcement action in respect of the failure has expired; and
(b) It does not constitute a contravention of any of the requirements of any enforcement notice or breach of condition notice then in force.[260]

---

256 TCPA 1990, s. 191(4).

257 TCPA 1990, s. 191(5). It must also specify the date of the application for the certificate. In the case of a use falling within one of the classes of the Use Classes Order the use must be identified by reference to that class.

258 TCPA 1990, s. 193(4); GDPO, art 24.

259 TCPA 1990, s. 191(2).

260 TCPA 1990, s. 191(3). As to the time limit for taking enforcement action, see para 12.34. Breach of condition notices are dealt with at para 12.21. In *Nicholson v Secretary of State for the Environment* [1998] JPL 553, it was held that the relevant time for deciding whether the time for taking enforcement action has expired is the time of the application under TCPA 1990, s. 191.

12.163 In addition, TCPA 1990, s. 191(6) provides that the lawfulness of any use, operations, or other matter for which a certificate is in force shall be 'conclusively presumed'. And under TCPA 1990, s. 191(7) the certificate will have effect as if it were a grant of planning permission in three instances; (a) for the purposes of obtaining a caravan site licence,[261] (b) for the purpose of obtaining a waste disposal licence[262] and (c) for the purposes of obtaining a waste management licence.[263] These are cases, where, in general, planning permission is a condition precedent to the issue of the relevant licence.

12.164 The Act makes it an offence if any person, for the purposes of procuring a particular decision on an application for a certificate, knowingly or recklessly makes a statement which is false or misleading in a material particular. It is likewise an offence if any person, with intent to deceive, uses any document which is false or misleading or withholds any material information.[264] In the case of such dishonesty, the local planning authority may revoke any certificate granted.[265]

12.165 There is a right of appeal to the Secretary of State against a refusal to grant a certificate, and this extends to any refusal in part; and to any modification or substitution of the use, operations, or other matter in question. The right of appeal also extends to a failure to give a decision within the prescribed form.[266]

12.166 The procedure under TCPA 1990, s. 191 calls for some observations. First, the provisions are notably wider in scope than the former certificate of established use. Application may now be made by 'any person' as opposed to persons having an interest in the land; the new procedure provides for determinations not merely in relation to the use of land, as formerly, but also in relation to operations and matters constituting a failure to comply with conditions. And the local planning authority may now modify a description in the application or substitute a fresh description. Second, as we have seen, the new provisions define in some detail the concept of lawfulness thus making it clear that the new certificate renders the use etc, not merely immune from enforcement but lawful. Third, as with certificates of established use, the local planning authority's decision is a purely judicial one and, if they are satisfied that the applicant's case is made out, they must grant a certificate. In *Panton v Secretary of State for the Environment, Transport and the*

---

261 Under the Caravan Sites and Control of Development Act 1960, s. 3(3).

262 Under the Control of Pollution Act 1974, s. 5(2).

263 Under the Environmental Protection Act 1990, s. 36(2)(a).

264 TCPA 1990, s. 194(1). The maximum penalty on summary conviction is a fine not exceeding the statutory minimum; on indictment to imprisonment for a term not exceeding two years or an unlimited fine or both: TCPA 1990, s. 194(2).

265 TCPA 1990, s. 193(7).

266 TCPA 1990, s. 195 as substituted by PCA 1991, s. 32 and Sch 7, para 32.

Regions,[267] the High Court provided some guidance as to how the local planning authority or Secretary of State should approach applications for certificates of lawfulness where the application is based on immunity through the passage of time.

12.167 First, they must ask and answer the question: when did the material change of use occur? To qualify, this would need to be before 1 July 1948,[268] by 31 December 1963, or at a date at least 10 years prior to the current application.

12.168 Second, if the material change of use took place prior to one of those dates, has that use been lost by operation of law, in one of three possible ways, ie by abandonment, the formation of a new planning unit,[269] or by a material change of use?

12.169 Third, if the decision maker is satisfied that the description of the use specified in the CLEUD application does not properly describe the nature of the use which resulted from the material change of use, the decision maker must modify or substitute each description so as to properly describe the nature of the change which occurred.

12.170 One of the difficulties that the Carnwath Report sought to resolve was the fact that the former established use, although immune from enforcement, was not regarded as lawful. In *LTSS Print and Supply Services Ltd v London Borough of Hackney*,[270] The Court of Appeal held that where an enforcement notice had been issued in respect of unauthorized development, there was no right to revert to a previous *established* use under TCPA 1971, s. 23(9) (which became TCPA 1990, s. 57(4))[271] since an established use was not lawful but merely immune from enforcement. It is clear that under the new provisions the previous use would be 'lawful' and there should be a right to revert. It was suggested in previous editions of this book that, providing a certificate of lawfulness is in force, the particular use etc, cannot be extinguished by abandonment.[272] This opinion requires re-appraisal as a result of the decision in *M & M (Land) Ltd v Secretary of State for Communities and Local Government*.[273] In this case, M purchased a site in respect of which a CLEUD had previously been issued for use as a 'scrap yard'. The local planning authority, however, later refused planning permission for works involving the redevelopment of the site as a scrap yard. On appeal the inspector was satisfied on the evidence that

[267] [1999] JPL 461. See also *Thurrock Borough Council v Secretary of State for the Environment, Transport and the Regions* [2002] EWCA Civ 226, [2002] All ER (D) 373 (Feb) where the Court of Appeal found that an inspector had misunderstood the *Panton* case.

[268] See para 7.01.

[269] See para 6.168.

[270] [1976] QB 663, [1976] 1 All ER 311. And see *Young v Secretary of State for the Environment* [1983] 2 AC 662, [1983] 2 All ER 1105.

[271] See para 7.01.

[272] See the discussion of the *Pioneer* case at para 6.176.

[273] [2007] EWHC 489 (Admin).

the scrap yard use had only ever been 'low key' but that in any event the activity had ceased some 10 years earlier. The inspector concluded that the use had been abandoned and since the proposed redevelopment was contrary to planning policy, he upheld the refusal of planning permission. M contended that it was not possible to abandon a use that was subject to a CLEUD. The court disagreed. Judge Mole QC, sitting as deputy judge, observed that s. 191(6) 'does no more and no less than declare conclusively that at the point in time that the certificate refers to, that particular use is lawful.' The judge felt that the certificate operated like a planning permission which makes a particular use lawful then is 'spent'.[274] This did not stand in the way of the permitted change of use being abandoned. The judge explained, 'A use permitted [by a planning permission] can be abandoned: a use that has been dignified by a certificate of lawful use can also be abandoned . . . '. In arriving at this conclusion, the court followed the interpretation of the decision of the House of Lords in *Pioneer Aggregates* (UK) *Ltd v Secretary of State for the Environment* as put forward by the Court of Appeal in *Cynon Valley Borough Council v Secretary of State for Wales*. This aspect of the *M & M Land* case was considered in chapter 6.[275] Similarly, in *White v Secretary of State for the Environment* [276] the Court of Appeal held that a use which became lawful on 1 July 1948 was capable of abandonment, so that resumption of the use constituted development for which planning permission was required. Such uses have always been regarded as 'lawful'.

12.171 It also seems to be the case that a certificate of lawfulness can be overridden by an enforcement notice. An authority on the issue is the decision of the Court of Appeal in *Staffordshire County Council v Challinor*.[277]

12.172 The borough council in 1994 granted a CLEUD for the use of a site as a plant hire yard and for the storage of recycled building materials. The site formed part of a larger area, 'Woodside', which had been in agricultural use. In 1996, the county council (as local planning authority for a county matter) refused to grant planning permission for the use of a large part of Woodside for uses in connection with the recycling of demolition and construction materials. This activity nevertheless continued and the county council issued an enforcement notice alleging a breach of planning control in that there had been a material change of use from agriculture to a 'waste transfer station'. An appeal against the notice was dismissed. When the notice was not complied with, the authority was granted an injunction and entered the land to secure compliance under s. 178 TCPA 1990. In an action by the landowners to recover the cost of compliance, the High Court held that the enforcement notice could not override the conclusive nature of the CLEUD as

[274] Relying on *Cynon Valley Borough Council v Secretary of State for Wales* [1986] 2 EGLR 191.
[275] See para 6.177.
[276] [1989] JPL 692.
[277] [2007] 2 EGLR 191.

s. 191(6) states that the lawfulness of the relevant use shall be 'conclusively presumed'. Thus activities within the scope of the CLEUD were not in breach of the enforcement notice. The council appealed.

12.173 Giving the leading judgment of the Court of Appeal, Keene LJ observed that it was well-established that, where existing use rights are not relied on as a ground of appeal against an enforcement notice, they cannot subsequently be relied on in a prosecution for non-compliance with an enforcement notice.[278] The position was the same with regard to proceedings for an injunction in support of an enforcement notice. Distinguishing the *Mansi* case, the court concluded that there was no general right to assert existing use rights at a time when the enforcement notice had come into effect after an appeal had been disallowed or had never been lodged. The existence of a CLEUD made no difference, as the certificate was only declaratory of the lawfulness of the use at a particular time. Specifically endorsing the *M & M (Land)* decision, Keene LJ explained that this was the reason why a use specified in a CLEUD could be abandoned. In enforcement cases there was no unfairness because there had been opportunity to raise the existing use on appeal, and if that opportunity had not been exploited, there was no injustice in disallowing the issue to be raised later. Accordingly, the decision of the trial judge was reversed and an injunction was granted to secure compliance with the enforcement notice. The decision is important because it illustrates the limitations of certificates of lawfulness.

12.174 Finally, must the local planning authority refuse to grant a certificate of lawfulness where the use has been carried on unlawfully under other legislation? In *R v Epping Forest District Council, ex p Philcox,*[279] the local planning authority had issued a certificate notwithstanding that the operations had been carried out contrary to the Environmental Protection Act 1990, s. 33 which imposed criminal liability for various waste management offences. The applicant argued that s. 191 of the 1990 Act had to be read in the context of the presumption that a person should not benefit from a breach of the law. The Court of Appeal held that where the plain words of the statute stated what was lawful, there was no room for the presumption; thus, despite the commission of a criminal offence the local planning authority were entitled to issue a certificate if the case for a lawful use under TCPA 1990, s. 191 had been made out.

Transitional provisions

12.175 Certificates of established use granted under the pre-existing legislation remain conclusive in relation to any matter stated in the certificate as at the date of the

---

[278] *Vale of the White Horse District Council v Treble Parker* [1997] JPL 660.

[279] (2000) 81 P & CR 361.

certificate.[280] It is therefore conclusive as respects any matters stated in it for the purpose of an appeal against any enforcement notice issued after the date specified in the certificate, assuming there has not been an unlawful material change of use or abandonment of a use since that date which may remove the immunity.

12.176 The PCA 1991 does not provide for the automatic conversion of certificates of established use to certificates of lawful existing use. This is presumably because the latter is regarded as a more valuable document than the former, but it is possible to submit an application to convert an established use certificate into a certificate of lawfulness. This must be made like any other application for a certificate of lawfulness. Although the local planning authority will not need to 'look behind' an established use certificate submitted in support of an application to convert, they may need to be satisfied that the established use cited in the certificate has continued to subsist.

Enforcement of planning control: development consent for nationally significant infrastructure projects under the Planning Act 2008

12.177 Provisions relating to enforcement under the new planning regime established by the PA 2008[281] are to be found in Part 8 of that Act. In general terms, criminal offences will be committed if development is carried out without development consent or in breach of the terms of the order granting consent. This is in contrast to enforcement under general planning control, where, as we have seen, it is not an offence to carry out unauthorized development. Under the 2008 Act regime, the local planning authority have rights of entry onto the land if they reasonably suspect that an offence has been committed; and there are time limits after which a person may not be charged with an offence. The local planning authority have power to serve an information notice if it appears to them that an offence may have been committed and the Act lays down offences in relation to such notices. If a person is found to have carried out unauthorized development, the local planning authority may serve notice on the guilty person requiring the situation to be remedied. If such notice is not complied with, the local planning authority may enter the land and carry out the works. The powers of the local planning authority include the right to apply to the court for an injunction restraining unauthorized development.

280 TCPA 1990, s. 192(4) as originally enacted, and unamended by the transitional powers in PCA 1991, s. 84(3).

281 The topic is discussed in chapter 8, Part 2.

Powers of enforcement

12.178 Powers of enforcement are vested in the 'relevant local planning authority'. Under s. 173 PA 2008, this will normally be the local planning authority for the area in which the land is situated. However, where the land is in an area where there is both a district and a county planning authority, if the unauthorized development involves a hazardous waste facility (under s. 14(1)(p) of PA 2008) the relevant authority will be the county. In any other case, it will be the district authority.

Offences

12.179 If no development consent is in force in respect of a development, then (under PA 2008 s. 160) a person will commit an offence if they carry out, or cause to be carried out, development for which consent is required. A person found guilty of an offence will be liable on summary conviction to a fine not exceeding £50,000, or on indictment, to a fine.

12.180 Further, under PA 2008 s. 161, if a person without reasonable excuse carries out, or causes to be carried out, development in breach of an order granting development consent, or fails to comply with the terms of such an order, they will be guilty of an offence.[282] It will be a defence for a person charged with an offence under s. 161 to prove that the breach or failure arose only because of an error or omission in the order, and a correction notice specifying the correction of the error or omission has been issued.[283] Persons found guilty of an offence under s. 161 will be liable to a fine on the same level as for s. 160, discussed above.

12.181 As with general planning control under TCPA 1990, there are time limits. Under the provisions of s. 162 PA 2008, a person cannot be charged with an offence under s. 160 or 161 after the end of a period of four years. In the case of an offence under s. 160, the four year period starts to run on the date on which the development was substantially completed. In the case of an offence under s.161 the four year period starts to run on whichever is the later of: (i) the date of substantial completion of the development; or (ii) the date on which the breach or failure to comply occurred. However, if within the four year period, an information notice[284] has been served or an injunction applied for, the time limit will be extended. The extended period will be the period of four years beginning with the

[282] No offence is committed under this section for failing to comply with the terms of a consent under the Coast Protection Act 1949 or a licence under the Food and Environmental Protection Act 1972 that is deemed to be granted by a development consent order. See PA 2008, ss. 143 and 144 respectively.

[283] There is a mechanism in Schedule 4 of PA 2008 for the correction of errors in development consent orders decisions. See para 8.232.

[284] See para 12.183.

date of service of the information notice or the application for an injunction; where both these eventualities have occurred, it will be the later of the two dates.

Rights of entry

12.182 Under s. 163 of the 2008 Act, if the local planning authority has reasonable grounds for suspecting that an offence has been committed under ss. 160 and 161 they may authorize a person to enter the land. Section 164 PA 2008 provides that a justice of the peace may issue a warrant authorising such a person to enter the land if there are reasonable grounds for suspecting that an offence has been committed and entry has been, or is likely to be, refused or the case is urgent. An offence will be committed by a person under s. 165 PA 2008 if they obstruct a person lawfully authorized to enter the land.

Information notices

12.183 By virtue of s. 167 PA 2008, where the local planning authority suspect that an offence under ss. 160 or 161 has been committed, they may serve an 'information notice' on any person who (a) is the owner or occupier of the land or has any other interest in it; or (b) is carrying out operations on the land or using it for any purpose. The information notice may require the recipient to provide information about operations being carried out, the use of the land or any other activities being carried on. The notice may also require information about the provisions of any order granting development consent for the land. The information notice, which must inform the recipient of the consequences of failure to respond, is complied with by giving the required information to the local planning authority in writing. Under the provisions of s. 168 PA 2008 there are offences relating to information notices. An offence will be committed under s. 168(1) if a person, without reasonable excuse, fails to comply with any requirement of an information notice within 21 days from when the notice is served. [285] There is a further offence under s. 168(4) if, in response to the notice, a person makes a statement that is false or misleading in a material respect, or reckless as to whether it be true or false.[286]

Notices of unauthorized development

12.184 Section 169 PA 2008 provides that where a person has been guilty of an offence under s. 160, the local planning authority may serve a 'notice of unauthorized development' requiring the person to remove the development and restore the land to its previous condition. The local planning authority may also serve such a

[285] A person guilty of such an offence will be liable on summary conviction to a fine not exceeding level 3 on the standard scale.

[286] The fine under this subsection is, on summary conviction, a fine not exceeding level 5 on the standard scale.

notice where a person has been found guilty of an offence under s. 161, ie where there has been a failure to remedy the breach or comply. A notice of unauthorized development must specify a period within which any steps are to be taken, and may specify different periods for different steps.

12.185 Under the terms of s. 170 PA 2008, if any of the steps in a notice of unauthorized development have not been taken before the end of the period of compliance with the notice, the authority must enter the land and carry out the required works, recovering from the owner the expenses reasonably incurred in so doing. A person commits an offence if they wilfully obstruct a person exercising powers under this section. [287]

Injunctions

12.186 The local planning authority may apply to the court for an injunction if they consider it necessary or expedient for any actual or apprehended offence under ss. 160 or 161 to be restrained.

[287] A person convicted of this offence will be liable on summary conviction to a fine not exceeding level 3 on the standard scale.

13

PLANNING AGREEMENTS AND OBLIGATIONS

13.01 The statutory system of planning control described in previous chapters has always been supplemented by provision for voluntary agreements between landowners and local planning authorities. TCPA 1990, s. 106 as originally enacted[1] provided that a local planning authori ty could enter into an agreement with any person interested in land in their area for the purpose of restricting or regulating the development or use of the land either permanently or for a limited period only. However this section was replaced by TCPA 1990, ss. 106, 106A, and 106B by virtue of PCA 1991, s. 12(1).[2] Those provisions represented a complete reworking of the legal framework relating to planning agreements, even to the extentof re-naming such agreements as planning 'obligations', in recognition of thefact that they may involve unilateral undertakings by the landowner.[3] It isnecessary first to trace the history of planning agreements and obligations to the present.

Planning agreements before PCA 1991

13.02 From 1948 to 1968 planning agreements could be made only with the approval of the Minister. The TCPA 1968 removed the need to obtain the Minister's

---

[1] Re-enacting TCPA 1971, s. 52. Planning agreements could be entered into under TCPA 1932, s. 34. See *A-G (ex rel Scotland) v Barratt Manchester Ltd* [1992] JPL 148.

[2] The new provisions came into force on 25 October 1991.

[3] As to 'unilateral' undertakings, see para 13.24.

approval, and there followed a great increase in the number of agreements made under what became TCPA 1990, s. 106.[4] Before 1968, there were, for instance, agreements to discontinue the sale of petrol from a badly sited garage on the opening of a new filling station under the same ownership, to restrict the use of holiday chalets to the summer months and to prevent their being used as permanent residence, and to regulate the use of caravan sites.

13.03 With the removal of ministerial control in 1968 many local planning authorities saw the opportunity to obtain 'gains' for the community which could not be secured by means of conditions attached to a grant of planning permission. There entered into the business of granting planning permission an element of bargaining, and in the development boom of the late 1960s and early 1970s many developers were ready to make concessions rather than court a refusal of permission and incur the delay involved in exercising the right of appeal to the Secretary of State. The type of 'gain' achieved in this way included such matters as the dedication of land to public use; provision of community buildings in large developments; to provide the local authority with land for local authority requirements, or to construct housing suitable for local authority requirements.[5] Gains of this kind represented purposes going well beyond traditional land use and amenity considerations.

13.04 The former TCPA 1990, s. 106 was often used, however, for the benefit of the developer. A proposed development might require improved means of access, provisions of new sewers, or other forms of infrastructure which involved the carrying out of work on land which was not under the control of the applicant for planning permission.[6] Under a section 106 agreement the developer could give enforceable undertakings to carry out the necessary work when he had obtained the power to do so or to reimburse the appropriate public authority for doing the work under statutory powers.

13.05 The controversy engendered by the use and abuse of the former TCPA 1990, s. 106 resulted in the Secretary of State asking his Property Advisory Group to review the matter. The Group in their report[7] urged that, with some exceptions, the practice of bargaining for planning gain should be regarded as unacceptable and recommended that it be discouraged. As a result the Secretary of State issued Circular 22/83 (which was replaced by subsequent circulars, as discussed below)

---

[4] The total number of agreements approved by the Minister in the four years 1956–9 was 83: the number approved in the 1960s was rather higher, but did not exceed 157 in any one year: see Jowell [1977] JPL 423.

[5] Jowell, above. And see 'The Use of Planning Agreements', Department of the Environment Research Report, HMSO, 1992.

[6] See para 8.101.

[7] 'Planning Gain', 1981.

which counselled that obligations should only be imposed where it would be unreasonable to grant a permission in the terms sought without such an obligation, and that a wholly unacceptable development should not be permitted just because of extraneous benefits offered by the developer.

Scope of s. 106 as originally enacted

13.06 A number of cases have addressed the issue of what was permissible in section 106 agreements under the TCPA 1990 as originally enacted. It will be recalled that this section, and its identically worded predecessor, TCPA 1971, s. 52, provided for agreements 'restricting or regulating the development of use of the land'. The precise ambit of this provision was a matter of uncertainty, as the case law reveals.

13.07 In *Bradford City Metropolitan Council v Secretary of State for the Environment*,[8] the council had imposed a condition requiring the widening of an existing road; this would have required the carrying out of works on land not owned or controlled by the developer. On appeal the Secretary of State held that the condition was illegal and expressed the view that the council should either have refused permission altogether or attempted to negotiate an agreement under what became TCPA 1990, s. 106. The Court of Appeal held that the condition was manifestly unreasonable.[9] Commenting on the possible use of TCPA 1971, s. 52 (which became TCPA 1990, s. 106), Lloyd LJ said, if the condition was manifestly unreasonable and so beyond the powers of the planning authority to impose it, whether or not the developers consented, it had to follow that it was also beyond the powers of the planning authority to include it in a section 106 agreement. But, said Lloyd LJ, there might be a case for a more limited agreement under s. 106. A contribution towards the cost of widening the road might well have been reasonable, due to the increased use of the road resulting from the development and the benefit to the occupiers of the residential development. 'There was all the difference in the world between a provision of a section [106] agreement requiring a contribution from a developer towards the cost of widening a highway and a provision which required the entire works to be carried out at his risk and expense.'

13.08 Likewise, in *R v Westminster City Council, ex p Monahan*[10] Kerr LJ said:

> Section [106] agreements undoubtedly facilitated the formulation of qualified planning permissions in comparison with the imposition of express conditions, and no doubt they simplified the procedural aspects of the planning process in many ways . . . But if a particular condition would be illegal—on the ground of manifest unreasonableness or otherwise—it could not acquire validity if it was embodied in a

[8] [1986] JPL 598, CA.

[9] The Court of Appeal followed the earlier decision *Hall & Co Ltd v Shoreham-by-Sea UDC* [1964] 1 All ER 1, [1964] 1 WLR 240, CA; see para 10.43.

[10] [1989] JPL 107, CA. See para 8.74.

section [106] agreement whether at the instance of the applicant himself or not. That in effect was equally the conclusion of Lloyd LJ in *Bradford*.

13.09 The remarks of both Lloyd and Kerr LJJ were obiter, but they afforded substantial authority for the proposition that—as with conditions in planning permission—a local authority could not under TCPA 1990, s. 106 lawfully require or agree to a provision that is manifestly unreasonable.[11]

13.10 It also seems that a section 106 agreement had to satisfy the test applied to conditions that the provisions must serve a planning purpose. In *R v Gillingham Borough Council, ex p F Parham Ltd*,[12] Roch J referred to the decision of the House of Lords in *Newbury District Council v Secretary of State for the Environment*[13] where Lord Scarman had said that 'a condition must fairly and reasonably relate to the provisions of the development plan and to planning considerations affecting the land'; that test, said Roch J, applied also to s. 106. In relation to conditions there is a further test namely that they must fairly and reasonably relate to the permitted development, that is, it must be related to planning needs arising from the actual purpose for which the permission has been granted.[14] Roch J held that this test did not apply to section 106 agreements.[15]

13.11 These authorities should now be viewed in the light of the decision of the Court of Appeal in *Good v Epping Forest District Council*.[16]

13.12 In *Good*, which concerned an agreement under TCPA 1971, s. 52, the court held that the powers of a local authority to enter into such an agreement were not controlled by the nature or extent of their powers to impose conditions. The two statutory powers were distinct. Thus an obligation in a planning agreement would not be ultra vires merely because the purpose could not be achieved by the imposition of a condition. This approach is surely to be favoured since if it were otherwise there would be little point in giving local authorities the power to make planning agreements or obligations. Such transactions are, after all, voluntary on the part of the landowner.

Enforcement of agreements under TCPA 1990, s. 106 as originally enacted

13.13 Planning agreements under TCPA 1990, s. 106 as originally enacted were normally made by deed and so the agreement was enforceable against the landowner

---

[11] For the meaning of 'manifestly unreasonable' in the context of conditions, see para 10.41.

[12] [1988] JPL 336.

[13] [1981] AC 578, [1980] 1 All ER 731, HL.

[14] See the account of *Newbury District Council v Secretary of State for the Environment* at para 10.36

[15] In *R v Wealden District Council, ex p Charles Church South East Ltd* [1989] JPL 837 Popplewell J agreed with Roch J in *Gillingham* on this issue. These judgments took a broader view of the scope of TCPA 1990, s. 106 than that expressed in Circular 22/83. And see *Safeways Properties Ltd v Secretary of State for the Environment* [1991] JPL 966.

[16] [1994] JPL 372.

who entered into it even if he had not provided any consideration. However in the case of enforcement against successors in title to the original owner, the wording of the old TCPA 1990, s. 106 was such that only *restrictive* covenants were enforceable against such parties. It was doubtful whether *positive* covenants—that is, those requiring the expenditure of money or labour by the owner—could be enforced against successors in title. This difficulty was overcome by the local authority either obtaining the necessary powers under a local Act of Parliament or making the covenants in the agreement expressly subject to an enabling provision in Local Government (Miscellaneous Provisions) Act 1982, s. 33.[17] The landowner was able to enforce the agreement both in respect of positive and restrictive covenants since the authority were parties to the original agreement. In *Avon County Council v Millard*,[18] the Court of Appeal held that the ordinary civil remedies for breach of contract were available to a local authority to enforce a section 106 agreement—in practice, this will normally mean an injunction.

13.14 The rule of law that a public authority cannot by agreement restrict the future exercise of its statutory powers, applies to planning agreements. In *Windsor and Maidenhead Royal Borough Council v Brandrose Investments Ltd*,[19] an agreement between a developer and the local authority under what became TCPA 1990, s. 106 envisaged the demolition of certain buildings in order to redevelop a site. Subsequently the council designated the site as a conservation area, which meant that special consent was required to demolish the buildings.[20] The Court of Appeal granted an injunction to prevent demolition without consent; there was nothing in the relevant statutory provisions to inhibit the council from using their statutory powers in designating a conservation area.[21] It seems quite clear that the local planning authority could not commit themselves by means of a section 106 agreement to grant planning permission not in accordance with the development plan. Moreover, it is doubtful whether the local planning authority could commit themselves to grant planning permission even in accordance with the development plan; other considerations apart, to do so would pre-empt the right of members of the public to make representations.[22] A developer may, of course, be reluctant to enter into commitments unless he is sure of planning permission, but this problem can be met by making the operation of the obligation conditional upon the grant of permission.

17 This device will no longer be necessary under the PCA 1991, see para 13.18.

18 (1985) 83 LGR 597.

19 [1983] 1 All ER 818, [1983] 1 WLR 509.

20 See para 16.119.

21 The decision included consideration of the obscurely worded TCPA 1990, s 106(4) which is not included in the substituted s. 106.

22 See para 8.10.

Discharge and modification of agreements under TCPA 1990, s. 106 as originally enacted

13.15 Restrictions imposed by agreements under the former s. 106 could be discharged or modified by application to the Lands Tribunal under the Law of Property Act 1925, s. 84.[23] The Tribunal's powers were limited to restrictive (ie negative) covenants. The PCA 1991 introduced new machinery for the discharge and modification of planning obligations, which will be considered later in this chapter.[24] Although the PCA 1991 expressly provides that LPA 1925, s. 84 does not apply to planning obligations, there would seem to be no reason why the section 84 procedure should not remain available for agreements entered into under TCPA 1990 as originally enacted and earlier legislation. The new machinery does not apply to such agreements.

13.16 It would not therefore seem to be possible to vary or amend an old-style planning agreement by means of a new-style planning obligation: *R v Merton London Borough Council, ex p Barker*.[25] The proper course would be to discharge the planning agreement by the appropriate means and then the parties should enter into an entirely fresh planning obligation under the new TCPA 1990, s. 106.

Planning obligations under PCA 1991

13.17 As stated at the beginning of this chapter, PCA 1991, s. 12(1) substituted new TCPA 1990, ss. 106, 106A, and 106B.

Scope of the new TCPA 1990, s. 106

13.18 TCPA 1990, s. 106(1) provides that any person interested in land in the area of a local planning authority may, by agreement or *otherwise*,[26] enter into an obligation (to be referred to as a 'planning obligation'):

(a) restricting the development or use of the land in any specified way;
(b) requiring specified operations or activities to be carried out in, on, under, or over the land;
(c) requiring the land to be used in any specified way;
(d) requiring a sum or sums to be paid to the authority on a specified date or dates or periodically.

[23] See *Re Beecham Group Ltd's Application* (1980) 41 P & CR 369.
[24] See para 13.32.
[25] [1998] JPL 440. The point was accepted by Latham J as arguable but it was not necessary for the decision in the case.
[26] This refers to a unilateral undertaking, discussed at para 13.24.

13.19 Subsection (2) provides that a planning obligation may:

(a) be unconditional or subject to conditions;
(b) impose any restriction or requirement mentioned in subsection 1(a) to (c) above, either indefinitely or for such periods as may be specified; and
(c) if it requires a sum or sums to be paid, require the payment of a specified amount or an amount determined in accordance with the instrument by which the obligation is entered into and if it requires the payment of periodical sums, require them to be paid indefinitely or for a specified period.

13.20 These provisions make it clear that planning obligations, unlike the former planning agreements, may comprise positive as well as restrictive covenants, thus avoiding the need to rely on other enabling legislation. Moreover under the old regime financial payments could only be required where they were incidental to restricting or regulating the use of the land: financial payments can now be required as a primary undertaking which is not necessarily related to the interest in the land the subject of the obligation. This means that a developer may undertake to contribute financially to off-site infrastructure—of course, the developer must himself have an interest in the land.

13.21 Some indication of the apparent scope of TCPA 1990, s. 106 is given by *R v Plymouth City Council, ex p Plymouth & South Devon Co-operative Society Ltd.*[27] In this case the Court of Appeal equated the tests for the materiality of a planning obligation with those for the validity of planning conditions. That aspect of the case will be dealt with later in this chapter. Nevertheless the court was prepared to take a broad view of what was permissible where major supermarket chains offered certain benefits in connection with the grant of planning permission. The community benefits offered by J Sainsbury plc included the construction of a tourist information centre, a bird-watching hide, and a static art feature on the site. Off-site they offered park-and-ride facilities and a financial contribution of £1 million towards infrastructure costs for a nearly industrial site—this was in recognition of the fact that the development of the superstore would cause a loss of industrial land in the locality. Tesco Stores Ltd offered, inter alia, a financial contribution to the provision of a crèche, a wildlife habitat on a site contiguous to the proposed development, a moving water sculpture on site, and the sale to the local authority of land for park-and-ride facilities.

13.22 So far as the benefits which were to be provided on site, the Court of Appeal held that there was not the slightest difficulty or room for argument because they made the development more attractive, which was surely in the public interest. As regards the off-site benefits, the offers of contributions towards the alleviation

[27] (1993) 67 P & CR 78.

of traffic problems in the way of park-and-ride facilities, and the £1 million offer by Sainsbury, both plainly had planning purposes.

13.23 A question that has arisen is whether the transfer of land can legally form the subject matter of a section 106 obligation. This was one of the issues in *R v South Northamptonshire District Council, ex p Crest Homes plc*[28] where section 106 agreements placed an obligation on developers to transfer certain land to the local authority for community purposes, eg as open space for a school. The Court of Appeal held that such obligation, providing it was expressed in a negative fashion, clearly fell within either TCPA 1990, s. 106(1)(a) 'restricting the development or use of the land in any specified way'; or TCPA 1990, s. 106(1)(c) 'requiring the land to be used in any specified way'. This principle, however, may not apply to a unilateral undertaking to transfer land which cannot, of itself, impose any restriction on the development and use of the land: *Wimpey Homes Holdings Ltd v Secretary of State for the Environment*.[29] Unilateral undertakings are considered below.

Unilateral undertakings

13.24 The provisions allow the developer to make a unilateral undertaking whereby he may promise to do or not do certain things if, eg planning permission is granted.[30] The purpose of this device is to enable the developer to break the deadlock that can occur at the appeal stage. For example, in one reported instance,[31] the local planning authority had refused permission for low-cost rural housing on land outside a village and for a scheme contrary to the policies in the development plan. At the inquiry, the applicants tabled a draft section 106 agreement in a format previously suggested by the authority as one that would overcome the objections to the development. Subsequently, the authority declined to accept the agreement on the basis that adequate provision for low-cost housing had been made elsewhere in the village. As a result, the applicants put forward a unilateral undertaking in the form of a planning obligation, based on the draft section 106 agreement and this was accepted by the inspector as dealing adequately with the local authority's objections. Once accepted and entered into in accordance with the statutory requirements for executing a planning obligation, a unilateral undertaking creates an obligation that is binding on the developer just as if it had been entered into bilaterally.[32]

28 [1995] JPL 200.
29 [1993] JPL 919.
30 See para 13.18.
31 [1992] JPL 101.
32 TCPA 1990, s. 106(3), as substituted.

13.25 The validity of unilateral obligation arose before the High Court in *South Oxfordshire Borough Council v Secretary of State for the Environment*.[33] Developers applied for planning permission to construct a golf course and clubhouse to provide funds to repair listed buildings in a village conservation area deemed by English Heritage to be of national importance. The developers offered an undertaking to use all reasonable endeavours to dispose of the site by way of a long building lease or otherwise and thereafter within a period of 20 years to utilize all relevant income for repairs to the listed buildings. Sir Graham Eyre QC (sitting as deputy judge) upheld the obligation notwithstanding that the money was to be put to a purpose, rather than being paid to the local authority. It fell therefore under paragraph (b) of TCPA 1990, s. 106(1) as opposed to paragraph (d).[34]

13.26 It should be noted that the purpose of such undertakings is to enable the developer to enter into a planning obligation as an *alternative* to doing so by agreement; they are not intended to replace the use of agreements. Indeed authorities are encouraged by the policy guidance to do their best to reach agreement by negotiation and it is only where the developer considers that negotiations are being unnecessarily protracted or unreasonable demands being made that he may wish to enter into a unilateral undertaking.

Formalities and enforcement

13.27 The Act provides that a planning obligation may only be entered into by an instrument executed as a deed and that it must state that it is a planning obligation under section 106. Further, it must identify the land; the person entering the obligation and his interest; and the local authority by whom the obligation is enforceable.[35] A copy of the deed must be given to the local authority by whom it is enforceable[36] and once these formalities are complete the planning obligation will be registrable as a local land charge under the Local Land Charges Act 1975.[37] It will then be enforceable by the authority against the person entering into the obligation and his successors in title.[38] However the deed creating the planning obligation may provide that a person shall not be bound by the obligation in respect of any period during which he no longer has an interest in the land.[39]

13.28 In 2002 an amendment was made to the General Development Procedure Order so as to require the local planning authority to include in the planning register the

33 [1994] 1 PLR 72.
34 See para 13.18.
35 TCPA 1990, s. 106(9).
36 TCPA 1990, s. 106(10).
37 TCPA 1990, s. 106(11).
38 TCPA 1990, s. 106(3).
39 TCPA 1990, s. 106(4).

details of any relevant planning obligations (or agreements under s. 278 of the Highways Act 1980) entered into or proposed.[40]

13.29 It seems that where a planning obligation or agreement purports to transfer land to a person not a party to it, there must be compliance with the Law of Property (Miscellaneous Provisions) Act 1989, s. 2.

13.30 Section 2 requires that a contract for the sale or other disposition of land must be in writing and signed by or on behalf of each party to the contract. In *Jelson Ltd v Derby City Council*,[41] the council entered into a section 106 agreement with a developer (J) under which J was required to transfer an affordable housing site to a housing association nominated by the council. Since, under the terms of the agreement, no housing association could be nominated until J had commenced development, there was therefore no signature of the intending purchaser as required by the Act of 1989. In the Chancery Division of the High Court, David Mackie QC held that the affordable housing provisions of the agreement were void. The Court, however, was prepared to apply the 'blue pencil' test and so the agreement remained in effect shorn of the offending provisions. The decision is an apt illustration of the fact that, despite the statutory context of TCPA 1990, section 106, agreements entered into under it are subject to the rules of the law of contract.

13.31 The position with regard to enforcement of planning obligations is made much clearer by PCA 1991. It is now specifically enacted that a planning obligation may be enforced by injunction.[42] Additionally, if any works required by the obligation have not been carried out, the local authority may enter the land on 21 days' notice, carry out the necessary works, and recover the costs.[43] It is an offence for any person to wilfully obstruct anyone seeking to enforce the terms of a planning obligation.[44] Any financial obligations on the part of the developer can be recovered as a civil debt and the Act enables regulations to be made providing that any sums to be paid or the expenses of the authority are to be a charge on the land.[45]

Modification and discharge of planning obligations

13.32 TCPA 1990, s. 106A provides that a planning obligation may be modified or discharged in only two possible ways. First, by agreement between the two parties

---

[40] T & CP (General Development Procedure) (Amendment) (England) Order 2002, SI 2002 No 828.

[41] [2002] JPL 203.

[42] TCPA 1990, s. 106(5).

[43] TCPA 1990, s. 106(6) and (7).

[44] TCPA 1990, s. 106(8). The maximum penalty on summary conviction is a fine not exceeding level 3 on the standard scale.

[45] TCPA 1990, s. 106(2).

to the obligation—this must be by an instrument executed as a deed[46]—and secondly, by application to the local planning authority under the procedure contained in TCPA 1990, ss. 106A and 106B.[47]

13.33 Under this procedure any person against whom a planning obligation is enforceable may apply to the local planning authority for the planning obligation to be modified or discharged.[48] The Act provides that such an application may be made at any time after the expiry of the 'relevant period' which is to be prescribed by regulations, or if no such period is prescribed, a period of five years from the date when the obligation was entered into.[49] On receipt of such an application the local planning authority may determine:

(a) that the planning obligation shall continue to have effect without modification;
(b) if the obligation no longer serves a useful purpose, that it shall be discharged; or
(c) if the obligation continues to serve a useful purpose, but would serve that purpose equally well if it had effect subject to the modifications specified in the application, that it shall have effect subject to those modifications.

13.34 The meaning of these provisions arose in *R (on the application of Garden and Leisure Group) v North Somerset Council*.[50]

13.35 A garden centre, GNR, sought permission to have its s. 106 agreement modified to allow it to sell a wider range of products including swimming pools, farm shop food, and outdoor pursuits clothing. There was a local plan policy restricting retail development in the countryside and the sale of goods from horticultural units. The council's planning committee resolved to approve the application as they considered that the modified section 106 agreement continued to serve its original purpose of regulating retail sales. The details regarding floorspace and range of products to be sold were referred to another committee and were yet to be determined when the application for judicial review was brought. The claimant, GLG, was a neighbouring garden centre who argued that the local planning committee had failed to apply the test in s. 106A of TCPA 1990 when it decided to grant the application.

13.36 Held: by Richards J that the planning committee had misunderstood the test under s. 106A in that they had failed adequately to focus on the question of whether the obligation would continue to secure compliance with local plan policy. The resolution was quashed.

---

[46] TCPA 1990, s. 106A(1)(a), (2).

[47] Law of Property Act, s. 84 (see para 13.15) is expressly excluded from application to planning obligations: s 106A(1).

[48] TCPA 1990, s. 106A(3).

[49] TCPA 1990, s. 206A(4). The regulations (see fn 52, below) do not prescribe a different period.

[50] [2003] EWHC 1605 (Admin).

13.37 The court considered that the proposed modifications had to be considered in their entirety. The purpose of the policy was a useful one, ie to prevent large-scale retail development in the countryside, but GNR's proposal went beyond what was capable of meeting the requirements of the policy. It could not have been rationally decided that the purpose of the obligation would be served equally well if the sale of additional goods were allowed. The council had argued that the application for judicial review should not be entertained as they had not yet made a decision amenable to judicial review. It was held that the decision was so amenable because the court, in its discretion, considered that a useful purpose would be served by such a challenge.[51]

13.38 The local planning authority are to give notice of their determination to the applicant within eight weeks from the date on which the application is received or such extended period as may be agreed.[52]

13.39 The application must be made on a form provided by the local planning authority which must identify the land, the relevant planning obligation, and the applicant's reasons for applying for modification or discharge. Any other persons against whom the obligation is enforceable must be notified and they may make representations; a certificate must accompany the application certifying that these requirements have been complied with. Further, the local planning authority must publicize the application in the manner prescribed by the regulations and invite representations.[53]

13.40 There is a right of appeal to the Secretary of State under s. 106B where the local planning authority either fail to give notice of their determination within the prescribed period or determine that the planning obligation shall continue without modification.[54] The appeal must be made within six months of the local planning authority's decision or within such longer period as the Secretary of State may allow. It must be made on the form provided by the Secretary of State and be accompanied by all relevant documents as prescribed by the regulations.[55] The Secretary of State must, if either the applicant or the authority so wish, give each of them an opportunity of appearing before and being heard by a person appointed by the Secretary of State for the purpose.[56] His decision on appeal is final.[57] It should be noted that neither the local planning authority nor the Secretary of

[51] *R (on the application of Burkett) v Hammersmith and Fulham London Borough Council* [2002] 2 PLR 90; see para 20.41.

[52] TCPA 1990, s. 106A(7). Town and Country Planning (Modification and Discharge of Planning Obligations) Regulations 1992, SI 1992 No 2832, reg 6.

[53] TCPA 1990, s. 106A(9). Planning Obligations Regs, regs 3, 4, 5.

[54] TCPA 1990, s. 106B(1).

[55] TCPA 1990, s. 106B(3). Planning Obligations Regs, reg 7.

[56] TCPA 1990, s. 106B(5).

[57] TCPA 1990, s. 106B(6).

State, in dealing with an application or appeal, have any jurisdiction to impose their own modifications—if the modifications in the application are unacceptable, it must be rejected.

NSIP development consent

13.41 Section 174 of PA 2008 permits the promoter of a nationally significant infrastructure project[58] to enter into a planning obligation (a 'development consent obligation') with local authorities, in the same way as developers applying for planning permission under TCPA 1990. Only the IPC or, where appropriate, the Secretary of State, will be able to modify or discharge a development consent obligation. A new s. 106C, inserted by s. 174 PA 2008, provides for legal challenges in connection with the modification or discharge of development consent obligations. The proceedings must be brought by way of judicial review within six weeks from the relevant date.

Policy guidance

13.42 The general policy is that local planning authorities may seek benefits where the benefit sought is related to the development and necessary to the grant of permission. They should ensure that the presence of extraneous benefits does not influence their decision on the planning application. If there is a choice between the imposition of conditions and entering into a planning obligation, the imposition of a condition is preferable because it enables the developer to appeal to the Secretary of State.

13.43 For many years the policy guidance was contained in Circular 1/97. That guidance provided a number of criteria as to the reasonableness of seeking a planning obligation from an applicant for planning permission. It depended on whether what is sought or offered:

(1) was needed to enable the development to go ahead, for example the provision of adequate access or car parking; or
(2) was necessary from a planning viewpoint and was so directly related to the proposed development and the use of the land after its completion that the development ought not to be permitted without it. The circular cited examples including the provision of social, educational, recreational, sporting, or other community provision, the need for which arose from the development; or
    (a) was designed in the case of mixed development to secure an acceptable balance of uses or secure the implementation of local plan policies, eg the inclusion of an element of affordable housing in a larger residential development; or

58 See para 8.168.

(b) was to offset the loss of or impact on any amenity or resource present on the site prior to development, eg in the interests of nature conservation.

13.44 The circular emphasized that if what was sought was in line with the guidance set out above, then a further test was to be applied, ie was the extent of what was sought fairly and reasonably related in scale and kind to the proposed development as well as being reasonable in all other respects?

13.45 It will be noticed that the language of the circular, with its emphasis on concepts such as reasonableness, proportionality, and necessity reflected the criteria applied by the courts to the validity of conditions.[59] In recent cases, however, the courts, when considering the materiality of planning agreements and obligations, have taken a much less stringent approach than that stated in the policy guidance.

13.46 Circular 1/97 was replaced by Circular 5/05. The new circular retains the policy tests from Circular 1/97 but places greater emphasis on the requirement for the obligation to be necessary in order to make the development acceptable in planning terms, and on the objective of sustainable development. The intention is that s. 106 should continue to be an impact mitigation or positive planning measure linked to planning necessity and should not be used for 'tax-like' purposes such as the capture of land value increases for purposes not directly necessary for development to proceed. The re-emphasis of the policy tests in Circular 1/97 seeks to discourage the offering by developers of facilities that are not required by the development, in order to make clear that planning permission is not being bought or sold.

13.47 In contrast to Circular 1/97, Circular 5/05 does not include a wide range of examples of the appropriate uses of planning obligations as this is not seen as a matter for national prescription. Rather it is a matter for the local community to decide, through its development planning processes, that development should comply with certain agreed policies. It is then perfectly acceptable to require development to contribute to those policies, where they are not addressed in the application itself and cannot be met by imposing planning conditions.

13.48 Local planning authorities will be required to include general planning obligation policies in the new-style DPDs, just as they were required to include them in the old-style development plans. The revised circular recommends that local planning authorities should set out in detail what they will expect their planning obligations to deliver in their SPDs.

13.49 The current circular encourages the use of unilateral obligations where it is possible for the developer to ascertain in advance the likely requirements of the local

59 See para 10.25.

planning authority. It seems this is likely to be increasingly the case where local planning authorities set out detailed policies, particularly those based on formulae and standard charges, as part of their LDF. Developers are encouraged to submit unilateral undertakings alongside their planning applications, in the interests of speed.

Materiality of planning obligations: the case law

13.50 In *R v Plymouth City Council, ex p Plymouth & South Devon Co-operative Society Ltd*,[60] the Court of Appeal held that all three of the 'Newbury' tests for the validity of a planning condition[61] applied to the question of whether a planning obligation was a material consideration when a local planning authority determined a planning application. However, crucially, Hoffmann LJ rejected a suggestion that, in order to be material, an offer of benefits by a developer had to be *necessary* in that it overcame what would otherwise have been a planning objection to the development; 'the fact that the principle of necessity is applied as a policy by the Secretary of State does not make it an independent ground for judicial review of a planning decision'. The benefits offered in this case, and which were upheld by the court, were considered earlier in this chapter.[62]

13.51 However the reference in the *Plymouth* case to the 'Newbury' tests appeared difficult to reconcile with the decision of the Court of Appeal in *Good v Epping Forest*[63] which, although it concerned a section 52 agreement, was nevertheless relevant to planning obligations. In the face of some uncertainty as to the scope of planning obligations, the House of Lords sought to lay down some authoritative guidance in *Tesco Stores Ltd v Secretary of State for the Environment*.[64]

13.52 Tesco and Tarmac both applied for planning permission to build a retail superstore at Witney, Oxon. A public local inquiry into both proposals was held. At the inquiry, the county council argued that, because of traffic congestion in the centre of Witney, development of either site would require the construction of a new road, referred to as the West End Link Road (WEL). As the highway authority lacked the neccessary funds, full private funding would be required at a cost of £6.6 million; Tesco offered to provide this. Rejecting the inspector's recommendations, the Secretary of State granted planning permission to Tarmac but not Tesco.

13.53 The Secretary of State relied principally on paragraphs B8 and B9 of Circular 16/91 (in similar terms to the current circular—see above). He considered that

60 (1993) 67 P & CR 78.
61 See para 10.30.
62 See above.
63 See para 13.11.
64 [1995] 2 All ER 636, [1995] 1 WLR 759.

the full funding of WEL was not fairly and reasonably related in scale to the proposed development; it was not needed to enable the development to go ahead nor was it otherwise so directly related to the proposed development that it ought not to be permitted without it. There was no evidence, given the distance between WEL and the development sites, of anything other than a marginal (less than 10 per cent) increase in town centre traffic; it would have been unreasonable to seek even a partial contribution from the developers. Tesco challenged the decision to refuse them planning permission on the ground, *inter alia*, that the Secretary of State had failed to have regard to a material consideration, ie their offer of full funding by way of a planning obligation.

13.54 Held: at first instance, by Nigel Macleod QC (sitting as deputy judge), that the Secretary of State had wrongly failed to treat Tesco's offer of funding as a material consideration which fairly and reasonably related to the proposed development; his decision would be quashed.

13.55 Tarmac appealed to the Court of Appeal who allowed the appeal and reinstated the decision of the Secretary of State. On appeal to the House of Lords at the instance of Tesco, their Lordships upheld the decision of the Court of Appeal that the Secretary of State had not erred in law in deciding as he did. Their Lordships considered that he had not disregarded Tesco's offer as immaterial but had given it due consideration; on the evidence before him he had clearly accorded it little weight.

13.56 Lord Keith said: 'An offered planning obligation which has nothing to do with the proposed development . . . will plainly not be a material consideration and could be regarded only as an attempt to buy planning permission. If it has some connection with the proposed development which is not de minimis, then regard must be had to it. But the extent, if any, to which it should affect the decision is a matter entirely within the discretion of the decision-maker and in exercising that discretion he is entitled to have regard to his established policy'.

13.57 Lord Hoffmann rejected the submission of counsel for Tarmac that Tesco's offer was not material because it did not have the effect of rendering acceptable a development which would otherwise have been unacceptable, ie the test of necessity. His Lordship said:

> The law has always made a clear distinction between the question of whether something is a material consideration and the weight which it should be given. This distinction . . . is only one aspect of a fundamental principle of British planning law, namely that the courts are concerned only with the legality of the decision-making process and not with the merits of the decision . . . The test of acceptability or necessity put forward by [counsel] suffers in my view from the fatal defect that it necessarily involves an investigation by the court of the merits of the planning decision.

13.58 The decision of the House of Lords would appear to have clarified the law in a number of respects:

(1) A planning obligation may be valid even if it fails the second of the *Newbury* tests for the validity of conditions (ie that they must fairly and reasonably relate to the permitted development). Lord Hoffmann said that the only tests for the validity of a planning obligation outside the express terms of section 106 are that it must be for a planning purpose and not be '*Wednesbury*' unreasonable[65] thus affirming the approach of the Court of Appeal in *Good v Epping Forest District Council.*[66] But validity is not the same thing as materiality and it is now clear that for a planning obligation offered by a developer to be material it must have some relevance to the proposed development, the weight given to it being entirely a matter for the discretion of the decision-maker.

(2) The notion that if a condition was manifestly unreasonable it followed that the same requirement in a planning obligation would also be unreasonable[67] is no longer tenable. In this respect Lord Hoffmann in the *Tesco Stores* case specifically endorsed the decision of the Court of Appeal in *R v South Northamptonshire District Council, ex p Crest Homes*[68] as representing the modern approach.

In that case, the local authority, faced with an alteration to the structure plan which contemplated residential development which would double the local population, decided that applicants for planning permission to build the new houses would be required to enter agreements to contribute to the necessary infrastructure, eg schools, community centres and a by-pass road etc. The authority calculated the cost of such works and allocated the burden among prospective developers in accordance with a formula. The formula was based on a percentage (20 per cent for residential, 17.5 per cent for commercial) of the enhanced value of the land added by the grant of planning permission. This was challenged by Crest Homes plc on the basis that the local authority were selling planning permissions or had unlawfully established what was in effect a local land development tax. The Court of Appeal, however, upheld the policy and considered that it was in accordance with the Secretary of State's circular. Henry LJ said:'Where residential development makes additional infrastructure necessary or desirable, there is nothing wrong in having a policy that requires major developers to contribute to the costs of infrastructure related to their development'.

---

65 See para 10.68.
66 See para 13.11.
67 See para 13.07.
68 [1995] JPL 200.

It seems fairly clear that a planning condition in the same terms would be unreasonable and invalid.

(3) It also seems clear as a result of the *Tesco Stores* case that the failure to comply with the requirements of the Secretary of State's policy guidance will not, as a matter of law, invalidate a grant of planning permission. The local planning authority would not be acting unlawfully if it failed to apply the Secretary of State's necessity test in considering whether a planning obligation should be sought. On the other hand, the local planning authority would not be acting unlawfully if it did, as a matter of policy, apply a necessity test. In these respects the *Tesco Stores* decision has raised fears in some quarters that the 'sale' of planning permissions by local authorities has been facilitated.

The reform of planning obligations

13.59 The government's Green paper of 2001, *Planning: Delivering a Fundamental Change*,[69] criticized the system of planning obligations as being over-complex, difficult to agree, and responsible, at least in part, for causing delays in the planning process. A consultation paper accompanying the Green Paper proposed a system of fixed tariffs—a proposal that engendered much opposition. In 2002 the government stated that legislative reform was not required and resolved to refine the negotiated system through further policy guidance. Then a consultation document in 2003[70] put forward a number of proposals for reforming the negotiated system and proposed a new optional planning charge.

13.60 In a quite separate development, the Barker Report, commissioned by the Treasury, was published in March 2004,[71] recommending that the government should introduce a type of charge, a 'planning gain supplement' (PGS) tied to the grant of planning permission so that development gains could be recouped for wider community benefits. This proposal was reminiscent of previous attempts to tax development gains, such as the development charge under TCPA 1947; development land tax under the Community Land Act 1975; and the Development Land Tax Act 1976 although the first two of those measures were more redistributive than the Barker proposals. Barker also recommended that the use of planning obligations could be scaled back to cover the direct impacts of development and the mitigation of its effects along with the provision of affordable and social housing. Accordingly, the Treasury announced in March 2004 that the introduction of a national PGS would be considered and a decision would be made at the end of 2005.

---

69 DTLR, 2001.

70 *Contributing to sustainable communities—a new approach to planning obligations*, ODPM, 2003.

71 *Review of Housing Supply*, HM Treasury, 2004, chaired by Kate Barker.

13.61 In June 2004, the ODPM stated that it would press ahead with implementing changes to the current negotiated system of planning obligations through a revised circular and a good practice guide, at the same time working up proposals for an optional planning charge. PCPA 2004, ss. 46 and 47 contained provisions enabling the Secretary of State to make regulations providing for the making of a 'planning contribution' (ie a payment in money or in kind) in relation to the use or development of land in the local authority's area. Although PCPA 2004 contained provisions for the repeal of s. 106, s. 106A, and s. 106B, the government indicated at the time that the s.106 regime would be re-enacted in the form of regulations as an alternative to the developer making a planning contribution. Thus under these proposals, the developer faced a choice—pay the charge or negotiate a s.106 obligation.

13.62 However the measures in PCPA 2004 relating to planning contributions were not implemented and in late 2007 the government announced that the PGS proposals were being abandoned. In a further twist to this long-running saga, the government indicated that there would be provisions in the forthcoming Planning Bill to empower local authorities to apply planning charges to new development, alongside negotiated contributions for site-specific matters. The income generated would be used to fund infrastructure identified through the development plan process, including contributions towards the costs of infrastructure of regional or sub-regional importance.

13.63 These proposals have now become reality in the Planning Act 2008 which provides for a Community Infrastructure Levy. This is considered below.

Community infrastructure levy (CIL)

13.64 The PA 2008, Part 11, makes provision for the introduction of a 'community infrastructure levy'. The government's rationale for the CIL has been explained as follows:[72]

> Generally, when land is granted planning permission for development, two things happen. First, the development has an impact on the local community, which needs to be mitigated if the development is to be sustainable (in the widest sense). And second, the value of the land may rise. The overall purpose of the CIL is to ensure that development contributes fairly to the mitigation of the impact it creates; to ensure that development is delivered, and in a more sustainable way. The fact that the value of land (or property) typically rises as a result of development means that contributions can be required without removing incentives to develop . . . The Government therefore believes that it is right that development itself should make

72 *The Community Infrastructure Levy*, DCLG 2008, paras 4 and 20.

more of a contribution to the infrastructure cost faced by local communities, and that the burden of contributing to development should be spread more fairly. It also believes that developers should have more certainty as to what they will be expected to contribute, thus speeding up the planning system.

13.65 It must be emphasized that the regime under s.106 TCPA 1990 discussed earlier in this chapter will be retained as the legal basis for negotiated agreements between developers and local authorities. Thus planning obligations will continue to provide the means of securing contributions from developers for those authorities choosing not to introduce the CIL. Nevertheless, the Government has stated that it will encourage local planning authorities to impose charges using the CIL, rather than relying on planning obligations, 'because of the clearer basis it provides for securing contributions from a wider range of developments and the additional safeguards and benefits it allows for.'[73]

CIL: the statutory provisions

13.66 The provisions in the 2008 Act regarding the levy are the skeletal—they pave the way for the Government to flesh out the provisions by making of regulations. Nevertheless, an important principle is established by s. 205(2) of PA 2008 which provides:

> [The] Secretary of State shall aim to ensure that the overall purpose of the CIL is to ensure that the costs incurred in providing the infrastructure to support the development of an area can be funded (wholly or partly) by owners or developers of land.

13.67 The Act provides in s. 205 (1) that the secretary of State may with the consent of the Treasury make regulation of a charge to be known as a CIL.

The charge

13.68 PA 2008, s.206 provides that the charging authority may charge CIL in respect of the use and development of the land in its area. Charging authorities, ie authorities which will be able to levy CIL, are to be local planning authorities responsible for the production of the local development plans for the area. In London, the charging authority is to be the Mayor of London and the CIL regulations may provide for other authorities to be charging authorities.

Liability

13.69 Section 208 of PA 2008 provides that where liability to CIL would arise in respect of proposed development, a person may assume the liability to pay the levy. A person

[73] Ibid, para 87.

assuming liability before the commencement of development becomes liable when, in reliance on planning permission, development is commenced.

13.70 Where liability is not assumed in this way, the owner or developer of the land is to be liable for CIL. 'Development', for the purpose of CIL liability, means 'anything done by way of or for the purpose of the creation of a new building, or anything done to or in respect of an existing building'. Regulations may, inter alia, exclude specified works or changes of use from this definition.

13.71 There are provisions in s. 210 enabling regulations to provide for exemptions to or reductions in CIL for charities

Amount

13.72 Under the provision of s. 211 charging authorities proposing to charge CIL must issue a document called a charging schedule setting out the CIL rates of the area. In setting rates, authorities are to have regard to the actual or expected costs of infrastructure, the economic viability of development, and other actual or expected sources of funding for infrastructure. The CIL regulations may make other provisions about setting rates; in particular as to the administrative costs in connection with CIL; and as to the values used, and documents produced, for other statutory purposes.

13.73 The CIL regulations may permit or require a charging schedule to adopt specified methods of calculation, eg by reference to description or purposes of development or other specified criteria. There may be provision for differential rates, a zero rate, increased rates or reductions. Charging authorities may revise a charging schedule.

Charging schedules

13.74 Under PA 2008, s. 212 charging authorities must appoint an examiner to examine their draft charging schedule. The person appointed must be independent of the authority and have appropriate qualification and experience. The draft submitted must be accompanied by a declaration that the charging authority has complied with the relevant procedural requirements and criteria; that the authority has used appropriate evidence; and it must contain any other matter prescribed by the CIL regulations. The charging authority must approve the declaration.

13.75 The examiner must consider the matters referred to in the previous paragraph. He may recommend that the draft schedule be approved; that it be approved with specified modifications; or that it be rejected. Regulations must provide for anyone to make representations about a draft charging schedule. Regulations must also provide for anyone who makes representations about a draft charging schedule to be heard by the examiner.

13.76 A charging authority may only approve a draft charging schedule if the examiner recommends approval and subject to any modifications recommended. The charging authority must approve the charging schedule.

13.77 An approved charging schedule may not take effect unless it has been published by the authority. There is, under s. 215, to be a right of approval on a question of fact relating to the calculation of the amount of CIL levied on proposed development.

Application

13.78 Section 216 of Act of 2008 provides that the CIL regulations must require authorities charging CIL to apply it, or cause it to be applied, to the funding of infrastructure. 'Infrastructure' includes:

(a) roads and other transport facilities;
(b) food defences;
(c) school and other educational facilities;
(d) medical facilities;
(e) sporting and recreational facilities;
(f) open spaces; and
(g) affordable housing (being social housing within Part 2 of the Housing and Regeneration Act 2008 and such other housing as the CIL regulations may allow).

13.79 The regulations may amend the above list so as to add, remove or vary items or exclude matters from the meaning of 'infrastructure'. Further, the regulations may specify works, installations and other facilities that are, or are not to be, funded by CIL; criteria for determining areas of land which may be funded; and what is to be, or not to be, treated as funding.

13.80 The regulations may require charging authorities to prepare and publish a list of projects that are to be, or may be, wholly or partially funded by the CIL; and they may include provision as to the circumstances in which a charging authority may or may not apply CIL to projects not included in the list. In making provision about funding, the regulations may permit CIL to be used, for example, to reimburse expenditure already incurred; or to include the provision for the giving of loans, guarantees, and indemnities. Under provisions of s. 217 PA 2008, the CIL regulations must include provision about the way in which CIL may be collected.

Enforcement

13.81 Under s. 218 of PA 2008, the CIL regulations must include provision about the enforcement of CIL, such as the consequences of late payment and the failure to pay. The section specifies a range of matters for which the regulations may include provision, such as the payment of interest and the imposition of penalties or surcharges. The regulations may also replicate or apply, with or without modifications, any enactment relating to the enforcement of a tax. There is also provision for regulations to create criminal offences, for example, offences relating to evasion or providing false or misleading information; and for the creation of land charges.

13.82 By virtue of s. 219, the regulations may require a charging authority to pay compensation in respect of loss or damage suffered as a result of enforcement action.

Procedure

13.83 Section 220 PA 2008 provides that the CIL regulations may include provision about the procedure to be followed in connection with CIL. It contains a number of example of matters the regulations may make provision about, including consultation; publicity; the form and content of documents; and the possibility of holding an examination in public.

The Secretary of State

13.84 Under the provision of s. 221 PA 2008, the Secretary of State may give guidance to a charging authority or other authority about any matter connected with CIL (including an examiner appointed under s. 212) and the authority must have regard to any guidance so given

Relationship with other powers

13.85 By virtue of s. 223 PA 2008, the CIL regulations may include provision about how certain powers are to be used or not used. These include planning obligations under s.106 TCPA 1990 and agreement under s. 278 of the Highways Act 1980. By this means, the CIL regulations could be used, should the Secretary of State think it necessary or expedient, to restrict the use of planning obligations and highway agreements in some way. However, under the Act, such a power can only be used in a prescribed set of circumstances, such as for complementing the main purpose of the CIL regulations; or preventing agreements, undertakings, or other transactions from being used to undermine or circumvent the CIL regulations.

13.86 It should be noted that, under the provision of s. 225 PA 2008, the provisions relating to the planning contributions in PCPA 2004, which were never brought into force, are to be repealed after Royal Assent. Similarly, powers in PCPA 2004 to repeal the TCPA 1990 s. 106 regime are also to be repealed.

14

PURCHASE NOTICES AND BLIGHT NOTICES

14.01 Planning control often prevents a landowner putting his land to the most profitable use. Until 1991 it was still possible to claim compensation under TCPA 1990, Part IV or Part V. But this was not always available and even these limited rights were removed by the Planning and Compensation Act.[1] This is reasonable enough; in the normal case, there remains a profitable use for the land, and the owner can either continue to use it for this purpose or sell the land to someone else at a reasonable price. To take an obvious example: however disappointing a refusal of planning permission for building development may be to the owner of agricultural land he can continue to use it for agriculture or sell it to someone who is prepared to use it for agriculture.

14.02 There are, however, some cases of hardship in which the Planning Acts recognize the need for some further remedy. For instance there may be no beneficial use for the land unless planning permission can be obtained for its development; a

[1] See para 21.31.

common example is the site of a building destroyed by fire. Such land is said to have become incapable of reasonably beneficial use, and TCPA 1990, Part VI, Chapter I enables the owner in certain circumstances to serve purchase notice requiring the appropriate local authority to purchase his interest.

14.03 Hardship may also arise where land is designated, say, in the development plan for some purpose which will ultimately involve its compulsory acquisition. The designation does not render the land incapable of reasonably beneficial use, but the threat of compulsory purchase may make it virtually unsaleable. This hardship is remedied to some extent by TCPA 1990, Part VI, Chapter II which enables certain owner-occupiers to serve a purchase order in these circumstances; this type of purchase notice is called a 'blight notice'.

Adverse planning decisions

14.04 TCPA 1990, Part VI, Chapter 1 applies where (a) planning permission has been refused or granted subject to conditions as a result of an application to the local planning authority; or (b) planning permission is revoked or modified; or (c) a discontinuance order is made under TCPA 1990, s. 97.[2]

14.05 In the first two of the above cases any owner of the affected land may serve a purchase notice if the following conditions are satisfied:[3]

(a) the land has become incapable of reasonably beneficial use in its existing state; and
(b) if permission was granted subject to conditions, that the land cannot be rendered capable of reasonably beneficial use by carrying out development in accordance with these conditions; and
(c) in any case (ie whether permission was refused or granted subject to conditions) that the land cannot be rendered capable of reasonably beneficial use by carrying out any development for which permission has been granted or for which either the local planning authority or the Secretary of State has undertaken to grant permission.

14.06 If a discontinuance order has been made, the conditions for the service of a purchase notice are:[4]

(a) that by reason of the order the land has become incapable of reasonably beneficial use; and

---

2 Or under TCPA 1990, Sch 9, para 1: see para 17.62.
3 TCPA 1990, s. 137(2), (3).
4 TCPA 1990, s. 137(2), (4).

(b) that it cannot be made capable of reasonably beneficial use by the carrying out of any development for which planning permission has been granted whether by that order or otherwise.[5]

14.07 The expression 'beneficial use' was explained by Widgery J in *Adams and Wade Ltd v Minister of Housing and Local Government*[6] as follows:

> The purpose [TCPA 1962, s. 129] is to enable a landowner whose use of his land has been frustrated by a planning refusal to require the local authority to take the land off his hands. The reference to 'beneficial' use must therefore be a reference to a use which can benefit the owner or the prospective owner and the fact that the land in its existing state confers some benefit or value upon the public at large would be no bar to the service of a purchase notice.

14.08 In many cases, therefore, the test will be an economic one—is the land in its existing state capable of yielding a reasonable return to its owner? In some cases—for example the site of a former building—it will usually be quite clear that there is no beneficial use in this sense. Where there is *some* beneficial use, it will be necessary to decide whether that use is reasonably beneficial. In the event of dispute, this will be largely a question of fact for the Secretary of State, and the court is not likely to interfere with his findings if he has applied the right tests.

14.09 Thus in *General Estates Co Ltd v Minister of Housing and Local Government*,[7] the company owned a site of about 11 acres. About half was let to a sports club at a rent of £52 a year; the rest was vacant but could be let for grazing at about £20 a year. The Minister concluded on these facts that the land had not become incapable of reasonably beneficial use. The company applied to the High Court for an order to quash the Minister's decision. The application was dismissed; it could not be said that the Minister's findings were so perverse as really to be outside his powers.

14.10 A similar approach was taken by the Court of Appeal in *Colley v Secretary of State for the Environment*.[8] A woodland site of just over two hectares was subject to a tree preservation order.[9] Estimated income from the sale of the timber was negligible and there would be no income from the sale of mature oaks for another 50 years. The court upheld the Secretary of State's refusal to confirm a purchase notice. He had not erred in law in regarding the land as capable of reasonably beneficial use as a commercial woodland. Evans LJ said whatever the Secretary of State may have taken 'reasonably beneficial' to mean, 'it cannot have been financial benefit, because

[5] For grant of planning permission by discontinuance order, see para 11.18.

[6] (1965) 18 P & CR 60.

[7] (1965) 194 Estates Gazette 202.

[8] (1998) 77 P & CR 190. A previous dispute regarding compensation for revocation of planning permission concerning the same site was settled by the House of Lords in *Canterbury City Council v Colley* [1993] AC 401, [1993] 1 All ER 591: see para 11.34.

[9] See para 15.02.

on the evidence this was non-existent on any sensible accounting basis. But it is not wrong in principle to say . . . that the concept is not synonymous with profit'.

14.11 In deciding what is a reasonably beneficial use it may be helpful to compare the value of the land in its existing state with the value it would have if developed in accordance with planning permission. There have been some expressions of doubt as to whether comparisons of this sort are legitimate. Thus, in *Brookdene Investments Ltd v Minister of Housing and Local Government,*[10] Fisher J asked: 'How can a use which would involve the carrying out of a development be relevant to an inquiry as to whether land has become incapable of reasonably beneficial use in its existing state?'

14.12 However it now seems clear that it is permissible to compare the value of the land in its existing state with the value which it would have if planning permission were granted for the limited range of development comprised in TCPA 1990, Schedule 3,[11] Part I. That seems to follow from TCPA 1990, s. 138(1) and (2) which, as amended by the PCA 1991,[12] provides that, for the purpose of deciding whether the basic conditions for the service of a purchase notice have been satisfied, no account is to be taken of any 'unauthorised prospective use' if it would involve the carrying out of development other than development within TCPA 1990, Schedule 3, Part I; and where the purchase notice follows a refusal or conditional grant of planning permission, the assumption of Schedule 3 development must not exceed certain limits set out in Schedule 10 to the Act.

14.13 The effect of TCPA 1990, s. 138(1), (2) as originally enacted was considered by the High Court in *Gavaghan v Secretary of State for the Environment.*[13] The decision remains of relevance to the amended TCPA 1990, s. 138.

14.14 The claimant had been refused planning permission to erect a dwellinghouse on some land adjoining a residential property known as Lower Court. He served a purchase notice on the council, but the council served a counter notice that they were unwilling to comply with it. On the matter being referred to the Secretary of State, he decided that the land could be rendered capable of reasonably beneficial use, because he considered it reasonable to conclude on the evidence that the owner of Lower Court was a prospective purchaser of the land to use it as curtilage land; the council had given an undertaking to grant planning permission for the change of use to curtilage land.

14.15 The claimant challenged the Secretary of State's decision on the ground that the change of use to curtilage land would be new development and so must be

---

10 (1970) 21 P & CR 545.

11 See Appendix 1.

12 TCPA 1990, s. 138(2) was amended by the PCA 1991 to take account of the repeal of TCPA 1990, Sch 3, Part II. For Sch 3 development, see ch 21 below.

13 [1989] JPL 596. An appeal against this decision was dismissed by the Court of Appeal, reported at [1990] JPL 273, [1990] 1 WLR 587.

disregarded under s. 138(1), (2) as originally enacted; further there was no evidence that the owner of Lower Court was a prospective purchaser.

14.16 Mr Lionel Read QC, sitting as deputy judge, held that although s. 138(1) required any prospective use involving new development to be disregarded in determining whether the basic conditions were satisfied, nevertheless the Secretary of State was entitled to have regard to any planning permission for other development which had actually been granted or which the local planning authority had undertaken to grant. But the Secretary of State had acted irrationally in concluding on the evidence that there was a prospective purchaser, and he should therefore have confirmed the notice.

14.17 On appeal to the Court of Appeal it was held that there was no evidence at all upon which the Secretary of State could have arrived at his decision on the latter point. Although the appeal was on this ground, the decision of the Court of Appeal by implication confirms the learned deputy judge's interpretation of TCPA 1990, s. 138.

14.18 Does it follow that land is incapable of reasonably beneficial use if in its existing state it is of substantially less value than it would be if permission were granted for Schedule 3 development? The question came before the Divisional Court in *R v Minister of Housing and Local Government, ex p Chichester RDC.*[14]

14.19 A piece of coastal land of about 2½ acres was subject to considerable erosion, and a large sum of money would be required to prevent further erosion. There were 14 bungalows on part of the land, and the remainder was divided into 17 plots which were let as caravan sites during the summer under temporary planning permissions. The owner applied for permission to develop the land for residential purposes; on this being refused he served a purchase notice. The Minister confirmed the notice on the ground that 'the land in its existing state and with the benefit of temporary planning permissions is of substantially less use and value to its owner than it would be if planning permission had been granted (without limitation as to time) for the rebuilding of the buildings which formerly stood there and have been demolished since 7 January 1937'.

14.20 The Chichester RDC applied to the High Court for an order to quash the Minister's confirmation of the purchase notice.

14.21 Held: the reason given by the Minister was not valid because the question was whether 'the land has become incapable of reasonably beneficial use in its existing state' and not whether the land was of less use to the owner in its present state than if developed.

14.22 The Divisional Court did not, however, go so far as to say that there should be no comparison of the value of the land in its existing state with the value which

14 [1960] 2 All ER 407, [1960] 1 WLR 587.

it would have after Schedule 3 development. Where the Minister erred in the *Chichester* case was in accepting the comparison with Schedule 3 as conclusive. The correct approach seems to be that approved, albeit somewhat reluctantly, by Fisher J in *Brookdene Investments Ltd v Minister of Housing and Local Government*[15]—namely, that a comparison with Schedule 3 values may be made; but, if it is made, it must be made along with other relevant facts, and it is for the Secretary of State to decide in each case how much weight is to be given to such comparison. Indeed, the proposition that Schedule 3 is essentially a compensatory provision with only a limited role in relation to purchase notices was accepted by Silber J in *Hudscott Estates (East) Ltd v Secretary of State for the Environment, Transport and the Regions*.[16]

'Any owner'

14.23 A purchase notice may be served by 'any owner of the land' who considers that the above conditions are satisfied. TCPA 1990, s. 336 provides that for this purpose the word 'owner' is to mean: 'a person, other than a mortgagee not in possession, who, whether in his own right or as trustee for any other person, is entitled to receive the rack-rent of the land or, where the land is not let at a rack-rent, would be so entitled if it were so let'. Although rack-rent is not specifically defined, this definition clearly excludes the owner of a reversion expectant on the termination of a long lease at a ground rent. For this reason it was contended in *London Corpn v Cusack-Smith*[17] that the context required a different meaning for the word 'owner'.

14.24 Land in the City of London was held by H on 99 years' lease at a ground rent. Following the destruction of the buildings H disclaimed liability for the rent under the Landlord and Tenant (War Damage) (Amendment) Act 1941, until the premises were rebuilt. Planning permission was subsequently refused for rebuilding and H served a notice under what is now s. 137 requiring the Corporation to purchase his interest; this notice was confirmed by the Minister.

14.25 Subsequently the freeholders served a notice requiring the purchase of their interest, but the Corporation contended that the freeholders were not within the definition of owner in s. 119 of the Act of 1947 now [TCPA 1990, s. 336]. The House of Lords (reversing a decision of the Court of Appeal) held that the word 'owner' must be given the meaning ascribed by s. 119(1).

14.26 The hardship in this case occurred because the lessees had exercised their right under the LT(WD)(A) 1941 to suspend payment of the ground rent and the

15 (1970) 21 P & CR 545.
16 (2001) 82 P & CR 71.
17 [1955] AC 337, [1955] 1 All ER 302.

Corporation had refused to permit rebuilding: a similar situation might arise where a building is destroyed by fire, and the lease contains a clause permitting abatement of the ground rent. In other cases, however, there will be less hardship, because the freeholder will be entitled to the ground rent even if the lessee's interest is acquired by a public authority.

Procedure

14.27 In the cases of adverse planning decisions, a purchase notice is served on the district council (or the London borough) for the area in which the land is situated.[18] The purchase notice must relate to the whole of the land subject to the adverse planning decision; it will be invalid if it relates only to a part.[19] If the council are willing to comply with the purchase notice, or if they have found another local authority or statutory undertaker who are willing to comply with it, they serve a notice to that effect; the authority in question are then deemed to have served notice to treat for the interest of the owner who served the notice.

14.28 If the council are not willing to comply with the notice and have not found another authority or statutory undertaker who would be willing to comply with it, the council must within three months forward the purchase notice to the Secretary of State and notify the owner accordingly. If the Secretary of State considers that the basic requirements are satisfied, he will do one of the following:

(a) confirm the notice, in which case the council are deemed to have served notice to treat;
(b) grant permission for the development in respect of which the application was made; or, if permission was granted subject to conditions, amend the conditions so far as is necessary to render the land capable of reasonably beneficial use;
(c) grant permission for some other development of either the whole or part of the land;[20]
(d) substitute another local authority or statutory undertaker for the council on whom the notice is served, in which case that authority or statutory undertaker are deemed to have served notice to treat.

14.29 A special situation arises where the land forms part of a larger area for which planning permission has been given; there may be a condition that the particular piece of land in question is to remain undeveloped or is to be laid out as amenity land,

---

18 TCPA 1990, s. 137(2).

19 *Cook and Woodham v Winchester City Council* [1995] JPL 240.

20 If he considers that this would make it capable of reasonably beneficial use: TCPA 1990, ss. 141(2), 142(3).

or the application for permission may show that this was contemplated. In these circumstances he may in his discretion refuse to confirm the notice.[21]

14.30 Whatever action the Secretary of State proposes to take he must give notice to the person who served the purchase notice, to the council on whom it was served, to the local planning authority, and to any other local authority or statutory undertaker whom he proposes to substitute for the council. Any of these parties then has the right to be heard at a public local inquiry or other hearing. This procedure also applies where the Secretary of State decides not to confirm a notice on the ground that the basic requirements have not been satisfied, but not apparently if he decides that the purchase notice should not be confirmed on the ground that the person who served it is not an 'owner'.

14.31 The Secretary of State must give his decision during the 'relevant period'; that is, nine months from the date of service of the purchase notice or within six months of the date on which a copy of the purchase notice was forwarded to him, whichever is the earlier. If he fails to do so, or if he fails to take any of the other courses of action open to him (see (b) and (c) above), the purchase notice is deemed to have been confirmed.[22]

14.32 In *Herefordshire County Council v Richard White*,[23] the Court of Appeal held that an owner had no right, once it was served, to amend a purchase notice. This may arise where there is an error in the original notice and the owner wishes to redeem the situation. The court ruled that there was no express provision in the Act for such a right, nor did it arise by necessary implication. At the same time it seems that there is nothing to prevent an owner from serving more than one purchase notice. Whether there has been an implied withdrawal of the first notice, where a subsequent notice has been served, would depend on the circumstances and the terms on which the second notice was served. The question would be determined by an objective analysis of the owner's conduct. Dyson LJ said: 'The question whether, having served notice A, an owner impliedly withdraws that notice if he subsequently serves notice B depends on the circumstances in which and the terms on which he serves notice B. If he merely serves notice B without any reference to notice A, he will ordinarily be taken to have impliedly withdrawn notice A. If he does so in response to an objection to the validity of notice A by the [local planning authority], the inference is irresistible that, by serving notice B *without more*, the owner is withdrawing notice A.'

---

[21] TCPA 1990, s. 142 re-enacting a provision originally introduced by the TCPA 1968 and designed to deal with the position revealed in *Adams and Wade Ltd v Minister of Housing and Local Government* (1965) 18 P & CR 60.

[22] TCPA 1990, s. 143(2).

[23] [2007] EWCA Civ 1204.

14.33 Of course, as Dyson LJ acknowledged, if, on the other hand, the owner states that he is serving notice B without prejudice to his contention that notice A is valid and that he will continue to rely on notice A until it has been adjudged to be invalid, then he would be making it clear that notice A is not being withdrawn.

Adverse planning proposals: blight notices

14.34 Blight notices relate to land which has become difficult to sell because of 'planning blight', that is, the threat of compulsory purchase implicit in some planning proposal. The scheme was first introduced by the TCPA 1959, but it has been considerably extended since then: there are now far more cases in which a blight notice can be served, and the conditions have been relaxed. There are, however, two important limitations. First, only certain classes of owner-occupier can serve a blight notice. Secondly, at least some part of the owner-occupier's land must be under threat of compulsory purchase; the scheme affords no protection to the person whose land is depreciated in value by a threat of compulsory purchase hanging over neighbouring land.

14.35 A blight notice may be served in respect of an hereditament or agricultural unit consisting wholly or partly of land falling within any of the following cases.[24]

Development plan documents

14.36 Land which is identified for the purposes of 'relevant public functions' by a DPD for the area in which the land is situated.

14.37 'Relevant public functions' are the functions of a government department, local authority, National Park authority, or statutory undertakers; the establishment or running by a public telecommunications operator of a telecommunications system.

14.38 For the purpose of the above provision, a DPD is a DPD, or a revision thereof, which has been adopted or approved under Part 2 of PCPA 2004; and a DPD, or revision thereof, which has been submitted to the Secretary of State for independent examination, unless withdrawn under s. 22 of PCPA 2004.

14.39 TCPA 1990 as originally enacted specified land included in a structure plan, local plan, or unitary development plan (for certain functions) as blighted land subject to the possible service of a blight notice. But these provisions were repealed by PCPA 2004, as from 28 September 2004—there are, however, transitional provisions in Schedule 8, para 16 of PCPA 2004; and for Wales in PA 2008, s.197.

---

[24] TCPA 1990, Sch 13.

This enables the blight notice procedure to apply to structure plans, local plans and UDPs in Wales until such time as superseded by an LDP under TCPA 1990.

Land affected by resolution of local authority or directions of the Secretary of State

14.40 Land earmarked by resolution of local authority or by a direction of the Secretary of State as land which may be required for the purposes of 'relevant public functions', ie the functions of a government department, local authority, National Park authority, or statutory undertakers; the establishment or running by a public telecommunications operator of a telecommunications system.

Compulsory purchase under special Act

14.41 Land authorized to be acquired by special Act.

New towns

14.42 Land within an area designated as the site of a new town. The blight notice may be served at any time after the draft designation order has been published. If subsequently the Secretary of State decides not to make the designation order, or modifies it so as to exclude the land in question, a blight notice cannot thereafter be served.

Slum clearance

14.43 Land which is either included in a clearance area under the Housing Act 1985, s. 289 or is land surrounded by or adjoining a clearance area which the local authority have determined to purchase.

General improvement area

14.44 Land indicated by information published under the Housing Act 1985, s. 257 as land which the local authority propose to acquire as part of a general improvement area.

Highways proposals in development plan

14.45 Land indicated in a development plan as required for the construction or improvement of a highway, other than land identified for purposes of 'relevant public functions' in a DPD, mentioned in the first paragraph above.

Orders for schemes for highways

14.46 Land indicated in an order or scheme under the Highways Act 1980 for the construction, alteration, or improvement of a highway.

Compulsory purchase order under highway land acquisition powers

14.47 Land subject to a compulsory purchase order under the Highways Act 1980, s. 250 for the acquisition of rights over highway land, but notice to treat has not yet been served. The blight notice can be served at any time after the order has been submitted to the appropriate Minister for confirmation; or, where the order is proposed by the Minister, after the draft order has been published. If the order is subsequently not confirmed or, in the case of a draft order is not made, a blight notice cannot thereafter be served.

Land affected by new street orders

14.48 Land affected by an order made under the Highways Act 1980, s. 188 or the Public Health Act 1925, s. 30 regarding the minimum widths of new streets or highways declared to be new streets.

Land in urban development areas

14.49 Land in an urban development area designated by the Secretary of State under the HA 1980.

Compulsory purchase orders

14.50 Land subject to a compulsory purchase order, but notice to treat has not yet been served.

14.51 The blight notice may be served at any time after the compulsory purchase order has been submitted to the appropriate Minister for confirmation; or, in the case of compulsory purchase by a government department, after the draft order has been published. If subsequently the compulsory purchase order is not confirmed (or, in the case of a government department, the order is not made) a blight notice cannot thereafter be served.

Acquisition under the Transport and Works Act 1992

14.52 Land authorized to be compulsorily acquired under the Transport and Works Act 1992, s. 2 or 3.

Land identified in national policy statements under the Planning Act 2008

14.53 Land in a location identified in an NPS as suitable (or potentially suitable) for a specified description of development. The compulsory acquisition of the land must be authorized by an order granting NSIP development consent (or the land must fall within the limits of deviation); or an application for an order granting NSIP development consent must seek authority to compulsorily acquire the land.

14.54 These categories of land are referred to in the Act as 'blighted land'.[25]

Who may serve notice

14.55 A blight notice under these provisions may be served by a person having an interest 'qualifying for protection'[26] namely:

(a) the resident owner-occupier of any hereditament;
(b) the owner-occupier of any hereditament with a net annual value not exceeding the prescribed limit;
(c) the owner-occupier of an agricultural unit.[27]

14.56 For this purpose 'owner-occupier' includes a lessee with at least three years to run as well as a freeholder.[28] 'Resident owner-occupier' is defined as 'an *individual* who occupies the whole . . . of the hereditament';[29] and for this reason in *Webb v Warwickshire County Council*[30] the Lands Tribunal held that the interest must be a strictly personal one abating on death with the result that a personal representative could not serve a blight notice.

14.57 The effect of this decision is modified by TCPA 1990, s. 161 which provides that a personal representative may serve a blight notice if the deceased owner would have been entitled to serve such a notice at the date of his death. It is a further condition that one or more individuals (to the exclusion of any body corporate) shall be beneficially interested in the proceeds of sale.

14.58 'Hereditament' means the land comprised in a hereditament included in the valuation list for rating purposes. As agricultural land is not included in the valuation list, the Act speaks in this connection of an agricultural unit, and this means land which is occupied as a unit for agricultural purposes.[31] With the abolition of domestic rating by the Local Government Finance Act 1988, residential property is no longer included in the valuation list. However as there is no limit of annual value for the service of a blight notice in respect of residential property, the need to arrive at an annual value for such property only arises in the case of a blight notice served in respect of non-domestic property of which some part is a dwelling.[32]

---

25 TCPA 1990, s. 149(1).
26 TCPA 1990, s. 49(2), (3).
27 As defined in TCPA 1990, s. 171.
28 TCPA 1990, s. 168(4).
29 TCPA 1990, s. 168(3).
30 (1971) 23 P & CR 63.
31 TCPA 1990, s. 171(1).
32 In such a case, the value of the residential part will be 5 per cent of the sum payable on compulsory purchase, as certified by the relevant valuation officer: TCPA 1990, s. 171(2).

14.59 In certain circumstances a mortgagee of such an interest may serve a blight notice.[33]

14.60 It will be appreciated that a blight notice can only be served in respect of business or other essentially non-residential premises if the net annual value does not exceed the prescribed limit or if the owner occupies some part of the premises as a dwelling. Investment owners have been excluded because:

> The value of an investment is affected by many factors. It would be well nigh impossible to determine whether the value of an investment property had changed because of some blighting effect of local authority proposals or because of some change in the market. Local authorities might therefore find themselves forced to buy an interest in property which had not really been blighted by their proposals. Moreover the time when the interest in property was offloaded on the local authority would be likely to depend, not upon any genuine need to realise capital, in order to enable a man to find a new roof for his head, as in the other case, but merely because at that particular date the changes in the market were such that the money might be more profitably invested in something else.[34]

14.61 In *Essex County Council v Essex Inc Congregational Church Union*,[35] the House of Lords had to consider an appeal concerning an attempt to serve a blight notice in respect of a church and church hall. The actual decision was that, in the circumstances, the Lands Tribunal had at the outset no jurisdiction to decide whether the respondents' interest in the property was 'qualified for protection' by purchase notice, and consequently that the Court of Appeal and the House of Lords had no jurisdiction either. The Lands Tribunal and Court of Appeal had, however, considered that they possessed this jurisdiction, and had decided that since the property was marked 'exempt' in the rating list this included it in the category of premises with a net annual value not exceeding the prescribed limit. The House of Lords stated that this decision, though there was in any case no jurisdiction to give it, was wrong.[36]

Service and effect of notice

14.62 The blight notice is to be served on the 'appropriate authority'—namely, the government department, local authority, or other body who are likely to acquire the land.[37] In the case of land blighted by an NPS under PA 2008, the appropriate authority is the statutory undertaker named as an appropriate person to carry out

---

33 TCPA 1990, s. 162.

34 Speech of Lord Chancellor on 27 April 1959 (215 HL Official Report (5th series) cols 1041–2).

35 [1963] AC 808, [1963] 1 All ER 326.

36 Provision is made for the valuation of exempt premises by the TCPA 1990, s. 171(3). The hereditament is to be assessed as if it were liable to rating.

37 TCPA 1990, s. 169.

the development specified in the NPS, or the Secretary of State where there is no such named statutory undertaker.

14.63 The person serving the notice is known as the claimant and he must serve a notice in the prescribed form.[38] This will state that the whole or some part of the hereditament or agricultural unit is 'blighted land',[39] that the claimant is entitled to an interest which qualifies for protection in the hereditament or unit, that he has made reasonable efforts to sell that interest, and that he has been unable to sell it except at a price substantially lower than he might reasonably have expected but for the threat of compulsory purchase. The requirement of a reasonable endeavour to sell no longer applies if the land is authorized by a special enactment to be compulsorily acquired or a compulsory purchase order is in force and in both cases the powers of compulsory acquisition remain exercisable.[40]

14.64 In the case of a hereditament, the notice must require the appropriate authority to purchase the whole of the claimant's interest. This applies even if part only of the hereditament is blighted; only where the claimant does not own the whole can the notice refer to less than the whole hereditament and even then it must require the authority to take the whole amount owned by the claimant.[41]

14.65 In the case of an agricultural unit, the rules are different. The threat of compulsory acquisition may extend only to a small part of the farm and might not cause difficulty in selling the farm as a whole. If, however, the effect is to render the farm unsaleable at a reasonable price, a blight notice may be served in respect of the 'affected area', that is, so much of the farm as is blighted land.[42] If the claimant can show that the whole or part of the 'unaffected area' would not be viable as a separate unit, then that land may also be included in the blight notice.[43]

14.66 If the appropriate authority are not willing to purchase the land they may within two months serve a counter notice specifying their objections.[44] There are in effect three main grounds on which the authority may object:

(1) that the conditions laid down in the TCPA 1990 have not been satisfied;
(2) that they do not intend to acquire any part of the hereditament or (in the case of an agricultural unit) any part of the affected area;

---

[38] For the prescribed form, see the General Regulations.
[39] See para 14.35.
[40] ie falling within TCPA 1990, Sch 13, paras 21 and 22. This amendment was made by PCA 1991, s. 70.
[41] TCPA 1990, s. 150(1), (2), (3).
[42] TCPA 1990, s. 158(2).
[43] TCPA 1990, s. 158(2).
[44] TCPA 1990, s. 151.

(3) that they do not intend to acquire any part of the hereditament or any part of the affected area within the next 15 years, but this only applies where the blight arises from the provisions of the development plan or in certain cases in which the land is indicated in the development plan for the construction or improvement of a highway.

14.67 In the case of an agricultural unit the authority may also object on the ground that they propose to acquire part only of the affected area.[45] In the case of land blighted by an NPS under the PA 2008, the appropriate authority is prevented from serving a counter-notice on the grounds of having no intention of carrying out the development.

14.68 The claimant may require the objections to be referred to the Lands Tribunal; unless the objection falls within class (2) or (3) above, it is for him to satisfy the Tribunal that the objection is not well founded. If the Tribunal are satisfied the objection is not well founded, they will declare the notice valid. If the authority upholds an objection that the authority intend to acquire part only of the affected area the Tribunal will declare the notice valid in relation to the part only.[46]

14.69 If no counter-notice has been served or if the notice has been declared valid, the appropriate authority will be deemed to have served notice to treat in respect of the hereditament or (in the case of an agricultural unit) either the affected area or such less area as the authority intended to acquire in any event.[47]

45 TCPA 1990, s. 158.
46 TCPA 1990, s. 153.
47 TCPA 1990, s. 154.

15

SPECIAL FORMS OF CONTROL

15.01 One of the objects of town and country planning is the preservation and enhancement of amenity—that is, the pleasant features of town and countryside. This is achieved partly through the control of development as described in earlier chapters; that is, the planning authority may refuse permission for development which would be detrimental to amenity or they may attach conditions designed to safeguard amenity. In addition to this general power of control planning legislation provides a number of special forms of control which are mainly concerned with preserving or improving the pleasant features of the town and country. The TCPA 1990 provides for the preservation and planting of trees; control over the display of outdoor advertising; and the proper maintenance of waste land. In addition the Hazardous Substances Act provides for the control of hazardous substances.

Tree preservation

15.02 The felling of trees is not development as defined in the TCPA 1990, but where it is considered desirable in the interests of amenity the felling or lopping of trees or woodlands can be controlled by making tree preservation orders (TPOs) under

TCPA 1990, s. 198. A tree preservation order may apply to a single tree, a group of trees, or to a substantial woodland. It may prohibit the felling, lopping, uprooting, wilful damage, or wilful destruction of the trees without the consent of the local planning authority; and in the case of woodlands, it may contain provisions as to the replanting of any area which is felled in the course of forestry operations permitted under the order.[1]

15.03 What is a tree? There is no definition of 'tree' in the TCPA 1990, but the use of the word 'tree' probably excludes bushes and shrubs and hedgerows as such; a hedgerow, however, may include trees. A gardening encyclopaedia[2] defines a tree as 'a woody plant normally with one stem at least 12 to 15 feet tall in maturity'. The same work defines a shrub as 'a perennial woody plant, branching naturally from its base without a defined leader (a single main shoot) and not normally exceeding 30 feet high'. In *Kent County Council v Batchelor*,[3] Lord Denning said in *woodland* a tree 'ought to be something over seven or eight inches in diameter': on that view, it would apparently not be an offence to fell smaller trees in a woodland covered by a tree preservation order. However in *Bullock v Secretary of State for the Environment*,[4] Phillips J treated Lord Denning's remark as obiter and declined to follow it; he held that there was no reason why anything that would ordinarily be called a tree should not be a 'tree' for the purposes of the legislation, and no reason why a coppice should not be the subject of a tree preservation order.

15.04 It seems that a tree may be 'wilfully destroyed' by negligence as well as deliberate intent. In *Barnet London Borough Council v Eastern Electricity Board*,[5] contractors laying electric cables damaged the root systems of six large trees all of which were subject to a tree preservation order; as a result, the life expectancy of the trees was shortened and they had been rendered less stable and a potential danger. The council prosecuted the Board but the magistrates dismissed the case on the ground that the reduction of the life expectancy of the trees by an uncertain period could not amount to destruction. The Divisional Court, however, held that a person wilfully destroyed a tree if he inflicted on it so radical an injury that in all the circumstances any reasonable forester would decide that it must be felled.

15.05 A tree preservation order will normally be made by the local planning authority[6] but in exceptional cases the Secretary of State may make an order.[7] Tree preservation orders no longer require the approval of the Secretary of State, but the local

1 TCPA 1990, s. 198.
2 *Encyclopaedia of Gardening* (Marshall Cavendish).
3 (1976) 33 P & CR 185.
4 (1980) 40 P & CR 246, [1980] JPL 461.
5 [1973] 2 All ER 319, [1973] 1 WLR 430.
6 TCPA 1990, s. 198.
7 TCPA 1990, s. 202.

planning authority must give notice of the making of the order and consider any objections.[8]

15.06 There are restrictions on the making of tree preservation orders where a Forestry Dedication Covenant is in force or where the Forestry Commissioners have made a grant under the Forestry Acts. In these circumstances an order may be made only if there is not in force some working plan approved by the Forestry Commissioners and they consent to the making of the order.[9] Moreover a tree preservation order cannot prohibit the cutting down of trees which are dying or dead or have become dangerous, nor may it prohibit felling in order to comply with a statutory obligation or to abate a nuisance.[10]

15.07 The decision of the Court of Appeal in *Perrin v Northampton Borough Council*[11] was concerned with the extent to which works to a tree subject to a TPO could be justified in order to abate a nuisance. TCPA 1990, s. 198(6)(b) permits 'the cutting down, uprooting, topping or lopping of any trees . . . so far as may be necessary for the prevention or abatement of a nuisance'.

15.08 The roots of a large oak tree subject to a TPO encroached on the claimant's land and were causing damage to the foundations of his property. The claimant applied for consent to fell the tree[12] but this application was refused by the local planning authority. The claimant challenged this decision, arguing that he was entitled to fell the tree as this was 'necessary' to abate a nuisance under the above-mentioned statutory provision. The local planning authority contended that felling was not necessary because other techniques, such as the construction of a root barrier, could achieve the same objective. At first instance, the court held that the existence of alternative engineering solutions was irrelevant because the word 'necessary' referred to the cutting down, etc of the tree and nothing more.

15.09 The Court of Appeal disagreed and held that the legislation did not, either expressly or by necessary implication, require so restrictive an approach to the construction of the statutory provision. As the underlying purpose of the legislation was to protect trees, it would be 'counter-intuitive' (per Blackburne J) to ignore other methods of preventing or abating the nuisance other than works to the tree itself, albeit that the works to the tree would be the minimum necessary.

---

[8] TCPA 1990, s. 199. The reasons that the local planning authority give for making the order can be brief: *Brennon v Bromsgrove District Council* [2003] EWHC 752 (Admin). A tree preservation order made in respect of land which is placed at Forestry Commission disposal or is managed or supervised by them does not prevent forestry operations undertaken by the Forestry Commission: TCPA 1990, s. 200 as substituted by PCPA 2004, s. 85.

[9] TCPA 1990, s. 200.

[10] TCPA 1990, s. 198(6). In *R v Brightman* [1990] 1 WLR 1255, it was held that the burden of proving that one or other of the exceptions applies with the person charged with the offence.

[11] [2007] EWCA Civ 1353.

[12] For TPO consents, See para 15.15.

15.10 In making and administering a tree preservation order the planning authority are concerned solely with considerations of amenity; they are not concerned with such matters as the economic value of the trees. Control over felling in the interests of the national economy was introduced, however, by the Forestry Act 1951 (now the Forestry Act 1967). Under that Act it is an offence to fell any tree without the consent of the Forestry Commissioners, except in certain specified cases.[13] The cutting down of a tree may therefore require the consent of the local planning authority under a tree preservation order and/or the consent of the Commissioners under the Forestry Act 1967.

Making the order

15.11 A tree preservation order is to be in the form (or substantially the form) prescribed by the Tree Preservation Regulations 1999.[14] In that year new regulations came into force replacing the Tree Preservation Regulations 1969, as subsequently amended, which were duly revoked.

15.12 A tree preservation order must specify the trees, groups of trees, or woodlands to which it relates; where the order relates to a group of trees, it must specify the number of trees in the group. The position of the trees or woodlands must be defined on a map attached to the order. In order to prevent felling before the order can be confirmed, the local planning authority may include in the order a direction under TCPA 1990, s. 201 that the order shall take effect provisionally on a specified date and this direction will continue in force for a maximum of six months.[15]

15.13 Notice that the order has been made must be served on 'persons interested' in the land affected by the order with a statement that objections and representations may be made to the local planning authority within 28 days. A copy of the tree preservation order must be made available for inspection at the offices of the authority.[16] 'Persons interested' in relation to land affected by the order means: every owner and occupier of the land and every other person whom the authority know to be entitled to fell any trees to which the order relates or to work by surface working any materials in, on, or under the land. Land affected by the order includes adjoining land.[17]

---

13 The exceptions are to be found partly in the Forestry Act 1967, s. 9 and partly in the Forestry (Exceptions from Restriction of Felling) Regulations 1951. They include the cutting down of small trees and felling which is necessary for the purpose of carrying out development in accordance with planning permission.

14 T & CP (Trees) Regulations 1999, SI 1999 No 1892, reg 2 and the schedule to the regulations. The 1999 regulations came into force on 2 August 1999 and have been amended by SI 2008 No 2260.

15 Tree Preservation Regs, reg 2. Further provision is made for the protection of trees in conservation areas by the TCPA 1990, s. 211; see para 16.124.

16 Tree Preservation Regs, regs 3 and 4.

17 Tree Preservation Regs, reg 1.

15.14 Once they have considered any objections or representations duly made, the authority may confirm the order with or without modifications. Notice of confirmation must be given to persons interested in the land affected by the order.[18] Once confirmed, the validity of the order can be questioned in High Court proceedings under s. 288 of the 1990 Act.[19]

Consents under the order

15.15 The procedure for obtaining consent to fell or top trees protected by a preservation order varies according to whether the Forestry Act 1967 also applies.

15.16 If the Forestry Act 1967 does not apply, the procedure will be that laid down in the tree preservation order and this procedure will be modelled on the provisions of the TCPA 1990 for obtaining planning permission. Application for consent must be made to the local planning authority, and the authority may refuse consent or grant it either unconditionally or conditionally.[20] The authority must give their decision within two months. If they fail to do so, or if the applicant is aggrieved by their decision, he may appeal to the Secretary of State who will deal with the matter in the same way as an appeal against refusal of planning permission.

15.17 If the Forestry Act 1967 applies, application is made to the Forestry Commissioners. If the Commissioners propose to grant a licence, they must consult the local planning authority; if that authority objects the application will be referred to the Secretary of State who will deal with it as if it had been referred to him under TCPA 1990, s. 7. If the Commissioners propose not to grant a licence, they need not consult the local planning authority and the applicant has no right of appeal, though he may have a right to compensation under the Forestry Act. The Commissioners may decide not to deal with the application themselves but to refer it to the local planning authority in which case the procedure laid down in the tree preservation order applies.[21]

15.18 If the matter comes before the Secretary of State in any of the ways mentioned above, his decision may be challenged in High Court proceedings under TCPA 1990, s. 288.[22]

15.19 The local planning authority may revoke or modify any grant of consent under the tree preservation order. The procedure is similar to that described in an earlier

---

[18] Tree Preservation Regs, regs 5 and 6.

[19] See para 20.07.

[20] The conditions may require the replacement of any tree or trees on site or in the near vicinity.

[21] Forestry Act 1951, s. 13.

[22] See para 20.07.

chapter for the revocation or modification of planning permission.[23] The planning authority will be liable to pay compensation for abortive expenditure.

Compensation

15.20 No compensation is payable for the making of a tree preservation order. In general, compensation is payable for loss or damage resulting from a refusal of consent or for the imposition of conditions.[24]

15.21 A claim for compensation must be submitted within 12 months of the local planning authority's decision, or that of the Secretary of State on appeal. No claim can be made for an amount of less than £500. The current Prescribed Form of Tree Preservation Order provides that no compensation shall be payable in respect of any loss of development value or other diminution in the value of the land as a result of the decision.

Replacement of trees

15.22 Provisions as to the replacement of trees are contained in TCPA 1990, s. 206. This section applies where a tree is removed or destroyed in contravention of the preservation order or is removed or destroyed or dies at a time when its cutting down is authorized without express consent because it is dead or dying or dangerous. In these circumstances the owner of the land must plant another tree of an appropriate size and species at the same place as soon as he reasonably can—unless, on his application, the local planning authority dispense with the requirement. The new tree will be subject to the original preservation order.

15.23 In the case of woodlands, it will suffice to plant the same number of trees on or near the land on which the trees stood or on such other land as may be agreed, and in such places as may be designated by the local planning authority.[25]

Enforcement

15.24 The effective enforcement of tree preservation orders has caused some difficulty. The TCPA 1947 provided that contravention of a tree preservation order should be an offence punishable by fine, and this was re-enacted in the TCPA 1962; the penalties were small and were not always an effective deterrent. Some early tree preservation orders provided for the service of enforcement notices requiring replanting, and this might well have proved an effective deterrent, but in 1953 the Minister advised local authorities that it was doubtful whether these enforcement

[23] See para 11.01.

[24] Prescribed Form of Tree Preservation Order, art 9. This restriction does not apply to orders made before 2 August 1999, when the current regulations came into force.

[25] TCPA 1990, s. 206(3).

provisions could be validly included in preservation orders. However when the Civic Amenities Act 1967 was passed penalties were increased and express provision made for enforcement notices. The Planning and Compensation Act 1991 further increased penalties and strengthened the enforcement provisions in a number of ways. These changes were in parallel, so far as relevant, to the changes made to enforcement provisions generally by the PCA 1991.

15.25 The relevant provisions are now to be found in the TCPA 1990 and may be summarized as follows:

(1) If any person contravenes a tree preservation order by cutting down, uprooting, or wilfully destroying a tree, or topping or lopping it in such a manner as to be likely to destroy it, he may be charged under TCPA 1990, s. 102 and may be fined, on summary conviction up to £20,000. The statutory maximum was previously £2,000. If the defendant is indicted before the Crown Court, the court may impose whatever fine it considers appropriate. On either summary conviction or indictment, the court may now have regard to any financial benefit which accrued to the defendant.[26] The offence is absolute in that knowledge of the order is not a requirement of the offence.[27]
(2) Any other contravention of a tree preservation order is an offence punishable by fine not exceeding level 4 of the standard scale.[28]
(3) If a landowner fails to comply with the requirements of TCPA 1990, s. 206 as to the replacement of trees, he is not guilty of an offence but the local planning authority may serve an enforcement notice under TCPA 1990, s. 207 requiring him to plant a tree or trees of such size and species as may be specified in the notice. An enforcement notice under TCPA 1990, s. 207 may also be served if a landowner fails to comply with any conditions of a consent given under a tree preservation order requiring the replacement of trees, although this might also be an offence under TCPA 1990, s. 210. An enforcement notice under TCPA 1990, s. 207 must be served within four years,[29] and there is a right of appeal to the Secretary of State.[30]

15.26 Where trees are required to be replaced under the above provisions, the PCA 1991[31] provides that a notice made by the local planning authority to enforce the

26 TCPA 1990, s 210(1), (2), (3), as amended by PCA 1991, s. 23.

27 *Maidstone Borough Council v Mortimer* [1980] 3 All ER 552. No offence is committed if the defendant's ignorance is due to the failure of the authority to place a copy of the order on deposit for inspection: *Vale of Glamorgan Borough Council v Palmer and Bowles* (1982) 81 LGR 678. The owner is liable for the acts of his servants but not for an independent contractor who had been expressly told not to touch the tree: *Groveside Homes Ltd v Elmbridge Borough Council* [1988] JPL 395.

28 TCPA 1990, s. 210(4).

29 TCPA 1990, s. 207(2).

30 TCPA 1990, s. 208, as amended.

31 PCA 1991, s. 23, amending TCPA 1990, s. 207.

duty to replant is required to specify a period at the end of which it is to take effect. The specified period shall be one of not less than 28 days beginning with the date of service of the notice. And the person on whom such a notice has been served may now appeal to the Secretary of State on an additional ground; namely, that in all the circumstances, the duty to plant a replacement tree should be dispensed with.[32] Further, where the local planning authority, under TCPA 1990, s. 209 enter the land to replant trees where an enforcement notice has not been complied with, it is now a criminal offence for any person to wilfully obstruct a person exercising that power.[33]

Planting of new trees

15.27 The provisions so far described are concerned with the preservation of existing trees and their replacement when felled or destroyed. The Civic Amenities Act introduced for the first time provisions designed to secure the planting of new trees. These provisions are now contained in TCPA 1990, s. 197. Under this section it is the duty of the local planning authority when granting planning permission for any development to consider whether it would be appropriate to impose conditions for the preservation and planting of trees and to make tree preservation orders in connection with the grant of planning permission.

Tree preservation orders: reform under the Planning Act 2008

15.28 As we have seen, under the existing system of TPOs, much of the detail of the law is contained in TCPA 1990, with procedural matters being prescribed by the Tree Preservation Regulations. Following a government consultation paper in 2007, *Tree Preservation Orders: Improving Procedures*, the Government decided to remove much of the detail regarding tree preservation controls from the primary legislation and to give the Secretary of State much wider powers to make regulations regarding trees.

15.29 Accordingly PA 2008, s. 192, repeals various provisions of TCPA 1990 relating to TPOs and enables these deleted matters to be included in regulations made by the Secretary of State. New ss. 202A–202G are inserted into TCPA 1990. These enable regulations to be made covering such matters as: the form and content of TPOs; the procedure to be followed in the making of TPOs; provisions regarding when TPOs are to take effect; the prohibited activities in relation to trees; the giving of consent for prohibited activities; provisions about the payment of compensation; and the maintenance of public registers. There is a transitional provision enabling the new regulations, when made, to apply to trees subject to existing TPOs.

---

32 TCPA 1990, s. 208, as amended.

33 Amended by PCA 1991, s. 23(5).

Hedgerows

15.30 Although, as we have seen, special controls apply to trees and woodlands, these have not, hitherto, extended to hedgerows. Hedgerows play an important part in conserving the natural beauty of the countryside and, of course, in providing habitats for birds and other wildlife. In recent years there has been concern that hedgerows are disappearing, mainly as a result of modern intensive farming methods.

15.31 Accordingly the Environment Act 1995, s. 97[34] empowers 'appropriate ministers'[35] to make regulations for 'the protection of important hedgerows in England and Wales'. The Hedgerow Regulations 1997[36] were made under these enabling powers—they came into force on 1 June 1997.

Scope of the Regulations

15.32 The Regulations apply to any hedgerow growing in, or adjacent to, any common land, protected land, or land used for agriculture, forestry, or the breeding or keeping of horses, ponies, or donkeys if either (a) the hedgerow has a continuous length of at least 20 metres; or (b) the hedgerow has a continuous length of less than 20 metres but intersects or joins another hedgerow at each end.[37] However the regulations do not apply to any hedgerow within the curtilage of or marking the boundary of a dwellinghouse.[38]

15.33 'Protected land', referred to above, means land managed as a nature reserve or notified as a Site of Special Scientific Interest.[39]

'Important' hedgerows

15.34 A hedgerow is 'important' if it, or the hedgerow of which it is a stretch, (a) has existed for 20 years or more; and (b) satisfies at least one of the criteria listed in Part II of Schedule 1 to the Regulations.[40]

15.35 The criteria are too lengthy and detailed to be quoted here but relate to hedgerows of archaeological or historical significance or which contribute to wildlife or landscape preservation. Anyone needing to establish whether any particular hedgerow is 'important' will need to consult the text of the Regulations.

15.36 The definition of an 'important' hedgerow is pivotal to the operation of the Regulations since it is prohibited to remove an important hedgerow except in accordance with the Regulations.

---

[34] The relevant provisions came into force on 21 September 1995.
[35] In England, the Secretary of State; in Wales, the Assembly.
[36] SI 1997 No 1160.
[37] Hedgerow Regulations 1997, SI 1997 No 1160, reg 3(1).
[38] SI 1997 No 1160, reg 3(3).
[39] SI 1997 No 1160, reg 2.
[40] SI 1997 No 1160, reg 4.

Removal of hedgerows

15.37 An owner who wishes to remove a hedgerow to which the Regulations apply (see above under *Scope of the Regulations*) must give the local planning authority a 'hedgerow removal notice'. The notice must be set out in the form prescribed by Schedule 4 to the Regulations. Removal of the hedgerow is prohibited unless a hedgerow removal notice has been received by the local planning authority and the authority have dealt with the notice as set out below.

15.38 Following receipt of the hedgerow removal notice, the local planning authority may notify the owner that the hedgerow can be removed, or serve on the owner a 'hedgerow retention notice' stating that the hedgerow may not be removed. If no hedgerow retention notice is served by the local planning authority within 42 days of receiving the removal notice, the owner is free to remove the hedgerow.[41] The removal must be carried out in accordance with the proposals in the hedgerow removal notice and within a period of two years commencing with the date of service of the removal notice.[42]

15.39 The Regulations impose an obligation on the local planning authority, before deciding whether to permit removal or require retention of hedgerows, to consult any parish council in England (or Community Council in Wales) where the hedgerow is situated.

Restrictions on the local planning authority's powers

15.40 It should be noted that the local planning authority only have power to serve a hedgerow retention notice in respect of an 'important' hedgerow as defined above. Indeed the Regulations expressly forbid them from serving such a notice in respect of a hedgerow which is not an 'important' hedgerow. Further, the authority *must* give such a notice in respect of an important hedgerow unless satisfied, having regard in particular for the reasons given for its proposed removal in the hedgerow removal notice, that there are circumstances which justify its removal.[43]

15.41 There is a right of appeal against a hedgerow retention notice to the Secretary of State.[44]

Permitted removal of hedgerows

15.42 Regulation 6 permits the removal of hedgerows in certain circumstances where no hedgerow removal notice need be given to the local planning authority.

---

41 SI 1997 No 1160, regs 5 and 6.
42 SI 1997 No 1160, reg 5.
43 SI 1997 No 160, reg 5.
44 SI 1997 No 1160, reg 9.

15.43 The removal of a hedgerow is permitted if required for any of the following purposes:

(a) to provide temporary access to land;
(b) to provide temporary access in emergencies;
(c) to provide access where another means of access is not available;
(d) for the purpose of national defence;
(e) for the carrying out of development for which planning permission has been granted or is deemed to be granted, but excluding permitted development under the General Permitted Development Order (with exceptions);[45]
(f) land drainage or flood defence works carried out under statutory powers;
(g) to prevent the spread of, or ensuring the eradication of, plant pest or tree pest under the relevant legislation;
(h) to carry out the functions of the Secretary of State in respect of any highway for which he is the highway authority;
(i) to carry out works to prevent obstruction of electricity installations under the relevant legislation;
(j) to manage the hedgerow by trimming, coppicing, etc.

Enforcement

15.44 The Regulations provide for the enforcement of the Regulations by prosecution, by replacement of the hedgerow, and by injunction. All or any of the enforcement methods may be used and an injunction may be sought in the case of an apprehended breach.

15.45 It is an offence to remove, intentionally or recklessly, or cause or permit to be removed, a hedgerow where that is prohibited by the Regulations. A person convicted may be liable on summary conviction to a fine not exceeding the statutory maximum or on indictment to a fine of unlimited amount—here, in fixing the level of the fine, the court may have regard to any financial benefit which has accrued to the defendant.[46]

15.46 Where it appears to the local authority that a hedgerow has been removed in contravention of the Regulations, the authority may require the owner to plant another hedgerow. This must be by notice in writing specifying the shrubs to be planted and the period in which this must be done. The authority have default powers to enter the land and carry out the work at the owner's expense.[47]

[45] The exceptions are Part II (development under local or private Acts or orders) and Part 30 (toll road facilities). For the GPDO, See para 7.12.
[46] SI 1997 No 1160, reg 7.
[47] SI 1997 No 1160, reg 8.

15.47 The local authority may apply to the court for an injunction to restrain any actual or apprehended breach under the Regulations. They have this right whether or not they have exercised any other powers under the Regulations.[48]

Further provisions

15.48 The Regulations contain further provisions requiring the local planning authority to maintain records[49] and to provide them with rights of entry.[50] There are also special provisions for hedgerows owned by local planning authorities and for hedgerows situated on ecclesiastical property, in regulations 15 and 16 respectively.

15.49 Because the Regulations only prevent the removal of 'important' hedgerows (although they apply to a wider category of hedgerows in order to achieve that objective), concern has been expressed that the regime will make only a limited contribution to hedgerow protection.

15.50 Dissatisfaction in some quarters with the current Regulations led to a government review of the 1997 Regulations. The report of the review includes simpler criteria for establishing the importance of hedgerows by reason of landscape, history, or wildlife significance and increased time for local authorities to consider hedgerow removal notices. It is anticipated that revised regulations will be made in due course.

High hedges: Anti-social Behaviour Act 2003

15.51 It should be noted that Part 8 of ASBA 2003 introduced controls to mitigate the problem of landowners growing very tall hedges—often using the evergreen Leylandii—and thereby causing a nuisance to neighbours. Under the relevant part of the Act, if the parties to such a dispute cannot settle it amicably, either party may refer it to the local authority. The hedge in question must be formed, wholly or predominantly, by a line of two or more evergreens; and rise to a height of 2 metres or more above ground level. The hedge must also act, to some extent, as a barrier to light or access; and the claimant's reasonable enjoyment of their domestic property must be adversely affected.[51]

15.52 If the authority consider that the complaint is justified, they may decide to abate the adverse effect by the service of a nuisance notice. Although the notice can require the hedge in question to be reduced, it cannot require it to be reduced to a height of less than 2 metres. The affected party has a right of appeal to the Secretary of State, who may quash or vary the notice. Failure to comply with the notice constitutes an

---

48 SI 1997 No 1160, reg 11.
49 SI 1997 No 1160, reg 10.
50 SI 1997 No 1160, regs 12, 13, and 14.
51 ASBA 2003, ss. 65(1) and 66(1). See further the High Hedges (Appeals)(England) Regs 2005, SI 2005 No 711, which came into force on 1 June 2005.

offence subject to fines of up to £1,000, and, on default, the authority has powers to enter the land and carry out the work, recovering the cost from the owner.

Outdoor advertising

15.53 The TCPA 1947 brought all outdoor advertising under control by introduction—as a general rule—that any outdoor advertisement required consent even if its display does not involve development. This system of control is now continued by the TCPA 1990. Advertisements displayed prior to 1 July 1948 were also brought under control, the local planning authority being empowered to 'challenge' any such advertisement by requiring the persons responsible for its display to make application for its retention. Provision is also made for areas of special control in which only certain limited classes of advertising are permitted, and the planning authority has no power to grant consent for anything outside these classes.

15.54 The system of advertising control is embodied in regulations made by the Secretary of State under TCPA 1990, s. 220.[52] The definition of advertisement for the purposes of the Act and of these Regulations is extremely wide and includes much else besides ordinary commercial advertising. The full definition in the TCPA 1990, as amended by PCA 1991, s. 24, is as follows: 'any word, letter, model, sign, placard, board, notice, awning, blind, device or representation, whether illuminated or not, in the nature of, and employed wholly or partly for the purpose of, advertisement, announcement or direction, and (without prejudice to the preceding provisions of this definition) includes any hoarding or similar structure used or designed or adapted for use, and anything else principally used or designed or adapted principally for use, for the display of advertisements'.[53]

15.55 Thus the legend 'Samuel Short, Family Butcher' on a shop fascia, or 'John Jones, Dental Surgeon' on a door place, will be advertisements as well as the large poster advertising a well-known national product. So will road traffic signs and election posters.

15.56 The question of what constitutes an 'advertisement' arose in two linked cases;[54] where powerful beams of light were projected into the night sky from the roofs of amusement centres, creating a floral pattern on the underside of the cloud base.

[52] The current regulations are the Control of Advertisements Regulations 2007, SI 2007 No 783. See also Circular 3/07 and *Outdoor Advertisements and Signs—a Guide for Advertisers*, DCLG, 2007.

[53] TCPA 1990, s. 336(1). For the purposes of the Regulations, however, 'advertisement' does not include anything employed wholly as a memorial or as a railway signal: or a placard or other object borne by an individual or animal: reg 2(1).

[54] *Newport Borough Council v Secretary of State for Wales*; and *Great Yarmouth Borough Council v Secretary of State for the Environment* [1997] JPL 650, per Rich J.

Disagreeing with a ruling of the Secretary of State that the beams of light did not constitute an advertisement, the court considered that the beams constituted a 'sign'. The light was being used for the purpose of advertisement and as a direction also; indeed the learned judge made comparisons with the Star of Bethlehem.[55]

15.57 More recently, in *Butler v Derby City Council*[56] the appellant was convicted for displaying a banner on his property, 2 metres by 1 metre in size, bearing the legend 'Save Five Lamps'. Below this appeared the logo of an environmental pressure group, 'Derby Heart'; and a telephone number and website address. Derby Heart opposed Derby City Council's road scheme proposals. At first instance the court held that the banner constituted a 'direction' and was therefore an advertisement for the purposes of TCPA 1990. This decision was upheld by the Divisional Court—the logo and contact details of the pressure group were advertising its existence. The words 'advertisement, announcement or direction' in s. 336 of TCPA 1990 were wide and not mutually exclusive; the banner therefore fell within the statutory definition. The question of whether a banner displaying only a political message (eg 'Stop the War'; 'Save the Whale', etc) could amount to an 'announcement' was left open by the court.

Principles of control

15.58 The powers of control conferred by the TCPA 1990 are to be exercised only in the interest of amenity (visual and aural) and public safety.[57]

15.59 There is an express ban on any condition amounting to censorship of the subject matter of any advertisement; and the consent is to be for the use of the site rather than for particular advertisements. There is, however, one exception: where application is made for the display of a particular advertisement, the authority may consider its contents so far—but only so far—as is necessary from the point of view of amenity and public safety.[58]

15.60 It is clear from all this that the planning authority is not entitled to consider such controversial questions as the economic value or social desirability of advertisements, nor even the substantial rates payable to the local authority in respect of many commercial advertisements.

15.61 In considering questions of amenity, the local planning authority are to consider the general characteristics of the locality, and special consideration is to be given to features of historic, architectural, cultural, or similar interests. Under the heading of public safety they are to consider the safety of persons using any road, railway, waterway (including coastal waters), docks, harbour, or airfield likely to

55 [1997] JPL 650 at 658.

56 [2005] EWHC 2835 (Admin).

57 TCPA 1990, s. 220(1); Advertisement Regs, reg 3(1) and (2).

58 Advertisements Regs, reg 3(4).

be affected by the display of advertisements; and in particular whether they are likely to obscure or hinder the interpretation of traffic signs, etc.[59] The authority must also consider whether the display of the advertisement in question is likely to hinder the operation of any security device (such as CCTV cameras), or any device for measuring the speed of vehicles (such as speed cameras).

15.62 Under the Regulations there are in effect three categories of advertisements. First, there are nine types of advertisement which are not subject to the general rule that outdoor advertising requires consent. Second, there are many advertisements which require consent, but are deemed to have received consent under the Regulations themselves. Finally there are those which do not come within either of the first two categories and thus require express consent from the local planning authority. We will deal with each of these categories in turn.

Advertisements excepted from control

15.63 Some nine types of advertisements are excepted from the general rule that all advertisements require either deemed or express consent. This status is different from deemed consent, in that excepted advertisements cannot be 'challenged' by the local planning authority as described below.

15.64 The nine classes of excepted advertisements are as follows:[60]

Class A: displayed on enclosed land and not readily visible outside the enclosure, or from any part of it over which the public has a right of way or a right of access.
Class B: displayed on or in a vehicle or vessel, unless it is being used primarily for the display of advertisements (rather than for conveying people or goods).
Class C: incorporated in and forming part of the fabric of a building, but not extending to an advertisement fixed to or painted on a building.
Class D: displayed on goods for sale (including a gas as liquid) or their container, provided it refers to the article for sale, is not illuminated, and does not exceed 0.1 square metres in area.
Class E: relating specifically to pending Parliamentary, European Assembly, or local government elections; or a referendum under the Political Parties, Elections and Referendums Act 2000.
Class F: required by standing order of either House of Parliament or by enactment.
Class G: approved traffic signs.
Class H: display of any national flag on a single flagstaff.
Class I: displayed inside a building and not within 1 metre of any external doors, windows, or other opening through which it is visible from outside.

---

59 Advertisements Regs, reg 3(1) and (2).
60 Advertisements Regs, Sch 2.

15.65 It is important to note that, although excepted from the provisions relating to consent, all the above classes of advertisements are subject to the standard conditions set out in Schedule 1 to the Regulations.[61]

Deemed consent

15.66 All advertisements (other than those falling within the excepted classes set out above) require consent under the Regulations, but some 16 classes of advertisements have the benefit of deemed consent; some of these classes are sub-divided with the result that large numbers of advertisements have deemed consent. The classes of advertisements with deemed consent are set out in Schedule 3 to the Regulations. They include, inter alia:

(1) Functional advertisements of local authorities, statutory and public transport undertakings.[62]
(2) Advertisements relating to the premises on which they are displayed, namely advertisements for identification, direction, or warning, subject to a maximum size of 0.75 metres or 0.3 square metres in an area of special control and other conditions[63]; business and professional name plates subject to a maximum size of 0.3 square metres and other conditions;[64] advertisements relating to religious, educational, recreational, medical, and other institutions, hotels, public houses subject to a maximum size of 1.2 square metres and other conditions.[65]
(3) Temporary advertisements relating to the sale or letting of premises,[66] sale of goods or livestock,[67] building work being carried out on the land,[68] local events of a non-commercial character;[69] each of these categories is subject to a variety of conditions.
(4) Advertisements on business premises with reference to the business carried on, the goods sold, or services provided; in the case of shops there are some conditions including a requirement that the advertisement must be on a wall containing a shop window.[70]

---

61 Advertisements Regs, reg 3(2).
62 Advertisements Regs, Sch 3, class 1.
63 Advertisements Regs, Sch 3, class 2A.
64 Advertisements Regs, Sch 3, class 2B.
65 Advertisements Regs, Sch 3, class 2C.
66 Advertisements Regs, Sch 3, class 3A.
67 Advertisements Regs, Sch 3, class 3B.
68 Advertisements Regs, Sch 3, class 3C. The building work must have planning permission: *R (on the application of Cal Brown Advertising Ltd) v Hounslow London Borough Council* [2001] EWCA 864 (Admin), [2001] All ER (D) 313 (Oct).
69 Advertisements Regs, Sch 3, class 3D.
70 Advertisements Regs, Sch 3, class 5.

(5) Advertisements on the forecourts of business premises; here again there are conditions.[71]

(6) Advertisements on the glazed surface of telephone kiosks, subject to conditions.[72] This new class was introduced in 2007.

15.67 The Secretary of State may in effect withdraw deemed consent by issuing—following a proposal by the local planning authority—a direction that the display of an advertisement of a class or description in Schedule 3[73] may not be undertaken in any particular area, or in any particular case, without express consent. Before making such a direction the Secretary of State must publish statutory notices and give notice to persons likely to be affected, and he must consider any objections received within a specified period.[74]

15.68 Furthermore the local planning authority may 'challenge' an advertisement displayed with deemed consent by issuing a discontinuance notice requiring the discontinuance of the display of an advertisement or the use of the site for that purpose. The person on whom it is served may apply to the local planning authority for express consent and, if consent is refused, appeal to the Secretary of State; the discontinuance notice will not take effect pending the outcome of these proceedings.[75] In *O'Brien v London Borough of Croydon*,[76] it was held that a discontinuance notice must be served on the person whose specific interests are promoted by the advertisement, that person being the 'advertiser' within regulation 8.

Express consent

15.69 Unless an advertisement is excepted from control or has deemed consent under the Regulations, application must be made to the local planning authority for express consent.[77] The authority may grant consent subject to certain standard conditions[78] and any other conditions they think fit or they may refuse consent; if they refuse consent or impose conditions, they must state their reasons for so doing.[79] The application must be made either electronically or in hard copy. Each consent will be for a period of five years unless the local planning authority specify either a longer or shorter period; if they specify a shorter period, they must state their reasons for so doing.[80] The authority may decline to determine an application for express

71 Advertisements Regs, Sch 3, class 6.
72 Advertisement Regs, Sch 3, class 16.
73 Other than class 12 or 13.
74 Advertisements Regs, reg 7.
75 Advertisements Regs, reg 8.
76 [1999] JPL 47.
77 Advertisements Regs, reg 9.
78 Advertisements Regs, Sch 2.
79 Advertisements Regs, reg 14(1).
80 Advertisements Regs, reg 14(7).

consent that is the same, or substantially the same, as one dismissed by the Secretary of State on appeal within the previous two years.[81]

15.70 If the local planning authority refuse consent or attach conditions, the applicant may appeal to the Secretary of State, but he may refuse to entertain an appeal against the standard conditions.[82] The procedure for appeals is based on that for appeals against refusal of planning permission.[83] The Secretary of State has the power to dismiss an appeal in the case of undue delay.[84]

15.71 The proposed display may involve development as defined in TCPA 1990, s. 55. It is not necessary to apply for planning permission—this is deemed to be granted by the consent under the Regulations.[85]

15.72 The Regulations contain provisions for the revocation or modification of consent similar to those in the TCPA 1990 for the revocation of planning permission.[86]

15.73 In 1999 amending regulations were made to the original 1992 Regulations,[87] inserting a new regulation 9A. This is now to be found in regulation 15 of the current 2007 Regulations. It enables the Secretary of State to call in any express application for advertisement consent made by an interested local planning authority. If the Secretary of State does not call in the application the local planning authority may determine the application themselves.

Enforcement of control

15.74 Any person who displays an advertisement in contravention of the Regulations is guilty of an offence punishable by a fine not exceeding level 3 on the standard scale and a daily fine of one tenth of level 3 on the standard scale.[88] The persons displaying an advertisement are deemed to include not only the person who puts it up, but also the person whose land it is displayed on and the person whose goods or business are advertised; in the latter two cases, however, it is a defence to show that the advertisement was displayed without knowledge or consent.[89]

15.75 In *Kingston-upon-Thames London Borough Council v National Solus Sites Ltd*,[90] the respondents displayed 11 different advertising posters on hoardings on six different

---

81 Advertisements Regs, reg 14(1)(c).
82 Advertisements Regs, reg 17.
83 The detailed provisions are set out in the Advertisements Regs, Sch 4.
84 Advertisements Regs, Sch 4.
85 TCPA 1990, s. 222. See para 7.84.
86 Advertisements Regs, regs 18, 19.
87 T & CP (Control of Advertisements) (Amendment) Regulations 1999, SI 1999 No 1810, with effect from 27 July 1999.
88 TCPA 1990, s. 224(3).
89 TCPA 1990, s. 224(4), (5). *John v Reveille Newspapers Ltd* (1955) 5 P & CR 95; *Wycombe District Council v Michael Shanly Group Ltd* [1994] 02 EG 112.
90 [1994] JPL 251.

dates without consent. The Divisional Court (per Glidewell LJ) held that the display from time to time of these different posters constituted 11 separate offences under the Advertisements Regulations. It is therefore open to the local authority in such a case to lay multiple informations thereby considerably increasing the possible penalty.

Areas of special control

15.76 The TCPA 1990 provides for the definition of areas of special control which may be '(a) a rural area, or (b) an area which appears to the Secretary of State to require special protection on the grounds of amenity'.[91] The language is curious since the purpose of defining a special area (whether rural or not) will be the protection of amenity rather than public safety. Perhaps the meaning is that rural areas may be freely defined as areas of special control, but there must be some really pressing reason for imposing special control in an urban area. By 1989 rather more than 45 per cent of the total land area of England and Wales had been defined as being within an area of special control.[92] The effect of special control is that only the following classes of advertisement may be displayed.[93]

(a) *without express consent*
  (i) any advertisement within the excepted classes;[94]
  (ii) advertisements specified as having deemed consent, with the exception of illuminated advertisements on business premises and advertisements on hoardings;[95]

(b) *with express consent*
  (i) structures for exhibiting notices of local activities;
  (ii) announcements or directions relating to nearby buildings and land, eg hotels and garages;
  (iii) advertisements required for public safety;
  (iv) advertisements which would be permitted under (a)(ii) above but for infringing the conditions as to height, number, or illumination; or a direction restricting deemed consent.

15.77 If the local planning authority consider that any area should be made subject to special control, they make an order to this effect. The order will require the Secretary of State's confirmation and, if there are any objections, the Secretary of State will hold a public inquiry before deciding whether or not to confirm the order.[96]

---

91 TCPA 1990, s. 221(3).

92 Circular 15/89.

93 Advertisements Regs, reg 20.

94 See para 15.60. The conditions for the specified classes are in some cases more stringent than in areas not subject to special control.

95 See para 15.66.

96 TCPA 1990, s. 221(6).

15.78 Where an order defining an area of special control is in force, it is the duty of the local planning authority to consider at least once in every five years whether it should be revoked or modified.[97]

Land adversely affecting amenity of neighbourhood

15.79 The powers of local planning authorities to secure the tidying up of unsightly pieces of land were, in 1990, considerably strengthened. The TCPA 1971, as originally enacted, enabled the local planning authority to deal with any 'garden, vacant site or other open land' which was in such a condition that it 'seriously injured the local amenities'. This was replaced by new provisions now to be found in TCPA 1990, s. 215. These enable the local planning authority to secure the *tidying* up of any land in their area which is in such a condition that it 'adversely affects' the amenity of the neighbourhood. In such a case the authority can serve a notice on the owner[98] and occupier requiring him to take the steps specified in the notice for remedying the condition of the land. Subject to a right of appeal to the local magistrates,[99] failure to comply with the notice is a punishable offence[100] and the planning authority may also enter upon the land and carry out the work at the expense of the defaulter.[101]

15.80 The Government has amended the General Regulations[102] in relation to land adversely affecting the amenity of a neighbourhood. The amended regulations provide that expenses incurred by a local authority in carrying out the works are to be a charge binding on successive owners of the land in question, taking effect as from the date on which the authority completes the work required to be done by the notice.

Hazardous substances

15.81 The normal processes of planning control provide some opportunities for regulating the presence on land of hazardous substances. Thus on an application for planning permission for industrial use or for storage the local planning authority could refuse permission or impose conditions controlling the presence of hazardous

---

[97] Advertisements Regs, reg 20(4).

[98] For definition of owner, see para 14.23.

[99] TCPA 1990, s. 217. Section 218 gives both the appellant and the local planning authority a right of appeal from the magistrates to the Crown Court.

[100] TCPA 1990, s. 216(2).

[101] TCPA 1990, s. 219.

[102] Town and Country Planning General (Amendment) Regulations 1997, SI 1997 No 3006 which came into force on 8 January 1998. See Circular 2/98—Prevention of Dereliction through the Planning System.

substances; however the lengthy procedures for enforcement might well result in delays which would be unacceptable where hazardous substances were concerned. Moreover once an industrial or storage use has been established, the introduction of hazardous substances would not be development at all.

15.82 In 1979 the Advisory Committee on Major Hazards recommended that development control under the Planning Acts should be extended to cover the use of hazardous substances; the Committee recommended this method of control in preference to a specialized system exercisable by the Health and Safety Executive because control by local planning authorities was perceived as involving the community.

15.83 The first legislative steps were taken in 1983 by amendments to the Use Classes and General Development Orders. Their effect was to remove the benefit of these Orders in cases of development involving a notifiable quantity of hazardous substances. But with the coming into force of the Planning (Hazardous Substances) Act 1990 (see below) the rationale for these amendments has been removed and the Orders have been further amended to delete references to hazardous substances.[103]

15.84 Comprehensive provision for controlling the presence of hazardous substances was first made by the Housing and Planning Act 1986 which added some new sections to the TCPA 1971. These provisions are now to be found in the Planning (Hazardous Substances) Act (P(HS)A) 1990, as amended by the Environmental Protection Act 1990 and the Planning and Compensation Act 1991. The Act came into force on 1 June 1992.

What are hazardous substances?

15.85 There is no definition of 'hazardous substances' in the Hazardous Substances Act. However the Act delegates to the Secretary of State the power to make regulations specifying the substances which are subject to control.[104] Provision is now made by the Planning (Hazardous Substances) Regulations 1992.[105] Some amendments to the Act and regulations have been made by the Planning (Control of Major-Accident Hazards) Regulations 1999, the 'COMAH Regulations'.[106] The purpose of the amendments is to give effect to Directive 96/82 on the control of major-accident hazards involving dangerous substances ('Seveso II').

---

103 Town and Country Planning (Use Classes) (Amendment) (No 2) Order 1992, SI 1992 No 659; Town and Country Planning General Development (Amendment) (No 2) Order 1992, SI 1992 No 658. The latter has been revoked and the amendment preserved in the consolidated General Permitted Development Order 1995.

104 Hazardous Substances Act, s. 5.

105 Planning (Hazardous Substances) Regulations 1992, SI 1992 No 656, as amended.

106 SI 1999 No 981.

15.86 The COMAH Regulations have themselves been further amended by the COMAH (Amendment) Regulations 2005.[107] This is to give effect to Directive 2003/105 which amends Directive 96/82 in various respects.

15.87 The 2005 revisions to the COMAH Regulations amend, inter alia, the quantities and classifications of dangerous substances set down in the COMAH Regulations 1999, which replaced the original list in the Regulations of 1992. The list is highly technical. Part 2 of the Schedule specifies named substances such as ammonium nitrate, chlorine, hydrogen, and acetylene; Part 3 relates to categories of substances not specifically named in Part 2. These are categorized according to whether the substance is toxic, oxidizing, explosive, flammable, or dangerous for the environment. In each case the regulations specify the qualifying quantities.

15.88 The essence of the control is that the presence of any hazardous substance on, over, or under land will require hazardous substances consent.[108] Consent will not be needed where the aggregate amount of the substance on the land and on other sites within 500 metres under the same control[109] is less than the controlled quantity.[110]

15.89 Where hazardous substances consent is required it will be necessary to apply to the hazardous substance authority for express consent,[111] but there are two forms of deemed consent.[112]

Hazardous substances authorities

15.90 Generally, the hazardous substances authority will be the district council, London Borough council, National Park Authority or, in Wales, the county or county borough council. The county council will be the authority in respect of land which is used for mineral working or refuse disposal in a non-metropolitan county.[113] In most cases therefore the hazardous substances authority will be the local planning authority under another name.[114]

15.91 Under the P(HS)A 1990 as originally enacted, special arrangements were made relating to the operational land of statutory undertakers but these provisions were repealed by the Environmental Protection Act 1990.

---

[107] SI 2005 No 1088, which came into force on 30 June 2005.
[108] See para 15.92.
[109] Two or more companies within the same group may be treated as a single person for this purpose: P(HS)A 1990, s. 39(3).
[110] P(HS)A 1990, s. 4(1), (2). COMAH Regs, reg 2 amends s 4 by adding to the control zone any other land which forms part of a single establishment.
[111] See para 15.92.
[112] See para 15.99.
[113] P(HS)A 1990, ss. 1, 3.
[114] See para 3.35.

Express consent

15.92 The procedure for obtaining express consent is to be prescribed by Part 3 of the Hazardous Substances Regulations.

15.93 The application must be made on a form prescribed by the Regulations, giving the requisite information and containing a site map and a substance location plan.[115]

15.94 The applicant is required to publish notice of the application in a form prescribed by the Regulations by advertisement in a local newspaper and by posting a site notice.[116] Members of the public then have 21 days in which to make representations to the authority. If the applicant is not the owner of the land, owners must be notified of the application and certificates of ownership (similar to those required by article 6 of the General Permitted Development Order in relation to a planning application) must be submitted with the application.[117] Any owners upon whom such notice is served also have 21 days within which to make representations.

15.95 The applicant for hazardous substances consent must pay a fee[118] and the authority must record the application in a register.[119] Before determining the application, the authority are required to consult with certain bodies[120] including the Health and Safety Executive. The Executive has an important role in advising authorities as to the nature of the threat posed by hazardous substances. Circular 4/00[121] counsels that any advice that consent should be refused in a particular case should not be overridden without the most careful consideration. Should an authority propose to do so, they are instructed to give the Executive 21 days' notice to allow them to seek that the application be called in by the Secretary of State.

15.96 When considering an application the authority are to have regard to any material considerations and in particular to:

(a) any current or contemplated use of the land;
(b) the way in which land in the vicinity is used or likely to be used;
(c) any planning permission that has been granted for development of land in the vicinity;
(d) the development plan;
(e) any advice given by the Health and Safety Executive.[122]

---

115 P(HS)A 1990, s. 7: Hazardous Substances Regs, reg 5 and Sch 2.
116 Section 7; Regs, reg 6(1) and Sch 2.
117 P(HS)A 1990, s. 87; Regs, reg 7 and Sch 2.
118 Hazardous Substances Regs, Part 7.
119 P(HS)A 1990, s. 28.
120 Hazardous Substances Regs, reg 10.
121 Annex A-5.
122 P(HS)A 1990, s. 9(2).

15.97 The authority may then grant consent either unconditionally or subject to such conditions as they think fit, or they may refuse consent. If granting consent the authority must include a description of the land to which it relates, a description of the hazardous substance or substances to which it relates, and in respect of each hazardous substance to which it relates, a statement of the maximum quantity allowed at any one time.[123]

15.98 If the authority refuse consent or grant it subject to conditions the applicant will be entitled to appeal to the Secretary of State. The Secretary of State must offer the appellant and the authority the opportunity of a public local inquiry or other hearing. The decision on the appeal may be given by the Secretary of State or delegated to the inspector. As mentioned above, the Secretary of State has power to call in an application before it is determined by the authority.[124]

Deemed consents

15.99 P(HS)A 1990, s. 11 provides for deemed consent for hazardous substances present on the land during the 'established period', that is the 12 months immediately preceding the 'relevant date'. The relevant date was the date the Act came into force, ie 1 June 1992. Owners of the land then had six months from that date to submit a claim for the deemed consent; in other words the control extends to existing sites when the Act came into force.

15.100 P(HS)A 1990, s. 12 provides that where the authorization of a government department is required for development by a local authority or statutory undertakers, the department in giving the authorization may direct that hazardous substances consent is deemed to have been granted.

15.101 The COMAH Regulations provide for deemed consents for hazardous substances for which hazardous substances consent was not required before the COMAH Regulations came into force.[125]

Revocation of consent

15.102 The hazardous substances authority may make an order to revoke or modify a hazardous substances consent if they consider it expedient so to do and also in certain defined circumstances; for example if there has been a material change of use of the land to which the consent relates.[126] The order will not take effect unless

123 P(HS)A 1990, s. 9(2).
124 P(HS)A 1990, s. 20.
125 COMAH Regs, reg 4.
126 P(HS)A 1990, s. 14.

and until confirmed by the Secretary of State[127] and there are provisions for compensation in some cases.[128]

15.103 Furthermore a hazardous substances consent is revoked if there is a change in the person in control of part of the land to which it relates unless application for continuation of the consent has previously been made to the authority. On such an application the authority may modify the consent in any way they think appropriate or they may revoke it, but there is provision for compensation to the person who was in control of the whole of the land.[129]

Enforcement

15.104 Contravention of hazardous substances control is an offence punishable on summary conviction by a fine not exceeding the statutory maximum or on indictment by a fine; if the offence continues thereafter, there may be a daily fine. In determining the amount of any fine, the court may have regard to any financial benefit which has accrued or appears likely to accrue to the offender.[130]

15.105 The hazardous substances authority may also issue a contravention notice similar to an enforcement notice under the TCPA 1990.[131]

Hazardous substances on Crown land

15.106 PCPA 2004, s. 79(3) provides that the P(HS)A 1990 binds the Crown.[132] The 2004 Act inserts new ss. 30A and 30B into the P(HS)A 1990 for hazardous substances present on Crown land.

15.107 Under these transitional provisions (which resemble those discussed above for when the P(HS)A 1990 was brought into force) the hazardous substances authority will be deemed to have granted hazardous substances consent where an appropriate Crown authority makes a claim before the end of six months after the date on which s. 79(3) comes into force.[133] The hazardous substance must have been present on Crown land for 12 months ending with the day before the commencement of s. 79(3),[134] and the quantity of the substance must not exceed the established quantity.

15.108 Further, P(HS)A 1990, s. 32 which provides for application for hazardous substances consent in anticipation of disposal of Crown land, is repealed.[135]

---

127 P(HS)A 1990, s. 15.
128 For the extent of the compensation liability, see P(HS)A 1990, s. 16.
129 P(HS)A 1990, ss. 17, 18, 19.
130 P(HS)A 1990, s. 23, as amended by the Planning and Compensation Act 1991, Sch 3, para 10.
131 P(HS)A 1990, ss. 24, 25. As to enforcement notices, see para 12.01.
132 For Crown land generally, see para 17.01.
133 P(HS)A 1990, s. 30B (1), (2), (4) and (11). Regulations are prescribed by SI 2006 No 1283.
134 Ibid, s. 30B(10).
135 PCPA 2004, s. 79(4).

16

BUILDINGS OF SPECIAL INTEREST AND CONSERVATION AREAS

Buildings of special interest

16.01 The preservation of buildings of special architectural or historic interest has long been regarded as an important objective of town and country planning. Thus schemes under the TCPA 1932 could provide for the preservation of such buildings. The TCPA 1947 enabled local authorities to make building preservation orders with the approval of the Minister. A building preservation order prohibited the demolition of, or the making of specified alterations to, the building without the consent of the local authority. Before approving the order, the Minister had to consider any objections or representations made by interested persons and, if need be, hold a public local inquiry. The system was thus fair and open, the case for giving the building special status was fully tested at the time, and thereafter the owner knew exactly what was prohibited without consent. The TCPA 1947 also provided for the listing of buildings by the Minister; where a building was listed, it became an offence to demolish or alter it without first giving notice to the local planning authority who could then consider whether to make a preservation order.

16.02 All this was changed by the TCPA 1968. The provisions as to building preservation orders were repealed, and instead it became an offence to demolish or alter a listed building without first obtaining 'listed building consent' from the local planning authority or the Minister.[1]

16.03 The system thus introduced in 1968 was continued under the TCPA 1971 with some significant changes under the later Acts. The legislation has now been consolidated in the Listed Buildings Act (LBA). The Planning and Compensation Act 1991 made a number of amendments to that Act which will be considered later in this chapter.

Administration of the system

16.04 After the General Election of 1992 the Department of National Heritage was set up to be responsible for a broad range of matters including tourism, sport, broadcasting, and conservation. As a result, a number of the responsibilities formerly entrusted to the Secretary of State were transferred to the Secretary of State for National Heritage (as he then was).[2] In 1997 the Department of National Heritage was renamed as the Department for Culture, Media and Sport.[3] The Secretary of State for Culture, Media and Sport was given general responsibility for conservation policy and also for the listing of historic buildings, discussed below. In addition, he was given responsibility for the issuing of notices where listed buildings have fallen into disrepair and the associated compulsory acquisition.[4] The ministerial powers and duties in relation to listed building control, such as decisions to call in applications for listed building consent,[5] remained with the Secretary of State.

16.05 As from 1 April 2005, as part of a package of proposed reforms discussed at the end of this chapter, English Heritage took over the administration of the listing system. This initial step did not require primary legislation. Ultimately, however, the intention is that all designation decisions will be devolved to English Heritage from the Secretary of State, subject to certain safeguards. This will require statutory amendment. The existing statutory framework is discussed below.

---

[1] Buildings subject to preservation orders under the old law are now deemed to be listed.

[2] Transfer of Functions (National Heritage) Order 1992, SI 1992 No 1311.

[3] Secretary of State for Culture, Media and Sport Order 1997, SI 1997 No 1744.

[4] See para 16.88. He also has certain reserve powers in respect of the designation of conservation areas, see para 16.103.

[5] See para 16.37.

Listing of buildings

16.06 The listing of buildings of special architectural or historic interest is the responsibility of the Secretary of State. He may compile lists of such buildings or he may give his approval (with or without modifications) to lists compiled by English Heritage or by other persons or bodies.[6] In compiling his own list the Secretary of State may act on his own initiative,[7] but he may—and often does—receive suggestions from the local planning authority and sometimes even from private individuals.

16.07 When considering whether to list a building the Secretary of State may consider not only the building itself but also: (a) the contribution which its exterior makes to the architectural or historic interest of a group of buildings, and (b) the desirability of preserving any features fixed to the building or contained within its curtilage.[8] The reference to features undoubtedly includes artefacts such as portrait panels and carvings inside the building provided they have been affixed to the premises so as to become part thereof.[9]

16.08 Before including buildings in the lists, the Secretary of State must consult English Heritage[10] and such other persons as he may consider appropriate as having a special knowledge of, or interest in, such buildings.[11]

16.09 The Secretary of State has placed a very wide interpretation on the words 'buildings of special architectural or historic interest'. The selections have not been limited to buildings of obvious aesthetic quality or those associated with well-known characters or events, but may include architecture typical of a certain period or illustrative of the work of particular architects.[12] Current government guidance as to the general principles to be applied to the selection of buildings for listing is grouped under five headings: (i) age and rarity; (ii) aesthetic merits; (iii) selectivity; (iv) national interest; and (v) state of repair.[13] Selectivity under (iii) is a recognition that listing needs to be selective where a substantial number of buildings of a similar type survive. The policy in such circumstances is to list only the most representative or significant examples.

---

6 Listed Buildings Act 1990, s. 1(1).

7 There is an interesting account of the workings of the system in *Amalgamated Investment and Property Co Ltd v John Walker & Sons Ltd* [1976] 3 All ER 509, [1977] 1 WLR 164.

8 Listed Buildings Act 1990, s. 1(3).

9 *Corthorn Land and Timber Co Ltd v Minister of Housing and Local Government* (1965) 63 LGR 490: and see para 16.15.

10 The requirement to consult the Commission does not apply in Wales.

11 LBA 1990.

12 See DCLG Circular 1/07, paras 6.9–6.16.

13 Ibid, paras 6.12–6.16.

16.10 Listed buildings are in practice (though not as a matter of statutory requirement)[14] classified as Grade I, Grade II*, or Grade II. Grade I buildings are buildings of exceptional interest. Grade II* buildings are particularly important buildings of more than special interest; and Grade II buildings are buildings of special interest which warrant every effort being made to preserve them.[15]

16.11 The Secretary of State is not statutorily required to consult the owner of a building that is intended to be listed, although in March 1995 the Secretary of State announced that in future there would be public consultation on all listing recommendations emerging from the English Heritage thematic survey of particular types of building. However on appeal against a refusal of listed building consent, the appellant may contend that the building is not of special architectural or historic interest and ought to be excluded from the list.[16]

16.12 If the Secretary of State decides that a building should be listed, he will notify the local planning authority who must then give notice to the owner and occupier;[17] the listing will also be recorded in the register of local land charges.[18] The secrecy with which buildings have been listed has caused problems in the past for intending purchasers and developers. Some protection is afforded by LBA 1990, s. 6. Where a planning application has been made, or permission has been granted, for development involving the demolition or alteration of a building, application may be made to the Secretary of State for a certificate that he does not intend to list the building; if he gives such a certificate, he is precluded from listing the building within the next five years.

16.13 The purpose of listing is to give guidance to local planning authorities in the performance of their functions under the LBA 1990 and also under the TCPA 1990 as well as to prohibit demolition or alteration;[19] this means that the local planning authority will be expected to give special consideration to listed buildings in deciding whether to give planning permission for nearby development and in the drafting of development plan policies.

16.14 Subject to certain exemptions considered later in this chapter[20] there appear to be no restrictions on the types of structure or erection which may be listed. Indeed in view of the wide meaning given to the word 'building' in TCPA 1990, s. 336[21]

---

[14] There is a reference to Grade II buildings in the Listed Buildings Regs, reg 5.

[15] See Circular 1/07, para 6.6.

[16] See para 16.38. The Secretary of State has indicated that he is willing to consider requests from owners for 'de-listing': see PPG 15, para 6.26.

[17] LBA 1990, s. 2(3).

[18] LBA 1990, s. 2(2).

[19] LBA 1990, s. 1(1).

[20] See para 16.49.

[21] See para 6.07.

(applied by LBA 1990, s. 91(2)), it would seem that such structures as village pumps, lych gates, and milestones may be included in such lists.

What is a listed building?

16.15 LBA 1990, s. 1(5) provides that, in addition to the building itself, the following are to be treated as part of the building:

(a) any object or structure fixed to the building;
(b) any object or structure within the curtilage of the building which, although not fixed to the building, forms part of the land and has done so since before 1 July 1948.

16.16 This definition has caused some problems. In the *Calderdale* case[22] a terrace of mill cottages was linked by a bridge to a mill which had been listed. At the date of listing, the mill and the cottages were in common ownership, but in 1973 the cottages had passed into the ownership of the borough council who now wished to demolish them. The question was whether the cottages were structures within the curtilage of the mill. The judgments of the Court of Appeal seem to have taken it for granted that the terrace, and each cottage within it, were structures for the purposes of what is now LBA 1990, s. 1(5). The court concentrated on two questions: whether the cottages were 'fixed' to the mill and whether they remained within the curtilage notwithstanding the division of ownership. It was held (1) that the terrace was a single structure and fixed to the mill by the bridge; (2) that the terrace had not been taken out of the curtilage by reason of the changes that had taken place. Stephenson LJ identified three factors which were relevant in determining whether a structure was within the curtilage of a listed building; (a) the physical layout of the listed building and the structure; (b) their ownership past and present; and (3) their use and function past and present.

16.17 The apparently wide-ranging effects of this decision have been considerably narrowed as a result of the later decision of the House of Lords in *Debenhams plc v Westminster City Council.*[23]

16.18 Debenhams were the owners of two buildings, the 'Regent Street building'; and the 'Kingly Street building'. They were separated by a street but linked by a tunnel and a bridge. The Regent Street building had been listed, but not the other. In order to claim certain exemptions for unoccupied listed buildings under the General Rate Act 1967, Debenhams claimed that the Kingly Street building fell

22 *A-G (ex rel Sutcliffe) v Calderdale Borough Council* (1982) 46 P & CR 399, [1983] JPL 310, CA.
23 [1987] AC 396, [1987] 1 All ER 51, HL.

within the definition of listed buildings in what is now s. 1(5) of the Listed Buildings Act.

16.19 The House of Lords considered that the important question was the meaning of 'structure' in s. 1(5). Lord Keith of Kinkel said that in its ordinary significance 'structure' certainly embraced anything built or constructed and so would cover any building; but in the present context 'structure' was intended to convey a limitation to such structures as were ancillary to the listed building itself, for example the stable block of a mansion house or a steading of a farm house, either fixed to the main building or within its curtilage.

16.20 Held: The Kingly Street building was not ancillary to the Regent Street building, and so was not included in the listing.

16.21 Although the House of Lords interpreted the word 'structure' in this context in a much narrower sense than that assumed by the Court of Appeal in the *Calderdale* case, that case is still good authority on the question of what is the curtilage of a listed building. Moreover, the actual decision in *Calderdale* might, in the very unusual circumstances of that case, have been correct since the cottages might be regarded as having originally been ancillary to the mill itself.[24]

16.22 The *Debenhams* case was followed in a decision of deputy judge Sir Graham Eyre, *Watts v Secretary of State for the Environment*.[25] A brick wall had formed a continuous structure between Bix Manor, a listed building, and a small barn. The wall had not been specifically listed but was demolished in order to provide access. The learned deputy judge said that the question was whether the wall constituted a structure ancillary to a listed building. It seems that at time of listing in 1985 the wall had formed part of the curtilage of a property separate from the listed building both in terms of ownership and physical occupation; thus it could not be said to serve the listed building nor was there any functional connection. He expressed concern that what he called a 'mere accident of ownership' should have such significance.

16.23 Indeed there is no doubt that the issue of what constitutes the 'curtilage' of a listed building can give rise to difficulty. The question arose again recently in *Skerritts of Nottingham Ltd v Secretary of State for the Environment, Transport and the Regions*.[26] 'Grimsdyke' was a large country house used as an hotel and situated in spacious grounds.[27] A stable block stood some 200 metres from the house.

---

24 See the comments in *Debenhams plc v Westminster City Council* (above) of Lords Keith of Kinkel and Mackay of Clashfern. See further *Watson-Smyth v Secretary of State for the Environment* [1992] JPL 451.

25 [1991] JPL 718.

26 [1999] JPL 932.

27 The property had once been the home of the librettist W S Gilbert.

Grimsdyke was listed but the stable block had not been listed in its own right. An enforcement notice was served alleging the removal, from the stable block, of the existing timber framed windows and their replacement with plastic double glazing, without listed building consent. The owners appealed to the Secretary of State who accepted the inspector's reasoning that the stable block was within the curtilage of a listed building. George Bartlett QC, sitting as deputy judge, allowed an appeal against this decision. The owners appealed to the Court of Appeal contending that the Secretary of State had erred in law in overlooking the principle (if there was such a principle) that the curtilage of a building was confined to a small area around that building.

16.24 Held: the appeal would be dismissed and the Secretary of State's decision upheld.

16.25 Walker LJ (with whom Alliott J and Henry LJ agreed) rejected the proposition that the curtilage of a building must always be small.[28] It was a question of fact and degree; the curtilage of a substantial listed building is likely to extend to what are or have been, in terms of ownership and function, ancillary buildings. It follows that the curtilage of a listed building could be a relatively large area, although no piece of land could ever be within the curtilage of more than one building.

16.26 Although the concept of curtilage may not be restricted by size, it must be part of the enclosure of the house or building to which it attaches. Thus in *Lowe v First Secretary of State*,[29] the owner of Arlesford Hall, a listed building, erected a 1.8 metre high, 650 metre chain fence alongside the driveway to the Hall. Tucker J held that the inspector had erred by taking into account the reason given by the owner for erecting the fence, which was to protect the land in his ownership. The curtilage could not possibly include the whole of the parkland setting in which the house lay, nor the driveway along which the fence was erected. The erection of the fence did not therefore constitute development within the curtilage of a listed building.[30]

16.27 In a later case, *Sumption v Greenwich London Borough Council*,[31] the meaning of 'curtilage' in connection with listed buildings was revisited. The owner of a listed property, Hillside House (which is part of the Greenwich World Heritage site), purchased a piece of land in order to extend the garden. The owner then erected a chestnut paling fence on the additional land thereby created; he later submitted a planning application to construct a wall in place of the fence. Planning permission was refused. The owner later applied for a CLOPUD under s. 192 TCPA 1990 to

28 A proposition based on *Dyer v Dorset County Council* [1989] JPL 451.
29 [2003] 08 EG 129 (CS).
30 Ie for the purposes of GPDO 1995, 'minor operations'—see para 7.24.
31 [2007] EWHC 2776 (Admin).

certify the lawfulness of the proposed works. This application was lodged two years after the land had been acquired. The local planning authority granted a certificate on the basis that the construction of the wall was permitted development, as a minor operation under Part 2, Class A of the GPDO. Neighbouring owners, S, challenged the issue of the certificate on the basis that the works involved 'development within the curtilage of, or to a gate, fence, wall or other means of enclosure surrounding a listed building'—in such circumstances, the development is not permitted.[32]

16.28 Collins J held that the curtilage of the listed building did extend over the land on which the wall was built. The learned judge said:

> It would, in my view, be well nigh impossible to contend that once the wall was erected and the garden use confirmed so that the land did indeed form part of the garden of Hillside House it was not within the curtilage. It does not seem to me to be relevant that the garden use has not formally been approved. What matters is what is in fact *the use being made of the land*. It is clearly capable of being used by the owner . . . I do not regard the historical lack of connection as being capable of carrying weight in the circumstances . . . the facts permit of only one conclusion, namely that the curtilage of Hillside House does extend over the land [Author's italics].

16.29 This decision is important because it confirms that the lack of historical connection is of little significance and what matters is the use being made of the land. In the case itself, the land was attached to the house and capable of being enjoyed with it. The court also held that, irrespective of the curtilage issue, the works were also excluded from permitted development as constituting the rebuilding of a means of enclosure to a listed building. The certificate of lawfulness was quashed.

16.30 As we have seen,[33] listed buildings control does not apply to chattels, but as the distinction between fixtures and chattels is always a matter of some difficulty it is not surprising that the issue has caused controversy in relation to listed buildings.

16.31 The issue arose in relation to the removal of Canova's statue 'The Three Graces' which stood in a listed tempietto at Woburn Abbey. The Secretary of State originally took the view that the statue was a fixture (and therefore part of the realty) but proposed not to take listed building enforcement action.[34] He subsequently decided, on further advice, that the statue was not part of the building under s. 1(5) of the Listed Buildings Act and therefore not subject to control. He considered that the correct test to be applied was the same as at common law to

---

32 Under Part 2, para A 1(d) GPDO 1995.

33 See para 16.15.

34 See para 16.66.

decide whether an article is a fixture, ie the degree of annexation and the purpose of annexation.[35] It seems that the degree of annexation was not great—the statue itself was freestanding and stood on a plinth attached to the floor but removable. As to the purpose of annexation, the fact that the tempietto was built to house the statue did not of itself mean that the statue became part of the building; the purpose of installing the statue in the tempietto was not to dedicate it to the land, or incorporate it into the land, but to show off the statue.[36] In arriving at this decision the Secretary of State had regard to the history of the statue and the way it had been treated by the owners.

16.32 In *Kennedy v Secretary of State for Wales*,[37] enforcement notices were issued against the removal from Leighton Hall, Powys, of a carillon clock and three bronze chandeliers without listed building consent. The chandeliers were original to the Great Hall and the clock rested on the second floor of the entrance tower 'by its own colossal weight'. In dismissing an appeal against the enforcement notices the Secretary of State relied on the test referred to in the previous paragraph. Before the High Court, the appellant argued, inter alia, that the inspector, in adopting the second limb of the test, had taken into account an irrelevance, viz that the clock was part of the Hall's historical folklore and its bells rang out across the countryside. Otton J held that there was no evidence that irrelevant considerations had been raised. The learned judge confirmed that the definition of a fixture was the same for listed building legislation as it was for any other area of law. As for the clock, the fact that it was free standing was not of itself conclusive that it was not a fixture.

16.33 In the past it has not been uncommon for a complex of buildings to appear as one entry in the statutory list. This can give rise to problems in determining what buildings were intended to be listed. In *City of Edinburgh Council v Secretary of State for the Environment*,[38] the list referred to 'Redford Barracks . . . (original buildings of 1909–1915 only)'. There was a riding school in the suite of buildings which was thought to have been built after 1915. Although it was mentioned elsewhere in the list, the Reporter concluded that the reference to 'original buildings' meant that the riding school was excluded from the list.

16.34 The House of Lords unanimously upheld the decision of the Second Division of the Court of Session that the Reporter's interpretation was wrong. The words of description in the list were ambiguous. They did not necessarily refer to a building constructed between 1909 and 1915, but could be interpreted as referring to the

35 Relying on the view of Lord Mackay of Clashfern in the *Debenhams* case; see para 16.17.
36 [1991] JPL 401.
37 [1996] EGCS 17. See also [1995] JPL 241, the *Time and Life Building* case.
38 [1998] JPL 224.

process of planning, conception, design, and completion of the architect's project.[39] Thus the riding school was part of the whole project and therefore comprised in the listing.

16.35 As Lord Hope noted: '[p]lainly it is desirable to compile the list with sufficient clarity and precision to avoid the kind of situation that has arisen here.' A matter which is perhaps left uncertain is the extent to which words of limitation in the description of the building in the list can override (in England) what is LBA 1990, s. 1(5).[40] Lord Hope appeared to indicate that this was possible but this view has been questioned.[41]

16.36 The wording of LBA 1990, s. 1(5)(a) is unqualified as to date. Accordingly it was held by Dyson J in *Richardson Developments Ltd v Birmingham City Council*[42] that, providing a building extension is a structure 'fixed to a [listed] building' under [LBA 1990, s. 1(5)(a)] and is ancillary to the listed building, it will be treated as listed even though added to the listed building after the date of listing. This decision confirms what was widely understood to be the case.

Listed building consent

16.37 LBA 1990, s. 9 makes it an offence to execute, without first obtaining listed building consent, any works for the demolition of a listed building or for its alteration or extension in a manner which would affect its character as a building of special architectural or historic interest; as we have seen, any object or structure fixed to the building and certain other objects or structures forming part of the land comprised within the curtilage are to be treated as part of the building.[43] In addition, where it is proposed to demolish a building, notice must be given to English Heritage to enable them to inspect and record details of the building.[44]

16.38 It is not always easy in practice to decide whether works to a listed building are properly classed as 'demolition' or 'alteration'—for many years it was generally assumed that the removal of part only of a listed building could be classed as 'demolition'.[45]

---

39 The architect was Harry B Measures.

40 Their Lordships were actually considering the Town and Country Planning (Scotland) Act 1972, s. 52(7). LBA 1990, s. 1(5) is discussed at para 16.15 above.

41 See the Case Editor's note at [1998] JPL 240.

42 [1999] JPL 1001.

43 See para 16.15.

44 LBA 1990, s. 8(2)(a), (b), and (c).

45 See eg *R v North Hertfordshire District Council, ex p Sullivan* [1981] JPL 752.

16.39 In *Shimizu (UK) Ltd v Westminster City Council*,[46] the question arose in connection with a claim for compensation under (now repealed) LBA 1990, s. 27. Qantas House was a listed building at the corner of Bond Street and Piccadilly, London. Listed building consent was granted for the demolition of the building with the exception of the facade and chimney breasts. A further application by Shimizu to demolish the chimney breasts (to provide more floor space) was refused, whereupon the company claimed compensation under section 27 of the LBA. For such a claim to succeed the proposed works had to be works of alteration, not demolition. If the definition of a listed building included 'any part of a building' as used in s. 336 of the principal Planning Act, then removal of that part would involve demolition and no compensation would be payable. The Lands Tribunal found for Shimizu but the Court of Appeal allowed the Council's appeal, holding that the removal of the chimney breasts constituted demolition. The Company appealed to the House of Lords. Held: (Lord Griffiths dissenting) the decision of the Lands Tribunal would be restored, ie the proposed works were works of alteration.

16.40 Lord Hope, with whom the majority of their Lordships agreed, rejected the previously accepted meaning of the word 'building' where it formed part of the expression 'listed building'. On his Lordship's analysis of the statutory provisions, there was no reason why the term 'listed building', where it appeared in the LBA 1990, had to be given the extended meaning. Thus 'demolition' must mean the demolition of substantially the whole of the listed building, not merely a part of it. His Lordship said: 'According to its ordinary meaning, the word 'demolish' when used in reference to a building means to pull the building down in other words to destroy it completely and break it up. I agree therefore with Millett LJ [in the Court of Appeal] when he said that demolition, with or without replacement, on the one hand and alteration on the other are mutually exclusive concepts.'

16.41 Although the claim for compensation under LBA 1990, s. 27 has now been abolished, the *Shimizu* case nevertheless has implications for listed building control.[47] Certainly it has not been welcomed by those responsible for the preservation of historic buildings. Presumably fewer proposals will now amount to demolition as defined by the House of Lords since what is required is the removal of the whole or substantially the whole of the building. One consequence is that the statutory obligation to notify English Heritage (formerly the duty was to notify the Royal Commission) of applications for proposed demolition of listed

---

46 [1997] JPL 523.

47 See Brainsby and Carter [1997] JPL 503, to whom the author is indebted, for a detailed analysis. The *Shimizu* decision also has implications for conservation areas: see para16.119.

buildings[48] is likely to apply to a reduced number of cases. The opportunity to record architectural and historic details may in some cases be lost.

16.42 Special provision is made for cases in which it is urgently necessary to execute works in the interests of safety or health or for the preservation of the building. The legislation does not expressly authorize such works, but provides that in the event of a prosecution for carrying out works without consent it shall be defence to prove all of the following matters: (a) that the works were urgently necessary in the interests of safety or health or for the preservation of the building; (b) that it was not practicable to secure safety or health or, as the case may be, to preserve the building by works of repair or works for affording temporary support or shelter; (c) that the works were limited to the minimum necessary; (d) that notice in writing justifying in detail the carrying out of the works was given to the local planning authority as soon as reasonably practicable.[49]

16.43 The prohibition against works which would affect the character of the building as one of special architectural or historic interest extends to works which do not fall within the definition of development[50] or which are permitted developments.[51] Thus the painting of the exterior of a building is permitted by the General Permitted Development Order[52] but may be held to affect the character of a listed building.[53] The prohibition also extends to works to the interior of the building if they affect the special character of the building.[54] There is no formal machinery by which the owner or occupier of a building can secure a formal determination as to whether his proposed works would affect the character of the building.[55] In the last resort, the question will be one of fact for the Secretary of State on appeal against a listed building enforcement notice or for the magistrates on a prosecution. In cases of doubt it may be helpful to discuss the matter with the local planning authority, but since the decision in *Western Fish Products Ltd v Penwith District Council,*[56] as affirmed by later cases, it is extremely doubtful that the advice of the planning officer would be binding on the authority.

---

48 LBA 1990; s. 8 has been amended to take account of the merger of English Heritage and the Royal Commission (Authorization of Works (Listed Buildings) (England) Order 2001, SI 2001 No 24).

49 LBA 1990, s. 9(3).

50 See para 6.01.

51 See para 7.01.

52 GPDO, Sch 2, Part 2, Class C.

53 *Windsor and Maidenhead Royal Borough Council v Secretary of State for the Environment* (1987) 86 LGR 402, [1988] JPL 410.

54 LBA 1990, s. 1(5).

55 The Secretary of State is under no statutory obligation to consider the point if taken on an appeal against refusal of listed building consent, but there appears to be nothing in law to prevent his doing so.

56 [1981] 2 All ER 204, 38 P & CR 7.

16.44 Originally a planning permission for development involving the demolition or alteration of a listed building might be so worded as to make it necessary to make separate application for listed building consent. This provision has now been repealed with the result that where development involves the demolition or alteration of a listed building, separate applications must be made for planning permission and listed building consent.

16.45 In *Chambers v Guildford Borough Council*,[57] it was held that the issue of whether a structure is listed under s. 1(5) LBA, and whether listed building consent is required for its removal, should not be litigated in court before an inspector has had the opportunity to consider it on appeal against a refusal of listed building consent. This was despite the fact that there was no statutory procedure in the LBA 1990 enabling a landowner to discover, in cases of doubt, whether listed building consent was required for intended works.

16.46 The dispute in the case concerned a Second World War pillbox situated in the grounds of a listed farmhouse which the owners wished to remove. In interpreting the legislation, McCombe J observed: 'It seems to me extraordinary that Parliament would envisage that a dispute of the present kind should be decided in High Court proceedings, then leaving other issues that may arise on an application to the usual planning process.' The proceedings were stayed by the judge pending the outcome of a fresh application for listed building consent and an appeal against a refusal thereon.

Exemptions from the effects of listing

16.47 There are certain exemptions from the effects of listing as discussed above.

1. *Ecclesiastical buildings*
   Churches can be listed—indeed many are thus designated—but they have always been regarded as exempt from the effects of listing, that is to say, no offence would be committed for the carrying out of unauthorized works. The only exception to this is in the case of the total demolition of a listed church.[58]
   Concern over the width of the exemption led, in 1987, to Parliament giving the Secretary of State powers to make a direction restricting the scope of the exemption.[59] The current provisions are to be found in LBA 1990, s. 60. The effect of that section is that listed building controls do not apply to the partial demolition, alteration, or extension of an ecclesiastical building which is for

57 [2008] EWHC 826 (QB).

58 *A-G (ex rel Bedfordshire County Council) v Howard United Reformed Church Trustees, Bedford* [1976] AC 363, [1976] 2 All ER 337, HL.

59 Housing and Planning Act 1986.

the time being used for ecclesiastical purposes, except in so far as the Secretary of State may otherwise provide by order.[60]

After lengthy public consultation, the Government announced in 1992 that an Order would be made restricting the ecclesiastical exemption in future to religious bodies which set up satisfactory internal systems of control as exemplified in a Government Code of Practice. The order in question, the Ecclesiastical Exemption (Listed Buildings and Conservation Areas) Order 1994,[61] came into effect on 1 October 1994. Under the terms of the order, the ecclesiastical exemption is retained for the Church of England, the Church in Wales, the Roman Catholic Church, the Methodist Church, the Baptist Union, and the United Reformed Church.[62] It follows that all other religious bodies will be subject to the general listed building controls.

The Order imposes some substantive limits on the exemption, however. Thus the exemption, where it applies, is restricted to (i) the church building itself and any object or structure within the building, and (ii) any object or structure fixed to the exterior of a church building or within the curtilage, but excluding objects or structures listed in their own right.[63] There are special provisions for Church of England cathedrals where, in general, the exemption extends to all objects or structures within the precincts.[64]

In 2004 the Government published a paper, *The Ecclesiastical Exemption: the Way Forward*, indicating that there would be no extension beyond the existing denominations operating their own controls under the exemption. The operation of the exemption would be reviewed from time to time.

2. *Scheduled ancient monuments*

   Buildings for the time being included in the schedule of monuments compiled and maintained under s. 1 of the Ancient Monuments and Archaeological Areas Act 1979 can be listed. However by virtue of LBA 1990, s. 61 the controls in the Act of 1979 take precedence and listed building controls do not apply.

---

[60] 'Ecclesiastical building' is not defined except that it does not include the residence of a minister of religion; s. 60(3). And see the *Howard* case, cited at fn 58 above, per Lord Cross at p 376. Some further proposals for the reform of the law relating to listed buildings were contained in *The Future of the Ecclesiastical Exemption*, DCMS, 2004.

[61] SI 1994 No 1771.

[62] SI 1994 No 1771, art 4. There are a number of other special cases; see art 6.

[63] Ecclesiastical Exemption Order, art 5.

[64] Ecclesiastical Exemption Order, art 5(2).

Procedure for obtaining consent

16.48 The procedure for obtaining listed building consent is modelled on that for obtaining planning permission, but there are some additional requirements as to publicity and consultation with the Secretary of State which illustrate the importance which is now attached to the preservation of buildings of special interest.

16.49 Any person may apply for listed building consent; but, whether or not he has an interest in the land, he must give notice of his application to every other person who has a sufficient interest[65] in the land.[66]

16.50 The application must be made on the standard application form published by the Secretary of State.[67] If the application involves either the demolition or (with minor exceptions) the alteration of a listed building the applicant must advertise the application stating where plans may be inspected; a notice to the same effect must also be displayed on or near the land. Any member of the public then has a period of 21 days in which to make representations.[68]

16.51 The Secretary of State has directed that in the case of demolition, the local planning authority must give notice of the application to certain national organizations.[69] The Secretary of State has also directed that the local planning authority must notify English Heritage of all applications for listed building consent which in the opinion of the authority affect the setting of any Grade I or Grade II* building.[70] In certain circumstances the requirement extends to Grade II (unstarred) buildings. It is submitted that these requirements are mandatory and not merely directory; failure to comply with them may result in a grant of listed building consent being quashed.

16.52 The Secretary of State may give directions calling in the application;[71] however if the local planning authority propose to grant consent, they must, in certain cases, notify the Secretary of State of their intention, and he then has a period of 28 days in which to consider whether or not to call in the application.[72]

16.53 In considering whether to grant listed building consent for any works, or whether to grant planning permission for development which affects a listed building or its setting, the Secretary of State and the local planning authority are required to have

---

65 Ie the fee simple or a tenancy with at least seven years to run. T & CP (Listed Buildings and Buildings in Conservation Areas) Regulations 1990, SI 1990 No 1519, reg 6(4).

66 SI 1990 No 1519, reg 6(1), (2).

67 SI 1990 No 1519, reg 3, as substituted by SI 2008 No 551.

68 SI 1990 No 1519, reg 5.

69 The direction is contained in Circular 1/01, para 15.

70 See Circular 1/01, para 8.

71 LBA 1990, s. 12.

72 LBA 1990, s. 13.

special regard to the desirability of preserving the building or its setting or any features of special interest which it possesses.[73] It is clearly the intention of Parliament that the desirability of preserving the building or its setting or special features should be the primary consideration, but it is also clear that it cannot be the sole consideration. For instance the economics of restoring a listed building has been recognized as a relevant consideration.

16.54 In *Kent Messenger Ltd v Secretary of State for the Environment*,[74] the applicants had appealed against the local planning authority's refusal of consent to demolish a listed building. The inspector accepted that restoration and repair would be uneconomic and recommended that consent be granted for demolition. The Secretary of State disagreed but failed to give adequate reasons for doing so. In the High Court Forbes J quashed the decision and remitted the case to the Secretary of State for reconsideration.

16.55 However in considering whether the restoration of a listed building would be an economic proposition, the Secretary of State is entitled, on the basis of evidence given at the inquiry, to take into account the extent to which the cost of restoration could be recouped by the redevelopment of the remainder of the site.[75]

16.56 At one time there was uncertainty as to whether, on an application for consent to demolish a listed building, it was relevant to consider the quality of the building proposed to be erected in its place. In *Kent Messenger Ltd v Secretary of State for the Environment*,[76] Forbes J left the question open, but the matter has now come before the House of Lords albeit indirectly. In *Save Britain's Heritage v Secretary of State for the Environment*,[77] the proposal in question was the redevelopment of the Mappin and Webb site in Mansion House Square, London. The site, which was included in a conservation area, comprised several listed buildings which were to be demolished to make way for a new building in the 'post-modern' style. The inspector and the Secretary of State found in favour of the proposal; the site, in their view, was unique and the design and quality of the replacement building would make a greater contribution to the architectural heritage than the retention of the existing buildings. The Court of Appeal[78] struck down this decision on the basis that the Secretary of State's decision had not given sufficient intelligible reasons for departing from the policy in the relevant circular[79] which provided for 'a presumption in favour of preservation'. The House of Lords reversed this

73 LBA 1990, s. 16(2).
74 [1976] JPL 372.
75 *Godden v Secretary of State for the Environment* [1988] JPL 99.
76 [1976] JPL372.
77 [1991] 2 All ER 10.
78 [1990] JPL 831.
79 Circular 8/87, para 89. This has now been replaced by PPG 15.

decision; it would always be possible to make an exception to the policy if the special circumstances of the case justified it.

16.57 In any case it may well be that where the listed building is in a conservation area, the quality of the proposed replacement building is a relevant consideration, because the planning authority are required to have special regard to the desirability of preserving or enhancing the character or appearance of the area.[80]

16.58 If the Secretary of State does not call in the application, the local authority may grant consent with or without conditions or they may refuse consent.[81] Where consent is granted for demolition of a listed building, the local planning authority may impose a condition that demolition shall not take place until a contract for carrying out works of redevelopment has been made, and planning permission has been granted for the redevelopment for which the contract provides.[82] Under the original provisions of LBA 1990, every listed building consent (whether for demolition or alterations) had to contain a condition to the effect that the consent would lapse if it was not acted upon within five years or such other period as may be stated in the consent. However under PCPA 2004, the duration of a listed building consent is to be reduced from five years to three, or such other period as may be determined by the local planning authority, and the period within which the works must be begun will be extended by one year if legal proceedings are brought to challenge the validity of the consent.[83] If consent is refused or granted subject to conditions, the applicant may appeal to the Secretary of State;[84] so too, if the authority fail to give a decision within the prescribed period.[85] The Act expressly provides that the grounds of appeal may include a claim that the building is not of special architectural or historic interest;[86] this is of considerable importance because, as noted earlier in this chapter, the owner or occupier cannot formally object to the listing of his building. Where a case comes before the Secretary of State (whether on appeal or on calling in) the applicant and the local planning authority have the right to a hearing.[87] The Secretary of State's decision

80 LBA 1990, s. 72. The quality of the proposed replacement building was held to be a relevant consideration in the case of an application for conservation area consent for the demolition of an unlisted building in *Richmond-upon-Thames London Borough Council v Secretary of State for the Environment* (1978) 37 P & CR 151, [1979] JPL 175: see para 16.120.

81 LBA 1990, s. 16(1).

82 LBA 1990, s. 17(3).

83 PCPA 2004, s. 51(4)(a), amending LBA 1990, s. 18.

84 LBA 1990, s. 20(1).

85 LBA 1990, s. 20(2). The prescribed period is eight weeks: Listed Buildings Regs, reg 3(4). PCPA 2004, s. 50(2) has inserted a new s. 20A into LBA 1990 to give the local planning authority and Secretary of State dual jurisdiction where the local planning authority have not determined the application within the eight-week period for an additional period where the case has gone to appeal. Corresponding provisions in relation to planning permission are discussed at para 8.102.

86 LBA 1990, s. 21(3).

87 LBA 1990, s. 22(2).

is final except that it can be challenged in High Court proceedings under LBA 1990, s. 63.

16.59 The Planning (Listed Buildings and Conservation Areas) (Amendment) (No 2) (England) Order 2004[88] reinstates the original time limit of six months for lodging listed building consent appeals with the Secretary of State. In 2003 the time limit had been reduced from six months to three months.

Amendments made by PCPA 2004

16.60 With regard to listed building consent, PCPA 2004 enabled the Secretary of State to make regulations with regard to such matters as the form and manner of applications; and the matters and documents to be included. The regulations had also to require that applications for listed building consent (of a prescribed description) must include a statement as to the design principles and concepts that have been applied; and a statement as to how issues relating to access have been dealt with.[89] These reforms are in parallel with the amendments made by PCPA 2004 to applications for planning permission. The requirement for a standard application form for applications for listed building consent has been brought into effect by statutory instrument. [90]

16.61 Listed building consent must not be granted, under s. 19 of LBA 1990 as amended by PCPA 2004, to the extent that it has effect to change a condition subject to which a previous listed building consent was granted by extending the time within which the works must be started.[91] Under s. 19, an application may be made to the local planning authority to discharge or vary conditions in a listed building consent—it corresponds to s. 73 of TCPA 1990 with regard to planning permission.[92]

16.62 A further reform which is equivalent to changes made by PCPA 2004 with regard to applications for planning permission is made by s. 43(3) of that Act. This section inserts two new provisions into LBA 1990 which enable the local planning authority to decline to determine a subsequent application for consent in certain circumstances,[93] and to decline to determine a twin-tracked application. This latter provision has not yet been brought into force.

---

88 SI 2004 No 3341. The measure was brought into force on 14 January 2005.

89 PCPA 2004, s. 42(6) and (7), amending the LBA 1990, s. 10.

90 Planning (Listed Buildings and Conservation Areas)(Amendment) (England) Regulations 2008, SI 2008 No 551, as from 6 April 2008.

91 PCPA 2004, s. 51(5), amending the LBA 1990, s. 19.

92 LBA 1990, s. 81A, as inserted by s. 43(3) of PCPA 2004. See, in relation to planning applications, para 10.99.

93 LBA 1990, s. 81B, as inserted by s. 43(3) of PCPA 2004. See, in relation to planning applications, para 8.134.

Revocation and modification

16.63 A listed building consent may be revoked or modified. The local planning authority may make an order for this purpose if they consider it expedient having regard to any material considerations,[94] or the Secretary of State may make the order himself. It is to be noted, however, that the power to revoke or modify only applies where the works authorized by the listing building consent have not been completed.[95]

16.64 In the normal case, the local planning authority must submit the order to the Secretary of State for confirmation, and he will if need be hold a public local inquiry or other hearing before deciding whether or not to confirm the order. But there is an alternative procedure which may be used where the persons affected have notified the local planning authority that they do not object to the order.[96]

16.65 Where listed building consent is revoked or modified, the local planning authority are liable for compensation for abortive expenditure and for any other loss or damage directly attributed to the revocation or modification.[97] Compensation is not payable where the persons affected by the order had notified the local planning authority that they did not object to the order.

Enforcement

16.66 The demolition or alteration of a listed building without consent, or in breach of the conditions attached to consent, is an offence punishable by fine and/or imprisonment. The Planning and Compensation Act 1991[98] increased the maximum fine on summary conviction from £2,000 to £20,000; moreover in determining the amount of any fine the court is to have regard to any financial benefit accuring from the offence. Previously this requirement only applied where a person was convicted on indictment.[99] Further, the maximum term of imprisonment has been increased from a period of six months to one of two years. It is similarly an offence to demolish a listed building without giving notice to English Heritage.[100]

---

94 LBA 1990, s. 23. A reference to having regard to 'the development plan and to any other' [material considerations] was deleted by PCPA 2004, s. 118 and Sch 6, paras 19, 21 and the word 'any' was inserted before 'material considerations' as from 28 September 2004.

95 LBA 1990, s. 24.

96 LBA 1990, s. 25.

97 LBA 1990, s. 28. The claim for compensation should be made to the local planning authority within six months of the date of the order: Listed Buildings Regs, reg 9.

98 LBA 1990, s. 57 and Sch 10, para 2.

99 A fine may thus be more suitable than imprisonment. See *R v Chambers* reviewed at [1989] JPL 229.

100 LBA 1990, s. 9. LBA 1990, s. 29 amends the National Heritage Act 1983 to provide that English Heritage may also prosecute for listed building offences.

Usually, of course, the actual work will be done by a contractor, but the owner will also be guilty of an offence if it can be shown that he caused the work to be done.

16.67 In *R v Wells Street Metropolitan Stipendiary Magistrate, ex p Westminster City Council*,[101] the Divisional Court held that the offence was one of strict liability, that is, the prosecution did not have to prove that the accused knew that the building was listed. The court considered that the issue was one of social concern and that the creation of strict liability would promote the objects of the legislation by encouraging greater vigilance; fears of injustice were all capable of being allayed by the discretion whether to prosecute or not and the discretion of the court to refrain from punishment.

16.68 It would seem that the prosecution should take care not to adduce too much evidence as to the defendant's intent, state of mind, motive, or knowledge. In *R v Sandhu*,[102] the defendant had been convicted after a lengthy Crown Court trial of carrying out unauthorized works at Hinault Hall, a listed building. The Court of Appeal struck down the decision. At the trial the court had heard detailed evidence to the effect that the accused had ignored his own surveyor's advice and had deliberately chosen to disregard the planning regulations. This evidence was held to be irrelevant and inadmissible in that it went beyond what was necessary to establish guilt under LBA 1990, ss. 7 and 9.

16.69 In *Sandhu* the evidence as to the accused was held to have prejudiced a fair trial—of course, such information may be relevant in arriving at an appropriate sentence.

16.70 In addition to prosecution, the local planning authority may issue a 'listed building enforcement notice' specifying the steps to be taken:

(i) for restoring the building to its former state; or
(ii) where such restoration would not be reasonably practicable, or would be undesirable, such further works as the authority consider necessary to alleviate the effect of the works carried out without consent;
(iii) for bringing the building to the state it would have been in if the terms and conditions of listed building consent had been complied with.[103]

16.71 Copies of the notice are to be served on the owner and occupier of the building and on any person having an interest in the building which is materially affected by the notice.[104] Any of these persons may appeal to the Secretary of State on a

---

101 [1986] 3 All ER 4, [1986] 1 WLR 1046.
102 [1997] JPL 853, CA.
103 LBA 1990, s. 38(1), (2). The effect of sub-para (ii) was considered in *Bath City Council v Secretary of State for the Environment and Grosvenor Hotel (Bath) Ltd* [1983] JPL 737 (roof of building in disrepair and patched with unsuitable materials before unauthorized repair works).
104 LBA 1990, s. 38(4).

number of specified grounds; these grounds include: (a) that the building is not of special architectural or historic interest and (b) that the matters complained of do not constitute a contravention of LBA 1990, s. 9, for instance that they do not affect the special character of the building.[105] There is a further right of appeal to the High Court on matters of law.[106]

16.72 Failure to comply with an enforcement notice is an offence punishable by fine; the penalties have been increased by the Act of 1990 in the same way as for the offence of carrying out works without consent, discussed above.[107] The local planning authority may also carry out the work themselves and recover the cost from the owner of the land.[108]

16.73 Can the authority require a listed building which has been demolished to be 'restored to its former state'? It could be argued that there is no longer a 'building' for the purpose of requiring steps for its restoration. The matter arose in *R v Leominster District Council, ex p Antique Country Buildings*.[109]

16.74 A sixteenth-century listed barn, which consisted of timbers held together with wooden pegs, was dismantled and sold to a firm whose intention was to export the timbers to the USA, where the barn would be reassembled. The council applied for a temporary injunction to prevent shipping, which was granted,[110] Hoffmann J rejecting the purchaser's contention that the barn was not a building within the meaning of the Act. In due course listed building enforcement notices were issued. On appeal against the notices the question arose as to whether the local planning authority had the power to require the barn to be re-erected. In the High Court, Mann J answered this question in the affirmative. Providing the structural components were still extant, re-erection could be lawfully required.

16.75 In the *Leominster* case over 70 per cent of the original timbers were extant. The judge recognized that there would be cases where, after demolition, all that was left of a listed building was rubble or ash. In such a case there was no power to require the owner to construct a replica. Nevertheless it was not a pre-requisite of the power to require restoration that all the original components were extant.

16.76 The *Leominster* case was applied in *R (on the application of Judge) v First Secretary of State*[111] where it was argued that the Secretary of State could not lawfully grant consent for the relocation of a listed statue (of Sir Samuel Sadler in Victoria Square,

---

105 LBA 1990, s. 39(1).

106 LBA 1990, s. 65.

107 LBA 1990, s. 43, as amended. See para 16.66 above. On subsequent convictions for non-compliance a daily fine may be imposed.

108 LBA 1990, s. 42.

109 [1988] JPL 554.

110 *Leominster District Council v British Historic Buildings and SPS Shipping* [1987] JPL 350.

111 [2005] EWHC 887.

Middlesborough) because, once moved, its component parts would become chattels, divorced from the land. Rejecting the contention, Sullivan J held that it was irrelevant to consider whether there had been a translation from realty to personalty. The word 'building' in the listed building legislation was capable of covering the statue which had been removed and re-located on a different spot.

16.77 It would seem that there is no time limit on the service of a listed building enforcement notice and an owner may be liable to enforcement action (but not prosecution) in respect of breaches of listed building control by his predecessors in title.[112]

16.78 Injunctive relief is also available. Where the local planning authority consider it necessary or expedient to restrain any actual or apprehended breach of listed building control, they may seek an injunction under s. 44A LBA 1990. This is so whether or not they have exercised, or are proposing to exercise, any of their other powers under LBA 1990. An example of a case where an injunction may be appropriate is the case of *Derby City Council v Anthony.*[113] Here the local planning authority sought an injunction to prevent an owner from demolishing a listed building before his application for consent to demolish the building had been determined. The owner was of the view that the building was in danger of imminent collapse; the local planning authority disagreed and considered that the security measures that they had specified in an urgent works notice met safety concerns. The court granted the injunction—there was no urgent need on the grounds of risk to the public to demolish the building.

Compensation

16.79 Refusal of listed building consent or the imposition of conditions may cause the owner of the building substantial loss in the sense of preventing him realizing some development value. Whereas there has never been any general right of compensation for such decisions, the Listed Buildings Act as originally enacted provided for a very limited right of compensation if certain conditions were satisfied.[114] Thus the claimant had to show that the value of his interest had been diminished by a decision of the Secretary of State (on appeal or on a called in application) to refuse or conditionally grant listed building consent for the proposed extension or alteration of a listed building. The proposed works must not have constituted development or must have been permitted development.[115]

---

[112] *Braun v Secretary of State for Transport, Local Government and the Regions* [2003] EWCA Civ 655.

[113] [2008] EWHC 895.

[114] LBA 1990, s. 27, now repealed. It was this right to compensation that was at issue in *Shimizu (UK) Ltd v Westminster City Council* [1997] JPL 523, see para 16.39.

[115] For permission by development order, see para 7.01.

The Planning and Compensation Act 1991, Schedule 19, repealed this right to compensation. **16.80**

Purchase notice

16.81 The refusal of listed building consent may render the land incapable of reasonably beneficial use. In such circumstances the owner may be able to serve a 'listed building purchase notice' on the planning authority. This procedure is available where listed building consent has been refused or granted subject to conditions or revoked or modified, and the owner claims that the following conditions are satisfied:[116]

(a) that the land has become incapable of reasonably beneficial use in its existing state;[117]
(b) if consent was granted subject to conditions (or modified by the imposition of conditions) that the land cannot be rendered capable of reasonably beneficial use by carrying out the works in accordance with these conditions;
(c) in any case (ie whether consent was refused or granted subject to conditions or revoked or modified) that the land cannot be rendered capable of reasonably beneficial use by carrying out any other works for which listed building consent has been granted or for which the local planning authority or the Secretary of State has undertaken to grant consent.

16.82 The procedure for the service of such purchase notices and the powers of the Secretary of State are similar to those for purchase notices in connection with refusal of planning permission.[118]

Building preservation notice (BPN)

16.83 A building preservation notice may be served to protect a building which is considered to be of special architectural or historic interest but which has not yet been listed as such and is in danger of being demolished or altered.[119] The notice remains in force for a maximum period of six months,[120] and whilst it is in force the building is protected in the same way as if it had been listed.[121]

16.84 Before serving the notice the local planning authority must request the Secretary of State to consider the listing of the building. They then serve notice on the owner and occupier explaining the position.[122] In case of urgency they may

116 LBA 1990, s. 32.
117 For the significance of this phrase, see para 14.04.
118 See para 14.27.
119 LBA 1990, s. 3(1).
120 LBA 1990, s. 3(3).
121 LBA 1990, s. 3(5).
122 LBA 1990, s. 3(2).

affix a notice to the building itself instead of serving notice on the owner and occupier.[123]

16.85 The notice ceases to have effect as soon as the Secretary of State decides to list the building or tells the local planning authority that he does not intend to list it. If he does not reach a decision within six months the notice automatically lapses.[124]

16.86 Application for listed building consent may be made whilst the building preservation notice is in force.

16.87 If the Secretary of State decides not to list the building or allows the building preservation notice to lapse, the local planning authority are liable for compensation in respect of loss or damage directly attributable to the making of the building preservation notice, and it is specifically provided that this compensation shall include damages payable for breaches of contract caused by the necessity of discontinuing or countermanding works to the building.[125]

Repair and acquisition of listed buildings

16.88 The listing of a building does not impose any direct obligation on the owners or occupiers for the repair of the building. But the Secretary of State and the local planning authority have two remedies if the building falls in to disrepair. First, s. 54 of the Listed Buildings Act[126] enables the local planning authority to take emergency action where a listed building is wholly or partly unoccupied and is in urgent need of repair; in such a case the authority can enter the building after giving seven days' notice[127] to the owner[128] and themselves carry out the necessary work.[129] The authority may subsequently serve notice on the owner to recover the cost; the owner may appeal against this notice to the Secretary of State on a number of grounds including hardship.

---

123 LBA 1990, s. 4.

124 LBA 1990, s. 3(3), (4).

125 LBA 1990, s. 29. It seems that loss or damage is not limited to what could reasonably have been foreseen but may include any loss or damage which is directly attributable to the building preservation notice: *Sample (Warkworth) Ltd v Alnwick District Council* [1984] JPL 670.

126 In London English Heritage has concurrent powers with the London borough council: LBA 1990, s. 54(7).

127 The notice must specify the works which the authority intend to carry out: LBA 1990, s. 54(6). It seems that the purpose of giving seven days' notice is to enable the owner to discuss the matter with the local authority and perhaps to volunteer to do the work for himself: *R v Secretary of State for the Environment, ex p Hampshire County Council* (1980) 44 P & CR 343, [1981] JPL 47 at 48, per Donaldson LJ.

128 The word 'owner' has the same meaning as in the TCPA 1990, s. 336: LBA 1990, s. 91(2). See para 14.23.

129 But only to the unoccupied parts: LBA 1990, s. 54(4).

16.89 In *R v Secretary of State for Wales, ex p Swansea City Council,*[130] the council issued a notice under LBA 1990, s. 54. The owner appealed to the Secretary of State claiming that the works were unnecessary and the amount unreasonable. The Secretary of State took the view that it was a prerequisite to the recovery of expenses that the works to which they related had to be definable as 'urgent works' for the purposes of LBA 1990, s. 54. The council applied to the High Court contending that expenses incurred in respect of works which appeared to the authority to be urgently necessary, and which were subsequently determined by the Secretary of State to have been necessary, but not urgently necessary, were recoverable. Dyson J allowed the application.

16.90 The Secretary of State has power to take action to secure the repair of any listed building[131] which is unoccupied and which is in urgent need of repair. In England (as distinct from Wales) he will authorize English Heritage to do the work.[132]

16.91 Secondly, where a listed building (whether occupied or unoccupied) is not kept in a reasonable state of preservation, either the Secretary of State, or a local authority may, under s. 47 of the Listed Buildings Act, acquire the building by compulsory purchase, together with any adjacent buildings required for preserving the listed building.[133] The power of compulsory purchase does not extend to ecclesiastical buildings exempt from control or to ancient monuments.[134]

16.92 Before starting the compulsory purchase the Secretary of State or the local authority must have served, at least two months previously, a repairs notice on the owner[135] of the building specifying the works considered necessary for the proper preservation of the building.[136] The notice does not impose any obligation on the owner to carry out the specified works, and it is presumably for this reason that there is no statutory provision for challenging it; the notice has been described as the 'harbinger of a compulsory purchase order and a useful checklist for the Secretary of State when he had to decide under s. 114 [of the Act of 1971] whether or not reasonable steps had been taken for the proper preservation of the building and thus whether he should confirm a compulsory purchase order'.[137] The Act does not expressly state that neither the Secretary of State nor the authority can proceed with compulsory purchase if the repairs are carried out, but it is submitted that this is the case.

130 [1999] JPL 524.
131 LBA 1990, s. 54(2).
132 LBA 1990, s. 54(2)(a).
133 LBA 1990, s. 47(7).
134 LBA 1990, ss. 60, 61. See para 16.47.
135 The word 'owner' has the meaning given by the TCPA 1990, s. 336.
136 LBA 1990, s. 48.
137 *Robbins v Secretary of State for the Environment* [1988] JPL 824, CA, per Glidewell LJ.

16.93 Where a local planning authority draw up a repairs notice they must specify only such works as are reasonably necessary for the preservation of the building; and in deciding whether to confirm a compulsory purchase order, the Secretary of State must consider whether the items specified in the repairs notice form a proper basis for a compulsory purchase order. In *Robbins v Secretary of State for the Environment*,[138] the House of Lords held that the relevant date for determining what works were required for the preservation of a listed building was not the date of the repairs notice, but the date that the building was listed. Their Lordships also held that even where the notice went further than the Act allowed, and required some element of restoration, as opposed to repair, it was not necessarily invalid. Further, it seems that the means of the owner are not relevant in specifying what works are reasonably necessary for the proper preservation of the building.[139]

16.94 In making a compulsory purchase order, the Secretary of State or the authority must go through the procedure laid down in the Acquisition of Land Act 1981, and the owner and any lessees will have the usual right of objection under that Act.[140] In addition there is a right of appeal to the magistrates on the ground that reasonable steps are being taken for properly preserving the building; if the magistrates are satisfied on this point, any further proceedings on the compulsory purchase order will be stayed.[141]

16.95 There are two bases of compensation for the compulsory acquisition of a listed building. Under what may be called the standard basis, it may be assumed for the purpose of assessing compensation that listed building consent would be granted[142] for (a) the alteration or extension of the building; or (b) the demolition of the building for the purpose of carrying out any development specified in TCPA 1990, Schedule 3, Part I.[143] This standard basis applies to any compulsory purchase of a listed building whether under LBA 1990, s. 47 or some other statutory powers.

16.96 These provisions place the owner of a listed building in a less favourable position than other owners whose land is compulsorily acquired. Of course the owner of a listed building need not ask for compensation to be assessed on the basis of assumptions about demolition and redevelopment; he can claim if he wishes the value of his building as it stands.

16.97 There is also a penal basis of compensation. The amount of compensation will be reduced where the building has been deliberately allowed to fall into disrepair for

138 [1989] 1 All ER 878, [1989] 1 WLR 201.

139 *Rolf v North Shropshire District Council* [1988] JPL 103. In this case the notice required works costing over £250,000.

140 LBA 1990, s. 47(2).

141 LBA 1990, s. 47(4).

142 LBA 1990, s. 49.

143 Schedule 3 development is explained at para 21.20.

the purpose of justifying its demolition and the redevelopment of the site or any adjoining land. In these circumstances the acquiring authority may include in the compulsory purchase order a 'direction for minimum compensation'. There is a right of appeal to the magistrates, who may quash the direction for minimum compensation. In any event the Secretary of State must be satisfied that the direction is justified. Where a direction for minimum compensation is confirmed, it is to be assumed in assessing compensation that planning permission would not be granted for development of the site and that listed building consent would not be granted for demolition or alteration of the building. This penal basis of compensation can only be applied to compulsory purchase under LBA 1990, s. 47.[144]

Conservation areas

16.98 Conservation areas are a more recent innovation. Prior to 1967, the emphasis was on the preservation of individual buildings as distinct from areas. Of course, under general planning powers, the local planning authority might, when considering an application for planning permission, consider the effect of the proposed development on the character of the surrounding area, and it would be wrong to belittle what has been done by many authorities to prevent unsuitable developments. But until 1967 no positive duty had been laid upon local planning authorities to take specific steps to safeguard the character of areas of special architectural or historic interest.

16.99 The Civic Amenities Act 1967 imposed such a duty for the first time; local planning authorities were required to determine which parts of their areas were of special architectural or historic interest, the character or appearance of which it was desirable to preserve or enhance, and to designate such areas as conservation areas. The relevant provisions of the Civic Amenities Act have been considerably extended over the years. The legislation is now contained in the Listed Buildings Act.

Designation of conservation areas

16.100 It is the duty of the local planning authority to determine from time to time which parts of their area should be treated as conservation areas.[145] In non-metropolitan areas the local planning authority for this purpose is the district council or unitary

144 LBA 1990, s. 50.

145 LBA 1990, s. 69(1). The decision to designate may be challenged by judicial review: *R v Canterbury City Council, ex p Halford* [1992] JPL 851. See also *R v Swansea City Council, ex p Elitestone Ltd* [1993] JPL 1019; and *R v Surrey County Council, ex p Oakimber* [1995] EGCS 120 where the designations were upheld. For a case where the designation was quashed, see *R (on the application of Arndale Properties Ltd) v Worcester City Council* [2008] EWHC 678.

council, but a county council may also designate conservation areas. In Greater London, English Heritage has concurrent powers with the London borough council.[146] The Secretary of State may also designate conservation areas but will probably do so only in exceptional cases.[147] It is also the duty of the local planning authority from time to time to review the past exercise of their functions in this respect and to consider whether new areas should be designated.[148]

16.101 The procedure for the designation of a conservation area is comparatively simple. The local planning authority determine—presumably by resolution of the council—that a specified area is a conservation area.[149] The Secretary of State's approval is not required, but the local planning authority must give him formal notice of the designation of any area as a conservation area, and they must publish notice in the *London Gazette* and the local press;[150] notice must also be entered in the local land charges register.[151] There are no provisions for the making of objections or representations at this stage by interested parties.[152] It seems that the local planning authority may subsequently cancel the designation of an area as a conservation area.[153]

16.102 Although there is no statutory requirement to this effect, local planning authorities have been recommended to establish conservation area committees and many authorities have done so; these committees are advisory to the authority, and the intention is that they should mainly consist of people who are not members of the council.[154]

The consequences of designation

16.103 The designation of a conservation area has a number of direct legalconsequences: the local planning authority must prepare a conservation area plan; there are special procedures for applications for planning permission, control of demolition of buildings, and felling of trees, and possible stricter controls over outdoor advertising. These matters are discussed later in this chapter. In addition LBA 1990, s. 72 provides that special attention shall be paid to the desirability of preserving

---

146 LBA 1990, s. 70(1).

147 LBA 1990, s. 69(3).

148 LBA 1990, s. 69(2).

149 LBA 1990, s. 69(1). In London, English Heritage also has power to designate conservation areas, but must first consult the London borough councils: LBA 1990, s. 70(1), (2).

150 LBA 1990, s. 70(5), (8). In England (as distinct from Wales) notice must also be given to English Heritage.

151 LBA 1990, s. 69(2).

152 See, however, the provisions mentioned below for the calling of a public meeting to consider the local planning authority's detailed proposals for safeguarding and enhancing the conservation area.

153 LBA 1990, s. 70(5).

154 See PPG 15, para 4.13.

or enhancing the character or appearance of the conservation area in the exercise, with respect to any buildings or other land in the area, of any powers under the Listed Buildings Act and some other legislation. The importance of this section was highlighted by the decision of the High Court in *Steinberg v Secretary of State for the Environment*.[155]

16.104 The local planning authority had refused planning permission for the erection of a dwellinghouse on a small piece of unused, derelict, and overgrown land in a conservation area. On appeal, the inspector identified as one of the main issues 'whether the proposed development would harm the character of the conservation area'. On this issue the inspector considered that the condition of the site detracted considerably from both the residential amenity and the visual character of the locality. The inspector allowed the appeal.

16.105 Two members of a neighbourhood association applied to the High Court to set aside that decision. Mr Lionel Read QC, sitting as deputy judge, held that the inspector had misdirected himself on a point of law. There was, said the learned deputy judge, a world of difference between the issue which the inspector had identified for himself—whether the proposed development would 'harm' the character of the conservation area—and the need to pay special attention to the desirability of preserving or enhancing the character or appearance of the area. The concept of avoiding harm was essentially negative. The underlying purpose of what is now s. 72 seemed to be essentially positive. The case was remitted to the Secretary of State.

16.106 The judgment was important because it emphasized the positive nature of the duty imposed by LBA 1990, s. 72 on the Secretary of State and local planning authorities to pay special attention to the desirability of preserving or enhancing the character or appearance of the conservation area.

16.107 The *Steinberg* ruling was followed in a number of cases[156] before the question came before the Court of Appeal in *Bath Society v Secretary of State for the Environment*[157] where Glidewell LJ sought to lay down some authoritative guidance as to the application of LBA 1990, s. 72. He held (1) that where a development proposal was in a conservation area, there were two statutory duties for the decision maker to perform; that imposed by LBA 1990, s. 72 as well as the duty to have regard to the development plan and any other material considerations; (2) the requirement to pay 'special attention' in LBA 1990, s. 72 should be the first consideration for the decision maker and it carried considerable importance and

155 [1989] JPL 258.

156 See eg *Harrow London Borough Council v Secretary of State for the Environment* [1991] JPL 137; *Ward v Secretary of State for the Environment* [1990] JPL 347.

157 [1991] JPL 663.

weight; (3) if the decision maker decided that the proposal would neither preserve nor enhance the character or appearance of the conservation area, then it would almost inevitably mean that it would have some detrimental, ie harmful effect. This would not necessarily mean that the application must be refused but it did mean, in the view of Glidewell LJ, that the development should only be permitted if it carried some advantage which outweighed the failure to satisfy the test under LBA 1990, s. 72.

16.108 The proposition at (3) above was not accepted by the Court of Appeal in *South Lakeland District Council v Secretary of State for the Environment*[158] since it appeared to ignore the possibility of a neutral proposal, ie one which was neither positive nor negative but which might still be said to preserve the character or appearance of the conservation area. Mann LJ said that 'the statutorily desirable object of preserving the character or appearance of an area was achieved either by a positive contribution to preservation or by development which left character or appearance unharmed, that is to say preserved'. These words were approved by the House of Lords;[159] Lord Bridge said:

> . . . where a particular development will not . . . where a particular development will not have any adverse effect on the character or appearance of the area and is otherwise unobjectionable on planning grounds, one may ask rhetorically what possible planning reason there can be for refusing to allow it. All building development must involve change and if the objective of [LBA 1990, s. 72] were to inhibit any building development in a conservation area which was not either a development by way of reinstatement or restoration on the one hand (positive preservation) or a development which positively enhanced the character or appearance of the area on the other hand, it would surely have been expressed in very different language from that which the draftsman has used.

16.109 It should be noted, however, that the cases discussed above were decided before TCPA 1990, s. 54A came into force.[160] In addition to the two statutory duties to which Glidewell LJ referred in the *Bath Society* case,[161] there is now a third, ie that the determination should be made in accordance with the development plan unless material considerations indicate otherwise. This was affirmed by David Keene QC, sitting as deputy judge, in *Heatherington (UK) Ltd v Secretary of State for the Environment*.[162] The decision related to LBA 1990, s. 66(1) although it would apply equally to s. 72.

---

158 [1991] JPL 654.

159 *South Lakeland District Council v Secretary of State for the Environment* [1992] 2 AC 141, [1992] 1 All ER 573.

160 See para 8.57.

161 See para 16.107.

162 [1995] JPL 228. And see *St Albans District Council v Secretary of State for the Environment* [1993] JPL 374.

16.110 In *Historic Buildings and Monuments Commission v Secretary of State for the Environment*,[163] English Heritage sought to challenge a decision of the Secretary of State that a uPVC plastic front door was in keeping with the character and appearance of a conservation area—the historic town of Wirksworth in Derbyshire. Counsel for English Heritage argued that the Secretary of State's inspector had not taken account of the planning history of the site and had set a dangerous precedent.

16.111 Dismissing these arguments, Gerald Moriarty QC, sitting as deputy judge, held that the inspector's decision was reasonable and within his planning judgment. It made no difference that the area was one where an Article 4 direction[164] had been made. Having found the development not to be harmful, the inspector did not consider that the question of precedent arose. The learned deputy judge concluded that even if it did arise, it 'was certainly a very trivial matter'.

Conservation area plan

16.112 The local planning authority are required to prepare proposals for the preservation and enhancement of the character and appearance of the conservation area.[165] This requirement was introduced by the Act of 1974 and, it is submitted, applies to conservation areas designated before the passing of that Act as well as to new conservation areas.

16.113 The proposals must be published and submitted to a public meeting in the area concerned; and, before finalizing the proposals the local planning authority must have regard to any views expressed by persons attending that meeting.[166]

16.114 The proposals put forward by the local planning authority are likely to involve the use of various powers under the Planning Acts, eg listing of buildings of special architectural or historic interest, the making of article 4(1) or 4(2) directions to restrict permitted development,[167] and the making of discontinuance orders to remove or modify non-conforming uses.[168]

163 [1997] JPL 424.
164 See para 7.60.
165 LBA 1990, s. 71(1).
166 LBA 1990, s. 71(2), (3).
167 See para 7.63.By circular 1/01, this obligation is restricted to development affecting a conservation area where the area to which the application relates exceeds 1,000 square metres, or the construction of any building more than 20 metres in height above ground level.
168 See para 11.15.

Control of development

16.115 Designation of an area as a conservation area does not preclude the possibility of new development within the area; what is important is that new developments should be designed in a sensitive manner having regard to the special character of the area. LBA 1990, s. 73 requires the local planning authority to advertise applications for planning permission for any new development which is likely to affect the character or appearance of a conservation area; it is for the local planning authority to decide whether the development would be of such a character and thus whether to advertise the application or not. The advertisement will take the form of a notice in the local press and the display of a notice on or near to the land to which the application relates. The public will then have the right to inspect the details of the application and to make representations to the local planning authority. In England (as distinct from Wales) the local planning authority must also send a copy of the notice to English Heritage.[169] When considering the application, the local planning authority must pay special attention to the desirability of preserving or enhancing the character or appearance of the area.[170]

16.116 Article 4(2) of the General Permitted Development Order 1995[171] gives local planning authorities enhanced powers to restrict, selectively, certain permitted development rights in conservation areas where the development would front a 'relevant location', that is, a highway, waterway, or open space.

16.117 The rights in question include: the enlargement, improvement or other alteration of a dwellinghouse; the alteration of a dwellinghouse roof; the erection of dwellinghouse porches and a number of other rights falling under Parts 1 and 2 of Schedule 2; also Class B of Part 31 of that Schedule (demolition of the whole or any part of any gate, fence, wall, or other means of enclosure) where the gate, etc is within the curtilage of a dwellinghouse.

16.118 The Secretary of State's approval is not required for an article 4(2) direction; however the order prescribes a procedure[172] whereby local residents must be notified by the authority and their representations taken into account in deciding whether or not to confirm the direction.

Control of demolition

16.119 The local planning authority may well see fit to protect some of the buildings in a conservation area by listing them as being of special architectural or historic

169 LBA 1990, s. 67(3) applied by s. 73(1).
170 See para 16.103.
171 See para 7.63.
172 GPDO, art 6.

interest under LBA 1990, s. 1.[173] There will, however, be many buildings in a conservation area which do not merit listing, but their demolition might detrimentally affect the general appearance of the conservation area. LBA 1990, ss. 74 and 75 prohibit (with some exceptions) the demolition of any building in a conservation area without special consent. For the purpose of controlling demolition, LBA 1990, s. 74 applies many of the provisions of the Listed Buildings Act relating to listed buildings, and until 1987 consent to demolish an unlisted building in a conservation area was known as listed building consent; it has now been re-named 'conservation area consent'. LBA 1990, s. 74 does not apparently extend to works of alteration. In an earlier edition of this book it was stated that LBA 1990, s. 74 probably prohibited partial demolition of a building in a conservation area without consent. But that view is no longer tenable as a result of the decision of the House of Lords in *Shimizu (UK) Ltd v Westminster City Council.*[174] It is clear now that consent would only be required for the total, or near total, demolition of an unlisted building in a conservation area.[175]

16.120 Many of the provisions relating to listed building consent apply to conservation area consent. Thus LBA 1990, s. 16(2), which requires the Secretary of State or the local planning authority to have special regard to the desirability of preserving the building or its setting,[176] will also apply to applications for conservation area consent to demolish an unlisted building. Moreover, as we have seen, there is always the duty imposed by LBA 1990, s. 72 to pay special attention to the desirability of preserving or enhancing the character or appearance of the area.[177] The effect of this was illustrated in *Richmond-upon-Thames London Borough Council v Secretary of State for the Environment,*[178] where the Secretary of State had refused consent to demolish an unlisted building on the ground that the proposed new building would intrude to an unacceptable degree into the conservation area; the High Court upheld the Secretary of State's decision: the function described in what is now LBA 1990, s. 72 could not be performed without seeing what was to be substituted and how it would fit into the conservation area.

16.121 Where consent is granted for demolition, the local planning authority may impose a condition that demolition shall not take place until a contract for carrying out works of redevelopment has been made, and planning permission has been granted for the redevelopment for which the contract provides.[179]

173 See para 16.06.
174 [1997] JPL 523. See para 16.39.
175 In 2001, the Government announced its intention to reverse, by legislative amendment, the *Shimizu* ruling in so far as it relates to conservation areas.
176 See para 16.07.
177 See para 16.103.
178 [1979] JPL 175.
179 LBA 1990, s. 17(3) applied by s. 74(3).

16.122 The local planning authority have power to prosecute and to issue an enforcement notice for breach of LBA 1990, s. 74 as in the case of listed buildings.[180] If consent to demolish is refused, the owner may be able to serve a purchase notice.[181]

16.123 LBA 1990, s. 74 does not apply to ecclesiastical buildings exempt from control[182] or to ancient monuments. Furthermore the Secretary of State may make a direction exempting certain classes of building.[183] He has in fact made a direction exempting some 11 classes of building: these include, inter alia, small buildings of up to 115 cubic metres, and buildings which the owner is required to demolish as a result of a statutory order.[184]

Trees in conservation areas

16.124 Under TCPA 1990, s. 211 anyone who wishes to cut down, top, lop, uproot, wilfully damage, or wilfully destroy[185] any tree in a conservation area must give notice of intention to the local planning authority. The authority then have six weeks in which to consider making a tree preservation order. The person concerned must not proceed with his intentions during this period of six weeks unless the authority have given specific consent in the meantime.[186]

16.125 The Secretary of State has power to specify exemptions from TCPA 1990, s. 211. Some five cases are currently exempted by the Town and Country Planning (Trees) Regulations 1999.[187]

Advertisements in conservation areas

16.126 The Secretary of State may make special provision in the Advertisement Regulations with respect to advertisements in conservation areas. To date no special regulations have been made with respect to advertisements in conservation areas.[188] The local planning authority may ask the Secretary of State for an order designating the whole or part of a conservation area as an area of special control,[189] if they feel that there are compelling reasons.[190] To some extent, however, LBA 1990, s. 72 may result in a higher standard of control in conservation areas because,

---

180 See para 16.37.
181 See para 16.81.
182 See para 16.47.
183 LBA 1990, s 74(3).
184 Circular 01/01.
185 For 'wilful destruction' of a tree, see the account at 15.04 above, of *Barnet London Borough Council v Eastern Electricity Board* [1973] 2 All ER 319, [1973] 1 WLR 430.
186 TCPA 1990, s. 211(3).
187 SI 1999 No 1892.
188 For conservation areas (and certain other areas) the Advertisement Regulations require express consent for certain classes but these are exceptions to the general provisions—see para 15.58.
189 See para 15.76.
190 PPG 19, para 22.

in considering any application for express consent, the local planning authority must pay special attention to the desirability of preserving or enhancing the character or appearance of the area.

Historic assets: proposals for reform

16.127 In March 2007 the Government issued a White Paper on heritage protection, *Heritage Protection for the 21st Century*, which was followed by a Draft Heritage Protection Bill for parliamentary scrutiny. The Bill, if enacted, would replace LBA 1990 and a number of other statutes, including the Ancient Monuments and Archaeological Areas Act 1979.

16.128 The Bill would set up a single system of designation on a 'Heritage Register'—there is to be one register for England and one for Wales. This unified register would replace the listing of buildings, the scheduling of ancient monuments, and so forth, and would comprise heritage structures, heritage open spaces, World Heritage Sites, and marine heritage sites. The basis for including assets on the register is their 'special historic, archaeological, architectural or artistic interest'. The responsibility for maintaining the register in England would lie with English Heritage; in Wales it would lie with the Welsh Ministers to keep up the Welsh register. There is to be consultation before an asset is placed on the register. During the consultation period, the asset is provisionally placed on the register and there is a right of appeal to the Secretary of State.

16.129 Once placed on the register, 'historic asset consent' would be required for the demolition, damage, destruction, removal, repair, or any alteration or addition, or any flooding or tipping alterations, affecting the special interest of a heritage structure. All such applications are to be handled by local planning authorities.

16.130 Two comments may be pertinent. First, the notion that these measures will reduce the number of consents which must be obtained is more apparent than real in most cases. As pointed out by Nigel Hewitson,[191] works to a listed building which also involve development as defined in TCPA 1990, s. 55 currently require both planning permission and listed building consent. Under the proposed system in the Bill, two consents would also be required: planning permission and historic asset consent. Second, the regime in the Bill provides for much greater openness in the procedures surrounding the designation of the asset. This is to be welcomed.

---

191 [2008] JPL 930, at p. 937.

17

SPECIAL CASES

Crown land

17.01 It is a general rule of English law that the Crown is not bound by a statute unless the statute so provides, whether expressly or by necessary implication. However since it is possible for the Crown and private persons to hold interests in the same land, TCPA 1947 made express provision as to the immunity of Crown land. These provisions are contained in Part XIII of TCPA 1990.

17.02 Part 7 of PCPA 2004 abolishes the immunity traditionally enjoyed by the Crown in matters of planning control. Before examining the scope of this major reform, it is necessary to examine the position of Crown land under the original provisions of TCPA 1990 as the immunity was not entirely total and a number of arrangements were put into place to accommodate planning controls.

17.03 Under these provisions a government department did not require planning permission to carry out development on land in which they had an interest and no enforcement notice could be served on the department. Other persons having an interest in Crown land, such as a lease from the Crown Estates Commissioners, who wished to carry out development could apply for planning permission in the normal way; if the 'appropriate authority' agreed, an enforcement notice could be served. (The 'appropriate authority' is defined in TCPA 1990, s. 293(2) and means the particular government department which controls the land in question and certain other bodies including the Duchy of Lancaster and the Duchy of Cornwall, according to circumstances, with the Treasury deciding any disputed cases.)

17.04 Similarly, government departments did not require listed building consent to carry out works to listed buildings, and no listed building enforcement notice could be served on the department. Any other person having an interest in the land had to obtain listed building consent; and if the appropriate authority agreed, a listed building enforcement notice could be served on any such person.

17.05 Although government departments were exempt from planning control, they were expected to consult local planning authorities before carrying out major development. The arrangements for such consultation were set out in Circular 18/84, Memorandum, Part IV. Rather than submitting a planning application, the department in question would consult the local planning authority. The proposals would usually be given publicity in the same way as for private developments, and opportunity was given for representations by members of the public.

17.06 The local planning authority could not veto development by government departments; but, where there was disagreement, the matter could be referred to the Secretary of State, and he could hold a procedure resembling a public inquiry. Such inquiries have been held in the past into the use of land by service departments, and, because of the concerns of local residents, into proposals for prisons and mental health institutions.

17.07 All these arrangements were subject to modification where national security was involved.

Planning permission, etc in anticipation of disposal of Crown land

17.08 Although the Crown did not require planning permission for its own development and the owner of a private interest in Crown land could apply for planning permission, there was a special problem where the Crown wished to sell land for private development. This was originally dealt with by an informal procedure whereby the local planning authority gave an opinion as to whether planning permission would be granted if a formal application were made. But this procedure did not bind the local planning authority or the Secretary of State in the event of a subsequent application or appeal; and in so far as the procedure was effective it deprived local people in certain cases of the opportunity to make representations. Ultimately this procedure was held to be unlawful in *R v Worthing Borough Council, ex p Burch*[1] and, following this decision, the Town and Country Planning Act 1984 was passed. That Act enabled Crown land to be sold or leased with planning permission already granted under proper statutory procedures; the relevant provisions were later incorporated into the TCPA 1990 and the LBA 1990.

17.09 Under these provisions the appropriate authority on behalf of the Crown could make an application for planning permission, listed building consent, or conservation area consent. A planning permission granted by virtue of these provisions applied (a) to development carried out after the land ceased to be Crown land; (b) so long as the land remained Crown land to a development carried out by virtue of a private interest in the land. Listed building consents and conservation area consents also applied only after the land ceased to be Crown land or a new private interest had been created.

Special enforcement notices

17.10 As we have seen,[2] where a person owning a private interest in Crown land carries out unauthorized development, the local planning authority can issue an enforcement notice provided the appropriate authority agree. But unauthorized development might be carried out on Crown land when no person was entitled to occupy it by virtue of a private interest. The TCPA 1990 enabled the local planning authority with the consent of the appropriate authority to issue a 'special enforcement notice'. Copies of the notice had to be served on persons alleged to have carried out the development, on any person occupying the land when the notice was issued, and on the appropriate authority. There was a right of appeal to the Secretary of State but only on the grounds that the matters alleged in the notice had not taken place or did not constitute development.

Continuance of uses instituted by the Crown

17.11 Since the Crown was not subject to planning legislation, any use of land begun by the Crown could lawfully be continued by a third party such as a purchaser of the land. TCPA 1990 enabled a local planning authority and the appropriate authority to enter into an agreement whereby a use of land instituted by the Crown was deemed to have been authorized by a planning permission granted subject to a condition requiring its discontinuance when the Crown ceased that use. The effect was that planning permission was normally required for the continuance of the use by anyone other than the Crown.

---

1 [1984] JPL 261.
2 See para 17.03.

Crown land: abolition of Crown immunity

17.12 The abolition of Crown immunity began some 18 years ago when, under the National Health Service and Community Care Act 1990, s. 60. Crown immunity for planning purposes was removed from health authorities as from 1 April 1991. Until then all the land and buildings of the NHS were vested in the Department of Health and were thus 'Crown land'.

17.13 In 1992 the Government announced that it was appropriate to bring Crown exemption under the planning system largely to an end. It was proposed that all Crown bodies should be required to apply to the local planning authority for planning permission, listed building consent, and hazardous substances consent in the normal way. There would be limited exemptions to this, principally where national or prison security were involved, or for trunk road proposals which were already subject to statutory procedures equivalent to planning procedures. No suitable opportunity for introducing the legislation arose in the intervening years; in fact the provisions relating to the abolition of Crown immunity were not in the Planning and Compulsory Purchase Bill as originally introduced into Parliament. The provisions were introduced by the Government at a much later stage.

17.14 Under PCPA 2004 'Crown land' is defined as land in which there is a Crown interest or a Duchy interest. However the definition of 'Crown interest' has been amended so as to exclude the reference to interests belonging to HM in right of the Crown or to a government department or held on trust for HM for the purposes of a government department.[3]

17.15 PCPA 2004 inserted a new s. 292A into TCPA 1990 which states that, subject to certain express provisions, TCPA 1990 binds the Crown. The PCPA 2004 also binds the Crown.[4] The PA 2008, s. 226 provides that the 2008 Act itself binds the Crown, subject to special provisions as specified. The express provision made in certain cases is discussed below.

National security

17.16 PCPA 2004, s. 80 amends s. 321 of TCPA 1990 and inserts a new s. 321A into that Act, relating to matters of national security in planning inquiries.

[3] TCPA 1990, s. 293 as amended by PCPA 2004, s. 79(4), Sch 3, para 6(1) and (2).

[4] Except Part 8—PCPA 2004, s. 111. The provisions came into force as from 7 June 2006. All relevant existing delegated legislation was applied to the Crown (with modifications) by the T & CP (Application of Subordinate Legislation to the Crown) Order 2006, SI 2006 No 1282.

17.17 In general, oral evidence in planning inquiries is heard in public and documentary evidence is open to public inspection.[5] However if the Secretary of State is satisfied that the public disclosure of information in a particular case would be contrary to the national interest, he may direct that the giving of evidence, etc may be restricted to such persons as he may specify.[6] But he may only do this in matters of (a) national security; and (b) the security of any premises or property.

17.18 The amendment made by PCPA 2004 provides that if the Secretary of State is considering giving such a direction as mentioned above regarding the national interest, the Attorney-General may appoint a person to represent the interests of any person who will be prevented from hearing or inspecting any evidence at the inquiry if the direction is given.[7] The Lord Chancellor may make rules as to the procedure to be followed before such a direction is given and as to the functions of the person to be appointed in such cases.

17.19 The above-mentioned provisions are also applied to inquiries relating to listed buildings and conservation areas;[8] and to inquiries under P(HS)A 1990.[9] By virtue of s. 81 of PCPA 2004, the provisions are adapted to Wales.

Urgent Crown development

17.20 PCPA 2004, s. 82(1) inserted a new provision[10] into the TCPA 1990 which applies if the appropriate authority certifies that development is of national importance and it is necessary that the development is carried out as a matter of urgency. In such a case the appropriate authority may, instead of applying for planning permission to the local planning authority, apply for such permission to the Secretary of State.

17.21 If the appropriate authority proposes to submit an application to the Secretary of State, it must publish in the local press a notice describing the proposed development, and stating that the authority proposes to submit the application to the Secretary of State.[11]

17.22 The appropriate authority must provide the Secretary of State with the documents necessary to assess the environmental effects as required by a normal planning application to which EIA[12] applies; and a statement of the authority's

---

5 TCPA 1990, s. 321(2).
6 Ibid, s. 321(3)(a) and (b).
7 Ibid, s. 321(5) as inserted by PCPA 2004, s. 80. See the Planning (National Security Directions and Appointed Representatives) (England) Rules 2006, SI 2006 No 1284.
8 LBA 1990, Sch 3, para 6A as inserted by PCPA 2004, s. 80(3).
9 HSA 1990, Sch, para 6A as inserted by PCPA 2004, s. 80(4).
10 TCPA 1990, s. 293A.
11 Ibid, s. 293A(3).
12 For EIA, See para 9.01.

grounds for making the application.[13] The Secretary of State may require the authority to provide him with such further information as he thinks necessary to enable him to come to a decision on the application.[14]

17.23 As soon as the Secretary of State receives the documents and other matters to which reference was made above, he must make copies available in the locality of the proposed development. (However this requirement does not apply to the extent that the document or other matter is subject to a direction under s. 321(3) of TCPA 1990, ie that public disclosure of the information would be contrary to the national interest.)[15] The Secretary of State must consult the local planning authority for the area and such other persons as specified by development order.[16]

17.24 In many respects an application under s. 329A of TCPA 1990 resembles a called in application under s. 77 of the Act;[17] thus the Secretary of State must have regard to the development plan, so far as material, and to any other material considerations.[18]

Urgent works relating to Crown land

17.25 PCPA 2004, s. 83 introduces similar provisions as discussed above (regarding urgent Crown development) for applications relating to works 'proposed to be executed in connection with any building which is on Crown land'.[19] This provision is wide enough to cover works proposed to be carried out by persons other than the Crown and the works in question need not necessarily be on Crown land.

Enforcement of planning control

17.26 Under the old regime enforcement proceedings could only be brought against the Crown with the consent of the appropriate authority. However s. 84 of PCPA 2004 inserts a new s. 296A into the TCPA 1990 which amends the position in that consent is no longer required for the service of an enforcement notice or stop notice.[20] Consent is, however, required for the taking of certain steps, ie entering the land, bringing proceedings, and the making of an application.[21] But there will be no criminal liability in connection with enforcement—the Act provides that 'no act or omission done or suffered by or on behalf of the Crown constitutes an offence'.[22]

---

13 TCPA 1990, s. 293(4)(a) and (b).
14 Ibid, s. 293A(6).
15 See para 17.16.
16 TCPA 1990, s. 293A(6)–(10).
17 See para 8.36.
18 TCPA 1990, s. 293A(11).
19 LBA 1990, s. 82B as inserted by PCPA 2004, s. 83.
20 TCPA 1990, s. 296A(6) as inserted by PCPA 2004, s. 84.
21 Ibid, s. 296A(5) as inserted by PCPA 2004, s. 84.
22 Ibid, s. 296A(1) as inserted by PCPA 2004, s. 84.

PCPA 2004 makes similar provision regarding listed buildings[23] and also hazardous substances.[24]

17.27 The enforcement of planning control is considered in chapter 12 above.

Tree preservation orders: forestry commissioners

17.28 Although the Forestry Commission is an emanation of the Crown, s. 85 PCPA 2004 substitutes a new s. 200 in TCPA 1990 which provides that the Forestry Commission will not be bound by a tree preservation order on their land, or on land placed at their disposal under the Forestry Act 1967; nor in respect of anything done in accordance with a plan of operations approved under a forestry dedication covenant within s. 5 of the Forestry Act 1967 or the conditions of a grant or loan made under s. 1 of the same Act.[25]

17.29 Controls exercised by the Forestry Commission over tree felling are discussed in chapter 15.[26]

Trees in conservation areas

17.30 Controls relating to trees in conservation areas are discussed in chapter 16.[27] It may be recalled that occupiers intending to fell or carry out certain other acts to a tree in a conservation area must notify the local planning authority who then have six weeks in which to consider making a tree preservation order. If the authority do not respond, the work does not require consent providing it is undertaken after the end of the six-week period and within two years. PCPA 2004, s. 86, amending s. 211 of TCPA 1990, places the Crown in the same position as any other occupier with regard to these controls.

Old mining permissions

17.31 Old mining permissions are discussed later in this chapter.[28] Originally the Crown was not required to register old mining permissions on its land as it was not subject to the PCA 1991 (which introduced the registration of old mining permissions regime). However s. 87 of PCPA 2004 applies the 1991 Act regime to Crown land by requiring registration before the date of commencement of s. 87(2) PCPA 2004.

---

23 LBA 1990, s. 82D as inserted by PCPA 2004, s. 84.
24 P(HS)A 1990, s. 30C as inserted by PCPA 2004, s. 84.
25 TCPA 2004, s. 200(1) and (2) as inserted by PCPA 2004, s. 85.
26 See para 15.15.
27 See para 16.124.
28 See para 17.72.

Purchase notices

17.32 Purchase notices are considered in chapter 14;[29] and listed building purchase notices in chapter 16.[30]

17.33 Under Schedule 3, para 1 of PCPA 2004 the Crown may serve a purchase notice.[31] The owner of a private interest in Crown land may also serve a purchase notice, but only if he first offers to dispose of his interest to the appropriate authority on equivalent terms, and the offer is refused by the appropriate authority. An offer is made on equivalent terms if the price payable for the interest is equal to the compensation which would be payable in respect of it if it were acquired in pursuance of a purchase notice.[32]

17.34 PCPA 2004, Schedule 3, para 2 makes corresponding provision with regard to listed building enforcement notices.[33]

Compulsory purchase

17.35 Compulsory purchase for planning purposes is discussed in chapter 3[34] and compulsory purchase in connection with the failure to repair listed buildings is considered in chapter 16.[35]

17.36 Under Schedule 3, paras 3 and 4 of PCPA 2004 Crown land becomes subject to compulsory acquisition but only if the appropriate authority agree to the acquisition.[36] PCPA 2004, Schedule 3, para 5 makes equivalent provision with regard to the compulsory purchase of listed buildings in need of repair.[37]

Applications for planning permission

17.37 Crown applications for planning permission before the coming into force of Part 7 of PCPA 2004 were considered earlier in this chapter.[38] PCPA 2004, Schedule 3, para 10 (which applies also to applications for CLOPUDs)[39] enables the Secretary of State to make regulations amending the previous provisions

---

29 See para 14.01.
30 See para 16.81.
31 Inserting a new s. 137A into the TCPA 1990.
32 TCPA 1990, s. 137A(4).
33 Inserting a new s. 32A into the LBA 1990.
34 See para 3.51.
35 See para 16.93.
36 Inserting a new s. 288(1A) into the TCPA 1990.
37 Inserting a new s. 47(6A) into the LBA 1990.
38 See para 17.01.
39 See para 6.179.

relating to the making and determination of such applications.[40] There are transitional provisions in Schedule 4 of PCPA 2004.

17.38 PCPA 2004, Schedule 3, para 11 makes equivalent provision for Crown applications for listed building or conservation area consent;[41] and para 12 makes like provision for applications for hazardous substances consent.[42]

Development by local authorities and statutory undertakers

17.39 Local authorities and statutory undertakers are subject to planning control and must therefore obtain planning permission for any development which they propose to carry out. But the system of planning control is modified in three special types of case: development by a local planning authority within their own area; development carried out on operational land by a statutory undertaker; and development by a local authority or statutory undertaker which requires the authorization of a government department.

Obtaining of planning permission by local planning authorities

17.40 TCPA 1990, s. 316 as originally enacted authorized the Secretary of State to make regulations governing the grant of planning permission for (a) development by the local planning authority of land within their area; (b) development by other persons of land owned by the local planning authority. The relevant procedures were introduced by the Town and Country Planning General Regulations of 1976; these procedures involved publicity and the passing of two resolutions. The Department of the Environment (as the ministry responsible for planning was then called) carried out a review of these procedures[43] and recommended a number of changes to the law with the object of ensuring fuller and more open debate about such development proposals and to increase public confidence in the accountability of local planning authorities.

17.41 Accordingly, PCA 1991, s. 20 substituted a new TCPA 1990, s. 316 and the Regulations of 1976 have been replaced by the General Regulations of 1992.[44] Under the new section an 'interested planning authority', in relation to any land, means any body which exercises any of the functions of a local planning authority in relation to that land; and for the purposes of the section, land is land of an authority if the authority have any interest in it.

40 Inserting a new s. 298A into the TCPA 1990.
41 Inserting a new s. 82F into the LBA 1990.
42 Inserting a new s. 31A into the P(HS)A 1990.
43 Reported at [1990] JPL 259.
44 Town and Country Planning General Regulations 1992, SI 1992 No 1492.

17.42 In essence these provisions make it clear that in general, TCPA 1990, Parts III,[45] VII[46] and VIII[47] will apply to land of interested planning authorities and its development by the authority or jointly with another person or by another person alone.[48] It means that applications by local planning authorities will be subject to the same statutory procedures, including publicity, as all other applications. Local planning authorities will be able to grant themselves planning permission for their own development proposals or for proposals to be carried out jointly with another person, unless the application is called in by the Secretary of State under TCPA 1990, s. 77.[49]

17.43 Where the proposal is for another party to develop land of an interested planning authority, and if it were not such land, the application would be determined by another body, the application must be determined by that body, unless called in by the Secretary of State.[50] Thus a county council wishing to dispose of school playing fields for residential development by a private developer will have to obtain planning permission from the district planning authority in whose area the land is situated.

17.44 Where a local planning authority grants itself permission, the application must not have been determined by a committee, sub-committee, or officer of the interested planning authority responsible for the management of any land or buildings to which the application relates.[51] The intention of this provision is to create a so-called 'Chinese Wall' within the authority.

17.45 The Regulations provide that a grant of planning permission by an interested planning authority shall enure only for the benefit of the applicant interested planning authority, except where the development is being carried out jointly with another person who is specified in the application as a joint developer. In such a case the permission shall enure for the benefit of the interested planning authority and the other person.[52]

17.46 In 1998 the Government made some amending regulations[53] which provide that the position stated in the above paragraph does not apply to a local planning authority that is the sole local planning authority for their area, eg a unitary

---

45 Development control; see chs 6–10 above.

46 Enforcement notices, stop notices, certificates of lawfulness; see ch 12 above.

47 Special controls, eg trees, advertisements etc; see ch 15 above.

48 TCPA 1990, s. 316, as substituted; General Regs, reg 2. For exceptions, see reg 2. And see Circular 19/92.

49 General Regs, reg 3. For called in applications, see para 8.36.

50 General Regs, reg 4.

51 General Regs, reg 10.

52 General Regs, reg 9.

53 Town and Country Planning General (Amendment) Regulations 1998, SI 1998 No 2800.

authority. Such authorities may now grant themselves planning permission which enures for the benefit of the land.

17.47 The procedures under the Regulations of 1976 were regarded by the courts as mandatory,[54] reflecting the considerable public disquiet concerning the development of local authority-owned land, particularly where the proposal was, say, for an out of town superstore which would be likely to have an impact on existing town centre businesses.

17.48 The procedures may have human rights implications. The matter arose in the well-known case of *R v Camden London Borough Council, ex p Cummins*,[55] where Ouseley J held that in granting planning permission for the development of their own land the local authority had not acted in a biased or predetermined manner. The application had been determined by Camden in full council, from which the General Regulations[56] did not require any interested councillor to be excluded. The councillors involved did not have a personal interest which would require them to be disqualified under the relevant code of practice and Ouseley J did not consider that they had acted with a closed mind or predetermined view.

17.49 There were also human rights considerations. The applicants further argued that: (a) Camden's determination of its own planning permission was a breach of a nearby resident's rights under article 6(1) ECHR[57] because the development would affect the views from her property; (b) the Secretary of State's refusal to call in the application was unlawful because article 6(1) could only be complied with by calling it in and having the factual disputes resolved by an inspector; and (c) the Secretary of State's policy of refusing to call in applications with only local importance, and the primary legislation preventing him from calling them in, were incompatible with article 6(1) of the Convention.

17.50 Ouseley J rejected the argument that the resident's civil rights were engaged or determined. There was no general property right to a view even if its obstruction reduced the value of the property in question. Significantly, however, the Court did not consider that the Secretary of State's refusal to call in the application was incompatible with article 6(1) which was complied with by the availability of judicial review.

---

54 *Steeples v Derbyshire County Council* [1984] 3 All ER 468, [1985] 1 WLR 256; see also *R v Lambeth Borough Council, ex p Sharp* (1984) 50 P & CR 284; *R v Sevenoaks District Council, ex p Terry* [1985] 3 All ER 226; and *R v Doncaster Metropolitan District Council, ex p British Railways Board* [1987] JPL 444.

55 [2002] EWHC 1116 (Admin).

56 See para 17.41.

57 See para 2.129.

Development by statutory undertakers

17.51 For the purposes of the TCPA 1990, the expression 'statutory undertaker' means 'persons authorised by any enactment to carry on any railway, light railway, tramway, road transport, water transport, canal, inland navigation, dock, harbour, pier or lighthouse undertaking, or any undertaking for the supply of hydraulic power and a relevant airport operator' (within the meaning of Part V of the Airports Act 1986).[58] A local authority may be a statutory undertaker; eg some local authorities provide public transport services and some are authorized to extend such services beyond their own boundaries.

17.52 Statutory undertakers who propose to carry out development must apply to the local planning authority for planning permission, but in relation to the operational land of statutory undertakers, some modifications are made by TCPA 1990, Part XI.

17.53 Under TCPA 1990 as originally enacted, if the application came before the Secretary of State (either because it was called in or on appeal against the decision of the local planning authority) the Secretary of State had to act jointly with the Minister responsible for the type of undertaking in question. In a reform made by PA 2008, s. 195, this will only apply, in England, where the Secretary of State or appropriate Minister so directs in relation to the relevant application or appeal.

Development requiring authorization of a government department

17.54 In many cases development by a local authority or statutory undertaker will require (apart from planning control) the authorization of a government department, eg the confirmation of a compulsory purchase order or consent for the borrowing of money. TCPA 1990, s. 90 enables the government department concerned to direct that planning permission shall be deemed to be granted. In practice, however, local authorities are expected to obtain planning permission by applying in the ordinary way.[59]

Minerals

17.55 As explained in an earlier chapter, the winning of minerals whether by underground or surface working constitutes development. As a physical operation, however, mineral working differs from other forms of development. In the erection of a building, for instance, the digging of foundations or the laying of bricks are only of value as part of the whole building; in mineral working,

---

58 TCPA 1990, s. 262(1).

59 See para 17.40.

however, the removal of each separate load is of value. As Lord Widgery CJ put it,[60] 'each shovelful or each cut by the bulldozer is a separate act of development'. Because of the special characteristics of mineral working, the Secretary of State is authorized to make regulations adapting and modifying the provisions of the TCPA 1990 in relation to mineral development.[61] The current regulations were made in 1995—they replace the Minerals Regulations of 1971.[62]

17.56 Another feature which distinguishes mineral working from other kinds of development is the physical damage to the land and the injury to the environment. The general power to impose conditions on the grant of planning permission has not always proved adequate to deal with the problems created by mineral working. As a result several new provisions were added to the TCPA 1971 by the Minerals Act 1981; these provisions are now to be found in the TCPA 1990.

17.57 The Planning and Compensation Act 1991, Schedule 1, applied the special provisions relating to mineral development discussed below to the deposit of mineral waste and in some instances to the deposit of refuse or waste materials generally. TCPA 1990, s. 336(1) (as amended) defines the 'depositing of mineral waste' as any process whereby a mineral working deposit is created or enlarged; the 'depositing of refuse or waste materials' includes the depositing of mineral waste.

Special provisions relating to mineral development

Mineral planning authorities

17.58 Many of the powers and duties of the local planning authority under the TCPA 1990 are exercisable in relation to minerals and mineral waste by the 'mineral planning authority', namely: (1) in a non-metropolitan county, the county planning authority or unitary authority; (2) in a metropolitan county or Greater London, the local planning authority, (3) in Wales, the local planning authority.[63]

Grant of temporary permission

17.59 TCPA 1990, s. 72 provides that, on a grant of planning permission, a condition may be imposed requiring the removal of a building or works or the discontinuance of any use of land at the expiration of a specified period. This provision does not apply to mineral workings or the deposit of mineral waste but is replaced by special provisions namely: (a) where the planning permission was granted before 22 February 1982, the development must cease not later than 60 years from that date; (b) in the case of a permission granted after that date, the development must

---

60 *Thomas David (Porthcawl) Ltd v Penybont RDC* [1972] 1 All ER 733, [1972] 1 WLR 354; affd [1972] 3 All ER 1092, 24 P & CR 309.

61 TCPA, s. 315.

62 Town and Country Planning (Minerals) Regs 1995, SI 1995 No 2863.

63 TCPA 1990, s. 1(4), (4B).

cease (unless some other period is specified) not later than 60 years from the date of the permission.[64]

Duration of planning permission

17.60 The normal rule has been that a grant of planning permission will lapse if development is not commenced within five years although that period was reduced to three years under PCPA 2004. This rule does not apply to a minerals permission granted or deemed to be granted subject to a condition that the development to which it related must be begun before the expiration of a specified period after the completion of other mineral development already being carried out by the applicant. For this purpose development is to be taken as having commenced on the earliest date on which any of the mining operations to which the planning permission relates began to be carried out.[65]

Aftercare conditions

17.61 Ever since the modern system of planning control was introduced in 1948, it has been standard practice of local planning authorities when granting permission for mineral workings to impose conditions relating to the restoration of the site after the minerals have been extracted. Since 1982 the mineral planning authority has had further powers; where planning permission is granted subject to a restoration condition, the authority may also impose an 'aftercare condition'. This is a condition requiring that such steps be taken as may be necessary to bring the land to the required standard for whichever of the following uses is specified in the condition: (1) use for agriculture, (2) use for forestry, (3) use for amenity. The condition may also specify an aftercare period during which the required steps are to be taken.[66]

Discontinuance orders

17.62 TCPA 1990, s. 102 enables a local planning authority to make a 'discontinuance order' in respect of any use of land, ie an order requiring a use of land to be discontinued, or imposing conditions on the continuance of the use, or requiring the removal or alteration of buildings, etc.[67] In relation to minerals and the deposit of refuse or waste materials, TCPA 1990, s. 102 enables the authority to make such an order in respect of mineral workings or waste disposal; such an order may include a restoration condition and an aftercare condition.[68] A discontinuance

64 TCPA 1990, Sch 5, para 1, as amended.
65 TCPA 1990, s. 91, as amended; Minerals Regs, reg 3.
66 TCPA 1990, Sch 5, para 2, as amended.
67 See para 11.15.
68 TCPA 1990, Sch 9, para 1, as amended.

order will not take effect unless and until confirmed by the Secretary of State; there are the usual procedures for the making and hearing of objections.[69]

Prohibition orders

17.63 Where it appears to the mineral planning authority that mineral working or the deposit of mineral waste has permanently ceased, they may make a prohibition order. The authority may assume that mineral working or depositing has permanently ceased only (1) where there has been no substantial working on the site of which the land forms part for at least two years; and (2) it appears on the available evidence that a resumption is unlikely. The order may prohibit the resumption of working or depositing and may impose any of the following requirements:

(a) removal of plant or machinery;
(b) to take specified steps for removing or alleviating injury to amenity;
(c) compliance with the conditions of the original planning permission;
(d) a restoration condition.

17.64 The order does not take effect unless and until confirmed by the Secretary of State; there are the usual procedures for the making and hearing of objections.[70]

Suspension orders

17.65 Where it appears to the mineral planning authority that the winning and working of minerals or the deposit of mineral waste has been temporarily suspended, they may make a suspension order; the authority may assume that working or depositing has been suspended only (a) where there has been no substantial working or depositing on the land of which the site forms part for at least 12 months, but (b) it appears likely on the available evidence that working or depositing will be resumed. The order will require that steps be taken for the protection of the environment. These steps may be for the purpose of:

(1) preserving the amenities of the area during the period of suspension;
(2) protecting that area from damage during that period; or
(3) preventing any deterioration in the condition of the land during that period.[71]

17.66 Provision is made for supplementary suspension orders. These may be made either for the purpose of imposing further requirements for the protection of the environment or revoking the suspension order or any previous supplementary order.[72]

---

69 TCPA 1990, s. 103. See para 11.20.
70 TCPA 1990, Sch 9, paras 3, 4, as amended.
71 TCPA 1990, Sch 9, para 5, as amended.
72 TCPA 1990, Sch 9, para 6.

17.67 A suspension order or supplementary suspension order will not take effect unless confirmed by the Secretary of State; opportunity must be given for objections and the Secretary of State will if need be hold a public local inquiry or other hearing. A supplementary suspension order which merely revokes the suspension order or a previous supplementary order does not require confirmation.[73] Suspension orders and supplementary orders must be registered as land charges.[74]

17.68 A suspension order does not prohibit a resumption of mineral working or the depositing of mineral waste but a person intending to recommence must give notice to the mineral planning authority.[75]

17.69 It will be the duty of the mineral planning authority to review suspension orders and supplementary suspension orders every five years.[76]

Enforcement notices

17.70 An enforcement notice may require the demolition or alteration of any unauthorized buildings or works or the discontinuance of any use of land.[77] The Minerals Regulations treat mineral development as a use for this purpose, and also for the purpose of what is now TCPA 1990, s. 179 so that the mineral operator can be prosecuted if he fails to comply with the enforcement notice.[78] Where mining operations are carried out without planning permission, the enforcement notice must be served within four years of the development being carried out.[79]

17.71 The Minerals Regulations do not apply the winning and working of minerals in connection with agriculture.[80]

Interim Development Order permissions

17.72 A particular problem dealt with by the PCA 1991[81] was that of old mining permissions granted between 1943 and 1948 under an Interim Development Order minerals permission, for the extraction of minerals or the deposit of mineral waste.[82] Such permissions contain only the most basic of conditions

---

73 TCPA 1990, Sch 9, para 7.

74 TCPA 1990, Sch 9, para 8.

75 TCPA 1990, Sch 9, para 10.

76 TCPA 1990, Sch 9, para 9.

77 See para 11.15.

78 Minerals Regs, reg 2.

79 TCPA 1990, s. 172(4). Since 'each shovelful or each cut by the bulldozer is a separate act of development', the four-year rule does little more than protect the mineral operator from any liability to restore the land; it certainly does not prevent the service of an enforcement notice to restrain further unauthorized working: *Thomas David (Porthcawl) Ltd v Penybont RDC*, above.

80 TCPA 1990, s. 315(4).

81 PCA 1991, s. 22 and Sch 2.

82 Deemed to be granted under Part III of the Act of 1947, s. 77.

and the danger is that, once implemented, they remain valid and can be reactivated at any time.

17.73 The PCA 1991 introduced a registration scheme. Any person who was the owner of land to which an old mining permission related, or who was entitled to any interest in a mineral to which such permission related, could apply to the mineral planning authority for the permission to be registered. Such applications had to be served on the authority before the end of a period of six months from when the relevant Schedule of the Act came into force; this meant that the application had to be made between 25 September 1991 and 24 March 1992.[83] Unless registered by that date such permissions lapsed without compensation.[84]

17.74 Where an application for registration is granted, the authority can impose any conditions which may be imposed on a grant of planning permission for the working of minerals or deposit of mineral waste, and must impose a condition that the development should cease not later than 21 February 2042.[85] There is a right of appeal against refusal of registration or the imposition of conditions to the Secretary of State.[86] In the case of dormant sites, ie where there had been no development 'to any substantial extent' for the two years preceding 1 May 1991, working cannot commence unless the permission has been registered and conditions approved by the mineral planning authority.[87] In the case of active sites, the permission will cease to have effect unless conditions are approved by the mineral planning authority within 12 months of the date of registration, or such longer period as is agreed with that authority.[88]

17.75 The Interim Development Order regime came before the House of Lords in *R v North Yorkshire County Council, ex p Brown*[89] and the Court of Appeal in *R v Durham County Council, ex p Huddleston*.[90] These cases are considered in Part 1 of chapter 9 above dealing with EIA.[91]

Minerals permissions granted from 1948 to 1982

17.76 The Environment Act 1995[92] continues the process commenced by the PCA 1991, discussed above, by providing for the initial review and updating of mineral

83 TCPA 1990, Sch 2, para 1(1) and (3).
84 TCPA 1990, s. 22(3), (4).
85 TCPA 1990, Sch 2, para 2(1). Guidance as to conditions is contained in MPG 9.
86 TCPA 1990, Sch 2, para 5(1).
87 PCA 1991, s. 22(3).
88 PCA 1991, Sch 2, para 2(4).
89 [1999] JPL 616.
90 [2000] 1 WLR 1484. See also *R v Somerset County Council, ex p Morris and Perry (Gurney Slade Quarry) Ltd* [2000] PLCR 117.
91 See para 9.01.
92 EA 1995, s. 96. And see MPG 14.

permissions granted on or after 1 July 1948 and before 22 February 1982, when the main provisions of the Minerals Act 1981 came into force. The EA 1995 also provides for the periodic review of all mineral permissions. These provisions are contained in Schedules 13 and 14 of the Act.

17.77 For the purpose of these provisions minerals sites are divided into Phase I sites and Phase II sites. In general terms Phase I sites are those situated within environmentally sensitive areas, including national parks and areas of outstanding natural beauty, where the relevant planning permissions attaching to all or the greater part of the site were granted before 1 April 1969. Phase II sites are those not in environmentally sensitive areas where the permissions attaching to the site or the greater part of the site were granted after 31 March 1969 and before 22 February 1982.[93] There is also a third category—dormant sites. These are Phase I or Phase II sites where no minerals development has been carried out to any substantial extent between 22 February 1982 and 6 June 1995.[94]

17.78 The minerals planning authority must, within three months of EA 1995, Schedule 13 coming into force, prepare and publish a list (the 'first list') of active Phase I and II sites and dormant sites in their area.[95] In the case of Phase I sites the list must specify a date by which any owner of the land or interest in a mineral (hereafter referred to as the 'owner') must apply to the authority to determine the conditions to which the permissions relating to the site are to be subject.[96] This date must be no later than three years from when Schedule 13 came into force.

17.79 The authority must then prepare and publish the 'second list', ie a list of active Phase II sites, again specifying a date by which owners may apply to determine conditions as above. This list must be prepared within three years of the coming into force of EA 1995, Schedule 13.[97] The application date must be no more than six years later.

17.80 The first list is crucial to the review mechanism. This is because planning permission relating to Phase I and II sites not included in the first list will lapse unless the owner has applied to be included within three months of the publication of the list.[98] If the site is not added to the list, the permission will lapse

---

93 EA 1995, Sch 13, para 2.

94 EA 1995, Sch 13, para 1, except under an interim development order or a development order.

95 EA 1995, Sch 13, para 3. Sch 13 and the other relevant provisions of the 1995 Act were brought into force on 1 November 1995 by virtue of SI 1995 No 2765.

96 EA 1995, Sch 13, paras 3, 9. For cases on the 'first list' see *R v North Lincolnshire Council, ex p Horticulture and Garden Sales Ltd* [1998] Env LR 295; and *Dorset County Council v Secretary of State for the Environment, Transport and the Regions* [1999] JPL 633.

97 EA 1995, Sch 13, para 4.

98 EA 1995, Sch 13, paras 6, 12.

in any event. The publication of the first list also effectively triggers the initial review and sets the timetable for what follows.

17.81 When the mineral planning authority receive applications in relation to active Phase I or II sites or dormant sites they must determine the conditions to which planning permissions are to be subject. Such conditions may include any condition which may be imposed on a minerals permission and may be in addition to, or in substitution for, any existing conditions.[99] There is a right of appeal to the Secretary of State against the authority's determination.[100] In certain circumstances compensation will be payable, ie where conditions are imposed on an active Phase I or Phase II site which restrict working rights, and where the effect of such restriction is to prejudice adversely, to an unreasonable degree, (i) the economic viability of operating the site, or (ii) the asset value of the site.[101] However there is no compensation payable in respect of dormant sites nor in respect of active sites where the conditions relate to the environmental impact of the development.

17.82 There are provisions in EA 1995, Schedule 13 allowing for the postponement of the date specified in the first or second list where the existing conditions attaching to active sites are satisfactory. This may be granted by the mineral planning authority on written application by the owner.[102]

17.83 The main distinction, however, between active sites and dormant sites is that in the case of the latter, planning permission lapsed when EA 1995, Schedule 13 came into force, unless an application to review the permission had been made and determined in accordance with the provisions of the Schedule. Planning permission relating to active Phase I and II sites, on the other hand, remains in force until the deadline for applications to review the permission has passed.

Periodic review of minerals permissions

17.84 TCPA 1990, s. 105[103] required mineral planning authorities to undertake periodic reviews of minerals sites in their area. This provision was repealed by the Environment Act 1995.[104]

17.85 The procedures under EA 1995, Schedule 14 closely follow EA 1995, Schedule 13, discussed above. In the case of Phase I and II sites the first periodic review will take

99 EA 1995, Sch 13, para 9. Such applications may be called in by the Secretary of State; para 13.
100 EA 1995, Sch 13, para 11.
101 EA 1995, Sch 13, paras 10, 15.
102 EA 1995, Sch 13, para 7.
103 As substituted by the PCA 1991, s. 21 and Sch 1, para 7.
104 EA 1995, s. 96(4), which was brought into force on 1 November 1995.

place 15 years after the initial review under the provisions of EA 1995, Schedule 13. Interim Development Order permissions[105] are to be first reviewed 15 years after conditions are determined under the provisions of PCA 1991, Schedule 2; in the case of any other site, the first review will take place 15 years after the grant of the most recent mineral permission relating to the site.[106] Following the first periodic review, the 1995 Act provides for second and subsequent reviews at 15-yearly intervals.[107]

Review of minerals permissions and EIA

17.86 As the regime for the review of mineral permissions introduced by the EA 1995 closely resembles the Interim Development Order regime in the PCA 1991, it is not surprising that it has raised the same concerns as to its adequacy with regard to the assessment of environmental effects.

17.87 The matter came before the High Court in *R v Oldham Metropolitan Council, ex p Foster*.[108] An old mineral permission had been granted in 1953 for the extraction of sand, clay, and gravel. The quarry was now a dormant site under the provisions of EA 1995, Schedule 13. The developers applied for the conditions to be determined and the council imposed numerous conditions on the basis of environmental concerns. The applicant argued that (a) the original planning permission was no longer subsisting as the working of the quarry in the 1950s had been carried out in breach of a condition that the site should be operated in accordance with an approved scheme; and (b) the council had acted unlawfully in failing to require an EIA, in accordance with the environmental effects regulations, before determining the conditions.

17.88 Held: the working of the quarry had been unlawful and the permission had lapsed in 1979.

17.89 Keene J also held that the determination of conditions was a 'development consent' to which the EIA Directive applied. He noted the implications of the House of Lords decision in *Brown*[109] and accepted that it was theoretically possible for the council to determine the conditions which themselves required all the remaining environmental information to be dealt with in such a way as to comply with the Directive. However this was not the actual case here.

---

105 See para 17.72.
106 EA 1995, Sch 14, para 3.
107 EA 1995, Sch 14, para 12.
108 [2000] Env LR 395.
109 See para 9.54.

The EIA Amendment Regulations

17.90 The Town and Country Planning (Environmental Impact Assessment) (England and Wales) (Amendment) Regulations 2000 (the 'EIA Amendment Regulations')[110] amend the EIA Regulations of 1999[111] following the decisions of the House of Lords and Court of Appeal respectively in the *Brown* and *Huddleston* cases.[112] These new provisions are intended to bring the review of old mining permissions within the scope of EIA requirements.

17.91 The new regulations apply to applications to Minerals Planning Authorities (MPAs) to determine the conditions to which planning permission is subject under (a) the Planning and Compensation Act 1991, Schedule 2, ie the Interim Development Order regime;[113] and (b) Environment Act 1995, Schedules 13 and 14, ie review of minerals permissions granted from 1948 to 1982.[114]

17.92 The regulations introduce a novel concept in planning law, the 'ROMP application'.[115] A ROMP application is an application to a relevant MPA to determine the conditions to which a mining permission is to be subject;[116] and 'ROMP development' is development which has yet to be carried out and is authorized by a planning permission in respect of which a ROMP application has been, or is to be, made.

17.93 The EIA Amendment Regulations 2000 apply the provisions of the principal EIA Regulations 1999[117] to ROMP applications. This is achieved by the insertion of a new regulation 26A into the Regulations of 1999,[118] with some modifications and additions. The main differences are:

(1) Where the applicant has received notice that an environmental statement is required, the period for writing to the MPA or Secretary of State is extended to six weeks, or such other period as may be agreed, instead of the usual three weeks.[119]
(2) Where the applicant has received notice that an environmental statement or additional information is required, a period must be specified within which these are required and by which the applicant must have complied with the

110 SI 2000 No 2867. The regulations came into force on 15 November 2000.
111 See para 9.01.
112 See paras 9.54 and 9.58.
113 See para 17.72.
114 See para 17.76.
115 (Sic) 'Registration of Old Mining Permissions'.
116 EIA Amendment Regs, reg 2(1).
117 See para 9.01.
118 EIA Amendment Regs, reg 2(5).
119 EIA Regs 1999, as amended, reg 26A(3) and (5).

publicity provisions in the EIA Regulations 1999, regulation 14(5). The period may be extended by agreement.[120]

(3) If the applicant fails to comply with the periods specified in paragraphs (1) and (2) above, minerals development shall be suspended until the requirements are met with.[121]

(4) The provisions in the EIA Regulations 1999 providing for a refusal of planning permission, or removing the duty of the authority to deal with the application, where there is a failure by the applicant to comply with specified time periods, do not apply to ROMP applications.[122]

17.94 Perhaps the most significant effect of the EIA Amendment Regulations 2000 is the modification of the deemed consent provisions in the PCA 1991 and EA 1995.[123] Thus where a ROMP application is in respect of a mineral planning permission authorizing development within Schedule 1 or 2 of the EIA Regulations ('EIA development'), then the deemed consent provisions to which reference was made above shall not operate to treat the authority as having determined the ROMP application.

17.95 Deemed consent will apply, however, where a screening direction or screening opinion has been adopted or made to the effect that the development is not EIA development.[124]

17.96 Where it falls to the MPA to determine an EIA application, the authority must give written notice of their determination of the ROMP application within 16 weeks of the date of receiving the ROMP application, or such extended period as may be agreed.[125]

17.97 If the MPA fail to give their decision within 16 weeks, or such extended period as agreed, the PCA 1991 and EA 1995 apply so as to give the applicant a right of appeal to the Secretary of State which must be exercised within six months from the expiry of the 16-week period, or such period as agreed.[126]

17.98 Under the ROMP Regulations 2000, EIA was only mandatory for minerals permissions where the application to determine the conditions was made on or after 15 November 2000. Where the application had been made before that date, mineral operators were merely encouraged to apply EIA requirements, ie EIA was voluntary. This arrangement has not worked well and there are a number of

---

120 EIA Regs 1999, reg 26A(16) and (17).
121 EIA Regs 1999, reg 26A(17).
122 EIA Regs 1999, reg 26A(4).
123 See para 17.73.
124 EIA Regs 1999, as amended, reg 26A(22).
125 EIA Regs 1999, reg 26A(24).
126 EIA Regs 1999, reg 26A(26).

'stalled reviews' where the operators are refusing to provide the requested environmental information. New regulations made in 2008[127] make EIA a statutory requirement for these applications—thus if the environmental information is not provided in a reasonable time, the planning permission will be automatically suspended. There is a duty on MPAs to make a prohibition order two years after automatic suspension.

Compensation provisions

17.99 As we have seen, planning authorities have extensive powers of control over the winning and working of minerals and the deposit of mineral waste.

17.100 In some cases these powers will be used to require the mineral operator to take steps to prevent or remedy damage to the environment. The minerals extraction industries have accepted that, in some circumstances, it would be reasonable that part of the cost of such preventive or remedial action should be borne by the mineral operator and that the planning authority should pay a reduced rate of compensation. To give effect to these principles the law was amended in 1981 to permit the payment of compensation on a reduced basis where mineral compensation requirements are satisfied; these provisions were contained in TCPA 1990, Schedule 11.

17.101 PCA 1991, s. 21 and Schedule 11 replace TCPA 1990, Schedule 11 and introduce a new TCPA 1990, s. 116. This is an enabling provision which gives the Secretary of State greater scope as to the way in which he may alter the calculation of reduced compensation.

17.102 New regulations, revoking those made in 1985, have been made.[128] The regulations define the circumstances in which compensation is not to be payable following the making of a modification or discontinuance order; they also modify TCPA 1990, s. 115 in its application to claims for compensation following the making of a prohibition, suspension, or supplementary suspension order where there are other interests in addition to those of the claimant.

[127] SI 2008 No 1556.

[128] T & CP (Compensation for Restrictions on Mineral Working and Mineral Waste Depositing) Regulations 1997, SI 1997 No 111.

18

PLANNING AND ENVIRONMENTAL CONTROLS

18.01 We saw in chapter 1 that early planning law was concerned largely with questions of amenity and the rational allocation of land uses. It long predated the contemporary concern with environmental protection and climate change. Since those early days there has emerged a substantial body of environmental protection law contained in various statutes including the Environmental Protection Act 1990 and the Pollution Prevention and Control Act 1990; and the planning legislation itself is now increasingly concerned with environmental objectives such as sustainable development. We are concerned in this chapter with the relationship between planning law and some of these other forms of environmental regulation.[1] There are three environmental regulatory regimes that are of particular significance to a consideration of planning controls. These are:

(1) Integrated Pollution Prevention and Control (IPPC) under the Pollution Prevention and Control Act 1999;
(2) Waste Management controls under Part II of EPA 1990; and
(3) the Contaminated Land regime under Part IIA of EPA 1990.

18.02 It should be noted that the administration of the first and second of the abovementioned regimes, ie IPPC and Waste Management has recently been integrated

---

1 For a brief but illuminating analysis of this 'grey area', see Thornton (2008) JPL 609.

by the Environmental Permitting (England and Wales) Regulations 2007[2] which came into force on 6 April 2008. Previously those operating industrial sites under IPPC were required to obtain a PPC Permit; and those engaged in the disposal or recovery of waste were required to do so under a Waste Management Licence. The new regulations replace these authorizations and provide for a single 'Environmental Permit' for either pollution or waste activities. In general the substance of the two regimes has not changed in terms of the standards prescribed and the activities regulated, although in addition to the new permits, the enforcement of the regimes has been unified.

18.03 We will also consider, in this chapter, the European Habitats Directive, Directive 92/43/EEC, as implemented into domestic law by the Conservation (Natural Habitats, etc) Regulations 1994.

IPPC

18.04 Before considering IPPC and the new environmental permits, to which reference was made above, it is necessary to consider the predecessor to IPPC, 'IPC'. The background to IPC is that, before 1990, releases from the major polluting industries to the three environmental media (air, water, and land) were subject to a fragmented regime involving various regulatory bodies. There were often overlapping controls so that, for example, one industrial spillage incident might fall under more than one system of control.

18.05 EPA 1990 introduced, under Part I, a system of 'integrated' pollution control. Under the Act, the most polluting industrial processes were brought under 'Integrated Pollution Control' (IPC) with the Environment Agency (EA)[3] being responsible for multi-media regulation of the most polluting processes ('Part A' processes). Other less polluting processes ('Part B' processes) fell under the control of local authorities as Local Authority Air Pollution Control (LAAPC). This latter system, as the name suggests, was limited to control over emissions to air only. Discharges to the other two media, falling outside Part A, were governed by water pollution and waste controls.

18.06 Those wishing to operate plants covered by Part A had to apply for an IPC Authorization from the EA. Principally the operator had to show that the Best Available Techniques Not Entailing Excessive Costs (BATNEEC) were to be applied so as to minimize pollution. The EA was required to include in the

[2] SI 2007 No 3538.

[3] Originally, and until 1996, the regulatory body was Her Majesty's Inspectorate of Pollution (HMIP).

authorization specific conditions that BATNEEC and other objectives of IPC were met. In addition to the specific conditions, there was an important implied condition under s. 7(4) of EPA 1990 that the operator must use BATNEEC to prevent or minimize harm to the environment. The main emission standards for the processes and substances prescribed under IPC were laid down in Process Guidance Notes, prepared by the enforcing authority. These covered the five main industrial sectors subject to IPC—fuel and power, metal, mineral, chemical, and waste disposal. There were enforcement powers available to the regulatory body for those operators who carried on a prescribed process without an authorization or in contravention of conditions.

18.07 Implementing Directive 96/61/EC (now replaced by Directive 08/1/EC), the Pollution Prevention and Control Act 1999 introduced a new regime—Integrated Pollution Prevention and Control (IPPC). Under IPPC, activities and installations which give rise to significant emissions to all environmental media are classified as Part A(1) activities—these are subject to the regulatory control of the EA. Activities which give rise to less significant emissions to all environmental media are known as Part A(2) activities—these are regulated by local authorities. Further, activities which are controlled in respect of emissions to the air only are called Part B activities. These are also controlled by local authorities. The new Environmental Permitting regime has broadly retained these categories and responsibilities.

18.08 Under IPPC, before April 2008 'PPC Permits' were granted as opposed Authorizations under the old IPC system. There are number of differences between the old system and the new, but the most well-known is that the requisite standard for the control of activities has become 'BAT', as opposed to the former BATNEEC. BAT is broader than BATNEEC and covers not only technology and techniques but extends to the design, building, maintenance, and decommissioning of the installation. Guidelines to establish what constitutes BAT are contained in BAT reference documents (known as 'BREF Notes') which impose European Union-wide standards. IPPC has been gradually phased in to cover existing installations subject to IPC. The activities covered by IPPC are now specified by the Environmental Permitting Regulations, Schedule 1 and include the metals, minerals, and chemical industries; and a range of similar activities.

18.09 Until recently new industrial installations subject to IPPC required a PPC Permit in order lawfully to commence operations. However as from 6 April 2008 existing PPC Permits have been converted into Environmental Permits and, of course, new installations will require an application for a new-style Permit. A new installation will also require planning permission or an NSIP development consent, as the case may be, as it will constitute 'development' under TCPA 1990—this is a consent to build the plant which may involve also a material change of use, depending on what the land was used for previously. The relationship between the environmental controls and the planning controls is a delicate one. The land use implications of proposed development are clearly 'material considerations' for the local planning authority in considering the planning application.[4] In *Gateshead Metropolitan Borough Council v Secretary of State for the Environment*,[5] the Court of Appeal indicated that the fact that planning permission had been granted for a development subject to IPC (it would apply equally to IPPC) did not amount to a restriction on the discretion of the pollution control authority to refuse the Authorization (or Permit) if it considered it appropriate to do so. It might be concluded from this that the prudent operator should seek the environmental consent first but the reality is that it may depend upon the circumstances of each case.

Waste management

18.10 'Waste management' includes not only the disposal of waste to landfills but also incineration, recycling, recovery operations, and some forms of energy production. The environmental problems caused by these activities should not be underestimated—landfill can lead to contamination of the soil, water pollution, and the build-up of unstable gases. Incineration causes air pollution and the disposal of hazardous wastes can involve danger to human health.

Planning controls over waste

18.11 Planning control has an important part to play in the regulation of waste management through the requirement of planning permission for waste development and with regard to the allocation, through development plans, of appropriate sites. Under s. 55(3)(b) TCPA 1990, the deposit of refuse and waste materials on land always constitutes a material change of use, notwithstanding that the site is already used for that purpose, if the superficial area of the deposit is extended or if the height is extended above the original ground level. Moreover, for the purposes of planning control, waste is described as a 'county matter' and the PCA 1991 required county authorities to prepare either a waste local plan or include their waste policies in a minerals local plan. Waste treatment and disposal facilities were key topics to be covered in the old-style structure plans.

18.12 PCA 1991, Schedule 1, applied the special provisions relating to mineral development[6] to the deposit of mineral waste and in many cases to the deposit of refuse or waste materials generally. Thus minerals planning authorities could, under these

---

4 See para 8.68.

5 [1994] JPL 255. The case is more fully discussed at para 8.93. See also PPS 23 *Planning and Pollution Control*, 2004.

6 See para 17.58.

provisions, impose aftercare conditions and make various orders previously only applying to minerals, eg prohibition orders and suspension orders.

18.13 PCPA 2004 brought further reform. County councils are now required to prepare a Minerals and Waste Development Scheme for any part of their area for which there is a district council. County councils which are unitary authorities will include their minerals and waste policies under their Local Development Scheme. The Act laid down transitional provisions whereby, in general, existing waste local plans were 'saved' for a period of three years until 28 September 2007. At regional level the Regional Spatial Strategy should incorporate a waste management strategy looking forward over a period of 15 or 20 years or so.

Environmental controls over waste

18.14 Waste management as an industry has been regulated by a licensing system originally introduced under Part II of EPA 1990. When that Act came into force the system was initially regulated by Waste Regulation Authorities (WRAs) mostly on a county council basis, with disposal being the responsibility of 'arm's length' local authority waste contractors (LAWDCs). However the Environment Act 1995 transferred the functions of the WRAs to the EA as from 1 April 1996. It had been the duty of WRAs to prepare a 'waste disposal plan'—these plans were essentially concerned with waste management policy and they did not directly address land use issues as does a development plan under planning law.

18.15 Waste disposal plans have been superseded by the adoption of the National Waste Strategy which contains a strategic overview of national waste policy and specifies targets for reducing the quantity of waste sent to landfill. The strategy embodies the 'proximity principle' that waste should be treated or disposed of as near as possible to its source. Further, under the Waste Emissions and Trading Act 2003, s. 32, local authorities in non-metropolitan areas of England are to develop a 'Joint Municipal Waste Management Strategy'. Under s. 29 of the Act, the Assembly in Wales may make regulations requiring local authorities to have a waste management strategy for their own areas.

18.16 Under Part II of EPA 1990 as originally enacted, a Waste Management Licence (WML) was required for the treatment, keeping, disposal, or recovery of 'controlled waste'. Controlled waste was renamed 'Directive waste' as from 1994. Such waste is defined as household, industrial, and commercial waste although the Waste Management Licensing Regulations 1994 prescribed a wide range of exemptions from the need for a WML. The EA was given a wide discretion to attach appropriate conditions to a WML; such conditions could relate to matters which must be complied with before the activities commence and after they have ceased. Thus a state of affairs was introduced where there was less need, than was formerly the case, for planning conditions to deal with such matters.

18.17 As with the PPC Permit regime, as from 6 April 2008, WMLs have been replaced by Environmental Permits. This will be considered more fully in the next section, but it should be noted that an Environmental Permit relating to a waste operation will be refused if the relevant site does not have planning permission or a certificate of lawfulness for waste development.[7]

Environmental permits

18.18 Under the Environmental Permitting Regulations only 'regulated facilities' require a permit. This definition includes[8] an IPPC installation; a waste operation; mobile plant, other than waste mobile plant; and waste mobile plant, unless exempt or excluded.

18.19 A single Environmental Permit can cover more than one regulated facility, but only where each facility shares the same regulator and operator; and, in general, where all the facilities are on the same site. As mentioned above, when the new regime came into force on 6 April 2008, existing PPC Permits and WMLs were automatically converted into Environmental Permits.

Exempt waste operations

18.20 As with the WML regime, a range of waste operations are exempt from the need for an Environmental Permit.[9] These include certain activities relating to the recovery or reuse of waste; a number of operations involving recycling; the storage or deposit of construction wastes in connection with building work; the storage of waste in a specified secure place; and the temporary storage of waste on the site where it is produced. It must be stressed, however, that exempt waste operations must be registered and also meet certain other criteria prescribed by the regulations. In addition they must not, unless specifically allowed, involve hazardous waste.

Regulatory bodies

18.21 The EA acts as regulator for part A(1) installations; Part A(1) mobile plant; and waste operations. Local authorities are the responsible regulatory body for Part A(2) installations; the Part B LAAPC regime; Part A(2) and Part B mobile plant; and waste operations carried out in association with Part A(2) or B installations or Part A(2) and Part B mobile plant.[10]

---

7 Environmental Permitting Regulations, sch 9, para 2, replacing s. 36(2) of EPA 1990.
8 Ibid, sch 3.
9 Environmental Permitting Regulations, reg 5.
10 Ibid, reg 32(1) and (2); sch 1, para 2; and sch 2, para 2.

18.22 The definitions of these installations, operations, and plant are largely the same as that laid down under the PPC regulations and are reproduced in Schedule 1 to the Environmental Permitting Regulations.

Contaminated land

18.23 In any consideration of the law relating to the development of land, it is impossible to ignore the regime in Part IIA of EPA 1990 relating to contaminated land. Many industrial sites may be affected by land contamination—the legacy of historic pollution—and as a result the planning process may be delayed, eg where a brownfield site has to be cleaned up before redevelopment can take place. Local planning authorities must take into account land contamination when preparing development plans; and when determining planning applications, they can impose conditions relating to such contamination. PPS 23, Annex 2 contains guidance on the relationship between the planning system and the contaminated land regime. New model planning conditions for development on land affected by contamination were issued in May 2008 and are to be found in the Annex. The Annex also prescribes good practice for local planning authorities in approaching land contamination issues.

18.24 In 1994 the Government issued a consultation paper, *Paying for our Past*, which set out policy objectives and proposed legislation for dealing with contaminated land. Statutory provisions were included in s. 57 of the Environment Act 1995 which were inserted into Part IIA of EPA 1990. In 2000, the government made the Contaminated Land (England) Regulations governing procedural matters and issued Circular 2/00 setting out guidance as to the implementation of the legislation. The 2000 regulations have now been replaced by the Contaminated Land (England) Regulations 2006.[11] The main legislative scheme came into force in England on 1 April 2000.

18.25 The contaminated land regime is not a permit-based 'command and control' system of environmental legislation. It deals, in the main, with historic pollution and the regime is concerned with: (1) identifying the land which is contaminated; (2) identifying who is responsible for the contamination; and (3) allocating the clean-up costs between the responsible persons. Essentially the core philosophy is that the polluter should pay the costs of alleviating land contamination and that land should be suitable for use.

---

11 SI 2006 No 1380. Revised guidance is contained in DEFRA Circular 1/06.

Definition of contaminated land

18.26 EPA 1990, s. 78A defines 'contaminated land' as: '. . . any land which appears to the local authority in whose area it is situated to be in such a condition, by reason of substances in, on or under that land, that: (a) significant harm is being caused or there is a significant possibility of such harm being caused; or (b) pollution of controlled waters is being, or is likely to be, caused'.[12] It follows that land which is polluted but poses no threat of harm to persons or the environment, will not be contaminated land within the meaning of the Act. 'Harm' is defined in s. 78(4) of EPA 1990 as: '. . . harm to the health of living organisms or other interference with the ecological systems of which they form a part and, in the case of man, includes harm to his property'.

18.27 Guidance in the Circular on the above provisions refers to the concept of a 'pollutant linkage'. This is the link between:

A contaminant or pollutant present in the ground, AND
A relevant receptor* (target); AND
A pathway which allows EITHER the contaminant to cause significant harm to the receptor; OR there is a significant possibility of such harm being caused to the receptor; OR pollution of controlled waters is being or is likely to be caused

*Table A of the Circular interprets 'receptor' as: human beings, property (buildings, crops, and animals) and sites protected by nature conservation legislation, eg SSSIs. Where such a linkage as described above is present, it must be 'significant', ie there must be a 'significant pollution linkage' (SPL) for the land to be classed as contaminated land. If there is a linkage but the harm is not significant, or if any element of the linkage described above is missing, then the land will not fall within the definition. Thus where there is a pollutant that is effectively sealed in the ground with no pathway permitting escape so as to cause significant harm to a receptor, in one sense the land might be described as contaminated, but it will not be 'contaminated land' under EPA 1990.

18.28 The Circular provides that in assessing the significance of the harm, the local authority should consider whether the harm caused to the receptor falls within the specified categories in relation to that receptor, eg in the case of humans, the types of damage specified are; serious injury, birth defects, and reproductive impairment. In the case of property, substantial damage to buildings or substantial loss in crop value would be required. In the case of protected nature conservation sites, what is required is any harm which results in an irreversible or substantial adverse

[12] When the relevant provision of the Water Act 2003 is brought into force, for subsection (b) the following wording will be substituted; 'significant pollution of controlled waters is being caused or there is a significant possibility of such pollution being caused.'

change to the functioning of the ecosystems which form a substantial part of the site.

18.29 If there is no actual significant harm the local authority must consider whether there is a 'significant *possibility* of significant harm' being caused. This involves a risk assessment paying particular attention to magnitude or consequences of the differing types of significant harm. It must take account of: the nature and degree of the harm; the susceptibility of the receptors; and the timescale within which the harm might occur. Significant possibility of significant harm is assessed 'on the balance of probabilities' except in the case of harm to human health where the risk must be medically unacceptable.

Identification of contaminated land

18.30 Under s. 78B of EPA 1990, the local authority is under a duty to inspect their area from time to time to identify contaminated land; and to decide whether such land should be designated as a 'special site'. Special sites are those where the actual or threatened contamination is serious, or the site is one where the required remediation would benefit from the expertise of the EA; thus special sites are regulated by the EA. In fact the majority of contaminated sites fall under the responsibility of local authorities.

18.31 Once land has been identified as being contaminated, the authority must serve a 'remediation notice' on the appropriate persons responsible for the remediation. This will specify the works required and the timescale within which such works must be completed. If the authority is satisfied that nothing by way of remediation could be specified, they must issue a 'remediation declaration' recording why they consider a remediation notice should not be served. If of the view that appropriate works are already being carried out, the authority must publish a 'remediation statement', specifying what has been done by way of remediation.

18.32 EPA 1990, s. 78F and the Circular designate who is to be responsible for remediation:

Class A persons—those who have caused or knowingly permitted the presence of contaminating substances in or under the land, ie the polluter is responsible;
Class B persons—the owner/occupier who will be responsible if no polluter (ie Class A person) can be found after reasonable inquiry.

18.33 Owners/occupiers could fall into both Class A and Class B if, for example, land is contaminated with more than one substance and they are Class A in relation to one substance and Class B in relation to the other. It should be noted, however, that the apportionment of the costs of remediation is a matter of some complexity and may involve the application of certain 'exclusion tests' as set out in the Circular.

18.34 We now turn to a consideration of the European Habitats Directive and its implementation in domestic law.

Planning control and natural habitats

18.35 The European Directive on the Conservation of Natural Habitats and the Wild Fauna and Flora (the 'Habitats Directive')[13] aims to conserve fauna and flora in their natural habitats as a part of ensuring 'biodiversity'. Biodiversity (or biological diversity) can best be defined as 'the sum total of life's variety on earth'.[14] In promoting the maintenance of biodiversity, account is to be taken of economic, social, cultural, and regional requirements in the European Community.[15]

18.36 The Habitats Directive provides for a Community-wide ecological network of special areas of conservation (SACs) to be set up under the title 'Natura 2000'. The network is to include special protection areas (SPAs) classified under the Directive on the Conservation of Wild Birds (the 'Birds Directive').[16]

18.37 Article 4 of the Habitats Directive provides a procedure whereby the European Commission is to establish, in agreement with member states, a draft list of sites of Community importance, identifying those which host one or more priority natural habitat types or priority species.[17] 'Priority' habitats and species are those in danger of disappearance and which are mainly found in the territory covered by the European Community. Once a site has been adopted in accordance with this procedure, the member state concerned is to designate that site as a special area of conservation. The habitats and species listed in the annexes to the Directive must then be maintained or restored at a 'favourable conservation status'.[18] Conservation status is said to be 'favourable' when the population of a species is maintaining itself on a long-term basis, the natural range of the species is not likely to be reduced for the foreseeable future, and there is, and will probably continue to be, a sufficiently large habitat to maintain its populations on a long-term basis.[19]

18.38 Under article 6 of the Directive, member states are enjoined to take appropriate steps to avoid the deterioration of habitats.[20] Further, any plan or project not directly connected with or necessary to the management of the site but likely to

13 92/43/EEC.
14 The United Kingdom is a signatory to the UN Biodiversity Convention 1992.
15 Habitats Directive, recitals.
16 79/409/EEC; Habitats Directive, art 3(1).
17 Habitats Directive, art 4(2).
18 Habitats Directive, art 4(4).
19 Habitats Directive, art 1.
20 Habitats Directive, art 6(2).

have a significant effect thereon, must have the implications for the site appropriately assessed. The proposal should only be permitted where it has been ascertained that it will not adversely affect the integrity of the site.[21] There is, however, a 'get out' in article 6(4) of the Directive which enables a project to proceed in spite of a negative assessment—there must, however, be imperative reasons of overriding public interest and the member state must take compensatory measures. Clearly such plans or projects as fall within the meaning of 'development' under domestic planning law[22] would be covered by the above provisions, but so might other activities excluded from development under domestic law, for example, a change from one type of agriculture to another.

Conservation (Natural Habitats, etc) Regulations 1994

18.39 The Habitats Directive has been implemented in the UK by the Conservation (Natural Habitats, etc) Regulations[23] referred to hereafter as 'the Nature Conservation Regulations'.

18.40 The Nature Conservation Regulations require that the Secretary of State and the nature conservation bodies shall exercise their functions under the existing legislation so as to secure compliance with the requirements of the Habitats Directive.[24] The existing legislation includes powers under the National Parks and Access to the Countryside Act 1949, the Countryside Act 1968, the Wildlife and Countryside Act 1981, and the Environmental Protection Act 1990. In fact the government's view is that the existing legislation will substantially meet most of its obligations under the Directive, the purpose of the Nature Conservation Regulations being to reinforce the existing measures in various respects.[25]

18.41 Essentially, under the Regulations, once a site has been adopted by the Commission as a site of Community importance, the Secretary of State is to designate the site as a SAC as soon as possible and within six years at the most.[26] The Regulations apply to both SACs and also SPAs under the Birds Directive[27]—these are collectively referred to in the Regulations as 'European Sites'.[28]

---

21 Habitats Directive, art 6(4).

22 See para 6.01.

23 SI 1994 No 2716, as amended by SI 1997 No 3055; and SI 2007 No 1843. See also Circular 6/05, *Biodiversity and Geological Conservation.*

24 Nature Conservation Regs, reg 3(2).

25 Department of the Environment Consultation Paper, 1993.

26 Nature Conservation Regs, reg 8(1).

27 See para 18.36.

28 Nature Conservation Regs, reg 10(1).

18.42 The Nature Conservation Regulations have a considerable impact on planning law. It will be recalled that development plans are required to include policies in respect of the conservation of the natural beauty and amenity of the land;[29] under the Regulations this is supplemented in that such policies must include policies encouraging the management of features of the landscape which are of major importance for wild flora and fauna.[30] Such features may include river banks, fences and walls, ponds or small woods which may be essential for the migration, etc of wild species.

18.43 With regard to European Sites there are, in certain circumstances, restrictions on the granting of planning permission; that is, both express permission and that permitted under development order. However the Regulations go further than this and require a review of existing permissions with a view to possible revocation or modification or the discontinuance of a use. There are, in addition, special provisions relating to Simplified Planning Zones and Enterprise Zones.[31] These matters will be considered more fully below.

Development affecting European sites

18.44 Regulation 48 of the Nature Conservation Regulations implements Article 6 of the Habitats Directive, which was discussed above.[32] The provision applies[33] to a grant of planning permission on an application under the TCPA 1990, Part III,[34] on an appeal under TCPA 1990, s. 78[35] or where permission is granted by the Secretary of State in relation to a purchase notice,[36] on an enforcement appeal,[37] or where it follows an order under TCPA 1990, s. 102 requiring the discontinuance of a use or the removal of buildings or works.[38]

18.45 Under regulation 48(1), a 'competent authority' (which includes the local planning authority or Secretary of State), before deciding whether to undertake, or give any consent, permission, or other authorization for a plan or project which:

(a) Is likely to have a significant effect on a European Site, either alone or combined with other proposals; and
(b) Is not directly connected with or necessary to the management of the site,

---

29 See para 5.01.
30 Nature Conservation Regs, reg 37(1).
31 See para 7.72 and 7.76.
32 See para 18.38.
33 By virtue of the Nature Conservation Regs, reg 54, as amended by SI 2007 No 1843.
34 See para 8.01.
35 See para 8.121.
36 See para 14.01.
37 See para 12.01.
38 See para 11.15.

must make an 'appropriate assessment' of the implications for the site in view of the site's conservation objectives.

18.46 It seems that the assessment referred to above does not correspond to an environmental assessment[39] although, of course, for some proposed development an assessment under the Environmental Impact Regulations will be required.[40] For the purposes of the assessment required by regulation 48(1), the competent authority must consult the appropriate nature conservation body[41] and, if they consider it appropriate, the opinion of the general public.[42]

18.47 In the light of the conclusions of the assessment, and subject to regulation 49 (explained below), the authority may agree to the plan or project *only having ascertained that it will not adversely affect the integrity of the European Site.*[43] The 'integrity' of a site is the coherence of its ecology, enabling it to sustain the habitat or species for which it was classified.[44]

18.48 It is clear that the above provisions impose a substantive restriction on the discretion of the local planning authority to grant planning permission where satisfied that a European Site would be significantly affected; in other words, the requirements of the Regulations cannot be overridden by policies in the development plan or other material considerations.

18.49 Regulation 49 provides a derogation. If the competent authority are satisfied that, there being no alternative solutions, the plan or project must be carried out for imperative reasons of overriding public interest (including those of a social or economic nature), they may agree to the proposal notwithstanding a negative assessment of the implications for the site.[45] However where the site hosts a priority natural habitat type or a priority species, the 'imperative' reasons referred to above must be either (a) reasons relating to human health, public safety, or beneficial consequences of primary importance to the environment, or (b) other reasons which in the opinion of the European Commission are imperative reasons of overriding public interest.[46]

18.50 Where a proposal is agreed to, notwithstanding a negative assessment of the implications for the site, the Secretary of State is placed under an obligation to

---

39 See para 9.01.
40 Circular 6/05, Part 1, B.
41 In England, Natural England.
42 Nature Conservation Regs, regs 48(3), (4).
43 Author's italics.
44 Circular 6/05, part 1, B.
45 Nature Conservation Regs, reg 49(1).
46 Nature Conservation Regs, reg 49(2), as amended by SI 2007 No 1843. Priority habitats and species are indicated by an asterisk in Annexes I and II of the Habitats Directive.

'secure that any necessary compensatory measures are taken to ensure that the overall coherence of Natura 2000 is protected'.[47]

18.51 One might ask what 'alternative solutions' the local planning authority or the Secretary of State are required to consider under regulation 49. The Government's view is that they should consider whether there are suitable alternative sites for the proposed development or different, practicable approaches which would have a lesser impact.[48]

Review of existing planning permissions

18.52 The Nature Conservation Regulations require the review of existing planning permissions for proposals which are likely to have a significant effect on a European Site, and which are not related to the management of the site.[49] The competent authority must follow a procedure similar to that relating to applications for permission in regulation 48 (above).[50]

18.53 The requirement to review existing permissions applies to any planning permission or deemed planning permission.[51] Fortunately there is a major limitation on this requirement in that it does not apply to permissions for development which has been completed, to development subject to a condition as to time of commencement which has elapsed, or to permission for a limited period that has expired.[52] The duty therefore relates to planning permissions which have not been fully implemented.

18.54 In reviewing any planning permission or deemed planning permission under the above procedure, the competent authority must consider whether any adverse effects could be overcome by entering into a planning obligation under TCPA 1990, s. 106[53] and, if they consider such effects might be overcome, invite those concerned to enter into such obligations.[54] In so far as the adverse effects cannot be overcome in this way, the authority is to use its powers to make an order under TCPA 1990, s. 97 to revoke or modify the planning permission[55] or under TCPA 1990, s. 102 or Schedule 9, paragraph 1, to secure the discontinuance of a use.[56]

---

47 Nature Conservation Regs, reg 53.
48 Circular 6/05 Part 1, B.
49 Nature Conservation Regs, regs 50(1), 51.
50 Nature Conservation Regs, reg 50(2).
51 Nature Conservation Regs, reg 55(1). See para 7.85, as to deemed planning permission.
52 Nature Conservation Regs, reg 55(1)(a), (b), and (c). By virtue of reg 55(2) the requirement does not apply to permission granted by development order or SPZ; but see paras 18.55 and 18.61.
53 See para 13.01.
54 Nature Conservation Regs, reg 56(1).
55 See para 11.01.
56 Nature Conservation Regs.

These procedures, however, are subject to the confirmation of the Secretary of State. Compensation may be payable.[57]

Permitted development rights

18.55 In relation to permitted development rights granted under the General Permitted Development Order,[58] the Nature Conservation Regulations provide that any permission so granted is subject to a condition that any development which:

(a) Is likely to have a significant effect on a European Site, and
(b) Is not directly connected with or necessary to the management of the site, shall not be begun until the developer has received written notification of the approval of the local planning authority.

18.56 The condition applies whether the development order was made before or after the commencement of the Regulations[59] and it applies to the continuance of development begun but not completed before such commencement.[60]

18.57 There is a specific provision whereby an application may be made to the appropriate nature conservation body for an opinion as to whether the development is likely to have such an adverse effect as mentioned in the previous paragraph. An opinion that the development is not likely to have such effect is conclusive of that question for the purpose of reliance on the planning permission granted by the development order.[61]

18.58 The procedure is prescribed by regulation 62. Under this provision, where a person intends to carry out development in reliance on a permission granted by development order, application may be made in writing to the local planning authority for their approval.[62] The application must be accompanied by a copy of any relevant notification by the appropriate nature conservation body and by the requisite fee.[63] A copy of the application must be sent to the appropriate nature conservation body and the local planning authority must take account of any representations made by them.[64] The authority may only give their approval if satisfied that the development will not adversely affect the integrity of the site.[65]

57 Nature Conservation Regs, reg 59.
58 See para 7.01.
59 Nature Conservation Regs, reg 60(1).
60 Nature Conservation Regs, reg 60(2).
61 Nature Conservation Regs, reg 61.
62 Nature Conservation Regs, reg 62(1).
63 Nature Conservation Regs, reg 62(2).
64 Nature Conservation Regs, reg 62(2).
65 Nature Conservation Regs, reg 62(6).

18.59 Regulation 64 deals with special development orders.[66] Any such order made after the commencement of the Regulations may not grant planning permission for development which is likely to have a significant effect on a European Site and which is not directly connected with or necessary to the management of the site. Any order made before the commencement of the Regulations shall cease to have effect of granting such permission, whether or not the development authorized by the permission has already begun.

18.60 A similar provision with regard to Local Development Orders was introduced into the 1994 regulations by an amendment in 2007.[67] Thus an LDO made on or after 21 August 2007 may not grant planning permission likely to have a significant effect on a European site which is not directly connected with or concerned with the management of the site.

Simplified planning zones and enterprise zones

18.61 Regulations 65 and 66 enact similar provisions in relation to SPZs and EZs[68] as that relating to special development orders, discussed above. Thus orders adopting or designating such schemes shall not have effect to grant planning permission for development adversely affecting a European Site; the same applies to orders already made. There is provision for compensation for abortive expenditure under TCPA 1990, s. 107 in such cases.[69]

66 See para 7.64.
67 SI 2007 No 1843, reg 5(36) inserting a new reg 64A into the 1994 regulations.
68 See paras 7.72 and 7.76.
69 Nature Conservation Regs, reg 67(1).

19

PLANNING APPEALS

19.01 Where the local planning authority give a decision on a planning application, there is a right of appeal to the Secretary of State, and from him a right of challenge in the courts on a point of law. Before determining such an appeal, the Secretary of State must afford either party, if they so wish, the opportunity to put their case before a person appointed for the purpose.

19.02 Similarly where listed building consent or conservation area consent are refused there is a right to appeal to the Secretary of State; if there is an appeal both the appellant and the local planning authority have the right to ask for a hearing. There is also a right of appeal against enforcement notices.

19.03 There are procedural rules, in some cases made by the Lord Chancellor under the Tribunals and Inquiries Act 1992, in others by the Secretary of State, governing the various classes of appeal. Originally such rules covered public inquiries, but in recent years regulations have been made to cover appeals by written representation and in 2000 rules were made relating to informal hearings. Planning appeals are also subject to the rules of natural justice, which will be discussed in the following chapter.

19.04 Under a reform made by the PA 2008, the Secretary of State will be required to determine the procedure by which certain appeal proceedings under TCPA 1990,

LBA 1990 and HSA 1990 should be dealt with—ie by written representations; a hearing; or a public local inquiry. These provisions are considered later in this chapter. Further, Schedule 11 of the 2008 Act provides for notices of appeal to be accompanied by such information as may be prescribed by development order. In addition, the schedule also provides for a development order to specify a time limit for appealing against a local planning authority's refusal of a certificate of lawfulness under ss. 191 or 192 of TCPA 1990.[1]

Appeals against planning decisions: preliminary

19.05 As we saw in an earlier chapter,[2] TCPA 1990, s. 78 confers a right of appeal against a refusal of planning permission or the imposition of conditions attached to a planning permission.[3] An appeal may also be made under TCPA 1990, s. 78 against the failure by the local planning authority to determine the application within the prescribed time limit; against outline planning permission;[4] and in relation to the refusal of various approvals under the General Permitted Development Order.[5] The TCPA 1990 provides that, before determining an appeal under s. 78, the Secretary of State is required, if either the appellant or the local planning authority so wish, to give each of them an opportunity of appearing before and being heard by a person appointed by the Secretary of State for the purpose, ie an inspector.[6] As we saw in an earlier chapter,[7] the vast majority of appeals are nowadays determined by inspectors, although in law the decision is that of the Secretary of State. Appeals determined by inspectors are called 'transferred appeals'; those determined by the Secretary of State are referred to as 'non-transferred appeals'.

19.06 If neither party wishes to exercise their right to a hearing, and the Secretary of State does not consider it necessary that an inquiry or hearing should be held, the appeal will be determined by the written representation procedure. If either party does wish to be heard, they must state their reasons and their preferred procedure. The Secretary of State will then decide whether an inquiry or hearing will be held.

19.07 Where the right to be heard is exercised, it is presently the Secretary of State's policy to promote the use of hearings rather than inquiries in appropriate cases. Hitherto, hearings have been conducted in accordance with an informal code

---

[1] See paras 6.179 and 12.157.
[2] See para 8.121.
[3] See DETR Circular 5/00 for guidance on the operation of the procedures.
[4] See para 8.29.
[5] See para 7.01.
[6] TCPA 1990, s. 79(2).
[7] See para 8.124.

of practice,[8] but in 2000 the Secretary of State made a set of statutory rules for the conduct of such proceedings.[9] Nevertheless there will continue to be cases where the inquiry will be the most appropriate forum, for example where there are a large number of objectors or where complex technical, legal, or policy issues are involved.

19.08 We are now in a position to consider the procedures involved in appeals by written representations; where a hearing is held; and where there is a public inquiry.

Written representation procedure

19.09 The written representation procedure is generally quicker, simpler, and cheaper than proceeding by way of inquiry; it is currently the preferred method of approximately over two-thirds of appellants. The TCPA 1990[10] empowers the Secretary of State to make regulations prescribing the procedure for this type of appeal—the current regulations are the Town and Country Planning (Appeals) (Written Representations Procedure) (England) Regulations 2000, the 'Written Representations Regulations'.[11]

19.10 The procedure may be summarized as follows:

(1) Where the appellant informs the Secretary of State that he wishes the appeal to be dealt with in this way, he should set out his case in full in his notice of appeal.
(2) The Secretary of State will, once he has received all the information necessary to enable him to entertain the appeal, immediately notify the appellant and the local planning authority of the 'starting date'.[12] This date is the point from which all other procedural steps in the regulations are calculated.
(3) Within two weeks of the starting date, the local planning authority are required to notify interested parties. Interested parties are: (a) any person notified or consulted in accordance with the Act or development order about the application giving rise to the appeal; and (b) any other person who made representations to the local planning authority about that application.[13] The local planning authority must also submit to the Secretary of State an appeals questionnaire and supporting documents.

---

8 Contained in Circular 2/88, Annex 2.
9 See para 19.13.
10 TCPA 1990, s. 323.
11 SI 2000 No 1648. See also Circular 5/00, Annex 1.
12 SI 2000 No 1648, reg 4.
13 SI 2000 No 1648, reg 5.

(4) Where the questionnaire does not comprize the local planning authority's full case, further representations must be submitted to the Secretary of State within six weeks of the starting date.[14] By this date, the Secretary of State must have received any further representations from the appellant.[15]

(5) Within nine weeks of the starting date each party should submit comments on the representations of the other parties.[16] Interested persons must submit any representations to the Secretary of State within six weeks of the starting date.

(6) The Secretary of State may proceed to a decision on the appeal taking into account only such written representations as have been submitted within the relevant time limits.[17]

19.11 Although there is no statutory basis for it in the case of written representation procedure, the inspector will visit the site.[18]

19.12 The written representation procedure is based on a very tight timetable. It is clearly prudent for the appellant to begin preparation of his case well before the last date for giving notice of appeal, as he is required to set out his case in the notice of appeal.

Hearings procedure

19.13 At a hearing the inspector leads a discussion about the issues raised by the appeal. Circular 5/00 says that a hearing is suitable for small-scale development; where there is little third party interest; where complex legal, technical, or policy issues are unlikely to arise; and where there is no likelihood that formal cross-examination will be needed.[19]

19.14 Hearings are conducted in accordance with the Town and Country Planning (Hearings Procedure) (England) Rules 2000, the 'Hearings Rules'.[20] The procedure may be summarized as follows:

(1) The Secretary of State will, once he has received all the information necessary to enable him to entertain the appeal, immediately notify the appellant and the local planning authority of the starting date.

---

14 SI 2000 No 1648, regs 5 and 6.
15 SI 2000 No 1648, reg 7.
16 SI 2000 No 1648, reg 7.
17 SI 2000 No 1648, reg 10.
18 See Circular 5/00, para 11.
19 Circular 5/00, para 3.
20 SI 2000 No 1626.

(2) The local planning authority must, as soon as practicable after being notified that a hearing is to be held, notify the Secretary of State and the appellant of any statutory party[21] who has made representations to them. Within two weeks of the starting date they must submit to the Secretary of State an appeals questionnaire and supporting documents and notify interested parties.[22]

(3) Within six weeks of the starting date the appellant and the local planning authority must submit their written hearing statement to the Secretary of State, and interested parties must submit any comments. The hearing statement must contain full particulars of the case including any documents to which they wish to refer.

(4) Within nine weeks of the starting date the appellant and local planning authority must submit copies of any final comments to the Secretary of State.[23] The hearing date must be arranged by the Secretary of State to take place within 12 weeks of the starting date or as soon as practicable thereafter.[24]

(5) The procedure at the hearing itself should be informal and parties are encouraged to submit a short summary of evidence on matters that they can agree.[25] The inspector may, if he considers it appropriate, adjourn the hearing to the site; otherwise the inspector may conduct a site visit during the hearing or after it has closed.[26] Submissions in respect of costs should be made at the conclusion of the hearing.

(6) If it becomes apparent during the hearing that the procedure is inappropriate, the inspector may, after consulting the parties, close the proceedings and arrange for an inquiry to be held.

(7) The inspector may disregard any representations received after the hearing has closed. If, after this, in the case of transferred appeals, the inspector proposes to take into consideration any new evidence or any new matter of fact (not being a matter of government policy) which was not raised at the hearing and which he considers to be material to his decision, he must not come to a decision without first notifying the persons entitled to appear at the inquiry who appeared at it of the matter in question, and affording them an opportunity of making representations to him or requesting the re-opening of the hearing—such representations or requests must be submitted to the Secretary of State within three weeks of the date of the notification.[27] There is a corresponding provision relating to non-transferred appeals where the Secretary

---

21 Ie those persons whose representations the local planning authority are required to take into account; see para 8.10.

22 Hearings Rules, r 4.

23 Hearings Rules, r 6.

24 Hearings Rules, r 7.

25 Circular 5/00, Annex 2(i).

26 Hearings Rules, r 12.

27 Hearings Rules, r 14.

of State is disposed to disagree with the inspector's decision in the circumstances outlined above.[28]

(8) Finally the Secretary of State, or the inspector, must notify the parties, including interested parties who appeared at the hearing, of his decision.

Public inquiries: preliminary

19.15 Where the appeal is to be determined following a public local inquiry, the procedure is regulated by the Town and Country Planning (Inquiries Procedure) (England) Rules 2000 (the 'Inquiries Procedure Rules');[29] or the Town and Country Planning (Determination by Inspectors) (Inquiries Procedure) (England) Rules 2000 (the 'Determination by Inspectors Rules').[30] The former govern procedure relating to non-transferred cases, the latter relating to transferred cases, which, as we have seen, constitute the great majority of cases.

19.16 The new Rules, which replace Rules made in 1992, have been made with the purpose of streamlining the appeal process. There are some innovations. These include the requirement that the local planning authority and appellant prepare a 'statement of common ground' upon matters which are agreed and forward it to the Secretary of State in advance of the inquiry. And in a break with long-established practice, at the inquiry the local planning authority are to 'open', that is, present their case first. In addition the Secretary of State is able to disregard any representations received after the close of the inquiry.

Public inquiries: transferred cases

Pre-inquiry procedure

19.17 As with written representations and hearings discussed above, a key concept in inquiry procedure is the 'starting date'—this is the point from which all other steps in the Rules are calculated. The starting date is defined by rule 2 of the Determination by Inspectors Rules as the date of (a) the Secretary of State's written notice to the appellant and the local planning authority that he has received all the documents required to enable him to entertain the appeal; or (b) the relevant notice, whichever the later. The 'relevant notice' is the Secretary of State's written notice informing the appellant and local planning authority that an inquiry is to be held.

---

28 Hearings Rules, r 13.
29 SI 2000 No 1624.
30 SI 2000 No 1625.

19.18 The procedure may be summarized as follows:

(1) On receipt of the relevant notice from the Secretary of State, the local planning authority must inform the Secretary of State and the appellant in writing of the details of any statutory party[31] who has made representations to them. The Secretary of State must, as soon as practicable thereafter, inform the appellant and local planning authority of the details of any statutory party who has made representations to him.[32]

(2) Within two weeks of the starting date, the local planning authority must submit to the Secretary of State an appeals questionnaire and supporting documents and notify interested parties.[33]

(3) The Secretary of State must notify the name of the inspector to every person entitled to appear at the inquiry.[34]

(4) No later than six weeks after the starting date, the local planning authority must serve their statement of case on the Secretary of State and any statutory party; and the appellant must serve his statement of case on the Secretary of State and any statutory party.[35] A 'statement of case' (often referred to as a 'rule 6 statement') comprises a written statement containing full particulars of the case which a party proposes to put forward at the inquiry, and a list of any documents to be referred to or put in evidence.

Under the previous rules made in 1992 the appellant was given a further three weeks for assessing the local planning authority's statement before he was required to serve his own. This provision has now been removed and the parties' respective statements must be served by the same deadline.

The Rules provide that the appellant and local planning authority may each require the other party to forward them copy of any document referred to in the list of documents included in that party's statement of case.[36]

(5) Within 12 weeks of the starting date the inspector may send to the appellant, local planning authority, and any statutory party a written statement of the matters which, for the purposes of the appeal, he particularly wishes to be informed.[37] Further, the inspector must hold a pre-inquiry meeting if he expects the inquiry to last for eight days or more, unless he considers it unnecessary. The purpose of such a meeting is to ensure that the inquiry is conducted efficiently and expeditiously.[38]

31 See para 8.10.
32 Determination by Inspectors Rules, r 4.
33 Inspectors Rules, r 4.
34 Inspectors Rules, r 5.
35 Inspectors Rules, r 6.
36 Inspectors Rules, r 6.
37 Inspectors Rules, r 7.
38 Inspectors Rules, rr 2 and 7.

(6) The Secretary of State must prepare a timetable for all inquiries that appear to him likely to last for eight days or more, which he may at any time vary.[39]

(7) Unless a lesser period of notice is agreed, the Secretary of State must give not less than four weeks written notice of the date, time, and place fixed by him for the holding of the inquiry to every person entitled to appear.[40] Rule 10 provides that the date fixed for the holding of the inquiry shall be not later than 20 weeks after the starting date, unless he considers such a date impracticable. Each principal party is only permitted one refusal of a date offered for the inquiry before the Secretary of State will proceed to fix a date.[41]

Inquiry procedure

19.19 The persons entitled to appear at the inquiry include: the appellant; the local planning authority; (if not the local planning authority) the county or district council in whose area the land is situated; any statutory party and any other person who has submitted a statement of case.[42] Beyond those expressly entitled by the Rules, the inspector may permit any other person to appear at the inquiry and such permission shall not be unreasonably withheld.

19.20 Where (a) the Secretary of State or the Historic Buildings and Monuments Commission has given the local planning authority a direction restricting the grant of planning permission; or (b) where the Secretary of State or any other Minister of the Crown, government department, or local authority has expressed in writing the view that planning permission should not be granted, any party may, not later than four weeks before the date of the inquiry, apply to the Secretary of State for a representative of any of the above-mentioned bodies to attend the inquiry—such a person shall not be required to answer any question which is directed at the merits of government policy.[43]

19.21 Any person entitled to appear at the inquiry and proposing to give, or calling another person to give, evidence by reading a proof of evidence must send a copy to the inspector together with any written summary, normally no later than four weeks before the date fixed for the holding of the inquiry. No written summary will be required where the proof of evidence contains no more than 1,500 words; however where a written summary is required, only the summary is to be read at the inquiry, unless the inspector permits or directs otherwise.[44]

39 Inspectors Rules, r 8.
40 Inspectors Rules, r 10.
41 Circular 5/00, Annex 3, para 26.
42 Determination by Inspectors Rules, r 11.
43 Inspectors Rules, r 12.
44 Inspectors Rules, r 14.

19.22 The 'statement of common ground' first appeared in the current Rules. It is a written statement prepared jointly by the local planning authority and the appellant containing agreed factual information.[45] The parties must ensure that the Secretary of State and any statutory party receive a copy of it, not less than four weeks before the date fixed for the holding of the inquiry.[46]

19.23 The hope is that the inclusion of agreed material in a statement of common ground will save time and expense at the inquiry. There are some matters upon which it will usually be possible to reach agreement; for example the nature of the proposal, the description of the site, and the relevant planning policies. It might also be possible to agree on technical matters such as traffic flows or design standards, possible planning conditions, or the content of a planning obligation should the appeal be successful.[47]

19.24 Except as otherwise provided by the Rules, the inspector shall determine the procedure at the inquiry.[48] The procedure may be summarized as follows:

(1) At the start of the inquiry the inspector will identify what he considers to be the main issues and any matters on which he requires further explanation.
(2) Unless the inspector otherwise directs, the local planning authority will 'open', ie present their case first, and the appellant will have the right of final reply. Each side will call their witnesses. The evidence may be given as in a court of law by question and answer, but it may be given instead by the witness reading his proof of evidence or summary as the case may be. Each witness may expect to be cross-examined by the other side and by any statutory party. The inspector has a discretion to allow other interested parties to ask questions of a witness. Questions may also be asked by the inspector.
(3) Statutory parties have the right to state their case and the inspector may allow other interested parties to make statements.
(4) The inspector may allow either or both parties to alter or add to any submissions in their statement of case, but must give the other party and any statutory parties an adequate opportunity of considering the fresh submissions, if necessary by adjourning the inquiry.
(5) The hearing is concluded by the parties making their closing submissions; where the Secretary of State expects the inquiry to last for eight or more days, any person making a closing submission must by the close of the inquiry provide the inspector with a copy of their submission in writing.

45 Inspectors Rules, r 2.
46 Inspectors Rules, r 15.
47 See Circular 5/00, Annex 3 (ii).
48 Determination by Inspectors Rules, r 16.

(6) Having closed the inquiry the inspector will visit the site in the company of the appellant, the local planning authority, and any statutory party. The inspector may also make an unaccompanied inspection of the land before or during the inquiry without notifying the persons entitled to appear at the inquiry.

Post-inquiry procedure

19.25 Under rule 18, when making his decision, the inspector may disregard any written representations or evidence received after the close of the inquiry.

19.26 If, after the close of the inquiry, the inspector proposes to take into consideration any new evidence or matter of fact (not being a matter of government policy) which was not raised at the inquiry and which he considers to be material to his decision, he must not come to a decision without first notifying the persons entitled to appear at the inquiry who appeared at it of the matter in question; and affording them an opportunity of making representations to him or of asking for the re-opening of the hearing—such representations or requests must be submitted to the Secretary of State within three weeks of the date of the notification.[49]

19.27 The inspector must notify his decision and the reasons for it, in writing, to (a) all persons entitled to appear at the inquiry who did appear; and (b) to any other person who, having appear at the inquiry, has asked to be notified of the decision.[50]

Public inquiries: non-transferred cases

19.28 As mentioned earlier in this chapter, where the Secretary of State determines the appeal on the recommendation of the inspector, the procedure is regulated by the Inquiries Procedure Rules.[51] These rules differ from the Determination by Inspectors Rules in the ways outlined below.

19.29 Where the Secretary of State causes a pre-inquiry meeting to be held, a special procedure is triggered under rule 5; pre-inquiry meetings will be held where the Secretary of State expects the inquiry to last for eight days or more, unless he considers it unnecessary. The rule will normally be invoked in the case of all inquiries to which the Code of Practice for Preparing for Major Planning Inquiries is applied.[52]

---

49 Inspectors Rules, r 18.
50 Inspectors Rules, r 19.
51 SI 2000 No 1624.
52 See Circular 5/00, Annex 4.

19.30 Where the Secretary of State decides to hold a pre-inquiry meeting, he must notify the parties of his intention and also provide a statement of the matters about which he particularly wishes to be informed. The purpose is to clarify the matters which the Secretary of State considers to be the key issues and to assist the parties in preparing for the inquiry. This notification is given when the parties are informed that an inquiry is to be held.

19.31 The local planning authority must publish notice of the local planning authority's intention to hold a pre-inquiry meeting and of the statement of matters about which the Secretary of State wishes to be informed.

19.32 Under rule 5 the appellant and the local planning authority must ensure that copies of their outline statements (ie statements of the principal submissions which they propose to put forward at the inquiry) have been submitted to the Secretary of State within eight weeks of the starting date. The Secretary of State may require other parties to provide an outline statement within four weeks of being so required.

19.33 The pre-inquiry meeting, or where there is more than one such meeting, the first such meeting, must be held within 16 weeks of the starting date.

19.34 The other main area where the Inquiries Procedure Rules differ from the Determination by Inspectors Rules is the post-inquiry procedure. Under the former, after the close of the inquiry, the inspector must make a written report to the Secretary of State including his conclusions and recommendations or his reasons for not making any recommendations.

19.35 After the close of the inquiry the Secretary of State may decide to differ from the inspector on a matter of fact this is a situation which cannot occur in a transferred appeal determined by the inspector.[53]

19.36 In the above situation rule 17 of the Inquiries Procedure Rules provides: if, after the close of the inquiry, the Secretary of State differs from the inspector on any matter of fact or takes into consideration any new evidence or matter of fact (not being a matter of government policy) and is for that reason disposed to disagree with the inspector's recommendation, he shall not come to a decision at variance with that recommendation without first notifying the persons entitled to appear and who appeared at the inquiry of his disagreement and the reasons for it, and affording them the opportunity of making written representations to him within three weeks (or where new evidence or new matters of fact have been taken into consideration) of asking for the re-opening of the inquiry.

[53] Inquiries Procedure Rules, r 17.

Appeals against planning decisions: finality of decision

19.37 As mentioned in an earlier chapter[54] the TCPA 1990 provides that the decision of the Secretary of State, or inspector in transferred cases, is final[55] except for the possibility of challenge under TCPA 1990, s. 288. That provision offers the only means whereby the validity of an appeal decision can be challenged, as TCPA 1990, s. 284(1) states that, save for challenge under TCPA 1990, s. 288, the validity of such decisions 'shall not be questioned in any legal proceedings whatsoever'.

Undue delay

19.38 The Planning and Compensation Act 1991, s. 18 introduced a new TCPA 1990, s. 79(6A). It provides that if at any time before or during the determination of an appeal it appears to the Secretary of State that the appellant is responsible for undue delay in the progress of an appeal, he may notify the appellant that the appeal is dismissed unless the appellant takes such steps as are specified to expedite the appeal. The notice shall specify a period within which such steps are to be taken, and if the appellant fails to take those steps within the specified period, the Secretary of State may dismiss the appeal.

19.39 The power to dismiss an appeal in the case of undue delay might be of some use in dealing with the practice of 'twin-tracking'. Here, two planning permissions in identical terms, A and B, are submitted to the local planning authority. The developer seeks determination of A while lodging an appeal against the non-determination of B after the relevant statutory period.[56] He will only proceed expeditiously with the appeal on B if planning permission is ultimately refused for A. If planning permission is granted for A, his appeal on B may be withdrawn.

Award of costs

19.40 The costs of a planning appeal, which in the case of major inquiries can be very considerable, are normally borne by the party that incurs them. In certain circumstances, however, costs may be awarded in favour of a party to an appeal.

19.41 The Local Government Act 1972, s. 250(5) allows orders to be made by the Secretary of State 'as to the costs of the parties at the inquiry and as to the parties

---

54 See para 8.121.
55 TCPA 1990, s. 79(5).
56 Additional measures in PCPA 2004 to address twin-tracking are discussed at para 8.135.

by whom such costs are to be paid, and every such order may be made a rule of the High Court on the application of any party named in the order'. The TCPA 1990 applies this provision to planning appeals decided by the Secretary of State when an inquiry has been held;[57] to planning appeals determined on inquiry by an inspector;[58] to planning appeals decided under the hearings procedure;[59] although this has not, as yet, been brought into force in relation to appeals decided under the written representation procedure.[60]

19.42 The above provision applies to certain other appeals under the TCPA 1990, and by LBA 1990, s. 89 to listed buildings appeals.

19.43 A provision introduced by the PCA 1991 is also of importance. It sometimes happens that, following an appeal, an inquiry is arranged, but one or other of the principal parties abandons their case before the opening of the inquiry. The other party is put to considerable wasted time and expense. TCPA 1990, s. 332A, inserted by PCA, s. 30, provides that if an inquiry is requested by either party, and arrangements are made but the inquiry does not actually take place, the Secretary of State has the power to require any party to pay any costs of any other party.

19.44 Previously the power to award costs applied only where the inquiry had been held. TCPA 1990, s. 322A applies also to hearings.

Criteria for the award of costs

19.45 The criteria for the award of costs by the Secretary of State are set out in Circular 8/93. Before an award of costs is made the following conditions will normally need to be met:

(1) one of the parties has sought an award at the appropriate stage of the proceedings (normally before the inquiry is concluded);
(2) the party against whom the costs are sought has acted unreasonably; and
(3) this unreasonable conduct has caused the party seeking costs to incur or waste expense unnecessarily, either because it should not have been necessary for the matter to be determined by the Secretary of State or because of the manner in which another party has behaved in the proceedings.[61]

19.46 The word 'unreasonable' is used in its ordinary meaning.[62] Circular 8/93 contains a summary of the criteria for the award of costs on the grounds of

57 TCPA 1990, s. 320(2). See para 19.28.
58 TCPA 1990, s. 320(2) and Sch 6, para 6(4). See para 19.17.
59 TCPA 1990, s. 322. See para 19.13.
60 See para 19.09.
61 Circular 8/93, Annex 1, para 6.
62 *Manchester City Council v Secretary of State for the Environment* [1988] JPL 774.

unreasonable behaviour.[63] Thus appellants are at risk of an award of costs against them if, for example, they: fail to comply with normal procedural requirements; fail to pursue or attend an inquiry or hearing; introduce new grounds of appeal, or new issues, late in the proceedings; withdraw the appeal after being notified of inquiry or hearing arrangements, without any material change in the circumstances; or pursue a case which obviously has no reasonable grounds of success, including one which flies in the face of national planning policies.

19.47 The grounds upon which local planning authorities may be at risk of an award of costs against them include, for example, if they: fail to comply with normal procedural requirements, including compliance with relevant regulations; fail to provide evidence, on planning grounds, to substantiate their reasons for refusing planning permission; fail to take into account relevant policy statements or judicial authority; refuse to discuss or provide information in respect of a planning application; at a late stage, introduce an additional reason for refusal or abandon a reason for refusal; and impose conditions which are unnecessary, unreasonable, unenforceable, imprecise, or irrelevant.

Application for costs

19.48 An application for costs should be made by a party before the inspector closes the inquiry or hearing. The other party has, of course, a right of reply. An application for costs made after the inquiry or hearing will be accepted only if the party applying for costs can show good reason for not having applied earlier.[64]

Listed building consent and conservation area consent appeals

19.49 The procedure on these types of appeals[65] is governed by the Rules described earlier in this chapter.

Determination of procedure

19.50 The Planning Act 2008, s. 196(1) inserts a new s. 319A into TCPA 1990 requiring the Secretary of State to determine the procedure by which certain appeal procedures under the Act should be considered.

19.51 The relevant procedures are, whichever appears to the Secretary of State to be more appropriate of: (a) a local inquiry; (b) a hearing; or (c) written representations. The Secretary of State must notify the appellant or applicant and the local

---

63 See Appendix to Circular 8/93.
64 Circular 8/93, Annex 5, paras 1 and 4.
65 See para 16.01.

planning authority of the determination as to the procedure selected within a prescribed period. The Secretary of State must publish the criteria that are to be applied in determining the method of appeal. The proceedings to which the section apply are:

(a) planning application called in by the Secretary of State under s. 77 TCPA 1990;
(b) an appeal under s. 78 TCPA 1990 against a decision of a local planning authority refusing, etc planning permission;
(c) an appeal under s. 174 TCPA 1990 against an enforcement notice issued by a local planning authority;
(d) an appeal under s. 195 TCPA 1990 against a decision of a local planning authority in relation to a certificate of lawfulness; and
(e) an appeal under s. 208 TCPA 1990 against a notice issued by a local planning authority under s. 207 TCPA 1990 relating to the replacement of trees.

19.52 The Secretary of State may by order amend the above list by adding or deleting particular proceedings or otherwise modifying it.

19.53 PA 2008, s. 196(2) makes similar provision as above with regard to certain proceedings under LBA 1990 by the insertion of a new s. 88D into that Act. The proceedings to which the section applies are:

(a) an application for listed building consent that is called in by the Secretary of State under s. 12 LBA 1990;
(b) an appeal under s. 20 LBA 1990 against a decision of a local planning authority refusing, etc planning permission; and
(c) an appeal under s. 39 LBA 1990 against a listed building enforcement notice issued by a local planning authority.

19.54 Further, PA 2008 s. 196(3) makes similar provision with regard to certain proceedings under the HSA 1990 by the insertion of a new s. 21A into that Act. The proceedings to which the section applies are:

(a) an application called in by the Secretary of State under s. 20 HSA 1990;
(b) an appeal under s. 21 HSA 1990 against a decision of a hazardous substances authority refusing, etc hazardous substances consent.

Payment of fees

19.55 A new s. 303ZA of TCPA 1990, inserted by PA 2008, s. 200, allows the Secretary of State to make regulations providing for the payment of fees in respect of appeals under TCPA 1990 and LBA 1990. The regulations may make provision [66] as to a range of matters in connection with the payment of the fees. The fee is to be

[66] For fees payable on a planning application, see para 8.32.

payable by the appellant and it is in addition to any fee payable to the appropriate authority under s. 303 of TCPA 1990.

Timetable for decisions

19.56 Schedule 2 of PCPA 2004 requires the Secretary of State to make timetables for certain decisions he has to make under TCPA 1990. The obligation applies to any decision which must be made by the Secretary of State himself in connection with (a) called in applications under s. 77 TCPA 1990[67] and with (b) planning appeals under s. 78. The obligation also applies to other decisions, 'connected decisions', ie one which the Secretary of State thinks is connected with a decision under (a) or (b) above, and the Secretary of State is required by virtue of any enactment to take the decision, or the Secretary of State by virtue of a power under any enactment directs that the decision be referred to him.

19.57 However the Secretary of State may specify, by order, decisions, or descriptions of decisions for which there is not to be a timetable.[68]

19.58 The Secretary of State must publish the timetables, and must notify the following persons in a particular case of the published timetable—the applicant or appellant (as the case may be) in relation to the decision; the local planning authority, and any other person who requests notification. The Secretary of State has powers to vary the timetable, but if he fails to take any step in accordance with the timetable, or the timetable as varied, he must give written reasons to the person he is required to notify of the timetable.

19.59 The Secretary of State must publish and lay before Parliament an annual report reviewing his perfomance under these provisions and explaining any failure to comply with a timetable.

[67] See para 8.36.

[68] See T & CP (Timetable for Decisions) (England) Order 2005, SI 2005 No 205 which came into force on 1 April 2005. The Order details those cases which will not be required to be subject to a timetable, ie because they are reliant on decisions made by others. It also excludes those decisions made by planning inspectors on the Secretary of State's behalf.

20

REVIEW BY THE COURTS AND THE OMBUDSMAN

20.01 It will be appreciated from previous chapters that the planning Acts invest both the local planning authority and the Secretary of State with wide discretionary powers in the making of decisions. Such discretion is subject to the powers of review and supervision of the High Court.

20.02 The court is not concerned with the merits, on planning grounds, of any particular decision, but rather with the question of legality—substantive or procedural. In reviewing legality, the court applies the doctrine of 'ultra vires' by which actions beyond the powers of the enabling statute will be quashed or declared to be a nullity and of no effect.

20.03 In most cases, against decisions of the local planning authority, the TCPA 1990 provides for an appeal by the applicant to the Secretary of State. Before reaching his decision the Secretary of State shall, unless the parties waive the right to a hearing, appoint an inspector to hold a public inquiry or hearing.[1] In nearly all cases now, however, the inspector will make the decision himself[2] and currently over 80 per cent of appeals are dealt with by way of written representations.

1 See para 19.15.
2 See para 8.124.

20.04 The decision of the Secretary of State (or his inspector with power to determine) in a planning appeal is expressed to be 'final'[3] but the TCPA 1990 has a statutory machinery whereby its legality may be challenged in the High Court on specified grounds amounting to substantive or procedural ultra vires within six weeks of the decision by any 'person aggrieved' by it.[4]

20.05 Apart from the statutory machinery for quashing a decision of the Secretary of State it has long been accepted that the legality of decisions of the local planning authority may be challenged in the High Court as part of that court's supervisory jurisdiction.[5] The remedies available by this method are: (i) a quashing order (formerly 'certiorari'); (ii) a prohibiting order (formerly 'prohibition'); and (iii) a mandatory order (formerly 'mandamus'). The remedies of declaration and injunction are also available. All these methods of challenge may be obtained by a claim for 'judicial review', however the claimant is required to have a sufficient interest in the matter concerned ('locus standi').

20.06 This chapter will deal first with the statutory review machinery under TCPA 1990 and then go on to consider judicial review. Lastly we will examine briefly the role of the Parliamentary and Local Commissioners ('ombudsmen'), who have powers to investigate maladministration by government departments and local authorities respectively.

Statutory review

20.07 As indicated above, s. 288 TCPA 1990 provides the only means by which the legality of a decision of the Secretary of State in a planning appeal may be challenged in the courts.[6]

20.08 The grounds of challenge under s. 288 fall into two branches. Under the first branch a decision may be challenged if it is not within the powers of the Act, ie ultra vires. The second branch refers to a failure to comply with 'the relevant requirements'; this extends to procedural requirements not necessarily to be found in the Act itself, such as the Inquiry Procedure Rules. The two branches clearly overlap but the main difference between them is that under the second branch the

[3] TCPA 1990, s. 79(5).

[4] TCPA 1990, s. 288. Actions may also be brought in the High Court under TCPA 1990, s. 187 (validity of old-style development plans); under PCPA 2004, s. 113 (validity of new-style development plans); and under TCPA 1990, s. 289 (validity of enforcement action). See chs 4, 5, and 12 above.

[5] *R v Hillingdon London Borough Council, ex p Royco Homes Ltd* [1974] QB 720.

[6] The machinery in s. 288 TCPA 1990 also covers other appeal decisions made under the Act including those made under s. 97 (revocation, etc orders—see ch 11 above); under s. 102 (discontinuance orders—see ch 11 above); under s. 177 (decision made under ground (a) in enforcement appeals—see ch 12, above); under s. 195 (CLEUDs and CLOPUDs respectively—see chs 6 and 12); and s. 198 (tree preservation orders—see ch 15 above).

defect must have resulted in 'substantial prejudice' to the applicant. However, even where a decision is ultra vires under the first branch, it seems the court still has a discretion whether or not to quash.[7]

20.09 The principles upon which the court may act under s. 288 were discussed by Forbes J in *Seddon Properties Ltd v Secretary of State for the Environment*,[8] subsequently approved by the Court of Appeal in *Centre 21 Ltd v Secretary of State for the Environment*.[9] The learned judge said that (1) the decision maker must not act perversely, thus if the decision is so unreasonable that no reasonable decision maker could ever have come to it, the courts can interfere;[10] (2) in reaching his conclusion the decision maker must not take into account irrelevant material or fail to take into account that which is relevant;[11] (3) the decision maker must abide by the statutory procedures, in particular those in the Inquiries Procedure Rules; and (4) the decision maker must not depart from the rules of natural justice. Natural justice is considered more fully below; as a ground of challenge it applies not only to statutory review currently under discussion but also to judicial review discussed later in this chapter.

Natural justice

20.10 There are two rules of natural justice: (i) the right to a hearing ('audi alteram partem') and (ii) no person shall be a judge in his own cause or the rule against bias ('nemo debet esse judex in propria causa'). The rules as applicable to planning appeals are now regarded as consisting of a general 'duty to act fairly' and the House of Lords has referred to the need for an objector to feel he has had a 'fair crack of the whip'.[12] We will now consider the application of the two rules in turn.

Right to a hearing

20.11 The requirements of this branch of the rule will be satisfied providing a party (a) knows the case against him and (b) is given a fair opportunity to state his views. For this reason an oral hearing is not necessarily required—indeed the planning legislation provides for planning appeals to be dealt with by way of written representations.

20.12 In the conduct of planning appeals, the requirements of the audi alteram partem rule are reflected in the Inquiries Procedure Rules.[13] Although the rules are an

7 *Miller v Weymouth and Melcombe Regis Corpn* [1974] 27 P & CR 468.
8 [1978] 42 P & CR 26.
9 [1986] JPL 914.
10 See the discussion of the '*Wednesbury*' principle in para 10.70.
11 See *Ashbridge Investments Ltd v Minister of Housing and Local Government* [1965] 1 WLR 1320.
12 *Fairmount Investments Ltd v Secretary of State for the Environment* [1976] 2 All ER 865.
13 See para 19.19.

expression of natural justice, they do not replace it, rather they complement it.[14] Nevertheless, where the rules have not been breached, it appears there is a heavy onus on the party alleging unfairness.[15] Disregard of the rules will not automatically render a decision ultra vires in the absence of substantial prejudice,[16] but where such disregard amounts to a substantive breach of natural justice, the court will quash the decision.[17]

20.13 As has already been said, each party must have had a 'fair crack of the whip'. In *Performance Cars Ltd v Secretary of State for the Environment*,[18] the applicant was provided with documents containing the local authority's case only on the morning of the inquiry and he requested an adjournment of 30 days to consider them. The inspector offered him a long lunch break to consider them; the Court of Appeal held that the procedure was unfair despite the absence of substantial prejudice.

20.14 The more informal atmosphere of a hearing, as opposed to an inquiry, raises the danger that a full and fair hearing may not take place, and that there is a risk of a less than thorough examination of the facts. In *Dyason v Secretary of State for the Environment*,[19] the appellant had been refused planning permission to carry out development at his ostrich farm. At the hearing the appellant called an expert witness to give his opinion on a business plan which the appellant had submitted in advance of the hearing. The expert had not seen the business plan in advance and explained to the inspector that he could offer no assistance as he had not seen it. The inspector provided no opportunity for a short adjournment to enable the expert witness to assist. The Court of Appeal held that the fair hearing required by the statute had not been provided. The absence of an accusatorial procedure, ie the opportunity to cross-examine witnesses, places an inquisitorial burden on the inspector. Although statutory rules governing the conduct of hearings have now been made,[20] the observations of the Court of Appeal in the *Dyason* case remain valid.

20.15 In the case of inquiries the Inquiries Procedure Rules confer a right of cross-examination on the main parties, but other parties may only cross-examine to the extent permitted by the inspector; his discretion here must be exercised fairly.[21]

---

[14] *Hyndburn Borough Council v Secretary of State for the Environment* [1979] JPL 536.
[15] *Rea v Minister of Transport* [1982] 47 P & CR 207.
[16] *Reading Borough Council v Secretary of State for the Environment* [1986] JPL 115.
[17] *Swinbank v Secretary of State for the Environment* [1987] 55 P & CR 371.
[18] [1977] 34 P & CR 92.
[19] [1998] JPL 778.
[20] See para 19.13.
[21] See *Bushell v Secretary of State for the Environment* [1981] AC 75; cf *Nicholson v Secretary of State for Energy* [1978] JPL 39.

20.16 The decision must not be based on a ground which was not before the parties and upon which they have had no opportunity to comment. Thus in *Fairmount Investments Ltd v Secretary of State for the Environment*,[22] a case under the Housing Act 1957, the inspector recommended, after a site visit, that the objectors' houses were structurally unsound and that rehabilitation would not be financially viable. This observation had not been made before or at the inquiry and the objectors had not had an opportunity to comment on it. The House of Lords held that a breach of natural justice had taken place.[23] The principle is reflected in the present Inquiries Procedure Rules which provide that if the Secretary of State disagrees with the inspector on any matter and is for that reason disposed to disagree with an inspector's recommendation he must invite the parties who were invited to appear and did appear to make representations. In cases where new evidence or facts have been taken into account he must reopen the inquiry if requested to do so by the appellant or the local planning authority. In other cases he has a discretion to reopen the inquiry which is subject to the rules of natural justice.[24] Where the Secretary of State disagrees with his inspector on a matter of fact, but no evidence was adduced at the inquiry upon which he could reasonably have based his decision, the court may overturn the decision.[25]

20.17 Proper, adequate, and intelligible reasons should be given for the decision. This requirement is not technically one of natural justice but is required by legislation in the case of planning inquiries.[26] The reasons can be briefly stated.[27] In a number of cases the courts have warned against scrutinizing too closely the wording of decision letters,[28] but nevertheless one of the most common grounds of challenge remains the adequacy of the reasoning contained in the decision letter.

20.18 The requirement to give reasons under the planning legislation was considered by the House of Lords in *Save Britain's Heritage v Secretary of State for the Environment*.[29] According to Lord Bridge, who gave the leading judgment in a unanimous decision, deficiency of reasons will only afford a ground for quashing a decision if the court is satisfied that the interests of the applicant have been substantially prejudiced by the deficiency. For example a developer might be substantially prejudiced where, having been refused planning permission, the planning considerations on which the decision is based are not explained sufficiently

---

22 [1976] 2 All ER 865.
23 And see *Furmston v Secretary of State for the Environment* [1983] JPL 49.
24 See para 19.25.
25 *Coleen Properties v Minister of Housing and Local Government* [1971] 1 All ER 1049.
26 Tribunals and Inquiries Act 1992.
27 *Bradley & Sons Ltd v Secretary of State for the Environment* [1983] 47 P & CR 374.
28 See for example *West Midlands Co-operative Society v Secretary of State for the Environment* [1988] JPL 121.
29 [1991] 2 All ER 10. The case is discussed at para 16.56.

clearly to enable him reasonably to assess his prospects of obtaining permission for some alternative development.

20.19 In a later case, *South Buckinghamshire District Council v Porter (No 2)*,[30] Lord Brown in the House of Lords summarized the proper approach to a 'reasons challenge' in the planning context. His Lordship said:

> The reasons for a decision must be intelligible and they must be adequate. They must enable the reader to understand why the matter was decided as it was and what conclusions were reached on the 'principal important controversial issues', disclosing how any issue of law or fact was resolved. Reasons can be briefly stated, the degree of particularity required depending entirely on the nature of the issues falling for decision. The reasoning must not give rise to a substantial doubt as to whether the decision-maker erred in law, for example by misunderstanding some relevant policy or some other important matter or by failing to reach a rational decision on relevant grounds. But such adverse inference will not readily be drawn. The reasons need only to refer to the main issues in the dispute, not to every material consideration. They should enable disappointed developers to assess their prospects of obtaining some alternative development permission, or, as the case may be, their unsuccessful opponents to understand how the policy or approach underlying the grant of permission may impact upon future such applications. Decision letters must be read in a straightforward manner, recognising that they are addressed to parties well aware of the issues involved and the arguments advanced. A reasons challenge will only succeed if the party aggrieved can satisfy the court that he has genuinely been substantially prejudiced by the failure to provide an adequately reasoned decision.

20.20 Although this guidance cannot be regarded as definitive or exhaustive, Lord Brown considered that it would focus attention on the main considerations when a party was contemplating a reasons challenge in the courts.

The rule against bias

20.21 This rule of natural justice, that no man shall be a judge in his own cause, has only limited application in planning. This is because decision makers are imbued with very wide discretion and may legitimately pursue a policy. Nevertheless it is the case that there should be no pecuniary interest or conflict of interest manifest in the circumstances in which a decision is made. Here the appearance of bias is sufficient to invalidate. Thus in *Hendon RDC, ex p Chorley*,[31] a member of the council committee dealing with a planning application was an estate agent acting for the applicants in connection with the property that was the subject matter of the application. He was present at the meeting that resolved to permit development, although apparently he took no part in the discussion. Certiorari was granted to quash the decision on the ground, inter alia, of bias.

---

[30] [2004] UKHL 33.
[31] [1933] 2 KB 696.

20.22 In *Steeples v Derbyshire County Council*,[32] the county council contractually bound itself to a development company whereby the council would use its best endeavours to obtain planning permission for a leisure centre. Webster J accepted that the council's decision to grant planning permission had been fairly made. However, to the reasonable man, who would be taken to know of all relevant matters including the council's potential liability in damages if permission were not granted, it would appear that the contract would have had a significant effect on the planning committee's decision. The judge held that the decision was void or voidable on the ground of a failure to comply with natural justice.[33] However a political predisposition in favour of a proposed development will not, without more, amount to bias.[34]

20.23 In the more recent case of *R v Bassetlaw District Council, ex p Oxby*,[35] the council had commissioned a report that identified a number of planning permissions granted by the council which had been affected by bias. Rather than revoke the consents under the provisions of TCPA 1990, s. 97,[36] the council resolved to bring judicial review proceedings to have the consents quashed. An unusual feature of the case is that the action was brought by the Leader of the Council. The Court of Appeal accepted the applicant's argument that it was not expedient to exercise the power of revocation since the permissions were affected by bias and should be quashed without payment of compensation.

Statutory review procedure

20.24 The court's powers under TCPA 1990 are limited to quashing the decision. There is no power to substitute its own decision or to modify or vary the Secretary of State's decision. Further, the whole decision is quashed and it was held in *Kingswood District Council v Secretary of State for the Environment*[37] that, following the quashing of a decision, the Secretary of State is under a duty to deal with the matter 'de novo', with, as it were, a clean sheet. He might therefore have to have regard to any further material considerations arising subsequently to his original decision. The Inquiries Procedure Rules deal with this possibility by requiring the Secretary of State to give the parties an opportunity to make further representations.[38]

---

32 [1984] 3 All ER 468.

33 Cf *R v St Edmundsbury Borough Council, ex p Investors in Industry Commercial Properties Ltd* [1985] 3 All ER 234, where a test of actual bias seems to have been applied.

34 *Franklin v Minister of Town and Country Planning* [1948] AC 87; *R v Amber Valley District Council, ex p Jackson* [1984] 3 All ER 501.

35 [1998] PLCR 283. See also *Corbett v Restormel Borough Council* [2001] 1 PLR 108.

36 See para 11.01. Revocation of planning permission may have rendered the council liable to compensation.

37 [1987] P & CR 153.

38 See para 19.25.

Time limits

20.25 The right to challenge under TCPA 1990, s. 288 is extinguished after six weeks from the date of the decision. The courts have interpreted such time limits strictly. Thus in *Smith v East Elloe RDC*,[39] the House of Lords held that an identically worded provision relating to a compulsory purchase order prevented a person aggrieved by the order from challenging its validity after the expiry of the time limit in circumstances where it had been made in bad faith.

20.26 Some years later a majority of the same court took the view that such 'privative' clauses could not prevent an application to the court out of time where a decision was ultra vires.[40] More recently, however, the courts have followed *Smith v East Elloe RDC*[41] and in *Griffiths v Secretary of State for the Environment*[42] the House of Lords held, Lord Scarman dissenting, that the six-week period runs from the date when the decision is made by the Secretary of State and not from when notice of it is received by the aggrieved person. It seems that the decision is made by the Secretary of State on the date stamped on the decision letter; in the case itself the letter took five days to arrive, thus reducing the time within which an application might be made to the High Court.

20.27 In *Okolo v Secretary of State for the Environment*,[43] the Court of Appeal held (in relation to a similar six-week rule in the Acquisition of Land Act 1981) that a time limit that is stated to be in weeks ends at midnight on the corresponding day of the week to that on which the period started. Thus, if a decision is made on a Monday and there are six weeks within which to challenge it, the six weeks ends on midnight on the Monday in six weeks' time.

Standing

20.28 Only 'persons aggrieved' by the Secretary of State's decision have standing ('locus standi') under TCPA 1990, s. 288. Historically the courts took a narrow view of the words—in *Buxton v Minister of Housing and Local Government*,[44] Salmon J held that adjoining landowners were not persons aggrieved; the words were confined to persons with legal grievances.[45] Later, in *Turner v Secretary of State for the Environment*,[46] it was held that if, at the inquiry, the inspector exercises his right

[39] [1956] AC 736.

[40] *Anisminic Ltd v Foreign Compensation Commission* [1969] 2 AC 147.

[41] *R v Secretary of State for the Environment, ex p Ostler* [1977] QB 122 where the Court of Appeal distinguished *Anisminic* on the ground that it referred to a judicial decision.

[42] [1983] 2 AC 51.

[43] [1997] JPL 1005.

[44] [1961] 1 QB 278.

[45] Salmon J's interpretation of person aggrieved was, in effect, restricted to the applicant for planning permission and parties entitled to be notified of the application.

[46] [1973] 28 P & CR 123. And see *A-G of Gambia v N'Jie* [1961] AC 617.

under the Inquiries Procedure Rules to invite third parties to appear and make representations, such persons may be persons aggrieved. In that case, Ackner J held that a local preservation society who had appeared at the inquiry at the grace of the inspector had sufficient locus standi under what is now s. 288. Subsequent decisions have continued the same approach.[47]

20.29 The current attitude of the courts is probably best exemplified by the reasoning of the Court of Appeal in the case of *Eco-Energy (GB) Ltd v First Secretary of State.* [48] Following an earlier decision, *Times Investment Ltd v Secretary of State for the Environment,* [49] Buxton LJ considered that 'persons aggrieved' under s. 288 were either (i) the appellant in the planning process; or (ii) someone who took a sufficiently active role in the planning process, eg a substantial objector, not just a person who objected and did no more about it; or (iii) someone who had a relevant interest in the land.

Judicial review

20.30 The availability of the statutory review procedure under s. 288 outlined above depends upon there having been an appeal to the Secretary of State. We have seen that 'persons aggrieved' by the decision of the Secretary of State can include third parties who have sufficient standing.[50]

20.31 However there will be many cases where the applicant for planning permission is content with the decision of the local planning authority and does not therefore appeal to the Secretary of State. In such a case a third party wishing to challenge the validity of the decision of the local planning authority may be able to bring a claim for judicial review under the provisions of the Supreme Court Act, s. 31 and Part 54 of the Civil Procedure Rules.

20.32 Under these rules the claimant must first make an application to the Administrative Court for permission to proceed with the claim. The claim for judicial review must be served on the defendant and on any other party whom the claimant considers to be directly affected; such parties may put forward summary grounds of defence. A pre-action protocol adopted in 2002 requires the claimant to give notice of the intended proceedings to the defendant, who must respond

---

47 *Bizony v Secretary of State for the Environment* [1976] JPL 306; *Hollis v Secretary of State for the Environment* [1982] 47 P & CR 351; and see *Wilson v Secretary of State for the Environment* [1988] JPL 540.

48 [2004] EWCA Civ 1566.

49 [1991] JPL 57.

50 See para 20.28.

in 14 days. The purpose of the procedure is to give the public authority the opportunity to reconsider its position.

20.33 In addition to having an arguable case, the applicant for judicial review must be able to show that he has sufficient standing and that he has acted promptly. These two additional matters are considered below.

Standing

20.34 The claimant seeking judicial review must have a 'sufficient interest' in the matter to which the application relates.[51] In *R v Inland Revenue Commissioners, ex p National Federation of Self-Employed and Small Businesses Ltd*,[52] the House of Lords held that issues of standing could not be divorced from the substantive merits of a case. This ruling has, in general, had a liberalizing effect and standing has been extended to such parties as adjoining landowners and ratepayers.[53]

20.35 In *R v Somerset County Council and ARC Southern Ltd, ex p Dixon*,[54] Sedley J affirmed the view that the rules relating to standing were essentially concerned with excluding 'busybodies and troublemakers'. Thus the applicant, who was a local resident, parish councillor, district council candidate, and member of various environmental bodies, was held to have sufficient interest. This decision should be contrasted with the slightly earlier ruling of Popplewell J in *R v North Somerset District Council, ex p Garnett and Persienne*.[55] Here both applicants lived locally and visited and enjoyed the site of the proposed development. Both had taken an active part in the objections but had made no written representations. Having set out the opposing arguments and referred to authority, Popplewell J held that the applicants had no sufficient interest, but did not give reasons.

20.36 More recently in *R (Kides) v South Cambridgeshire District Council*,[56] the claimant sought to challenge a grant of planning permission for housing development and she raised a legal ground of no personal interest to her—namely, affordable housing. In the High Court, Ouseley J refused the claimant permission to proceed with that particular ground on the basis that she was a mere busybody in relation to this issue—it was 'merely a means of creating difficulties for the landowner,

[51] Supreme Court Act 1981, s. 31(3).

[52] [1981] 2 All ER 93. See also *Covent Garden Community Association Ltd v Greater London Council* [1981] JPL 183; and *R v Inspectorate of Pollution, ex p Greenpeace Ltd (No 2)* [1994] 4 All ER 329.

[53] But see *R v Secretary of State for the Environment, ex p Rose Theatre Trust Co* [1990] 1 QB 504.

[54] [1997] JPL 1030.

[55] [1997] JPL 1015. See also *R v North West Leicestershire District Council, ex p Moses* [2000] JPL 733.

[56] [2002] EWCA Civ 1370.

developer and Council'. The Court of Appeal disagreed. Jonathan Parker LJ could not see how it could be just to debar a litigant who had a real and genuine interest in obtaining relief from relying on grounds, which may be good grounds, in which she has no personal interest. He said: 'It seems to me that a litigant who has a real and genuine interest in challenging an administrative decision must be entitled to present the challenge on all available grounds.'

Time limits

20.37 An application for permission to proceed with judicial review must be brought '(a) promptly; and (b) in any event not later than three months after the grounds to make the claim first arose'.[57] The court may, however, grant an extension of time having regard to any substantial prejudice caused by the delay'.

20.38 Although the position has now changed, a few years ago the courts took the controversial view that, in order for such challenges to be made promptly, they must be brought within six weeks. The controversy began with the decision in *R v Ceredigion County Council, ex p McKeown*[58] where an application for judicial review was lodged one day before the expiry of the three-month time limit. In refusing the application, Laws J held that there had been inexcusable delay. It was nearly impossible to conceive of a case, in the view of the learned judge, where leave for judicial review would be granted when the application was lodged more than six weeks after the planning permission had been granted. Thus the period for bringing judicial review proceedings was aligned with that for statutory review, as discussed above.

20.39 Further, in *R v Leicester City Council, ex p Safeway Stores*,[59] the council, on 20 May 1998, resolved to approve an application for approval of reserved matters. An application for permission to apply for judicial review was made on 29 July 1998. Dyson J dismissed the application on the ground of undue delay even though, at the time of the application, the council had not issued a formal grant of approval. The court took the view that time may run from the date of the authority's resolution, which could in theory be revoked due to a change of mind, rather than from the date of the decision letter.

20.40 Dyson J felt that the court should not adopt a more generous approach to resolutions than to formal grants, as in the real world, parties do rely on resolutions. The learned judge also held that the six-week period referred to in some planning cases and the three-month period referred to in [Part 54][60] were outer time periods.

---

57 Rule 54.5(1), CPR.
58 [1998] 2 PLR 1.
59 [1999] JPL 691. And see *R v Bristol City Council, ex p Anderson* [2000] PLCR 104.
60 As to the six-week period, see para 20.25.

It was necessary in each case to have regard to the facts in deciding whether an application had been made promptly; in this case Dyson J had no doubt that the applicants had not proceeded promptly.

20.41 It is hardly an exaggeration to say that the decision of Laws J in the *Ceredigion* case[61] and the subsequent decisions based upon it caused great uncertainty. The matter has now been considered by the House of Lords in *R v Hammersmith and Fulham London Borough Council, ex p Burkett*[62]—their Lordships' decision has restored a measure of certainty to the law.

20.42 Mr and Mrs Burkett brought judicial review proceedings relating to the proposed re-development of the former gasworks site at Imperial Wharf, Fulham. In September 1999 the council resolved to grant planning permission. The Burketts commenced judicial review proceedings on 6 April 2000 and the planning permission was issued on 12 May 2000. The application failed before both the High Court and Court of Appeal on the basis that the proceedings had been brought out of time. The Court of Appeal held that where the same objection affects the initial resolution as will affect the eventual grant of permission, it is at the date of the resolution that the grounds for the application first arise. On the issue of promptness, the Court considered that six weeks would be quite long enough in some cases to meet the demands of promptness; in others it would not be; and yet in other cases it might be too long. The 'six weeks rule' in s. 288 TCPA 1990 should be kept in mind 'as a touchstone of varying usefulness'.

20.43 The House of Lords disagreed with the approach of the Court of Appeal. Lord Steyn (with whom Lords Slynn, Hope, Millett, and Phillips agreed) held that time ran, not from the date of the resolution, but from the date of the grant of planning permission. This was because a resolution will not necessarily ripen into an actual grant of permission, and unlike a grant, gives rise to no rights and obligations. His Lordship said: 'The court has jurisdiction to entertain an application by a citizen for judicial review in respect of a resolution before or after its adoption. But it is a jump in legal logic to say that he *must* apply for such relief in respect of the resolution on pain of losing his right to judicial review of the actual grant of planning permission which does affect his rights. Such a view would also in tension with the established principle that judicial review is a remedy of the last resort.'

20.44 On the issue of delay, Lord Steyn rejected the notion that the three-month time limit prescribed by the rules could be contracted by judicial decision to six weeks—this was a 'misconception'. Doubts were also expressed by Lords Steyn and Hope

---

61 See fn 58 above.
62 [2002] UKHL 23.

as to whether 'promptness' was defined with sufficient certainty so as to comply with European law and also the ECHR.

Correction of errors under Part 5 of PCPA 2004

20.45 PCPA 2004, Part 5, contains new provisions enabling the Secretary of State or an inspector (ie the 'decision-maker') to correct an error in a decision letter without being exposed to the expensive and possibly lengthy procedures of a challenge in the High Court. The remedy is only available in cases of statutory review under TCPA 1990.[63]

20.46 The error in question must be a 'correctable error' under the provisions of the Act, ie an error (a) which is contained in any part of the decision document which records the decision, but (b) which is not part of any reasons given for the decision.[64]

20.47 The decision-maker may correct the error if he receives a written request to do so from any person, or if he informs the applicant in writing of the error and that he is considering making the correction.[65] He must also inform the local planning authority of the fact. Under s. 56 of PCPA 2004 as originally enacted, the decision maker had to obtain the written consent of the applicant, and if the applicant was not the owner, the consent of the owner. However, this requirement will be removed in England by s. 184 of PA 2008.

20.48 The correction process must be commenced within the six-week period in which the High Court challenge under TCPA 1990 must be brought.[66] It would seem that once the period has elapsed without High Court proceedings having been commenced, or steps taken under Part 5, the decision cannot be corrected.

20.49 As soon as practicable after making a correction, or deciding not to make a correction, the decision maker must issue a written notice specifying the correction (a 'correction notice'), or giving notice of a decision not to correct.[67] The decision-maker must give the correction notice to the applicant; if the applicant is not the owner, the owner; the local planning authority; and if the correction was requested by another person, that person.[68]

---

63 PCPA 2004, ss. 56–9. For statutory review, see para 20.07.
64 Ibid, s. 59(5).
65 Ibid, s. 56(2).
66 See para 20.26.
67 PCPA 2004, s. 57(1).
68 Ibid, s. 57(2).

20.50 If a correction is made, the original decision is to be regarded as not having been made, and the decision is taken for all purposes as having been made on the date the correction was issued. But if a correction is not made, the original decision continues to have full force and effect.[69] A correction notice itself becomes an action on the part of the Secretary of State the validity of which is challengeable in the High Court under TCPA 1990.[70]

The ombudsman remedy

Parliamentary Commissioner for Administration

20.51 In the 1960s there was a widespread feeling that parliamentary control was an insufficient safeguard against maladministration by government departments. To allay such fears the Parliamentary Commissioner Act 1967 created the office of Parliamentary Commissioner for Administration or 'ombudsman',[71] appointed by the Crown and responsible to Parliament. The ombudsman's function is to investigate individual complaints of injustice in consequence of maladministration by government departments and produce a report in each case.

20.52 The Act of 1967 does not define 'maladministration' but it would seem to relate to the way in which a decision is arrived at. It was memorably defined by the Lord President of the Council in the parliamentary debates which led to the passing of the 1967 Act as covering 'bias, neglect, inattention, delay, incompetence, arbitrariness and so on'.

20.53 There has been criticism that the ombudsman's powers are too limited. Thus he cannot, in the absence of special reasons, investigate actions in respect of which the complainant may take action in the courts. Complaints must be made via a Member of Parliament and generally must be brought within 12 months from the date the citizen first became aware of the maladministration. He has no power to order that a decision be altered; nevertheless, an adverse report may put pressure on a department to improve its procedures for the future. Where there is no maladministration, he cannot question a decision on its merits, even where it is based on a mistake of fact or is unreasonable.[72]

---

[69] Ibid, s. 58(1) and (2).

[70] Ibid, s. 58(3). There are corresponding provisions relating to High Court challenges arising out of enforcement (see ch 12 above); decisions under the LBA 1990 (see ch 16 above); and decisions under the P(HS)A 1990 (see ch 15 above)—PCPA 2004, s. 58(4)–(6).

[71] 'Grievance man'. As to the meaning of 'maladministration' see *R v Local Commissioners for the North and East Area of England, ex p Bradford Metropolitan City Council* [1979] QB 287.

[72] PCA 1967, s. 12(3).

20.54 Over the years a number of complaints have been brought against the government department responsible for planning. The reports reveal that where maladministration has been found, the greatest single cause for complaint has been delay, followed by, inter alia, complaints concerning the handling of planning inquiries, the refusal to award costs, alleged failures to enforce planning control, and refusals to call in planning applications.

20.55 In *R v Parliamentary Commissioner for Administration, ex p Balchin*,[73] a successful challenge was made of a decision of the Parliamentary Commissioner. The Commissioner's finding that no maladministration was involved in the local authority's handling of a highways acquisition was overturned by Sedley J and the Commissioner was required to reconsider his decision.

Local Commissioners for Administration

20.56 The Local Government Act 1974 introduced two Commissioners for Local Administration, one for England and one for Wales, with responsibility for providing Local Commissioners ('Local Ombudsmen') on a regional basis. Their function is to investigate complaints by members of the public of injustice as a consequence of maladministration by local authorities. They also provide and publish appropriate guidance to local authorities on good administrative practice. Before providing such guidance they must consult with local authority associations.[74]

20.57 The Local Ombudsmen are specifically excluded from dealing with matters where the complainant has a right of appeal to a tribunal or Minister or a right of redress in the courts.[75] They cannot investigate actions of local authorities which affect all or most of the inhabitants of the local authority concerned.[76] There is, as in the case of the Parliamentary Commissioner, a 12-month limitation period. Complaints may be made either directly to the Local Ombudsman or through a member of the local authority concerned. The Act of 1974 requires that reports of investigations should be publicized by various means at the local level.

20.58 Of the many matters that have been found to be maladministration causing injustice by local planning authorities, unreasonable delay, the giving of incorrect information or misleading advice and poor liaison between the various agencies in local authorities figure strongly. Since 1978 local authorities have had a power to pay compensation, as opposed to payments on an 'ex gratia' basis.

---

73 [1997] JPL 917.

74 PCA 1967, s. 12A.

75 LGA 1974, s. 26(6).

76 It seems that the 12-month limitation period may be enforced strictly—see *Bradford* case at fn 71 above.

21

PLANNING COMPENSATION

21.01 So far in this book we have dealt with the purposes and machinery of planning control. But planning control has been perceived as involving certain financial problems which are called the 'Compensation-Betterment Problem'. Put quite simply, this is the problem of what is to be done about (a) owners whose property is reduced in value by action taken under planning legislation; and (b) owners whose property is increased in value by such action.

The historical background

Compensation for planning restrictions

21.02 English law has adopted two contrasting principles with compensation for the deprivation of rights over land. On the one hand the courts insisted that property shall not be compulsorily acquired without full compensation—unless Parliament provides to the contrary. As was said in *A-G v De Keyser's Royal Hotel Ltd*:[1] 'It is a well-established principle that, unless no other interpretation is possible, justice requires that statutes should not be construed to enable the land of a particular individual to be confiscated without payment.'

1 [1920] AC 508.

21.03 Or, as it was put in the later case of *Belfast Corpn v OD Cars Ltd*:[2] 'The intention to take away property without compensation is not to be imputed to the legislature unless it is expressed in unequivocal terms.'

21.04 On the other hand compensation is not payable for restrictions on the user of property unless Parliament expressly so provides. Through Public Health Acts and similar legislation, Parliament has either directly restricted the user of land or authorized local authorities to do so. In only a few cases, however, has it been thought necessary to provide for the payment of compensation.[3]

21.05 Strictly speaking the restrictions imposed by planning legislation fall within the second category: in other words planning legislation restricts an owner's use of his property but it does not take away the property from him. On the other hand some of the restrictions imposed or authorized by the Planning Acts go far beyond anything in, say, the Public Health Acts. They can be fairly said to take away rights in property.

21.06 The building regulations may restrict the way in which a man develops his land, but under planning legislation the appropriate authorities may forbid him to develop at all.[4]

21.07 Until 1947 at least, Parliament recognized that many planning restrictions were in effect confiscatory of property rights. For the purposes of compensation, planning restrictions were divided into those which were confiscatory and those which were merely regulatory and thus akin to public health restrictions.

21.08 The Acts of 1909 to 1925 provided for compensation to any person 'injuriously affected' by any provisions in any planning scheme subject, inter alia, to the following exceptions:

(a) no compensation was payable for any provision in a scheme which could have been imposed as a byelaw without payment of compensation;
(b) provision might be made in the scheme itself for excluding compensation in respect of restrictions on the density, height, or character of buildings, if the Minister was satisfied that it was reasonable to exclude compensation having respect to the situation and nature of the land.

21.09 The same approach was adopted in the TCPA 1932. Compensation was payable to persons whose property was injuriously affected by any provisions in the scheme or by the carrying out by the responsible authority of any work under the scheme. As under earlier legislation the scheme might exclude compensation for certain restrictions; the list of matters in respect of which compensation could be excluded

---

[2] [1960] AC 490, [1960] 1 All ER 65.
[3] See *Belfast Corpn v OD Cars Ltd*, above.
[4] Building regulations may prevent development where the site is too small to satisfy the requirements as to space about buildings, but this is exceptional.

was extended to restrictions on the use of land or buildings if these were needed for the protection of health or the amenities of the neighbourhood.

Betterment

21.10 'Betterment' has been defined as 'any increase in the value of land (including the buildings thereon) arising from central or local government action, whether positive, eg by the execution of public works or improvements, or negative, eg by the imposition of restrictions on other land'.[5] The word 'betterment' is sometimes used to describe not only the increase in value of the property but also the amount of such increase in value recovered from the owner.

21.11 Betterment resulting from positive action by a public authority has been recovered in a number of different ways, of which the most common is a set off against compensation received by the owner for land compulsorily acquired under the scheme of development.[6]

21.12 The advent of planning legislation in 1909, however, raised the problem of betterment in a new form. Earlier statutes had been concerned only with betterment resulting from positive action in the form of public works. Planning control, however, produces betterment in a different way. If building is prohibited or restricted on certain land—for instance, land to be kept in a green belt or open space—two results may follow. First, adjoining land on which building is to be permitted may be increased in value because of the amenity created by the green belt or open space. Second, the restriction on the amount available for development may intensify the demand for land on which building will be permitted.

21.13 Without the compulsory purchase of large areas of building land, betterment resulting from planning control can only be recovered by a direct charge on the land concerned. The Acts of 1909 to 1925 adopted this method and authorized the recovery of one half of any increase in the value of property due to the coming into operation of a scheme. It is believed that no betterment was ever recovered under these Acts.

21.14 The TCPA 1932 went further and provided for the recovery of 75 per cent of any increase in value due either to the coming into operation of a scheme or the execution of works by the responsible authority under the scheme. The TCPA 1932 had not been in force seven years when the Second World War broke out, and by 1942 only 5 per cent of England and 1 per cent of Wales were subject to operative schemes. It is difficult to judge whether the TCPA 1932 would have been a success

---

[5] Final Report of the Expert Committee on Compensation and Betterment (Uthwatt Committee), para 260.

[6] See the Land Compensation Act 1961, ss. 7–9.

over a longer period, and whether enough could have been raised by way of betterment to meet the liability for compensation. The historical precedents in relation to betterment were certainly not encouraging, and the liability to compensation deterred authorities from full use of their powers of planning control.

21.15 In 1941 the Government appointed what came to be known as the Uthwatt Committee to consider a number of matters including compensation and betterment. The Committee recommended what was in effect the nationalization of the development rights in land outside built-up areas. The land would remain in private ownership, but development would require the consent of the State which would thereupon acquire the land, if necessary by compulsory purchase, either for development by a public authority, or for re-sale or lease to a private developer.[7]

The TCPA 1947 solution

21.16 The TCPA 1947 in some respects went even further than the Uthwatt Committee had recommended. In effect it nationalized the development rights in all land, including land in built-up areas. On the other hand it did not provide for the acquisition by the state of all land required for development purposes. Although extensive powers of compulsory purchase were conferred upon public authorities, land required for private development would not normally be acquired by the State; instead the existing owner would, so to speak, re-acquire the development rights by paying a 'development charge'.

21.17 The word 'nationalization' was not used in the TCPA 1947; nor indeed was it expressly provided that the development rights in land should be transferred to the State. But the transfer of development rights to the state was clearly enough the underlying theory. In practice this was achieved in the following ways:

(a) development must not be carried out without planning permission;
(b) if permission was refused or granted subject to conditions, the owner of the land was not entitled to compensation because he no longer possessed the development rights;
(c) if permission was granted for development, the owner would pay a development charge representing the difference in the value of the land with the benefit of that permission and its existing use value;
(d) if the land were compulsorily acquired, the compensation would be limited to existing use value;
(e) as a measure of compensation for the loss of development rights landowners were entitled under TCPA 1947, Part VI to make a claim for a once-for-all payment from the Government.

[7] Uthwatt Report, para 56.

21.18 Under Part VI, TCPA 1947, s. 58 provided for a global sum of £300 million as compensation generally for loss of development value. The owner of a freehold or leasehold interest could submit a claim for compensation for loss of development value representing the difference between the 'unrestricted' and 'restricted' values of his interests on 1 July 1948. The unrestricted value was that which the interest would have had if the TCPA 1947 had not been passed; the restricted value was its value on the assumption that permission would not be granted for any development other than Third Schedule development (which is described below).

21.19 The claims were not, in fact, paid out because the new government which came into office in 1951 decided to replace the financial provisions of the TCPA 1947 by a different scheme; this was effected by the Acts of 1953 and 1954.

Third Schedule development

21.20 In this review of the financial provisions of the TCPA 1947, it must be noticed that certain forms of development, considered to be within the existing use of land, were exempted from the 'nationalization' scheme. These developments were set out in detail in the TCPA 1947, Schedule 3 and for this reason were originally referred to as 'Third Schedule development'. The Third Schedule to the TCPA 1947 became the Third Schedule to the TCPA 1962, then Schedule 8 to the TCPA 1971, but in the TCPA 1990 it is Schedule 3; it will therefore be referred to henceforth as 'Schedule 3 development'. However, as will be seen later in this chapter, the PCA 1991 has repealed most of Schedule 3 as it appeared in the TCPA 1990 as originally enacted. Schedule 3 development may be described as development consistent with, or required for, the existing use of the land or building in question. For instance the conversion of a large house into flats is development and requires planning permission,[8] but the house remains in residential use.

21.21 It must be emphasized that Schedule 3 development requires planning permission. But under the TCPA 1947 it did not attract development charges and in assessing loss of development value any potential development of this kind was included in the existing use or restricted value of the land. Moreover, even under the TCPA 1947, compensation was payable if planning permission was refused or granted subject to conditions for certain forms of Schedule 3 development.[9]

The TCPA 1954 solution

21.22 In November 1952 the Government published a White Paper announcing a drastic revision of the financial provisions of the TCPA 1947. The Government

---

[8] TCPA 1990, s. 55(3)(a).

[9] This right to compensation has finally been removed by the Planning and Compensation Act 1991. See para 21.35.

proposed in effect to hand back to private ownership the development rights in land as they existed immediately before the TCPA 1947, but not as altered for better or worse by the operation of planning control since that date.

21.23 These proposals were put into effect by the TCPA 1953—an emergency measure to deal with the more urgent problems—and by the TCPA 1954. These two Acts did not affect the powers of control over development provided by the TCPA 1947, but the financial consequences of granting or refusing permission were altered. If permission were granted, the owner no longer had to pay a development charge.[10] If permission were refused or granted subject to conditions, then (with some exceptions) owners of legal interests in the land were entitled to compensation, provided a claim for loss of development value had been established under TCPA 1947, s. 58. Similarly if land were compulsorily acquired, the compensation was to include the amount of the TCPA 1947, s. 58 claim as well as the existing use value. In consequence of all this, the obligation to pay the £300 millon in one lump sum was abolished, the full amount of the established claim being available to provide compensation as and when a loss of development value was actually incurred—namely when planning permission was refused or granted subject to conditions or when land was compulsorily acquired.

21.24 The established claim, or what was left of it after certain other payments to mitigate the effects of the TCPA 1947 had been made, was then converted into an 'unexpended balance of established development value'. This provided the basis of compensation for restrictions on development (other than Schedule 3 development) imposed on or after 1 January 1955 until the scheme was finally abolished by the PCA 1991. Compensation for restrictions on Schedule 3 development continued to be payable under the rules originally established by the TCPA 1947 until these were also abolished by the PCA 1991.[11]

21.25 There were, therefore, until the reforms of 1991, two sets of rules for compensation for planning restrictions—namely one scheme for restrictions on Schedule 3 development, and another more complex scheme for restrictions on what was known as 'new development', that is, development outside Schedule 3.

21.26 Compensation for restrictions on new development was payable only if there was an unexpended balance and this existed only if a claim had been established under TCPA 1947, s. 58 and the amount of the compensation did not exceed the unexpended balance. No new claims could be made under TCPA 1947, s. 58 and there was no provision for increasing the amount of the established claims to take account of the decline in the value of money. And, of course, the landowner was

10 This liability was abolished by the TCPA 1953 with effect from November 1952.
11 See para 21.35.

denied any increase in development value resulting from the development plan zoning—often a very substantial item indeed.

21.27 For these reasons the TCPA 1954 was in its turn subjected to a good deal of criticism, and in 1959 Parliament decided to revert to full market value (including the benefit of any enhancement due to the development plan) as the basis of compensation for compulsory purchase. The TCPA 1954 was left untouched in relation to compensation for planning restrictions; these provisions were re-enacted in all the Planning Acts up to 1990. As mentioned above, the PCA 1991 has now repealed them and these repeals will be considered later in this chapter.

Land Commission and Community Land

21.28 Following the General Election of 1964, a fresh attempt was made to deal with the compensation-betterment problem. This resulted in the Land Commission Act 1967. The Act set up a Land Commission with power to acquire land for development at current use value plus an increment to the owner. At the same time a Betterment Levy was imposed on development value, initially at a rate of 40 per cent of the net development value. But the scheme had hardly got into its stride when, following the change of government in 1970, the Land Commission Act was repealed.

21.29 The Labour Government which came to office in 1974 made yet another attempt to deal with the problem of land values. This last attempt was embodied in the Community Land Act 1975 and the Development Land Tax Act 1976. The objective of the Community Land scheme, according to a White Paper,[12] was to enable the community to control the development of land in accordance with its needs and priorities. For this purpose it was local authorities who were enabled to acquire land for development, whereas development land tax was payable whenever development value was realized. However the Community Land Act was repealed in 1980 following the return of a Conservative Government, but the development land tax was retained. In the economic climate of the early 1980s it was considered to be a discouragement to development, and in his 1985 Budget speech the Chancellor of the Exchequer announced its abolition in respect of all chargeable transfers and events arising on or after 19 March 1985.

The compensation-betterment problem after 1991

21.30 The Planning and Compensation Act 1991 finally abolished the right to compensation for restrictions on new development and Schedule 3 development and this will be discussed below.

[12] Cmnd 5730, para 16.

Planning and Compensation Act 1991

21.31 The TCPA 1990 as originally enacted expressly preserved the limited rights to compensation for planning restrictions referred to earlier in this chapter. However in 1986 a government consultation paper[13] had proposed their repeal and this proposal was carried through by PCA 1991, s. 31 which came into effect on 25 September 1991. A little more will be said about these repeals below.

Compensation for restrictions on new development—repealed

21.32 As explained earlier in this chapter,[14] compensation for restrictions on new development depended on the existence of an unexpended balance of established development value. There were further conditions: (1) the claim had to be triggered by a refusal or conditional grant of planning permission on or after 1 January 1955; (2) the claimant's interest must have been depreciated as a result; (3) compensation must not have been excluded under the Act. The exclusions were very broad and often meant that the entitlement to compensation was the exception rather than the rule.[15]

21.33 Another problem was that, by the 1980s, the amounts paid in compensation were extremely small, being effectively tied to land values prevailing in 1954. Moreover, where compensation had been paid and the land was subsequently developed, the Secretary of State could require it to be repaid. This depended upon the registration in the local land charges registry of a 'compensation notice' which could apportion the payment as between different parts of the land.[16] These elaborate procedures could hardly be justified by the very small (and diminishing) number of claims.

21.34 The provisions were widely regarded as anachronistic and virtually obsolete and their repeal in 1991 was long overdue.

Compensation for restrictions on Schedule 3 development—repealed

21.35 The concept of Schedule 3 development was explained earlier in this chapter. Before the reforms of 1991, Schedule 3 was divided into three parts. Part I, which remains, comprises development for which compensation was not available; Part II,

13 Compensation Provisions in the Town and Country Planning Acts (1986).

14 See para 21.22.

15 See the 8th edition of this book, ch 21.

16 Similar provisions are retained, however, in the case of compensation for the revocation or modification of planning permission. See TCPA 1990, ss. 111, 112.

which has been repealed, comprised development for which compensation was available.[17] Part III contains certain supplementary provisions.

21.36 The compensation under Part II was payable on the refusal or conditional grant of planning permission by the Secretary of State for development falling under Part II. The value of the interest had to be less than it would have been but for the decision and the claim had to be submitted to the local planning authority within six months of the decision unless an extension of time was agreed. Of the various classes of development under Part II the most notable was the enlargement, improvement, or other alteration of certain prescribed buildings to certain limits of cubic content and gross floor space.

21.37 With the repeal of TCPA 1990, s. 114 and PCA 1991, Schedule 3, Part II, compensation is no longer payable, but it is important to note that Part I of Schedule 3 (and certain additional restrictions in PCA 1991, Schedule 10) are expressly preserved. They remain relevant for certain purposes, including, in particular, the following:

(1) In deciding whether, for the purposes of confirming a purchase notice, land has become incapable of reasonably beneficial use.[18]
(2) In assessing compensation for depreciation in connection with an order revoking or modifying planning permission where it may be assumed that planning permission would be granted for development under Part I of Schedule 3.[19]

21.38 The proposal to repeal the entitlement to compensation under PCA 1991, Schedule 3, Part II was first made by the government in the consultation paper of 1986. There were two particular problems. First, the entitlement was open to abuse in that there was an incentive for developers to seek permission for unacceptable development in the hope of receiving substantial compensation. This was particularly so in areas of high and rising land values where the increase in capital value of the proposed development might significantly exceed the building costs. The problem was highlighted in the early 1980s by the ruling of the Court of Appeal in *Peaktop Properties (Hampstead) Ltd v Camden London Borough Council*[20] where it was held that the cubic content enlargement tolerance under what was paragraph 3 of Part II applied to a whole block of flats and so applications to build another story on an existing block fell within the Schedule. That case led to a number of speculative applications to build penthouse flats. Although an amendment in 1985[21] attempted to deal with this problem by (in general)

17 See the 8th edition of this book, ch 20, where the provisions were discussed in full.
18 See para 14.04.
19 See para 11.24.
20 (1983) 46 P & CR 177.
21 Town and Country Planning (Compensation) Act 1985, s. 1(2).

excluding the enlargement of a block of flats which would result in an increase in the number of dwellings, it was felt that a problem remained.

21.39 A second, and related, difficulty was that the government felt that local planning authorities were simply unwilling to refuse planning permission because of the potential liability for compensation. As a result their development control powers were attenuated particularly in areas of environmental sensitivity.

21.40 As indicated above, TCPA 1990 Schedule 3, Part I remains in force for certain purposes. It is reproduced at the end of this chapter, together with certain surviving supplementary provisions in Part III and Schedule 10.

Compensation for other planning restrictions

21.41 The reforms of 1991 do not affect the right of certain types of owner to serve a purchase notice or blight notice if, in either case, the necessary conditions are satisfied.[22] If the notice is confirmed the owner's interest will be purchased and compensation for the value of the land paid.

21.42 The TCPA 1990 provides for compensation to be paid consequent upon a number of other adverse planning decisions. These instances have been dealt with in earlier chapters but are summarized below.

(1) Compensation may be payable under TCPA 1990, ss. 107 and 108 where a planning permission is revoked or modified. Similarly TCPA 1990, s. 115 provides for compensation in respect of depreciation caused by the making of a discontinuance order under TCPA 1990, s. 102. See chapter 11 above.
(2) Compensation may be payable under the Listed Buildings Act 1991, s. 28 where listed building consent is revoked or modified. See chapter 16 above.
(3) Compensation may be payable for loss or damage caused by a building preservation notice under LBA 1991, s. 29. See chapter 16 above.
(4) Compensation may be payable under TCPA 1990, s. 186 for loss or damage attributable to the prohibition contained in a stop notice. See chapter 12 above.
(5) Compensation may be payable for a refusal of consent under a tree preservation order by virtue of TCPA 1990, s. 208. See chapter 15 above.
(6) Compensation may be payable for the revocation or modification of a hazardous substances consent under the P(HS)A 1990, s. 16. See chapter 15 above.

22 See para 14.01.

APPENDIX 1

Schedule 3 TCPA 1990
Development Not Constituting New Development

Part I
Development Not Ranking For Compensation Under s. 114

1. The carrying out of—
   (a) the rebuilding, as often as occasion may require, of any building which was in existence on 1 July 1948, or of any building which was in existence on 1 July 1948, or of any building which was in existence before that date but was destroyed or demolished after 7 January 1937, including the making good of war damage sustained by any such building;
   (b) the rebuilding, as often as occasion may require, of any building erected after 1 July 1948 which was in existence at a material date;
   (c) the carrying out for the maintenance, improvement or other alteration of any building, of works which—
      (i) affect only the interior of the building, or do not materially affect the external appearance of the building, and
      (ii) are works for making good war damage

   so long as the cubic content of the original building is not substantially exceeded.
2. The use as two or more separate dwellinghouses of any building which at a material date was used as a single dwellinghouse.

Part II (repealed)

Part III
Supplementary Provisions

9. Where after 1 July 1948—
   (a) any buildings or works have been erected or constructed, or any use of land has been instituted, and
   (b) any condition imposed under Part III of this Act, limiting the period for which those buildings or works may be retained, or that use may be continued, has effect in relation to those buildings or works or that use,

   this Schedule shall not operate except as respects the period specified in that condition.
10. (1) Any reference in this Schedule to the cubic content of a building shall be construed as a reference to that content as ascertained by external measurement.
   (2) For the purposes of paragraph 1 the cubic content of a building is substantially increased or exceeded—
      (a) in the case of a dwellinghouse, if it is increased or exceeded by more than one-tenth or 1,750 cubic feet, whichever is the greater; and
      (b) in any other case, if it is increased or exceeded by more than one-tenth.
11. (Repealed)
12. (1) In this Schedule 'at a material date' means at either—
      (a) 1 July 1948; or
      (b) the date by reference to which this Schedule falls to be applied in the particular case in question.

(2) Sub-paragraph (1)(b) shall not apply in relation to any buildings, works or use of land in respect of which, whether before or after the date mentioned in that sub-paragraph, an enforcement notice served before that date has become or becomes effective.

13. (1) In relation to a building erected after 1 July 1948 which results from the carrying out of any such works as are described in paragraph 1, any reference in this Schedule to the original building is a reference to the building in relation to which those works were carried out and not to the building resulting from the carrying out of those works.

(2) This paragraph does not apply for the purposes of sections 111 and 138.

Schedule 10
Condition Treated as Applicable to Rebuilding and Alterations

1. Where the building to be rebuilt or altered is the original building, the amount of gross floor space in the building as rebuilt or altered which may be used for any purpose shall not exceed by more than ten per cent the amount of gross floor space which was last used for that purpose in the original building.
2. Where the building to be rebuilt or altered is not the original building, the amount of gross floor space in the building as rebuilt or altered which may be used for any purpose shall not exceed the amount of gross floor space which was last used for that purpose in the building before the rebuilding or alteration.
3. In determining under this Schedule the purpose for which floor space was last used in any building, no account shall be taken of any use in respect of which an effective enforcement notice has been or could be served or, in the case of a use which has been discontinued, could have been served immediately before the discontinuance.
4. (1) For the purposes of this Schedule gross floor space shall be ascertained by external measurement.

   (2) Where different parts of a building are used for different purposes, floor space common to those purposes shall be apportioned rateably.
5. In relation to a building erected after 1 July 1948 which is a building resulting from the carrying out of any such works as are described in paragraph 1 of Schedule 3, any reference in this Schedule to the original building is a reference to the building in relation to which those works were carried out and not to the building resulting from the carrying out of those works.

APPENDIX 2

Planning Act 2008

Commencement

Section 241

(1) The following provisions of the Act come into force on the day on which this Act is passed—

(a) The provisions of Part 1 to 9 (except section 194(2) to (5) and paragraph 7 of schedule 7) which—

(i) confer powers to make orders (other than orders granting, or making changes to orders granting, development consent), regulations or rules, or

(ii) make provision about what is (or is not) permitted to be done, or what is required to be done, in the exercise of any such power;

(b) Part 11, except section 206, 211(7), 224 and 225;

(c) this Part, except section 238.

(2) Nothing in subsection (1)(a) affects the operation of s.13 of the Interpretation Act 1978 (c.30) in relation to this Act.

(3) Execpt as provided for by subsection (1)(a) the provisions listed in subsection (4) come into force on such day as may be appointed by order made by –

(a) the Welsh Minsters, in relation to Wales;

(b) the Secretary of State, in relation to England.

(4) The provisions are—

(a) sections 183, 185, 187, 188, 191(1) and (3), 192, 193 and 197 to 200;

(b) paragraphs 1, 2(1) and (2), 3(1), (2) and (4) and 4 to 6 of Schedule 7;

(c) Schedules 8 and 11;

(d) the repeals in—

(i) TCPA 1990 (except those in Schedules 1 and 1A to that Act);

(ii) The Environmental Protection Act 1990 (c.43);

(iii) The Planning and Compensation Act 1991 (c.34);

(iv) sections 42(3) and 53 of PCPA 2004.

(5) Section 186 and the repeal in Schedule 1A to TCPA 1990 come into force on such a day as the Welsh Ministers may by order appoint.

(6) Sections 194(2) to (5), 201, 202, 203 and 225 (together with related entries in Schedule 13), and paragraph 7 of Schedule 7, come into force at the end of two months beginning with the day on which this Act is passed.

(7) Sections 204 comes into force in accordance with subsection(5) of that section.

(8) The other provisions of this Act come into force on such day as the Secretary of State may by order appoint.

(9) The powers conferred by this section are exercisable by statutory instrument.

(10) An order under this section may—

(a) appoint different days for different purposes (including different areas);

(b) contain transitional, transitory or saving provision in connection with the coming into force of this Act.

INDEX